Higher National Computing Tutor Resource Pack

Higher National Computing Tutor Resource Pack

Patrick Hall

Bruce Hellingsworth

Howard Anderson

Newnes

OXFORD AMSTERDAM BOSTON LONDON NEW YORK PARIS
SAN DIEGO SAN FRANCISCO SINGAPORE SYDNEY TOKYO

Newnes
An imprint of Elsevier Science
Linacre House, Jordan Hill, Oxford OX2 8DP
225 Widlwood Avenue, Woburn, MA 01801-2041

First edition 2003

British Library Cataloguing in Publication Data
A catalogue record for this book is available from the British Library

ISBN 0 7506 54244

Composition by Scribe Design, Gillingham, Kent
Printed and bound in Great Britain

Contents

1	**Hardware and networks**	1-1
	1.1 Assignment: hierarchy of design	1-1
	1.2 Moore's law: is it true?	1-2
	1.3 Enrichment material	1-3
	1.4 Tutor's notes and resources	1-10
	1.5 Practical task	1-13
	1.6 Assignment: PC specification	1-15
	1.7 Practical DOS	1-17
	1.8 Enrichment material	1-27
2	**Systems analysis**	2-31
	Rationale	2-31
	2.1 Introduction to the systems analysis models	2-31
	2.2 Requirements analysis	2-32
	2.3 Systems analysis models	2-34
	SSADM	2-48
	Object-oriented analysis (OOA) development	2-52
	Unified Modelling Language (UML)	2-55
	Data modelling	2-60
3	**Software constructs and tools**	3-79
	3.1 Business models	3-79
	3.2 Programming methodology	3-113
	3.3 Problem-solving theory	3-226
4	**Computing solutions**	4-239
	4.1 Information and contemporary applications	4-239
	4.2 Information processing tools	4-252
	4.3 Evaluation measures	4-279
5	**Quality management principles**	5-285
	Rationale	5-285
	5.1 System analysis and design tools	5-285
	5.2 Software quality assurance	5-322
	5.3 Professional standards	5-333

6 Networks 6-339
6.1 Impact of communications technology 6-339
6.2 Cost and security 6-351
6.3 Tutor's resources 6-374
6.4 Network assignment 6-374

Appendix A Hex, binary and other number bases 6-377
Appendix B ASCII and Unicode 6-381
Appendix C Searching the Internet 6-382

1 Hardware and networks

1.1 Assignment: hierarchy of design

In *Higher National Computing*, the idea of hierarchy of design is introduced via an analogy with bricks being used to build a town.

In computing in general, it is very important that students understand the hierarchical nature of systems and their design. Gone are the days when monolithic designs were commonplace; modern products benefit from the ideas of layered, modularized designs. This has led to the much improved ability to modify parts, extend their functionality and flexibility and to improve reliability.

The object of this assignment is to foster the concepts of the hierarchy of design.

Assignment

The tables below show the example for hierarchy of design given in *Higher National Computing*.

Your assignment is to provide a second example of the hierarchy of design leaving the computer hardware and software elements in place.

Example repeated from the book for convenience.

of bricks and towns	*of computer hardware*	*of computer software*
Bricks. Study what a brick is made of, how it is made, how strong it is, what will it cost	1s and 0s, simple digital circuits and how logical arithmetic can be performed with a circuit	Boolean logic
Walls. Study how to mix cement, how to lay bricks to make a wall, how strong is a wall	How a sequence of logical operations can be achieved with a circuit, how to add, subtract, perform logical AND and OR operations etc.	How to perform arithmetic with simple numbers
How to make several walls into a building with spaces for windows and doors etc. How to build a roof	How to store many logical instructions and feed them in sequence to a circuit that can execute them	How to perform arithmetic with multiple digit numbers
How to install all the services a building needs, water, electricity, gas, heating etc. and to move in the carpets, furniture etc.	How to accept human inputs by devices such as a keyboard and to display outputs using devices like a colour monitor	How to handle data such as text and to edit it, i.e. move a sentence within a paragraph
How to build a row of houses, provide street lighting, public access etc.	How to provide a complete set of devices such as a mouse, keyboard, printer, CPU etc. and to make them all connect correctly	How to present a complete set of facilities in a wordprocessor
How to plan a town, provide libraries, shops, hospital, bus station etc.	A complete PC	How to control the entire machine: the operating system

Example answer

of car design	*of computer hardware*	*of computer software*
How petrol burns, its chemistry and physical properties. The metallurgy of engine parts	1s and 0s, simple digital circuits and how logical arithmetic can be performed with a circuit	Boolean logic
Design of wheels, gears, pistons etc., their individual characteristics and limitations	How a sequence of logical operations can be achieved with a circuit, how to add, subtract, perform logical AND and OR operations etc.	How to perform arithmetic with simple numbers
How to make an engine from individual components, how much power it produces, how fuel efficient it is	How to store many logical instructions and feed them in sequence to a circuit that can execute them	How to perform arithmetic with multiple digit numbers
How to assemble the engine, gearbox, wheels, seats, body shell and all the other components into a complete car	How to accept human inputs by devices such as a keyboard and to display outputs using devices like a colour monitor	How to handle data such as text and to edit it, i.e. move a sentence within a paragraph
How the complete car performs, how acceptable it is as a product to customers in terms of comfort, performance, reliability etc.	How to provide a complete set of devices such as a mouse, keyboard, printer, CPU etc. and to make them all connect correctly	How to present a complete set of facilities in a word processor
The complete design and manufacturing details for mass production of the car	A complete PC	How to control the entire machine: the operating system

1.2 Moore's law: is it true?

Moore's law

In 1965, Gordon Moore was the Research Director of the electronics company Fairchild Semiconductor. Some 3 years later he was to become one of the founders of Intel. He made an interesting prediction based on what had happened up to that time with memory chips (not microprocessors). He noticed that memory doubled in capacity every 18–24 months. He then predicted this would continue, leading to an exponential growth in size and hence computing power. Market trends have shown it to have come true up until now with memory and with microprocessors; there are predictions that it will fail in the future but these predictions have themselves failed in the past as they have been made many times.

It seems that Dr Moore thinks it is still true. See http://developer.intel.com/update/archive/issue2/feature.htm for what he says. Notice, however, that in some people's eyes the 'law' has changed. It originally referred to the density of transistors on a piece of silicon. This is closely related to RAM capacity but many people take it to mean 'processor speed'. Transistor density is only one of the many factors that contribute to processor speed. You should also notice that Dr Moore refers to Intel products, not surprising considering he is a co-founder of the company, but as the market place is very competitive and other companies products are comparable, it is reasonable to extrapolate his results to other firms.

There must be a limit to this improvement. This limit is often called a 'wall' and has been predicted for some time. At any one time, the technical difficulties that must be overcome to make ever better semiconductors are very severe. It is not always obvious that they will be overcome. Trying to foretell the future is always very dangerous! This is especially true for processor speed; simple predictions related to clock speed do not take into account developments such as pipelining and superscalar architectures. These developments have had an enormous effect on execution speed, and it is this speed that is important, not clock speed.

Moore's second law

There is the corollary to Moore's law, named by some as Moore's second law. He points out that as transistor density improves, the cost of the research and production increases dramatically. In the period

1965 to 1995, the costs increased by a factor of about 1000, what was $12 000 became $12 million. It may be that the real 'wall', the final limit to CPU execution speed or RAM capacity, will be an economic one, and the cost of manufacture may rise to such an extent that components become too expensive. See http://www.imakenews.com/techreview/ e_article000003598.cfm.

Internet traffic

In a paper that can be found at http://www.research.att.com/~amo/doc/internet.moore.pdf, the case is made that Moore's law seems to apply to Internet traffic as well.

1.3 Enrichment material

Assembly and machine code

Tutor's note: In Unit 1 of *Higher National Computing*, the writing of assembly language programs is not required. The purpose of the description below is to reinforce the ideas of machine code, of programs stored in the same address space as data and the fetch–execute cycle. A detailed description of all parts of the assembly program is not presented or required, indeed some of the usual assembler directives etc. are deliberately left out for clarity. The assembler used (A86) is shareware and available from the author, Eric Isaacson, at http://eji.com/index.htm or 416, E. University Ave. Bloomington, IN 47401-4739. The assumption has been made that students are already familiar with ASCII and hex.

All PC processors 'work' on machine code. Machine code is a series of instructions and data stored in RAM and processed an instruction at a time. Although it is quite possible to enter machine code directly into memory and execute it, it is not a productive way to carry out the business of computing! Most programs are written in a high level language (e.g. C++, Java), the program is then translated via a complex process to produce the required machine code. An alternative method appropriate to some specific problems is to use an assembler. This is a method that requires knowledge specific to the processor and operating system in use. It involves typing the code as mnemonics into a text editor, using a program called an 'assembler' to translate the mnemonics into machine code then using the operating system to load and execute the program.

At the DOS prompt you may see the following sequence of events:

```
C:\progs> edit trp1.asm
C:\progs> a86 trp1.asm trp1.com
C:\progs> trp1
```

- The first line starts the text editor and allows the text to be added in the usual way.
- The second line calls the assembler program (A86 in this case) to work in the input file trp1.asm and to output the machine code into file trp1.com.
- The last line asks DOS to load and execute the program.

Example: program trp1.asm

```
top:          jmp start
buffer:       db 'Mary had a little lamb',10,13,0
start:        mov si,buffer
L1:           mov dl,[si]      ;get first character
              cmp dl,0         ;see if end of string
              jz finprint      ;finish if end of string
              mov ah,2         ;initialise subroutine int21 DOS call next
              int 021          ;write char
              inc si           ;point to next char
              jmp L1           ;back for more chars
finprint:     int 020          ;back to DOS
```

The assembler runs and produces the machine code, in this case, file trp1.com.

Hex dump of trp1.com

```
E9 19 00 4D 61 72 79 20 68 61 64 20 61 20 6C 69    ;e..Mary had a li
74 74 6C 65 20 6C 61 6D 62 0A 0D 00 BE 03 01 8A    ;ttle lamb.../.._
14 80 FA 00 74 07 B4 02 CD 21 46 EB F2 CD 20       ;._u.t.'.I!FeoI
```

As you can see, the machine code (written in hex bytes) does not seem to mean very much!

As assembly is a simple process of converting mnemonics directly to machine code; it can be reversed, the machine code can be 'turned back' to assembly code. The table below shows the result of this process and provides a comment on what most of the bytes mean. The contents column contains the hex bytes from trp1.com.

Address	*Contents*	*Mnemonic*	*Comments*
0100	E91900	JMP 011C	;Jump to the first instruction after the data
0103	4D	M	;data
0104	61	a	;data
0105	72	r	;data
0106	79	y	;data
0107	20	(space character)	;data
0108	68	h	;data
0109	61	a	;data
010A	64	d	;data
010B	20	(space character)	;data
010C	61	a	;data
010D	20	(space character)	;data
010E	6C	l	;data
010F	49	I	;data
0110	74	t	;data
0111	74	t	;data
0112	6C	l	;data
0113	65	e	;data
0114	20	(space character)	;data
0115	6C	l	;data
0116	61	a	;data
0117	6D	m	;data
0118	62	b	;data
0119	0A	(line feed)	;data
011A	13	(carriage return)	;data
011B	00	(0 used as end of string marker)	;data
011C	BE0301	MOV SI,103	;point to start of data at address 103
011F	8A14	MOV DL,[SI]	;get the data pointed to in DL processor register
0121	80FA00	CMP DL,00	;test to see if data is last in the string
0124	7407	JZ 012D	;if so, jump to last instruction in program
0126	B402	MOV AH,02	;put 2 into AH register, required for DOS function 2 call next
0128	CD21	INT 21	;call DOS into 21 function 2 to write character to screen
012A	46	INC SI	;point to next character in data string at next address
012B	EBF2	JMP 011F	;go back to address 11F to start again
012D	CD20	INT 20	;terminate program and return to DOS CLI (the DOS prompt)

Note

- Data and instructions all occupy the same address space, so the string 'Mary had a little lamb' is stored next to the code used to process it.
- The program uses two calls to the operating system, one to terminate the program and one to write individual characters to the screen. This is common in computing, few if any programs 'do it all'; services offered by the operating system are used all the time. If this program were written to make no use of operating system calls, other things would have to be determined, e.g. the address in memory of the video hardware, the address of the last character written to the screen, the number of rows and columns available on the screen etc. Once this data was known, the program would have to keep track of them all and possibly do some calculation to determine if the string would fit on the screen etc. For this program, the system software does it all for us. The DOS system call will itself call a BIOS system call. The BIOS 'knows' about the detailed shape of each letter, if it has serifs etc., and how to convert this shape to the pattern of dots (pixels) to be displayed.
- There seem to be gaps in the addresses. This is not so, it is just that some instructions take up more than one address location. For instance, starting at address 011C there is the machine code instruction BE 03 01 which when unassembled, gives the mnemonic MOV SI, 103. This instruction takes up the addresses 011C, 011D and 011E so the next instruction starts at address 011F. Some instructions only occupy one byte, for instance at address 012A the instruction to add 1 to the SI register has the machine code 46 only.

Enrichment material

Logic and logic gates

The core of a digital computer is logic.

Logic is a branch of mathematics that revolves around the idea of a proposition. A proposition is a statement that is either true or false, it has no other possible values.

The proposition 'you are running' may well be not true as you read this page but as a proposition, it has only the possibility of being true or false. The argument that you are perhaps sitting down has no value, you are either running or not, the proposition 'you are running' is either true or false. In computers, propositions are translated into 'the circuit is on' or perhaps 'the circuit is at 5 volts', a situation that is easy to build using logic 'gates', circuits that have the property of having only one of two possible states. There is a shorthand for propositions, the use of letters A, B, C etc. For instance, proposition A may be 'you are running' and proposition B may be 'it is not raining now'. In this case, B = 0 means it is raining because the proposition is false.

It is common to use a '1' for true and '0' for false. (It is becoming common for electrical power switches to be marked 1 for on and 0 for off.)

Logical states can be combined using gates, or dedicated circuits. A circuit that tests if two logical inputs are both 'on' or 'true' or '1' (all the same value!) is called an AND gate and will produce an output of 1 only if both the inputs have the value 1, otherwise the circuit will produce a value of 0. This can be summarized on a truth table like this:

Input A	*Input B*	*Output*
0	0	0
0	1	0
1	0	0
1	1	1

A physical circuit that behaves this way is called an AND gate. Such gates can be made in silicon from simpler components such as transistors.

The common logic gates have two inputs and the most common have names, i.e. AND, OR, NAND, NOR, XOR etc. and an even simpler one that has one input and one output, the NOT gate (often known as an inverter). The truth tables for these are below.

NOT

Input	*Output*
0	1
1	0

Inputs		*Outputs*				
A	B	AND	OR	NOR	NAND	XOR
0	0	0	0	1	1	0
0	1	0	1	0	1	1
1	0	0	1	0	1	1
1	1	1	1	0	0	0

NAND means 'Not AND' and you can see from the table that whenever the AND function has the output 1, the NAND function has the output 0 and vice versa. NOR is similar, it has the opposite value to the OR function because it means 'Not OR'. The XOR function means Exclusive OR, the output is similar to the OR function except when both inputs = 1.

Circuits can be built using logic gates and to draw these circuits, symbols are used. Unfortunately there are many 'standard' symbols used, but the ones used in Figure 1.1 are at least in common use.

Logic gates are combined to make larger and more complex circuits. A simple example is given in Figure 1.2.

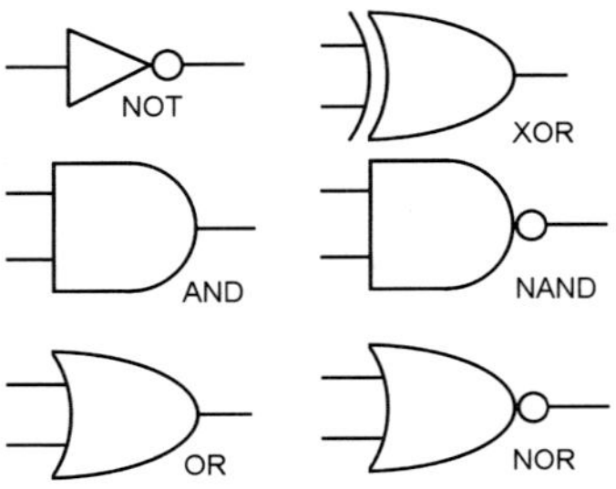

Figure 1.1

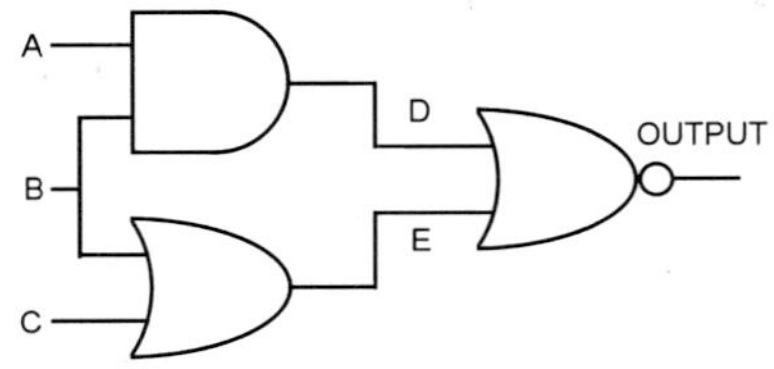

Figure 1.2

The output from this circuit can be shown on a truth table.

A	*B*	*C*	*D* = *A AND B*	*E* = *B OR C*	*OUTPUT* = *D NOR E*
0	0	0	0	0	1
0	0	1	0	1	0
0	1	0	0	1	0
0	1	1	0	1	0
1	0	0	0	0	1
1	0	1	0	1	0
1	1	0	1	1	0
1	1	1	1	1	0

This means the output will only be a 1 if

A = 0 and B = 0 and C = 0

or

A = 1 and B = 0 and C = 0

The circuit has three. Since $2^3 = 8$, there are eight different combinations of 1s and 0s on the three inputs. That is why there are eight lines in the truth table.

Arithmetic with circuits

An addition in decimal is 1 + 1 = 2 but written in binary is 1 + 1 = 10. If we set out this in columns we get:

	1
+	1
1	0

where the 1 on the left is carried over to the next column. This is the notation normally used for addition etc.

If we were to write all the possible additions of two binary digits, we would get:

	1
+	1
1	0

	1
+	0
0	1

	0
+	1
0	1

	0
+	0
0	0

These can be summarized on a truth table like this:

Numbers to be added		*Outputs*	
A	*B*	*Sum*	*Carry*
0	0	0	0
0	1	1	0
1	0	1	0
1	1	0	1

(As we are using binary numbers, they can be treated as logical propositions as they can only have values of 1 or 0.)

You should be able to see that the Sum output has the same truth table as the XOR function and the Carry output has the same truth table as the AND function. This means that we can draw a circuit that will add two binary digits and output the result, i.e. the sum and carry. The resulting circuit is called a half adder (see Figure 1.3).

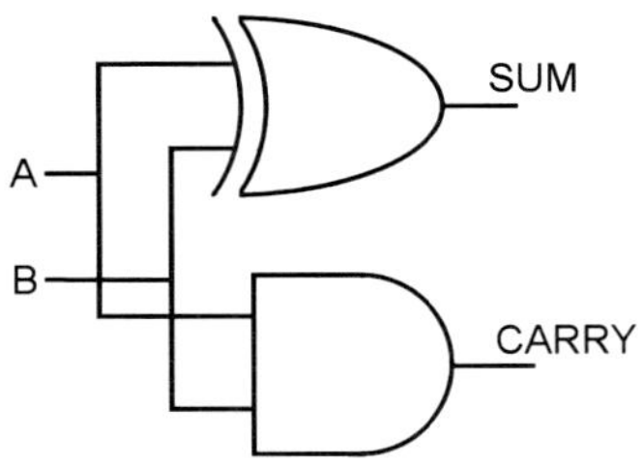

Figure 1.3 *Half adder*

This circuit is fine if all we need to add is just two binary digits but if we need to add say 2 bytes together, we need a circuit that will cope with a carry from the previous column. Consider the addition of 01 and 11:

1	1
0	1
Carry 1	
	0

The sum in the right-hand column is 1 + 1 = 0 but we will need to carry 1 over to the next column. If we want a circuit that will add the next column, it will require three inputs, i.e. to add the 1 and 0 and the 1 carried over from the previous column. This can be done by using two half adders joined together as shown in Figure 1.4. The result is called a full adder.

We can now use seven full adders and one half adder to add to 8 bit bytes to give an 8-bit result with a carry. In Figure 1.5, each full or half adder is shown as a square symbol.

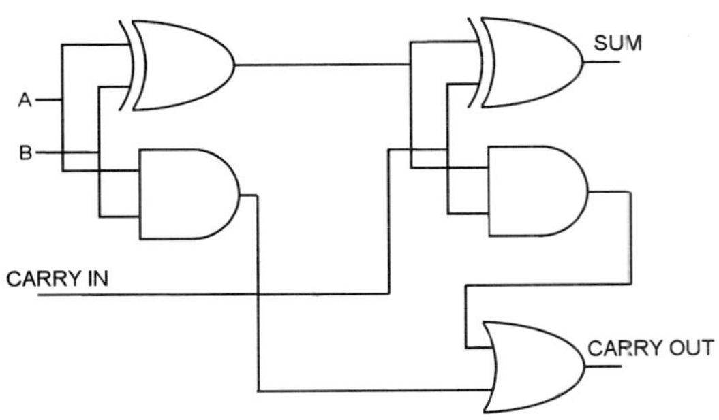

Figure 1.4

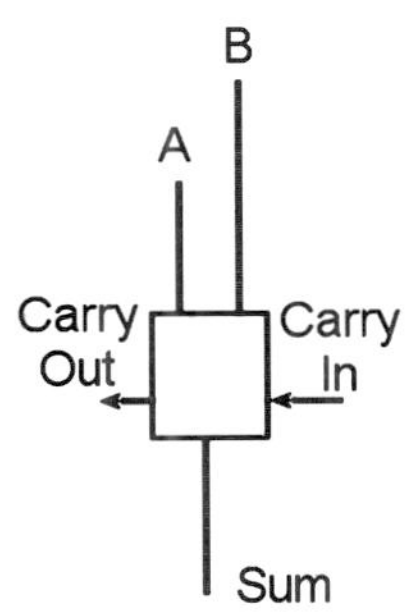

Figure 1.5

These are connected as shown in Figure 1.6.

If we supply the values 147 and 235 as binary values 10010011 and 11101001 we should get the result 382. Eight bits will not hold the value 382 so the result will be 256 (represented as the carry bit) and 126 as the binary pattern 01111110. The carry out from each addition is connected to the carry in of the next adder. This is shown in Figure 1.7.

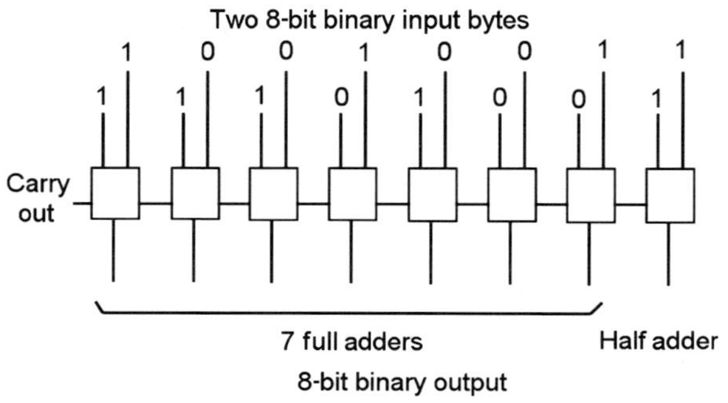

Figure 1.6

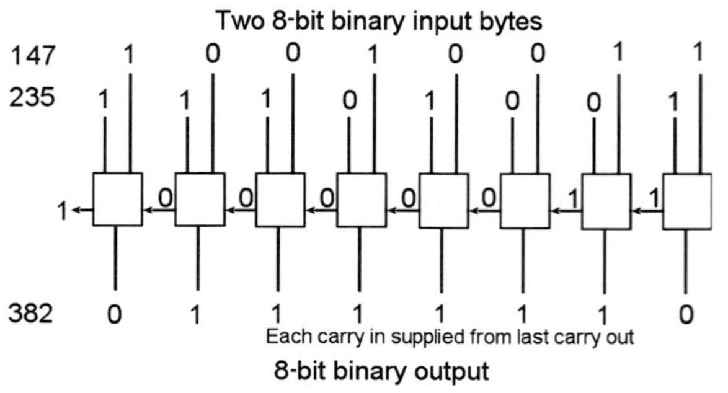

Figure 1.7

Address decoder

An 'address' in memory is simply a way of thinking about how memory chips are connected. If a RAM chip has 14 address lines we could place the value 10110100110110 on these lines. If the chip is set to 'read', the data that appears on the data bus is said to be 'at' address 10110100110110. The binary value 10110100110110 is 11 574 in decimal so when 10110100110110 is applied to the chip we can think about the address 11 574.

As $2^{14} = 16\,384$ in decimal, the chip can store 16 384 values because that is the number of different addresses that is possible using 14-bit binary. If we need more memory than 16 384 bytes then we could use, say, four chips and connect them with two more 'address' lines. This would give an address bus of 16 lines so a total addressable memory of $2^{16} = 65\,536$ or 64 kb of memory. The circuit in Figure 1.8 shows this arrangement.

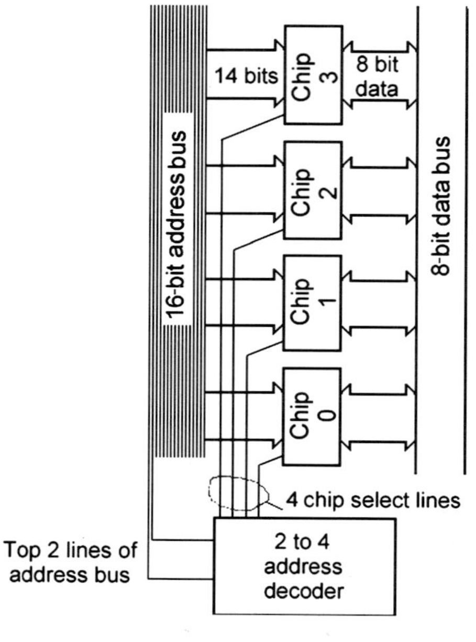

Figure 1.8

The additional two lines are not connected to the chips as they only have 14 lines each; instead they are connected to a two to four address decoder and the four output lines from this circuit are connected to the 'chip enable' lines on the RAM chips. This has the effect of 'turning the chip on' but the decoder is so arranged that only one chip is enabled at any one time.

The truth table for the decoder is simple to work out and is shown below.

Inputs		*Outputs*			
A	B	Line 3 A AND B	Line 2 A AND NOT(B)	Line 1 NOT(A) AND B	Line 0 NOT(A) AND NOT(B)
0	0	0	0	0	1
0	1	0	0	1	0
1	0	0	1	0	0
1	1	1	0	0	0

The behaviour is that with any value applied to inputs A and B, only one line can be on at once.

The circuit for the decoder is easy to work out. Line 3 simply requires a single AND gate. The other lines are connected to AND and NOT gates as in Figure 1.9.

$\bar{A}$ is the symbol for NOT (A)

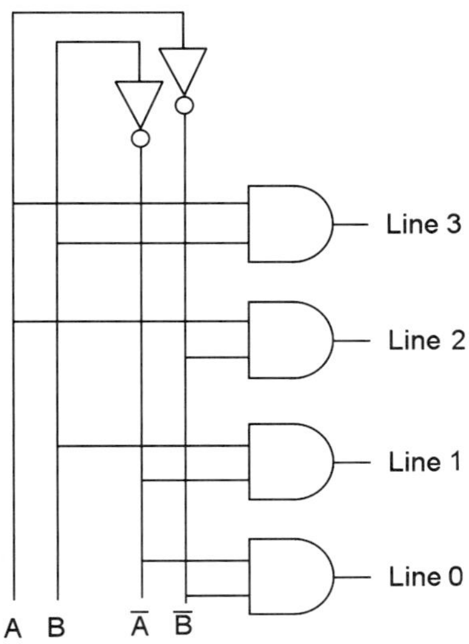

Figure 1.9

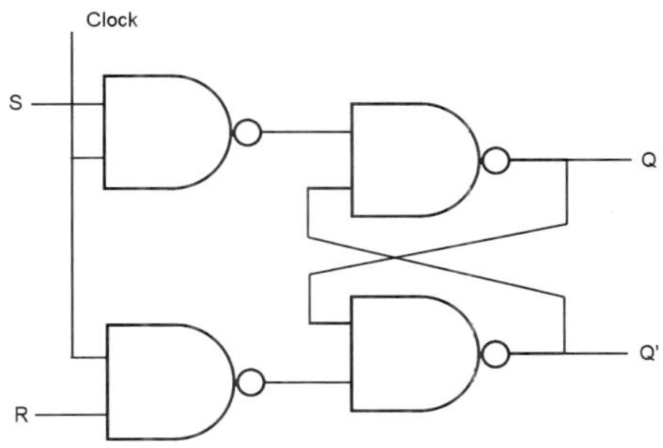

Figure 1.10 *Clocked RS flip-flop*

Figure 1.11 *Clock signal*

Circuits with memory: flip-flops

Circuits such as these show an output almost immediately an input is applied; remember that although circuits are fast, nothing happens instantaneously. When the inputs are changed, the output changes, i.e. they have no memory. If more complex circuits are designed where the outputs feed back into the input side, a degree of memory can be achieved. The circuit in Figure 1.10 is called a flip-flop, the output will remain the same until requested to change.

The clock of the RS flip-flop has nothing to do with the gadget on the wall that tells you when it is lunch time! In logic circuits, a clock is simply a series of 1s and 0s otherwise known as a square wave (see Figure 1.11).

When the clock = 0, the output of the left-hand gates both = 1 (see the truth table for a NAND gate). This means the circuit will remain in whatever state it is currently in regardless of the logic on lines S and R. When the clock = 1, whatever logic levels are applied to S and R can reach the righ-hand gates. If clock = 1, S = 1 and R = 0 the output Q will be Set to 1. If clock = 1, S = 0 and R = 1, the output Q is Reset to 0. You can think of this as an RS or Reset–Set flip-flop. If clock = 1 and S = 0 and R = 0 nothing changes. The other state where clock = 1, S = 1 and R = 1 is not allowed as the output will be indeterminate.

Since S = 1 and R = 1 are not allowed and S = 0 and R = 0 has no effect, a simple modification of the RS flip-flop can be made to eliminate these states. An inverter or NOT gate is inserted between S and R such that when S = 1, R must = 0 and when S = 0, R must = 1. This is known as a D-type flip-flop, its behaviour is very simple, if clock = 1 the circuit 'remembers' whatever logic state is applied to D. If clock = 0, the output remains at what it was, i.e. it is a simple 1-bit memory (see Figure 1.12).

This circuit can be used to store a single binary digit. If eight of these are arranged with a common clock signal, it can be used to store a whole byte of information (see Figure 1.13).

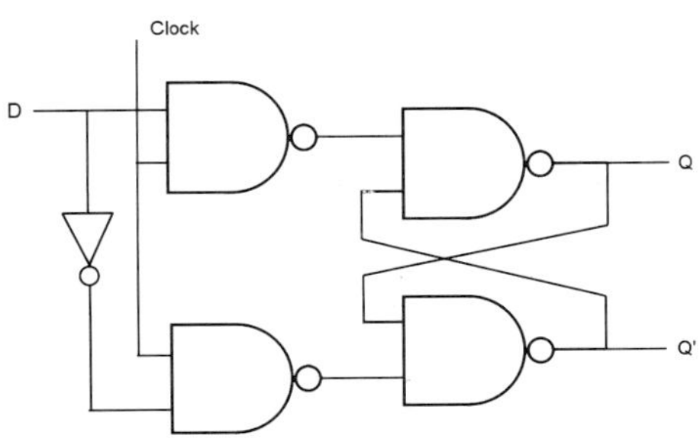

Figure 1.12 *D-type flip-flop*

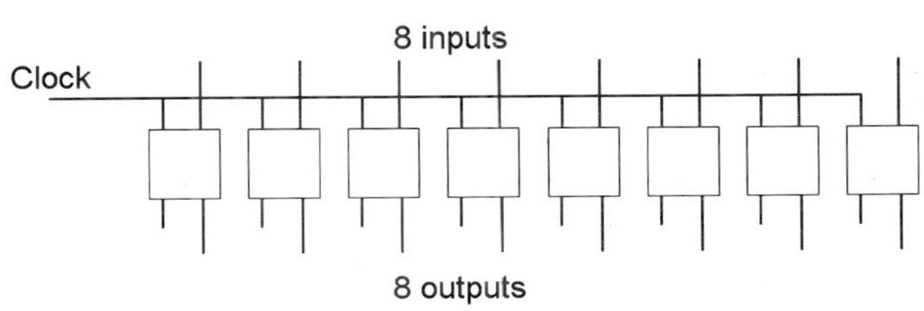

Figure 1.13 *Simple byte store using 8 D-type flip-flops*

1.4 Tutor's notes and resources

Internet search on display types

A set of URLs are shown here. They have been selected because the latest technical information is available in this fast developing area, as always with computing publications, staying current is a severe problem. The best way to gain the latest information is often directly from the manufacturers or research institute. The links below are mainly from these organizations.

There has been a large increase in the use of LCD screens on desktop machines; many people prefer the image quality whilst benefiting from the saving in desk space. Even if you do not see them in colleges and universities, if a close watch is made of television reports covering the finance institutions and other heavy users of computers, such flat panel displays are seen to be quite common.

Organization	*URL*
Arun Display Technologies	Glossary of display device terms http://www.arundisplay.co.uk/glossary/index.htm
ePanorama.net	Video display technology page http://www.epanorama.net/videodisplay.html
zdnet (Ziff Davis)	Non-LCD display technology http://www.zdnet.co.uk/pcmag/supp/1998/mobile/23.html
Display Technology Alliance	Latest information on display technologies http://195.212.30.14/
IBM research	Latest information on display technologies from IBM Research http://www.research.ibm.com/cross_disciplines/display_tech.shtml
Hitachi	Introduction to Monitor & Flat Panel Display Technology from Hitachi http://www.hitachidisplays.com/how_monitors/
PC Technology guide	PC Technology guide to displays http://www.pctechguide.com/07panels.htm
Sharp	The principles behind LCD technology from Sharp http://sharp-world.com/sc/library/lcd_e/index_2e.htm
PCguide.com	PC Guide: Monitors http://www.pcguide.com/ref/crt/index-c.html
Rensselaer Polytechnic Institute	Display technology, CRT against LCD http://nina.ecse.rpi.edu/tft/research_summary/sld007.htm

Practical task: image quality

How good is a photographic image on a PC?

There are several ways to answer this. The first is to consider the PC as the end point in a complete imaging system starting with some form of camera and ending with a displayed image. This approach will involve some complex mathematics that will be used to demonstrate some tricky ideas; these include modulation transfer functions, image processing algorithms and human perception. To pursue this route it is suggested that some study is made of http://www.users.qwest.net/~rnclark/scandetail.htm. In this, Roger Clark shows the results of some detailed experiments and relates them to the relevant theory. A little of this theory is presented below.

The second way is simply to conduct some simple tests and ask humans to make subjective judgements about image quality. This approach is not rigorous but at least involves the real customer of PC images, the viewer. Typical image properties to consider are:

- Resolution
- Contrast

Image resolution

A typical PC shows images at a resolution of about 70–100 dpi or dots per inch. Images that have finer detail will not look any better than the screen on which they are presented.

Let's check the screen resolution: measure the screen of your PC and find out the slot pitch (also called the dot pitch) of the screen. If you do not have the technical specification of the monitor, search the Internet using the model number and make. Say you were using a 15" monitor, this will typically have an 11" visible width. If the slot pitch is a typical 0.28 mm this equates to (1/0.28 * 25.4) or about 91 slots per inch. If the screen resolution is set to 1024 * 768 then you have 1024 pixels spread over the 11" so that will give 1024/11 = 93 pixels per inch. This result seems to match the 70–100 figure above but remember that whatever the screen resolution set, you can never see more pixels than there are slots on the screen.

Image contrast
This depends on the original image, the monitor settings and the light levels around the monitor. Assuming no light is glaring from the screen and a 'good' image is being displayed, adjust the PC brightness and contrast to maximize the image quality. Now consider what you are seeing. A photographic image with good contrast often looks sharper than a low contrast image that contains much detail. In this sense, sharp means 'contains fine detail'.

Modulation transfer function or MTF
A little theory may help here: consider an image of a set of black solid objects against a white background, say a set of black painted window bars with a white screen behind them. The window bars have a sharp edge. If we draw a graph of the light intensity coming from the image, we should get something like graph 1 (see Figure 1.14), i.e. sudden changes from white to black due to the edges of each bar. In fact we would get something more like graph 2 (see Figure 1.15), there would not be a very sharp change from white to black owing to the properties of the imaging system. The change from white to black and back again is the modulation of the light coming from the image. The accuracy with which this modulated signal is transferred over an imaging system is called the 'Modulation Transfer Function' or mtf of the system. If there were no loss of quality (impossible), there would be an mtf of 100%, i.e. the modulation of the original is the same as the modulation of the viewed image.

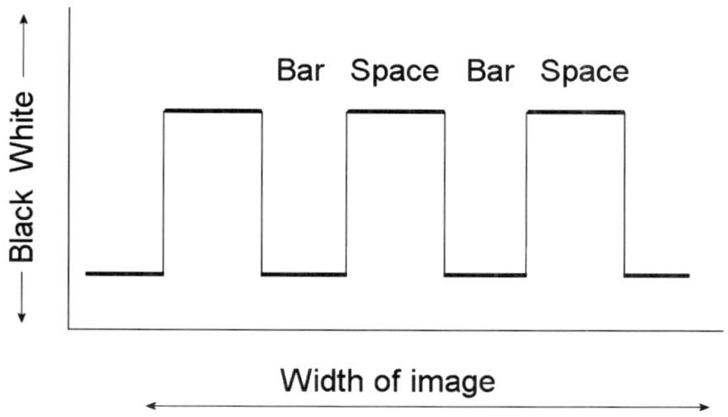

Figure 1.14

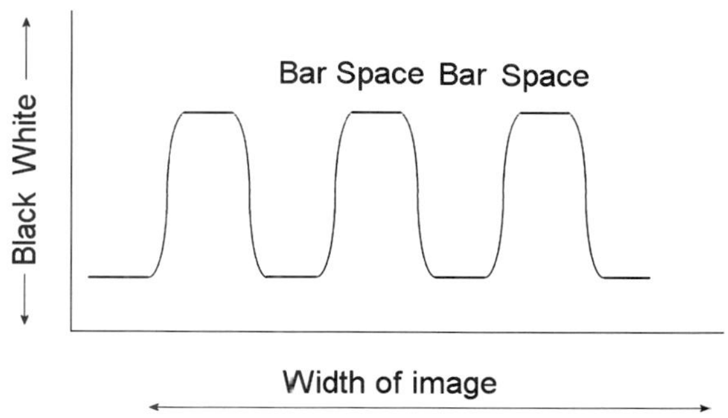

Figure 1.15

A square wave can be made by adding an infinite number of sine waves of varying amplitude, wavelength and phase. For all practical purposes, the square wave in graph 1 can be made up of 8 or 10 sine waves, each with shorter wavelengths than the previous one. In this case the 'wavelengths' are spatial, not the wavelength of the illumination. You can consider that an imaging system will transit or transfer different spatial wavelengths with different degrees of success so some systems will transmit the short ones well, some will transmit the long ones well. Unfortunately in technology, you can never get things to do everything at once. A system with an mtf of near 100% at one spatial wavelength will not give that performance at the other end of the scale. Generally you will get imaging systems that transfer either good contrast or good detail but not both together. Good detail implies a high mtf at short wavelengths. Many camera and film manufacturers will cheat in this process, giving higher contrast images that are not as sharp as can be achieved but they look sharp because human visual perception will mistake contrast for resolution. Military intelligence or surveillance photographs that must contain maximum detail will often look quite 'flat', i.e. have low contrast. The wave in graph 2 can be thought of as a square wave with the shorter spatial wavelengths missing. Adding more sine waves of shorter wavelengths would 'sharpen' the corners of the square wave.

Practical scanning task
Use a reasonable quality 35 mm camera to take a photograph of a well-lit daytime scene that contains much detail and have it printed at a standard photographic outlet at 6" by 4" on glossy paper. If possible, use a digital camera to photograph the same scene at the same time. Such a picture is shown in monochrome in Figure 1.16 but the coloured version can be seen at www.bh.com/manuals/0750654244.

Scan the photograph at different resolution settings and compare the results when displayed on the PC screen. On most PCs, it will not be practical to scan the entire image, simply select one area. If you scan the entire image, you will get uncompressed file sizes as set out in this table. Remember that trucolor uses 3 bytes per pixel to give 224 = 16.7 million colours.

Resolution in dpi	*No. of pixels*	*No. of tricolour bytes*	*Mbytes*
100	240 000	720 000	1
200	960 000	2 880 000	3
300	2 160 000	6 480 000	6
400	3 840 000	11 520 000	11
600	8 640 000	25 920 000	25
1200	34 560 000	103 680 000	99
4800	552 960 000	1 658 880 000	1582

File sizes for uncompressed 6" by 4" scanned images.

Example scans

The whole image in Figure 1.16 was scanned with the software set at 100 dpi. Looking at the coloured version from the Internet rather than the monochrome ones here, does it look good quality to you in terms of resolution and contrast?

Figure 1.16

The gravestone that appears closest was selected as the test scan area at higher resolutions. Using a magnifying glass on the original photograph, it is easy to read the number 34A down the left-hand side of the stone. Is this visible in the scanned images? At 200 dpi it is just a blur, at 400 dpi you can persuade yourself that you can read it but it is not until 1200 dpi that it comes closer to what it looks like on the original. For this reason, it is important that you carry out your own experiments so you have the original to compare with the scanned images. Compare your results with the images presented on Roger Clark's site at http://www.users.qwest.net/~rnclark/scandetail.htm.

Now answer the questions

What resolution is required of images to be displayed on a PC screen?
What resolution is required for printed digital photographs?
Is there any benefit to be gained from having a high-resolution camera?

The 'closest' gravestone is shown here in two ways. One with the result scaled to demonstrate the difference in image resolution (see Figure 1.17) and the other to demonstrate the fact that PCs will display images pixel for pixel so the 200 dpi scan will look much smaller than the 1200 dpi one as it contains fewer pixels (see Figure 1.18).

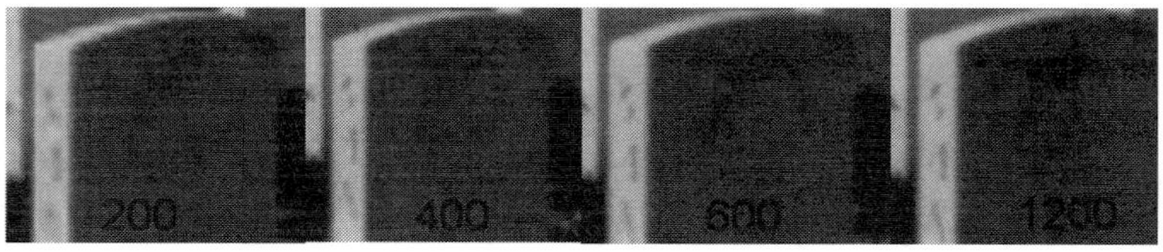

Figure 1.17

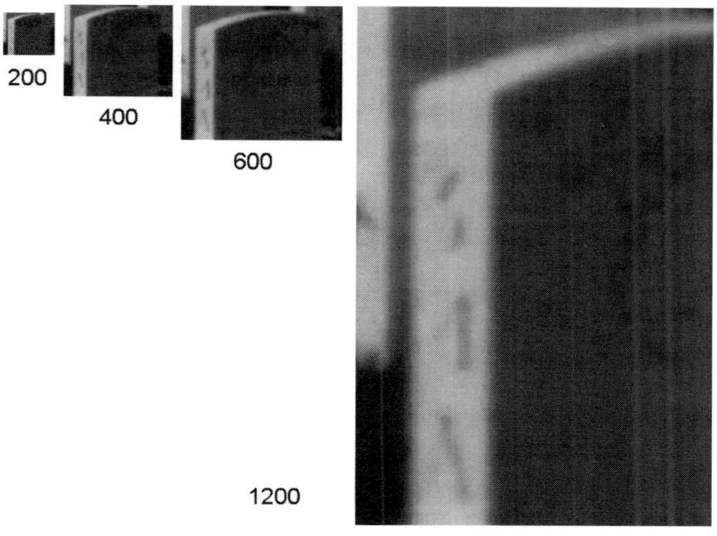

Figure 1.18

Technical image details

Camera Nikon F601 with Sigma 24-80 zoom lens, Fuji 200 print film, printed on 6" by 4" glossy paper. Scanned using an Umax Ultra 600S scanner set at various resolutions.

The image is of Tyne Cot cemetery in Belgium, it contains 11 871 graves and commemorates 34 888 more men who died in the Ypres Salient from 16 August 1917 to the end of the Great War of 1914–1918. It is one of the most poignant places on earth.

1.5 Practical task

PC speed

For this practical task you will need to obtain and install the benchmark software called WinBench from Ziff Davis at http://www.zdnet.com/etestinglabs/ and follow the benchmark link. You must only use the software under the conditions outlined in their licence agreement. (WinBench® is a registered trademark and WinMark is a trademark of Ziff Davis Publishing Holdings Inc., an affiliate of eTesting Labs Inc., in the US and other countries.)

In the HNC computing book, much was made of the fact that CPU clock speed is a poor indicator of PC performance if used on its own. This practical task will demonstrate this idea in numbers.

Practice results analysis

Once you have the WinBench software, open the Benchmark Results Viewer, choose the File menu option and then choose 'Sample Winbench.ztd'. This is a file of benchmark results from ZDnet's research office. Once opened, you should see a long list of benchmark results for several different computers. Again using the File menu option, choose 'Create Excel Spreadsheet' and you will see the same results presented in Excel.

In Excel, after having inserted a new worksheet, highlight the rows labelled:

- WinBench 99/CPUmark 99, WinBench 99/Business Disk
- WinMark 99 (Thousand Bytes/Sec)
- System Info/CPU Clock Speed

Copy them using edit->copy (or CTRL C), swap to the new worksheet then paste them into your new worksheet using edit->paste (or using CTRL V).

The data will have several columns that contain superscripted references to notes etc. You should select and delete these columns. If you then reorder the rows, you should end up with something like the data below.

System Info/CPU Clock Speed	266	150	233	400	200	400	333	400	266	233	117
WinBench 99/CPUmark 99	20.1	14.1	6.93	30.4	18.3	30.8	25.4	31.6	17.8	13.1	9.14
WinBench 99/Business Disk	2280	1330	1230	2290	2110	5340	3300	2920	2090	1720	1360
WinMark 99 (Thousand Bytes/Sec)											

It is now simple to make graphs (Excel insists on calling them charts) to display the results. What to do:

- Highlight the rows CPU Clock Speed and Business Disk WinMark 99 (you can select non-adjacent rows by holding down CTRL when you click the mouse)
- Choose the chart wizard
- Choose XY Scatter as the chart type

With a little format adjustment, you should get a graph like the one shown in Figure 1.19.

Still in Excel, if you right click on one of the diamond symbols on the chart, Excel will offer the menu shown in Figure 1.20:

When you choose 'add trendline', choose the linear option. You should get the result shown in Figure 1.21.

From these results, you will see that for the 400 MHz CPU clock speed machines, the benchmark figures vary considerably. If CPU clock speed were a predictor of performance, you would get a very close fit of data to the linear trendline.

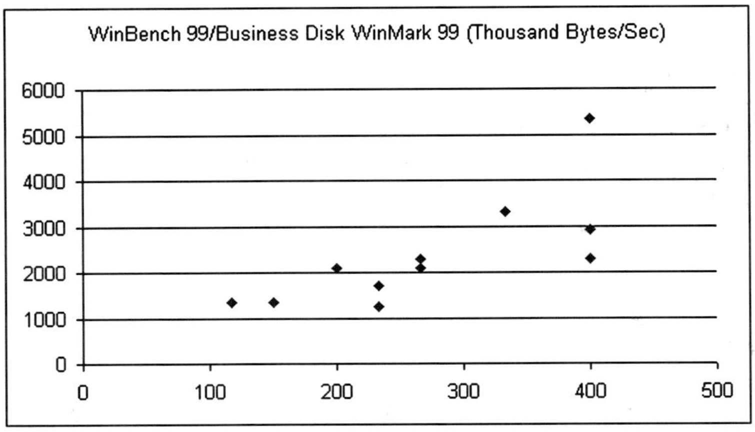

Figure 1.19

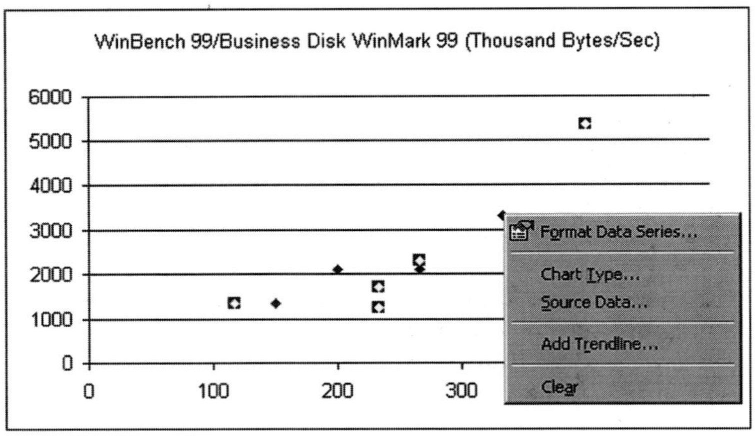

Figure 1.20

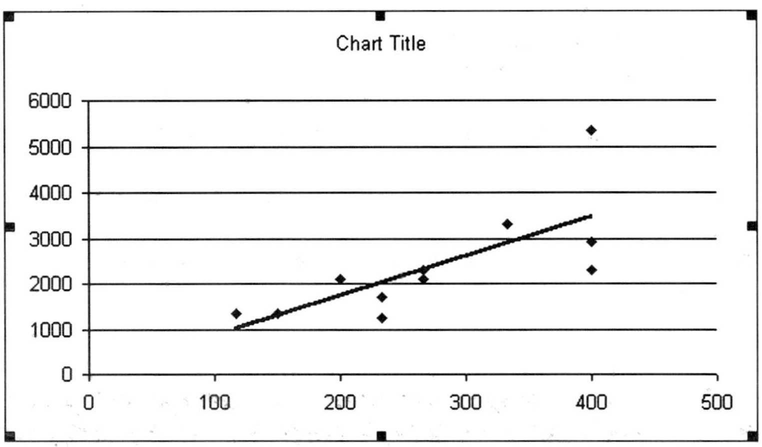

Figure 1.21

If you read the help file material that comes with the WinBench software, you will see that Ziff Davis insists that any quoted benchmark is accompanied by precise details of the machine being tested. This is recognition that simple indicators such as CPU speed are indeed unreliable.

What you should do next

Install and run the benchmarking software on as many different machines as possible and save the results. In the Benchmark Results Viewer, you can merge your results with those of the sample data. The instructions on how to do this are quite clear in the Benchmark Results Viewer helpfile under merge.

Questions to be answered

1. It is often said that fitting more memory to a PC makes it run faster. Is this true or is it only true about the speed that Windows runs? To find out, run the benchmark software on the same machine but with different amounts of RAM fitted and plot the results on a graph.
2. Does a machine fitted with an SCSI drive offer better performance than one fitted with an IDE disc drive?
3. Does fitting a graphics card with large amounts of RAM improve performance?

1.6 Assignment: PC specification

Having completed unit 1 of the HNC computing book, students should be confident that they can specify machines to suit a variety of end users. They should also be able to communicate effectively with IT hardware specialists when dealing with the finer detail of machine specification, installation and commissioning. This assignment is intended to build on the confidence.

The assignment

You should specify computing equipment to satisfy the needs of the user set out below. In your recommendations, you should supply such calculations and other evidence that the equipment you specify meets the needs of the user. Cost is not always the highest priority, sometimes it will be performance, capacity or reliability but to overspecify is easy if you are not paying the bill. As the 'consultant' for this user, you must spend their money wisely.

The user

Suckit and Sea are a marine research organization that specializes in the study of wrecks on the sea bed. Their divers and other technical staff research actual wrecks whilst their London-based office staff research historical evidence to aid the location of previously unknown wrecks. They make their profit in a variety of ways that include marine salvage, the making of television documentaries and guided tours of famous wreck sites. Unfortunately business has been slow recently so money is tight. Following a serious fire that destroyed their offices, their five full-time historical research staff based in London require equipment that will scan old documents borrowed on short-term loan. These handwritten texts with images are then stored in an indexed and searchable database. As many of the scanned images are not suitable for Optical Character Recognition (OCR) treatment, staff read any text on the scanned versions of the documents and key that into their machines, images are processed to remove as much extraneous material as possible using some very sophisticated but CPU intensive image processing software. Further work is then carried out to add wreck data to modern maps.

The equipment must be able to scan documents at an adequate resolution and to store them such that they are available across the company Intranet along with the modern map data.

An initial meeting yielded the following approximate figures:

- Five staff working 35 hours/week allowing for a minimum of 20 and a maximum of 100 documents processed each week per person.
- A few of the documents are 1 m^2, many are at least 400 mm by 275 mm whilst most are the old foolscap size of 13" by 8" (330 mm by 203 mm).
- The estimated total number of documents that are to be processed following the fire is 8000.

Considerations

Scanners

It would probably not be economical to purchase a scanner capable of handling 1 m^2 documents as there are likely to be only a few of these (maps), this work should be subcontracted to a specialist scanning company.

The remaining documents are at or below A3 size so A3 scanners should be adequate. Their resolution need be no better than to resolve the fine ink-strokes of hand drawn maps. Experiments are best to determine this figure but a value of 300 dpi (12 dots/mm) has been estimated as being sufficient.

Amount of data

Eight thousand documents are to be stored. If the assumptions below are valid, there will be approximately 95 Gbytes of stored data. If a further 5 Gbytes of other data and software are allowed, storage on the file server must be at least 100 Gbytes allocated to the project.

40% of the scanned images are 400 mm by 275 mm
50% old foolscap size of 13" by 8" (330 mm by 203 mm)
10% 1 m^2

Number of files	*Width*	*Height*	*per image*	*Total all images*	*With 50% image compression*	*Mbytes*	*Gbytes*
3200	400	275	15 840 000	50 688 000 000	25 344 000 000	24 170	24
4000	330	203	9 646 560	38 586 240 000	19 293 120 000	18 399	18
800	1000	1000	144 000 000	115 200 000 000	57 600 000 000	54 932	54
				Totals			
				204 474 240 000	102 237 120 000	97 501	95

Image sizes using 12 dots per mm (300 dpi) scans.

Network

The choice of peer to peer or fileserver would favour a fileserver approach as a single store can be used for the large amount of data and standard PCs used to access that data. Data transmission rates over the network must be sufficient to transfer the largest files efficiently. The 1 m^2 map yields files of 69 Mbytes with 50% compression. As 69 Mbytes is approximately 700 Mbits, a 100 Mbit/sec connection would give a transfer time of 7 seconds for such a file if the network was doing nothing else and the entire bandwidth was achievable. This is unlikely so at least 15 seconds would be required to move such a large file. The extra cost of running a faster connection should be considered but the relatively low number of large files may allow a 100 Mbit/sec connection. As this speed is becoming the 'standard' in offices, it should be a low cost solution.

Computers

At least five machines are required with sufficient performance to run the scanning software, run the image processing software and store temporary images before transmission for storage on the fileserver. Image processing can take up much CPU time so a very fast CPU and chipset should be specified. This requirement may be able to be relaxed if some of the image processing could be run automatically as a batch job overnight whilst unattended. Machines with 1.7 MHz CPUs are becoming available but the section on benchmarking and elsewhere should convince anyone that relying on CPU speed alone is not a good predictor of speed. If you look at the graph in Figure 1.22, nor is price. From one manufacturer, the costs of machines with different CPU speeds are plotted. They do not take into account the different disc drives etc. fitted but do show there is considerable scope for saving if a small reduction is allowed in CPU speed. When careful analysis of published benchmarking data is carried out, a good performance can be obtained without paying the premium for the fastest machines on the market. From just the data below, machines with a 1.2 GHz CPU speed seem to be about the average price of £1000 (without taking account of peripherals).

Printers

If the larger maps are to be printed at low cost, the only real alternative on the market are the A1 size six colour inkjet printers. It may be that very little printing is required as the data is viewable on screen. Some prints may be required for discussions at meetings etc. A dedicated bureau would probably meet the demand for larger prints. There are many A3 colour inkjet printers now available for low cost, one of these may be sufficient to produce a low number of smaller copies.

Archiving

A recordable CD-R drive will allow approximately 650 Mbytes of data per CD, each disc costing less than £1.

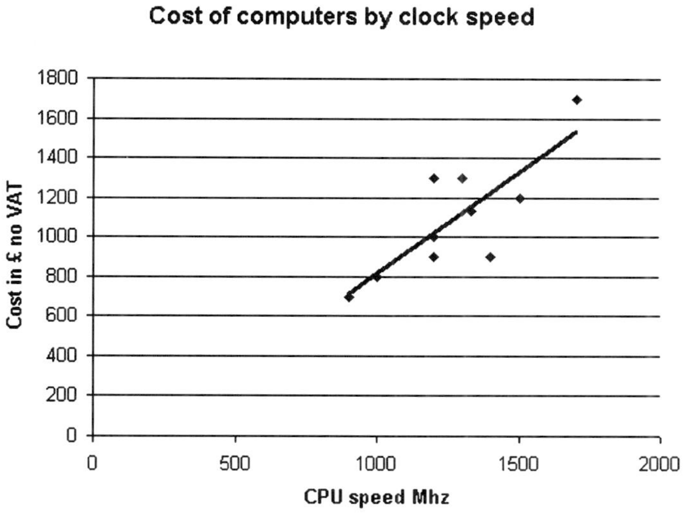

Figure 1.22 *Graph of desktop computers against CPU speed*

1.7 Practical DOS

MS-DOS, the Microsoft Disc Operating System

When running Windows 95/98, open an MS-DOS window with Start>Programs>MS-DOS prompt.

You will have to press the ENTER key at the end of every DOS command line. None of the commands in DOS are case sensitive, capitals or lower case will work just the same.

You should now have a prompt on the screen that looks something like:

C:\WINDOWS>

This prompt is easily changed, as will be shown later.

The first command most people use is:

dir

which shows the files or directories on the disc. A directory is like a drawer in a filing cabinet, a location in which files may be logically grouped. DOS uses a 'tree' structure for its directories.

The command dir may produce something that looks like this (the files will be different on each machine):

```
Volume in drive C has no label
 Volume Serial Number is 3AF0-1303
 Directory of C:\WINDOWS

.              <DIR>             03/11/00  10:18 .
..             <DIR>             03/11/00  10:18 ..
SYSTEM         <DIR>             03/11/00  10:18 SYSTEM
WINSOCK   DLL          21,504    03/11/00  10:23 WINSOCK.DLL
WIN       INI           9,500    24/05/01   9:51 WIN.INI
HWINFO    EXE         110,592    23/04/99  22:22 HWINFO.EXE
NETDET    INI           7,885    23/04/99  22:22 NETDET.INI
PIDGEN    DLL          27,616    03/11/00  10:23 PIDGEN.DLL
PSETUP    BMP          13,054    29/11/00  14:22 PSETUP.BMP
HELP           <DIR>             03/11/00  10:23 HELP
LICENSE   TXT          32,424    23/04/99  22:22 LICENSE.TXT
SUPPORT   TXT             845    23/04/99  22:22 SUPPORT.TXT
.         .       .        .
(some filenames deleted to save space)
.         .       .        .
```

```
WINFILE     INI              0     21/05/01  14:42  winfile.ini
JUNK        TXT              0     24/05/01  15:08  junk.txt
ZDBUI       INI              2     01/06/97  20:33  zdbui.ini
WB99        INI          1,164     22/05/01  14:05  wb99.ini
ZDBUI32     INI             43     22/05/01  14:05  zdbui32.ini
            272  file(s)  108,383,679  bytes
            29  dir(s)       2,236.43  MB  free
```

Each of the lines in this example shows a directory. Yours may look somewhat different. You can see what is inside a directory such as windows with the command:

dir \system

but you may not be able to read that fast! Sometimes, the listing of files in a directory is too long to fit on the screen and will 'scroll off' the top of the screen. In this case you can alter the action of the dir command with a switch as in the following example command:

dir \system /p

/p is the switch to say page the directory output. Another switch is /w which says show a wide directory listing, e.g.
dir \system /w

For very long lists of files you can combine them with a command like this

dir \system /w /p

Notice the direction of the slash characters \ or / in the examples. You cannot use them the other way around. To say this command, the \ character is called a 'slash' and the / character is called a 'switch'. Much confusion exists around the names of these characters, some people use the term 'back slash' for the \ character. As long as you realize that \ is used for directory or pathnames and that / is used to change the result of commands you should be OK. Other operating systems and the Internet use / instead of \ so you must be careful!

Wildcards

The command:

dir \windows*.exe

should produce a list of all files in the windows directory that end in .exe, the * character is a wildcard which will replace any group of characters.

```
Volume  in  drive  C  has  no  label
 Volume  Serial  Number  is  3AF0-1303
 Directory  of  C:\WINDOWS

HWINFO      EXE        110,592     23/04/99  22:22  HWINFO.EXE
MPLAYER     EXE        159,744     23/04/99  22:22  MPLAYER.EXE
CLSPACK     EXE         49,424     07/04/00   9:34  CLSPACK.EXE
DOSREP      EXE         89,147     23/04/99  22:22  DOSREP.EXE
DRWATSON    EXE        139,264     23/04/99  22:22  DRWATSON.EXE
EXPLORER    EXE        180,224     23/04/99  22:22  EXPLORER.EXE
.           .          .          .
(some  filenames  deleted  to  save  space)
.           .          .          .
WSCRIPT     EXE         90,162     03/11/00  12:32  wscript.exe
ISUNINST    EXE        306,688     29/10/98  16:45  IsUninst.exe
OPENMAIL    EXE        131,584     12/09/97   0:00  OPENMAIL.EXE
CTREGRUN    EXE         41,984     11/10/99   1:01  CTREGRUN.EXE
OADIST      EXE        490,096     08/04/97   9:27  oadist.exe
```

```
ENSCFG32     EXE          421,888      23/09/99  14:05  ENSCFG32.EXE
ENSMIX32     EXE          230,400      29/09/99  16:15  ENSMIX32.EXE
STARTER      EXE           32,768      26/05/99  17:10  STARTER.EXE
ST5UNST      EXE           71,680      23/04/99  22:22  ST5UNST.EXE
UNINST~1     EXE           53,834      02/05/01  11:22  Uninstall.exe
REGCLE~1     EXE          770,560      02/05/01  11:22  RegCleanr.exe
             92 file(s)    12,281,472 bytes
             0 dir(s)       2,236.58 MB free
```

The command

dir system\n*

uses the wildcard to give a listing of all files starting with 'n' and with any extension in the system directory.

```
Volume in drive C has no label
 Volume Serial Number is 3AF0-1303
 Directory of C:\WINDOWS\SYSTEM

NDSWAN16     DLL            1,728      03/11/00  10:23  NDSWAN16.DLL
NDSWAN32     DLL           24,576      23/04/99  22:22  NDSWAN32.DLL
NETAPI       DLL          106,704      03/11/00  10:23  NETAPI.DLL
NETDI        DLL          317,872      03/11/00  10:23  NETDI.DLL
NETOS        DLL           27,680      03/11/00  10:23  NETOS.DLL
NDIS         VXD          166,029      23/04/99  22:22  NDIS.VXD
NDIS2SUP     VXD           23,744      23/04/99  22:22  NDIS2SUP.VXD
NDISWMI      SYS           16,480      23/04/99  22:22  NDISWMI.SYS
.            .        .         .
(some filenames deleted to save space)
.            .        .         .
NWGDI        DLL           40,464      22/04/98  15:33  NWGDI.DLL
NWIPXSPX     DLL           41,088      09/01/96  13:17  NWIPXSPX.DLL
NWLOCALE     DLL           43,760      07/10/97  11:12  NWLOCALE.DLL
NWNET        DLL          225,328      28/08/97   9:19  NWNET.DLL
NWSHELLX     DLL          172,032      19/11/99   9:37  NWSHELLX.DLL
NWSIPX32     DLL           25,088      19/03/98  13:36  NWSIPX32.DLL
NWSLOG       DLL           13,568      23/11/99  10:51  NWSLOG.DLL
NWSRVLOC     DLL            8,704      01/04/98  13:30  NWSRVLOC.DLL
NWAPP32      DLL          323,584      31/10/98  23:40  NWAPP32.DLL
NDPP95       DLL           61,440      23/11/99  16:03  NDPP95.DLL
NDPSPROP     DLL          118,784      08/12/99  12:23  NDPSPROP.DLL
             50 file(s)     5,048,072 bytes
             0 dir(s)       2,236.54 MB free
```

The command

dir system*.exe

should produce all the .exe files like this:

```
Volume in drive C has no label
 Volume Serial Number is 3AF0-1303
 Directory of C:\WINDOWS\SYSTEM

CFGWIZ32     EXE           65,536      23/04/99  22:22  CFGWIZ32.EXE
DPLAYSVR     EXE           29,968      09/09/99      7:00  DPLAYSVR.EXE
DDHELP       EXE           39,184      09/09/99      7:00  DDHELP.EXE
ICWSCRPT     EXE          151,040      16/11/00   8:39  icwscrpt.exe
ACTMOVIE     EXE           36,864      23/04/99  22:22  ACTMOVIE.EXE
ADDREG       EXE          32A,768      23/04/99  22:22  ADDREG.EXE
```

```
CLICONFG    EXE          37,136     23/04/99  22:22  CLICONFG.EXE
CMDL32      EXE          49,152     23/04/99  22:22  CMDL32.EXE
CMMGR32     EXE          12,288     23/04/99  22:22  CMMGR32.EXE
.           .       .        .
(some  filenames  deleted  to  save  space)
.           .       .        .
USER        EXE         549,760     19/04/00  13:02  USER.EXE
UNAXA       EXE          47,616     03/11/00  13:56  UNAXA.EXE
CONVDSN     EXE           7,680     11/07/97   0:00  CONVDSN.EXE
MAPISP32    EXE          10,000     26/03/98   0:00  MAPISP32.EXE
MAPISRVR    EXE          38,160     26/03/98   0:00  MAPISRVR.EXE
CNFNOT32    EXE         131,344     26/03/98   0:00  CNFNOT32.EXE
ATI2CWXX    EXE          25,088     13/07/99  14:46  ATI2CWXX.EXE
ATIIISXX    EXE          13,056     03/06/99  14:17  ATIIISXX.EXE
ATIIPRXX    EXE          94,208     29/06/99  16:57  ATIIPRXX.EXE
DPMW32      EXE          28,672     20/05/99   7:15  DPMW32.EXE
            87  file(s)   5,410,180  bytes
            0  dir(s)     2,236.53  MB  free
```

The DOS filing system

Imagine a room that contains a row of eight filing cabinets, each one of which has four drawers. If each cabinet were numbered 1–8 and each drawer were marked A, B, C or D, then a file labelled 'Bloggs' could be called:

R498\5\C\Bloggs

to denote room number 498, cabinet number 5 and drawer C, in which the file is stored. Under DOS, the file system works in the same way. A file may be called

a:\lotus\c152.wk1

which means that it exists on the A: drive in directory LOTUS and the filename is C152.WK1. The line shown above is called a 'pathname' and is sometimes required when using DOS, although you often leave out the drive letter and the directory name. If you were in room 498 with the filing cabinets, it would not be necessary to refer to the room number all the time. In the same way with DOS, if one drive is 'current', say the C: drive, then you do not have to include it in the pathname. The language used here is that C: is the default drive. If you do include it, it will still work OK. For example, if the prompt says C:\> and you issue the command:

dir C:\windows

it will have the same effect as:

dir \windows

Changing directory

You can make any directory current by the change directory command, e.g.:

cd \windows\system

and the prompt should change to:

C:\WINDOWS\SYSTEM>

to indicate that a different directory is current. If you now issue the command:

dir

it will have the same effect as before, i.e. a listing of the files in c:\ WINDOWS \SYSTEM directory, but now you can work on files in this directory, deleting, renaming etc. without constantly having to include the whole pathname to refer to files. PLEASE DO NOT MODIFY ANY WINDOWS OR SOFTWARE FILES IN THESE DIRECTORIES.

To change back to the 'root' directory, issue the command:

cd \

where the \ character is short for 'root'.

Earlier it was stated that a drive can be the default, i.e. the one 'switched on'. A similar thing happens with default directories. If you have changed directory to, say, the Windows directory, the prompt will be C:\WINDOWS>. If you now type the command:

dir system

it will give you the directory listing for the c:\windows\system directory. If, however, you were still in the root directory and issued the same command, it would look for a directory called system inside the root directory. On a standard installation of Windows, the directory C:\system does not exist, so the output will not be what you may expect.

Regardless of which drive or directory is current, you can always use a fully qualified pathname which is the posh name for including all the details and not assuming that anything is the default.

To use the above example, if you use the command:

dir c:\windows\system

it will always work (on a standard machine) because all the details are present. Note especially the leading \ character as this means 'start at the root directory'. You should see that:

dir c:windows\system

will look for a directory called windows\system inside the directory you happen to be in, but:

dir \windows\system
will look from the root directory. Of course if you are in the root directory, both commands will work the same! Try them both from a directory that is not the root.

Some useful variations of the dir command

dir /od	will put files in order of date (dir / order date)
dir /o-d	will put files in reverse order of date
dir /on	will put files in order of name (dir / order name)
dir /o-n	will put files in reverse order of name
dir /os	will put files in order of size (dir / order size)
dir /o-s	will put files in reverse order of size
dir /ad	will list directories only (dir / attribute directory)
dir /a-d	will list files only (dir / attribute -directory, i.e. no directories)

You may combine these such as:

dir /a-d /od

which will list files only in date order:

dir *.txt /s

will list all files on the disc that have a .txt extension, the /s means include subdirectories.

DOS prompt

The C:\WINDOWS > prompt is made up of three parts. The first is the drive letter C: (you must have the colon), the second is the \WINDOWS directory name and the last is the prompt itself, the > character. If the prompt shows as C:\> then the current directory is \ or the 'root' directory. The file system used with DOS is similar to other operating systems and is known as a 'tree' structure, but like all computer trees, it has its root at the top!

File extensions

Files usually have a file extension such as fred.txt or fred.doc. The extension is used to show what kind of data is inside the file.

In many instances, DOS does nothing special with file extensions, they are for your use or use by programs such as Word, but program and system files have special extensions that you should not use for your files until you know exactly what they mean.

Examples are:

- .exe (executable program)
- .com (compact executable program)
- .sys (system)
- .dll (dynamic link library, executable program code)
- .bat (batch file)
- .bin (binary file)

Other common extensions you may see:

- .doc (document as used by Microsoft Word)
- .xls (Excel spreadsheet)
- .mdb (Access Database)
- .txt (text file)
- .bmp (bitmapped graphics file)
- .jpg (joint photographic expert group graphics file)

there are many many others.

Pipes, filters and IO redirection

I/O redirection

I/O means Input Output. It may come as a surprise but DOS does not show the result of commands on the screen nor does it read from the keyboard! You might argue that you can see the output but in fact DOS writes to something called STDOUT (Standard Output) which is the screen unless you tell it otherwise. It reads from STDIN (Standard Input) which happens to be the keyboard unless you tell it otherwise. All errors are sent to STDERR, which is usually the screen.

The dir command can be redirected into a file with the command:

```
dir > dirlist.txt
```

The > character redirects the output from STDOUT to the file called dirlist.txt. The result is that you will not see the dir listing on the screen as usual, it will be in a text file that was created by the command. If the file had been there before, the old contents will now be lost and overwritten by the new dir listing details. If you did not want this to happen, you can add the results to the end of the file with the command:

```
dir > dirlist.txt
```

where the > characters mean 'append to' following the redirection.

Question

How would you make a file called football.txt that contains:

- a list of all files that start with the word 'foot'
- files to be in date order
- files to be from all subdirectories on the disc

Answer

Use the command:

```
dir \foot*.* /s > football.txt
```

The part that says dir \foot*.* will search from \, the root directory and look for all files that start with foot but end with anything and have any extension. The /s is called switch s and makes the dir command look in all subdirectories. Finally the > redirects the output to the file called football.txt.

Question
How would you make a file called mywork.txt containing all the names of the files on a floppy disc in size order.

Answer
Use the command:

dir a:\ /s > myfile.txt

It is interesting to note that Windows 95/98 will not do this simple service but in old fashioned DOS it is very simple. Once the file is created you can load it into any editor you wish, even Word.

Pipes
A pipe in the language of operating systems is a means of connecting the output of one program to another. DOS contains a command called sort that, as the name suggests, will sort a list of words. You can use the sort command from the DOS prompt but it is not very useful. Try this command:

sort (and press ENTER)

Type a few lines of words such as:

burt
anne
joe
jim
fred

then type CTRL Z, the ASCII End of File character.
The result should be:

anne
burt
fred
jim
joe

i.e. all the names are in alphabetical order.
The real use of this program is as a 'filter' when a command is 'piped' to the sort program.
Try this command:

dir /a-d | sort

the dir /a-d command will work as above but the result will be piped into the sort command with the | character. This is called the pipe character and is usually above the \ character to the left of the z key.

NB. In a DOS window, some keyboard maps do not yield the same characters as are marked on the keys. The pipe character is ASCII 124 and can be obtained by holding down the ALT key, keying 124 on the *numeric keypad* then releasing the ALT key. If you try the command below and the system responds with the message 'Too many parameters Find' it is because you have the wrong character used for the | symbol.

The command:

dir /a-d | find 'foot'

will send the output of the dir command into the find program (a filter program) and look for all occurrences of the string 'foot' in the listing. Try the command for strings that you know are present.

The DOS wildcard does not work correctly. If you want all files that contain the string 'fred', the command dir *fred.* should work but does not, it gives all the files on the machine. You can get the result you want by using:

dir | find 'fred'

Because the output of the command is piped to the find program which looks for strings in lines of text.
This method can be very useful if you need to find a file made on a given date but you cannot remember the name. The command:

dir /s | find '14/09/98'

will look in all subdirectories and then search in each line for the string '14/9/98'. You need care here because DOS is capable of displaying the date in different formats. You may find the date 14th September 1998 looks like 14/9/98 or 9/14/98 in US format or 14-09-98 etc.
Of course if you use the command:

dir /s | find '14/09/98' > mylist.txt

the output will be sent to a file called mylist.txt, a feature Windows 95/98 does not possess.
If you are feeling adventurous, you can combine all these things. A command such as:

dir c:*sys*.* /s | find '98' | sort > c:\this year.txt

will make a file called year.txt, in alphabetical order, of all filenames that contain the string 'sys' in the name and the string '98' somewhere in the dir line.

Other DOS commands

Other DOS commands that are useful are md, rd, copy, move, ren, del, undelete, type, more and attrib as shown below.

MD

MD is short for Make Directory. The command:

md a:\exam

will make a directory on the a: drive inside the \ (root) directory. The command:

md a:\exam\cp

will make a directory called cp inside the a:\exam directory if it exists.

RD

RD is short for Remove Directory. The command:

rd a:\exam

will remove the directory only if it contains nothing. The command DELTREE will remove a directory and all its contents including subdirectories, it is therefore a dangerous command!

Copy

The copy command will of course copy files and will obey the default drive and directory rules as described above.
The command:

copy c:\mywork\flist.txt c:\archive

will copy the file named flist.txt no matter what drive or directory is current. The command:

copy flist.txt c:\archive

will look for the file in the current directory.

If you use the copy command with only one parameter like this

copy c:\junk.txt

it will copy the named file into whatever drive and directory is current. The copy command will also allow renaming on copy. The command:

copy a:\junk.txt h:\fred.txt

will copy the file and rename in one command. This can be dangerous if you use misspelled directory names. If you intend to copy all .txt files to a directory on A: called a:\mybook but you make a typing error in the command. You type:

copy *.txt a:\mbook

by accident (leaving out the y). The effect is not what you want because you will find that the last file in the .txt list will be in the a:\ (root) directory and it will be called mbook, i.e. you will have only one incorrectly named file not a whole group of them!

Move

The move command works in a similar way to the copy command except that it will not take one parameter. If you need to move a file into the current directory you can use a command like this:

move c:\junk.txt .

where the . character is shorthand for 'this directory'.

The move command is also used to rename directories and can also rename in the same manner as the copy command with the same dangers.

Ren

the ren command is used to rename files (not directories) like this:

ren c:\junk.txt junk.doc

Del

The del command is the same as erase and will remove a file from the directory listing. It does not remove the file from the disc as it can be recovered. If a file is secret and you do not wish it to be seen. The only safe way to delete is to overwrite it first with non-secret data then delete it.

For a file called junk.txt, the command:

del junk.txt

will delete the name entry from the directory but leave the file on disc.

Type and More

The type command sends files to STDOUT. In plain language, you can send a file to the screen to look at with a command like:

type c:\myfile.txt

If the file is too long, you can pipe it to the more command with:

type c:\myfile.txt | more

which will page the results to the screen, or you can use IO redirection using the command:

more <> myfile.txt

where the redirection is from a file not to a file.

Tasks for you

Devise the DOS commands for these items: for floppy discs, DO NOT turn on the A: drive by using the command A: and pressing enter, instead you should issue the commands from the DOS directly from whatever drive is current.

1. Obtain the file list in wide format for the c:\netscape directory.
2. Obtain the file list for files in c:\netscape that have an .exe extension.
3. Obtain the file list for a floppy in drive A: root directory.
4. Obtain a list of all files on the C: drive with an .INI extension.
5. Obtain a list of all directories on drive C: (not files).
6. Obtain the file list for all directories on your H: drive that have today's date (useful when you forget what you called a file!).
7. Obtain a fully sorted list of all files in the windows directory and its subdirectories that start with 'W'.
8. Obtain a list of all files on C: that have a .BMP extension and write the result to a file called bmpfiles.txt on your H: drive.
9. Obtain a file list of all files on the C:\ drive that have a date in 1997 and have the string 'ETS' in the filename (hint: wildcards will not work).
10. Use IO redirection to create a:\fred.txt that contains a file list of all files only on h:\.
11. Copy a file called A:\fred.txt to h:\ but remember, do not turn on the A: drive.
12. Make a directory on the H: drive called exam.
13. Copy a file called A:\fred.txt to h:\exam directory and rename it to fred.bak in the same command.

Changing the prompt

The prompt actually shown on the screen can be changed using the DOS command prompt.

If you issue the command:

prompt $p

the prompt will change to C:\ so the > character will disappear. If you issue the command:

prompt $g

the C:\ part will disappear but the > character will reappear. The command:

prompt pg

will turn them both on at once. This is the condition most computers start with. The prompt command can be made to display the date, time or other characters. Try a selection of these:

$t	time
$_	move to next line
$d	date
$p	current directory
$g	> character
$q	= character
$h	backspace and delete one character

For the adventurous, try this prompt:

prompt pqthhhhhhg

which should result in the prompt containing the current directory followed by the time and finishing with the > character. The six $h are to backspace and delete the hundreds of a second from the time. Restore it to normal with prompt pg.

Answers to exercise

1. Obtain the file list in wide format for the c:\netscape directory: dir /w c:\netscape
2. Obtain the file list for files in c:\netscape that have an .exe extension: dir c:\netscape*.exe
3. Obtain the file list for a floppy in drive A: root directory: dir a:\

4. Obtain a list of all files on the C: drive with an .INI extension: dir /s c:*.ini
5. Obtain a list of all directories on drive C: (not files): dir /ad /s c:\
6. Obtain the file list for all directories on the C: drive that have today's date (useful when you forget what you called a file!): dir /s c:\ | find '24/10/01'
7. Obtain a fully sorted list of all files in the windows directory and its subdirectories that start with 'W': dir /on c:\windows\w*.*
8. Obtain a list of all files on C: that have a .BMP extension and write the result to a file called bmpfiles.txt in the C: root directory: dir /s c:*.bmp > c:\bmpfiles.txt
9. Obtain a file list of all files on the C:\ drive that have a date in 1997 and have the string 'ETS' in the filename (hint: wildcards will not work): dir /s c:\ | find 'ETS' | find '/97'
10. Use IO redirection to create a:\fred.txt that contains a file list of all files only on h:\: dir h:\ > a:fred.txt
11. Copy a file called A:\fred.txt to h:\ but remember, do not turn on the A: drive: copy a:\fred.txt h:\
12. Make a directory on the H: drive root directory called exam: md h:\exam
13. Copy a file called A:\fred.txt to h:\exam directory and rename it to fred.bak in the same command: copy a:\fred.txt h:\fred.bak

DOS to unix conversion

The table below shows the most basic set of commands for users who need some practice in moving from a DOS to a Unix shell environment.

Any of the Unix shells are far more powerful than the DOS command line interpreter, COMMAND.COM. Both DOS and Unix will allow pipes, filters and I/O redirection but as Unix was built that way from the start, a more reliable environment is available. DOS uses the \ character to separate directory elements, Unix uses the / character.

Command	*DOS command*	*Unix command*
Directory, short format	dir /w	ls
Directory, long format	dir	ls -la
Directory, one page at a time	dir /p	ls -la | more
Clear screen	cls	clear
Change directory	cd path	cd path
Make directory	md path	mkdir path
Copy files	copy file1 file2	cp file1 file2
Move files	move file1 file2	mv file1 file2
Rename files	rename file1 file2	mv file1 file2
Delete files	del	rm
Delete empty directory	rmd r directory	rm -r directory
Show current directory	cd	pwd
Display a text file	type file	cat file
Help	help	man
Change file attributes	attrib	chmod
Print a file	print file1	lpr file1

1.8 Enrichment material

NTFS and other disc filing systems

The HNC computing book described the FAT (File Allocation Table) system of keeping track of files on a disc. This was chosen because the FAT is very common and is simple to understand. Unfortunately it suffers from significant weaknesses so has been replaced to a large extent by other disc filing systems. Some of the more significant are described here. There are a considerable number of different file systems, references to many of them can be found at http://www.penguin.cz/~mhi/fs/Filesystems-HOWTO/Filesystems-HOWTO.html or if that page has moved, search for the file 'Filesystems-HOWTO.html'. When last tried, www.google.com returned links to numerous copies of this file.

FAT formatted discs can be read and written to by PCs as well as Macintosh machines, many kinds of Unix operating systems and numerous other small computer systems. Although this system has many weaknesses, it is a victim of its own success, it is so common it 'will not go away'.

The smallest allocation unit on a FAT disc is the cluster. This leads to wasted space as a small file must occupy at least one cluster. With a cluster size of 64, this means 32 Kb of space is used regardless of the file size.

Size in MB	*Sectors per cluster*	*Bytes per cluster*
Maximum		
16–32	2	1 024
32–127	4	2 048
128–255	8	4 096
256–511	16	8 192
512–1023	32	16 384
1024–2048	64	32 768
2048 to 4096 (NT only)	128	64 536

Virtual FAT (VFAT)

Windows 95 was offered with a 32-bit file system driver with long filename support. This is a variant of FAT and is (unofficially) known as VFAT.

VFAT allows long filenames whilst keeping the 8.3 filename structure of the FAT system. Long names are stored as additional hidden directory entries.

FAT32

Windows 95 Service Release 2 introduced FAT32, a modification of the older FAT16 allowing more efficient disc allocation with 32-bit disc addressing. FAT16 is limited to 2 Gb partitions, FAT32 caters for very large partitions, up to 127 Tb. Root directory can grow to any size unlike FAT16 which has a fixed number of root entries (65 536 or 2^{16}). It is an inefficient system, searching large discs is very slow and compatibility with other systems is limited; however, it was only ever intended as a stop-gap between FAT16 and NTFS.

HPFS

This is the High-Performance File System introduced with OS/2. HPFS uses two-way links in its structure, each entry points to the last and the next entry whereas a FAT uses a single direction linked list, each entry points only to the next. Directories are sorted and placed on a balanced tree starting at the middle of the disc to reduce average access times. Partition sizes up to 64 Gb can be used together with long filenames.

HPFS is not suited to small discs but is a powerful and flexible file system. An enhanced version, HPFS386, is included with OS/2 Warp Server.

NTFS

This is Windows NT native file system.

Key features:

- Volumes up to 16 Eb in size can be supported. An exabyte is 10^{18} bytes. As a Gb is 10^9, an Eb is 10^9 Gb or a gigagigabyte!
- NTFS offers journaling, a system related to rollback in databases. A journal in this case is a file that logs system activity; in the event of a system crash, this log can be used to complete or undo recent changes.
- Offers full multi-user security based on Access Control Lists. This system is used to control permissions to file, directories etc. and is more flexible than Unix style permissions.
- Filenames are stored in Unicode, allowing multi-language filenames.
- Files can contain multiple data streams, i.e. one name points to several data areas. As Macintosh files are stored in two pieces (resource and data fork), Mac files are easily stored in NTFS.
- NTFS versions are not all backward compatible, NT version 3.x cannot read version 4 NTFS file system.
- NTFS can 'talk' to a number of other file systems allowing reading and writing of files to/from systems such as Macintosh HFS or Sun's Network Filing System (NFS) etc.

NTFS uses a B-tree. Tree data-structures can be searched very much faster than simple arrays or lists.

Unix and Linux

It has been said that computing standards are fine things, there are so many to choose from! Since its original popularity was gained in the academic world, the Unix world has split into many pieces so there are a large number of 'standard' versions of Unix. What is presented here is a typical Unix disc file system.

Under Unix a disc can be split into logical parts in a way similar to disc partitions under DOS, each physical disc may have one or more logical 'discs'. Each logical disc is split into four parts:

1. The Boot Block containing code that is loaded and run by the BIOS. This is essentially a loader program that loads and starts the rest of the system.
2. The Super Block describes the logical disc to the system, it contains:
   - size of the file system
   - number of free blocks on the system
   - a list of free blocks
   - an index to next free block
   - the size of the inode list
   - number of free inodes
   - a list of free inodes
3. The third block is a set if inodes. Each inode contains pointers to the actual disc blocks used by one file. A directory (folder under Windows) is treated as a file, i.e. a file of filenames.
4. The fourth block is the data block that actually contains the files. The blocks are 512 or 1024 bytes in size. Compare this with DOS that uses a standard 512-byte block.

Unix refers to the superblock very frequently so a copy is loaded in RAM to make this faster. When a change is made, the RAM copy is updated right away but the disc copy may not be updated until a short time later. If the system crashes in between, the disc copy of the superblock will not reflect the actual disc structure. This will cause trouble on system restart! Users can force the system to write the RAM copy to the disc but this is done as part of the system shutdown procedure anyway.

Under DOS and its FAT, files were just files. Under Unix, all files must record 'who' owned them as Unix was a multi-user system from the start. This implies that each file also has a set of read/write/execute permissions allocated to it, these permissions are stored in a number with each permission level stored as 1 bit.

CDFS

Unlike hard drives that store binary data in concentric tracks, data on CD is stored in a continuous 'track' up to 6 km long. This track is read from the inner part of the disc first as a continuous stream. If data is added at a later date, a second 'track' is added to the end of the first but is treated as a separate item. Each set of recorded data is called a 'session', some older CD-ROM drives will not read multi-session discs, i.e. those that have data added.

There are many different formats used to store music, photos and data on CD. Each format is described in a confusingly named 'Book', each one has a 'Colour'. You may hear of a 'Yellow Book' CD. This simply means a data CD. The main ones are shown in the table below. This is another case where there are so many standards to choose from! The 'standard' ISO9660 CD format will not work with long filenames, it only accepts the old DOS 8.3 format filename. Microsoft has introduced an extension to the ISO9660 format, this is called Joliet. You should not be surprised to find that not all CD-ROM drives will read all discs under all operating systems. The CD market is one of the least standardized of the computing areas.

'Book' colour	*CD format*
Red	Digital audio (CD-DA)
Yellow	Digital data (CD-ROM): ISO 9660 (also known as High Sierra*)
Green	CD-Interactive (CD-I)
Orange	CD-Recordable (CD-R), CD-Rewriteable (CD-RW)
White	Photo CD, Video CD and others

*ISO9660 is also known as 'High Sierra' after a meeting to attempt to sort out standards held at the High Sierra Hotel near Lake Tahoe in the USA. Unfortunately, the result was another standard to add to the set.

Consider the amount of data to be stored on a CD. (Remember CDs were designed to store music.)

CD quality music is sampled at a rate of 44.1 kHz, i.e. 44 100 times a second, a 16-bit (2 byte) sample of the sound wave is stored. Stereo has two channels and CDs will store 74 minutes (or 74 * 60 = 4440 seconds) of music, therefore:

sample rate * sample size * number of stereo channels * number of seconds = number of bytes to store

or

44100 * 2 * 2 * 4440 = 783 216 000 bytes or about 747 Mbytes of data.

Data CDs usually store about 650 Mbytes of data, the difference between 747 and 650 is taken up by more error correction code. Although music CDs also have error correction, if a music CD loses a byte or two from physical damage to the CD surface, the worst that can happen is a slight noise in the music. Data CDs cannot tolerate even a single bit error (especially in executable files) so better error correction is required to allow for the inevitable damage to the disc surfaces.

DVD

DVDs use the Universal Disk Format or UDF. Although they look like CDs, they are very different. Whilst a CD can store 650 Mbytes of data (or a little more if pushed), a DVD can store up to 17 Gbytes of data, almost 27 times as much. UDF is also used on CD-R and CD-RW discs in 'packet writing mode'. This makes more efficient use of disc space and is somewhat quicker:

17 Gbyte = $17 * 1024^3$, 650 Mbyte = 650 * 10242

so $17 * 1024^3/650 * 1024^2 = 26.78$ or about 27 times.

DVD works in a similar way to CDs. Both have indentations on the surface of a disc called lands and pits but a DVD has multiple layers.

Different DVD formats have different storage capacities, these are summarized as:

DVD-5 (12 cm, SS/SL): 4.38 gig (4.7 G) of data, over 2 hours of video
DVD-9 (12 cm, SS/DL): 7.95 gig (8.5 G), about 4 hours
DVD-10 (12 cm, DS/SL): 8.75 gig (9.4 G), about 4.5 hours
DVD-14 (12 cm, DS/ML): 12.33 gig (13.24 G), about 6.5 hours
DVD-18 (12 cm, DS/DL): 15.90 gig (17 G), over 8 hours
DVD-1 (8 cm, SS/SL): 1.36 gig (1.4 G), about half an hour
DVD-2 (8 cm, SS/DL): 2.48 gig (2.7 G), about 1.3 hours
DVD-3 (8 cm, DS/SL): 2.72 gig (2.9 G), about 1.4 hours
DVD-4 (8 cm, DS/DL): 4.95 gig (5.3 G), about 2.5 hours
DVD-R (12 cm, SS/SL): 3.68 gig (3.95 G)
DVD-R (12 cm, DS/SL): 7.38 gig (7.9 G)
DVD-R (8 cm, SS/SL): 1.15 gig (1.23 G)
DVD-R (8 cm, DS/SL): 2.29 gig (2.46 G)
DVD-RAM (12 cm, SS/SL): 2.40 gig (2.58 G)
DVD-RAM (12cm, DS/SL): 4.80 gig (5.16 G)

Details of UDF can be found at http://www.osta.org/html/ostaudf.html.

2 Systems analysis

Rationale

By way of an introduction students will learn:

- why software development techniques are required in the analysis/design process
- how to apply software analysis techniques for a given 'real world' specification based on an appropriate lifecycle model
- the different approaches to analysis and make comparisons about different models that are used within the software engineering environment today
- the techniques involved in 'fact finding' for a systems investigation and how to record/present follow-up documentation for a prospective customer
- the basic data modelling techniques, including functional modelling development and graphical representations (for example, entity-relationship diagrams) and how to implement such designs into a simple rational database system.

The unit provides a foundation of systems analysis and design by covering the required analysis skills for both commercial and technical applications. It also provides an underlying structure by developing the key skills required within the field of software engineering.

Students will need to be exposed to a variety of learning activities and assignments covering both theoretical and practical aspects of the unit. Students need to be able to produce documentation to a professional standard that would need to include graphical representations, and should be able to analyse the requirements of a proposed system, document the outcomes and communicate the results to a prospective customer. They should be aware of information systems in use within industry and be able to design and implement a simple relational database system, which could be based on documented analysis developed under systems investigation.

This unit is designed to integrate analysis techniques with practical applications in order for students to use information technology to document, analyse, design and implement systems being investigated.

2.1 Introduction to the systems analysis models

Rapid Software Prototyping – additional information

Background

A Rapid Software Prototype is a dynamic visual model providing a means of communication for both the customer and developer. It is more effective than textual documents or static models for displaying limited working applications of the proposed system. A prototype contains the following characteristics:

- A functional model can be displayed after a small amount of work.
- Provides a flexible base as modifications can easily be implemented.
- Provides the end user with an overview of the proposed system that shows the key components before full implementation.
- Prototype activities are completed quickly incurring small costs and time constraints.
- A prototype does not always provide a true representation of the complete system.

Benefits of the prototype model

- Any misunderstandings between the software developers and the end users are highlighted early in the development process.
- Missing functional components may be detected.
- Components that are difficult to use or confusing may be identified.
- A limited working system is available for end users, developers and management.
- It serves as a basis for developing the complete system specification.

From Pressman

> The prototyping principle, as presented by Pressman, focuses on building a sequence of prototypes until the requirements are understood, thereby assisting the customer or developer. The collection of requirements is the first step in this process. The next step is to develop a quick design. This design is focused only on the parts of the system that the user is concerned with and is turned into a prototype. Next, the user tests the prototype and a new discussion concerning the requirements for the system takes place. This cycle of talking to the customer, building a prototype, and then testing it is continued until all parties involved feel that the requirements are complete.

Rapid Software Prototyping is basically a systems analysis technique that provides a base for an accurate and complete set of functional requirements for the proposed system. It overcomes the problem that the traditional lifecycle model has in that the user can view a physical model early in the development process and not at the final testing phase. But it does have its drawbacks, such as adequate prototyping skills; mistaken concepts concerning definitions, objectives and functional requirements; it can lead to 'short cuts' within the full working application; premature delivery of the software product and its associated documentation; and problems with standardization and uniformity especially if fourth generation languages are used as generic tools during development.

See: http://www.shu.ac.uk/schools/cms/rapid.software.prototyping/

2.2 Requirements analysis

Suggested solution for Exercise 2.2.1 – College Admission System

1. Group size 3 to 4 students

This is a simulation with one elected person acting as the chair (project manager) and others forming system analysts, programming and technical support etc. roles. One member is elected to take the minutes for the meeting and outline the agenda. It is important that students know about the roles they are taking on. It may be advantageous for the students to research the roles (i.e. what is the main role of a systems analyst? etc.) prior to setting up the committee structure.

Agenda

Team members – introduce each other and specify roles
Apologies for absence
Review of the user requirements
Specify the functional requirements and constraints
Specify any ambiguous statements, missing components and platitudes
Any other points of interest

Minutes

These should reflect the discussions held in the meeting by stating who said what and the suggested solutions and/or any resulting conclusions.

2. Functional requirements

- Details of new students entered
- Student details stored on a student file
- Course check (to see if it is available)
- Enrolment – details entered into the registered file
- Display suitable message if course not available
- Produce invoice for appropriate course fee
- Produce partially completed enrolment forms
- Produce course information

3. Non-functional requirements (constraints)

- Run on the existing college network
- Only 300 kb of disk space is available
- System is to respond in less than 1 second

4. Obvious omissions

- How are incorrect inputs by the operator handled?
- When/how is the operator going to select required options?
- How is data to be entered (see platitudes below)?
- Invoices, courses and enrolment forms are to be printed, these require different paper requirements, how is the operator notified of this? Are different printers required?

Platitudes

- Be easy for the operator to use

6. Resulting questions

- What precise details are to be entered by the operator for new students?
- What file structure is required?
- How is the operator told if the required course is available so that the enrolment can proceed?
- Is a written message enough to tell the operator that a course does not exist or should some audible sound be added alerting the user?
- What precise details need to be displayed on the invoice?
- What precise details need to be displayed on the enrolment form?
- What precise details need to be displayed on the course printout. Does the cost need to be displayed along with the examination board etc.?
- How are the past students to be linked to the system in order to print out course information to previous enquiries?
- What type of user interface is required for the system, for example is a Windows environment required via mouse input or would another input medium be required like a touch screen etc.?
- What are the operational capabilities of the current Apple network system?
- Is it really necessary for the system to respond in less than one second? It is not a real time system. A wait of 2/3 seconds would normally seem appropriate

There may be many more points to add to the list as there is no one fixed solution. The main requirement here is for students to work in groups, grasp the first principles of analysing the problem and understand the importance of providing a sound base, which is clear, concise and unambiguous, for developing potential computer systems. The rule here is that students first understand the problem before trying to provide a solution.

Requirements analysis exercise – the Bess and Bailey Department Store

Goods order system

Outlined is part of the user requirements for the Bess and Bailey Department Store Goods Ordering System:

> The department store requires a system to handle its goods ordering system. Order requisitions are set up from within the various departments and sent to the purchasing office for processing. The purchasing office acknowledges the orders from the departments by date stamping them before checking their contents. If there is a problem with the order, for example the description, quantity required, date, etc. are erroneous, the order requisition is returned to the issuing department for amending. If the order requisition is OK the supplier name for the required goods to be ordered is added to the requisition from the Supplier Database. If no supplier exists the requisition is stored in a Pending Database and quotations are produced to send to prospective suppliers. Returned quotations from suppliers are added to the Supplier Database and the most suitable one added to the order requisition. Full details about the completed requisition are added to the Purchase Database. Copies of the completed requisition need to be sent to the following:
>
> - supplier of the goods
> - department requiring the purchase
> - goods in department
>
> When the order is in the department store from the supplier the Purchase Database is updated to show that the goods have been received.

The system is to be installed on the company's existing VAX mini computer system running under a VMS operating system. It needs to be easy to use and incorporates a small number of well-defined principles.

Required steps

1. Within your allocated groups organize and carry out a meeting to analyse the information. The meeting should have a specified agenda and minutes written.
2. Ascertain from the information the following:
   (i) Functional requirements
   (ii) Non-functional requirements
   (iii) Any obvious omissions
   (iv) Platitudes
3. Construct a suitable set of questions that can provide a basis for an interview with the customer.

Suggested solution

1. This follows the layout for the previous College Admission System.
2. (i) Functional requirements
   - Order requisitions raised from within departments
   - Purchasing department acknowledges the requisitions
   - Purchasing department checks the requisitions
   - Incorrect requisitions returned to the issuing department
   - Obtain supplier name from database
   - Produce quotations for new suppliers
   - Maintain supplier database
   - Full details added to the purchase database
   - Completed requisitions sent to various departments
   - Record details of orders received

   (ii) Non-functional requirements
   - Operate on the existing VAX computer system
   - Run the application under the VMS operating system

   (iii) Obvious omissions
   - When a requisition is received by the purchasing office and date stamped the department raising the order should be notified that it has been received
   - If no existing supplier exists there may be a time delay for ordering the goods. The department issuing the requisition needs to be informed of this as they may need to make alternative arrangements
   - Full details of the completed requisition need to be specified. For example, what precise information is required to be stored for each order?
   - How is the purchase office informed that the goods have arrived so the purchase order database can be updated?

   (iv) Platitudes
   - The system should be 'easy to use'
   - Incorporates a small number of well-defined principles

Points for discussion

- What details are required on the order requisition from the issuing department?
- How is the requisition sent from the department store to the purchase office (i.e. is it electronic or manual?)
- Is there a time period for waiting for quotations to be returned from potential suppliers?
- What is meant by the 'most suitable quotation'?
- Would a mouse driven HCI be the best form of program display?
- What training needs to be given to the users of the system?
- Are any security features required for the system (passwords, IDs etc.)

2.3 Systems analysis models

Yourdon data flow diagrams

Note: These exercises have been completed within the Select Yourdon CASE tool environment. Full details about the techniques used are contained in their user documentation. In order for the diagrams to be fully syntactically correct additional information needs to be added, for example Store Balancing and Group Node BNF structures. Once all the refinements have been completed they need to be checked for consistency to ensure all the 'parent–child balancing' links are correct.

Solution to Exercise 2.3.1 – Bess and Bailey Dog Kennels

(i) Context diagram

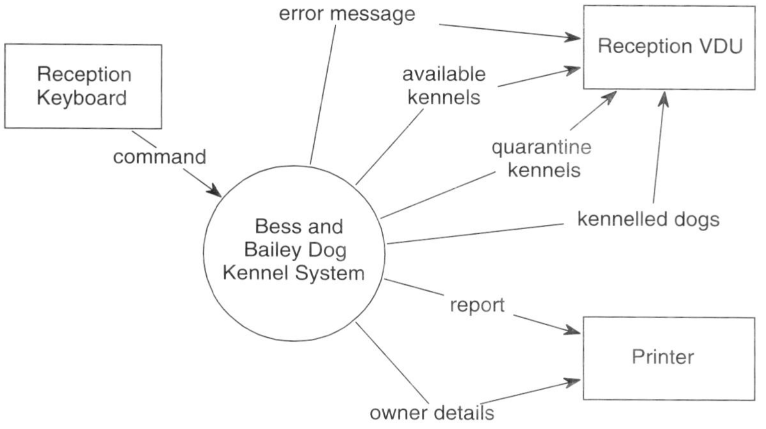

Figure 2.1 *Bess and Bailey Kennel system context diagram*

Check results for the context diagram

Project: C:\SELECT\SYSTEM\BBDC01\
Title : Bess and Bailey Dog Kennels
Date: 13-Dec-2000 Time: 11:45

Checking DOG1.DAT

No Errors detected, No Warnings given.

---- End of report ----

(ii) First refinement

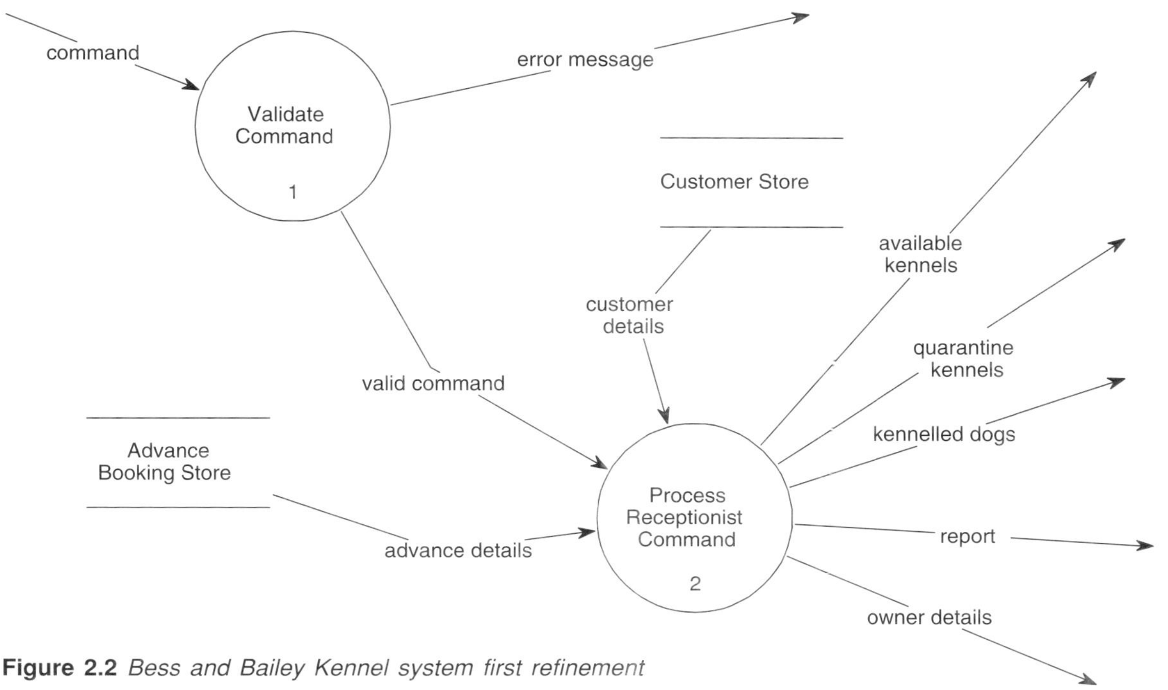

Figure 2.2 *Bess and Bailey Kennel system first refinement*

Test of the first refinement:

Project: C:\SELECT\SYSTEM\BBDC01\
Title : Bess and Bailey Dog Kennels
Date: 13-Dec-2000 Time: 12:3

Checking DOG2.DAT

No Errors detected, No Warnings given.

---- End of report ----

Store balancing requirements (only one input from the stores, but they still need to be added to the BNF clause)

Project: C:\SELECT\SYSTEM\BBDC01\
Title : Bess and Bailey Dog Kennels
Date: 13-Dec-2000 Time: 12:3

Name: **Customer Store**
Type: Store
Bnf: customer details
This item is used on the following diagrams:
DOG2.DAT Bess and Bailey Dog Kennel System
Last changed: DEFAULT 13-Dec-2000 12:22:25

---- End of report ----

Project: C:\SELECT\SYSTEM\BBDC01\
Title : Bess and Bailey Dog Kennels
Date: 13-Dec-2000 Time: 12:4

Name: **Advance Booking Store**
Type: Store
Bnf: advance details
This item is used on the following diagrams:
DOG2.DAT Bess and Bailey Dog Kennel System
Last changed: DEFAULT 13-Dec-2000 12:21:19

---- End of report ----

Note: The system will need a central database that will contain information on the kennels, which are set aside for quarantine, which have dogs in (and who they are) and which are free to use. This database will be the hub of most of the kennel commands and booking requirements and in respect to this it will be introduced in the second refinement.

Second refinement

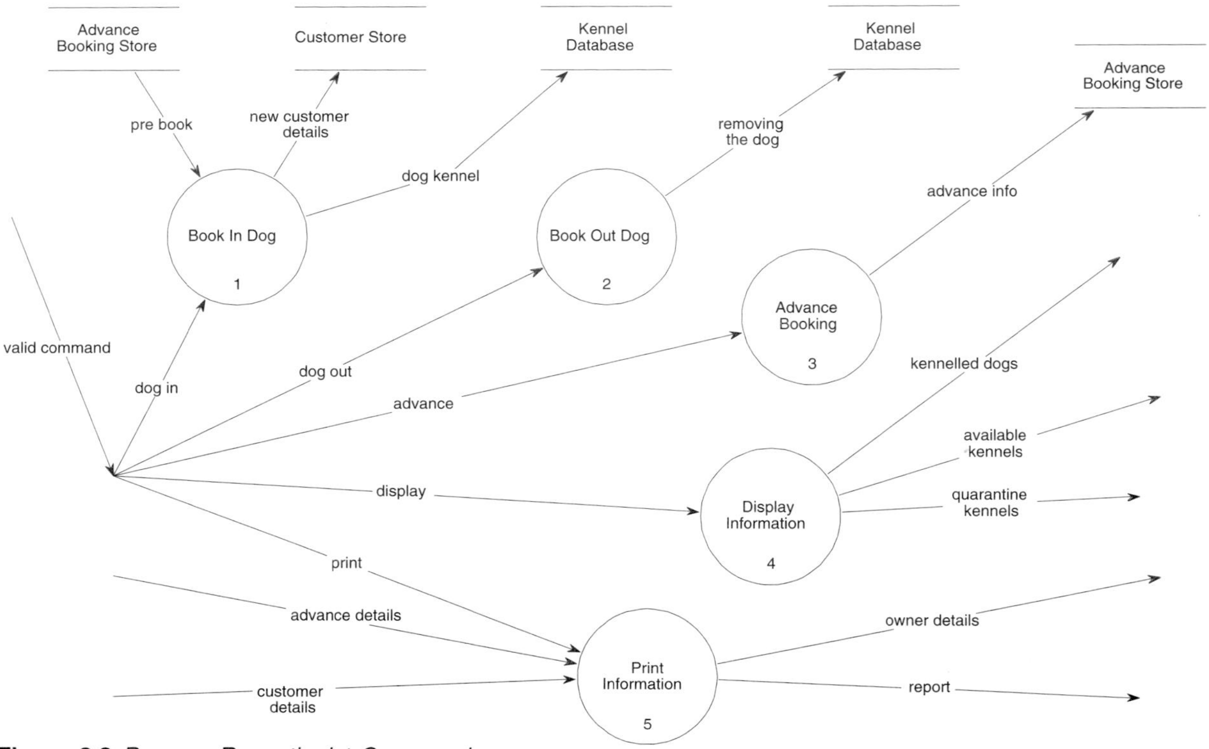

Figure 2.3 *Process Receptionist Command*

Check on the Process Receptionist Command

```
Project: C:\SELECT\SYSTEM\BBDC01\
Title  : Bess and Bailey Dog Kennels
Date: 19-Dec-2000 Time: 18:3

Checking DOG3 .DAT

No Errors detected, No Warnings given.

---- End of report ----
```

Process 4 (Display Information) and Process 5 (Print Information) require further refinements. Processes 1, 2 and 3 require no further refinements so their Process Specifications (PSPECS) are shown below. Remember you can continue to decompose the diagrams until a process is detailed enough to become a Process Specification (PSPEC).

(iii) Process specification for the Book In Dog Process

```
@IN  = dog in
@IN  = pre book
@OUT = dog kennel
@OUT = new customer details

@PSPEC 0.2.1 Book In Dog

   On receiving the dog in command do:
        check the Advanced Booking Store to ascertain the pre book
        requirements for the customer (if any)
        and
        update the Kennel Database by sending the new dog kennel data
        and
        update the Customer Store by sending the new customer details

@
```

Process specification for the Display Available Kennels Process

```
@IN  = dog out
@OUT = removing the dog

@PSPEC 0.2.2 Book Out Dog

   On receiving the dog out command do:
        update the Kennel Database by removing the dog
        from the kennels it had occupied

@
```

Process specification for the Display Available Kennels Process

```
@IN  = advance
@OUT = advance info

@PSPEC 0.2.3 Advance Booking

        On receiving the advance command do:
          send the customer advance info to the Advance Booking Store
@
```

Note: All the PSPECs should be checked, full details of these will be shown in the final consistency check.

Group Node BNF requirements for the valid command data flow

```
Project: C:\SELECT\SYSTEM\BBDC01\
Title  : Bess and Bailey Dog Kennels
Date: 20-Dec-2000 Time:  9:2

Name: valid command
Type: Discrete flow
Bnf:  [ dog in | dog out | advance | display | print ]
This item is used on the following diagrams:
    DOG2.DAT    Bess and Bailey Dog Kennel System
    DOG3.DAT    Process Receptionist Command
Last changed: DEFAULT        19-Dec-2000 19:06:01

---- End of report ----
```

The BNF statement shows an 'or' situation and the receptionist can enter one command or another and not all of them at the same time.

Store balancing – Modification to the Advance Booking Store and Customer Store

```
Project: C:\SELECT\SYSTEM\BBDC01\
Title  : Bess and Bailey Dog Kennels
Date: 20-Dec-2000 Time:  9:3

Name: Advance Booking Store
Type: Store
Bnf:  [ advance details | pre book | advance info ]
This item is used on the following diagrams:
    DOG2.DAT    Bess and Bailey Dog Kennel System
    DOG3.DAT    Process Receptionist Command
Last changed: DEFAULT        13-Dec-2000 13:15:40

---- End of report ----
```

```
Project: C:\SELECT\SYSTEM\BBDC01\
Title  : Bess and Bailey Dog Kennels
Date: 20-Dec-2000 Time:  9:3

Name: Customer Store
Type: Store
Bnf:  [ customer details | new customer details ]
This item is used on the following diagrams:
    DOG2.DAT    Bess and Bailey Dog Kennel System
    DOG3.DAT    Process Receptionist Command
Last changed: DEFAULT        19-Dec-2000 18:49:42

---- End of report ----
```

Third refinement: Display information on the receptionist's VDU

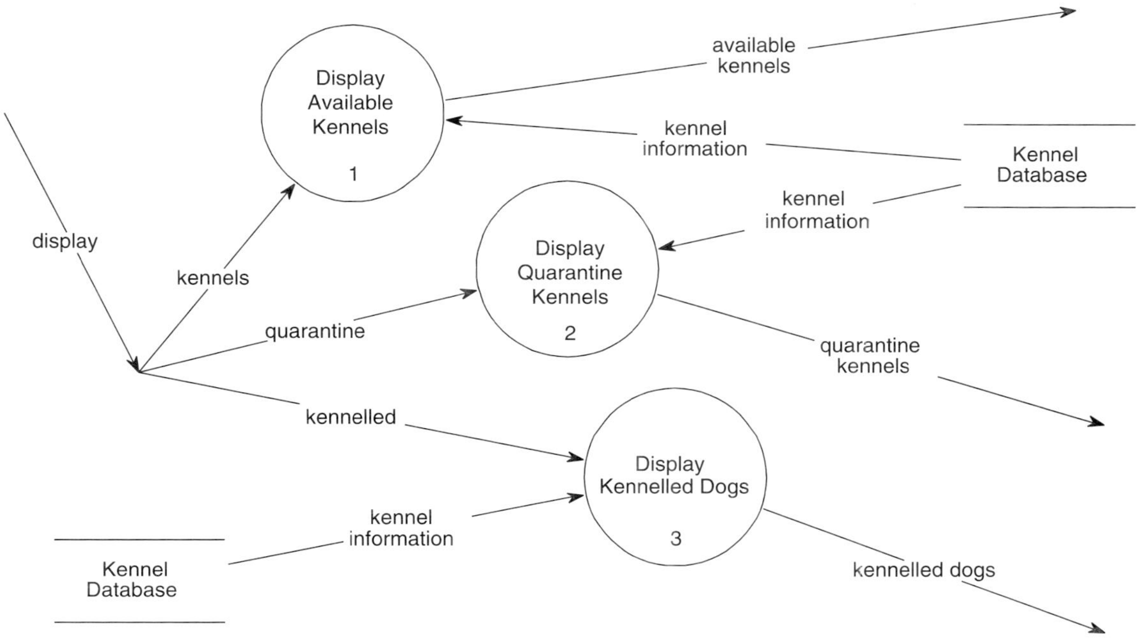

Figure 2.4 *Display Information*

Check of the Display Information refinement

```
Project: C:\SELECT\SYSTEM\BBDC01\
Title  : Bess and Bailey Dog Kennels
Date: 19-Dec-2000 Time: 17:0

Checking DOG5.DAT

No Errors detected, No Warnings given.

---- End of report ----
```

Group node requirements

```
Project: C:\SELECT\SYSTEM\BBDC01\
Title  : Bess and Bailey Dog Kennels
Date: 19-Dec-2000 Time: 17:1

Name: display
Type: Discrete flow
Bnf:  [ kennels | quarantine | kennelled ]
This item is used on the following diagrams:
     DOG3.DAT    Process Receptionist Command
     DOG5.DAT    Display Information
Last changed: DEFAULT        19-Dec-2000 17:04:35

---- End of report ----
```

Store balancing requirements

```
Project: C:\SELECT\SYSTEM\BBDC01\
Title  : Bess and Bailey Dog Kennels
Date: 19-Dec-2000 Time: 17:1

Name: Kennel Database
Type: Store
Bnf:  [ dog kennel | dog out kennel | kennel information ]
This item is used on the following diagrams:
    DOG3.DAT    Process Receptionist Command
    DOG5.DAT    Display Information
Last changed: DEFAULT        19-Dec-2000 17:04:57

---- End of report ----
```

Process specification for the Display Available Kennels process

```
@IN  = kennel information
@IN  = kennels
@OUT = available kennels

@PSPEC 0.2.4.1 Display Available Kennels

  on receiving the kennels display command do:
        obtain the kennel information from the Kennel Database
        and determine the available kennels for display on the VDU screen

@
```

Process specification for the Display Quarantine Kennels process

```
@IN  = kennel information
@IN  = quarantine
@OUT = quarantine kennels

@PSPEC 0.2.4.2 Display Quarantine Kennels

  On receiving the quarantine command do:
     obtain the kennel information data from the Kennel Database
        and determine the quarantine kennels that have been reserved

@
```

Process specification for the Display Kennelled Dogs process

```
@IN  = kennel information
@IN  = kennelled
@OUT = kennelled dogs

@PSPEC 0.2.4.3 Display Kennelled Dogs

  On receiving the kennelled command do:
        obtain the kennel information from the Kennel Database
           and determine the kennelled dogs (i.e. the dogs in the
                 kennels at the present time) for displaying on the
                 receptionist's VDU
@
```

Fourth refinement: Print Information to the receptionist's printer

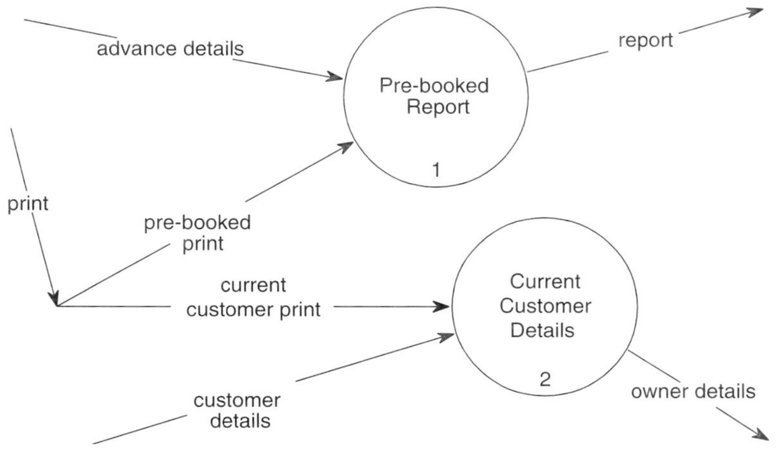

Figure 2.5 *Print Information*

Check on the Print Information refinement

```
Project: C:\SELECT\SYSTEM\BBDC01\
Title  : Bess and Bailey Dog Kennels
Date: 19-Dec-2000 Time: 17:2

Checking DOG4.DAT

No Errors detected, No Warnings given.

---- End of report ----
```

Group node requirements

```
Project: C:\SELECT\SYSTEM\BBDC01\
Title  : Bess and Bailey Dog Kennels
Date: 19-Dec-2000 Time: 17:2

Name: print
Type: Discrete flow
Bnf:  [ pre-booked print | current customer print ]
This item is used on the following diagrams:
      DOG3.DAT    Process Receptionist Command
      DOG4.DAT    Print Information
Last changed: DEFAULT        19-Dec-2000 16:50:54

---- End of report ----
```

Process specification for the Current Customer Details process

```
@IN  = current customer print
@IN  = customer details
@OUT = owner details

@PSPEC 0.2.5.2 Current Customer Details

  On receiving the current customer print command do:
    obtain the customer details from the Customer Store and
       produce the owner details of the people who currently
          have dogs in the kennels (the details to include name, address
          and telephone number)
@
```

Process specification for the Pre-booked Report process

```
@IN  = advance details
@IN  = pre-booked print
@OUT = report

@PSPEC 0.2.5.1 Pre-booked Report

  On receiving the pre-booked print command do:
        obtain advance details of people who have pre-booked
        from the Advance Booking Store and
                  produce a corresponding report to be printed out.
@
```

(v) Final diagram consistency check

```
Project: C:\SELECT\SYSTEM\BBDC01\
Title  : Bess and Bailey Dog Kennels
Date: 19-Dec-2000 Time: 19:1

Report: Diagram Consistency checking

This report contains a consistency check of all the diagrams in the project.

Checking DOG1.DAT
   No Errors detected, No Warnings given.
Checking DOG2.DAT
   No Errors detected, No Warnings given.
Checking DOG3.DAT
   No Errors detected, No Warnings given.
Checking DOG4.DAT
   No Errors detected, No Warnings given.
Checking DOG5.DAT
   No Errors detected, No Warnings given.
Checking PDOG10.DAT
   No Errors detected, No Warnings given.
Checking PDOG11.DAT
   No Errors detected, No Warnings given.
Checking PDOG4.DAT
   No Errors detected, No Warnings given.
Checking PDOG5.DAT
   No Errors detected, No Warnings given.
Checking PDOG6.DAT
   No Errors detected, No Warnings given.
Checking PDOG7.DAT
   No Errors detected, No Warnings given.
Checking PDOG8.DAT
   No Errors detected, No Warnings given.
Checking PDOG9.DAT
   No Errors detected, No Warnings given.

---- End of report ----
```

End of the Bess and Bailey Dog Kennels System.

Suggested solution to Exercise 2.3.2 – College MIS System

(i) Context diagram

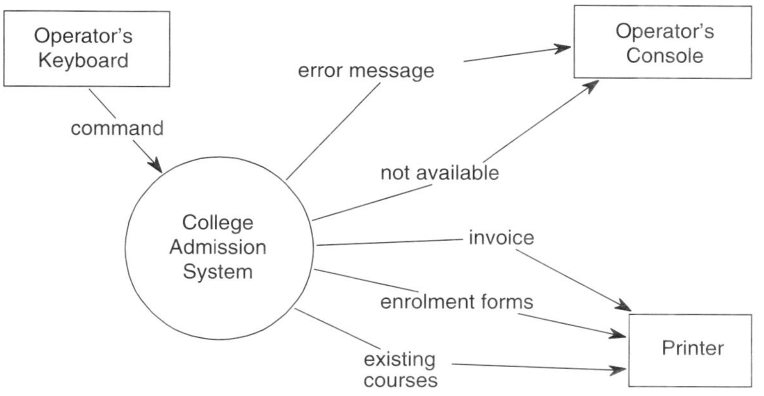

Figure 2.6 *College Admission System context diagram*

Check of CONTEXT diagram:

Project: C:\SELECT\SYSTEM\COLLEGE\
Title : College Admission System
Date: 20-Dec-2000 Time: 11:0

Checking COLLEGE1.DAT

No Errors detected, No Warnings given.

---- End of report ----

(i) First refinement – College Admission System

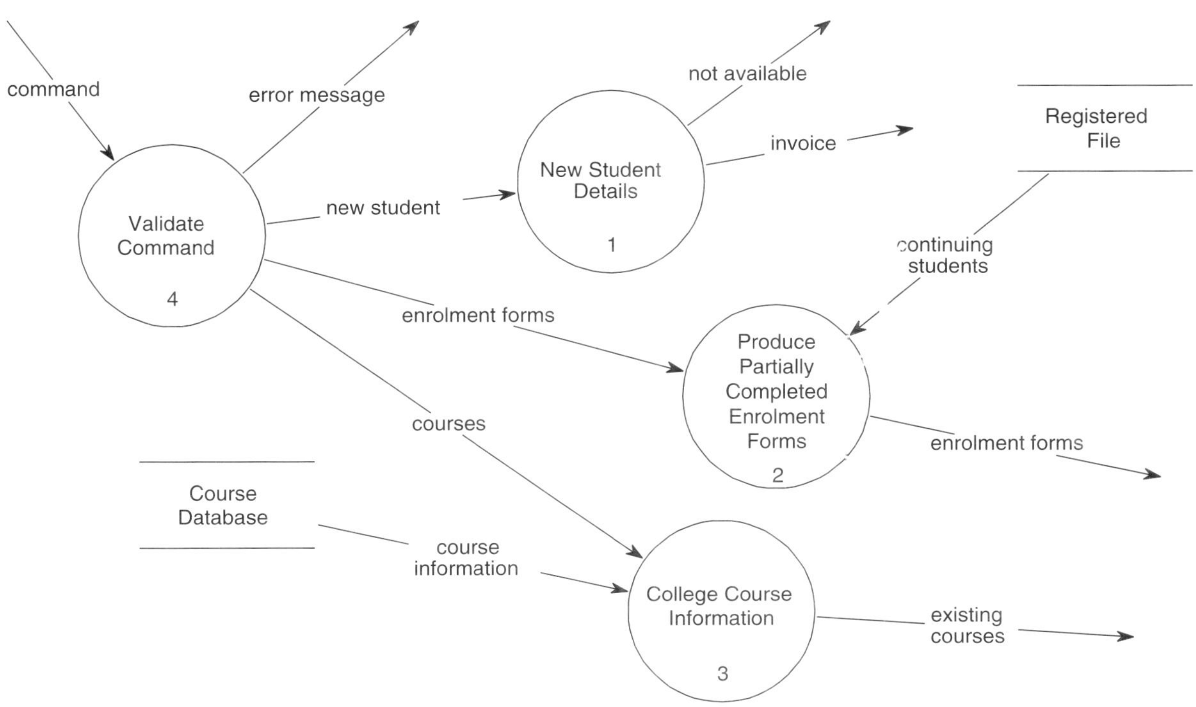

Figure 2.7 *College Admission System*

Check for the College Admission System refinement

```
Project: C:\SELECT\SYSTEM\COLLEGE\
Title  : College Admission System
Date: 20-Dec-2000 Time: 11:2

Checking COLLEGE2.DAT

No Errors detected, No Warnings given.

---- End of report ----
```

Store balancing for the Course Database

```
Project: C:\SELECT\SYSTEM\COLLEGE\
Title  : College Admission System
Date: 20-Dec-2000 Time: 11:2

Name: Course Database
Type: Store
Bnf:  course information
This item is used on the following diagrams:
    COLLEGE2.DAT College Admission System
Last changed: DEFAULT        20-Dec-2000 11:21:04

---- End of report ----
```

Note. The Registered File is also used in the first refinement diagram, but unlike the Course Database this needs to have input information added when new students are registered. Therefore the store balancing for this store will be shown after the next refinement.

(ii) Process Specifications for the Validate Command, Produce Partially Completed Enrolment Forms and College Course Information (these do not require any more refinement)

```
@IN  = continuing students
@IN  = forms
@OUT = enrolment forms

@PSPEC 0.2 Produce Partially Completed Enrolment Forms

  On receiving the forms command from the operator do:
        obtain continuing students information from the
        Registered File and produce partially completed
        enrolment forms for issuing to the continuing students

@
```

```
@IN  = course information
@IN  = courses
@OUT = existing courses

@PSPEC 0.3 College Course Information

  On receiving the courses command for the operator do:
        obtain the course information for the Course
        Database and produce lists of existing courses
        to be printed off for appropriate students
@
```

```
@IN  = command
@OUT = courses
@OUT = error message
@OUT = forms
@OUT = new student

@PSPEC 0.4 Validate Command

    On receiving the command from the operator do:
        if the command is not valid then
                display an error message
        else
                accept a valid command from
                        courses
                    or  forms
                    or  new student
@
```

(iii) Refinement for the New Student Details process

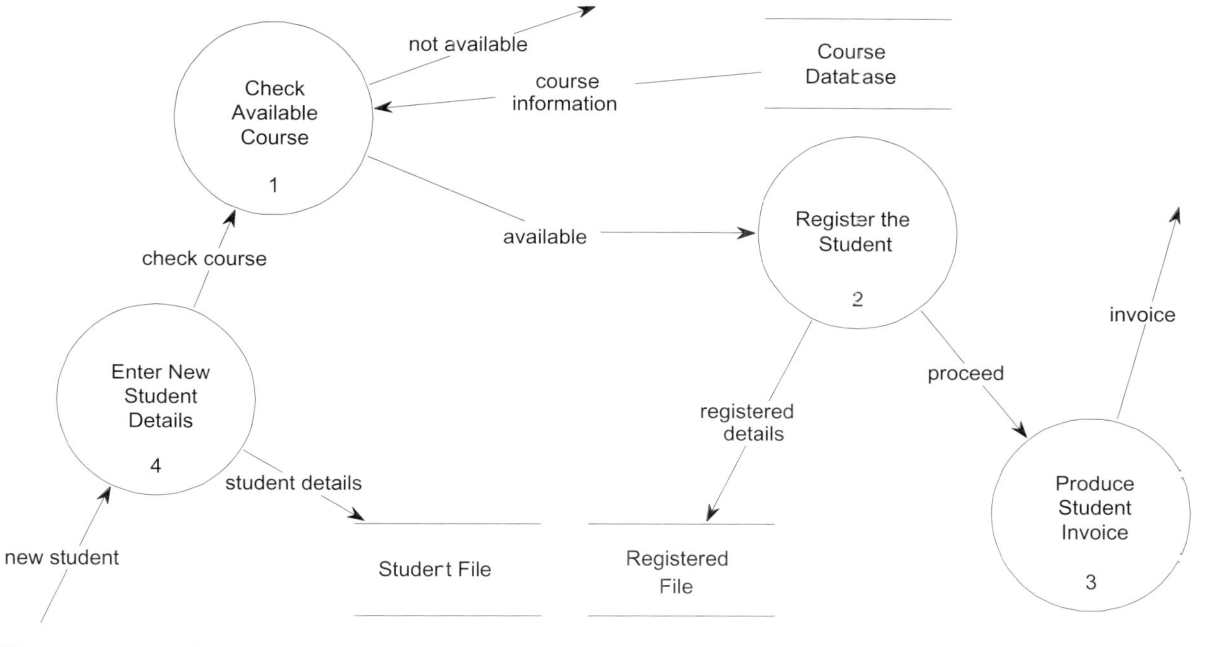

Figure 2.8 *New Student details*

Refinement check

```
Project: C:\SELECT\SYSTEM\COLLEGE\
Title  : College Admission System
Date: 20-Dec-2000 Time: 12:0

Checking COLLEGE2.DAT

No Errors detected, No Warnings given.

---- End of report ----
```

Store balancing for the Registered File

```
Project: C:\SELECT\SYSTEM\COLLEGE\
Title  : College Admission System
Date: 20-Dec-2000 Time: 12:0

Name: Registered File
Type: Store
Bnf:  [ continuing students | student details ]
This item is used on the following diagrams:
    COLLEGE2.DAT College Admission System
    COLLEGE3.DAT New Student Details
Last changed: DEFAULT        20-Dec-2000 11:51:33

---- End of report ----
```

Store balancing for the Student File

```
Project: C:\SELECT\SYSTEM\COLLEGE\
Title  : College Admission System
Date: 20-Dec-2000 Time: 12:3

Name: Student File
Type: Store
Bnf:  student details
This item is used on the following diagrams:
    COLLEGE3.DAT New Student Details
Last changed: DEFAULT        20-Dec-2000 12:21:33


---- End of report ----
```

(iv) Process specification for the Check Available Course process

```
@IN  = check course
@IN  = course information
@OUT = available
@OUT = not available

@PSPEC 0.1.1 Check Available Course

On receiving the check course command do:
        obtain the course information from the Course Database
        if the course exists and there are places then
                send an available message
        else
                send a not available message for display on the VDU screen
@
```

Process specification for the Enter New Student Details process

```
@IN  = new student
@OUT = check course
@OUT = student details

@PSPEC 0.1.4 Enter New Student Details

   On receiving the new student command do:
       obtain the new student details and send them to
       the Student File
       then send a check course message to proceed with the registration
@
```

Process specification for the Register the Student process

```
@IN  = available
@OUT = proceed
@OUT = registered details

@PSPEC 0.1.2 Register the Student
  On receiving the available command do:
    obtain the registered details about the student
    and course and send them to the Registered File
        then
    proceed to produce an invoice

@
```

Process specification for the Check Available Course process

```
@IN  = proceed
@OUT = invoice

@PSPEC 0.1.3 Produce Student Invoice

   On receiving the proceed message do:
       produce an invoice for printing out to the student

@
```

Note. All individual PSPECS should be checked to ensure they are syntactically correct. They must contain the data flows within the body of the explanation.

An example check of the Produce Student Invoice PSPEC

```
Project: C:\SELECT\SYSTEM\COLLEGE\
Title  : College Admission System
Date: 20-Dec-2000 Time: 13:0

Checking PCAS7.DAT

No Errors detected, No Warnings given.

---- End of report ----
```

Which has the same syntax as the diagram checks.

(v) Consistency check of all diagrams

```
Project: C:\SELECT\SYSTEM\COLLEGE\
Title  : College Admission System
Date: 20-Dec-2000 Time: 12:5

Report: Diagram Consistency checking

This report contains a consistency check of all the diagrams in the project.

Checking COLLEGE1.DAT
   No Errors detected, No Warnings given.

Checking COLLEGE2.DAT
   No Errors detected, No Warnings given.

Checking COLLEGE3.DAT
   No Errors detected, No Warnings given.

Checking PCAS1.DAT
   No Errors detected, No Warnings given.

Checking PCAS2.DAT
   No Errors detected, No Warnings given.

Checking PCAS3.DAT
   No Errors detected, No Warnings given.

Checking PCAS4.DAT
   No Errors detected, No Warnings given.

Checking PCAS5.DAT
   No Errors detected, No Warnings given.

Checking PCAS6.DAT
   No Errors detected, No Warnings given.

Checking PCAS7.DAT
   No Errors detected, No Warnings given.


---- End of report ----
```

End of the College Admission system.

SSADM

Additional information

Main characteristics

Standard framework for analysis and design:

- A structured framework methodology
- Main tasks include modules, stages, steps and activities

® SSADM is a registered trademark

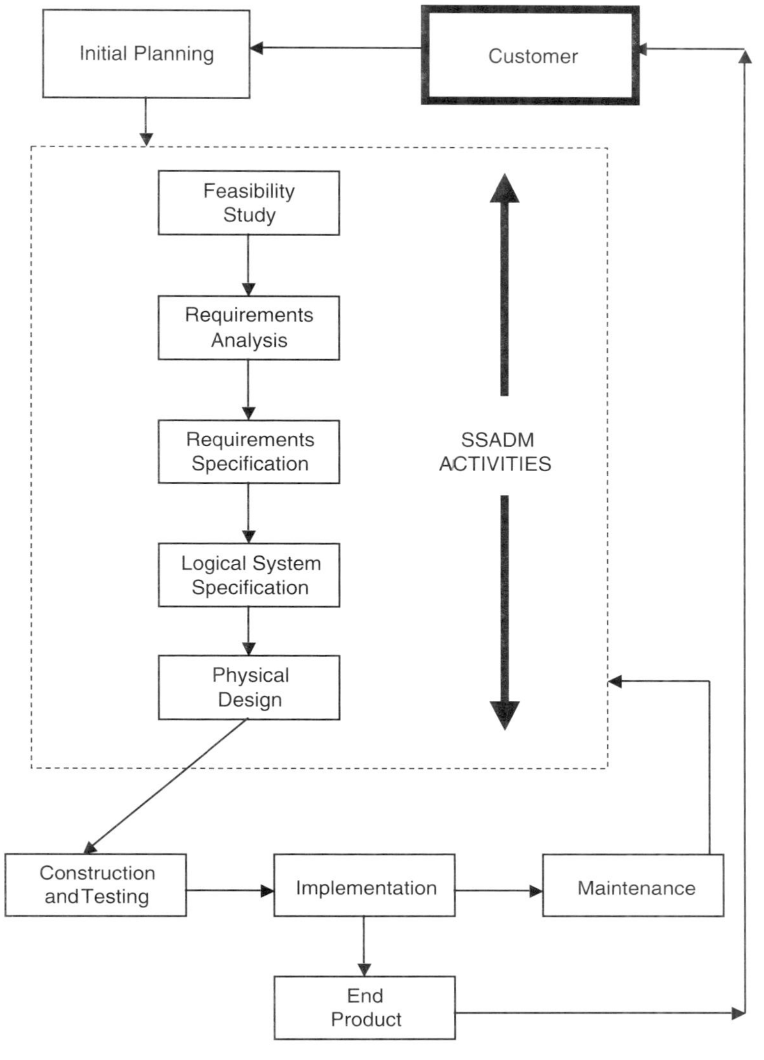

Figure 2.9 *Outline of SSADM (Structured Systems Analysis and Design Method)*

Standardization of development documentation:

- Standard documentation includes diagrams, forms or reports (SSADM is used extensively within UK government departments and industry, since the release of version 4 the UK government IT agency (CCTA) formalized SSADM into a British Standard)
- Provides a common analysis and design strategy, so any person who understands SSADM will be able to review any documentation from any SSADM development process

Powerful set of development tools and techniques:

- Provides a number of structured techniques to aid the development process, such techniques include:
  - Dataflow Modelling (DFM). This assists the analysis process by producing diagrammatic representations of what the system should do. The diagrams are hierarchical in structure starting with a basic outline (context diagram) and refining through with a greater level of detail
  - Logical Data Modelling (LDM). Here the real life entities and their associated attributes are used to model the files and records within an information system
  - Entity Behaviour Modelling (EBM). An event is an occurrence that changes an entity or associated records in any way. EBM models any unexpected events by introducing concepts of error checking. The view wherein an information system is reflective of processing transactions is handled, for example for a customer's bank account where the balance and overdraft values may alter after certain transactions. These events are modelled in an Entity Life History (ELH) diagram that demonstrates the order in which the event may occur

- Available CASE tools to implement the required structures into a standard format and ensure the syntax meets the requirements of the British Standard (BS 7738)

Once completed the three techniques need to be checked against each other by carrying out rigorous validation checks to ensure the final model is a true representation of the proposed software system.
Table 2.1 shows the permissible links between SSADM symbols.

Table 2.1

	Process	Data store	External entity
Process	yes	yes	yes
Data store	yes	no	no
External entity	yes	no	yes

For example, Figure 2.10 is not acceptable.

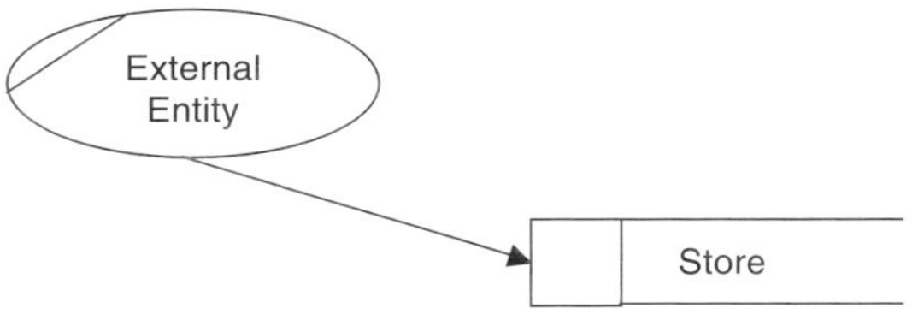

Figure 2.10

Rule: A process must always be present to access a data store.

Note that two external entities can be directly linked. This is shown in Figure 2.11.

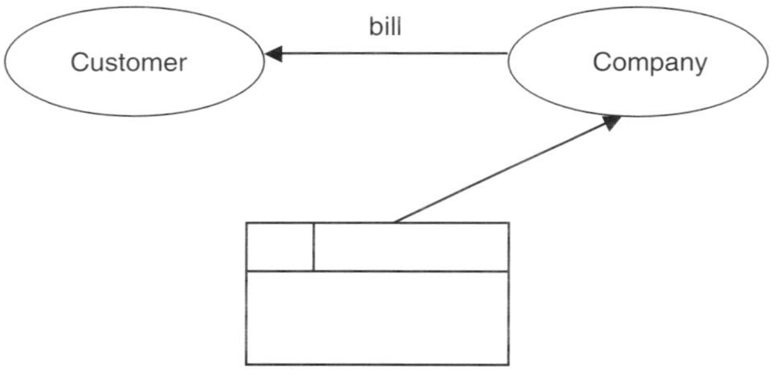

Figure 2.11

Suggested solution to Exercise 2.3.6

Bess and Bailey Department Store Customer Order System

Additional exercise

Bernese Mountain Dog Club Member Event Request System

Outlined below are the system requirements:

> The Bernese Mountain Dog Club (BMDC) requires a system to record details from members about the various events that it secludes. Members can make a request for events to be carried out by the club or modify existing events. Initially all member requests are checked by the club secretary, who first checks the member details (i.e. to ensure they are fully paid up members etc.) then records the request for safe keeping. The request is then added as an agenda item for the next committee meeting. The committee members will discuss the request and if adopted it will be stored in the event's file and the member notified. If the request is not adopted then the member is notified as to why it has been rejected.

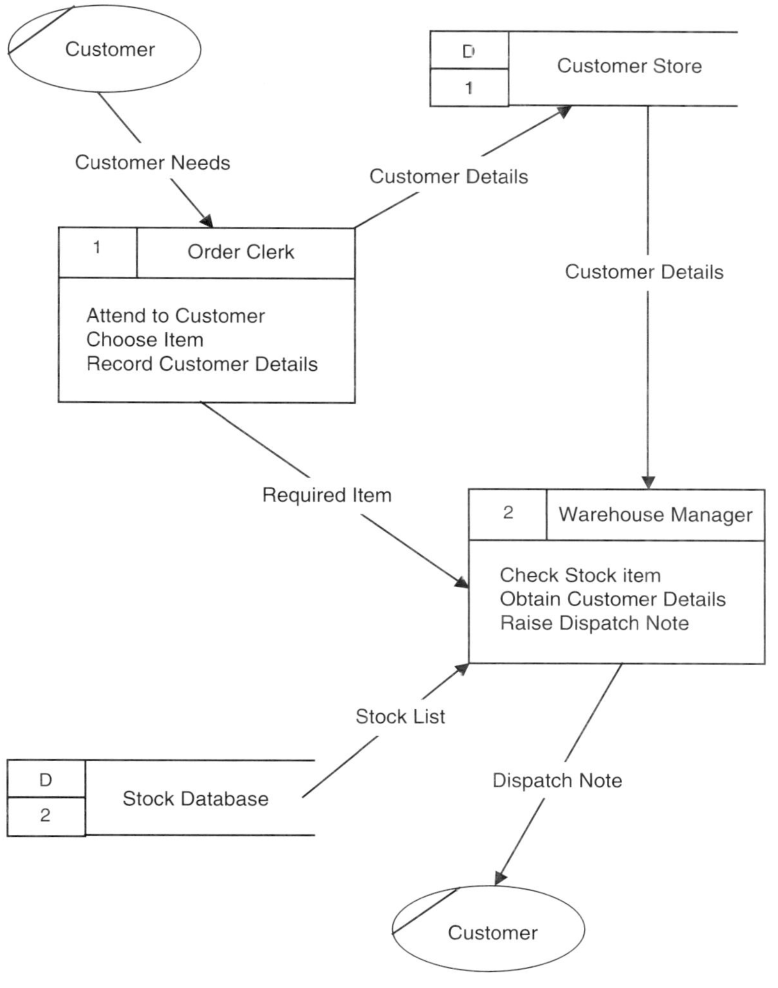

Figure 2.12 *Bess and Bailey Department Store Customer Order System*

Analyse the above requirements and:

1. Complete an SSADM context diagram.
2. Refine the context diagram to fully represent the requirements

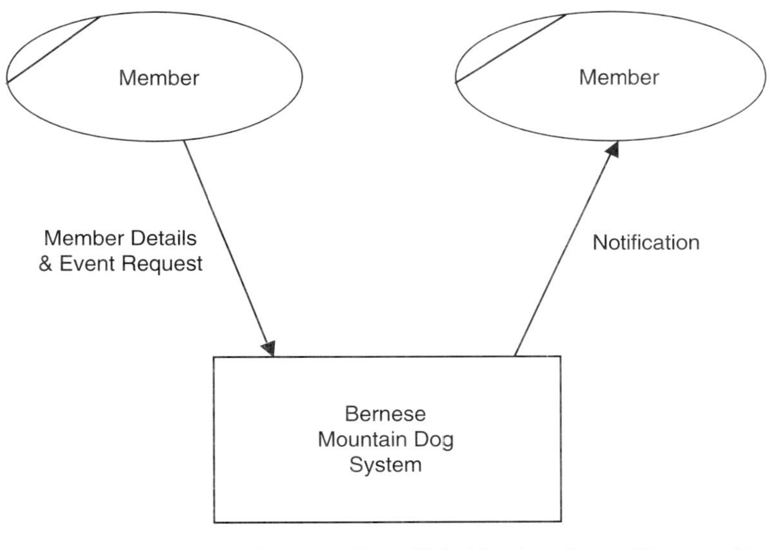

Figure 2.13 *Bernese Mountain Dog Club Member Event Request System context diagram*

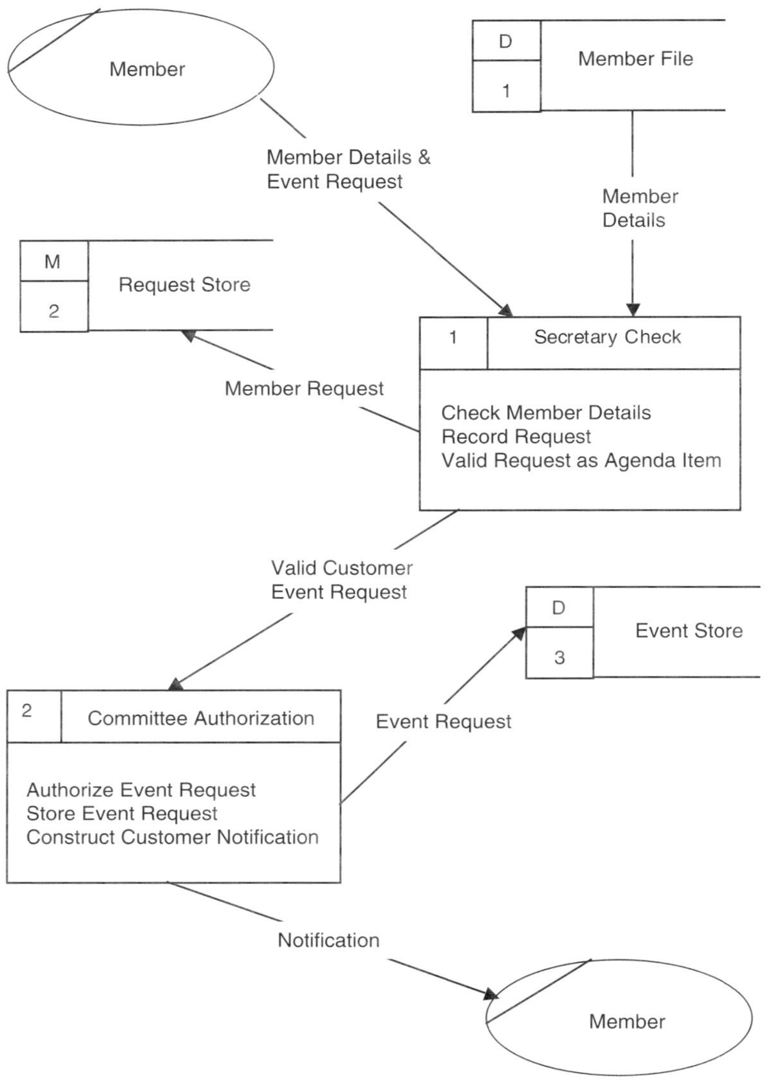

Figure 2.14 *Refinement of the context diagram*

Object-oriented analysis (OOA) development

Suggested solution to Exercise 2.3.3 – Seminar Organization

(i) Textual analysis

An organizer needs to keep and update information on a seminar devoted to canine health. The seminar is made up of several sessions, each run by different speakers. The speakers running the sessions have to produce a booklet for their own slot. Each session has a chairperson and that person is only allocated this role once. Information about the speakers who produce the booklets needs to be recorded; each booklet is written by one speaker only and speakers are required to produce only one booklet. For the seminar presentation purposes, a person can be a chairperson or a speaker.

(ii) The required classes are determined from the textual analysis and are shown underlined above. The required classes to be presented are:

- organiser
- seminar
- session
- speaker
- booklet
- chairperson

(iii) Associations

organiser and seminar (one to one association as there is only one seminar and one organizer)
seminar and session (one to many association as there is only one seminar, but each seminar can be divided into many sessions)
session and speaker (one to one association as each session is run by different speakers)
session and chairperson (one to one association as each person is allocated this role once only)
speaker and booklet (one to one association as each speaker is responsible for only one session and one booklet only needs to be produced for each slot
booklet and session (one to one association as all booklets are unique for each session)

(iv) Inheritance
The only inheritance factor comes from the fact that a person can be a chairperson or a speaker. Both are human and must contain common characteristics. Person could be classified as an abstract parent of a chairperson and speaker as no instances of it need to be created (i.e. we do not require a person object).

(v) Associated text

Class: Organizer
'There is only one instance of this class, it is the orchestrating instance'

Class: Seminar
Responsibilities: Record the overall theme of the seminar on canine health

Class: Session
Responsibilities: Record the session topic, venue, date and time

Class: Person
Responsibilities: Record the name, address, telephone number and e-mail address and allocated session of the speaker or chairperson

Class: Speaker (inherits from Person)
Responsibilities: Record the session topic

Class: Chairperson (inherits from Person)
Responsibilities:

Class: Booklet
Responsibilities: Record title of booklet and content information

(vi) Class-association diagram

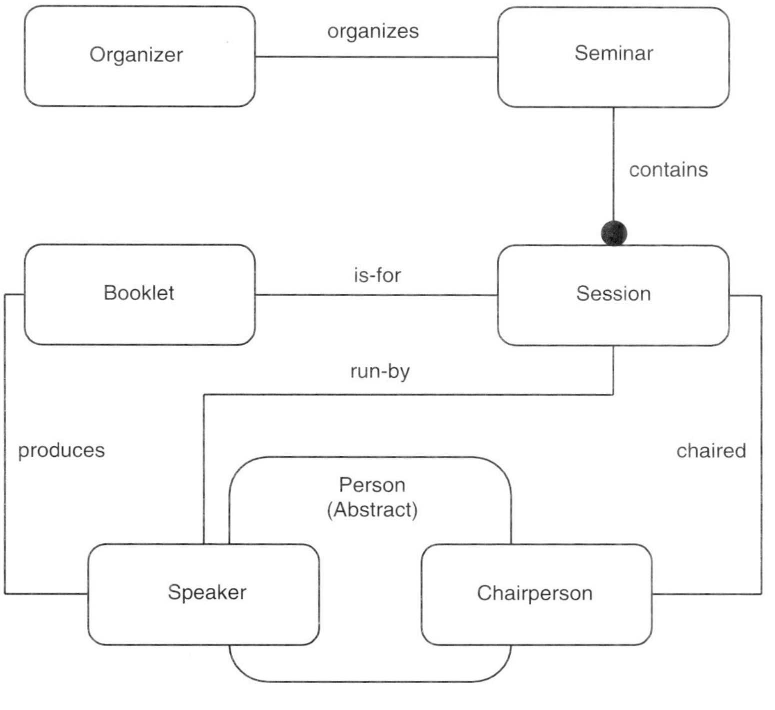

Figure 2.15

Example analysis problem

Ruddles University – Software Engineering Programme

The following is an extract from a negotiated statement of requirements:

> The computing school of the Ruddles University requires a system to keep information about the special Software Engineering Programme (SEP) it is setting up. The programme consists of a number of lectures, each taken by a single lecturer. A lecturer can take more than one lecture slot. Students need to register for each lecture slot and they can attend as many as they want. Students requiring formal certification for the Software Engineering Programme will need to take (and pass) a single examination at the end of the year. One lecturer has the responsibility of writing the examination paper.

Carry out the following analysis of the statement of requirements:

(i) Perform a textual analysis to ascertain any candidate objects
(ii) Select the required classes to be presented
(iii) Ascertain any associations that exist
(iv) Specify the inheritance factors contained within the text
(v) Produce associated text to outline the class responsibilities
(vi) Complete a class-association diagram

Suggested solution

(i) Textual analysis

The computing school of the Ruddles University requires a system to keep information about the special Software Engineering Programme (SEP) it is setting up. The programme consists of a number of lectures, each taken by a single lecturer. A lecturer can take more than one lecture slot. Students need to register for each lecture slot and they can attend as many as they want. Students requiring formal certification for the Software Engineering Programme will need to take (and pass) a single examination at the end of the year. One lecturer has the responsibility of writing the examination paper.

(ii) Required classes

- Computing school (Organizer, but not part of the SEP)
- Software Engineering Programme (SEP)
- Lecture
- Lecturer
- Student
- Examination

(iii) Associations:

SEP and Lecture (one to many association as there are many lecturers associated with the SEP)
Lecturer and Lecture (one to many association as each lecture requires only one lecturer, but lecturers can attend more than one lecture)
Lecture and Student (many to many association as many students can attend a single lecture and students can attend many lecturers)
Lecturer and Examination Paper (one to one association as one lecturer is assigned to write a single examination paper)
Student and Examination Paper (one to many association as there is only one examination paper which can be taken by many students)

(iv) Inheritance
As Lecturer and Student share some common characteristics which they could inherit from an abstract class Person.

(v) Associated text

Class: SEP
'There is only one instance of this class, it is the orchestrating instance'

Class: Lecture
Responsibilities: Record the title, date, time, location, register and lecturer

Class: Person
Responsibilities: Record the name and e-mail address

Class: Lecturer (inherits from Person)
Responsibilities: Record the room, phone, subject discipline

Class: Student
Responsibilities: Record the course, personal tutor, examination requirements

Class: Examination
Responsibilities: Record the date, time, duration, location

(vi) Object diagram

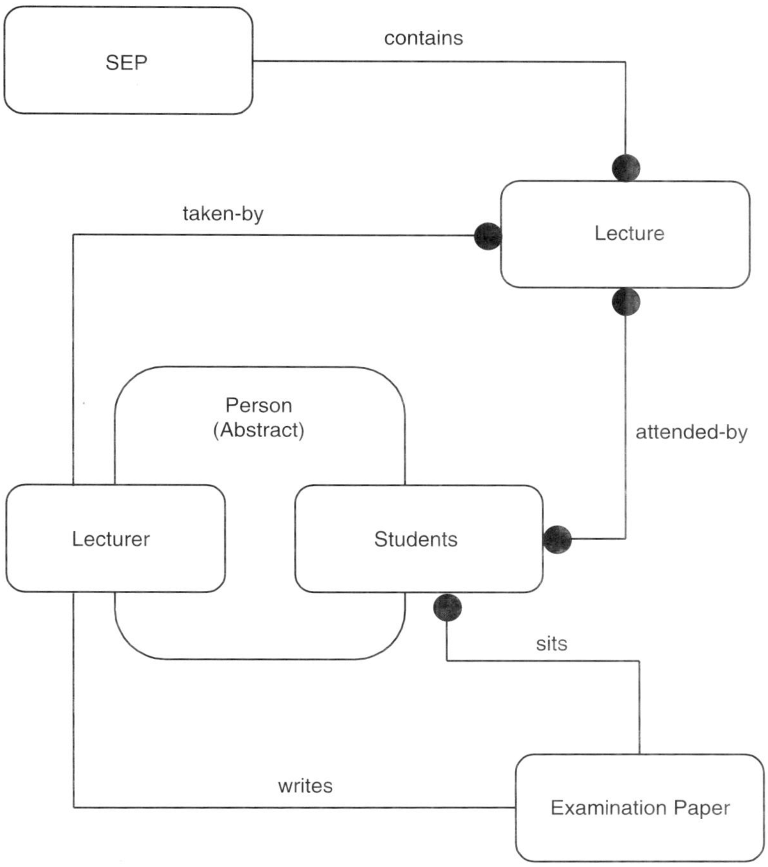

Figure 2.16 *Software Engineering Programme*

Unified Modelling Language (UML)

The UML model provides an industry standard development language which is ideally suited to the design requirements of modern object-oriented languages like Java.

It was adopted by the Object Management Group (OMG) as a standard in 1997.

See: http://www.omg.org/

Like most other analysis tools UML provides a set of diagrammatic techniques to visualize the relationship of elements between interrelated processes.

UML views

- Use-case view. A view showing the functionality of the system as seen by external actors
- Logical view. A view showing how the functionality is designed inside the system, in terms of the system's static structure and dynamic behaviour
- Component view. A view showing the organization of code components
- Concurrency view. A view that addresses the problems of communication and synchronization that are present in a concurrent system
- Deployment view: A view showing the deployment of the system into the physical architecture with actual computers and associated nodes.

Review of basic diagram structures

Class diagram

Frog
colour: String type: String location: String size: Real

Remember some basic conventions here, for example a lead capital for class names.
Creating two instances of the Frog class gives:

    Frog kermit = new Frog();
    Frog slimey = new Frog();

Creates two Frog objects:

Object diagrams

The convention is to start objects with a lowercase letter.

kermit
colour = "green" type = "Greenback" location = "UK" size = 7.5

slimey
colour = "brown" type = "Bullfrog" location = "US" size = 18.75

Suggested solution for Exercise 2.3.4 – Bernese College

(i) Textual analysis:

The Bernese College wants to improve its marketing strategy by setting up an Intranet website primarily to contain a computerized prospectus. The prospectus will contain course information that can be viewed by lecturers, managers, non-teaching staff and students. The college courses are made up of modules that are classified at three different levels: foundation, intermediate and advanced. Students will take three years (full-time) to complete the course starting at the foundation level. Foundation modules need to be assessed by incorporating level one key skills. Intermediate modules need to be assessed by directed coursework and Advanced modules will incorporate 'A' level examinations.

The prospectus needs to provide a list of lecturers, courses and modules with a more detailed description of the syllabus content of the modules. Information about individual lectures should include their location, main subject disciplines and telephone extension as well as the modules that the lecturer tutors. Each course is allocated a unique identifier and is made up of a number of modules at the required level. The management responsibilities of the prospectus need to add and/or remove lecturers and courses from the system. Each course is allocated a course director, who is also a lecturer, who has the responsibility for running the course and updating the course information contained in the prospectus.

Some of the above candidate identifiers for classes can be ignored as they are not relevant. For example, Students do not need to appear in the prospectus and are not relevant to the analysis model.

The main classes to be considered are:

Website, Prospectus, Lecturer, Course, Module (a super class for the Foundation, Intermediate and Advanced modules)

Note a Course Director is also a Lecturer (so it does not require a separate class, but its presence will be specified within an association). Courses are allocated a unique identifier (which can locate the course within the prospectus).

(ii) Relationships

Website contains a Prospectus
Lecturer listed in a Prospectus
Lecturer (Course Director) directs a Course
Lecturer tutors a Module
Course specified in the Prospectus
Module contained in a Course

(iii) Responsibilities:

Prospectus. Update course lists, update lecturer lists, display lecturers, display courses
Lecturer. Record location, subject disciplines, phone extension, current modules

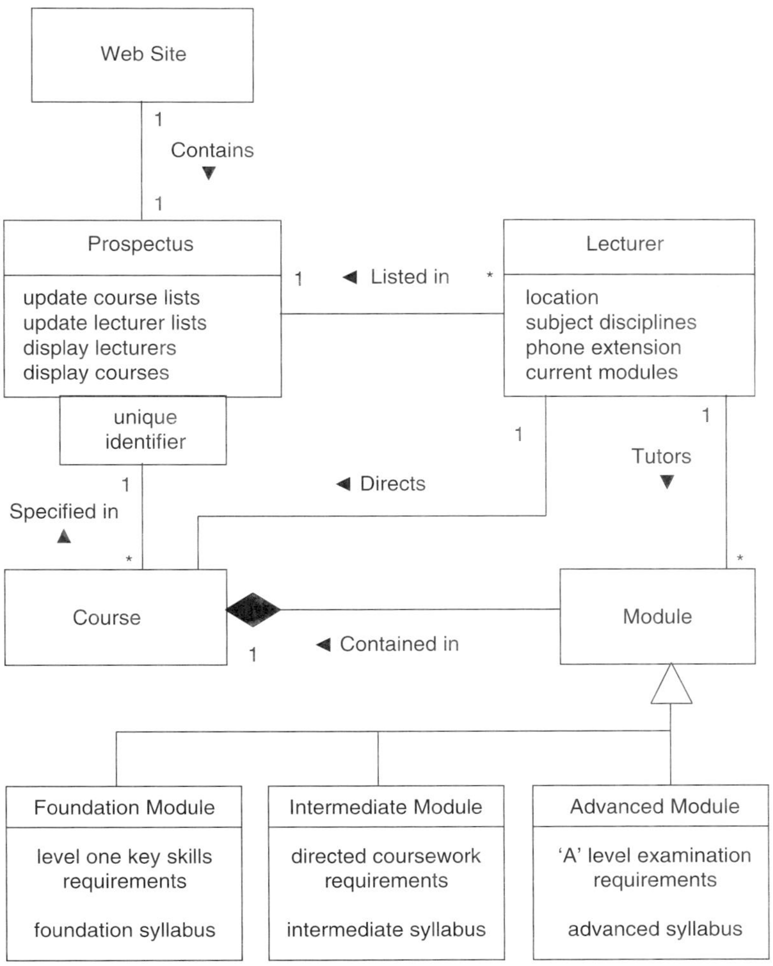

Figure 2.17

Foundation module. Record level one key skills requirements, foundation syllabus content
Intermediate module. Record directed coursework requirements, intermediate syllabus content
Advanced module. Record 'A' level examination requirements, advanced syllabus content

(iv) Class diagram

Additional example

Below is a statement of requirements for the Rio Corner Shop:

> The Rio Corner Shop requires a system to keep information about its newspaper daily delivery service. Each daily delivery involves several rounds, with each round being assigned a unique delivery person. Each round contains customers within given road boundaries. The deliveries consist of different types of newspaper product (local newspapers, national newspapers and news magazines). A customer may order several kinds of newspaper product for delivery and each newspaper product may be ordered by many customers.

Complete the following tasks:

1. Analyse the text to establish the classes to be presented
2. Establish any associations that may exist
3. Specify any inheritance factors contained within the text
4. Produce associated text to outline the class responsibilities
5. Complete a class-association diagram

Suggested solutions

1. Possible classes (obtained from textual analysis)
   DailyDeliveryService, PaperRound, DeliveryPerson, Customer,
   Newspaper, LocalNewspaper, NationalNewspaper, NewsMagazines

2. Associations
   DailyDeliveryService & PaperRound
   (Each daily delivery consists of many rounds 1:n)
   PaperRound & DeliveryPerson
   (Each round has one delivery person and each delivery person is allocated only one round 1:1)
   PaperRound & Customer
   (Each single paper round has many customers 1:n)
   Customer & Newspaper
   (A customer may order several kinds of newspaper product for delivery and each newspaper product may be ordered by many customers m:n)

3. Inheritance

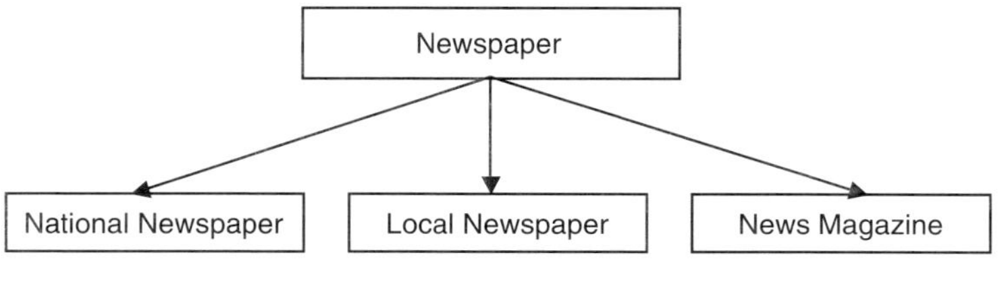

Figure 2.18

   All inherit from Newspaper

4. Responsibilities
   DailyDeliveryService. An orchestrating instance (only one instance of this)
   PaperRound. Records the delivery name, area and the delivery person
   DeliveryPerson. Records the name, address and telephone number
   Customer. Records the customer name, address and telephone number, delivery requirements
   Newspaper. An abstract class for all paper deliveries. Records the paper name, price
   LocalNewspaper. (Subclass of Newspaper) Records the delivery area

NationalNewspaper. (Subclass of Newspaper) Records the additional supplements
NewsMagazines. Records the magazine edition

5. Class-association diagram to represent the system (see Figure 2.19)
This example is going to look a little deeper into the requirements of the attributes and operations, below is a basic diagram to outline a full class structure:

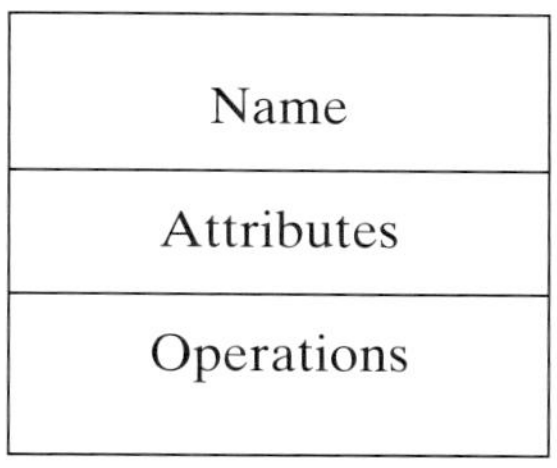

And remember that:

+ expresses public data and
– expresses private data

The operations will be implemented as methods within a class structure.

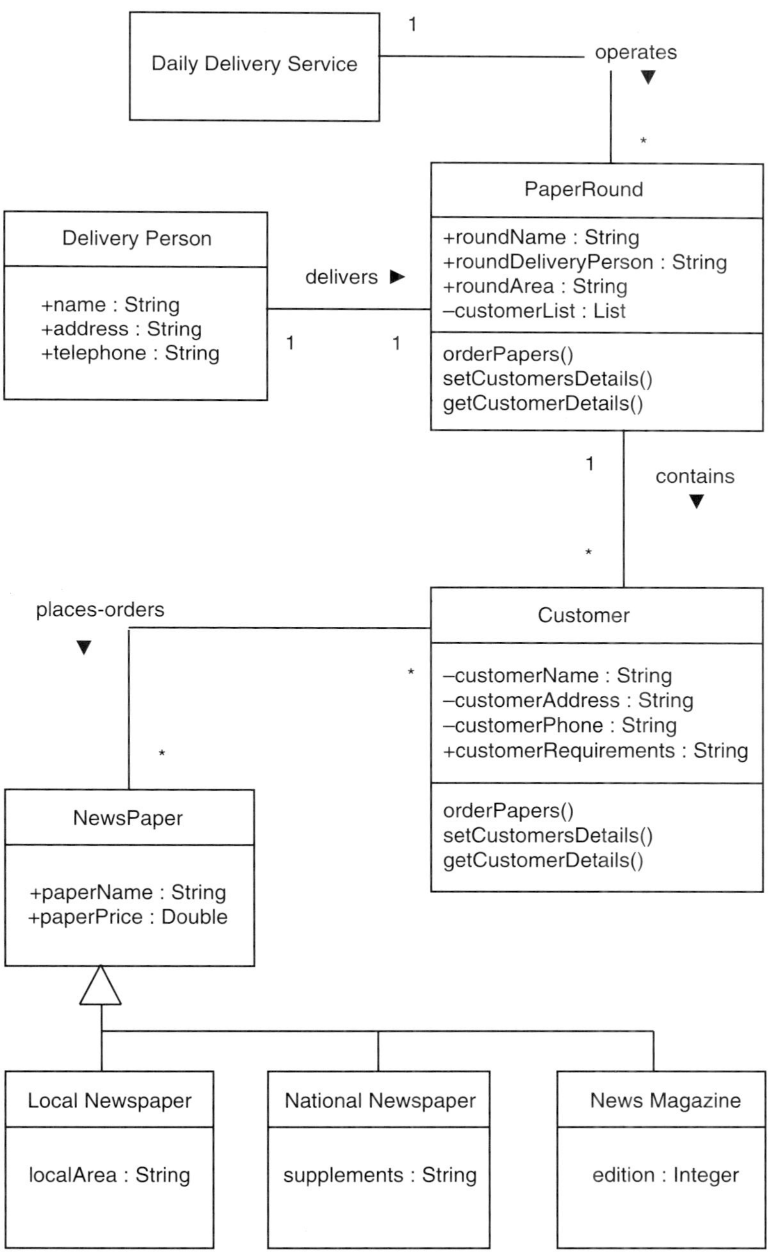

Figure 2.19 *Class-association diagram*

Data modelling

Additional information

Data models

A data model will represent the complete set of entities and relationships for a given system. It can be divided into the following stages:

1. A conceptual model of the data representing major objects and relationships
2. A refined model with any redundant components removed
3. A normalized model that is ready for conversion to a physical database

Normalization has three main aims:

1. To find and group together all the properties that are associated with a particular object
2. To remove any redundant information. For example, there is no point in storing a person's name, address, telephone number, e-mail address, etc. in multiple locations within a database
3. To provide unique identification for individual records. For example, you need to make sure when you delete a record from a particular table that it is the correct record

Symbols used:

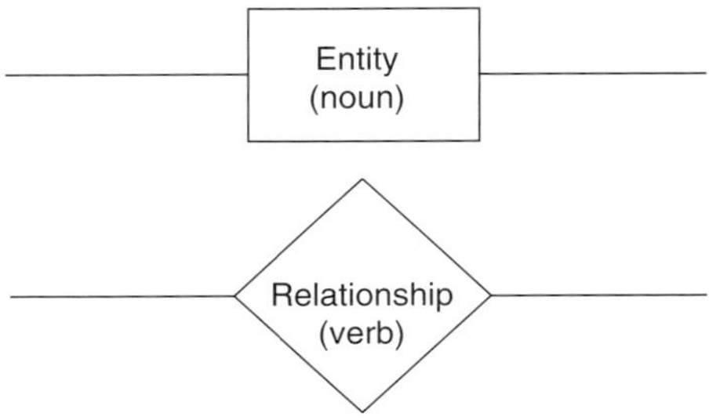

Figure 2.20

Attributes. These represent the 'Data Item Occurrences' that a particular real world entity contains

Cardinality. Specifies the degree of the relationship (1:1, 1:m, m:1 and m:n)

Quality aspects within database systems

Data integrity ensures that the overall data quality within a database system is maintained. It refers to the degree to which data is:

- accurate
- available when it is needed
- used correctly
- providing a correct relationship to other data

Two types of data integrity constraints that need to be evident within a database management system are:

- Inter-record integrity – data types and component values need to be consistent among all entries made in a column of a database table. For example, dates appearing in the same column must always be entered in the same way
- Referential integrity – references between database records must be valid. You need to make sure the referenced data does actually exist

Approaches to data modelling

1. Top-down design:
   - identify entities
   - determine attributes of the entities
   - determine the relationships and the associated degrees

2. Bottom-up design:
   - obtain existing information from within an organization
   - from the attribute data obtained group into required entities
   - determine the nature of the relationships

The examples shown in the book and the support material use the top-level design as it leads to a data model that is well organized. But this method can lead to problems if important data is left out. The bottom-up method does have the advantage that it helps ensure that no important details are left out. Within industry it is possible that some analysts will use a combination of both methods which can be validated against each other to ensure completeness and sound organizational structure.

Entity relationship diagrams

These are used as a graphical technique to document the logical design of the database. They can be used to represent the entire logical database scheme or certain user views within the system that contain more detailed information.

Database implementation

The aim of the systems analysis unit is not to teach practical database applications, these are covered by the data analysis and database unit, but to provide the analysis ground work (the conceptual model), develop the design model (logical model) and give a taster of how the model can be implemented.

However, if some students have not yet studied the database unit they will need some basic skills in implementing the analysis/design model.

Microsoft Access lays down the following steps for designing a database:

1. Determine the purpose of your database
2. Determine the tables you need in the database
3. Determine the fields you need in the tables
4. Identify fields with unique values
5. Determine the relationships between tables
6. Refine your design
7. Add data and create other database objects
8. Use Microsoft Access analysis tools

Step 1 determines the purpose of the database. What are its essential characteristics, how is it going to be used, who is going to use it, what information is required from it and what are the essential characteristics.

Step 2 the tables can be developed from the entities developed from within the conceptual model.

Step 3 the fields and their characteristics can be ascertained from the conceptual model attribute diagram where the domains can be used as a base for the required data type.

Step 4 the primary key defined within the attribute diagram can be used as a unique identifier.

Step 5 they are contained within the entity-relationship diagram along with their associated degrees.

Step 6 the logical model will ensure the correct relationship characteristics are maintained by assigning foreign keys. Once the tables, fields and relationships have been designed, it's time to study the design and detect any flaws that might remain. It is easier to change the database design now, rather than after you have filled the tables with data.

Step 7 you can now add the data to the tables (and any forms, queries, macros etc.).

Exercise 2.3.5

Morgan Software House

(i) Entities

Programmer, Terminal, Systems, Office, Manual, Manager

(ii) Relationships

Manager and Office. 1:1 relationship as each office has only one manager and a manager is allocated to only one office

Manager and Programmer. 1:n relationship as a single manager is in charge of many programmers and each programmer is responsible to one manager

Office and Terminal. 1:n relationship as each single office can contain up to 10 terminals.

Programmer and Terminal. 1:1 relationship as each individual programmer is allocated their own terminal and each terminal is used by a single programmer only

Programmer and System. 1:n (or m:n) relationship as programmers can work on one or more systems. There is no mention in the brief if the systems are worked on by individual programmers or open to many programmers
Terminal and Manual. 1:1 relationship as each terminal has its own manual and each manual contains the specification of an individual terminal.

Note: Although there must be a relationship between Office and Programmer there is no mention of this in the specification. So it is not included within the list of possible associations.

(iii) Entity-relationship diagram

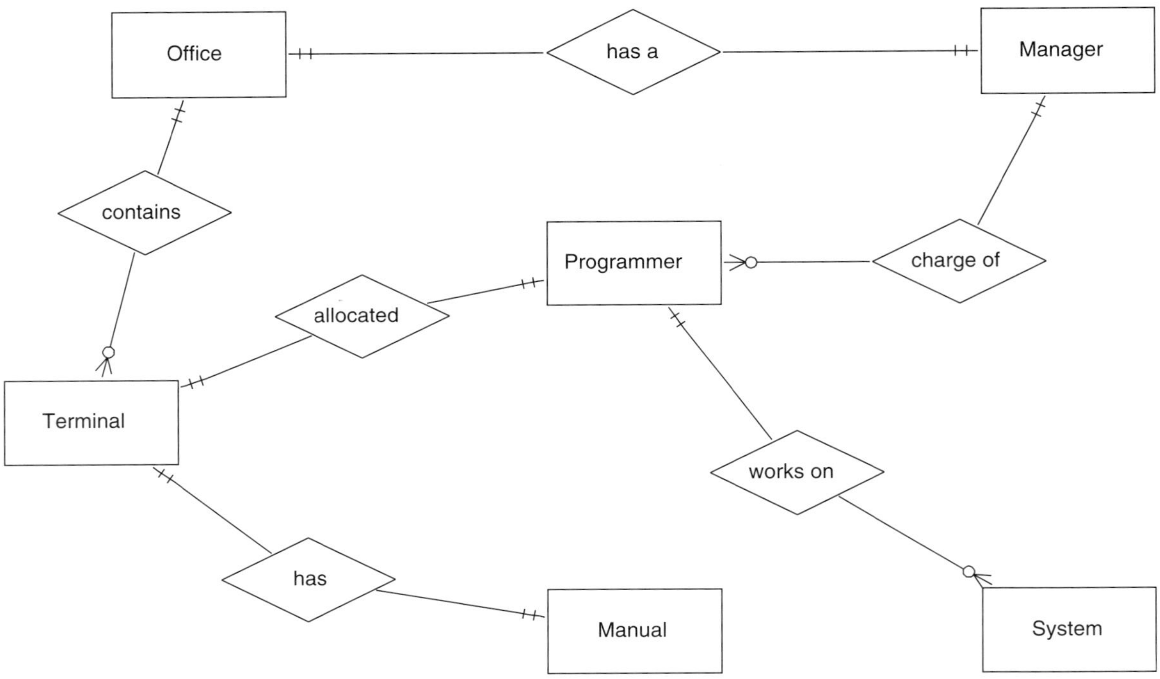

Figure 2.21 *Morgan Software House entity-relationship diagram*

(iv) Attribute diagram – Programmer

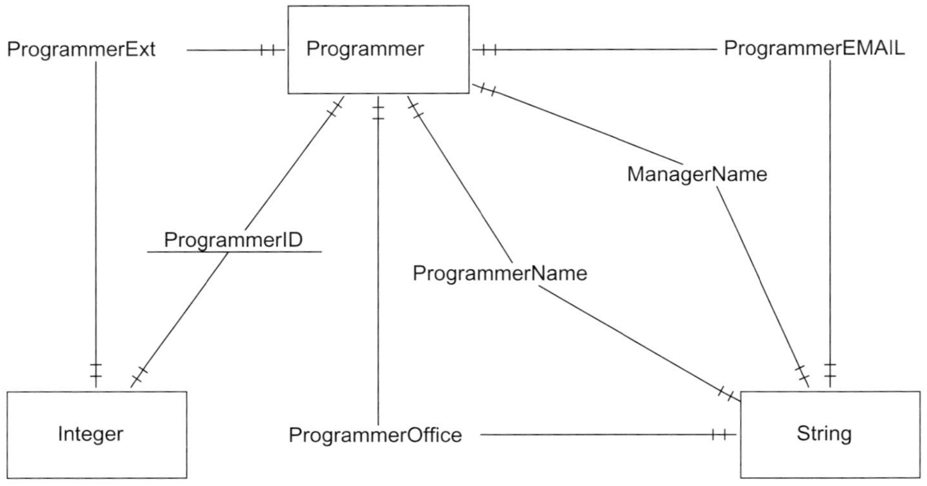

Figure 2.22 *Possible attributes for Programmer*

Attribute diagram – Manager

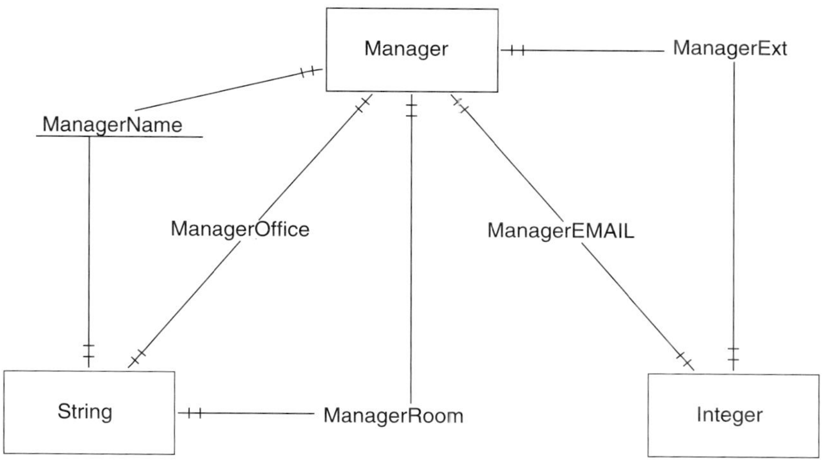

Figure 2.23 *Possible attributes for Manager*

Note: As ManagerName is the primary key of Manager and it has been allocated as a foreign key of Programmer this specifies the 1:n relationship between Manager and Programmer.

Solution to Exercise 2.3.6

Extract from a College Management System

(i) Entity-relationship diagram

Figure 2.24 *Relationship between Course Director and Student (l:n)*

(ii) Attribute diagram – Course Director

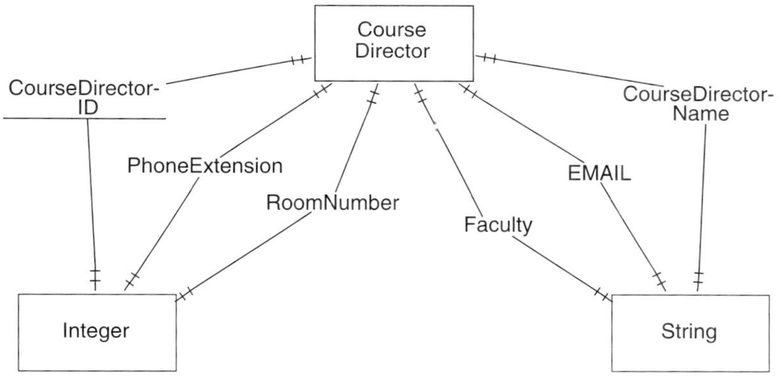

Figure 2.25 *Attribute diagram for Course Director*

(iii) Attribute diagram – Student

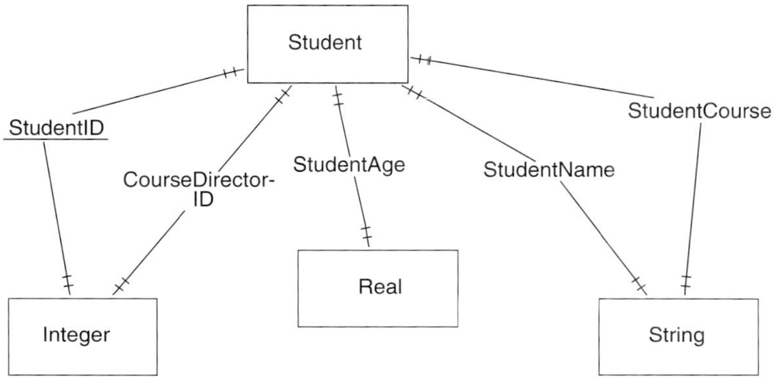

Figure 2.26 *Attribute diagram for Student*

(iv) Database – Student Table

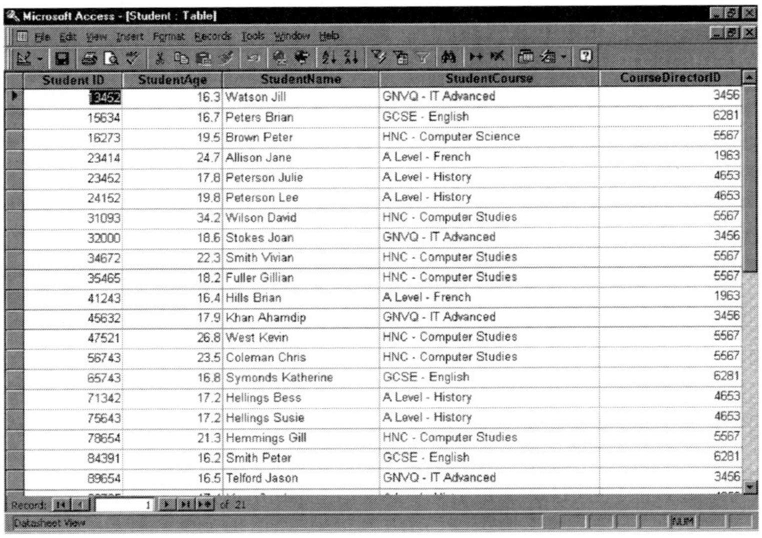

Microsoft Access - [Student : Table]

Student ID	StudentAge	StudentName	StudentCourse	CourseDirectorID
13452	16.3	Watson Jill	GNVQ - IT Advanced	3456
15634	16.7	Peters Brian	GCSE - English	6281
16273	19.5	Brown Peter	HNC - Computer Science	5567
23414	24.7	Allison Jane	A Level - French	1963
23452	17.8	Peterson Julie	A Level - History	4653
24152	19.8	Peterson Lee	A Level - History	4653
31093	34.2	Wilson David	HNC - Computer Studies	5567
32000	18.6	Stokes Joan	GNVQ - IT Advanced	3456
34672	22.3	Smith Vivian	HNC - Computer Studies	5567
35465	18.2	Fuller Gillian	HNC - Computer Studies	5567
41243	16.4	Hills Brian	A Level - French	1963
45632	17.9	Khan Ahamdip	GNVQ - IT Advanced	3456
47521	26.8	West Kevin	HNC - Computer Studies	5567
56743	23.5	Coleman Chris	HNC - Computer Studies	5567
65743	16.8	Symonds Katherine	GCSE - English	6281
71342	17.2	Hellings Bess	A Level - History	4653
75643	17.2	Hellings Susie	A Level - History	4653
78654	21.3	Hemmings Gill	HNC - Computer Studies	5567
84391	16.2	Smith Peter	GCSE - English	6281
89654	16.5	Telford Jason	GNVQ - IT Advanced	3456

Record: 1 of 21

Figure 2.27

(v) Database – Course Director Table

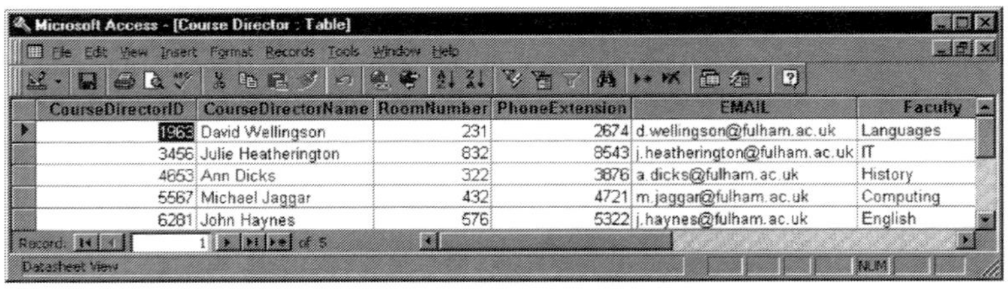

Microsoft Access - [Course Director : Table]

CourseDirectorID	CourseDirectorName	RoomNumber	PhoneExtension	EMAIL	Faculty
1963	David Wellingson	231	2674	d.wellingson@fulham.ac.uk	Languages
3456	Julie Heatherington	832	8543	j.heatherington@fulham.ac.uk	IT
4653	Ann Dicks	322	3876	a.dicks@fulham.ac.uk	History
5567	Michael Jaggar	432	4721	m.jaggar@fulham.ac.uk	Computing
6281	John Haynes	576	5322	j.haynes@fulham.ac.uk	English

Record: 1 of 5

Figure 2.28

(vi) Sorting Course Director Table into faculty order

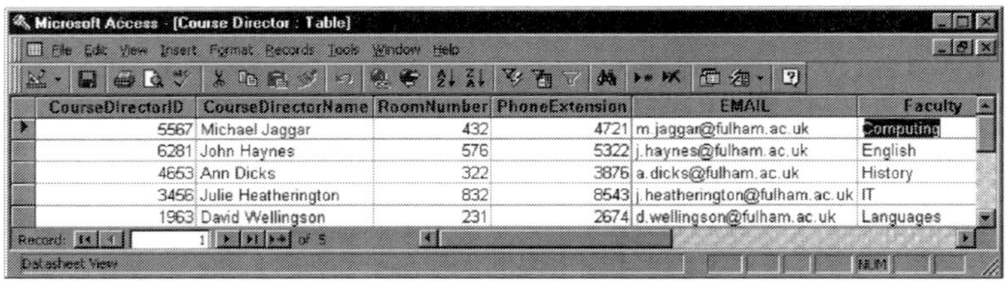

Microsoft Access - [Course Director : Table]

CourseDirectorID	CourseDirectorName	RoomNumber	PhoneExtension	EMAIL	Faculty
5567	Michael Jaggar	432	4721	m.jaggar@fulham.ac.uk	Computing
6281	John Haynes	576	5322	j.haynes@fulham.ac.uk	English
4653	Ann Dicks	322	3876	a.dicks@fulham.ac.uk	History
3456	Julie Heatherington	832	8543	j.heatherington@fulham.ac.uk	IT
1963	David Wellingson	231	2674	d.wellingson@fulham.ac.uk	Languages

Record: 1 of 5

Figure 2.29

(vii) Applying a filter (Selecting: Records, Filter, Advanced Filter/Sort)

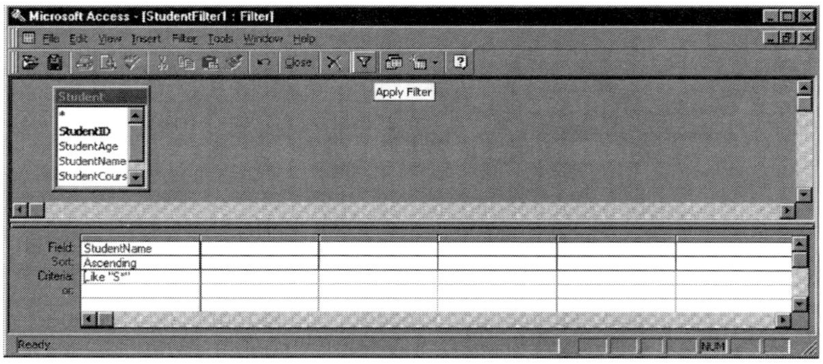

Figure 2.30

(viii) Result of the filter sort

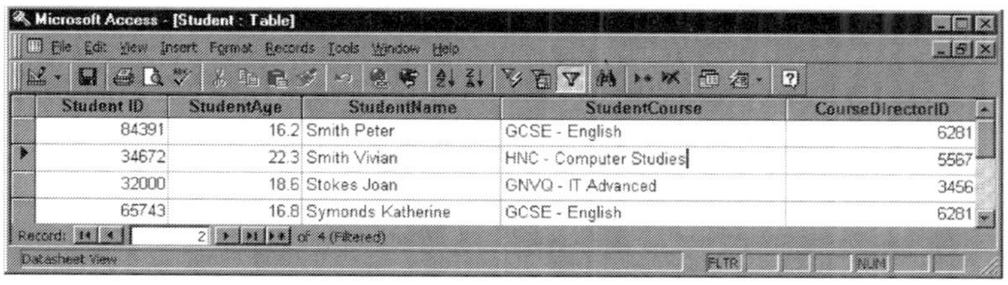

Figure 2.31

(ix) Form view – selecting a record from the Course Director Table (selecting the down arrow next to the New Object Button – just to the left of the help button – then selecting Autoform and scrolling to the required record)

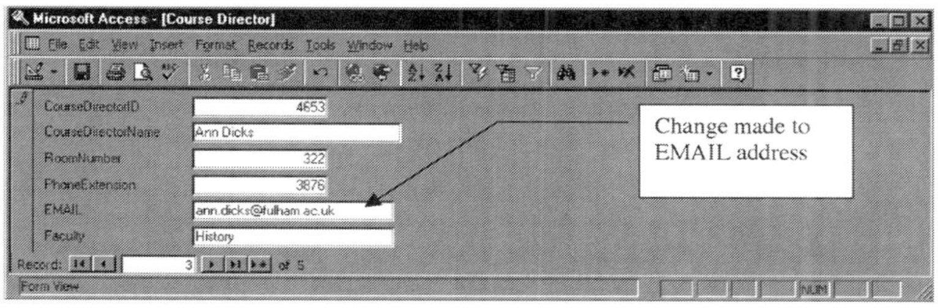

Figure 2.32

(x) Check on result

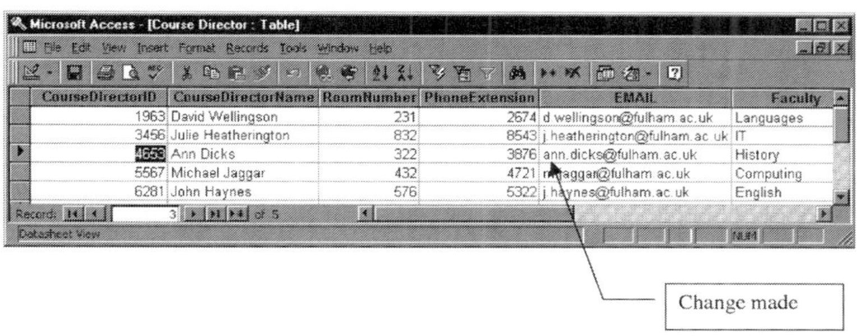

Figure 2.33

(xi) New record added to the Student Table

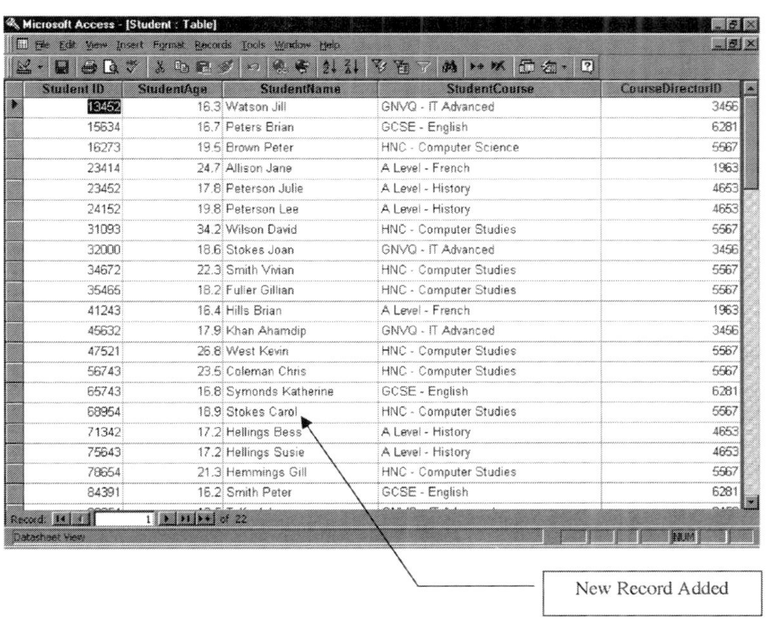

Figure 2.34

(xii) Relationship established

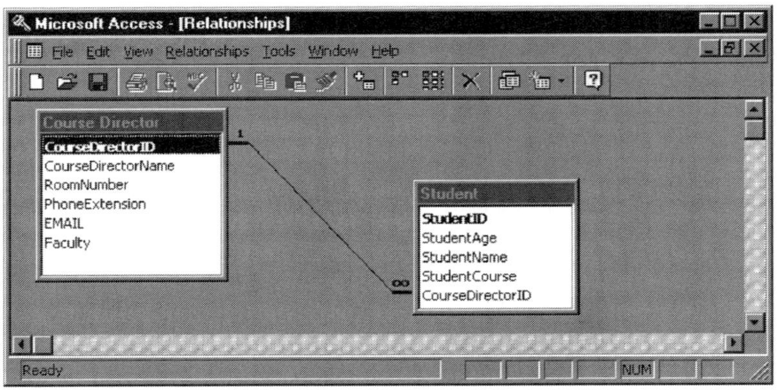

Figure 2.35

Note: As the primary key of the Course Director Table has been assigned as a foreign key of the Student Table the 1:n relationship is established and the relationship is added automatically.

(xiii) Query – Student Names v. Courses

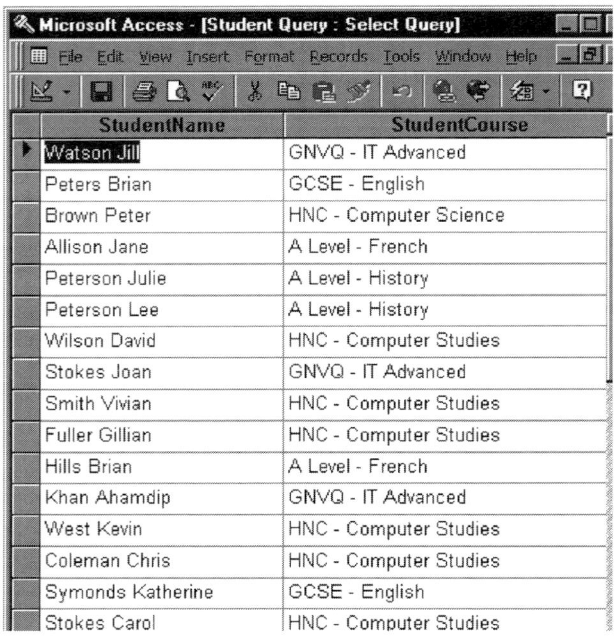

Figure 2.36

(xiv) Report of Course Director's name and e-mail address

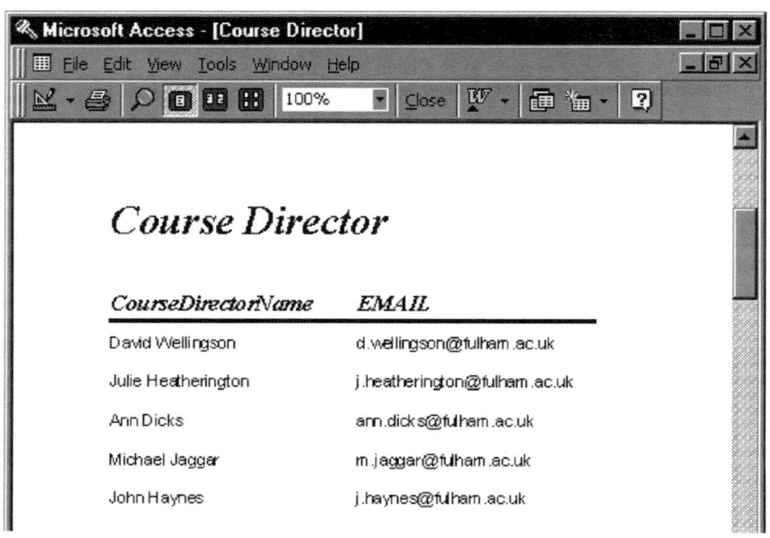

Figure 2.37

Note: Both Queries and Reports are obtained through the Database dialog box. For example, selecting the Reports tab gives:

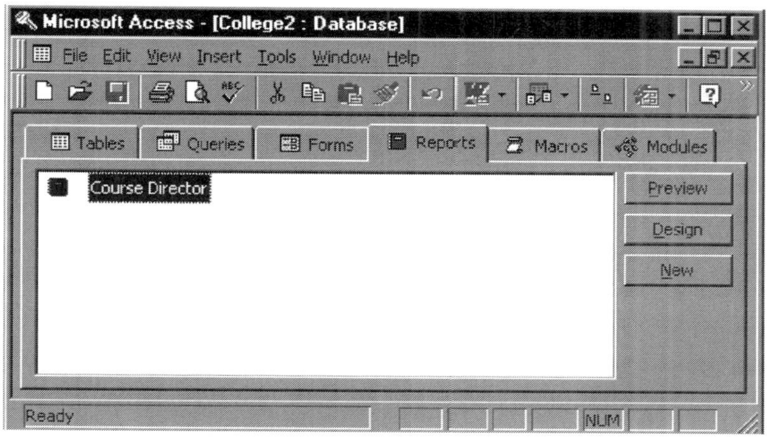

Figure 2.38

You then select new and use the wizard to obtain the required report – i.e. for student names and age

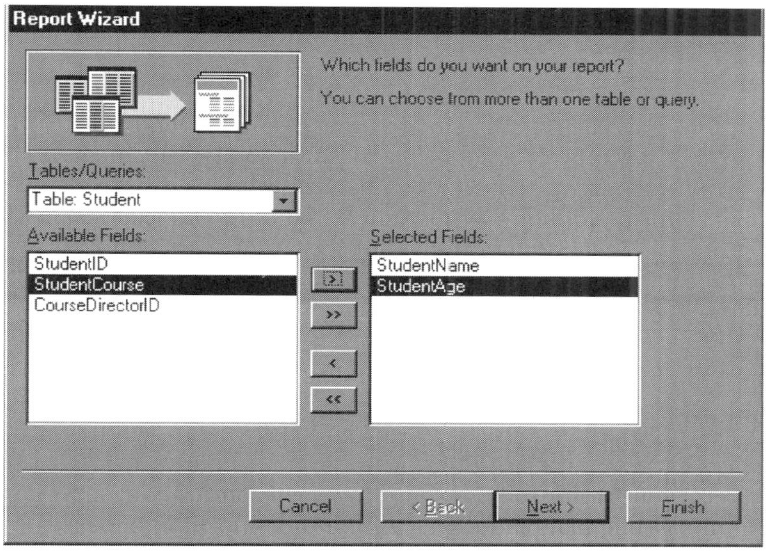

Figure 2.39

Gives the table:

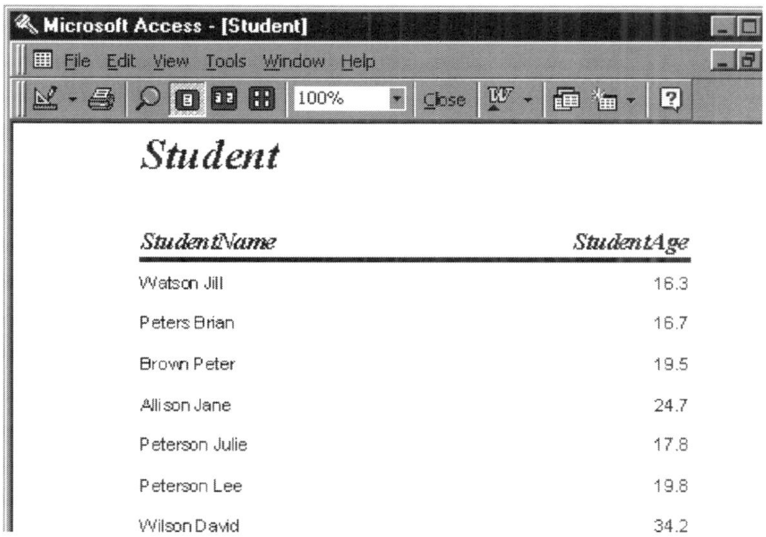

Figure 2.40

Additional exercise 1

Bailey University System

Part of a conceptual model for the Bailey College System is outlined below:

> The university requires all part-time staff to sign a contract for a given tutoring role. Contracts are unique in that each staff member signs one contract and a contract is for one staff member only. The staff are responsible for tutoring more than one student, but each student is tutored by a single member of staff. Students can attend more than one specified course and each course can be attended by many students.

Develop the conceptual model to:

1. Select some suitable entities
2. Outline some attributes for the entities
3. Establish the relationships between the entities and their degrees

Produce attributes for a logical model

4. Modify the conceptual attributes to produce a logical model
5. Using a CASE tool application construct an entity-relationship diagram
6. Test the diagram to ensure it is syntactically correct
7. For each of the entities construct attribute diagrams with suitable domains

Implementation

8. Construct a database table for the student entity type and include some sample data.

SQL (Structured Query Language)

The final part of this exercise is to use SQL to:

9. Select two columns from the student table

   Using the: Select ....
   From ....

10. Select from two columns within the student table given precise field data

    Using the: Select ....
    From ....
    Where ....

Suggested solution for the Bailey University System (additional exercise 1)

1. Suitable entities:

   CONTRACT – STAFF – STUDENT – COURSE

2. Attributes:

Staff	<u>StaffNumber</u>, StaffName, Department, Status
Contract	<u>ContractNumber</u>, ContractType
Student	<u>StudentID</u>, StudentName, StudentAge, Course
Course	<u>CourseCode</u>, CourseTitle, StaffNumber

3. Relationships:

Entity	*Relationship*	*Degree*	*Entity*
CONTRACT	IsFor	1:1	STAFF
STAFF	Tutors	1:n	STUDENT
STUDENT	StudiesA	m:n	COURSE

4. Logical model

STAFF	StaffNumber, StaffName, Department, Status, ContractNumber
CONTRACT	ContractNumber, ContractType, StaffNumber
STUDENT	StudentID, StudentName, StudentAge, Course, StaffNumber
COURSE	CourseCode, CourseTitle, StaffNumber

The identifier of CONTRACT (ContractNumber) has been posted to STAFF and the identifier of STAFF (StaffNumber) has been posted to CONTRACT. As each occurrence of StaffNumber identifies a unique STAFF record and each occurrence of ContractNumber identifies a unique CONTRACT record this represents the 1:1 relationship IsFor.

The identifier of STAFF (StaffNumber) has been posted as a foreign key of STUDENT. As each occurrence of StaffNumber identifies a unique STAFF record but may participate in any number of STUDENT records this represents the 1:n relationship Tutors.

For fully implementing the design it would be necessary to split the m:n relationship (StudiesA) into two 1:n relationships. Here ENROLMENT is introduced for this function.

STUDENT	StudentID, StudentName, StudentAge, Course, StaffNumber
ENROLMENT	StudentID, CourseCode
COURSE	CourseCode, CourseTitle, StaffNumber

5. CASE tool representation

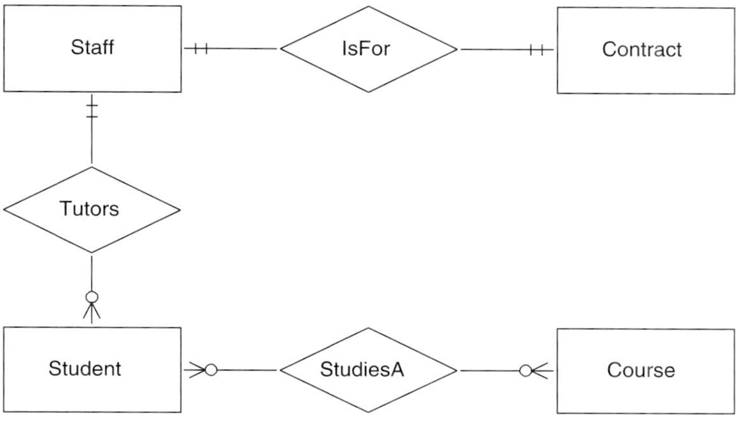

Figure 2.41 *Entity-relationship diagram – Bailey University*

6. Syntax check

```
Project: C:\SELECT\SYSTEM\BAIL1\
Title  : Bailey University System
Date: 10-Apr-2001 Time:  9:2

Checking BAILEY1.DAT

No Errors detected, No Warnings given.

---- End of report ----
```

7. Attributes

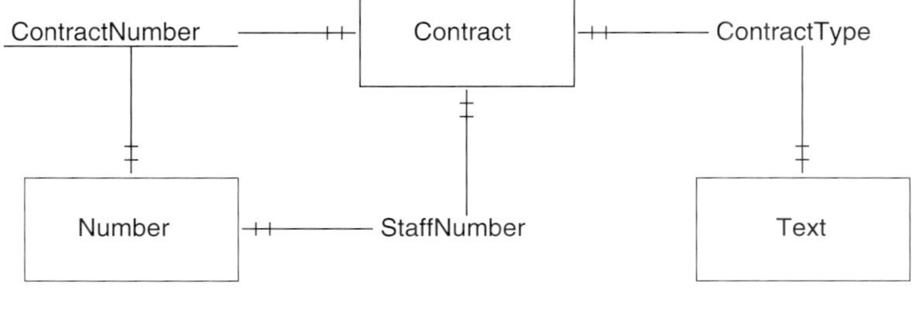

Figure 2.42 *Contract attributes and their domains*

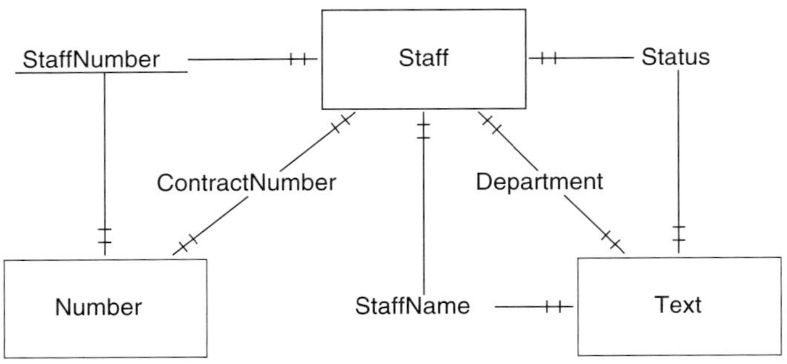

Figure 2.43 *Staff attributes and their domains*

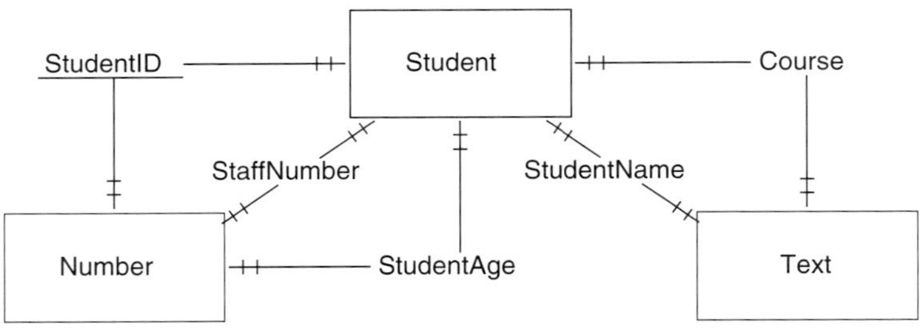

Figure 2.44 *Student attributes and their domains*

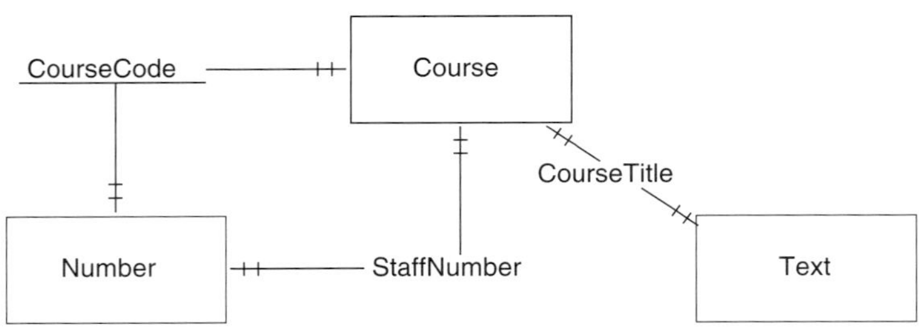

Figure 2.45 *Course attributes and their domains*

CASE tool consistency check

Project: C:\SELECT\SYSTEM\BAIL1\
Title : Bailey University System
Date: 10-Apr-2001 Time: 9:5

Report: Diagram Consistency checking

This report contains a consistency check of all the diagrams in the project.

Checking BAILEY1.DAT
No Errors detected, No Warnings given.

Checking CONTRACT.DAT
No Errors detected, No Warnings given.

Checking COURSE.DAT
No Errors detected, No Warnings given.

Checking STAFF.DAT
No Errors detected, No Warnings given.

Checking STUDENT.DAT
No Errors detected, No Warnings given.

---- End of report ----

8. Student table

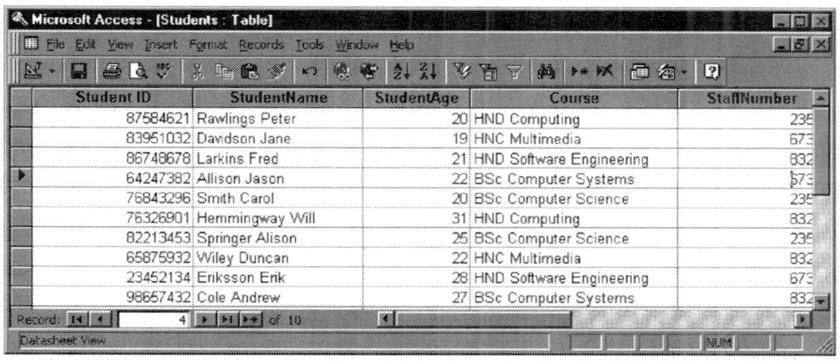

Student ID	StudentName	StudentAge	Course	StaffNumber
87584621	Rawlings Peter	20	HND Computing	235
83951032	Davidson Jane	19	HNC Multimedia	673
86748678	Larkins Fred	21	HND Software Engineering	832
64247382	Allison Jason	22	BSc Computer Systems	673
76843296	Smith Carol	20	BSc Computer Science	235
76326901	Hemmingway Will	31	HND Computing	832
82213453	Springer Alison	25	BSc Computer Science	235
65875932	Wiley Duncan	22	HNC Multimedia	832
23452134	Eriksson Erik	28	HND Software Engineering	673
98657432	Cole Andrew	27	BSc Computer Systems	832

Figure 2.46

9. SQL (Structured Query Language)
   Setting up from the Design View within Queries.

   SELECT StudentName, StaffNumber
   FROM Students;
   produces

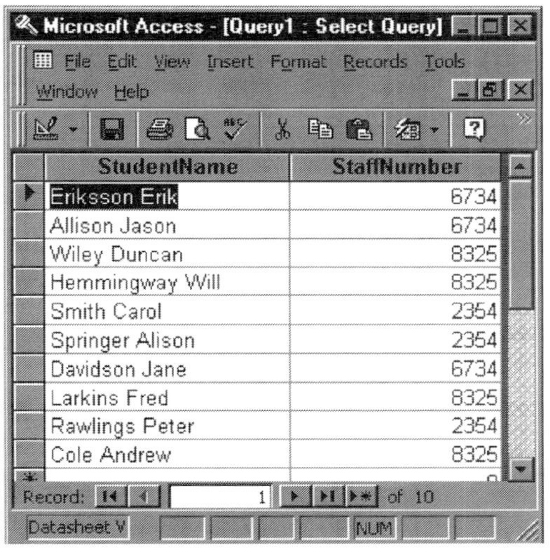

StudentName	StaffNumber
Eriksson Erik	6734
Allison Jason	6734
Wiley Duncan	8325
Hemmingway Will	8325
Smith Carol	2354
Springer Alison	2354
Davidson Jane	6734
Larkins Fred	8325
Rawlings Peter	2354
Cole Andrew	8325

Figure 2.47

10. Using the WHERE statement
    SELECT StudentName, StaffNumber
    FROM Students
    WHERE StaffNumber = 8325;

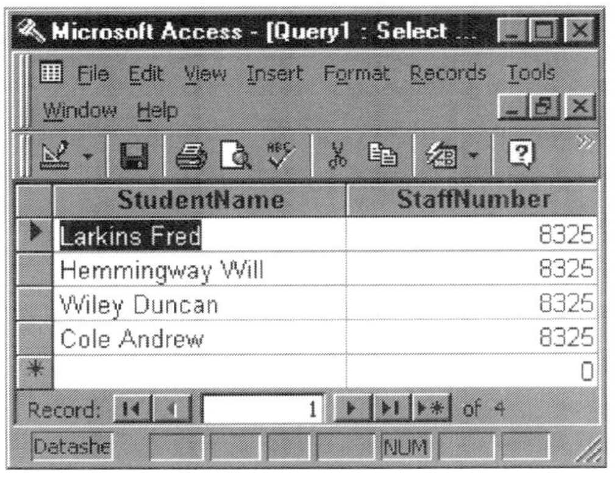

StudentName	StaffNumber
Larkins Fred	8325
Hemmingway Will	8325
Wiley Duncan	8325
Cole Andrew	8325
	0

Figure 2.48

Additional exercise 2

Morgan Tennis Club

Extract from the negotiated statement of requirements:

> The Morgan Tennis Club requires a simple database system for the booking of tennis courts for its members. Information for the following three main areas needs to be considered:
>
> Members
> Courts
> Booking
>
> Each member who makes a booking is given a booking number for a specified court. The system needs the following:
>
> - information about the member making a booking
> - each booking needs to record the member and court details
> - the court needs to record details of when and how long it is booked for
>
> Members can make a number of bookings for which a single court is assigned. All members are classified into their respective leagues (which are Premier, Division 1, Division 2 or Division 3).
> The club has 10 courts of various types. They can be grass, sand or hard courts. Two courts are to be allocated to the Premier players only.

Analyse the extract above and complete the following components. Use appropriate CASE tools for constructing the entity-relationship and attribute diagrams.

(i) Create an entity-relationship diagram to represent this system
(ii) Consider some attributes for each entity
(iii) For each entity create database tables containing some sample data
(iv) For the member table ensure the names are in ascending order
(v) Apply a filter to list all the members whose surname starts with a 'C'
(vi) Display a form view of a particular record for the member table. Change the field entry for one of the attributes
(vii) Add a new record to the member table
(viii) Show the relationship that exists between the entities
(ix) Set up a query to produce a subset of one of the tables, for example Members Names v League Status
(x) Produce a report for each table
(xi) Set up a macro to display the Member report, maximized and with a beep

Suggested solution for the Morgan Tennis Club (additional exercise 2)

(i) Entity-relationship model
From the question:
A Member can make several Bookings and a number of Bookings can be made by a single Member (thus establishing a 1:n relationship)
Many bookings are made for a specified Court and each single Court can be booked several times (thus establishing a 1:n relationship)

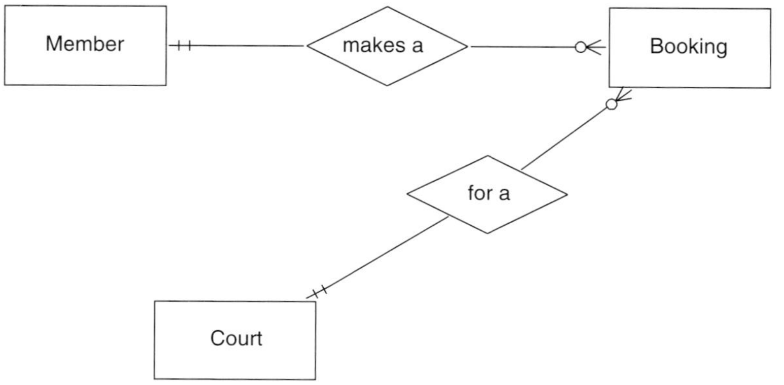

Figure 2.49 *Entity-relationship diagram – Morgan Tennis Club*

(ii) Attributes
Member: (<u>MemberNumber</u>, Name, Address, Telephone, LeagueStatus)
Booking: (<u>BookingNumber</u>, Date, Time, Single, PartnerName, MemberNumber, CourtNumber)
Court: (CourtNumber, CourtName, CourtType, Allocation, InService)

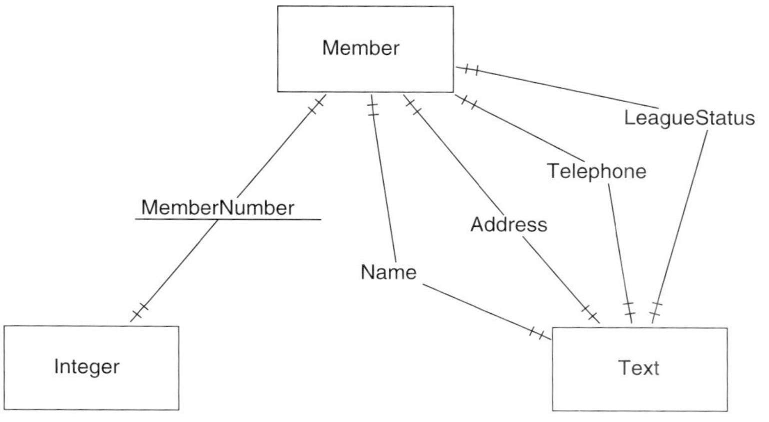

Figure 2.50 *Attribute diagram: Member*

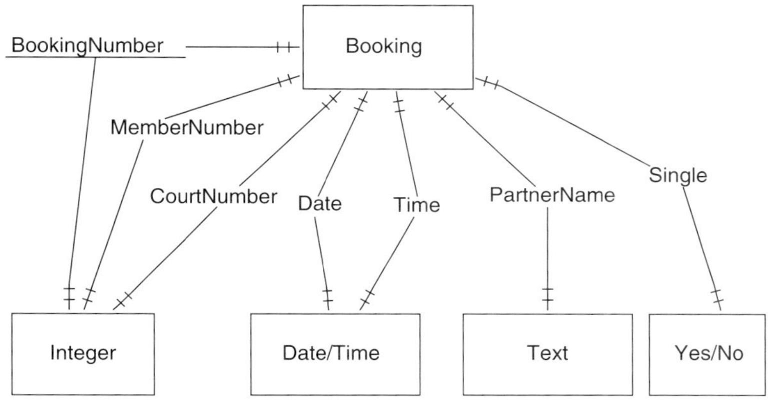

Figure 2.51 *Attribute diagram: Booking*

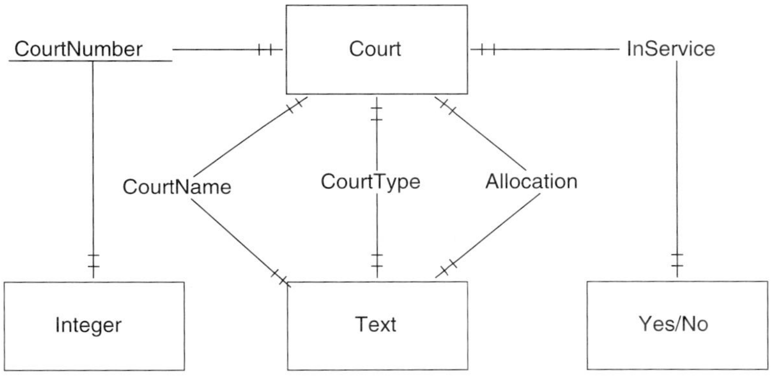

Figure 2.52 *Attribute diagram: Court*

(iii) Database tables

For the Member table it is best to create about 25 records to make it more realistic for applying the filter.

Remember the club has 10 courts. They can be grass, sand or hard courts.

Note that the relationships (and their associated degrees) defined in the design need to be implemented within the database application.

I have included 12 bookings in the Booking table.

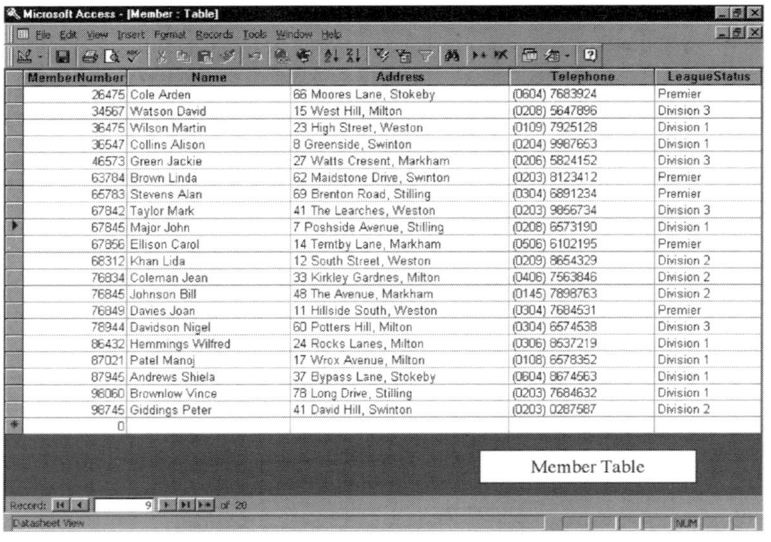
Microsoft Access - [Member : Table]

MemberNumber	Name	Address	Telephone	LeagueStatus
26475	Cole Arden	66 Moores Lane, Stokeby	(0604) 7683924	Premier
34567	Watson David	15 West Hill, Milton	(0208) 5647896	Division 3
36475	Wilson Martin	23 High Street, Weston	(0109) 7925128	Division 1
36547	Collins Alison	8 Greenside, Swinton	(0204) 9987653	Division 1
46573	Green Jackie	27 Watts Cresent, Markham	(0206) 5824152	Division 3
63784	Brown Linda	62 Maidstone Drive, Swinton	(0203) 8123412	Premier
65783	Stevens Alan	69 Brenton Road, Stilling	(0304) 6891234	Premier
67842	Taylor Mark	41 The Learches, Weston	(0203) 9856734	Division 3
67845	Major John	7 Poshside Avenue, Stilling	(0208) 6573190	Division 1
67856	Ellison Carol	14 Terntby Lane, Markham	(0506) 6102195	Premier
68312	Khan Lida	12 South Street, Weston	(0209) 8654329	Division 2
76834	Coleman Jean	33 Kirkley Gardnes, Milton	(0406) 7563846	Division 2
76845	Johnson Bill	48 The Avenue, Markham	(0145) 7898763	Division 2
76849	Davies Joan	11 Hillside South, Weston	(0304) 7684531	Premier
78944	Davidson Nigel	60 Potters Hill, Milton	(0304) 6574538	Division 3
86432	Hemmings Wilfred	24 Rocks Lanes, Milton	(0306) 8637219	Division 1
87021	Patel Manoj	17 Wrox Avenue, Milton	(0108) 6578352	Division 1
87945	Andrews Shiela	37 Bypass Lane, Stokeby	(0604) 8674563	Division 1
98060	Brownlow Vince	78 Long Drive, Stilling	(0203) 7684632	Division 1
98745	Giddings Peter	41 David Hill, Swinton	(0203) 0287587	Division 2
0				

Member Table

Record: 9 of 20

Figure 2.53

Booking table:

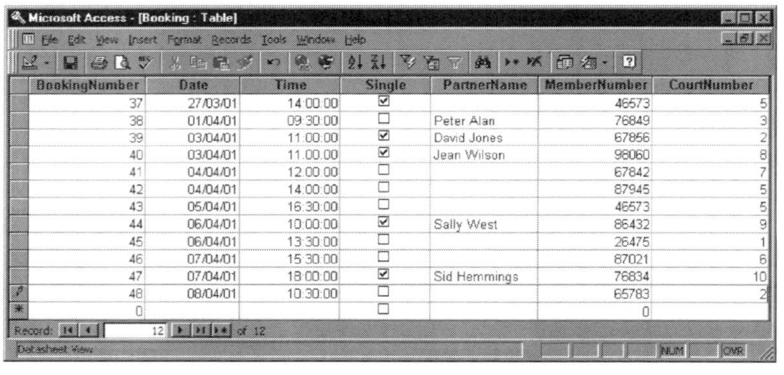
Microsoft Access - [Booking : Table]

BookingNumber	Date	Time	Single	PartnerName	MemberNumber	CourtNumber
37	27/03/01	14:00:00	☑		46573	5
38	01/04/01	09:30:00	☐	Peter Alan	76849	3
39	03/04/01	11:00:00	☑	David Jones	67856	2
40	03/04/01	11.00.00	☑	Jean Wilson	98060	8
41	04/04/01	12:00:00	☐		67842	7
42	04/04/01	14:00:00	☐		87945	5
43	05/04/01	16:30:00	☐		46573	5
44	06/04/01	10:00:00	☑	Sally West	86432	9
45	06/04/01	13:30:00	☐		26475	1
46	07/04/01	15:30:00	☐		87021	6
47	07/04/01	18:00:00	☑	Sid Hemmings	76834	10
48	08/04/01	10:30:00	☐		65783	2
0			☐		0	

Record: 12 of 12

Figure 2.54

Court table:

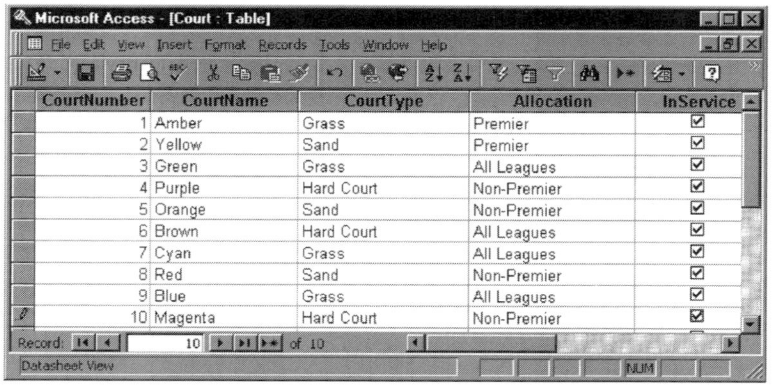
Microsoft Access - [Court : Table]

CourtNumber	CourtName	CourtType	Allocation	InService
1	Amber	Grass	Premier	☑
2	Yellow	Sand	Premier	☑
3	Green	Grass	All Leagues	☑
4	Purple	Hard Court	Non-Premier	☑
5	Orange	Sand	Non-Premier	☑
6	Brown	Hard Court	All Leagues	☑
7	Cyan	Grass	All Leagues	☑
8	Red	Sand	Non-Premier	☑
9	Blue	Grass	All Leagues	☑
10	Magenta	Hard Court	Non-Premier	☑

Record: 10 of 10

Figure 2.55

(iv) Member names in ascending order

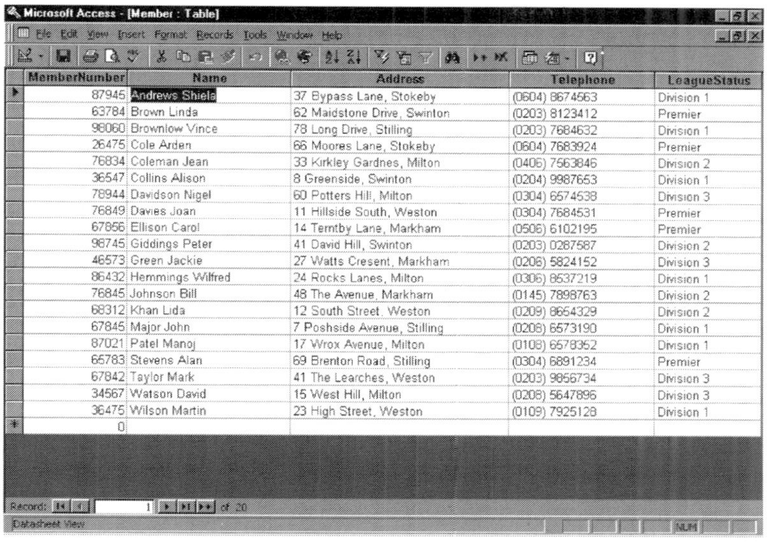

MemberNumber	Name	Address	Telephone	LeagueStatus
87945	Andrews Shiela	37 Bypass Lane, Stokeby	(0604) 8674563	Division 1
63784	Brown Linda	62 Maidstone Drive, Swinton	(0203) 8123412	Premier
98060	Brownlow Vince	78 Long Drive, Stilling	(0203) 7684632	Division 1
26475	Cole Arden	66 Moores Lane, Stokeby	(0604) 7683924	Premier
76834	Coleman Jean	33 Kirkley Gardnes, Milton	(0406) 7563846	Division 2
36547	Collins Alison	8 Greenside, Swinton	(0204) 9987653	Division 1
78944	Davidson Nigel	60 Potters Hill, Milton	(0304) 6574538	Division 3
76849	Davies Joan	11 Hillside South, Weston	(0304) 7684531	Premier
67856	Ellison Carol	14 Terntby Lane, Markham	(0506) 6102195	Premier
98745	Giddings Peter	41 David Hill, Swinton	(0203) 0287587	Division 2
46573	Green Jackie	27 Watts Cresent, Markham	(0206) 5824152	Division 3
86432	Hemmings Wilfred	24 Rocks Lanes, Milton	(0306) 8637219	Division 1
76845	Johnson Bill	48 The Avenue, Markham	(0145) 7898763	Division 2
68312	Khan Lida	12 South Street, Weston	(0209) 8654329	Division 2
67845	Major John	7 Poshside Avenue, Stilling	(0208) 6573190	Division 1
87021	Patel Manoj	17 Wrox Avenue, Milton	(0108) 6578352	Division 1
65783	Stevens Alan	69 Brenton Road, Stilling	(0304) 6891234	Premier
67842	Taylor Mark	41 The Learches, Weston	(0203) 9856734	Division 3
34567	Watson David	15 West Hill, Milton	(0208) 5647896	Division 3
36475	Wilson Martin	23 High Street, Weston	(0109) 7925128	Division 1
0				

Figure 2.56

(v) Applying a filter (Selecting: Records, Filter, Advanced Filter/Sort)

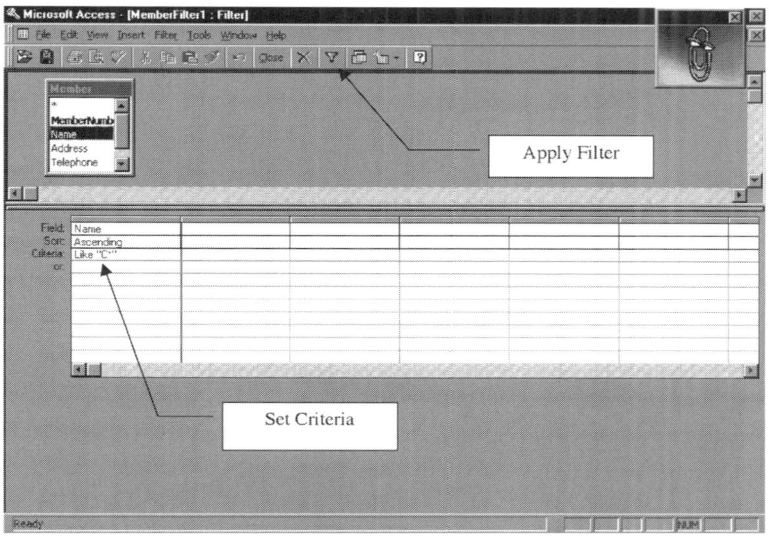

Figure 2.57

Produces

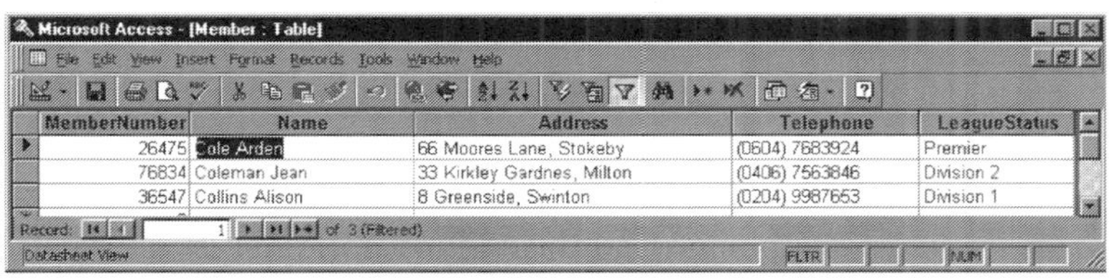

MemberNumber	Name	Address	Telephone	LeagueStatus
26475	Cole Arden	66 Moores Lane, Stokeby	(0604) 7683924	Premier
76834	Coleman Jean	33 Kirkley Gardnes, Milton	(0406) 7563846	Division 2
36547	Collins Alison	8 Greenside, Swinton	(0204) 9987653	Division 1

Figure 2.58

(vi) Form view

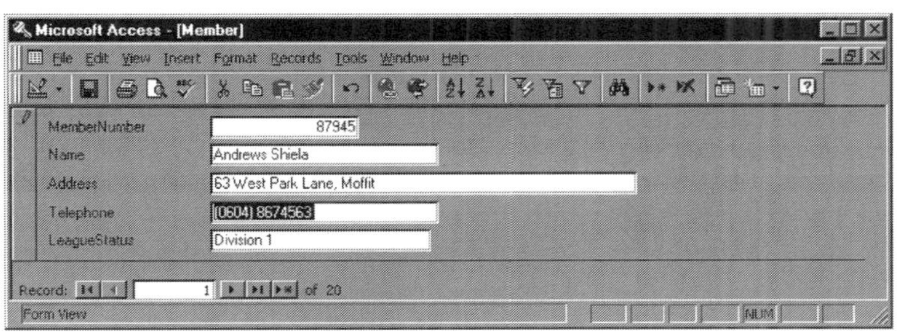

Figure 2.59

(vii) New record for Jill Milton added (also note the changes made in (vi))

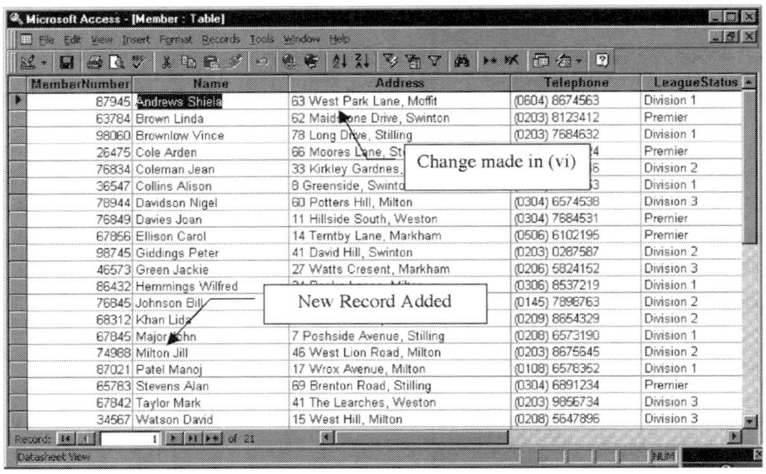

Figure 2.60

(viii) Establish relationships

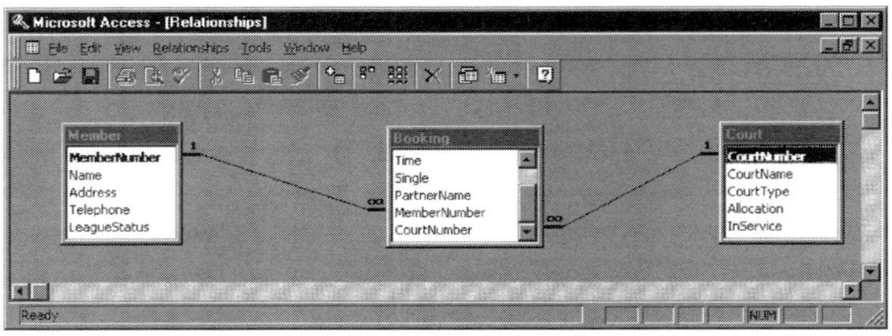

Figure 2.61

(ix) Subset names v. league status (select the Query tab from the main page)

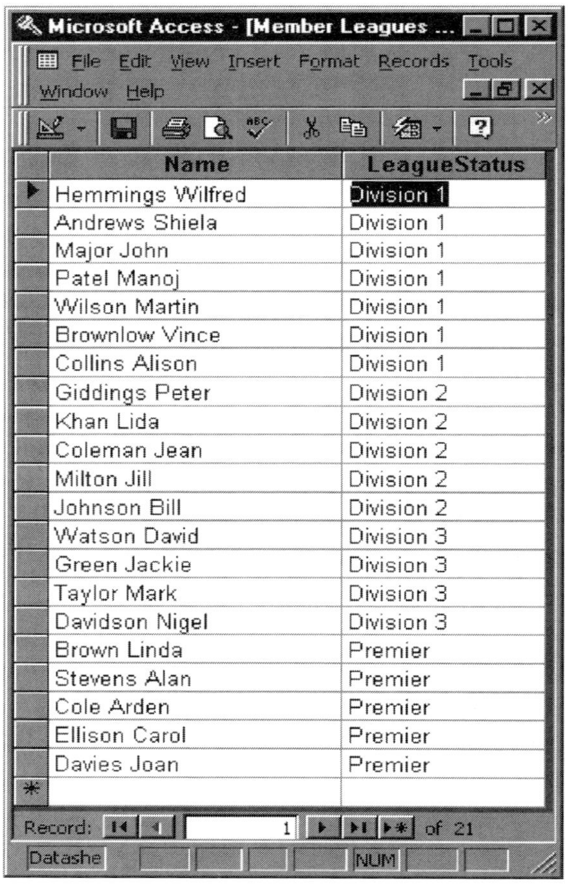

Figure 2.62

(x) Reports – shown in Figure 2.63 is the Member Report
Note: It may be necessary to adjust the design so the headings line up.

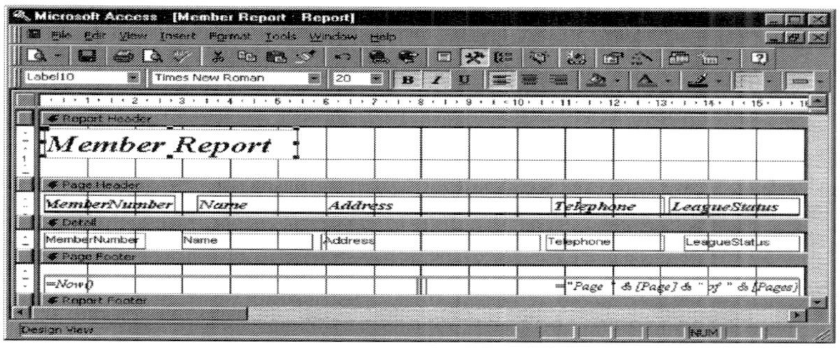

Figure 2.63

Member report

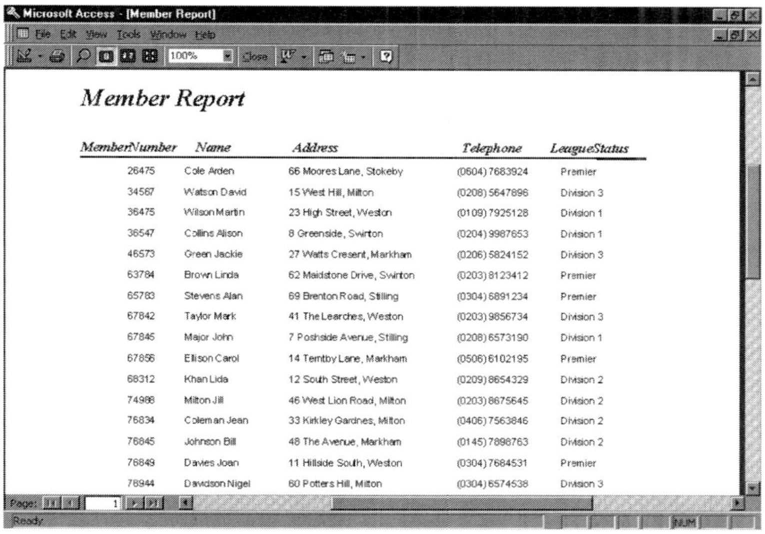

Member Report

MemberNumber	*Name*	*Address*	*Telephone*	*LeagueStatus*
26475	Cole Arden	66 Moores Lane, Stokeby	(0604) 7683924	Premier
34567	Watson David	15 West Hill, Milton	(0208) 5647896	Division 3
36475	Wilson Martin	23 High Street, Weston	(0109) 7925128	Division 1
36547	Collins Alison	8 Greenside, Swinton	(0204) 9987653	Division 1
46573	Green Jackie	27 Watts Cresent, Markham	(0206) 5824152	Division 3
63784	Brown Linda	62 Maidstone Drive, Swinton	(0203) 8123412	Premier
65783	Stevens Alan	69 Brenton Road, Stilling	(0304) 6891234	Premier
67842	Taylor Mark	41 The Learches, Weston	(0203) 9856734	Division 3
67845	Major John	7 Poshside Avenue, Stilling	(0208) 6573190	Division 1
67856	Ellison Carol	14 Temtby Lane, Markham	(0506) 6102195	Premier
68312	Khan Lida	12 South Street, Weston	(0209) 8654329	Division 2
74988	Milton Jill	46 West Lion Road, Milton	(0203) 8675645	Division 2
76834	Coleman Jean	33 Kirkley Gardnes, Milton	(0406) 7563846	Division 2
76845	Johnson Bill	48 The Avenue, Markham	(0145) 7898763	Division 2
76849	Davies Joan	11 Hillside South, Weston	(0304) 7684531	Premier
76944	Davidson Nigel	60 Potters Hill, Milton	(0304) 6574538	Division 3

Figure 2.64

(xi) Macro (outlined in Figure 2.65) is the design for the Macro – called Macro1

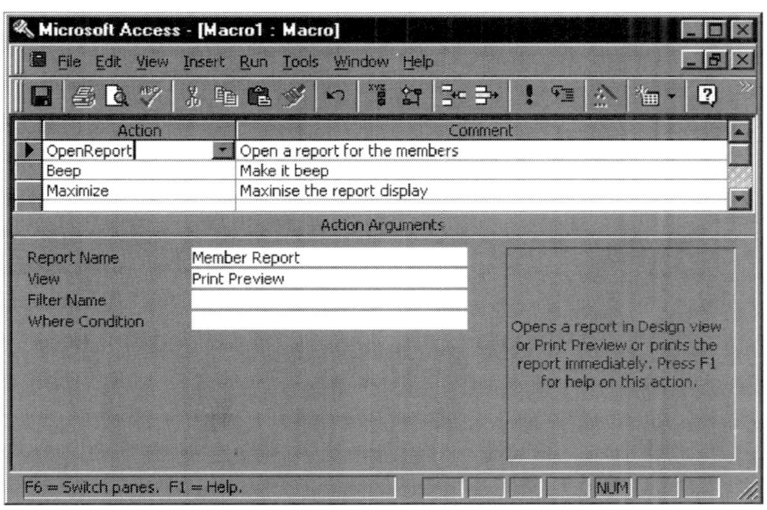

Figure 2.65

3 Software constructs and tools

3.1 Business models

Exercise 1: Decorating a room

This exercise investigates the cost of decorating a room. The walls have to be painted and the floor carpeted. The room has no window – perhaps it is the bathroom of a modern high-profile marina development – but does have a door. The door is not going to be painted or varnished. It is the one thing about the bathroom decor that the new residents approve of.

This is not a difficult problem to code as a spreadsheet, but does provide good practice in following a formal design methodology. The exercise is then extended by the inclusion of an input table.

Designing the mathematical model for the room

The model has to calculate the cost of both painting the walls of the room, excluding the door, and of buying a carpet to cover the entire floor. These two expenses are required independently and so there are two output variables for the model:

Output variable
PaintCost: The price of paint for the room
CarpetCost: The price of carpet for the room

Figure 3.1 shows an exterior perspective of the room, as if it were a separate office within an open plan area, rather than a wireframe view.

From this it can be seen that three input variables are needed to specify the volume and shape of the room:

Length: The length of the room
Width: The width of the room
Height: The height of the room

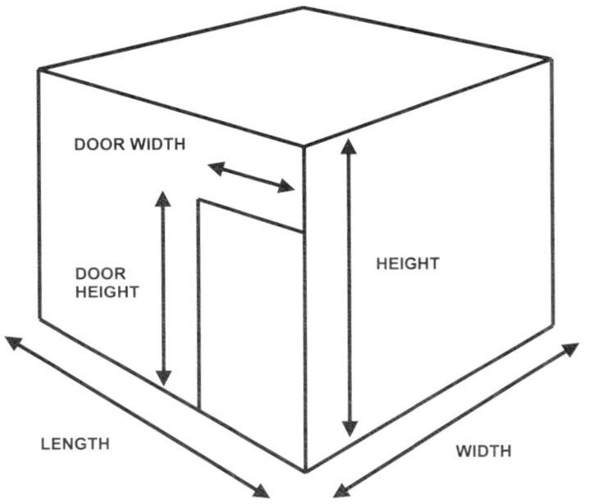

Figure 3.1 *Decorating a room*

Part of the surface area of the walls will be lost as it will be occupied by the door. Calculating the area of this excised section of wall area requires a knowledge of the dimensions of the door. The height and width of the door will be input variables:

DoorHeight:	The height of the door
DoorWidth	The width of the door

Just calculating the total wall area, and the area of the floor, is not sufficient. In order to obtain the cost of carpet and paint required to decorate the room it is necessary to be able to enter the basic cost of the materials.There are two further input variables:

Paint:	The cost of unit area of paint
Carpet:	The cost of unit area of carpet

Altogether the mathematical model will therefore make use of seven input variables:

Input variables

Length:	The length of the room
Width:	The width of the room
Height:	The height of the room
DoorHeight:	The height of the door
DoorWidth	The width of the door
Paint:	The cost of unit area of paint
Carpet:	The cost of unit area of carpet

Next the process variables for the model have to be decided. Calculating the total wall area will clearly involve separate calculations for the long and the short walls of the room. Each of these will require a process variable:

LongWall:	The area of a long wall of the room
ShortWall:	The area of a short wall of the room

In addition the area of the door will need to be subtracted, as this is not being painted. A third process variable is involved:

Door:	The area of the door

The total area of the walls is not of course an output variable for the model. What the user requires is costs, not areas. The wall area is clearly a process variable:

Walls:	The total area of the walls

The final process variable is the floor area, needed to allow the cost of the carpet to be calculated:

Floor:	The area of the floor

It is important to realize that deciding what process variables should be included in any model is to some extent a matter of personal choice. After all, one very long equation could be written which calculates the required answer all by itself! The nature of a spreadsheet, with its multiplicity of small cells, does, however, encourage a calculation to be broken down into individual stages. And this also makes it easier for other people to follow what is taking place. In addition separate calculations of a series of process variables facilitate extending a spreadsheet model to do other things. An example in the current model would be the modification of the spreadsheet to calculate the cost of painting the door. This will be far easier to incorporate if the process variable DoorArea has been employed in the existing model.

Taking this into account, the following is the set of process variables adopted for this model:

Process variables

LongWall:	The area of a long wall of the room
ShortWall:	The area of a short wall of the room
Door:	The area of the door

Walls: The total area of the walls
Floor: The area of the floor

The equations required for the model can now be introduced. From the diagram it can be seen that the area of the long wall can be found if the length of the room is multiplied by the height. This gives the first model of the equation:

LongWall = Length × Height

Similarly the area of the short wall is calculated as the product of the room's width and its height:

ShortWall = Width × Height

The area of the door is obtained by multiplying its height and width together:

Door = DoorHeight × DoorWidth

The total area of the walls can now be calculated. There will be four walls, two long and two short. The area of all four can be found by adding the long wall area and short wall area together and doubling this answer. Then the area of the door has to be subtracted. All of this is done by the equation:

Walls = 2 × (LongWall + ShortWall) – Door

Now the area of the floor is needed. This is another rectangle, with sides given by the values of the input variables Length and Width. The equation required for the floor area is:

Floor = Length × Width

The two output variables can finally be calculated. The cost of painting the walls is given by multiplying the wall area by the cost of a unit area of paint:

PaintCost = Walls × Paint

In the same way the cost of carpeting the floor is the product of the floor area and the unit carpet cost:

CarpetCost = Floor × Carpet

The complete set of equations is:

LongWall = Length × Height
ShortWall = Width × Height
Door = DoorHeight × DoorWidth
Walls = 2 × (LongWall + ShortWall) – Door
Floor = Length × Width
PaintCost = Walls × Paint
CarpetCost = Floor × Carpet

Mathematical model for the room

The complete mathematical model, including the assumption that has been made, is:

Output variables
PaintCost: The price of paint for the room
CarpetCost: The price of carpet for the room

Input variables
Length: The length of the room
Width: The width of the room
Height: The height of the room
DoorHeight: The height of the door

DoorWidth The width of the door
Paint: The cost of unit area of paint
Carpet: The cost of unit area of carpet

Process variables
LongWall: The area of a long wall of the room
ShortWall: The area of a short wall of the room
Door: The area of the door
Walls: The total area of the walls
Floor: The area of the floor

Equations
LongWall = Length × Height
ShortWall = Width × Height
Door = DoorHeight × DoorWidth
Walls = 2 × (LongWall + ShortWall) – Door
Floor = Length × Width
PaintCost = Walls × Paint
CarpetCost = Floor × Carpet

Assumption The door does not have to be painted.

Coding the model

The model is now coded as a spreadsheet. The actual design of the sheet depends upon choices made by the programmer. Which cells are used for different headings and variables is not decided by the model itself. As a result superficially different spreadsheets can be produced from the same model.

First the headings for the input variables are placed on the sheet as follows. 'Length' is added to cell A3, 'Width' to cell B3, 'Height' to cell C3, 'DoorHeight' to cell A5, 'DoorWidth' to cell B5, 'Paint' to cell C5 and 'Carpet' to cell D5. Test data is then entered beneath each of these headings. This means that in the subsequent equations to be placed on the sheet the following cell references will apply:

Input variable Length has cell reference A4
Input variable Width has cell reference B4
Input variable Height has cell reference C4
Input variable DoorHeight has cell reference A6
Input variable DoorWidth has cell reference B6
Input variable Paint has cell reference C6
Input variable Carpet has cell reference D6

After this the headings for the process variables are entered. 'LongWall' is entered into cell A10, 'ShortWall' into B10, 'Door' into C10, 'Walls' into D10 and 'Floor' into E10. The cell references for the process variables are now:

Process variable LongWall has cell reference A11
Process variable ShortWall has cell reference B11
Process variable Door has cell reference C11
Process variable Walls has cell reference D11
Process variable Floor has cell reference E11

The headings for the two output variables are placed on the sheet. 'PaintCost' is added to A15 and 'CarpetCost' to B15. The references are:

Output variable PaintCost has cell reference A16
Output variable CarpetCost has cell reference B16

The equations of the model can now be added to the appropriate process and output cells. Input and process variable names are replaced in these equations with the cell references shown above.

The equation:

LongWall = Length × Height

now appears, in cell A11, in the coded form of:

= A4 × C4

The equation:

ShortWall = Width × Height

now appears, in cell B11, in the coded form of:

= B4 × C4

The equation:

Door = DoorHeight × DoorWidth

now appears, in cell C11, in the coded form of:

= A6 × B6

The equation:

Walls = 2 × (LongWall + ShortWall) – Door

now appears, in cell D11, in the coded form of:

= 2 × (A11 + B11) – C11

The equation:

Floor = Length × Width

now appears, in cell E11, in the coded form of:

= A4 × B4

The equation:

PaintCost = Walls × Paint

now appears, in cell A16, in the coded form of:

= D11 × C6

Finally the equation:

CarpetCost = Floor × Carpet

now appears, in cell B16, in the coded form of:

= E11 × D6

The spreadsheet appears with its equations as shown in Figure 3.2.

Typical results are shown in Figure 3.3.

One-input tables

We use spreadsheets in 'what if' situations where we vary the data we are using to see how the results change. For example, you might have created a complicated mathematical model of a convoy of lorries driving across a suspension bridge. The model can calculate all the forces of tension and compression present in the bridge structure, compare this with the known strengths of the materials

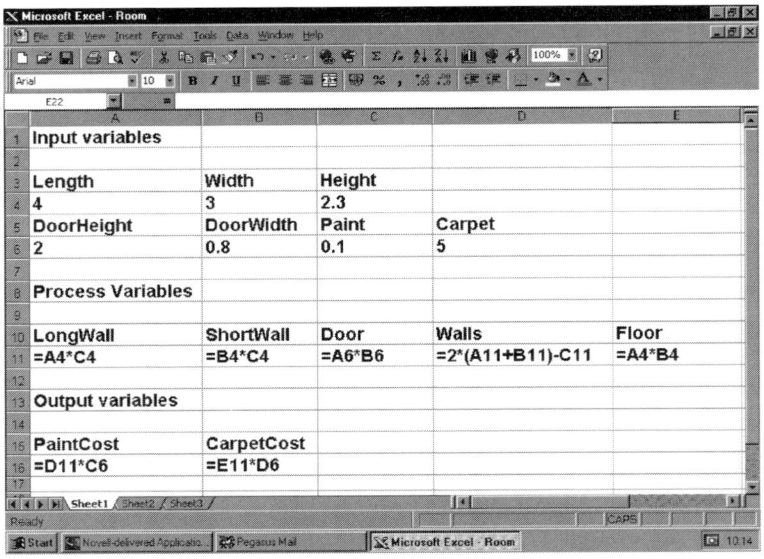

	A	B	C	D	E
1	Input variables				
2					
3	Length	Width	Height		
4	4	3	2.3		
5	DoorHeight	DoorWidth	Paint	Carpet	
6	2	0.8	0.1	5	
7					
8	Process Variables				
9					
10	LongWall	ShortWall	Door	Walls	Floor
11	=A4*C4	=B4*C4	=A6*B6	=2*(A11+B11)-C11	=A4*B4
12					
13	Output variables				
14					
15	PaintCost	CarpetCost			
16	=D11*C6	=E11*D6			
17					

Figure 3.2

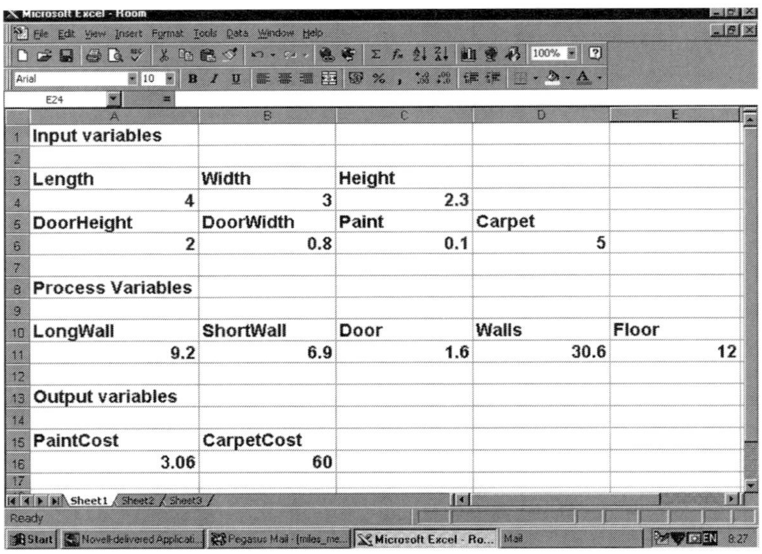

	A	B	C	D	E
1	Input variables				
2					
3	Length	Width	Height		
4	4	3	2.3		
5	DoorHeight	DoorWidth	Paint	Carpet	
6	2	0.8	0.1	5	
7					
8	Process Variables				
9					
10	LongWall	ShortWall	Door	Walls	Floor
11	9.2	6.9	1.6	30.6	12
12					
13	Output variables				
14					
15	PaintCost	CarpetCost			
16	3.06	60			
17					

Figure 3.3

used in its construction and then predict when the bridge will collapse. The model is then coded into Microsoft Excel. The engineer types in 1, 2, 3 . . . as the number of lorries and waits for 'Bridge now in river' to pop up somewhere on screen.

Of course it would be much easier if the spreadsheet simply created the set of test data 1, 2, 3 . . . automatically, or any other range of values required. All the person, using the spreadsheet would then have to do would be to type:

- The initial value of the range of test data
- The final value of the range
- The increment from one item of test data to the next.

Here is how such a range of test data can be set up in Excel. We shall use an extremely simple range of data, just 1, 2 . . .12. These values will be placed in cells A4 to A15. (The cell range A4A15.) First go to cell A4 and enter the value 1. Press Enter or click somewhere else on the sheet to make sure that it has been entered. Then highlight A4 and go to the Edit menu. From this menu select Fill and then Series. The 'Fill dialogue box' will appear. On this box select columns (as opposed to rows), then make sure that the 'step value' is 1 and the 'stop value' is 12. Finally click on OK. The range of test values will appear in cells A4 to A15.

This is how test data can be set up, but we need to see how it can be used in a model. The model we shall code is extremely simple. It just uses one equation:

Number = $N \times 5$

Provided that N is given the values 1, 2 . . .12 this equation will generate the five times table. We begin by placing numerical values of 1 and 5 into cells A1 and B1 and the equation:

= A1 × B1

into cell B3. This will calculate just one answer for the five times table:

1 * 5 = 5

The answer appears in cell B3. At this point we create a one-value input table from the column of test data that we have already established. This input table will replace the cell A1 in the equation in B3. First we highlight the cells A3 to B15. Then we click on the Data menu and select Table. A dialogue box appears and for 'Column Input Cell' we enter A1, because it is the value in A1 that we want extended to be over the whole range 1–12. Now the spreadsheet shows the equation worked out for all the values (see Figure 3.4).

If from Tools, then Options, the formulas are selected rather than calculated values, the sheet will look like Figure 3.5.

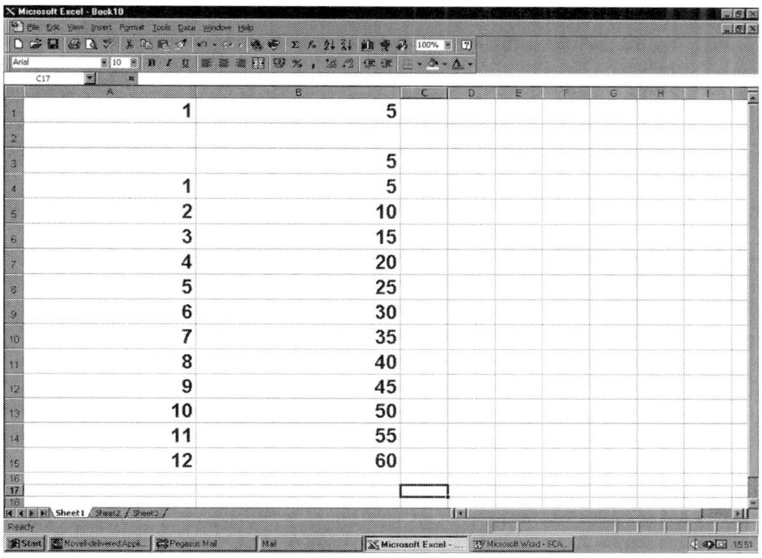

Figure 3.4 *One-value input table*

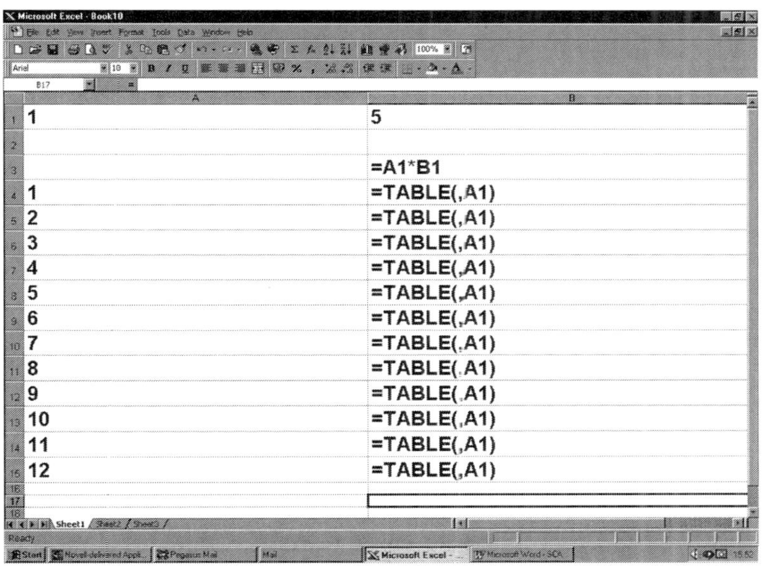

Figure 3.5 *One-value input table showing formulas*

Two-input table

In the examples considered up to this point only one series of values has been used. Sometimes we might want to calculate answers using two series of numbers. Suppose (to take a very easy example) we want to know the areas of rugs that can have lengths of 4, 5, 6 or 7 feet and widths of 2, 3 or 4 feet. You can see immediately that (for people who can't multiply quickly) a ready reckoner like that in Figure 3.6 would be useful:

This ready reckoner is taking two sets of inputs, the lengths along the top and the widths down the left-hand side. In the same way a two-input table can be created in Excel.

First enter the values for the lengths 4, 5, 6 and 7 into the cell range B4E4. Then enter the values for the widths into the cell range A5A7. Note that we are entering these values manually in this example. The earlier method using Edit/Fill/Series could of course be used instead.

Now enter the calculation, a simple multiplication, into the cell where the row and column of the table intersect. This is cell A4. The cell's references for the length and width have to be two cells not lying within the table. In this example the cells A1 and A2 have been chosen. So the calculation in A3 is

$= A1 \times A2$

	4	5	6	7
2	8	10	12	14
3	12	15	18	21
4	16	20	24	28

Figure 3.6 *A ready reckoner*

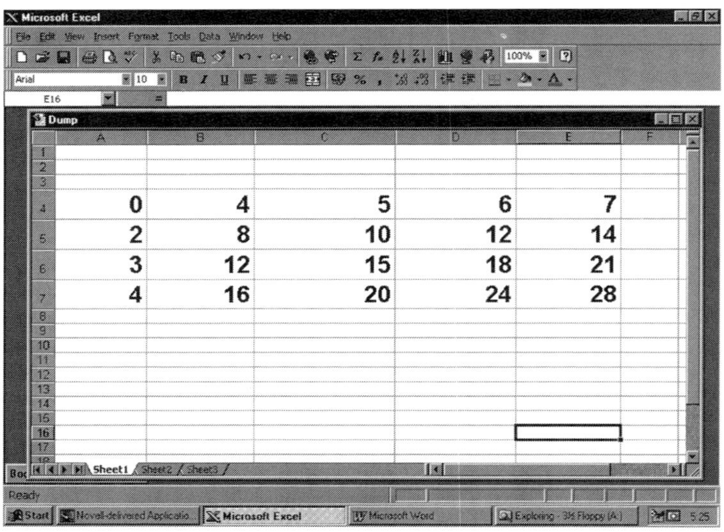

Figure 3.7 *Two-value input table*

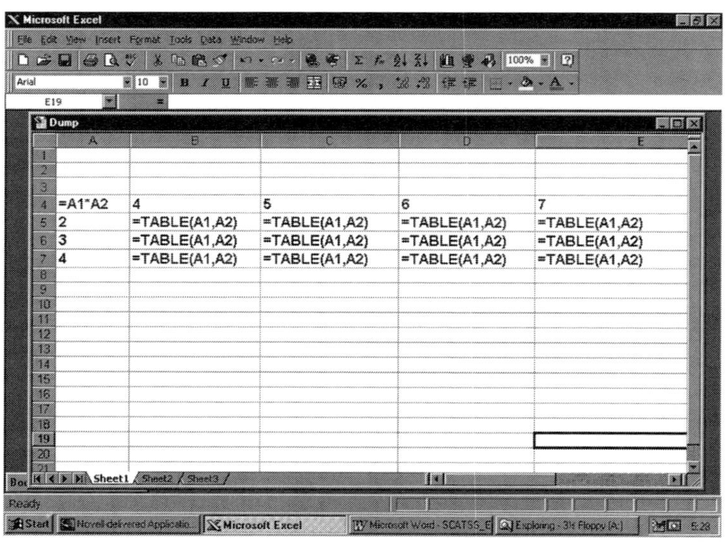

Figure 3.8 *Two-value input table showing formulas*

Now highlight the whole table. (This can be tricky!) Go to the Data menu and choose Table. Enter A1 and A2 as the Row Input cell and Column Input Cell and click OK.

Adding an input table to the room spreadsheet

The room spreadsheet can now be modified by using a one-value input table to allow a range of carpet prices to be considered. Here are the stages required for the modification of the original sheet.

First, identifying text is placed in cells D13 and E13. This is 'Carpet' and 'CarpetCost' again. The text will indicate on the sheet where a range of carpet prices will appear.

Next, the arbitrary value of 5 is entered into cell D15. This is highlighted and the Edit menu selected. From Edit, the Fill and Series menus are followed. On the last of these Select Columns is chosen and then appropriate values entered for the step value and stop value. The numbers picked here are 3 and 17, to give a range of carpet unit area costs of 5, 8, 11, 14 and 17. Clicking on OK then shows these values on the sheet.

The equation to calculate the total cost of the carpet, as given originally, is = E11 × D6. This is typed into cell E14. (A value of 60 will appear here, as before.) The range of values is now introduced into this equation by highlighting the cell range D14E19. The Data menu is selected, and Table from this. D6 is entered as the column input cell. When OK is clicked the full range of overall carpeting costs appears (Figure 3.9).

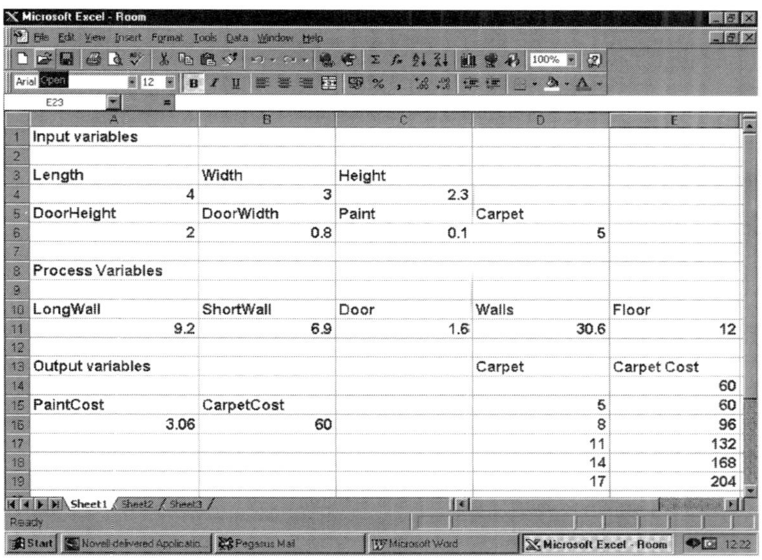

	A	B	C	D	E
1	Input variables				
2					
3	Length	Width	Height		
4	4	3	2.3		
5	DoorHeight	DoorWidth	Paint	Carpet	
6	2	0.8	0.1	5	
7					
8	Process Variables				
9					
10	LongWall	ShortWall	Door	Walls	Floor
11	9.2	6.9	1.6	30.6	12
12					
13	Output variables			Carpet	Carpet Cost
14					60
15	PaintCost	CarpetCost		5	60
16	3.06	60		8	96
17				11	132
18				14	168
19				17	204

Figure 3.9

Exercise 2: Running a lemonade stall

Saffron and Saskia, the rector's twins, help at the village fête by running a homemade lemonade stall. They sell three different strengths of lemonade, Fruity, Super and Lite. These differ solely in the proportions of lemon juice, citric acid and sugar which they add to the mixture:

A glass of Fruity contains 20 ml of lemon juice, 10 g of citric acid and 30 g of sugar.
A glass of Super contains 30 ml of lemon juice, 20 g of citric acid and 40 g of sugar.
A glass of Lite contains 20 ml of lemon juice, 10 g of citric acid and 10 g of sugar.

Saffron can buy sugar at 70p per half kilo and lemon juice at £1.50 for a litre bottle at the local supermarket. However, the cost of citric acid depends upon the chemical supplier Saskia chooses. They decide to design a spreadsheet model which will allow them to type in plausible sales figures for the three types of lemonade and then adjust the price per glass to seek the level of profit they are likely to achieve.

Designing the mathematical model for the lemonade prices

There is only one output variable for this model. The twins just want to know how much money their stall will generate:

Output variable
TotalProfit   The money made by the stall (in pounds)

The price of both sugar and lemon juice is fixed by the price in the supermarket Saffron has chosen, but Saskia is able to enter the cost of the citric acid they will need. This will be an input variable for the model:

CostAcid   The cost (in pence) of 1 g of citric acid

The price they charge for each type of lemonade will also be something that they can adjust in order to maximize their predicted profit. Each of the drinks, Fruity, Super and Lite, will require its own input variable to allow this flexibility:

PriceFruity   Price charged (in pence) for one glass of Fruity
PriceSuper   Price charged (in pence) for one glass of Super
PriceLite   Price charged (in pence) for one glass of Lite

The number of each type of drink sold will also be an input variable. This will permit the twins to run the model several times with different test data:

NumFruity   Number of glasses of Fruity
NumSuper   Number of glasses of Super
NumLite   Number of glasses of Lite

Input variables
The complete set of input variables is:

CostAcid   The cost (in pence) of 1 g of citric acid
PriceFruity   Price charged (in pence) for one glass of Fruity
PriceSuper   Price charged (in pence) for one glass of Super
PriceLite   Price charged (in pence) for one glass of Lite
NumFruity   Number of glasses of Fruity
NumSuper   Number of glasses of Super
NumLite   Number of glasses of Lite

Process variables in the model will be needed to calculate the cost of a particular drink from the price of its ingredients. A separate variable is associated with each of the three types of lemonade:

CostFruity   Cost of making one glass of Fruity (in pence)
CostSuper   Cost of making one glass of Super (in pence)
CostLite   Cost of making one glass of Lite (in pence)

As the price of each type is available as an input variable, combining this with the calculated cost allows the profit for a single glass of Fruity, Super or Lite to be calculated, again as a distinct process variable:

ProfitFruity   Profit on one glass of Fruity (in pence)
ProfitSuper   Profit on one glass of Super (in pence)
ProfitLite   Profit on one glass of Lite (in pence)

Finally the total profit for each drink, taking into account all of the drinks of that type sold, can be allocated a further variable:

TotalFruity   Total profit made on all glasses of Fruity (in pence)
TotalSuper   Total profit made on all glasses of Super (in pence)
TotalLite   Total profit made on all glasses of Lite (in pence)

Process variables
Altogether there will be nine process variables:
CostFruity   Cost of making one glass of Fruity (in pence)
CostSuper   Cost of making one glass of Super (in pence)
CostLite   Cost of making one glass of Lite (in pence)

ProfitFruity	Profit on one glass of Fruity (in pence)
ProfitSuper	Profit on one glass of Super (in pence)
ProfitLite	Profit on one glass of Lite (in pence)
TotalFruity	Total profit made on all glasses of Fruity (in pence)
TotalSuper	Total profit made on all glasses of Super (in pence)
TotalLite	Total profit made on all glasses of Lite (in pence)

The equations for the model can now be developed, beginning with the cost of individual drinks. First the unit costs of lemon juice and of sugar are derived from the description of the problem.

The price of a litre of lemon juice is £1.50. Dividing £1.50 by 1000 gives the cost of 1 ml of lemon juice as 0.15p.

The price of a half kilo of sugar is 70p. Dividing 70 by 500 therefore gives the cost of 1 g of sugar. These numbers cancel easily! Dividing 70 by 5 gives 14. So the price of 1 g of sugar is 0.14p.

The cost of each of the separate drinks is calculated from these figures as follows.

A glass of Fruity contains 20 ml of lemon juice and 30 g of sugar. This will cost (20 × 0.15 + 30 × 0.14)p, or 7.2p. A glass of Fruity also contains 10g of citric acid. The equation giving the cost of one glass of Fruity becomes:

CostFruity = 10 × CostAcid + 7.2

A glass of Super contains 30 ml of lemon juice and 40 g of sugar. This will come to (30 × 0.15 + 40 × 0.14)p, or 10.1p. Super also contains 20 g of citric acid and so the equation giving the cost of a glass is:

CostSuper = 20 × CostAcid + 10.1

A glass of Lite has 20 ml of lemon juice and 10 g of sugar. This amount costs (20 × 0.15 + 10 × 0.14)p, or 4.4p. As Lite has 10 g of citric acid the equation for the cost of a glass is:

CostLite = 10 × CostAcid + 4.4

Knowing the cost of each drink, the profit per glass can be calculated from the input price:

ProfitFruity = PriceFruity – CostFruity
ProfitSuper = PriceSuper – CostSuper
ProfitLite = PriceLite – CostLite

From these individual profits, and the input numbers of drinks sold, the total profit for each type of drink is found by multiplication:

TotalFruity = ProfitFruity × NumFruity
TotalSuper = ProfitSuper × NumSuper
TotalLite = ProfitLite × NumLite

The three profits for the three types of drink can now be added to give an overall profit for the lemonade stall. At this point the result is converted from pence to pounds:

TotalProfit = (TotalFruity + TotalSuper + TotalLite)/100

The set of equations is:

CostFruity = 10 × CostAcid + 7.2
CostSuper = 20 × CostAcid + 10.1
CostLite = 10 × CostAcid + 4.4
ProfitFruity = PriceFruity – CostFruity
ProfitSuper = PriceSuper – CostSuper
ProfitLite = PriceLite – CostLite
TotalFruity = ProfitFruity × NumFruity
TotalSuper = ProfitSuper × NumSuper
TotalLite = ProfitLite × NumLite
TotalProfit = (TotalFruity + TotalSuper + TotalLite)/100

Mathematical model for lemonade stall

The complete model is therefore:

Output variable

TotalProfit	The money made by the stall (in pounds)
Input variables	
CostAcid	The cost (in pence) of 1 g of citric acid
PriceFruity	Price charged (in pence) for one glass of Fruity
PriceSuper	Price charged (in pence) for one glass of Super
PriceLite	Price charged (in pence) for one glass of Lite
NumFruity	Number of glasses of Fruity
NumSuper	Number of glasses of Super
NumLite	Number of glasses of Lite

Process variable

CostFruity	Cost of making one glass of Fruity (in pence)
CostSuper	Cost of making one glass of Super (in pence)
CostLite	Cost of making one glass of Lite (in pence)
ProfitFruity	Profit on one glass of Fruity (in pence)
ProfitSuper	Profit on one glass of Super (in pence)
ProfitLite	Profit on one glass of Lite (in pence)
TotalFruity	Total profit made on all glasses of Fruity (in pence)
TotalSuper	Total profit made on all glasses of Super (in pence)
TotalLite	Total profit made on all glasses of Lite (in pence)

Equations

CostFruity = 10 × CostAcid + 7.2
CostSuper = 20 × CostAcid + 10.1
CostLite = 10 × CostAcid + 4.4
ProfitFruity = PriceFruity – CostFruity
ProfitSuper = PriceSuper – CostSuper
ProfitLite = PriceLite – CostLite
TotalFruity = ProfitFruity × NumFruity
TotalSuper = ProfitSuper × NumSuper
TotalLite = ProfitLite × NumLite
TotalProfit = (TotalFruity + TotalSuper + TotalLite)/100

Coding the model

This model is coded by first placing the text identifying the seven input variables on the spreadsheet. Cell A3 is given the text 'PriceFruity', cell B3 the text 'PriceSuper', cell C3 the text 'Price Lite', cell D3 the text 'CostAcid', cell A5 the text 'NumFruity', cell B5 the text 'NumSuper' and cell C5 the text 'NumLite'. This means that the following cell references apply for the input variables:

Input variable PriceFruity has cell reference A4
Input variable PriceSuper has cell reference B4
Input variable PriceLite has cell reference C4
Input variable CostAcid has cell reference D4
Input variable NumFruity has cell reference A6
Input variable NumSuper has cell reference B6
Input variable NumLite has cell reference C6

The nine process variables are identified on the spreadsheet by the following text. 'CostFruity' is placed in A10, 'CostSuper' in B10, 'CostLite' in C10, 'ProfitFruity' in A12, 'ProfitSuper' in B12,

'ProfitLite' in C12, 'TotalFruity' in A14, 'TotalSuper' in B14 and 'TotalLite' in C14. The cell references for the process variables are:

Process variable CostFruity has cell reference A11
Process variable CostSuper has cell reference B11
Process variable CostLite has cell reference C11
Process variable ProfitFruity has cell reference A13
Process variable ProfitSuper has cell reference B13
Process variable ProfitLite has cell reference C13
Process variable TotalFruity has cell reference A15
Process variable TotalSuper has cell reference B15
Process variable TotalLite has cell reference C15

The single output variable is represented by 'TotalProfit' in E10 and has cell reference E11.

Now the equations of the model are added to the sheet. For each equation the variable names used in the model are replaced by the cell references specified in the two lists above.

The equation:

CostFruity = 10 × CostAcid + 7.2

is entered in cell A11 in the modified version:

= 10 × D4 + 7.2

The equation:

CostSuper = 20 × CostAcid + 10.1

is entered in cell B11 in the modified version:

= 20 × D4 + 10.1

The equation:

CostLite = 10 × CostAcid + 4.4

is entered in cell C11 in the modified version:

= 10 × D4 + 4.4

The equation:

ProfitFruity = PriceFruity – CostFruity

is entered in cell A13 in the modified version:

= A4 – A11

The equation:

ProfitSuper = PriceSuper – CostSuper

is entered in cell B13 in the modified version:

= B4 – B11

The equation:

ProfitLite = PriceLite – CostLite

is entered in cell C13 in the modified version:

= C4 – C11

The equation:

TotalFruity = ProfitFruity × NumFruity

is entered in cell A15 in the modified version:

= A13 × A6

The equation:

TotalSuper = ProfitSuper × NumSuper

is entered in cell B15 in the modified version:

= B13 × B6

The equation:

TotalLite = ProfitLite × NumLite

is entered in cell C15 in the modified version:

= C13 × C6

The similarity of these equations allows easy replication of cell content with copy and paste. Finally the equation:

TotalProfit = (TotalFruity + TotalSuper + TotalLite)/100

is entered in cell E11 in the modified version:

= (A15 + B15 + C150/100

(This cell is formatted for currency.)
The spreadsheet appears with its equations as shown in Figure 3.10.

It appears with typical calculated results as shown in Figure 3.11

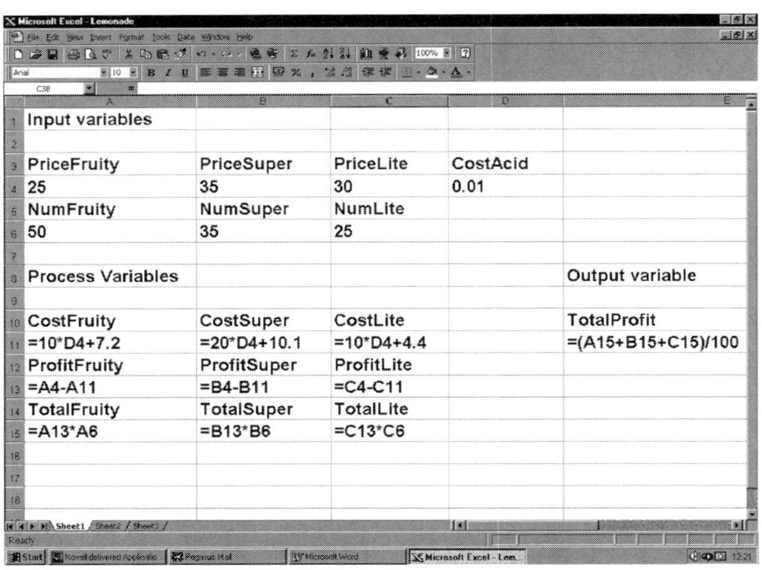

	A	B	C	D	E
1	Input variables				
2					
3	PriceFruity	PriceSuper	PriceLite	CostAcid	
4	25	35	30	0.01	
5	NumFruity	NumSuper	NumLite		
6	50	35	25		
7					
8	Process Variables				Output variable
9					
10	CostFruity	CostSuper	CostLite		TotalProfit
11	=10*D4+7.2	=20*D4+10.1	=10*D4+4.4		=(A15+B15+C15)/100
12	ProfitFruity	ProfitSuper	ProfitLite		
13	=A4-A11	=B4-B11	=C4-C11		
14	TotalFruity	TotalSuper	TotalLite		
15	=A13*A6	=B13*B6	=C13*C6		
16					
17					
18					

Figure 3.10

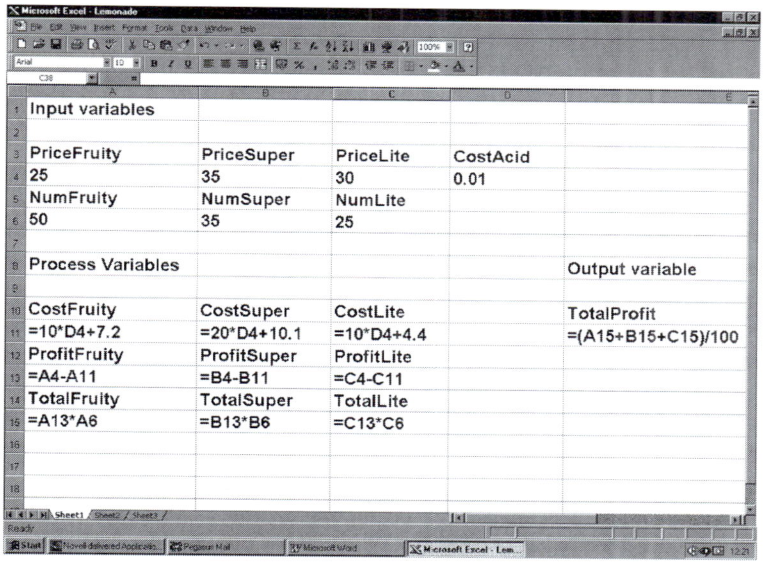

A	B	C	D	E
Input variables				
PriceFruity	PriceSuper	PriceLite	CostAcid	
25	35	30	0.01	
NumFruity	NumSuper	NumLite		
50	35	25		
Process Variables				Output variable
CostFruity	CostSuper	CostLite		TotalProfit
=10*D4+7.2	=20*D4+10.1	=10*D4+4.4		=(A15+B15+C15)/100
ProfitFruity	ProfitSuper	ProfitLite		
=A4-A11	=B4-B11	=C4-C11		
TotalFruity	TotalSuper	TotalLite		
=A13*A6	=B13*B6	=C13*C6		

Figure 3.11

Exercise 3: Educational building bricks

Following a severe downturn in the secondary and higher educational market, Williams Educational decide to focus all future investment on early learning materials. Their greatest hope rests upon the potential of a set of talking educational bricks. When piled up by toddlers these bricks make whimsical observations like 'Ooh. That's heavy!' and 'Oh dear. I don't like red cubes.' In addition bricks sense when they have not been handled for more than 24 hours and emit a high pitched persistent chirrup. The marketing department at Williams Educational claim that this will prevent bricks from being easily lost. (The design team is also considering whether the bricks should be Bluetooth enabled so that they can interface with the 'Williams Bionic Baby', also under development.)

The microprocessor and long-life battery for each brick are sealed inside a strong shell made of thermosetting plastic and which has one of three possible shapes, a rectangular block, a long cylindrical rod or a cube. To aid children design stable structures the bricks all have the same basic dimensions. The blocks and rods have identical length. The width of a block, diameter of a rod and edge of a cube are also equal. Thus only two dimensions define the entire three shapes.

The bricks are packed in boxed sets. A spreadsheet model is required which will calculate the profit made per box. This will allow Williams Educational to choose the best combination of block-, rod- and cube-shaped bricks. Only the cost of plastic is to be considered by this initial model as a supplier for the electronic circuits has yet to be established.

Designing the mathematical model for the educational bricks

There is only one output variable in the model. The profit on a set of educational bricks is required

Output variable

Profit Profit made on one set

In order to calculate the profit on a set of bricks, the model will have to take into account the price for which a set will be sold. This will be an input variable in the model:

Price Price charged for one set

In addition the number of each of the different shapes of brick included in the set must be entered into the model to help calculate the total quantity of thermosetting plastic required. Three more input variables are required for this:

NumBlock Number of blocks in set
NumRod Number of rods in set
NumCube Number of cubes in set

As described above, only two numbers are needed to define the size of the bricks. Both require their own input variable:

Length	Length of block or rod
Width	Width of block, diameter of rod, side of cube

These measurements are assumed to be in centimetres.
Finally the cost of thermosetting plastic is required as an input to the model:

CostPlastic	Cost of 1 litre of thermosetting plastic

Input variables
The complete set of input variables is:

Price	Price charged for one set
NumBlock	Number of blocks in set
NumRod	Number of rods in set
NumCube	Number of cubes in set
Length	Length of block or rod
Width	Width of block, diameter of rod, side of cube
CostPlastic	Cost of 1 litre of thermosetting plastic

The volumes of the three individual brick shapes are not required specifically as output from the model, but they are needed in order to be able to calculate the total volume of plastic used to produce a set of bricks. Each will have its own process variable:

VolBlock	Volume of a block
VolRod	Volume of a rod
VolCube	Volume of a cube

The volume of particular brick types, together with the number of that type in the set, allow the total volume of those bricks to be calculated. A separate subtotal is assigned to a process variable for each:

TotalBlock	Total volume of all blocks
TotalRod	Total volume of all rods
TotalCube	Total volume of all cubes

These subtotals permit the total volume of plastic used in the set to be held by a further process variable:

VolSet	Total volume of whole set

A knowledge of the volume of plastic then enables the cost to be calculated:

CostSet	Cost of set of blocks

Process variables
The process variables form this set in the model:

VolBlock	Volume of a block
VolRod	Volume of a rod
VolCube	Volume of a cube
TotalBlock	Total volume of all blocks
TotalRod	Total volume of all rods
TotalCube	Total volume of all cubes
VolSet	Total volume of whole set
CostSet	Cost of set of blocks

Referring to Figure 3.12 will help in constructing the three equations which give the volumes of individual bricks.

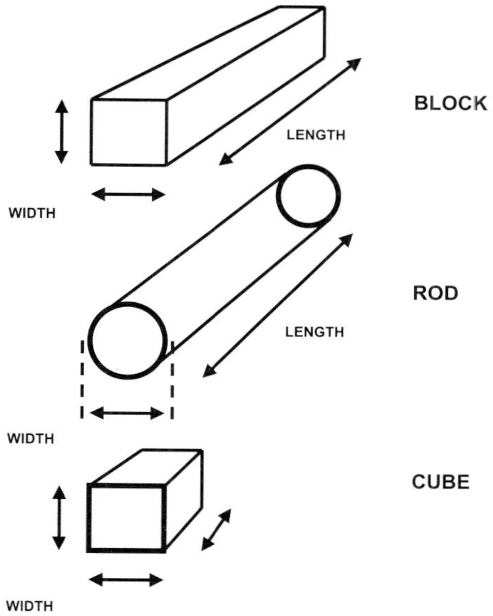

Figure 3.12 *Educational building bricks*

A block is a square prism in shape, the volume of which can be calculated by multiplying its length by its area of cross-section. The latter is simply Width × Width, or alternatively Width^2. The equation for the volume is:

$$\text{VolBlock} = \text{Length} \times \text{Width}^2$$

This result will be in cubic centimetres, as will be the values found below for the rod- and cube-shaped bricks.

A rod is a cylinder. Its volume is found by multiplying its length by the circular cross-section. The radius of the circle can be seen to be (Width/2) and so the equation for the volume is:

$$\text{VolRod} = \text{Length} \times \pi \times (\text{Width}/2)^2$$

The third brick shape is a cube, the volume of which is found by raising a side to the third power:

$$\text{VolCube} = \text{Width}^3$$

The total volume of all the blocks in the set is now found by multiplying the volume of an individual block by the number of blocks:

$$\text{TotalBlock} = \text{VolBlock} \times \text{NumBlock}$$

The total volume of rods and cubes is calculated by similar equations:

$$\text{TotalRod} = \text{VolRod} \times \text{NumRod}$$
$$\text{TotalCube} = \text{VolCube} \times \text{NumCube}$$

The volume of plastic used for the entire set of bricks is now found by adding the three subtotals together:

$$\text{VolSet} = \text{TotalBlock} + \text{TotalRod} + \text{TotalCube}$$

This total will be in cubic centimetres. Dividing by 1000 converts the value to litres. Then multiplying by the cost of a litre of plastic results in the total cost of the set of bricks:

$$\text{CostSet} = \text{VolSet} \times \text{Cost Plastic}/1000$$

The profit made on a set of bricks is found by subtracting the cost from the price charged:

$$\text{Profit} = \text{Price} - \text{CostSet}$$

These equations are sufficient to calculate values for all of the process variables and the single output variable:

VolBlock = Length $\times$ Width^2
VolRod = Length $\times$ π $\times$ (Width/2)^2
VolCube = Width^3
TotalBlock = VolBlock $\times$ NumBlock
TotalRod = VolRod $\times$ NumRod
TotalCube = VolCube $\times$ NumCube
VolSet = TotalBlock + TotalRod + TotalCube
CostSet = VolSet $\times$ Cost Plastic/1000
Profit = Price – CostSet

Mathematical model for the building bricks

The complete mathematical model is:

Output variable

Profit	Profit made on one set

Input variables

Price	Price charged for one set
NumBlock	Number of blocks in set
NumRod	Number of rods in set
NumCube	Number of cubes in set
Length	Length of block or rod
Width	Width of block, diameter of rod, side of cube
CostPlastic	Cost of 1 litre of thermosetting plastic

Process variables

VolBlock	Volume of a block
VolRod	Volume of a rod
VolCube	Volume of a cube
TotalBlock	Total volume of all blocks
TotalRod	Total volume of all rods
TotalCube	Total volume of all cubes
VolSet	Total volume of whole set
CostSet	Cost of set of blocks

Equations

VolBlock = Length $\times$ Width^2
VolRod = Length $\times$ π $\times$ (Width/2)^2
VolCube = Width^3
TotalBlock = VolBlock $\times$ NumBlock
TotalRod = VolRod $\times$ NumRod
TotalCube = VolCube $\times$ NumCube
VolSet = TotalBlock + TotalRod + TotalCube
CostSet = VolSet $\times$ Cost Plastic/1000
Profit = Price – CostSet

Coding the model

Text is added to the spreadsheet to identify the input variables. 'Price' is placed in cell A3, 'NumBlock' in cell B3, 'NumRod' in cell C3, 'NumCube' in D3, 'Length' in A5, 'Width' in B5 and 'CostPlastic' in C5. This means that test data is then entered according to these cell references:

Input variable Price has cell reference A4
Input variable NumBlock has cell reference B4
Input variable NumRod has cell reference C4
Input variable NumCube has cell reference D4
Input variable Length has cell reference A6
Input variable Width has cell reference B6
Input variable CostPlastic has cell reference C6

The location of process variables is also identified by text on the sheet. 'VolBlock' is added to cell A10, 'VolRod' to B10, 'VolCube' to C10, 'VolSet' to D10, 'TotalBlock' to A12, 'TotalRod' to B12, 'TotalCube' to C12 and 'CostSet' to D12. The cell references for the process variables are then:

Process variable VolBlock has cell reference A11
Process variable VolRod has cell reference B11
Process variable VolCube has cell reference C11
Process variable VolSet has cell reference D11
Process variable TotalBlock has cell reference A13
Process variable TotalRod has cell reference B13
Process variable TotalCube has cell reference C13
Process variable CostSet has cell reference D13

The output variable for the model is indicated by 'Profit' in cell A17 and has cell reference A18.
The equations can now be added to the appropriate cells in the coded form shown, using the correct cell references to replace variable names.
The equation:

$$\text{VolBlock} = \text{Length} \times \text{Width}^2$$

is placed in cell A11 in the modified form:

$$= \text{A6} \times \text{B6}^2$$

The equation:

$$\text{VolRod} = \text{Length} \times \pi \times (\text{Width}/2)^2$$

is placed in cell B11 in the modified form:

$$= \text{A6} \times \pi \times (\text{B6}/2)^2$$

The equation:

$$\text{VolCube} = \text{Width}^3$$

is placed in cell C11 in the modified form:

$$= \text{B6}^3$$

The equation:

$$\text{TotalBlock} = \text{VolBlock} \times \text{NumBlock}$$

is placed in cell A13 in the modified form:

$$= \text{A11} \times \text{B4}$$

The equation:

$$\text{TotalRod} = \text{VolRod} \times \text{NumRod}$$

is placed in cell B13 in the modified form:

= B11 × C4

The equation:

TotalCube = VolCube × NumCube

is placed in cell C13 in the modified form:

= C11 × D4

The equation:

VolSet = TotalBlock + TotalRod + TotalCube

is placed in cell D11 in the modified form:

= A13 + B13 + C13

The equation:

CostSet = VolSet × Cost Plastic/1000

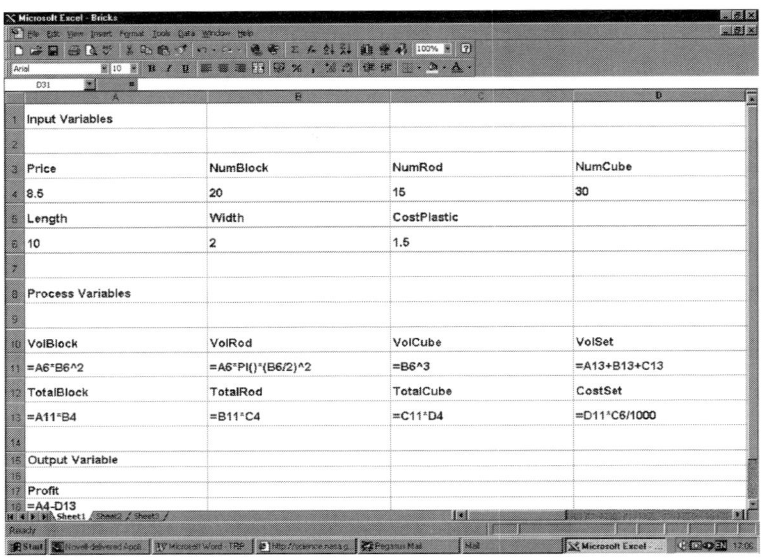

	A	B	C	D
1	Input Variables			
2				
3	Price	NumBlock	NumRod	NumCube
4	8.5	20	15	30
5	Length	Width	CostPlastic	
6	10	2	1.5	
7				
8	Process Variables			
9				
10	VolBlock	VolRod	VolCube	VolSet
11	=A6*B6^2	=A6*PI()*(B6/2)^2	=B6^3	=A13+B13+C13
12	TotalBlock	TotalRod	TotalCube	CostSet
13	=A11*B4	=B11*C4	=C11*D4	=D11*C6/1000
14				
15	Output Variable			
16				
17	Profit			
18	=A4-D13			

Figure 3.13

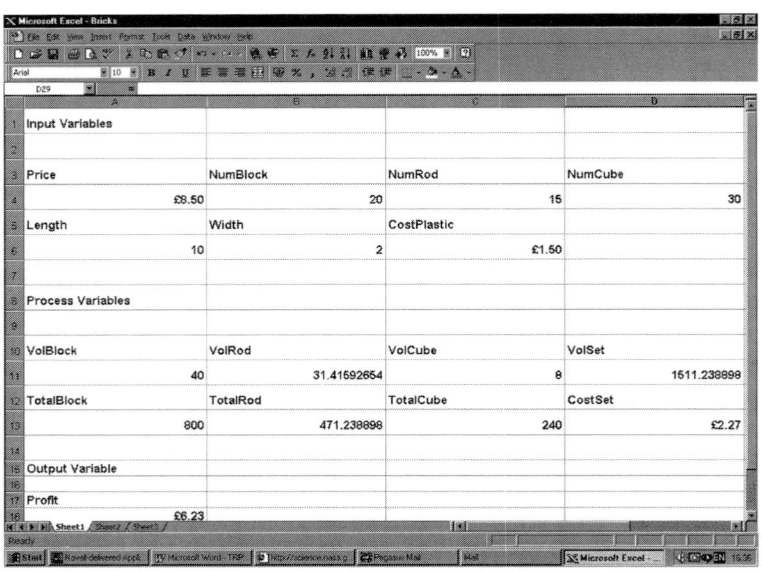

	A	B	C	D
1	Input Variables			
2				
3	Price	NumBlock	NumRod	NumCube
4	£8.50	20	15	30
5	Length	Width	CostPlastic	
6	10	2	£1.50	
7				
8	Process Variables			
9				
10	VolBlock	VolRod	VolCube	VolSet
11	40	31.41592654	8	1511.238898
12	TotalBlock	TotalRod	TotalCube	CostSet
13	800	471.238898	240	£2.27
14				
15	Output Variable			
16				
17	Profit			
18	£6.23			

Figure 3.14

is placed in cell D13 in the modified form:

= D11 × C6/1000

The equation:

Profit = Price – CostSet

is placed in cell A18 in the modified form:

= A4 – D13

The spreadsheet appears with its equations as shown in Figure 3.13.
Typical values are calculated as shown in Figure 3.14.

Extending the model

After he has played with a prototype set of blocks for some weeks the managing director of Williams Educational realizes that the reason his model of the Lloyd's Insurance building keeps falling over is that, no matter how many blocks he lays sideways, they never quite equal the height of the column of rods he has constructed. Blutack does not help. After discussing this problem (via e-mail) with the company's accountant he gradually understands that this is because the variable Length in the spreadsheet model is not necessarily a multiple of Width. Immediately he demands that the spreadsheet should not allow this situation to occur. How can the spreadsheet model be modified to ensure this?

The spreadsheet requires the addition of a condition which will check whether the width entered divides exactly, without any remainder, into the length. This can be tested using the Mod operator, which returns the remainder for a division. For example, 23 MOD 7 returns 2, because 3 multipled by 7 is 21, which is 2 less than 23. Similarly 50 MOD 13 is 11. If MOD returns a value of zero, then the division performed has been exact and the larger number is a multiple of the smaller.

The condition required for the educational bricks is:

IF Length MOD Width = 0 THEN [Values satisfactory] ELSE [Values unacceptable]

This is coded as the following Microsoft Excel condition, entered into cell B1:

= IF(MOD(A6,B6) = 0, 'OKAY', 'ERROR')

The portion of the sheet with this modification is shown in Figure 3.15.

This condition is then tested. A length of 10 cm and width of 2 cm is acceptable because 10 is a multiple of 2 (see Figure 3.16).

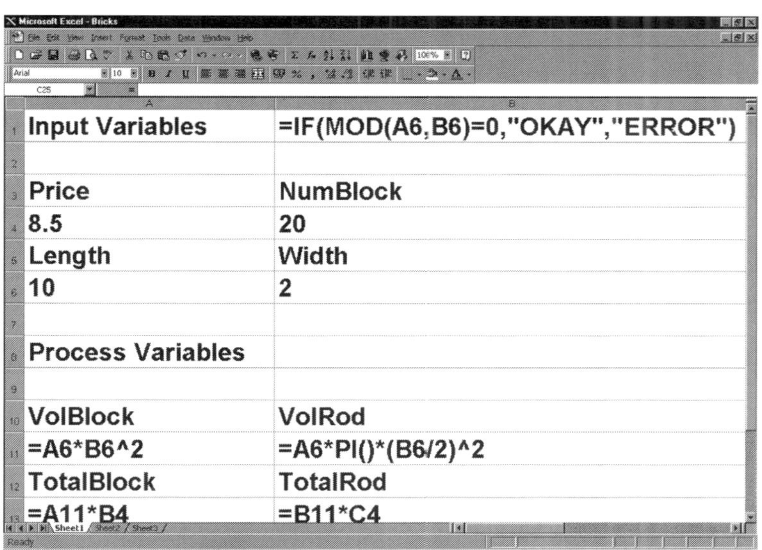

Figure 3.15

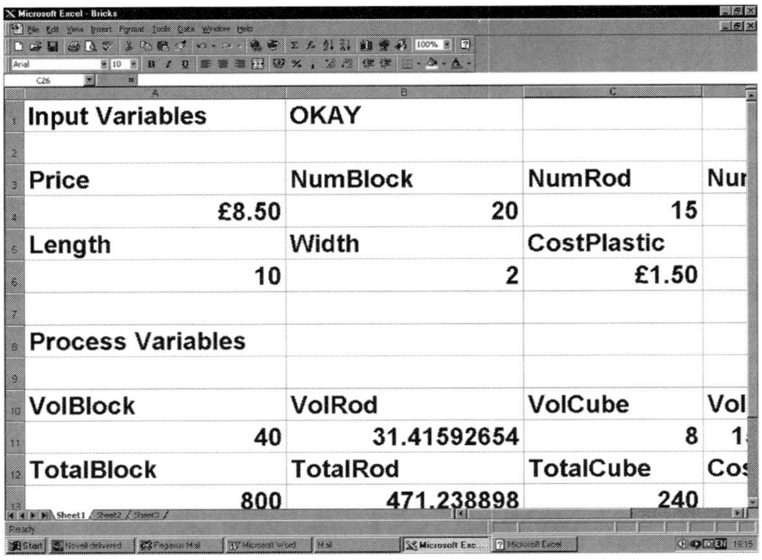

Figure 3.16

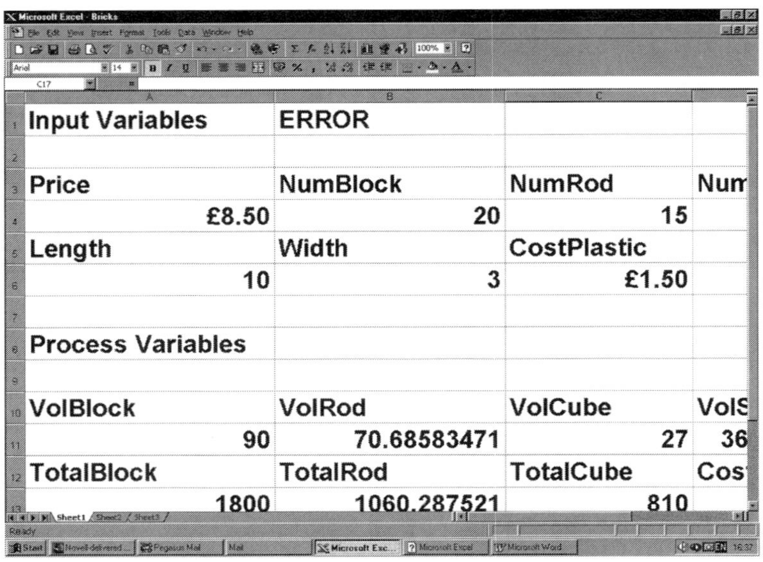

Figure 3.17

However a length of 10 cm and width of 3 cm is not appropriate because 10 is not a multiple of 3 (and the Lloyd's building will fall over again...) (see Figure 3.17).

Exercise 4: Constructing a concrete swimming pool

This exercise uses a spreadsheet to calculate the volume of concrete required to construct the buried shell of a garden swimming pool.

The geometry involved is not difficult and should encourage students to investigate different models. One approach would be to subtract an 'inner' volume from an 'outer'. This could lead to an interesting situation in which small quantities are raised to a power, reducing their impact on the result and introducing explicitly the need for simplifying assumptions.

The model developed here includes an important assumption, namely that the volume of a relatively complicated three-dimensional shell can be approximated as the product of surface area and thickness. There is an opportunity for a lecturer to discuss the concept of simplifying assumptions and the relevance of particular assumptions in a given model. Ways in which assumptions affect the plausibility of results can be debated.

Designing the mathematical model for the pool

The model will have just one output variable:

Output variable

Volume: The volume of concrete required for all the faces

The shape selected for the pool in this particular exercise is shown in the perspective diagram (Figure 3.18). It is a rectangular pool with a bottom that slopes uniformly from a shallow to a deep end. The dimensions defining the pool are shown on this diagram. They are the length and width of the pool and its depths, shallow and deep, at either end.

Also shown on the diagram is the 'slant' length of the bottom side. It is important to realize that this is not an independent dimension of the pool. Once the length has been decided, and the depths at both ends, the value for this slant length is uniquely fixed. This will be shown in the development of the equations for the mathematical model below.

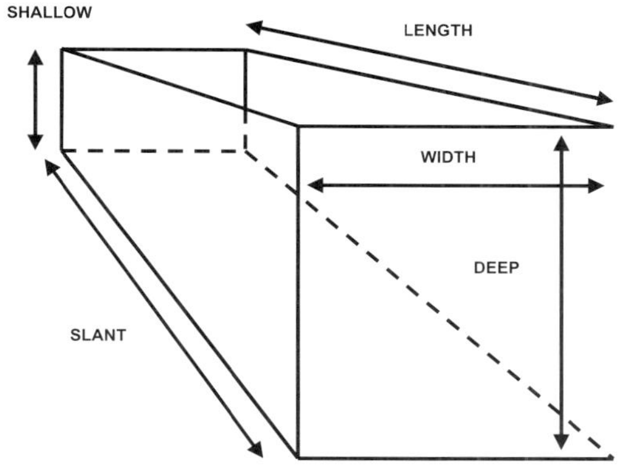

Figure 3.18 *Perspective view of swimming pool*

Not shown on the diagram is the thickness of the concrete shell forming the pool. On the scale of this diagram it would be difficult to indicate it. The considerable difference in magnitude between the thickness of the concrete and the other dimensions of the pool does, in fact, become one of the important assumptions of the model.

Input variables

The complete list of input variables for the model is therefore:

Length: The length of the pool
Width: The width of the pool
Shallow: The depth of the pool at the shallow end
Deep: The depth of the pool at the deep end
Thickness: The thickness of the concrete walls

Some of the process variables needed for the model of the pool can be identified if the different faces of the concrete shell are considered. These are shown on this further diagram (Figure 3.19). A process variable is assigned for the area of each of these surfaces.

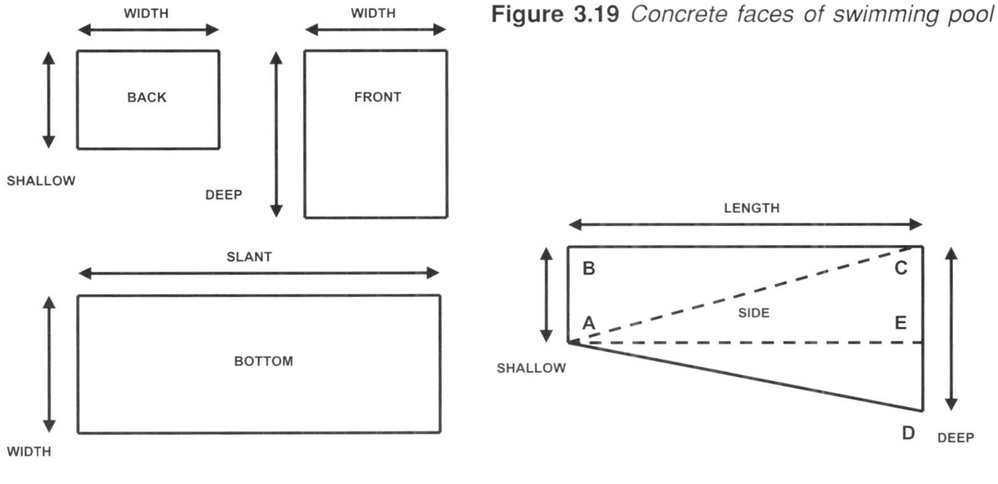

Figure 3.19 *Concrete faces of swimming pool*

The five separate faces of the concrete shell will be three rectangles and two trapezia. One face will be a small rectangle corresponding to the shallow end of the pool. This is labelled ‘Back’ on the diagram. The name is an arbitrary choice, relating solely to the way that the perspective diagram has been drawn.

Similarly a larger rectangle is labelled ‘Front’ and corresponds to the face at the deep end of the pool.

The floor of the pool, called ‘Bottom’ on the diagram, is the third rectangle.

Both long faces of the pool will be a trapezium, shown as ‘Side’ on the diagram. The two parallel edges of the shape correspond with the shallow and deep ends of the pool, while the top and bottom edges will not be parallel but instead diverge as the pool deepens. As both faces are identical, only one diagram is shown for both.

Including these faces as process variables in the model gives this initial list:

Back:	The area of the concrete side at the shallow end
Front:	The area of the concrete side at the deep end
Bottom:	The area of the bottom of the pool
Side:	The area of either of the two long sides of the pool

Another process variable included in the model represents the total surface area of all five faces of the pool’s concrete shell:

Area:	The total area of all the concrete faces of the pool

A final process variable is required for the calculation of the slant edge of the bottom of the pool:

Slant:	The length of the sloping bottom of the pool

Process variables
The complete list of process variables is:

Slant:	The length of the sloping bottom of the pool
Back:	The area of the concrete side at the shallow end
Front:	The area of the concrete side at the deep end
Bottom:	The area of the bottom of the pool
Side:	The area of either of the two long sides of the pool
Area:	The total area of all the concrete faces of the pool

The equations for the model can now be constructed. It is quite a simple model and many of the equations are only calculations of areas of rectangles. For example, the area of the rectangular face at the shallow end of the pool is found by multiplying the width of the pool by its depth at the shallow end:

Back = Width × Shallow

Similarly the area of the face at the deep end is found by multiplying the width by the depth at this end:

Front = Width × Deep

The area of the bottom of the pool is calculated by multiplying the slant length by the width:

Bottom = Slant × Width

This equation is not complete in itself, of course, because it includes the process variable Slant. Below, however, this variable will itself be defined as a combination of input variables.

The area of a trapezium is calculated as half of the sum of the parallel sides multiplied by the distance between them. This leads to the equation:

Side = Length × (Shallow + Deep)/2

The expression used is a standard textbook equation. However, if students have not encountered this before it might be easier to consider the area of the face as consisting of the two separate triangles ABC and ACD. For each of these the area will be given by the familiar equation:

(Height × Base)/2

For the triangle *ABC* this becomes:

(Length × Shallow)/2

For the triangle *ACD* the area is:

(Length × Deep)/2

Adding together the area of the two triangles now gives this equation for Side:

Side = (Length × Shallow)/2 + (Length × Deep)/2

Factorizing out the common expression of Length/2 leads to:

Side = Length × (Shallow + Deep)/2

This was the equation given above.
At this point the total area of all of the faces can be included in a single equation:

Area = Back + Front + Bottom + 2 × Side

The additional factor of 2 is required because there are two identical long sides in the concrete shell of the pool.

The equation needed for the volume of the concrete is now added to the model. This equation involves an important simplifying assumption which makes the model far easier. Provided that the thickness of the concrete shell is very small compared with its overall surface area, the volume of the shell can be calculated just by multiplying the area by the thickness. It would be possible to show this formally, by constructing an accurate equation and showing that certain terms were neglibile. However, this additional work would almost defeat the purpose of making the assumption. It should be possible to envisage intuitively the tiny volumes that have been ignored along the edges where faces intersect, and to realize their relative insignificance.

Of course it is important to state clearly in the model any assumptions that have been made. This allows others to appraise objectively any results gained from the model. (Perhaps this is something generally lacking from popular debate about global warming?)

The equation for the volume of the concrete is:

Volume = Area × Thickness

One final equation is required. This will calculate a value for Slant. The equation can be found by applying Pythagoras to the triangle *AED*. In this triangle the process variable Slant is represented by the hypotenuse *AD*, and so it can be seen that:

$(\text{Slant})^2 = (AE)^2 + (ED)^2$

However, *AE* is equal to Length, and *ED* is equal to (Deep – Shallow). The equation becomes:

$(\text{Slant})^2 = \text{Length}^2 + (\text{Deep} - \text{Shallow})^2$

If the square root of both sides of this equation is taken we have a final expression for Slant:

$\text{Slant} = (\text{Length}^2 + (\text{Deep} - \text{Shallow})^2)^{0.5}$

At this point the set of equations can be seen to be complete because they all involve on their right-hand side either input variables or process variables which are themselves the left-hand side of other equations in the model.

The complete set of equations for the model is therefore:

$\text{Slant} = (\text{Length}^2 + (\text{Deep} - \text{Shallow})^2)^{0.5}$
Back = Width × Shallow
Front = Width × Deep

Bottom = Slant × Width
Side = Length × (Shallow + Deep)/2
Area = Back + Front + Bottom + 2 × Side
Volume = Area × Thickness

Mathematical model for concrete swimming pool

The final form of the mathematical model can be stated as:

Output variable

Volume:	The volume of concrete required for all the faces

Input variables

Length:	The length of the pool
Width:	The width of the pool
Shallow:	The depth of the pool at the shallow end
Deep:	The depth of the pool at the deep end
Thickness:	The thickness of the concrete walls

Process variables

Slant:	The length of the sloping bottom of the pool
Back:	The area of the concrete side at the shallow end
Front:	The area of the concrete side at the deep end
Bottom:	The area of the bottom of the pool
Side:	The area of either of the two long sides of the pool
Area:	The total area of all the concrete faces of the pool

Equations

$\text{Slant} = (\text{Length}^2 + (\text{Deep} - \text{Shallow})^2)^{0.5}$
Back = Width × Shallow
Front = Width × Deep
Bottom = Slant × Width
Side = Length × (Shallow + Deep)/2
Area = Back + Front + Bottom + 2 × Side
Volume = Area × Thickness

Assumption

The equation given for the volume is sufficiently accurate, provided that the value of Thickness is very small when compared with the value of Area.

Coding the model

The model can now be coded. The way in which a particular model is coded as a spreadsheet will obviously be decided by the person entering it. There is no unique coding, and so what is illustrated below is fairly arbitrary. It should, however, offer some guidance.

First headings for the input variables are placed on to the sheet. 'Length' is placed in cell A3, 'Width' in B3, 'Shallow' in C3, 'Deep' in D3 and 'Thickness' in E3. Test values are also added in the cells immediately beneath each of the headings. The appropriate cell references for each of the input variables are therefore:

Input variable Length has cell reference A4
Input variable Width has cell reference B4

Input variable Shallow has cell reference C4
Input variable Deep has cell reference D4
Input variable Thickness has cell reference E4

Next, headings for the process variables are entered on to the spreadsheet. 'Slant' is placed in A8, 'Back' in B8, 'Front' in C8, 'Bottom' in D8, 'Side' in E8 and 'Area' in F8. The cells references for each of these process variables are:

Process variable Slant has cell reference A9
Process variable Back has cell reference B9
Process variable Front has cell reference C9
Process variable Bottom has cell reference D9
Process variable Side has cell reference E9
Process variable Area has cell reference F9

The heading for the single output variable Volume is added to A13 and so:

Output variable Volume has cell reference A14

Each of the equations is now placed in the cell corresponding to the appropriate process, or output, variable. These equations will be logically the same as in the model but of course the variable names that appear in the equations will be replaced by the cell references that have been chosen according to the lists above. The equations therefore appear in a slightly modified form:

The equation:

$$\text{Slant} = (\text{Length}^2 + (\text{Deep} - \text{Shallow})^2)^{0.5}$$

now appears, in cell A9, in the coded form of:

$$= (\text{A4}^2 + (\text{D4} - \text{C4})^2)^{0.5}$$

The equation:

$$\text{Back} = \text{Width} \times \text{Shallow}$$

now appears, in cell B9, in the coded form of:

$$= \text{B4} \times \text{C4}$$

The equation:

$$\text{Front} = \text{Width} \times \text{Deep}$$

now appears, in cell C9, in the coded form of:

$$= \text{B4} \times \text{D4}$$

The equation:

$$\text{Bottom} = \text{Slant} \times \text{Width}$$

now appears, in cell D9, in the coded form of:

$$= \text{A9} \times \text{B4}$$

The equation:

$$\text{Side} = \text{Length} \times (\text{Shallow} + \text{Deep})/2$$

now appears, in cell E9, in the coded form of:

$$= \text{A4} \times (\text{C4} + \text{D4})/2$$

The equation:

Area = Back + Front + Bottom + 2 × Side

now appears, in cell F9, in the coded form of:

= B9 + C9 + D9 + 2 × E9

The equation:

Volume = Area × Thickness

now appears, in cell A14, in the coded form of:

= F9 × E4

Figure 3.20 is a screen dump showing how the sheet appears, with settings adjusted to show formulas. The numerical result from the test data used is shown in Figure 3.21.

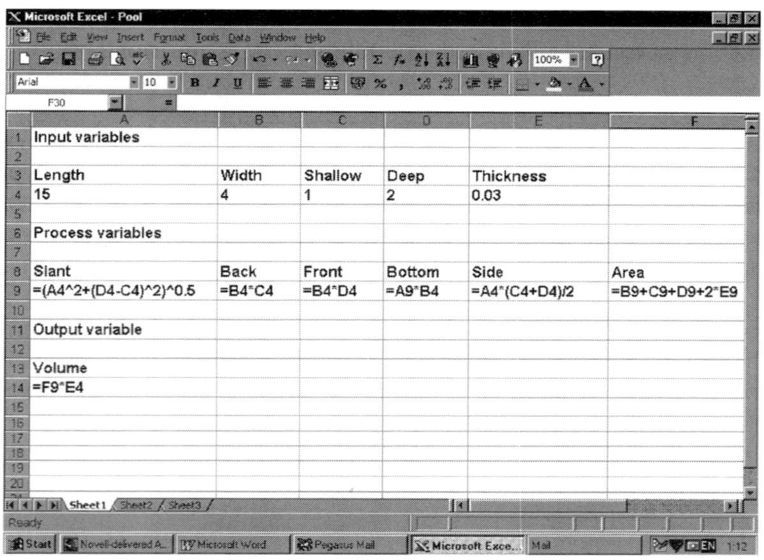

Figure 3.20

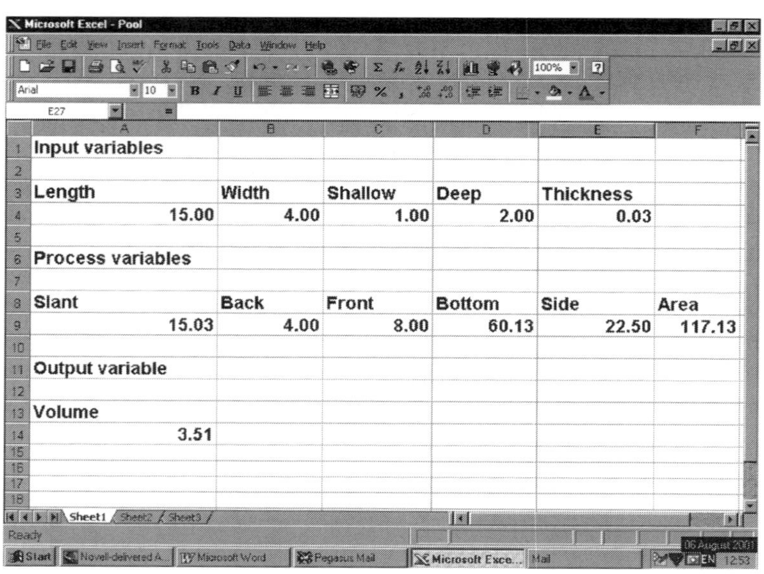

Figure 3.21

Exercise 5: The displacement of a barge

In this exercise the student has to design a model that will predict whether a rectangular barge will float or sink. The barge is a simple box shape, a cuboid, and is made of a material that weighs 600 kg per square metre. It floats in fresh water with a density of 1000 kg per cubic metre. (Dimensions of the barge are assumed to be in metres also.)

The exercise implies a knowledge of simple physics. Archimedes' principle would have to be explained – an object continues to sink in water until the weight of water that has been pushed out of the way is equal to the weight of the object itself.

An astute student should query the logic of this model. An assumption is made that the weight of the displaced water does equal the weight of the barge. This is then used, via reasonably simple algebra, to calculate the depth to which the barge must settle into the water in order for the displacement to be the same as its own weight. If this depth is less than the 'height' of the barge itself then it is assumed that the barge is floating. Of course this model holds true only up to the moment the barge sinks. Once it is fully immersed the weight of displaced water is less than the barge's weight. This contradicts one of the assumptions. The model is correct only up to the point when the barge sinks.

Designing the mathematical model for the barge

The spreadsheet needs only to inform the user whether a particular barge will float or sink. It does not have to present any other information about what happens to the barge. The model that will be developed could be modified to give further details of the situation, like the amount of freeboard as the barge settles into the water, but as the problem is stated this is not required. As a consequence there is no need to include specific output variables. The only information given to the user will take the form of text printed out by a condition.

Figure 3.22 shows the rudimentary appearance of the barge. It is a flat box, a cuboid.

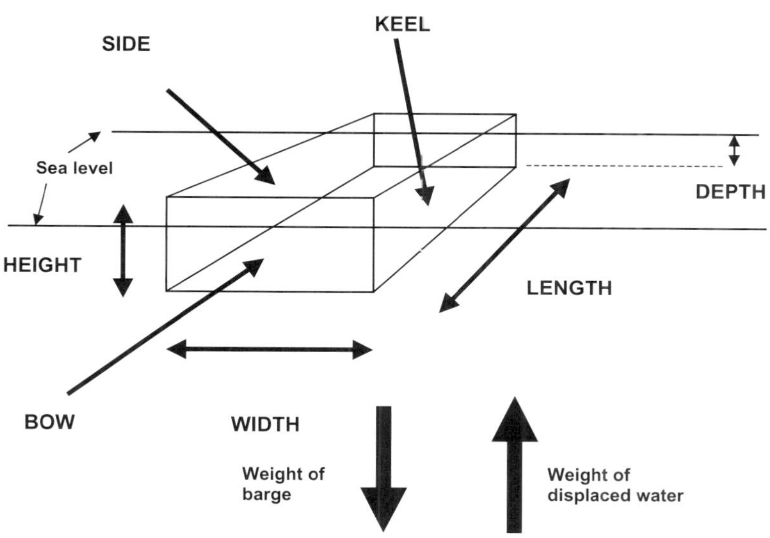

Figure 3.22 *Diagram for a displacement of a loaded barge*

Here an assumption could have been made, although it is not in this example. A real barge (think of the ones that are towed along the Thames and pass by Tate Modern and the South Bank Centre) will actually be oval ended. But such an oval cross-section will be fairly close to a rectangle, given the typical ratio of length to width. So the assumption would be: the barge can be regarded as a cuboid.

Treating it as a simple cuboid means that its size is completely defined by its length, width and height. These will be the only values required by the model, as the weight per unit area of the material from which the barge is constructed has been given as a constant in the problem. And so there are only three input variables.

Input variables
Length: Length of barge
Width: Width of barge
Height: Height of barge

As stated, the model will be based upon the principle that Archimedes famously enunciated about the weight of water displaced by a floating body. This will always be equal to the weight of the body itself. This means that the model will need to calculate the weight of the barge. And this can be calculated only if the total surface area of the barge is first known.

Finding the surface area of a cuboid consists simply of adding the areas of the separate rectangular faces. These distinct surface areas will be process variables in the model. From the diagram it can be seen that the faces are:

Side: Area of one side of barge
Bow: Area of bow (also equal to area of stern)
Keel: Area of bottom of barge

The total area of the faces will be a further process variable:

Hull: Total area of barge's hull

Once this area is known the weight of the barge can be calculated directly from a knowledge of the weight per unit area of the material used for its construction. This weight will be another process variable in the model:

BargeWeight: Weight of barge

According to Archimedes this weight is equal to the weight of displaced water, which is also included as a process variable:

WaterWeight: Weight of displaced water

It may be felt that there is a certain redundancy here, and that distinct process variables are not required for both the weight of the barge and the weight of the displaced water. This is true. The variable BargeWeight would suffice. However, including both variables does make the physics of the situation explicit as an equation in the model, namely that the weight of a floating object is equal to the weight of the liquid it displaces. Remember that it is important that a model is clearly understood by others.

The weight of the displaced water can be related to its volume, a further variable:

WaterVolume: Volume of displaced water

Finally, the volume of displaced water can be directly related to the depth to which the barge sinks. Obviously when a value is obtained for this depth it will be known whether the barge is floating:

Depth: Depth to which barge sinks in water

Process variables
The complete list of process variables in the model is:

Side: Area of one side of barge
Bow: Area of bow (also equal to area of stern)
Keel: Area of bottom of barge
Hull: Total area of barge's hull
BargeWeight: Weight of barge
WaterWeight: Weight of displaced water
WaterVolume: Volume of displaced water
Depth: Depth to which barge sinks in water

The equations for the model can now be established. From the diagram it can be seen that the three rectangular areas, Side, Bow and Keel, are obtained by multiplying the respective edges of the barge. This gives the three equations:

Side = Length × Height

Bow = Width × Height

Keel = Length × Width

The total area for the barge's hull is now twice the sum of the long and the short faces of the cuboid, to which is added the area of the bottom face. It is assumed that the barge is totally open and so the variable Keel does not have to be doubled to include a deck:

Hull = 2 × (Side + Bow) + Keel

The weight of the barge is now found by multiplying its surface area by 600, the value stated originally in the description of the problem:

BargeWeight = 600 × Hull

At this point Archimedes' principle appears formally in the model as the equation of the barge's weight with the weight of the water displaced:

WaterWeight = BargeWeight

The volume of the water (in cubic metres) is now found by dividing this weight by 1000:

WaterVolume = WaterWeight/1000

The displaced water can also be thought of as a cuboid with an area of cross-section equal to Keel and a thickness given by Depth, as indicated by the diagram. The volume of this cuboid will be Keel multiplied by Depth. This will equal WaterVolume, leading to the equation:

WaterVolume = Keel × Depth

Rearranging this equation gives the equation required for the process variable Depth:

Depth = WaterVolume/Keel

Now all the process variables are defined by equations, the set of which is therefore complete:

Side = Length × Height
Bow = Width × Height
Keel = Length × Width
Hull = 2 × (Side + Bow) + Keel
BargeWeight = 600 × Hull
WaterWeight = BargeWeight
WaterVolume = WaterWeight/1000
Depth = WaterVolume/Keel

Finally a single condition decides whether or not the barge floats. This is the self-evident statement that floating is equivalent to depth of immersion not exceeding the total height of the barge.

Condition
IF Depth > Height THEN [Barge sinks] ELSE [Barge floats]

Mathematical model for the barge

The complete model for the barge is:

Input variables

Length:	Length of barge
Width:	Width of barge
Height:	Height of barge

Process variables

Side:	Area of one side of barge
Bow:	Area of bow (also equal to area of stern)
Keel:	Area of bottom of barge
Hull:	Total area of barge's hull
BargeWeight:	Weight of barge
WaterWeight:	Weight of displaced water
WaterVolume:	Volume of displaced water
Depth:	Depth to which barge sinks in water

Equations

Side = Length × Height
Bow = Width × Height
Keel = Length × Width
Hull = 2 × (Side + Bow) + Keel
BargeWeight = 600 × Hull
WaterWeight = BargeWeight
WaterVolume = WaterWeight/1000
Depth = WaterVolume/Keel

Condition

IF Depth > Height THEN [Barge sinks] ELSE [Barge floats]

Coding the model

The text 'Length', 'Width' and 'Height' are placed in cells A3, B3 and C3, respectively. This means that:

Input variable Length has cell reference A4
Input variable Width has cell reference B4
Input variable Height has cell reference C4

Test data is entered into these three cells

Text identifying the process variables is now added. 'Hull' is added to cell A8, 'BargeWeight' to B8, 'WaterWeight' to C8, 'WaterVolume' to D8, 'Side' to A10, 'Bow' to B10, 'Keel' to C10 and 'Depth' to D10. This gives these cell references for the process variables:

Process variable Hull has cell reference A9
Process variable BargeWeight has cell reference B9
Process variable WaterWeight has cell reference C9
Process variable WaterVolume has cell reference D9
Process variable Side has cell reference A11
Process variable Bow has cell reference B11
Process variable Keel has cell reference C11
Process variable Depth has cell reference D11

For the output of the spreadsheet, the text 'Is barge afloat?' is added to cell A13.

The equations are now added to the cells representing the process variables, substituting the relevant cell references for variable names.

The equation:

Side = Length × Height

now appears, in cell A11, as the code:

= A4 × C4

The equation:

Bow = Width × Height

now appears, in cell B11, as the code:

= B4 × C4

The equation:

Keel = Length × Width

now appears, in cell C11, as the code:

= A4 × B4

The equation:

Hull = 2 × (Side + Bow) + Keel

now appears, in cell A9, as the code:

= 2 × (A11 + B11) + C11

The equation:

BargeWeight = 600 × Hull

now appears, in cell B9, as the code:

= 600 × A9

The equation:

WaterWeight = BargeWeight

now appears, in cell C9, as the code:

= B9

The equation:

WaterVolume = WaterWeight/1000

now appears, in cell D9, as the code:

= C9/1000

The equation:

Depth = WaterVolume/Keel

now appears, in cell D11, as the code:

= D9/C11

Finally, the condition:

IF Depth > Height THEN [Barge sinks] ELSE [Barge floats]

appears in cell A14 as the Excel code:

= IF(D11>C4, ‘No’, ‘Yes’)

The coded sheet appears as shown in Figure 3.23.

The model can now be tested with data which shows the barge both floating and sinking. In the two screen dumps (Figures 3.24 and 3.25) narrowing the width of the barge makes it sink.

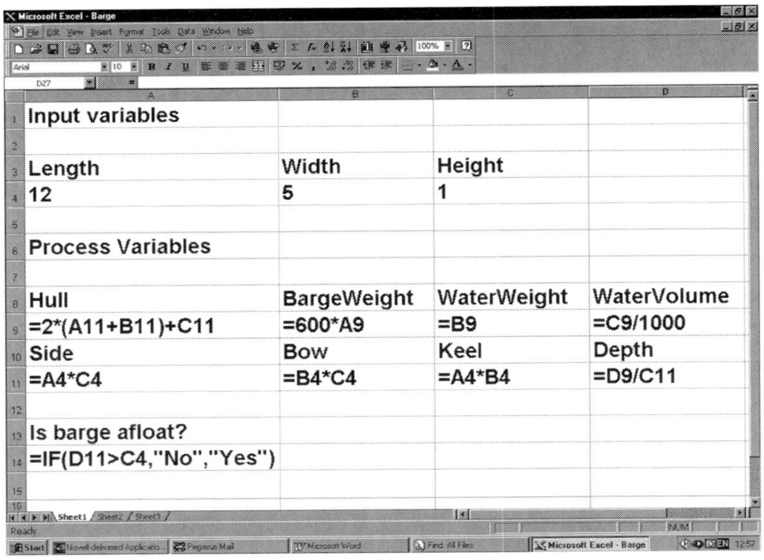

	A	B	C	D
1	Input variables			
2				
3	Length	Width	Height	
4	12	5	1	
5				
6	Process Variables			
7				
8	Hull	BargeWeight	WaterWeight	WaterVolume
9	=2*(A11+B11)+C11	=600*A9	=B9	=C9/1000
10	Side	Bow	Keel	Depth
11	=A4*C4	=B4*C4	=A4*B4	=D9/C11
12				
13	Is barge afloat?			
14	=IF(D11>C4,"No","Yes")			

Figure 3.23

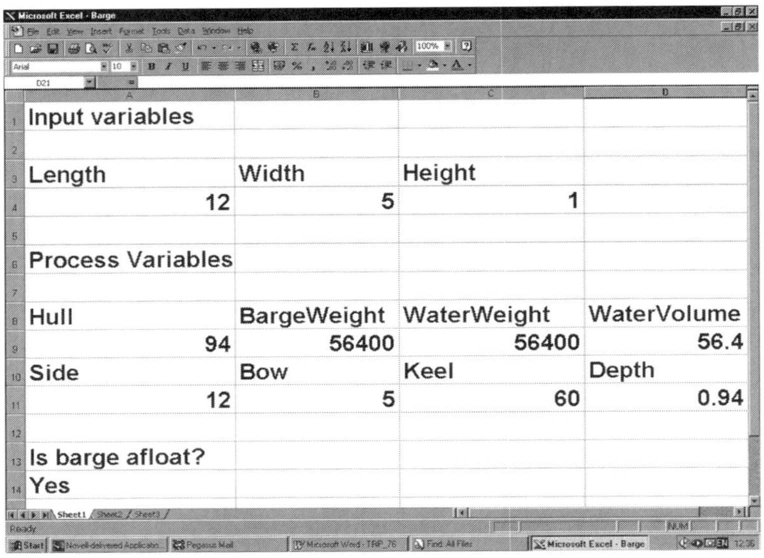

	A	B	C	D
1	Input variables			
2				
3	Length	Width	Height	
4	12	5	1	
5				
6	Process Variables			
7				
8	Hull	BargeWeight	WaterWeight	WaterVolume
9	94	56400	56400	56.4
10	Side	Bow	Keel	Depth
11	12	5	60	0.94
12				
13	Is barge afloat?			
14	Yes			

Figure 3.24

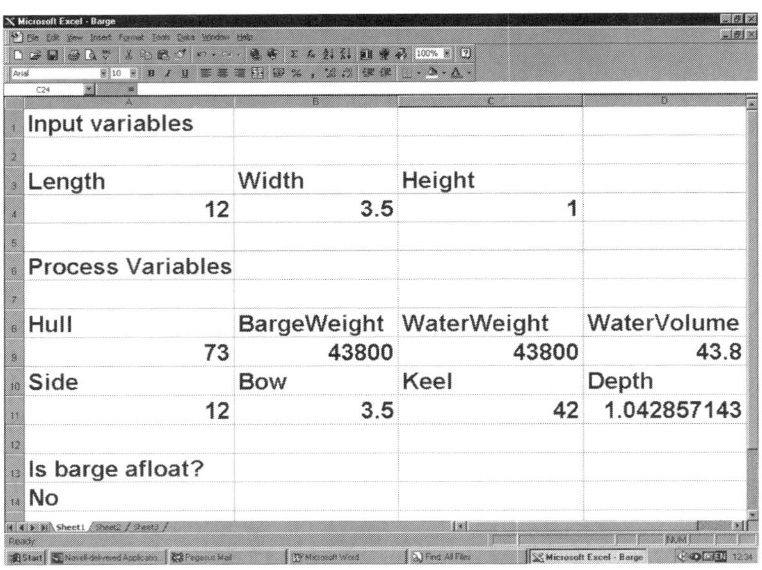

	A	B	C	D
1	Input variables			
2				
3	Length	Width	Height	
4	12	3.5	1	
5				
6	Process Variables			
7				
8	Hull	BargeWeight	WaterWeight	WaterVolume
9	73	43800	43800	43.8
10	Side	Bow	Keel	Depth
11	12	3.5	42	1.042857143
12				
13	Is barge afloat?			
14	No			

Figure 3.25

3.2 Programming methodology

Exercise 1: Investigating prime numbers

> This is the first in a series of seven programming exercises in which a computer solution is produced for a given problem. When adapting this material for groups of students the problem-solving aspect of the exercise should be emphasized. Although a complete solution is given here, learning will always take place more effectively when a student has had the opportunity to think through a problem for her/himself. Active encouragement should be given for alternative algorithms to be explored, or a different coding provided for the algorithm developed in the exercise.
>
> Computing is not rote learning!
>
> Three separate programs are included in this exercise, each developing on the one before.

A prime number has no factors other than 1 and itself.

Prime numbers were an early fascination for mathematicians and have continued to intrigue many people since ancient times. There is no end to the list of primes and generating the next higher becomes an increasing test of computational power and algorithmic ingenuity. The late astronomer Carl Sagan whimsically suggested in his science fiction novel *Contact* a hidden pattern in the distribution of prime numbers might be a deliberate clue about the origin of the Universe, hard-wired into its very fabric by some lofty race of meta-beings. (Carl omitted to say whether these were the white mice posited by Douglas Adams.)

Prime numbers also allow excellent problem-solving and programming opportunities for students. How can a program be written that will test whether a given number is prime or, instead, composite? (A composite number, unlike a prime, is the product of factors other than 1 and itself.)

The Sieve of Eratosthenes

A possible way of introducing this problem-solving exercise to a group of students is to return to a class exercise that some of them will recall from early days at school. It is called the Sieve of Eratosthenes.

Eratosthenes was born in 276 BC in Cyrene, which is now in Libya. The breadth of Eratosthenes' interests would deserve the title of polymath although it appears that his contemporaries considered him more as a jack of all trades. He was particularly interested in geodesy and calculated the circumference of the Earth by comparing the length of the shadow cast at noon in two different places, Aswan (then Syene) and Alexandria. He correctly assumed that the Sun was sufficiently distant for its rays to be regarded as effectively parallel, and hence that relatively simple geometry could relate the distance between the two separate shadows to the Earth's circumference. (The accuracy of his result, a quarter of a million stadia, depends upon modern interpretation of how long a stadia actually was.)

His work in mathematics included solid geometry and, of course, prime numbers. His 'sieve' is a very effective practical illustration of the concept.

Students should be issued with copies of a 'hundred square'. This is a table of ten rows and columns with all the integers from 1 to 100 marked in the individual cells (see Figure 3.26).

Students are now invited to strike out all the numbers into which 2 divides exactly. The cell containing 2 itself is left intact. A very obvious pattern results (see Figure 3.27). (Young children do this sort of thing with different coloured crayons).

Moving from left to right along the top row of the hundred square it can be seen that the next number to use as a divisor for the others in the square is 3. So now all the multiples of 3 are deleted from the square (see Figure 3.28).

The number 4 is no longer present on the top row. As a result the next number to use as a divisor is 5. This removes further multiples from the square (see Figure 3.29).

Already it can be seen that the prime numbers up to 47 have been highlighted by this process. Just one more deletion of multiples is required, this time multiples of 7, in order to leave the square with just prime numbers (see Figure 3.30).

The algorithm that has been demonstrated by this graphical process consists of discovering prime numbers by dividing a set of integers initially by 2 and then by 3, then 5, and sucessively by other primes as they are generated by the algorithm itself. It is used in the third of the example programs given below. First, however, a much simpler algorithm is used to test whether a particular number is prime or not.

Students should be encouraged to investigate the design of a simple prime-testing algorithm of their own, and then perhaps given the one shown here as an exercise in coding.

1	2	3	4	5	6	7	8	9	10
11	12	13	14	15	16	17	18	19	20
21	22	23	24	25	26	27	28	29	30
31	32	33	34	35	36	37	38	39	40
41	42	43	44	45	46	47	48	49	50
51	52	53	54	55	56	57	58	59	60
61	62	63	64	65	66	67	68	69	70
71	72	73	74	75	76	77	78	79	80
81	82	83	84	85	86	87	88	89	90
91	92	93	94	95	96	97	98	99	100

Figure 3.26

1	2	3	X	5	X	7	X	9	X
11	X	13	X	15	X	17	X	19	X
21	X	23	X	25	X	27	X	29	X
31	X	33	X	35	X	37	X	39	X
41	X	43	X	45	X	47	X	49	X
51	X	53	X	55	X	57	X	59	X
61	X	63	X	65	X	67	X	69	X
71	X	73	X	75	X	77	X	79	X
81	X	83	X	85	X	87	X	89	X
91	X	93	X	95	X	97	X	99	X

Figure 3.27

1	2	3	X	5	X	7	X	X	X
11	X	13	X	X	X	17	X	19	X
X	X	23	X	25	X	X	X	29	X
31	X	X	X	35	X	37	X	X	X
41	X	43	X	X	X	47	X	49	X
X	X	53	X	55	X	X	X	59	X
61	X	X	X	65	X	67	X	X	X
71	X	73	X	X	X	77	X	79	X
X	X	83	X	85	X	X	X	89	X
91	X	X	X	95	X	97	X	X	X

Figure 3.28

1	2	3	X	5	X	7	X	X	X
11	X	13	X	X	X	17	X	19	X
X	X	23	X	25	X	X	X	29	X
31	X	X	X	35	X	37	X	X	X
41	X	43	X	X	X	47	X	49	X
X	X	53	X	55	X	X	X	59	X
61	X	X	X	65	X	67	X	X	X
71	X	73	X	X	X	77	X	79	X
X	X	83	X	85	X	X	X	89	X
91	X	X	X	95	X	97	X	X	X

Figure 3.29

1	2	3	X	5	X	7	X	X	X
11	X	13	X	X	X	17	X	19	X
X	X	23	X	X	X	X	X	29	X
31	X	X	X	X	X	37	X	X	X
41	X	43	X	X	X	47	X	X	X
X	X	53	X	X	X	X	X	59	X
61	X	X	X	X	X	67	X	X	X
71	X	73	X	X	X	X	X	79	X
X	X	83	X	X	X	X	X	89	X
91	X	X	X	X	X	97	X	X	X

Figure 3.30

Testing whether a number is prime or composite

The algorithm consists of dividing the number by every integer from 2 onwards until a factor is found or until half the size of the number is reached. The advantage of this algorithm is that it is very easy to code, requiring little more than a single conditional loop. A flag is used to help govern the condition for exit from this loop. A flag value of True indicates that the number being tested is prime. A value of False means that it is not. Initially it is assumed that the number is prime.

1. Enter number
2. Initialize a flag as True
3. Initialize factor as 1
4. Increment factor
5. If factor divides exactly into number set flag to False
6. If flag is false go to step 8
7. If factor is less than half the number repeat from step 4
8. If flag is true number is prime else composite

This algorithm can be coded as follows:

```
Option Explicit
Private Sub Command1_Click()

'Checking whether a number is prime

'Declare number being tested
Dim intNumber As Integer

'Declare possible factor of number
Dim intFactor As Integer

'Declare exit flag
Dim Flag As Boolean

'Request number
intNumber = Val(InputBox("Enter a number"))

'Check possible factor
Flag = True
intFactor = 1
Do
intFactor = intFactor + 1
If intNumber Mod intFactor = 0 Then Flag = False
Loop Until Flag = False Or intFactor > intNumber / 2

'State result
Print intNumber; " is ";
If Flag = True Then
Print "prime"
Else
Print "composite"
End If

End Sub
```

A typical display for the program is shown in Figure 3.31. Four numbers have been tested in turn. They are 17, 40, 97 and 29.

Program documentation

First the program's objective is indicated by an initial comment:

```
Option Explicit
Private Sub Command1_Click()
'Checking whether a number is prime
```

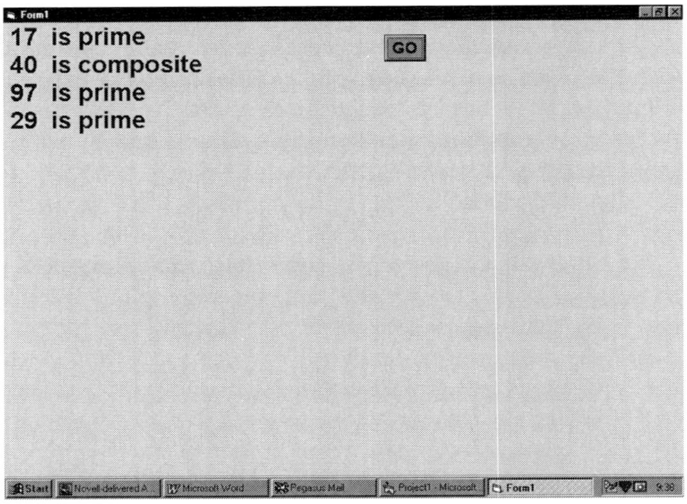

Figure 3.31

The potential prime number is represented by the variable intNumber. This is declared at the beginning of the program:

```
'Declare number being tested
Dim intNumber As Integer
```

The number that will be test-divided into intNumber is intFactor: this is also declared:

```
'Declare possible factor of number
Dim intFactor As Integer
```

The final declaration is for the Boolean variable, Flag:

```
'Declare exit flag
Dim Flag As Boolean
```

The InputBox function is now used to assign the number chosen by the user to the appropriate variable, intNumber (the use of Val is not required in later versions of Visual Basic):

```
'Request number
intNumber = Val(InputBox("Enter a number"))
```

After this the conditional loop which tests whether intNumber is prime can begin. It will divide intNumber by increasingly large potential factors to see if one of them will divide into it exactly. If this does happen the fact will be registered by resetting the value of the Boolean variable Flag to False, to indicate that intNumber is not prime. First, however, Flag is set to True. This is rather like the principle of 'innocent until proven guilty':

```
'Check possible factor
Flag = True
```

The test factor is then initialized as 1. This value is chosen because the value of intFactor will be incremented at each repeat of the loop. It needs to begin with a value of 2, for the first repeat, because this is the first possible factor with which a number should be tested in the Sieve of Eratosthenes:

```
intFactor = 1
```

The loop which tests intNumber now begins:

```
Do
```

The test factor is incremented:

```
intFactor = intFactor + 1
```

The modular division operator, Mod, is used to see if the factor divides exactly into the number being tested. Mod does not give the number of times that one number divides into another, but just the remainder of such a division. It is precisely what is required here. If the remainder is zero it means that intFactor has divided into intNumber an exact number of times, and is therefore really a factor of it.

So if Mod returns a value of zero the number cannot be prime, and the flag has to be set to a value of False:

```
If intNumber Mod intFactor = 0 Then Flag = False
```

The exit condition from the Do loop has two parts:

1. If the value of Flag becomes False, there is no point in the loop repeating any more times because the number is now known to be composite and further tests are irrelevant.
2. If the possible factor has increased to the point where it is bigger than half the number itself there is also no longer any reason to continue testing. A number cannot be divided exactly by a factor which is now as large as this:

```
Loop Until Flag = False Or intFactor > intNumber / 2
```

Once the loop is finished it will be known whether intNumber is prime or composite. This will depend solely upon whether the Flag is True or False. Print statements within an If Then Else structure can place appropriate text on the display:

```
'State result
Print intNumber; " is ";
If Flag = True Then
Print "prime"
Else
Print "composite"
End If

End Sub
```

Testing a range of numbers

The program just illustrated allows a particular number to be tested to see if it is prime. However, it is more likely that somebody would want to know how many primes there were up to some particular limit. For example, if you typed in 20 as the upper value, the program should detect and display the primes 2, 3, 5, 7, 11, 13, 17 and 19. If instead you typed 40 it should show 2, 3, 5, 7, 11, 13, 17, 19, 23, 29, 31 and 37.

It is quite easy to modify the existing program so that this can be done. All that basically is required is that the upper value should be entered, and a For loop introduced to check numbers up to this point.

Here is the modified program:

```
Option Explicit
Private Sub Command1_Click()

'Determine primes within a selected range

'Declare possible factor of number
Dim intFactor As Integer

'Declare exit flag
Dim Flag As Boolean

'Declare upper value
Dim intRange As Integer

'Declare loop control variable
Dim intCounter As Integer

'Request upper value
```

```
intRange = Val(InputBox("Enter upper value for range"))

For intCounter = 2 To intRange

'Check possible factor
Flag = True
intFactor = 1
Do
intFactor = intFactor + 1
If intCounter Mod intFactor = 0 Then Flag = False
Loop Until Flag = False Or intFactor > intCounter / 2

'State result
If Flag = True Then
Print intCounter; " is "; "Prime"
End If

Next intCounter

End Sub
```

Figure 3.32 shows the program generating the prime numbers in the range 2–50.

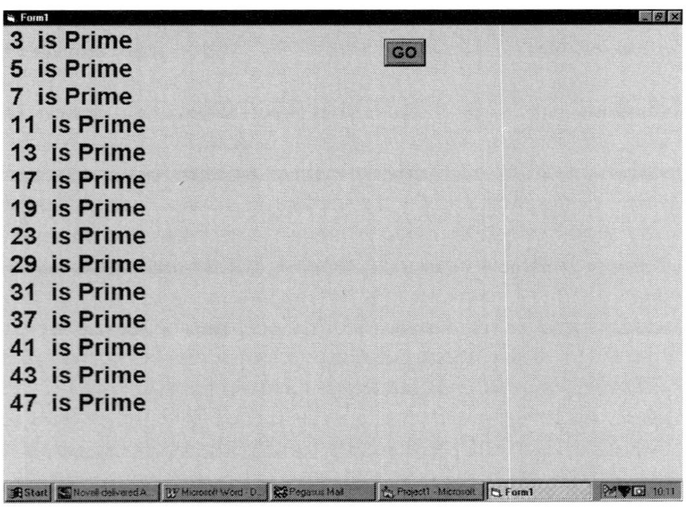

Figure 3.32

Program documentation
The descriptive comment indicates the program's function:

```
Option Explicit
Private Sub Command1_Click()

'Determine primes within a selected range
```

The variables intFactor and Flag are declared as before:

```
'Declare possible factor of number
Dim intFactor As Integer

'Declare exit flag
Dim Flag As Boolean
```

A new variable, intRange, is declared to represent the number determining the range over which primes should be sought. This, together with the loop control variable intCounter, is the equivalent of intNumber in the previous version of the program:

```
'Declare upper value
Dim intRange As Integer

'Declare loop control variable
Dim intCounter As Integer
```

The user is then asked to type in a value for intRange:

```
'Request upper value
intRange = Val(InputBox("Enter upper value for range"))
```

Once this value has been entered, the program continues as two nested loops. The outer loop is a For loop which looks in turn at each integer in the range specified by the user:

```
For intCounter = 2 To intRange
```

Within this outer loop the successive values of intCounter are tested to see if they are prime using code which is closely similar to the previous program. Throughout, the variable intNumber of the earlier code is replaced by intCounter.

First the variables Flag and intFactor are initialized:

```
'Check possible factor
Flag = True
intFactor = 1
```

Then a conditional loop resets the value of Flag to False if intCounter is not prime:

```
Do
intFactor = intFactor + 1
If intCounter Mod intFactor = 0 Then Flag = False
Loop Until Flag = False Or intFactor > intCounter / 2
```

If the current value of intCounter is prime this will be detected by the Flag as being True. The prime number discovered can then be displayed:

```
'State result
If Flag = True Then
Print intCounter; " is "; "Prime"
End If
```

Prime numbers encountered will continue to be displayed until the loop ends:

```
Next intCounter

End Sub
```

Using an array to determine prime numbers

The method for determining primes that has been adopted in this example works reasonably efficiently but students should always be encouraged to evaluate their work critically. It would therefore be appropriate at this point for the lecturer to question whether it was felt that this was the best possible method for generating a list of primes.

Some students might observe that the prime numbers are only being placed on the display. They are evanescent and not available for further use. They are not being stored in an array which allows them to be recalled according to their subscript.

Ideally any discussion should be discreetly steered towards the usefulness of an array in this context. An array does, in fact, allow a far more efficient algorithm to be designed. Students should be encouraged to think again about the way in which they would check whether a given number was prime or composite. After some discussion it should become apparent that an effective method to decide whether a number is prime or not is to test for division just by the prime numbers smaller than the number itself. For example, it can be shown that 17 is prime simply by testing it for division by 2, 3, 5, 7, 11 and 13. There is no need to try to divide by 4, 6, 8, 9, 10, 12, 14, 15 and 16. In fact as numbers being tested become larger and larger the primes themselves are more spaced out, and so an algorithm which insists upon dividing by all the intervening composite numbers becomes increasingly less efficient.

How much of this discussion should be led by the lecturer, and how much a group will achieve in a brainstorming session, will depend on circumstance. However, it should lead to the development of an algorithm which adopts a 'bootstrapping' approach to generating a list of primes. If it assumed that 2 is prime, then 3 can be tested by dividing just by 2. This adds 3 to the list of primes, which is now (2, 3). The next integer, 4, is tested by dividing by 2. It immediately fails this test and so the list of primes remains as (2, 3). The next integer, 5, is then test-divided first by 2 and then by 3. These tests show that 5 is prime and so the list becomes (2, 3, 5). Now 6 is tested. It is eliminated as a possible prime because 2 divides exactly into it. The list remains as (2, 3, 5), but when 7 is tested it becomes (2, 3, 5, 7). Once students have worked, manually, through a list like this they will appreciate this algorithm:

1. Make 2 the first element of a list of prime factors
2. Make 2 the first number to be tested
3. Increment number to be tested
4. Check if factor divides into number exactly
5. If it does, repeat from step 3
6. If it does not select next prime factor in list and repeat from step 4
7. If end of list add number to list of primes and repeat from step 3 with first factor

This algorithm can be coded in Basic as shown here:

```
Option Explicit
Private Sub Command1_Click()

'Using array of primes to generate
'further members

'Declare prime array
Dim intPrimes(100) As Integer

'Initial member of array
intPrimes(1) = 2

'Total of known primes
Dim intTotal As Integer
intTotal = 1

'Range to check
Dim intNumber As Integer

'Declare loop control variables
Dim intCounter1 As Integer
Dim intCounter2 As Integer
'Declare exit flag
Dim Flag As Boolean
'Request range from user
intNumber = InputBox("Enter upper value for range")

'Show that 2 is prime
Cls
Print "Prime 1 is 2"

'Outer loop checks successive numbers in selected range

For intCounter1 = 3 To intNumber

'Inner loop checks if current number is prime
intCounter2 = 0
Flag = True
```

```
Do
intCounter2 = intCounter2 + 1
If intCounter1 Mod intPrimes(intCounter2) = 0 Then Flag = False
Loop Until intCounter2 = intTotal Or Flag = False

'Add new prime to array
If Flag = True Then
intTotal = intTotal + 1
intPrimes(intTotal) = intCounter1
Print "Prime"; intCounter2 + 1; " is ";
Print intPrimes(intTotal)
End If

Next intCounter1

End Sub
```

A typical screen display for the program is shown in Figure 3.33. The range to be tested here is 3–50.

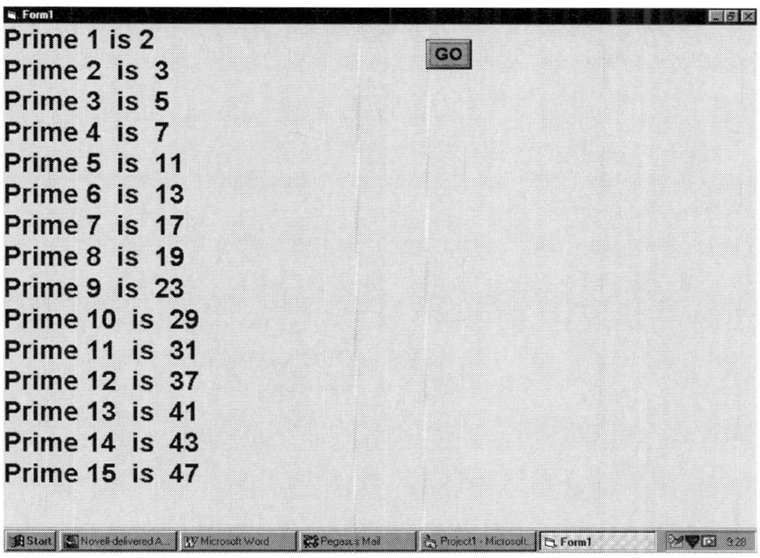

Figure 3.33

Program documentation

The program begins with Option Explicit and with comments to indicate what is achieved by the code:

```
Option Explicit
Private Sub Command1_Click()

'Using array of primes to generate
'further members
```

An array is then declared to store prime numbers as they are identified. The size of the array chosen here is quite arbitrary. It is assumed that 100 prime numbers will be sufficient to demonstrate that the algorithm is reasonably efficient:

```
'Declare prime array
Dim intPrimes(100) As Integer
```

The algorithm requires that initially just the first prime number, 2, is known. This is assigned to the first location of the array, intPrimes():

```
'Initial member of array
intPrimes(1) = 2
```

The total number of known prime numbers, intTotal, must always be available to the algorithm. The value of intTotal is constantly updated as new primes are discovered, but it must be initialized as 1 before any fresh primes are found. This is because at the beginning of execution of the program the prime number 2 is present in the intPrimes() array:

```
'Total of known primes
Dim intTotal As Integer
intTotal = 1
```

The user can choose over what range of numbers primes should be detected. This is done by assigning a value to the variable intNumber, which will be used subsequently in a For loop determining how many integers should be tested. First this variable must be declared:

```
'Range to check
Dim intNumber As Integer
```

Two loop control variables are needed, as the program will use two nested loops:

```
'Declare loop control variables
Dim intCounter1 As Integer
Dim intCounter2 As Integer
```

The inner loop of the nested pair is conditional, and a flag is required as part of the exit condition from it:

```
'Declare exit flag
Dim Flag As Boolean
```

At this point all the variables required by the program have been declared. The user is now prompted to enter the range over which integers will be tested. The InputBox function is used to assign a value to intNumber:

```
'Request range from user
intNumber = InputBox("Enter upper value for range")
```

Before any new primes are determined, the fact that 2 is already known as a prime is displayed:

```
'Show that 2 is prime
Cls
Print "Prime 1 is 2"
```

The nested loops which calculate whether successive integers are prime or not can now begin. The outer loop is a simple unconditional For loop which inspects each integer in turn. The upper limit of this loop is the value of intNumber which has been entered by the user. The loop begins with a value of 3, the next integer after the known prime, 2. The loop is controlled by the variable intCounter1, the value of which will be the number being tested to see if it is prime:

```
'Outer loop checks successive numbers in selected range

For intCounter1 = 3 To intNumber
```

The inner, conditional loop is a Do loop and requires a counter to determine how many times it has repeated. This is the variable intCounter2 and it is initialized as zero before the loop begins:

```
'Inner loop checks if current number is prime
intCounter2 = 0
```

Exit from the inner loop is determined by a double condition. One component of this is to decide whether the number being checked, intCounter1, is prime. The value of the Boolean variable, Flag, is used to monitor this. An assumption is made that intCounter1 is prime until it is proved not to be. The value of Flag is therefore initialized as True to indicate that intCounter1 is prime:

```
Flag = True
```

The conditional loop then begins:

```
Do
```

Immediately within the loop the counter, intCounter2, is incremented:

```
intCounter2 = intCounter2 + 1
```

This counter will identify each prime number in turn that is held in the array. These primes will be given by intPrimes(intCounter2). Of course when the program begins there will only be one prime in the array, intPrimes(1), which will be equal to 2. However, as the program continues to execute, the number of primes in the array will constantly increase as new prime numbers are found.

A check can now be carried out to see if the current prime selected by the value of intCounter2 will divide into the integer being tested. This is given by the value of the control variable for the outer loop, intCounter1. The test whether the former divides exactly into the latter is to check whether the remainder, given by using Mod, is equal to zero. If the remainder is zero then clearly intCounter1 is composite, not prime. Should this be the case the value of the Boolean flag variable is changed from True to False. A value of False means that intCounter1 is not prime:

```
If intCounter1 Mod intPrimes(intCounter2) = 0 Then Flag = False
```

The inner loop will test whether intCounter1 is prime by dividing it in turn by each of the primes held in the array. As soon as a division occurs with zero remainder the loop should exit. There is no need to test with other primes from the array. Immediate exit from the loop is achieved by including in the exit condition the expression Flag = False. This condition will be satisfied as soon as it is known that intCounter1 is composite.

The other part of the exit condition is that all the known primes have been tested as possible divisors of intCounter1. This will be the case when the counter for the inner loop, intCounter2, equals the current total of primes, intTotal.

The overall condition for exit from the inner loop is therefore:

```
Loop Until intCounter2 = intTotal Or Flag = False
```

As soon as a prime is discovered it must be added to the array, intPrimes(). This is an essential part of the algorithm. The condition for this is that the Boolean flag has remained True by the end of the inner loop:

```
'Add new prime to array
If Flag = True Then
```

First the total number of primes is increased by 1:

```
intTotal = intTotal + 1
```

This new value of intTotal is then the relevant subscript in the intPrimes() array for the addition of the newly discovered prime. The value of the new prime, intCounter1, is therefore assigned to the array location intPrimes(intTotal):

```
intPrimes(intTotal) = intCounter1
```

The discovery of this next prime number is added to the list of primes that is progressively displayed for the user:

```
Print "Prime"; intCounter2 + 1; " is ";
Print intPrimes(intTotal)
```

The if block following the condition then ends:

```
End If
```

Finally the outer loop ends:

```
Next intCounter1
```

This is the end of the Visual Basic code:

```
End Sub
```

Further exercises involving prime numbers

The whole subject of prime numbers is a fascinating area for problem solving using computational methods. There are many topics within the theory of primes where various ideas and conjectures, although plausible, have yet to be solved by traditional mathematics. Naturally it should not be assumed that a watertight mathematical proof can be produced by a computer. Nevertheless some of the unresolved conjectures provide excellent opportunities for the programmer to investigate the patterns superimposed upon the sequence of integers by the occurrence within it of prime numbers.

Here are some (arbitrarily selected) conjectures which could be explored by computer:

1. Goldbach's conjecture states that every even integer greater than 2 is the sum of two primes.
   The integer 20, for example, is equal to the sum of 7 and 13. The integer 24 is the sum of 11 and 13. Similarly 40 is equal to 17 plus 23.
   Students could be challenged to write a program which accepts the input of an even integer greater than 2 and then determines two prime numbers which add together to give this number.
   (Good opportunities exist here for validation of user input. The number accepted must be greater than 2. It must also be even.)
2. The twin primes conjecture assumes that there are an infinite number of primes which differ only by 2.
   Examples are 3 and 5, 5 and 7, 11 and 13. Students could be invited to develop a program which prints out a sequential list of such pairs. (They need not be asked for an infinite list, just a nice long one.)
3. Similar to the twin primes conjecture is the idea that primes occur in arithmetic progressions. This means that sets of consecutive prime numbers differ by the same amount, like 251, 257, 263 and 269. These four primes all differ by 6, but after 269 the next prime is 271 and the pattern is broken.
   Students could search for such progressions.
4. Another conjecture is that if a number is chosen at random and squared, and the same number plus one also squared, there will always be at least one prime number in the range created by the two squares.
   For example, if the number chosen is 6 then the range will be (6×6) to (7×7), or 36–49. Primes in this range are 37, 41, 43 and 47.

Just one of these topics is developed further here as a computer solution. Any of them would provide an invigorating exercise for discussion and practical investigation by students.

The last conjecture is chosen. To reiterate, this is the suggestion that if any integer, n, is chosen, there will be at least one prime number in the range defined by the square of this number and the square of the number one greater than it. It must be stressed that the program does not prove the conjecture but just provides particular examples of it. Of course if the program did indicate that no primes were found in the range generated by a selected value for n, then this would be a counter-example which disproved the conjecture. In other words the program can falsify the conjecture, in the spirit of Karl Popper, rather than verify it. Nevertheless in the real world you would be more likely to triple check the algorithm and its coding instead of writing to academic journals.

The program is developed from the second program given previously:

```
Option Explicit
Private Sub Command1_Click()

'Determine primes located between
'n squared and (n+1) squared

'Declare value for n
Dim intNumber As Integer

'Declare possible factor of number
Dim intFactor As Integer
```

```
'Declare exit flag
Dim Flag As Boolean

'Declare range limit variables
Dim intLower As Integer
Dim intUpper As Integer

'Declare loop control variable
Dim intCounter As Integer

'Request value for n
intNumber = InputBox("Enter value for 'n' ")

'Determine values for range limits
intLower = intNumber ^ 2
intUpper = (intNumber + 1) ^ 2

'Show range being checked
Cls
Print "Range checked is "; intNumber; "squared"
Print "to ("; intNumber; " + 1) squared"
Print

'Loop locates primes in range
For intCounter = intLower To intUpper
'Check possible factor
Flag = True
intFactor = 1
Do
intFactor = intFactor + 1
If intCounter Mod intFactor = 0 Then Flag = False
Loop Until Flag = False Or intFactor > intCounter / 2

'State result
If Flag = True Then
Print intCounter; " is "; "Prime"
End If

Next intCounter

End Sub
```

In Figure 3.34 the program is being demonstrated with a value for '*n*' of 8.

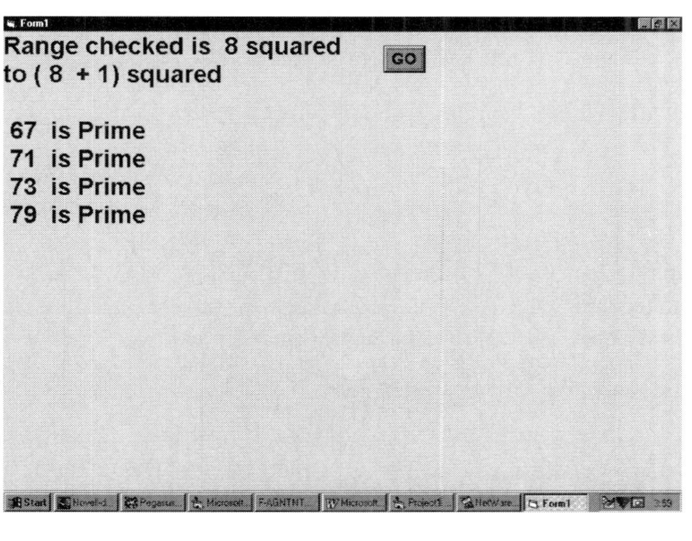

Figure 3.34

Program documentation

The code begins in the usual way with appropriate comments to introduce it:

```
Option Explicit
Private Sub Command1_Click()

'Determine primes located between
'n squared and (n+1) squared
```

A variable, intNumber, to represent the value of '*n*' is declared:

```
'Declare value for n
Dim intNumber As Integer
```

The integer variable, intFactor, and Boolean variable, Flag, are declared as in the first two programs above:

```
'Declare possible factor of number
Dim intFactor As Integer

'Declare exit flag
Dim Flag As Boolean
```

Two further variables, intLower and intUpper, are then introduced to define the range over which primes will be detected:

```
'Declare range limit variables
Dim intLower As Integer
Dim intUpper As Integer
```

A loop control variable is required:

```
'Declare loop control variable
Dim intCounter As Integer
```

After this the user is asked to type in the value of '*n*', represented in the program as intNumber:

```
'Request value for n
intNumber = InputBox("Enter value for 'n' ")
```

The values of '*n* squared' and '*n* + 1' squared can now be calculated from the values of intLower and intUpper:

```
'Determine values for range limits
intLower = intNumber ^ 2
intUpper = (intNumber + 1) ^ 2
```

The user is reminded of the range of numbers being tested for the existence of primes. The definition of the range, rather than the actual numerical values for intLower and intUpper, is shown as this stresses the point of the exercise:

```
'Show range being checked
Cls
Print "Range checked is "; intNumber; "squared"
Print "to ("; intNumber; " + 1) squared"
Print
```

A For loop now checks all the numbers between intLower and intUpper:

```
'Loop locates primes in range
For intCounter = intLower To intUpper
```

The body of this loop is now identical to the second of the examples given above:

```
'Check possible factor
Flag = True
intFactor = 1
Do
intFactor = intFactor + 1
If intCounter Mod intFactor = 0 Then Flag = False
Loop Until Flag = False Or intFactor > intCounter / 2

'State result
If Flag = True Then
Print intCounter; " is "; "Prime"
End If

Next intCounter

End Sub
```

Exercise 2: Finding perfect numbers

> This second programming exercise gives further opportunity for students to develop their skills in algorithm design and coding. However, it would be wise to allow plenty of time for them to investigate the concept of perfect numbers before expecting an algorithm and program to appear. Perfect numbers are unlikely to have been encountered before and many will wish to toy with various numbers, and their factors, using pencil and paper. An initial spreadsheet model is also a possibility.

Prime numbers are well known. Less familiar than the concept of primes is that of the perfect number. This is one where all of the factors of the number, including 1 but not the number itself, are equal to the number when they are added together.

The smallest perfect number is 6. This has factors of 1, 2 and 3:

$1 + 2 + 3 = 6$

The next perfect number after 6 is 28. This has factors of 1, 2, 4, 7 and 14:

$1 + 2 + 4 + 7 + 14 = 28$

Note that all factors of the number, except itself, are included in the sum. It is not restricted to prime numbers. For example, the prime factors of 28 are 1, 2 and 7 and these obviously do not add together to give 28:

$1 + 2 + 7 = 10$

Discovering perfect numbers is a good problem-solving exercise. Perfect numbers are fairly thinly spread, far more so than are primes, and so it would probably be practical to illustrate the concept to students by giving only the example of 6. They should then be able to deduce that 28 is also a perfect number. The next number after this, however, is 496, and it is hard to imagine this perfect number being detected quickly without the use of a computer:

$1 + 2 + 4 + 8 + 16 + 31 + 62 + 124 + 248 = 496$

The exercise is therefore a good example of the progression from a paper-based activity to one in which the student has to think algorithmically about the problem involved.

Finding a perfect number

Two programs are developed which allow numbers to be tested to see if they are perfect. In the first, a specific number is entered and the program determines whether or not it is perfect. The factors of the number are displayed as well as their total, and so the user can easily check whether this total is equal to the number itself.

In the second program all the numbers within a selected range are displayed which match the criterion of sum of factors equalling the number. This program does not display all the factors for each number checked, and so is more appropriate for locating perfect numbers quickly.

Both programs are based upon the same algorithm. A For loop counts up sequentially to half the size of the number being tested. Each value of the loop control variable is checked in turn to see if it divides into the number. If it does it is added to a running total. At the end of the loop this running total is compared with the number itself. If they are the same, the number is perfect.

This method can be stated a little more formally as an algorithm:

1. Input number to be tested
2. Set sum of divisors to zero
3. Initialize divisor as 1
4. If divisor divides exactly into number add it to sum
5. Increment divisor by 1
6. If divisor is not greater than half the number repeat from 4
7. If sum is equal to the number, the number is perfect

In fact the algorithm coded in this program is slightly different from the one given here, as will be explained in the program documentation.

```
Option Explicit
Private Sub Command1_Click()

'Checking whether a number is perfect

'Declare number being tested
Dim intNumber As Integer

'Declare factor
Dim intFactor As Integer

'Declare total
Dim intTotal As Integer

'Include 1 as a factor in the total
intTotal = 1

'Declare text string for display
Dim strResult As String

'Request number
intNumber = Val(InputBox("Enter a number"))

'Display 1 as a factor
Cls
Print "Sum of factors is:"
Print 1;

'Loop finds remaining factors and their total
For intFactor = 2 To intNumber / 2

If intNumber Mod intFactor = 0 Then

'Display factor
Print " + "; intFactor;

'Add factor to total
intTotal = intTotal + intFactor
```

```
End If

Next intFactor

'Display total
Print " = "; intTotal

'Remove unnecessary display
If intTotal = 1 Then Cls

'Decide result
If intTotal = intNumber Then
strResult = ""
Else
strResult = "not"
End If

'Display result
Print intNumber; " is "; strResult; " a perfect number"

End Sub
```

Here the program is used to test the number 30 and show that it is not perfect (see Figure 3.35). (Though Douglas Adams aficionados will probably think it does quite nicely all the same.)
When the number 28 is tested it is shown to be perfect (see Figure 3.36).

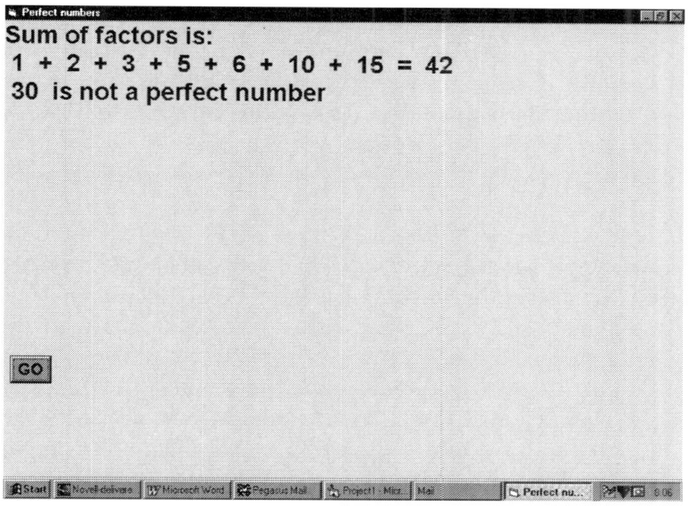

Figure 3.35

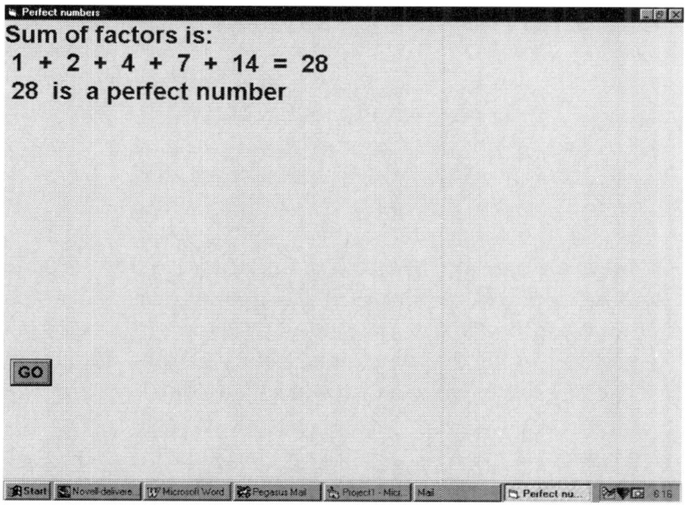

Figure 3.36

Program documentation

After Option Explicit and an initial comment, the variable which will hold the number to be tested, intNumber, is declared:

```
Option Explicit
Private Sub Command1_Click()

'Checking whether a number is perfect
'Declare number being tested
Dim intNumber As Integer
```

A further integer variable, intFactor, is then declared. This will represent all possible factors of intNumber and will also take the role of a loop control variable:

```
'Declare factor
Dim intFactor As Integer
```

In order to determine whether the number chosen by the user is perfect or not the total sum of all its factors is required. This sum will be held in the variable intTotal:

```
'Declare total
Dim intTotal As Integer
```

The total of all the factors will be at least 1, since this number will always divide into any other. It is therefore possible to initialize intTotal as 1. Doing this in fact helps to produce an easily formatted display of the factors on the screen, as will be explained subsequently:

```
'Include 1 as a factor in the total
intTotal = 1
```

The display is also made simpler to create if a text string is available. This is the variable strResult:

```
'Declare text string for display
Dim strResult As String
```

After these declarations have been made the program proper begins. First the user selects the number to be tested. It is assigned by the InputBox function to intNumber. Note again here the use of Val, unnecessary in later versions of Visual Basic.

```
'Request number
intNumber = Val(InputBox("Enter a number"))
```

The display of the factors of the number chosen starts here, a little vacuously, by indicating that 1 is, in fact, a factor of whatever has been entered (the fact that a number is now on the screen makes it possible, in the For loop which follows, to format the sequence pleasantly with alternating plus signs and factors):

```
'Display 1 as a factor
Cls
Print "Sum of factors is:"
Print 1;
```

The loop which determines the factors of intNumber now begins. It is controlled by the variable intFactor, which should be interpreted as representing potential factors as well as actual ones. To which category a particular factor belongs is decided in the loop body.

The values given to intFactor will begin at 2 and range all the way to half the size of intNumber. Obviously a number cannot have a factor (other than itself) which is greater than half of it:

```
'Loop finds remaining factors and their total
For intFactor = 2 To intNumber / 2
```

Within the loop the Mod operator is used to check whether intFactor divides into intNumber. If there is no remainder Mod will return zero, and this is used in the condition which decides whether a factor has been encountered:

```
If intNumber Mod intFactor = 0 Then
```

First the factor is displayed. The use of a plus sign makes explicit that the total of the factors is being calculated. Semicolons are used to place the addition horizontally on the screen:

```
'Display factor
Print " + "; intFactor;
```

Also within the body of the If condition the factor intFactor is added on to the running total, intTotal:

```
'Add factor to total
intTotal = intTotal + intFactor
```

The condition ends, and then the For loop:

```
End If

Next intFactor
```

The addition shown on the display is completed by printing the value of intTotal:

```
'Display total
Print " = "; intTotal
```

As shown in the screen dumps above this does create an effective display. However, if the number being tested is prime it can be seen that a rather pointless arithmetical statement, 1 = 1, will appear. To avoid this, the display is fudged quite blatantly by a duplicitous application of the Cls statement. It all happens too fast for the user to notice:

```
'Remove unnecessary display
If intTotal = 1 Then Cls
```

Finally the program must state whether the number that has been tested is perfect or not. The 'not' here is actually placed into the text string, strResult, introduced above. If the number is perfect strResult is made equal to the empty string "". If the number is not perfect then strResult is made equal to "not". The condition, of course, is whether the total of the number's factors, intTotal, is equal to the number itself, intNumber. The code required to generate the correct string for strResult is:

```
'Decide result
If intTotal = intNumber Then
strResult = ""
Else
strResult = "not"
End If
```

The number can then be described appropriately

```
'Display result
Print intNumber; " is "; strResult; " a perfect number"

End Sub
```

Extending the perfect numbers program

The program just developed is good fun to play with but it would be unlikely to help find the next perfect number after 28. Perfect numbers are just too well spaced out on the number line to be likely to be selected by accident.

Before long students will want to develop a variant of the program which will test over a range of numbers to try and find further perfect numbers. This can be done by modifying the existing program to include a further For loop. A lower and upper limit for the range of this loop can be chosen by the user and all the numbers within this range tested to see if they are perfect.

```
Option Explicit
Private Sub Command1_Click()

'Checking a range for the
'presence of perfect numbers

'Declare number being tested
Dim intNumber As Integer

'Declare factor
Dim intFactor As Integer

'Declare total
Dim intTotal As Integer

'Declare range variables
Dim intLower As Integer
Dim intUpper As Integer

'Request range from user
Do
intLower = InputBox("Enter lower value")
intUpper = InputBox("Enter upper value")
Loop Until intLower < intUpper
'Indicate range of search
Cls
Print "Checking the range "; intLower;
Print " to "; intUpper; ":"
Print

For intNumber = intLower To intUpper

'Initialise total
intTotal = 0

'Loop finds total of factors
For intFactor = 1 To intNumber / 2

'Add factor to total
If intNumber Mod intFactor = 0 Then
intTotal = intTotal + intFactor
End If

Next intFactor

'Identify perfect number
If intTotal = intNumber Then
Print intNumber; "is a perfect number"
End If

Next intNumber

End Sub
```

The program shown in Figure 3.37 is checking the range 1 to 30. As expected, the numbers 6 and 28 are both discovered to be perfect.

Significantly increasing the range being tested, so that it is now 1 to 500, detects only one further perfect number, 496. This indicates just how scarcely populated the integers are with perfect numbers (see Figure 3.38).

Once a new perfect number has been found, the previous program can be used to show all of the factors (see Figure 3.39).

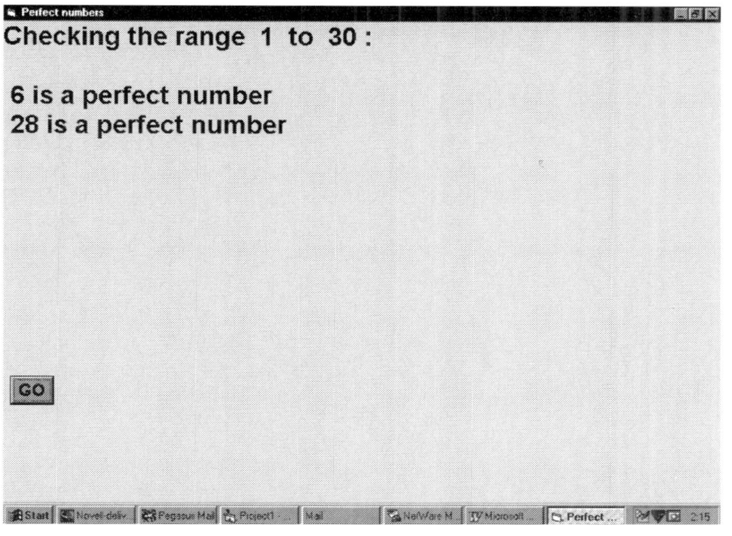

Figure 3.37

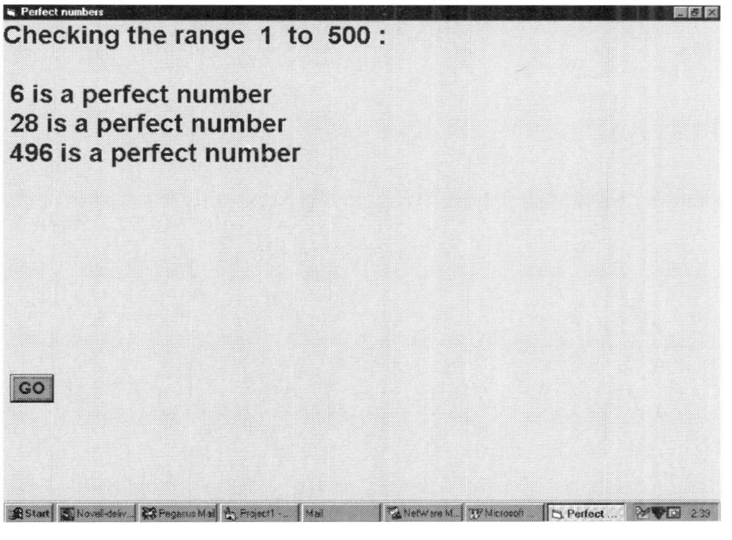

Figure 3.38

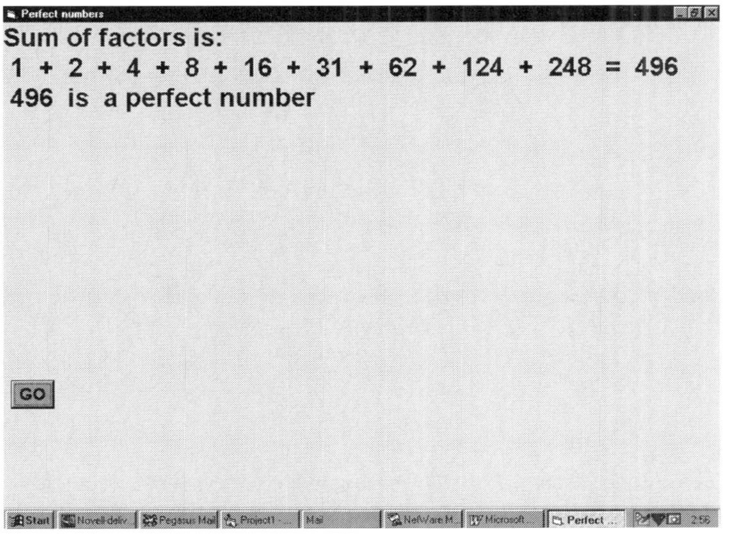

Figure 3.39

Program documentation

As in the previous version of the program, comments show what will be achieved by the code:

```
Option Explicit
Private Sub Command1_Click()

'Checking a range for the
'presence of perfect numbers
```

Again variables, intNumber and intFactor, are used to represent the number being tested and its putative factors:

```
'Declare number being tested
Dim intNumber As Integer

'Declare factor
Dim intFactor As Integer
```

A variable representing the total of the factors is needed again:

```
'Declare total
Dim intTotal As Integer
```

As the user can now select the range over which numbers will be tested, variables are required that define the lower and upper values. These are intLower and intUpper:

```
'Declare range variables
Dim intLower As Integer
Dim intUpper As Integer
```

The user's choice of range is validated to make sure that the lower value is less than the upper:

```
'Request range from user
Do
intLower = InputBox("Enter lower value")
intUpper = InputBox("Enter upper value")
Loop Until intLower <intUpper
```

The range is then confirmed by being displayed on the screen:

```
'Indicate range of search
Cls
Print "Checking the range "; intLower;
Print " to "; intUpper; ":"
Print
```

A For loop then follows controlled by intNumber, which varies over the range of values that has been selected:

```
For intNumber = intLower To intUpper
```

As many numbers are going to be checked to determine whether they are perfect, the sum of the factors of any given one of them must be reset to zero for each repeat of the loop:

```
'Initialise total
intTotal = 0
```

Nested within the outer loop is the same For loop as in the previous example, but without the print statement that displayed all the factors as they were found:

```
'Loop finds total of factors
For intFactor = 1 To intNumber / 2
```

As before each factor of intNumber is added to intTotal:

```
'Add factor to total
If intNumber Mod intFactor = 0 Then
intTotal = intTotal + intFactor
End If
```

The inner loop then ends:

```
Next intFactor
```

After the end of the inner loop, but still within the overall loop that is checking the whole range of numbers selected by the user, the sum of the factors is compared with the current value of intNumber. If these match, a perfect number has been found and it is displayed:

```
'Identify perfect number
If intTotal = intNumber Then
Print intNumber; "is a perfect number"
End If
```

The outer loop, and the program, then end:

```
Next intNumber

End Sub
```

Exercise 3: Palindromic numbers

> This third exercise in using a computer to explore numerical patterns is possibly more difficult than the two that have preceeded it. In dealing with an unusual idea, the 'palindromic number', it will give students a good opportunity to develop problem-solving and algorithmic skills. There is also an obvious need to break down a large problem into a series of subtasks, giving experience of top-down design.
>
> The exercise is divided into a series of short programs of gradually increasing difficulty. Each of these will provide the possibility of alternative algorithms and coding.

A palindrome is something which is the same when it is read from back to front. The example invariably given in children's puzzle books is:

MADAM I'M ADAM

(Presumably Eve couldn't work out who he was.) Read back to front this becomes:

MADA M'I MADAM

Provided that you are prepared to move the two spaces and the apostrophe to the right places, this is the same sentence as before.

Generating a palindromic sentence like this is not easy. The palindromic form has therefore appealed to many artists as a challenge. Palindromes appear in music, one of the most striking being a section of Alban Berg's opera *Wozzeck*, where precisely the same musical structure unwinds in reverse after a central point has been passed. Palindromes have also been introduced into arithmetic. Many years ago Martin Gardner, in his Mathematical Diversions column in the Scientific American, introduced the topic of palindromic numbers.These also read the same in reverse, as, for example, the number 747. A fascinating development of the palindromic form in arithmetic, though, is that when a number is not initially palindromic it can be turned into a palindromic form by reversing it and adding. For example:

145 is not a palindrome
145 + 541 = 686
686 is a palindrome.

Sometimes more than one stage of reversal and addition is required:

278 is not a palindrome
278 + 872 = 1150
1150 + 511 = 1661
1661 is a palindrome

Many numbers which are initially non-palindromic will require just one stage of reversal and addition in order to produce a palindrome. Others might require two or more stages. However, Martin Gardner observed that there is at least one number which never seems to produce a palidromic form, no matter how many times it is reversed and added to itself. Discovering a number which does not appear to turn into a palindrome after sufficient reversals and additions is clearly a problem for which the number-crunching ability of a computer is an advantage. This is also a (rather simple) illustration of the way that computers can be used in mathematical research, a fairly 'hot' topic as the legitimacy of such an approach to mathematical proof is disputed. (See, for example, the discussion of the 4-colour theorem.)

This exercise is an example of the way that a problem has to be broken down into subtasks. Clearly before a number can be tested to see if it is a palindrome there must be a routine which simply reverses any numbered entered.

Reversing a number

A trivial solution to this problem can be considered briefly, and then rejected. This accepts the input of a number as a string and then uses one of Basic's string-handling functions, Mid$, to place the individual letters into an array. The array elements are then displayed again but in reverse order.

```
Option Explicit
Private Sub Command1_Click()
'Palindromic numbers
'Version 0

Dim strNumber As String
Dim strLetter(20) As String
Dim intLength As Integer
Dim intCounter As Integer

PicDisplay.Cls

'Prompt user to enter number
strNumber = InputBox("Enter number", , , 6500, 5500)

'Determine length of number
intLength = Len(strNumber)

'Place letters in array
For intCounter = 1 To intLength
strLetter(intCounter) = Mid$(strNumber, intCounter, 1)
Next intCounter

'Display in reverse order
For intCounter = intLength To 1 Step -1
PicDisplay.Print strLetter(intCounter);
Next intCounter

PicDisplay.Print

End Sub
```

Program documentation

Comments indicate the program's function:

```
Option Explicit
Private Sub Command1_Click()
'Palindromic numbers
'Version 0
```

Four variables are declared. The number entered by the user is represented by strNumber. The number of digits in this number will be assigned to intLength. An array, strLetter(), is used to hold the separate digits, and intCounter is used as a loop control variable:

```
Dim strNumber As String
Dim strLetter(20) As String
Dim intLength As Integer
Dim intCounter As Integer
```

The user is prompted to enter the number and it is assigned to strNumber:

```
PicDisplay.Cls

'Prompt user to enter number
strNumber = InputBox("Enter number", , , 6500, 5500)
```

The Len string function is used to determine the length of the string that has been entered, and hence the number of digits in the user's choice. This value is assigned to intLength:

```
'Determine length of number
intLength = Len(strNumber)
```

The value of intLength is then used to make a For loop repeat exactly the number of times required to place each character (i.e. digit) of strNumber into the strLetter() array. The Mid$ function systematically extracts the digits:

```
'Place letters in array
For intCounter = 1 To intLength
strLetter(intCounter) = Mid$(strNumber, intCounter, 1)
Next intCounter
```

The contents of the array are now printed out in reverse order by a second For loop which uses Step to search through the array locations backwards:

```
'Display in reverse order
For intCounter = intLength To 1 Step -1
PicDisplay.Print strLetter(intCounter);
Next intCounter

PicDisplay.Print

End Sub
```

This method could be developed into the required program but it is extremely inelegant and should be used to demonstrate only how *not* to proceed with a problem of this sort. Ignore the 'Pretty is what works' mindset! Instead we need to find a completely arithmetical solution to the problem in which we avoid the use of strings and arrays.

Identifying the individual digits of a number

In order to reverse the order of the digits in a number we need first to be able to identify each of the digits in turn. For example, given the 4-digit number 5281 we have to find a way of decomposing it into the separate digits 5, 2, 8 and 1. Once we can extract these distinct digits we can then consider the problem of rearranging them into reverse order.

The first digit, 5, of 5281 can be obtained as the integral part of the answer when 5281 is divided by 1000. The remainder will be 281. If this in turn is divided by 100, and the integral part taken, the digit 2 is obtained. The process can be continued to extract all of the original number's digits in turn:

Dividing 5281 by 1000 gives 5 as the integral part of the answer with 281 as the remainder.
Dividing 281 by 100 gives 2 as the integral part with 81 as the remainder.
Dividing 81 by 10 gives 8 as the integral part with 1 as the remainder.
Dividing 1 by 1 gives 1 as the integral part with 0 as the remainder.

There is clearly a regular pattern here which can be written formally as an algorithm. Initially we restrict the number entered to four digits, but subsequently this restriction will be removed:

1. Input a 4-digit number
2. Initialize divisor as 1000
3. Initialize counter as 0
4. Increment counter
5. Divide number by divisor
6. Display integral part of answer
7. Assign the remainder as the new value of the number
8. Divide the divisor by 10
9. If counter is less than 4 repeat from 3

This algorithm can be simplified when a simple pattern is seen which links the value of the divisor to the value of the counter. Initially we have:

Counter = 1 ... Divisor is 1000
Counter = 2 ... Divisor is 100
Counter = 3 ... Divisor is 10
Counter = 4 ... Divisor is 1

There is, of course, no need to have the counter conventionally counting up in this way. Alternatively this would work perfectly well:

Counter = 3 ... Divisor is 1000
Counter = 2 ... Divisor is 100
Counter = 1 ... Divisor is 10
Counter = 0 ... Divisor is 1

Or, better still:

Counter = 3 ... Divisor is 10 ^ Counter
Counter = 2 ... Divisor is 10 ^ Counter
Counter = 1 ... Divisor is 10 ^ Counter
Counter = 0 ... Divisor is 10 ^ Counter

This is the method adopted in the following program, which will accept the input of a 4-digit number and then display in turn each its digits, in descending order. This program does not yet reverse a number, or produce a palindromic form, but it is a step towards that goal:

```
Option Explicit
Private Sub Command1_Click()
'Palindromic numbers
'Version 1

Dim intNumber As Long
Dim intCopy As Long
Dim intDivisor As Long
Dim intCounter As Integer

PicDisplay.Cls
```

```
'Prompt user to enter number
intNumber = Val(InputBcx("Enter number", , , 6500, 5500))

'Assign value to working variable
intCopy = intNumber

For intCounter = 3 To 0 Step -1

'Calculate value of divisor
intDivisor = 10 ^ intCounter

'Display first digit of number
PicDisplay.Print Int(intCopy / intDivisor)

'Remove first digit from number
intCopy = intCopy Mod intDivisor

Next intCounter

End Sub
```

Program documentation

The program begins with identifying comments:

```
Option Explicit
Private Sub Command1_Click()
'Palindromic numbers
'Version 1
```

Four variables are declared. The number entered by the user will be assigned to intNumber. A copy of this is made because in later versions of the program the original number will need to be retained. The copy is represented by intCopy. A third variable, intDivisor, is required for the division specified in the original algorithm above. Finally a loop counter is needed. This is intCounter:

```
Dim intNumber As Long
Dim intCopy As Long
Dim intDivisor As Long
Dim intCounter As Integer
```

The user is prompted to enter the number:

```
PicDisplay.Cls

'Prompt user to enter number
intNumber = Val(InputBox("Enter number", , , 6500, 5500))
```

A copy is made of the number entered:

```
'Assign value to working variable
intCopy = intNumber
```

A For loop now repeats four times, with the loop control variable taking in turn the values 3, 2, 1 and 0. This matches the algorithm immediately above:

```
For intCounter = 3 To C Step -1
```

The value of the divisor is directly related to the loop control variable so that it has the successive values of 1000, 100, 10 and 1:

```
'Calculate value of divisor
intDivisor = 10 ^ intCounter
```

The digits of the original number entered are now displayed in turn by dividing, at each repeat of the loop, the current value of the divisor into the copy of the number. The decimal part is ignored by the use of Int. Only the first digit of the copy is shown:

```
'Display first digit of number
PicDisplay.Print Int(intCopy / intDivisor)
```

The copy is then truncated by using the Mod function. Effectively this is reassigning to the copy the remainder after each successive division by 1000, 100, 10 and 1, as described above:

```
'Remove first digit from number
intCopy = intCopy Mod intDivisor

Next intCounter

End Sub
```

Screen dumps now illustrate how this program converts a four digit number into its successive digits (see Figures 3.40 and 3.41).

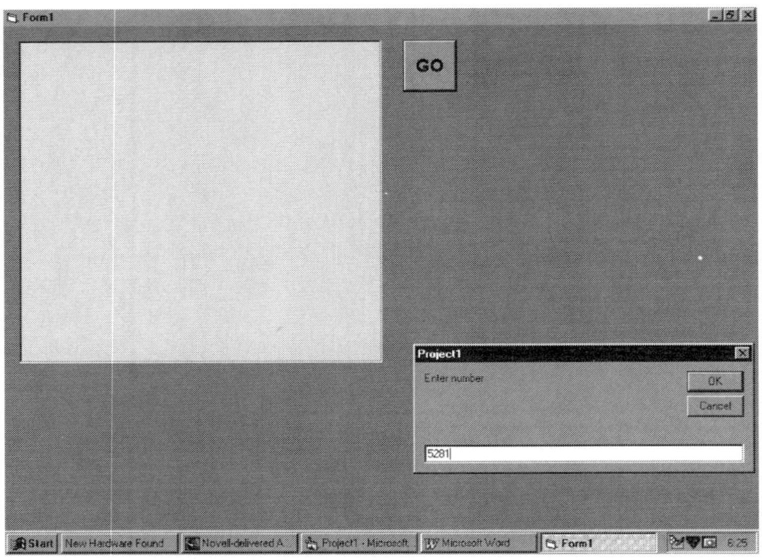

Figure 3.40

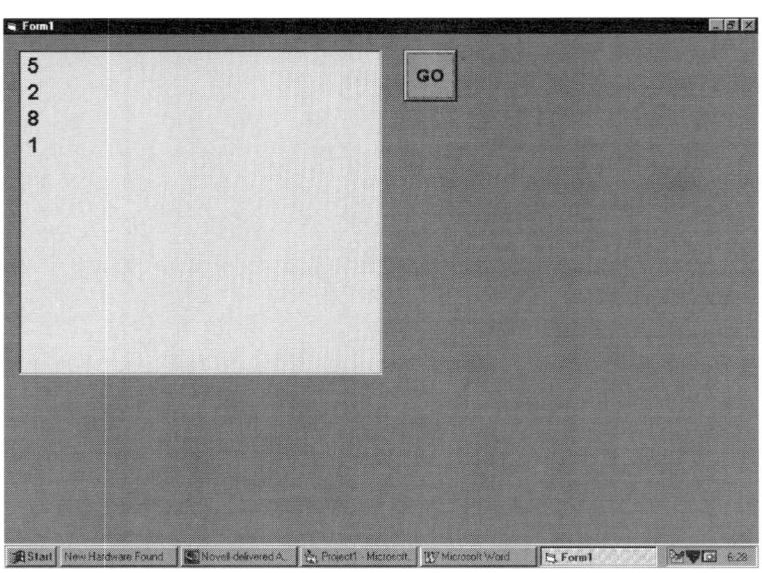

Figure 3.41

Rearranging the digits

The program given will remove the digits from any 4-digit number entered by the user and present them separately. So entering 5281 will produce the sequence 5, 2, 8 and 1. However, the program does not reassemble these digits into the reversed number 1825. In order to do this, each of the digits has to be assigned a place value:

The digit 5 must become 5 units.
The digit 2 must become 2 tens.
The digit 8 must become 8 hundreds.
The digit 1 must become 1 thousand.

This is equivalent to stating that:

The digit 5 must be multiplied by 1.
The digit 2 must be multiplied by 10.
The digit 8 must be multiplied by 100.
The digit 1 must be multiplied by 1000...
And then all four numbers are added together.

Showing this as an equation we have:

$$1825 = (1 \times 1000) + (8 \times 100) + (2 \times 10) + (5 \times 1)$$

This is equivalent to the rearranged equation:

$$1825 = (5 \times 1) + (2 \times 10) + (8 \times 100) + (1 \times 1000)$$

Showing the equation like this reflects the way in which 5, 2, 8 and 1 have been generated by the previous program. It should be fairly obvious that the same For loop which stripped the individual digits from the number entered by the user can be extended so that each digit is multiplied by the appropriate power of 10. This is what happens in the program below:

```
Option Explicit
Private Sub Command1_Click()
'Palindromic numbers
'Version 2

Dim intNumber As Long
Dim intCopy As Long
Dim intReverse As Long
Dim intDivisor As Long
Dim intCounter As Integer

PicDisplay.Cls

'Prompt user to enter number
intNumber = Val(InputBox("Enter number", , , 6500, 5500))

'Assign copy to working variable
intCopy = intNumber

For intCounter = 3 To 0 Step -1

'Calculate value of divisor
intDivisor = 10 ^ intCounter

'Calculate reversed number
intReverse = intReverse + Int(intCopy / intDivisor) * 10 ^ (3 - intCounter)

'Remove first digit from number
intCopy = intCopy Mod intDivisor
```

```
Next intCounter

'Display reversed number
PicDisplay.Print intReverse

End Sub
```

Program documentation

The same variables are declared as in the previous program. The number entered is represented by intNumber and a copy of it is assigned to intCopy. The number which repeatedly divides into the copy is again intDivisor, and a loop control variable intCounter is required. However, there is an additional variable, intReverse, which represents the new, reversed number which is constructed by the loop:

```
Option Explicit
Private Sub Command1_Click()
'Palindromic numbers
'Version 2

Dim intNumber As Long
Dim intCopy As Long
Dim intReverse As Long
Dim intDivisor As Long
Dim intCounter As Integer
```

As before the user is prompted to enter a number, which is assigned to intNumber, and an additional copy is assigned to intCopy:

```
PicDisplay.Cls

'Prompt user to enter number
intNumber = Val(InputBox("Enter number", , , 6500, 5500))

'Assign copy to working variable
intCopy = intNumber
```

The copy of the number is successively divided by intDivisor which takes values of 1000, 100, 10 and 1, as determined by the loop variable, intCounter, which has progressive values of 3, 2, 1 and 0:

```
For intCounter = 3 To 0 Step -1

'Calculate value of divisor
intDivisor = 10 ^ intCounter
```

Although in the previous version of the program each separate digit was displayed as Int(intCopy / intDivisor), in this version these digits must be reassembled into a reversed number. As illustrated in the example above the digits have to be multiplied by 1, then 10, then 100 and finally 1000. These powers of 10 can be generated inside the loop by raising 10 to the power (3 – intCounter). The successive values of this expression will be 0, 1, 2 and 3 as the loop repeats. This means that they produce exactly the power of ten required at each repeat of the loop. The expression 10 ^ (3 – intCounter) creates precisely the place value needed to reverse the sequence of the digits. All that is then required is that intReverse builds up the running total of the values created:

```
'Calculate reversed number
intReverse = intReverse + Int(intCopy / intDivisor) * 10 ^ (3 -
intCounter)
```

Finally the digit is removed from intCopy:

```
'Remove first digit from number
intCopy = intCopy Mod intDivisor
```

```
Next intCounter
```

The reversed number can then be displayed:

```
'Display reversed number
PicDisplay.Print intReverse

End Sub
```

The screen dump in Figure 3.42 shows the result.

Figure 3.42

Counting the digits in a number

This program reverses only a four digit number but has been developed in this way purely for simplicity. It is quite clear from the program that only a slight alteration would allow numbers of any length to be reversed. This is the line of code where the number 3 has appeared in a For statement. If a five digit had to be reversed, the number in the For statement would be 4. Generally if the number has N digits the For statement will contain $N - 1$. So what is needed is a routine which counts the number of digits in a number. The program below does this, as indicated by the two screen dumps (Figures 3.43 and 3.44) which accompany it:

```
Option Explicit
Private Sub Command1_Click()
'Palindromic numbers
'Version 3

Dim intNumber As Long
Dim intCopy As Long
Dim intDigits As Integer

PicDisplay.Cls

'Prompt user to enter number
intNumber = Val(InputBox("Enter number", , , 6500, 5500))

'Assign copy to working variable
intCopy = intNumber

'Loop counts number of digits
Do
```

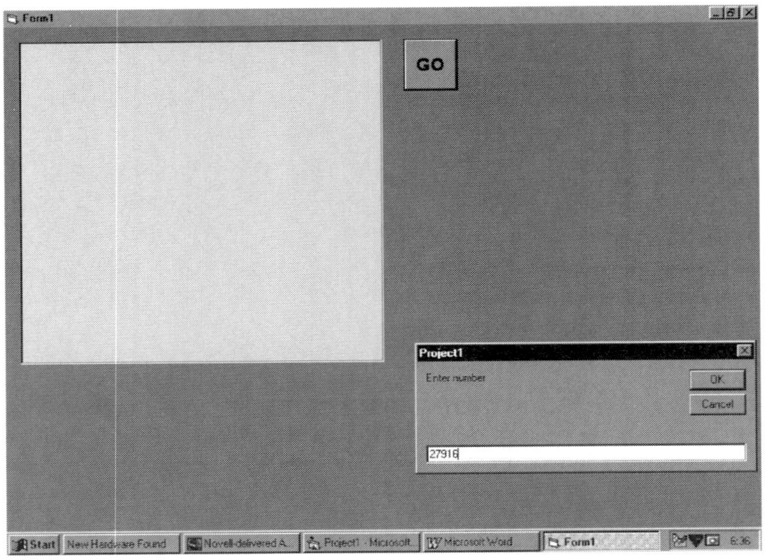

Figure 3.43

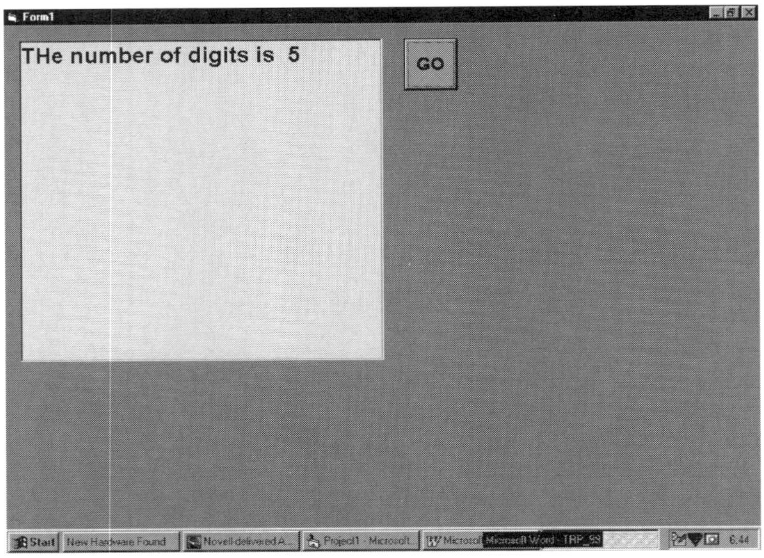

Figure 3.44

```
intDigits = intDigits + 1
intCopy = Int(intCopy / 10)
Loop Until intCopy = 0

'Display number of digits
PicDisplay.Print intDigits

End Sub
```

Program documentation

In keeping with the variable names used in the other programs, the number entered by the user is declared as intNumber and a copy of it as intCopy. A new variable introduced is intDigits. This will be a count of the number of digits in the number entered:

```
Option Explicit
Private Sub Command1_Click()
'Palindromic numbers
'Version 3

Dim intNumber As Long
Dim intCopy As Long
Dim intDigits As Integer
```

The user enters a number which is assigned to intNumber and copied to intCopy:

```
PicDisplay.Cls

'Prompt user to enter number
intNumber = Val(InputBox("Enter number", , , 6500, 5500))

'Assign copy to working variable
intCopy = intNumber
```

A conditional loop then follows in which intDigits acts as a counter:

```
'Loop counts number of digits
Do
intDigits = intDigits + 1
```

At each repeat of this loop intCopy is reduced by one digit. This is done by dividing by 10 and then discarding the decimal place by operating on intCopy with Int. For example, if the number entered by the user is 752, intCopy will be 75.2, reduced to 72, at the end of the first repeat of the loop. At the second repeat it is 7.2, reduced to 7. At the end of the third repeat it is 0.7, reduced to 0. The exit condition is therefore that intCopy becomes equal to zero. At this point the value of the counter, intDigits, will be equal to the number of digits in the number entered:

```
intCopy = Int(intCopy / 10)
Loop Until intCopy = 0

'Display number of digits
PicDisplay.Print intDigits

End Sub
```

Reversing a number of any length

Merging the last two programs now produces code which will reverse a number of any length:

```
Option Explicit
Private Sub Command1_Click()
'Palindromic numbers
'Version 4

Dim intNumber As Long
Dim intCopy As Long
Dim intDigits As Integer
Dim intReverse As Long
Dim intDivisor As Long
Dim intCounter As Integer

PicDisplay.Cls

'Prompt user to enter number
intNumber = Val(InputBox("Enter number", , , 6500, 5500))

'Assign copy to working variable
intCopy = intNumber

'Loop counts number of digits
intDigits = -1
Do
intDigits = intDigits + 1
intCopy = Int(intCopy / 10)
Loop Until intCopy = 0
```

```
'Assign second copy to working variable
intCopy = intNumber

For intCounter = intDigits To 0 Step -1

'Calculate value of divisor
intDivisor = 10 ^ intCounter

'Calculate reversed number
intReverse = intReverse + Int(intCopy / intDivisor) * 10 ^ (intDigits -
intCounter)
'Remove first digit from number
intCopy = intCopy Mod intDivisor

Next intCounter

'Display reversed number
PicDisplay.Print intReverse

End Sub
```

This program is illustrated by the two screen dumps (Figures 3.45 and 3.46).

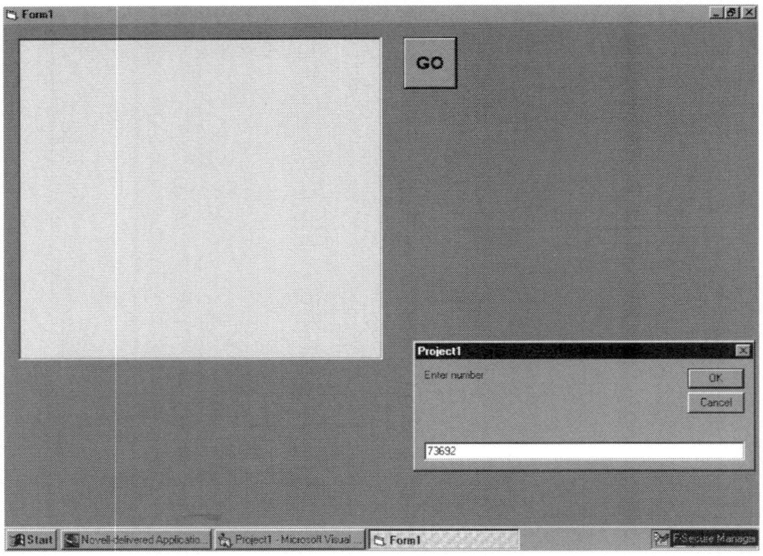

Figure 3.45

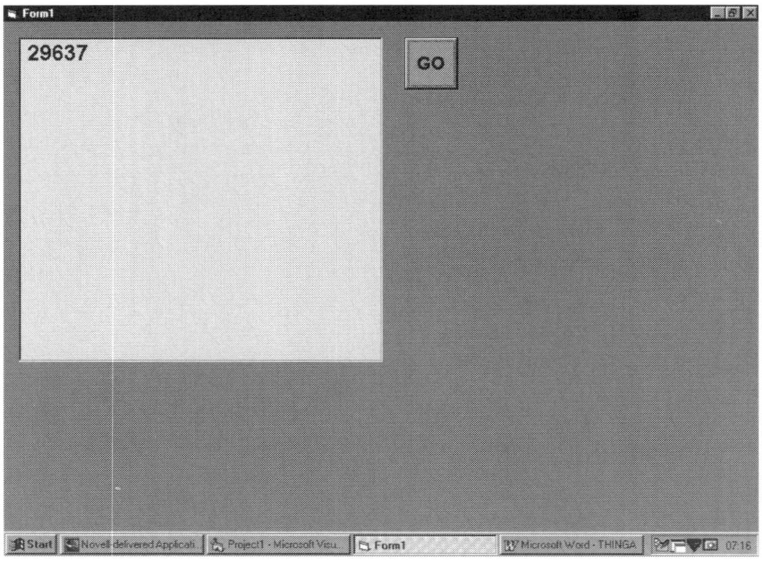

Figure 3.46

Program documentation

The program begins with the declaration of the same variables as in the previous two programs:

```
Option Explicit
Private Sub Command1_Click()
'Palindromic numbers
'Version 4

Dim intNumber As Long
Dim intCopy As Long
Dim intDigits As Integer
Dim intReverse As Long
Dim intDivisor As Long
Dim intCounter As Integer

PicDisplay.Cls
```

Again the user enters the number to be reversed and a copy is made:

```
'Prompt user to enter number
intNumber = Val(InputBox("Enter number", , , 6500, 5500))
```

Working with the copy of the original number, the same routine as in the last program counts the number of digits and assigns the value to intDigits. However, as this is initialized as –1 its final value will be one fewer than the actual number of digits. This is because the loop which will subsequently construct a reversed number requires a value one fewer, as explained earlier:

```
'Assign copy to working variable
intCopy = intNumber

'Loop counts number of digits
intDigits = -1
Do
intDigits = intDigits + 1
intCopy = Int(intCopy / 10)
Loop Until intCopy = 0
```

Another copy of the original number is needed. This is because the current copy has been reduced to zero by the counting routine:

```
'Assign second copy to working variable
intCopy = intNumber
```

Now the For loop which constructs a reversed number can be used. It is just like the previous version, except that the loop is controlled by the value of intDigits, not 3:

```
For intCounter = intDigits To 0 Step -1

'Calculate value of divisor
intDivisor = 10 ^ intCounter

'Calculate reversed number
intReverse = intReverse + Int(intCopy / intDivisor) * 10 ^ (intDigits -
intCounter)

'Remove first digit from number
intCopy = intCopy Mod intDivisor

Next intCounter
```

```
'Display reversed number
PicDisplay.Print intReverse

End Sub
```

Searching for palindromic numbers

At this point the original problem can be tackled. A program is written which determines the number of stages required to produce a palindromic form from any number entered:

```
Option Explicit
Private Sub Command1_Click()
'Palindromic numbers
'Version 5

Dim intNumber As Long
Dim intCopy As Long
Dim intDigits As Integer
Dim intReverse As Long
Dim intDivisor As Long
Dim intStages As Integer
Dim Flag As Boolean
Dim intCounter As Integer

PicDisplay.Cls

'Prompt user to enter number
intNumber = Val(InputBox("Enter number", , , 6500, 5500))

'Initialise count of stages
intStages = 0

'Initialise exit flag
Flag = False

'Loop tests for palindromic number
Do

PicDisplay.Print "Testing "; intNumber
'Assign copy to working variable
intCopy = intNumber

'Initialise number of digits
intDigits = -1

'Initialise reversed number
intReverse = 0

'Loop counts number of digits
Do
intDigits = intDigits + 1
intCopy = Int(intCopy / 10)
Loop Until intCopy = 0

'Assign second copy to working variable
intCopy = intNumber

For intCounter = intDigits To 0 Step -1

'Calculate value of divisor
intDivisor = 10 ^ intCounter
```

```
'Calculate reversed number
intReverse = intReverse + Int(intCopy / intDivisor) * 10 ^ (intDigits -
intCounter)

'Remove first digit from number
intCopy = intCopy Mod intDivisor

Next intCounter

'Test if number is palindromic
If intNumber = intReverse Then
PicDisplay.Print "Number is a palindrome"
Flag = True
Else
PicDisplay.Print intNumber; " + "; intReverse; " = ";
intNumber = intNumber + intReverse
PicDisplay.Print intNumber
intStages = intStages + 1
End If

'Show number of stages required
PicDisplay.Print "Number of stages "; intStages

Loop Until Flag = True

End Sub
```

The program is shown in operation in Figure 3.47.

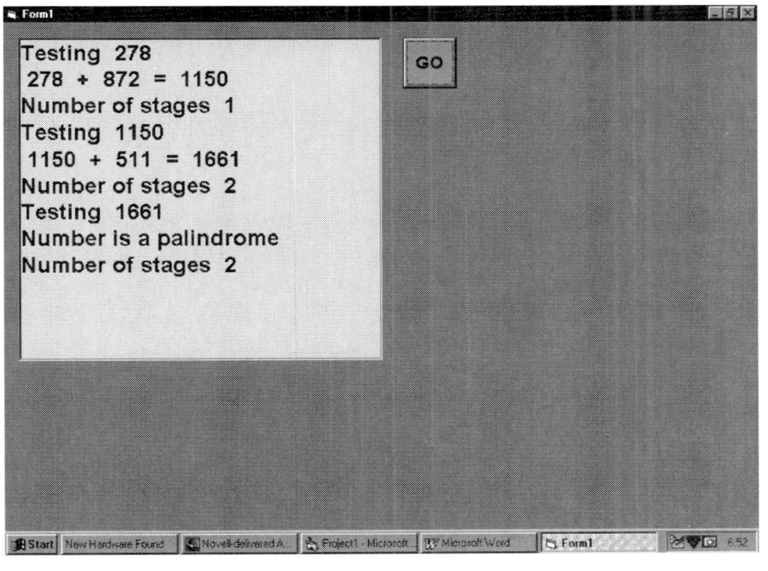

Figure 3.47

Program documentation

This program is very similar to the code developed so far, but has significant additions. A new conditional loop is intoduced which counts the number of times a number has to be reversed and added to itself before a palindromic form is created. This loop has a counter, intStages, which will indicate the number of repeats required to produce the palindrome, and a Boolean variable, Flag, which governs exit from the loop. These both have to be added to the initial declarations:

```
Option Explicit
Private Sub Command1_Click()
'Palindromic numbers
'Version 5
```

```
Dim intNumber As Long
Dim intCopy As Long
Dim intDigits As Integer
Dim intReverse As Long
Dim intDivisor As Long
Dim intStages As Integer
Dim Flag As Boolean
Dim intCounter As Integer

PicDisplay.Cls
```

After the user has entered the number to be tested, the two additional variables are initialized. The number of stages is initalized as zero and the exit flag is set to False. A value of True will subsequently indicate that a palindromic form has been found:

```
'Prompt user to enter number
intNumber = Val(InputBox("Enter number", , , 6500, 5500))

'Initialise count of stages
intStages = 0

'Initialise exit flag
Flag = False
```

The additional loop then begins:

```
'Loop tests for palindromic number
Do
```

The number currently being tested is indicated. Recall that if it takes several stages for a palindrome to be created a series of numbers will be tested. A working copy of the number is made:

```
PicDisplay.Print "Testing "; intNumber
'Assign copy to working variable
intCopy = intNumber
```

In the earlier program only one number had to be reversed. In this extended version, however, there might be many numbers which have to be reversed before a final palindromic form can be established. This means that both the variable intDigits, the number of digits in the current number being reversed, and intReverse, the new reversed number that is created, will have to be reinitialized within the overall conditional loop:

```
'Initialise number of digits
intDigits = -1

'Initialise reversed number
intReverse = 0
```

As in the previous program the number of digits in the number is counted by a loop:

```
'Loop counts number of digits
Do
intDigits = intDigits + 1
intCopy = Int(intCopy / 10)
Loop Until intCopy = 0
```

A second copy of the number is then used to create the reversed number, again as before:

```
'Assign second copy to working variable
intCopy = intNumber
```

```
For intCounter = intDigits To 0 Step -1

'Calculate value of divisor
intDivisor = 10 ^ intCounter

'Calculate reversed number
intReverse = intReverse + Int(intCopy / intDivisor) * 10 ^ (intDigits -
intCounter)

'Remove first digit from number
intCopy = intCopy Mod intDivisor

Next intCounter
```

At this point additional code is included. First the reversed number is compared with the original. If they are equal a palindromic form has been created. This is stated, and the value of Flag is reset to True so that the conditional loop will end:

```
'Test if number is palindromic
If intNumber = intReverse Then
PicDisplay.Print "Number is a palindrome"
Flag = True
```

However if intNumber and intReverse are not equal a palindromic form has not been reached. If this is the case the addition of the number to its reverse is shown on the display:

```
Else
PicDisplay.Print intNumber; " + "; intReverse; " = ";
intNumber = intNumber + intReverse
PicDisplay.Print intNumber
```

The number of stages required to produce a palindrome is increased by 1:

```
intStages = intStages + 1
End If
```

The number of stages taken so far is displayed:

```
'Show number of stages required
PicDisplay.Print "Number of stages "; intStages
```

If a palindrome has not been created the loop repeats:

```
Loop Until Flag = True

End Sub
```

Exercise 4: Decoding secret messages

Decyphering intercepted military communications has an important place in the history of computing. Students will be aware of Alan Turing's work at Bletchley Park and the development there of the early Colossus computer. Simple programs which can translate substitution codes are also an interesting problem for the student to attempt. In this exercise three decoding programs are developed. Each tackles a substitution code, but these are of increasing difficulty.

In the first program a simple shift of letters a fixed number of places to the left or right is assumed. The number of places must be entered in order for the message to be decoded. The second program is an extension of the first. Again all the letters have been shifted by the same amount. However, this time the program decides for itself what this standard shift is. It does this by assuming that the most common letter in the message must be an 'e'. The third program is more complicated still. It does not require all the letters to have been shifted in a regular fashion. Instead it compares the frequencies of the letters in the coded message with standard letter frequencies in language generally. It can therefore handle random substution. A letter 'e' might become 'f', but 'g' might become 'w' and 'b' become 'a'.

All three programs assume that lower case letters are used and that there are no spaces between words. Extending the code to eliminate both assumptions is left as a further challenge

A simple substitution code

Young children sometimes like to play at being spies and leave messages for each other in which all the letters have been moved in a regular fashion. For example, if all the letters are shifted one place to the right, the alphabet:

A B C D E F G H I J K L M N O P Q R S T U V W X Y Z

becomes instead:

B C D E F G H I J K L M N O P Q R S T U V W X Y Z A

(Note the wrap-around, with Z becoming A.)

Using this code the message:

THE CAT SAT ON THE MAT

is changed into:

UIF DBU TBU PO UIF NBU

This is suitably opaque and when fallen into enemy hands will produce doubt and confusion. (Naturally a code like this is of little practical use, but does give an opportunity for some interesting programming.)

A simple substitution program is easy to write, consisting of little more than taking the ASCII values of letters and adding or subtracting a fixed number to each. Here is such a program.

Program listing

```
Option Explicit
Private Sub Command1_Click()

'Decoding a message by simple substitution
'Letter shift decided by user

'Text entered by user
Dim strPassage As String

'Code for letter
Dim intCode As Integer

'Regular shift on all letters
Dim intShift As Integer

'Code for substituted letter
Dim intNewcode As Integer

'Loop counter
Dim intCounter As Integer
```

```
'Request text passage from user
Cls
strPassage = InputBox("Enter text")

'Request letter shift
intShift = InputBox("Enter number of places to shift")

'Display original text
Print
Print "Original text was:"
Print strPassage
Print

'Display decoded text
Print "Decoded text is:"

For intCounter = 1 To Len(strPassage)

'Find ASCII code of original letter
intCode = Asc(Mid$(strPassage, intCounter, 1))

'Generate substituted letter
intNewcode = intCode + intShift

'Wrap around if value outside range
If intNewcode <97 Then intNewcode = intNewcode + 26
If intNewcode > 122 Then intNewcode = intNewcode - 26

'Display decoded letter
Print Chr$(intNewcode);

Next intCounter

End Sub
```

The program is shown in Figure 3.48 in operation. First the coded message is entered.

The program requests the number of places through which each letter should be shifted in order to decode the message (see Figure 3.49).

The decoded message is then displayed (see Figure 3.50).

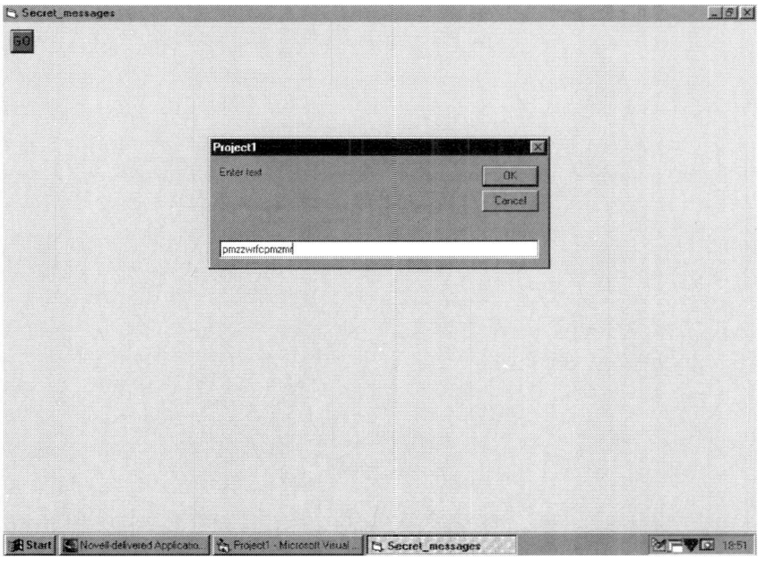

Figure 3.48

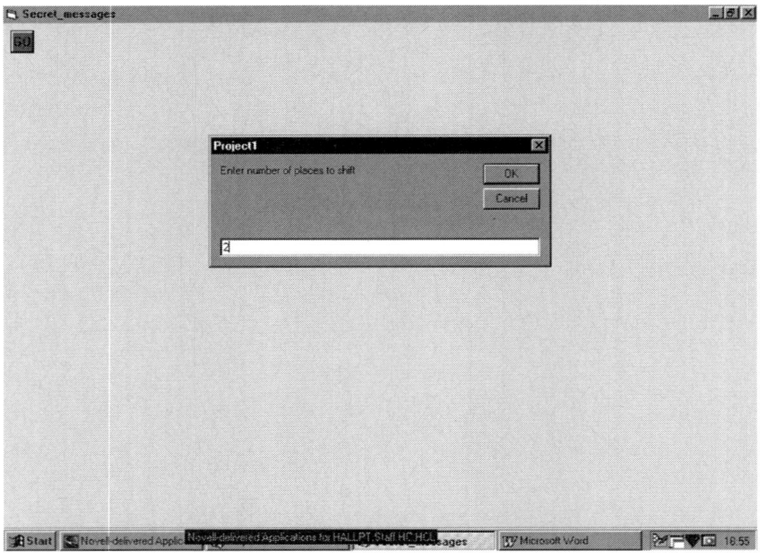

Figure 3.49

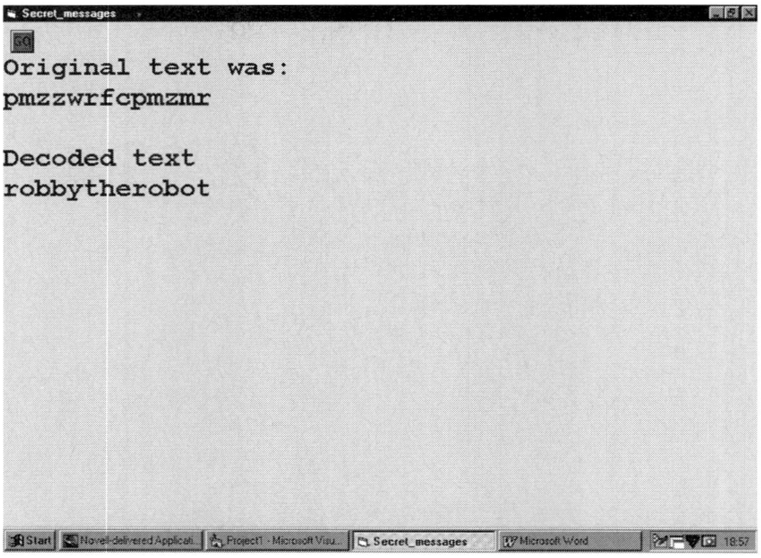

Figure 3.50

Program documentation

The program begins with comments that indicate what it will do:

```
Option Explicit
Private Sub Command1_Click()

'Decoding a message by simple substitution
'Letter shift decided by user
```

The text passage entered by the user will be assigned to a variable strPassage, which is declared here:

```
'Text entered by user
Dim strPassage As String
```

Part of the decoding involves determining the ASCII value for each character in the string. This is assigned to a variable called intCode. The variable is declared:

```
'Code for letter
Dim intCode As Integer
```

The number of places by which letters are displaced by the decoding has to be entered by the user and will be assigned to the variable intShift. This is declared:

```
'Regular shift on all letters
Dim intShift As Integer
```

The ASCII value for the decoded letter will be assigned to intNewcode:

```
'Code for substituted letter
Dim intNewcode As Integer
```

The last declaration in the program is for the loop control variable that will be employed:

```
'Loop counter
Dim intCounter As Integer
```

The user's coded message is now assigned to strPassage using Visual Basic's InputBox:

```
'Request text passage from user
Cls
strPassage = InputBox("Enter text")
```

The program also needs to be given the number of places by which each letter should be shifted:

```
'Request letter shift
intShift = InputBox("Enter number of places to shift")
```

Decoding can now take place. First the original coded message is displayed again:

```
'Display original text
Print
Print "Original text was:"
Print strPassage
Print
```

Text indicates that the decoded message follows:

```
'Display decoded text
Print "Decoded text is:"
```

A For loop now examines all the letters in the message:

```
For intCounter = 1 To Len(strPassage)
```

The ASCII of individual letters is assigned to intCode. The Mid$ function identifies each letter in the coded message in turn and the value of its ASCII is obtained for intCode:

```
'Find ASCII code of original letter
intCode = Asc(Mid$(strPassage, intCounter, 1))
```

The ASCII of the decoded letter is found by adding the amount by which letters have to be shifted to the ASCII held in intCode:

```
'Generate substituted letter
intNewcode = intCode + intShift
```

A problem can occur at this point if the shift takes the decoded letter outside the range of ASCII values representing the alphabet.

Suppose that letters are decoded by shifting three places to the left. Then we have for example:

a(97) decodes as (94) altered to x(120)
b(98) decodes as (95) altered to y(121)
c(99) decodes as (96) altered to z(122)

d(100) decodes as a(97)
e(101) decodes as b(98)
f(102) decodes as c(99)

It can be seen that incorrect ASCII is generated for values less than 97. However, the codes can be corrected by adding 26:

a(97) decodes as (94).
94 + 26 = 120.
Code altered to x(120)

b(98) decodes as (95)
95 + 26 = 121
Code altered to y(121)

c(99) decodes as (96)
96 + 26 = 122
Code altered to z(122)

From this it is clear that if the ASCII is less than 97 a correction is required. This correction involves adding 26.

Similarly if decoding involves shifting by four to the right we have:

s (116) decodes as x (120)
t (117) decodes as y (121)
u (118) decodes as z (122)
w (119) decodes as (123) altered to a (97)
x (120) decodes as (124) altered to b (98)
y (121) decodes as (125) altered to c (99)
z (122) decodes as (126) altered to d (100)

So here if the ASCII generated by the decoding is greater than 122 there must be a subtraction of 26 to generate the correct ASCII code.

These two potential corrections are performed by the code:

```
'Wrap around if value outside range
If intNewcode <97 Then intNewcode = intNewcode + 26
If intNewcode > 122 Then intNewcode = intNewcode – 26
```

The decoded letter can then be displayed:

```
'Display decoded letter
Print Chr$(intNewcode);
```

By the end of the loop the whole message has been decoded:

```
Next intCounter

End Sub
```

Determining the shift

This program works perfectly well provided that the constant shift of all letters, to the left or to the right, is known. If it is not, the program will not work unless a successful guess is made about what this shift is.

Guessing is not impossible. If the coded message is sufficiently long, then there is a good chance that the most frequently occurring letter in the message will represent 'e'. This is the most commonly used letter in English. All that needs to be done then is to determine how much the coded letter must be shifted to become 'e'. This same shift is then applied to all letters in the message in the hope that intelligible content will emerge.

The following program does precisely this. It is largely based upon the program above, with additional code to decide which of the letters in the message appears most often.

Program listing

```
Option Explicit
Private Sub Command1_Click()

'Decoding a message by simple substitution
'Letter shift determined by most common letter

'Text entered by user
Dim strPassage As String

'Code for letter
Dim intCode As Integer

'Regular shift on all letters
Dim intShift As Integer

'Code for substituted letter
Dim intNewcode As Integer

'Array to hold letter frequencies in text entered
Dim intFrequency(26)

'Location to increment in intFrequency()
 Dim intLocation As Integer

 'Largest frequency value
 Dim intMax As Integer

 'Most common letter
 Dim intCommon As Integer

 'Loop counter
Dim intCounter As Integer

'Request text passage from user
Cls
strPassage = InputBox("Enter text")

'Determine frequencies of letters in text passage
For intCounter = 1 To Len(strPassage)
intLocation = Asc(Mid$(strPassage, intCounter, 1)) - 96
intFrequency(intLocation) = intFrequency(intLocation) + 1
Next intCounter

'Find most common letter
intMax = 0
For intCounter = 1 To 26
If intFrequency(intCounter) > intMax Then
intMax = intFrequency(intCounter)
intCommon = intCounter
End If
Next intCounter

'Calculate letter shift
intShift = intCommon - 5

'Display letter shift
Print
Print "Letters are shifted "; Abs(intShift); " to ";
If Sgn(intShift) = 1 Then
```

```
Print "right."
Else
Print "left."
End If

'Display original text
Print
Print "Original text was:"
Print strPassage
Print

'Display decoded text
Print "Decoded text is:"

For intCounter = 1 To Len(strPassage)

'Find ASCII code of original letter
intCode = Asc(Mid$(strPassage, intCounter, 1))

'Generate substituted letter
intNewcode = intCode + intShift

'Wrap around if value outside range
If intNewcode <97 Then intNewcode = intNewcode + 26
If intNewcode > 122 Then intNewcode = intNewcode - 26

'Display decoded letter
Print Chr$(intNewcode);

Next intCounter

End Sub
```

Figure 3.51 shows the program in operation. First a carefully coded message is entered.

The program will not work unless the message does contain plenty of examples of the letter 'e'. Hence the insulting 'Ee Tone. You're an eejit'. (Less punctuation and spaces, of course.) Should this ever be read by my cousin, distinguished expert in tropical medicine, Dr Anthony Hall, I trust he will realize it is meant whimsically.

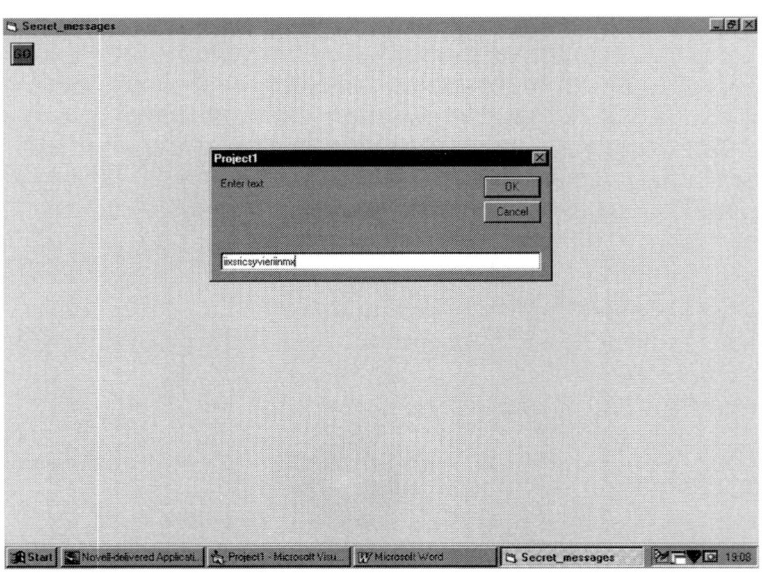

Figure 3.51

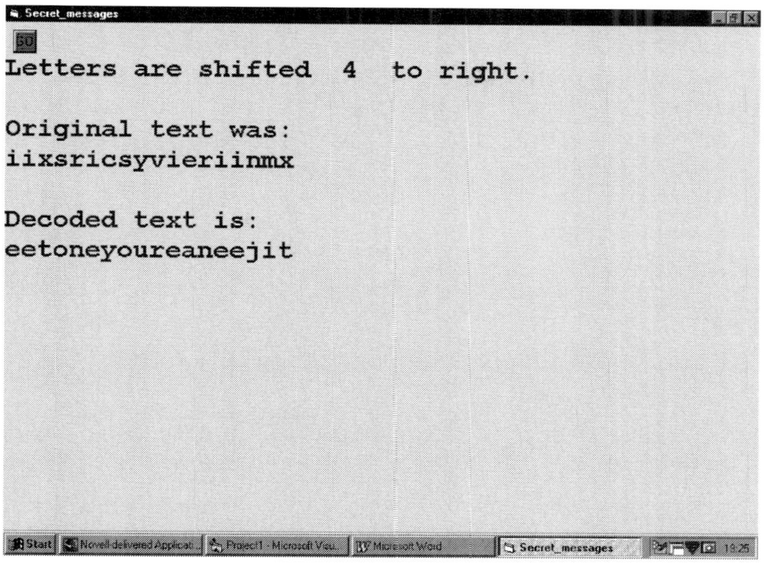

Figure 3.52

Program documentation

The program begins with comments that state its purpose:

```
Option Explicit
Private Sub Command1_Click()

'Decoding a message by simple substitution
'Letter shift determined by most common letter
```

As in the previous program the variables strPassage, intCode, intShift and intNewcode are declared:

```
'Text entered by user
Dim strPassage As String

'Code for letter
Dim intCode As Integer

'Regular shift on all letters
Dim intShift As Integer

'Code for substituted letter
Dim intNewcode As Integer
```

At this point new code is introduced. First an array, intFrequency(), is required to store the number of occasions each letter of the alphabet will appear in the coded message:

```
'Array to hold letter frequencies in text entered
Dim intFrequency(26)
```

A variable, intLocation, is declared which will identify the particular array location in intFrequency() which has to be updated:

```
'Location to increment in intFrequency()
 Dim intLocation As Integer
```

Determining the most common letter involves the use of the variable intMax:

```
'Largest frequency value
 Dim intMax As Integer
```

The most common letter in the message is identified as intCommon:

```
 'Most common letter
Dim intCommon As Integer
```

A loop control variable is needed as before:

```
'Loop counter
Dim intCounter As Integer
```

The user enters the coded message:

```
'Request text passage from user
Cls
strPassage = InputBox("Enter text")
```

Additional code in the program now finds out which is the most common letter. This is done in two stages. First the number of times each letter appears in the message is entered into the intFrequency() array. Then the intFrequency() array is examined to see which letter is the most frequent.

The array will hold its data like this:

Number of times 'a' occurs is assigned to intFrequency(1)
Number of times 'b' occurs is assigned to intFrequency(2)
Number of times 'c' occurs is assigned to intFrequency(3)
[Remaining locations]
Number of times 'z' occurs is assigned to intFrequency(26)

This means that when a letter 'a' is found in the message the variable, intLocation, which identifies array locations must be given a value of 1. When the letter 'b' is found intLocation must be 2. The letter 'z' has to generate 26.

In the loop below the letters are found using the Mid$ function as Mid$(strpassage, intCounter,1). The ASCII value for the letter is then obtained with Asc. Finally 96 must be subtracted as the ASCII for 'a' is 97. The value is then assigned to intLocation:

```
'Determine frequencies of letters in text passage
For intCounter = 1 To Len(strPassage)
intLocation = Asc(Mid$(strPassage, intCounter, 1)) - 96
```

Each value of intLocation found in this way is used to increment the corresponding location in the intFrequency() array:

```
intFrequency(intLocation) = intFrequency(intLocation) + 1
```

By the end of the loop the number of times each letter occurs in the message is held in the array:

```
Next intCounter
```

Once the array values are all complete intFrequency() can be examined to see which array location has the highest value. This will correspond to the most frequently occurring letter in the coded message.

The highest value is found by using the additional variable intMax. This is assigned an initial value of zero and then compared with each array location in turn. If the content of the location is greater than intMax its value is simply assigned to it. In this way by the time the last location is checked intMax will have the highest value.

First intMax is initialized:

```
'Find most common letter
intMax = 0
```

A For loop then checks each of the 26 locations of the intFrequency() array:

```
For intCounter = 1 To 26
```

If the array location is greater than the current value of intMax, its value is assigned to intMax. This means that intMax will always be equal to the greatest array value so far encountered:

```
If intFrequency(intCounter) > intMax Then
intMax = intFrequency(intCounter)
```

It is important that the actual value of the loop control variable is also recorded. This is the important information as it represents the letter itself, rather than the number of occurrences. The value of the counter is assigned to intCommon:

```
intCommon = intCounter
End If
```

By the end of the loop the value of intCommon represents the most common letter in the message:

```
Next intCounter
```

It is here that the assumption is made that the most common letter in the message must be 'e'. As explained above this might easily be an incorrect assumption for a short message. However, if the letter is 'e' the appropriate substitution shift will be generated by subtracting the position for 'e' in the array, 5, from intCommon:

```
'Calculate letter shift
intShift = intCommon - 5
```

The amount letters have to be shifted is then displayed to indicate how the message is being decoded. The absolute value of the shift, without sign, is shown, but then an If Then Else structure adds the further 'right' or 'left' according to whether the sign is plus or minus:

```
'Display letter shift
Print
Print "Letters are shifted "; Abs(intShift); " to ";
If Sgn(intShift) = 1 Then
Print "right."
Else
Print "left."
End If
```

The program code is then identical to the previous version of the program. First the original message is shown:

```
'Display original text
Print
Print "Original text was:"
Print strPassage
Print
```

A loop then decodes and displays each letter in turn:

```
'Display decoded text
Print "Decoded text is:"

For intCounter = 1 To Len(strPassage)

'Find ASCII code of original letter
intCode = Asc(Mid$(strPassage, intCounter, 1))

'Generate substituted letter
intNewcode = intCode + intShift

'Wrap around if value outside range
If intNewcode <97 Then intNewcode = intNewcode + 26
If intNewcode > 122 Then intNewcode = intNewcode - 26
```

```
'Display decoded letter
Print Chr$(intNewcode);

Next intCounter

End Sub
```

Random substitution

In the examples of substitution codes considered so far the problem has been made relatively easy by the way in which a regular substitution has been assumed. If 'a' is replaced by 'd' then 'b' will be replaced by 'e' and all other letters will be similarly coded by a shift of three places forward, with appropriate wrap-around for 'x', 'y' and 'z'. In reality of course spies are far more cunning than this and will avoid such an obvious pattern.

A totally random substitution pattern might appear impossible to crack. However, if the message is long enough the frequencies of substituted letters in the message should match the frequencies of the original letters in English generally. For example, 'e' is the most common letter in English. So if 'y' appears most frequently in the coded message a good assumption is that 'y' has been substituted for 'e' throughout. Similarly 't' is the second most commonly occurring letter. So if 'k' is the second most common in the coded message it is assumed that 'k' represents 't'.

The order of letters according to their frequency depends upon the textual material used to generate the data. Slightly different orderings appear on the Internet. The one adopted here is:

e t a o i n s h r d l u c m f g y p w b v k x j q z

Here is a program which decodes using this method.

```
Option Explicit
Private Sub Command1_Click()

'Decoding a message according to
'standard letter frequencies

'Standard frequencies of letters in English
Dim strStandard As String
strStandard = "etaoinshrdlucmfgypwbvkxjqz"

'Text entered by user
Dim strPassage As String

'Array to hold letter frequencies in text entered
Dim intFrequency(26, 2) As Integer

'Location to increment in strFrequency
Dim intLocation As Integer

'Loop counters
Dim intCounter As Integer
Dim intDecode As Integer

'Copy variable for sort routine
Dim intCopy As Integer

'Flag for sort routine
Dim Swap As Boolean

'Place codes into frequency array
For intCounter = 1 To 26
intFrequency(intCounter, 1) = intCounter
Next intCounter
```

```
'Request text passage from user
strPassage = InputBox("Enter text")

'Determine frequencies of letters in text passage
For intCounter = 1 To Len(strPassage)
intLocation = Asc(Mid$(strPassage, intCounter, 1)) - 96
intFrequency(intLocation, 2) = intFrequency(intLocation, 2) + 1
Next intCounter

'Sort frequency array into descending order
Do
Swap = False
For intCounter = 1 To 25
If intFrequency(intCounter, 2) <intFrequency(intCounter + 1, 2) Then
Swap = True

intCopy = intFrequency(intCounter, 1)
intFrequency(intCounter, 1) = intFrequency(intCounter + 1, 1)
intFrequency(intCounter + 1, 1) = intCopy
intCopy = intFrequency(intCounter, 2)
intFrequency(intCounter, 2) = intFrequency(intCounter + 1, 2)
intFrequency(intCounter + 1, 2) = intCopy
End If
Next intCounter
Loop Until Swap = False

'Replace letter totals with conversion code
For intCounter = 1 To 26
intFrequency(intCounter, 2) = Asc(Mid$(strStandard, intCounter, 1))
Next intCounter

'Show letter conversion table
Cls
Print
Print "Conversion is:"
For intCounter = 1 To 26
Print Chr$(intFrequency(intCounter, 1) + 96); " = ";
Print Chr$(intFrequency(intCounter, 2)); "     ";
If intCounter Mod 4 = 0 Then Print
Next intCounter
Print
Print

'Display original text
Print "Original text was:"
Print strPassage
Print

'Display decoded text
Print "Decoded text is"
For intCounter = 1 To Len(strPassage)
intLocation = Asc(Mid$(strPassage, intCounter, 1)) - 96
intDecode = 0
Do
intDecode = intDecode + 1
Loop Until intLocation = intFrequency(intDecode, 1)
Print Chr$(intFrequency(intDecode, 2));
Next intCounter

End Sub
```

Program documentation

The program begins with the usual Option Explicit to ensure that all variables are declared and comments are included to indicate what the program does:

```
Option Explicit
Private Sub Command1_Click()

'Decoding a message according to
'standard letter frequencies
```

A series of declarations and initializations then follows. First the sequence of most commonly occurring letters in English is assigned to the string strStandard. Obviously a choice has to be made here of the source of letter frequencies to be adopted:

```
'Standard frequencies of letters in English
Dim strStandard As String
strStandard = "etaoinshrdlucmfgypwbvkxjqz"
```

Next a string, strPassage, is declared which will be used to hold the coded text passage typed in by the user:

```
'Text entered by user
Dim strPassage As String
```

A two-dimensional array, intFrequency(), is used as a look-up table for the decoding that the program will perform. It has 26 pairs of locations corresponding to the 26 letters of the alphabet. In each pair the first location will represent a letter in the coded message and the second location what the letter becomes after decoding. The reason for this is explained in detail below.

It might be thought that the intFrequency() array should hold the letters themselves, and therefore be declared as type string. However, during the initial stages of decoding the same array is also used to hold the total number of each different letter in the message. This means that it has to be an integer array. It is relatively easy, of course, to identify letters by numbers via the use of ASCII codes:

```
'Array to hold letter frequencies in text entered
Dim intFrequency(26, 2) As Integer
```

The code which will be developed to identify locations in the intFrequency() array is fairly complicated and is made easier to design and comprehend if an additional integer variable, intLocation, is available to hold temporary values:

```
'Location to increment in strFrequency
Dim intLocation As Integer
```

Two loop control variables are required. Throughout most of the program a single variable, intCounter, is sufficient, but a second variable, intDecode, is required for a final nested loop:

```
'Loop counters
Dim intCounter As Integer
Dim intDecode As Integer
```

The fundamental rationale of the program relies upon being able to examine a series of individual letter totals and arrange them into descending order. They can then be compared with the standard frequencies of letters in English held in this program in the string strStandard. The program therefore requires a routine to compare the different letter totals and place them into order. A standard sorting routine, known as a bubble sort, is used. This requires two additional variables. The first, intCopy, is used as a temporary store for values in the intFrequency() array and is defined as being of type integer. The second variable, Swap, acts as a flag to indicate when the bubble sort is complete. It is therefore convenient to define it as a Boolean:

```
'Copy variable for sort routine
Dim intCopy As Integer
```

```
'Flag for sort routine
Dim Swap As Boolean
```

At this point all the declarations that the program will require are complete and the decoding routines can begin. First letter codes are placed into the intFrequency() array. In the program lower case letters are represented by numbers from 1 to 26, rather than the 97 to 122 which would be expected from the ASCII codes for lower case letters. This is done in order to relate the letters directly to the subscript of the array, without the need for frequent subtraction of 96.

A slight complication arises from the fact that, when relative frequencies of letters in the coded message are matched with the order of the most common letters in English words, the intFrequency() array will have to be sorted. This inevitably alters the order of array locations and means that array subscripts can no longer be used to identify letters. Suppose, for example, that there are six letter 'd's in the message entered by the user. After initial processing of the input string the value stored in the fourth location of the intFrequency() array will be 6, because d is the fourth letter of the alphabet. Similarly if there are five letter 'c's in the message the value that will be held in the third location of the array will be 5. However, after sorting into order of relative frequencies it is possible that the value of 6 will move into the third location of the array and the value of 5 will be shifted into the fourth location. If the array subscripts are being used to identify the letters it will now seem that the message contained six letter 'c's and five letter 'd's. Relying upon the array subscript to identify letters will lead to corruption of the data held in the intFrequency() array.

A solution to this problem is to make the array two dimensional, as indicated in the documentation above. It has 26 paired locations. In each of these the first location holds the code representing the letter and the second location the number of times the letter appears in the message entered. The array can now be sorted, according to the values held in the second location, without losing the information identifying the corresponding letters. These letter codes will be safely held in the first location of each pair and not be scrambled in the way that the array subscripts will be.

Of course the letter codes have to be placed into the first location of each pair. This is done quite simply by a For loop. This is controlled by the loop variable, intCounter, which takes values from 1 to 26. For each repeat of the loop the first location in the array is identified as intFrequency(intCounter,1). This just has to be assigned the value of the loop counter itself, intCounter:

```
'Place codes into frequency array
For intCounter = 1 To 26
intFrequency(intCounter, 1) = intCounter
Next intCounter
```

After this, the user is prompted to enter the coded message. It is assigned to the string, strPassage, by the use of the InputBox function. (Note that, unlike the use of InputBox in some of the other example programs, the default position of the dialogue box is not adjusted. This is because the entire form will be cleared before the decoded message is displayed.)

```
'Request text passage from user
strPassage = InputBox("Enter text")
```

Another For loop is now used to examine the message character by character and record the total number of times each particular letter appears. The range for the loop control variable is determined by the total number of letters in the message, strPassage. This is given by the length of string function, Len:

```
'Determine frequencies of letters in text passage
For intCounter = 1 To Len(strPassage)
```

The variable intLocation is now used for the first time to identify array locations. For each letter of strPassage in turn intLocation must select which location of the intFrequency() array should be incremented. For example, if a letter 'a' is encountered in the string, location 1 of intFrequency() should be incremented. If 'b' is found, location 2 should be incremented, and this pattern continues through to letter 'z', for which location 26 should increase.

Successive letters in strPasssage are first identified by the Mid$ function. This scans through strPassage, checking each character in turn as determined by the value of intCounter. Just one character is selected by the final 1. The ASCII value for the letter located is given by the use of the Asc function. This will differ, of course, from the corresponding array subscript for the letter by 96. For example, the ASCII for letter 'a' is 97, but the array subscript should be 1. A value of 96 therefore has to be subtracted before the final value is assigned to intLocation:

```
intLocation = Asc(Mid$(strPassage, intCounter, 1)) - 96
```

At this point the intFrequency() array can be incremented. The appropriate array pair is now inden-tified by intLocation. It is the second location of the pair which has to be increased by 1:

```
intFrequency(intLocation, 2) = intFrequency(intLocation, 2) + 1
```

The For loop then ends. When it has repeated the number of times determined by the length of the input string strPassage, all the letters in the coded meassge will have been identified and the relevant totals updated in the second locations of the intFrequency() array:

```
Next intCounter
```

As soon as all the letter totals have been recorded in the array, it has to be sorted into descending order to match the sequence of the most common letters held in strStandard. A comment indicates this:

```
'Sort frequency array into descending order
```

The sorting routine used in the program is a bubble sort. Although not a particularly efficient algorithm, this is relatively easy to understand. A bubble sort uses two nested loops. The inner loop compares items two at a time and swaps them into correct order if they are not already ordered. The inner loop usually has to repeat several times before all items are sorted. For this reason an outer loop is needed in order to keep repeating the inner one until no more swapping is required. The outer loop detects whether this is the case by the use of a flag the value of which is altered each time any swap takes place. The flag is reset each time the outer loop repeats. If it then remains unchanged, this indicates that no swapping has occurred and that all of the items are sorted into the correct order. An unchanged flag value can therefore be used to determine exit from the outer loop.

In this program the flag used to govern exit from the outer loop is Swap. It is a Boolean variable and is initally set to False. This value indicates that no swapping has yet occurred. If Swap remains as False by the end of the outer loop the bubble sort is complete:

```
Do
Swap = False
```

The outer loop has to be conditional because there is no way of determining in advance how many times it has to repeat before the intFrequency() array will be completely sorted. This will depend only upon the letter content of the secret message. This is why a Do loop has been employed for the outer loop. However, the inner loop is unconditional. The number of comparisons, between one array location and the one following it, will be exactly one fewer than the total number of the array locations present. This is because the first location can be compared with the second, the second with the third, and similarly up until the final comparison between the penultimate location and the last. The last location obviously cannot be compared with a non-existent location lying outside the array entirely.

As there are 26 array locations in intFrequency(), corresponding with the 26 letters of the alphabet, the number of times the inner loop has to repeat is 25. This is therefore the upper limit for the loop control variable, intCounter, of a conditional For loop:

```
For intCounter = 1 To 25
```

Within this inner loop pairs of successive array locations of the intFrequency() array are considered in turn. These are identified by the subscripts intCounter and intCounter +1. As letter totals are being checked for the sorting routine, the subscript will need to be followed by 2. The two array locations are therefore intFrequency(intCounter, 2) and intFrequency(intCounter + 1, 2). The sorting routine is designed to rearrange the array into descending order and so it is only when the first location is less than the one which follows it that any swapping is required. The condition which has to be satisfied for a swap to take place is therefore:

```
If intFrequency(intCounter, 2) <intFrequency(intCounter + 1, 2) Then
```

Several lines of code then follow as the action for this condition. First the Swap flag has to be set to True to indicate that a swap has been necessary. This is an essential feature of the routine as the value of True subsequently makes the For loop repeat and check if any further swapping is required:

```
Swap = True
```

After this the contents of the two array locations identified by subscript values of intCounter and intCounter + 1 have to be exchanged. This is done in two stages, first for the letter code in position 1 and then for the letter total in position 2.

The way in which the array contents are swapped around will be familiar to anybody who has ever cooked in a small kitchen. You have to move the tofu from the top of the fridge to the draining board before you can shift the pasta from the microwave to the top of the fridge. Then you can put the tofu in the microwave. Although the draining board isn't a designated cooking area when your mother visits it's impossible to cook without it. In other words to move two items around you need three locations to put them. One, the draining board, is a temporary location.

It is the same with the problem of swapping the content of two array locations. In addition to the locations themselves a third place is required to hold values briefly while the swapping takes place. This is the function of the intCopy variable in the program.

The letter codes held in the two array positions are therefore exchanged by the following process. First the letter code in the first array location is placed in the 'spare location' by assigning it to intCopy. (Note that the fact that it is a letter code is indicated by the final 1 in the brackets):

```
intCopy = intFrequency(intCounter, 1)
```

Next the letter code in the second array location is moved into the corresponding place in the first array location by assigning intFrequency(intCounter + 1, 1) to intFrequency(intCounter, 1). This assignment overwrites the value that was initially present but this does not matter because it is also present in intCopy:

```
intFrequency(intCounter, 1) = intFrequency(intCounter + 1, 1)
```

Finally the original value in the first array location, which has been safely duplicated in the spare location, intCopy, is assigned to the second array location:

```
intFrequency(intCounter + 1, 1) = intCopy
```

At the end of these three stages the letter codes have been swapped between the first and second array locations. Precisely the same three stages are now carried out again, this time in order to exchange the letter totals between the two array locations. The code is identical, except that the final 1 in the brackets is now replaced by a 2. This indicates that the array content is a letter total rather than a letter code:

```
intCopy = intFrequency(intCounter, 2)
intFrequency(intCounter, 2) = intFrequency(intCounter + 1, 2)
intFrequency(intCounter + 1, 2) = intCopy
```

This is the end of the condition and so End If is required:

```
End If
```

The inner, unconditional loop also ends:

```
Next intCounter
```

Finally the outer loop will end if no swaps have taken place, indicating that the array is completely sorted:

```
Loop Until Swap = False
```

Once the intFrequency() array has been sorted into order it can be turned into a 'look-up' table to decode the secret message. First it is important to remember what data is currently present in the array. It consists of 26 paired locations. The first location of each pair contains a letter code from 1 to 26 which identifies the lower case letters from a to z. The second location of a pair holds the number of times this letter has appeared in the coded message. The order in which these values appear reflects the relative frequency of the letters in the message. This means that the letter codes in the first location of each pair do not appear in their original order of 1 through to 26 but instead also correspond to the relative frequency of the letter in the message.

To convert the intFrequency() array into a look-up table all that needs to be done is overwrite the letter totals with the ASCII codes of the letters in the string strStandard. The most common letter in the message will be in the first location of the array. The ASCII code for 'e' will need to be placed into this location. The second most common letter will be in the second location. The letter 't' from strStandard must be inserted here.

As the most common letters in English are already conveniently held in the appropriate order in strStandard, a single loop is sufficient to copy the ASCII codes from this string to intFrequency(). As the loop control variable, intCounter, takes values from 1 to 26 it matches each time the location in intFrequency() with the appropriate letter from strStandard. The locations in the array are identified as intFrequency(intCounter, 2). The corresponding letters in the string, strStandard, are given by the use of the Mid$ function as Mid$(strStandard, intCounter,1). The ASCII codes of the letters are found using Asc. Note that although the letter codes for the letters in the message are in the range 1 to 26, as already explained, full ASCII codes from 97 to 122 will appear in the intFrequency(intCounter,2) positions.

The loop which converts the array into a look-up table is therefore:

```
'Replace letter totals with conversion code
For intCounter = 1 To 26
intFrequency(intCounter, 2) = Asc(Mid$(strStandard, intCounter, 1))
Next intCounter
```

The look-up table can now be displayed. First a heading is placed on the Visual Basic form:

```
'Show letter conversion table
Cls
Print
Print "Conversion is:"
```

A single For loop then displays the letter identified by the first location of the intFrequency() array followed by the decoded letter identified by the second location. As the first location values are in the range 1 to 26, 96 must be added to generate the ASCII values required. Then, for both ASCII codes, Chr$ is used to show the letter itself.

Semicolons are used to format the display of the conversion table. In addition an extra Print statement is included after every fourth pair of letters. This creates a neater table format provided that a non-proportional font is chosen for the Visual Basic form. These Print statements are selected by a simple condition involving the expression intCounter Mod 4. This will have a value of zero each time the value of intCounter is a multiple of 4:

```
For intCounter = 1 To 26
Print Chr$(intFrequency(intCounter, 1) + 96); " = ";
Print Chr$(intFrequency(intCounter, 2)); "   ";
If intCounter Mod 4 = 0 Then Print
Next intCounter
Print
Print
```

Beneath the table the uncoded message is repeated:

```
'Display original text
Print "Original text was:"
Print strPassage
Print
```

After this the decoded message is displayed. First a heading is shown:

```
'Display decoded text
Print "Decoded text is"
```

The message is then decoded by two nested loops. The outer loop is an unconditional For loop. The loop control variable, intCounter, has an upper value given by the number of characters in strPassage:

```
For intCounter = 1 To Len(strPassage)
```

Each letter in the message is identified in turn by the Mid$ function as Mid$(strPassage, intCounter, 1). The corresponding letter code is then found by obtaining the ASCII code with the Asc function and subtracting 96. The value obtained is assigned to the variable intLocation:

```
intLocation = Asc(Mid$(strPassage, intCounter, 1)) - 96
```

The inner loop of the nested pair then uses a conditional loop to match the letter code assigned to intLocation with the appropriate letter code in the intFrequency() array. As a result of the sorting process these codes will have been scrambled from their original sequential pattern. This makes the use of a conditional loop inevitable.

The counter used for the inner loop is initialized outside the loop, and immediately incremented in the loop body:

```
intDecode = 0
Do
intDecode = intDecode + 1
```

The value of intDecode then keeps increasing until a match occurs between the value of intLocation and the letter code identified by intDecode in intFrequency(). The inner loop then exits:

```
Loop Until intLocation = intFrequency(intDecode, 1)
```

At this point the correct pair of coded/decoded letters has been found in the look up table. This is because the letter code held by intLocation corresponds to the letter being checked in the original, coded message. If this matches the letter code identified by intDecode in the array, then the ASCII code identified by the same value of intDecode, intFrequency(intDecode, 2), gives the decoded letter. This can be displayed using Chr$. A semicolon means that the letters of the decoded message will appear as continuous text:

```
Print Chr$(intFrequency(intDecode, 2));
```

The outer loop, and the program, then both end:

```
Next intCounter

End Sub
```

Note again that the program assumes that the user will avoid using spaces in the message. No allowance has been made for the ASCII value of a space, although a slight modification in the form of a simple additional condition could achieve this.

Advanced Exercise 5: The mathematical billiard ball

On page 160 of Higher National Computing, a mathematical puzzle is given as an example of methods that can be adopted in problem solving. The puzzle involves a rectangle which has been divided into a number of squares. The squares define the size of the rectangle. A typical rectangle might, for example, consist of four rows and three columns of squares. The squares also define the path of a 'mathematical billiard ball' which, following perfect Newtonian mechanics on a frictionless horizontal surface, begins at the bottom left-hand corner and traces a diagonal path across the rectangle. The ball bounces at a perfect 45 degree grazing angle each time it hits one of the sides of the rectangle. Eventually it will reach one of the corners and stop (or rather fall into a mathematical pocket).

The rectangle's corners (vertices) are labelled A, B, C and D, beginning in the bottom left-hand corner and proceeding anticlockwise.

The problem is to determine whether there is any pattern linking the number of rows and columns in the rectangle with the vertex where the ball finally disappears.

When this exercise is attempted with students, using pencils and plenty of paper, it invariably becomes remarkably addictive. Various ideas and predictions are soon tested and the problem does seem to encourage group working (Figures 3.54 to 3.57).

However, some students observe a pattern immediately (or perhaps remember the game from their days at school) and need to be quarantined from the others. It is, perhaps, for these students that this programming exercise can be introduced as useful extension material.

Before the program is developed some initial ideas need to be considered.

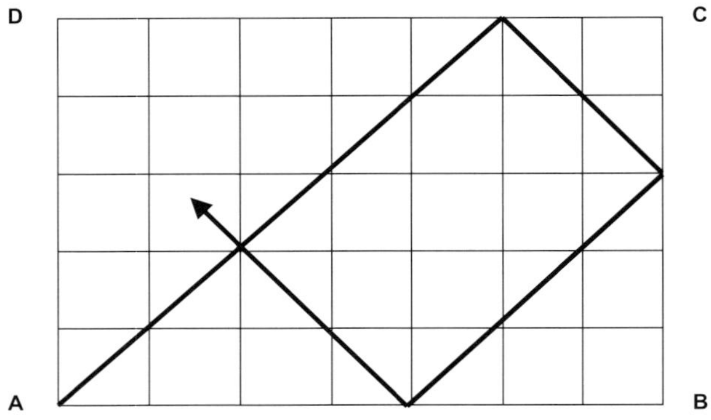

Figure 3.53 *A mathematical billiard ball*

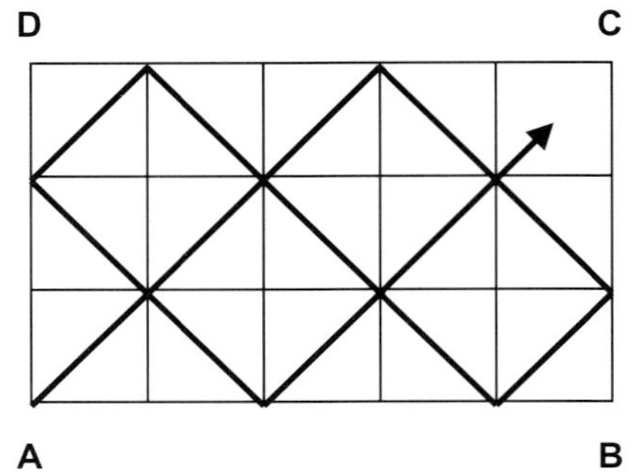

Figure 3.54 *3 rows and 5 columns: vertex reached is C*

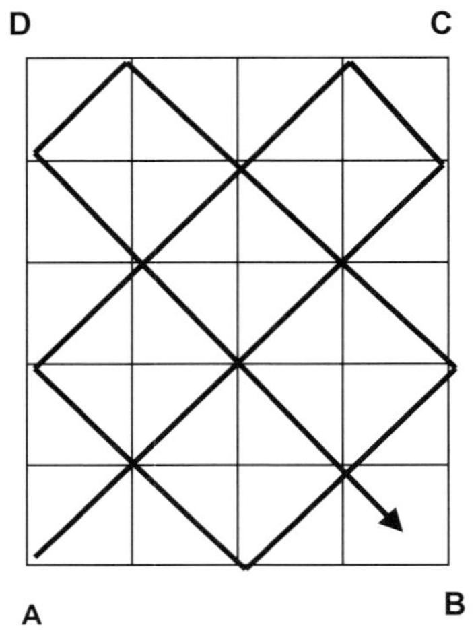

Figure 3.55 *5 rows and 4 columns: vertex reached is B*

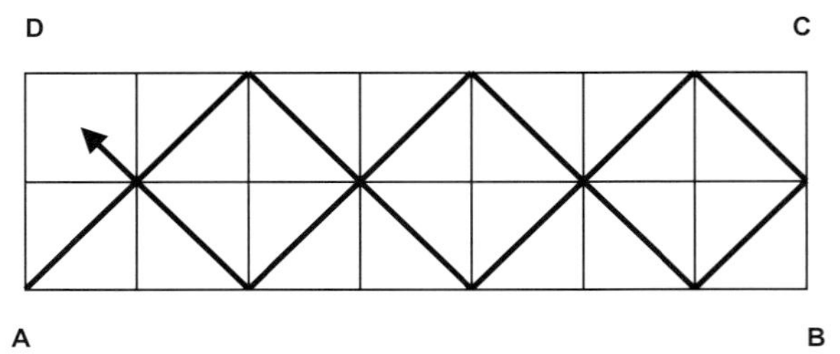

Figure 3.56 *2 rows and 7 columns: vertex reached is D*

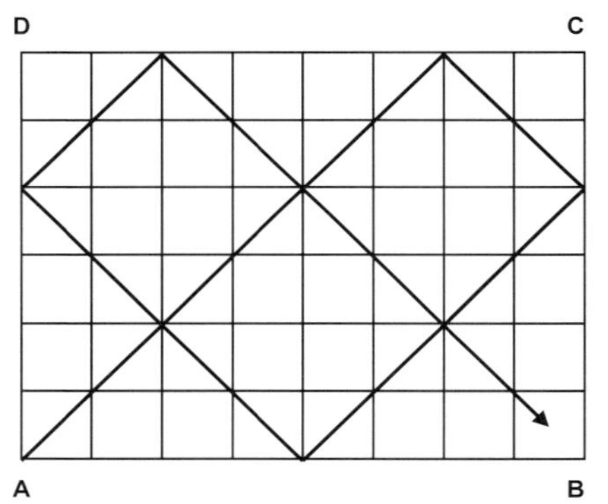

Figure 3.57 *6 rows and 8 columns: vertex reached is B*

Billiard ball space

In order to visualize the way in which the trajectory of the imaginary billiard ball is controlled it is best to think of a 'billiard ball space'. This is a little microworld consisting only of the ordered pairs of coordinates which correspond to the interior of the rectangle.

For example, if the user has entered a rectangle which has three rows and two columns the internal space will consist of the ordered coordinate pairs:

(0,0), (1,0), (2,0)
(0,1), (1,1), (2,1)
(0,2), (1,2), (2,2)
(0,3), (1,3), (2,3)

This is the totality of this particular billiard ball space, just a set of 12 ordered pairs (see Figure 3.58).

Note that we have a discrete space here. We are not concerned with fractional coordinates, or the spaces between the points. Our billiard ball does a neat quantum jump from one point to another. It is not real billiards.

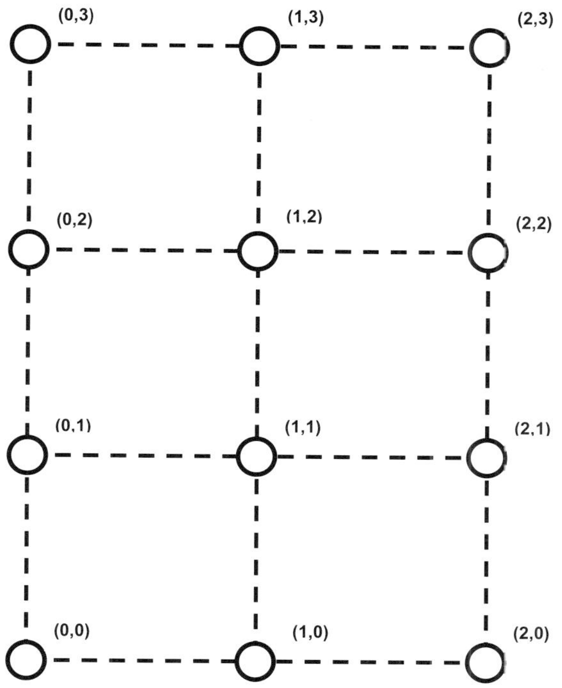

Figure 3.58 *Typical microworld for the billiard ball*

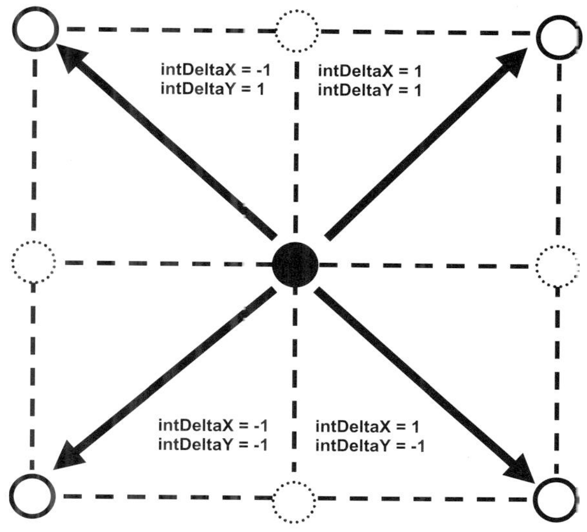

Figure 3.59 *Velocity components in billiard ball space*

The billiard ball is located within this space by its *x*- and *y*-coordinates. In the program these will be (intXgrid, intYgrid). For example, if the ball is at the bottom left-hand corner of the grid it will have coordinate values:

intXgrid = 0
intYgrid = 0

The program monitors the position of the ball within its private world by keeping track of intXgrid and intYgrid.

Moving the ball
In addition to being located in its world, the ball is also moving within it. It has a velocity. It is a very limited kind of velocity, however, because there are so few places that the ball can move towards (see Figure 3.59). (If the purist wishes to dispute the term 'velocity' as only distance and direction are involved, and not explicitly time, then accept that each repeat of the overall controlling loop can be considered as a time step.)

If we ignore the more involved situation of a ball reaching the boundary of the rectangle, it can move to just one of the four possible neighbouring points in its billiard ball space. Remember that it only moves diagonally. It can get to one of these points by doing one of the following:

Move right and up: increasing its x-coordinate by 1 and increasing its y-coordinate by 1
Move right and down: increasing its x-coordinate by 1 and decreasing its y-coordinate by 1
Move left and up: decreasing its x-coordinate by 1 and increasing its y-coordinate by 1
Move left and down: decreasing its x-coordinate by 1 and decreasing its y-coordinate by 1

There are no other ways in which the billiard ball can move. These four possible moves are represented in the program by two further variables intDeltaX and intDeltaY. The 'delta' indicates the variables' function. They act as increments to the *x*- and *y*-coordinates. Of course by including a minus sign an increment can also decrease the value. The values for intDeltaX and intDeltaY are related to the diagonal moves, as shown on the diagram.

Bouncing the ball
Incrementing intXgrid and intYgrid by intDeltaX and intDeltaY within a simple loop will make the billiard ball travel along a straight line until it begins to move out of its microworld. It can be kept

within the rectangle by reflecting it off the boundaries. This is done by reversing the sign of intDeltaX if the ball reaches either the left or the right side of the rectangle and similarly by reversing the sign of intDeltaY if it reaches the top or the bottom.

Reaching a vertex

Eventually the ball will reach one of the corners (vertex) of the rectangle. At this point the loop which is moving the ball will have to end and the vertex which has been reached displayed for the user. One way in which this could be done is by having a series of conditions which, in pseudocode, would appear like this:

If *x*-coordinate is Left and *y*-coordinate is Bottom Then Vertex is A
If *x*-coordinate is Right and *y*-coordinate is Bottom Then Vertex is B
If *x*-coordinate is Right and *y*-coordinate is Top Then Vertex is C
If *x*-coordinate is Left and *y*-coordinate is Top Then Vertex is D

This is not the method that has been adopted in this program, however. Instead a code is generated for the billiard ball which merges its *x*- and *y*-coordinates into a single number. This number will have a unique value for each position of the ball.

In effect it is converting the two-dimensional billiard ball space into a single-dimensional parametic space. It follows that each of the four corners of the rectangle will also have a unique value. All that needs to be done is to compare the parametric value for each position of the ball with the values known to hold for the four vertices. It will be immediately realized, then, if a vertex has been reached. The precise identity of the vertex, the letter to be displayed, will also be available.

The way in which the parametic value is obtained is extremely simple. The single digit for the *x*-coordinate and the single digit for the *y*-coordinate are turned into a 2-digit number. This is done by multiplying the *x*-coordinate by 10 and adding the *y*-coordinate. Provided that the *x*- and *y*-coordinates remain less than 10 this will generate a unique parametric value for all possible coordinates. For example, if intXgrid is 5 and intYgrid is 3 the parametric value for the ball's position will be 53. Similarly intgridX = 3 and intYgrid = 7 will generate a parametric value of 37.

The parametric values for the four vertices are placed into an array. They are therefore easily checked against the particular parametric value for the ball by a single loop embedded within the outer loop that is bouncing the ball around the rectangle.

We can now consider the program itself.

Program listing

The program code for the first version of mathematical billiards is as follows:

```
Option Explicit
Private Sub Command1_Click()

'Mathematical billiards
Cls

'Variables defining rectangle dimensions
Dim intRows As Integer
Dim intColumns As Integer

'Grid variables for billiard ball
Dim intXgrid As Integer
Dim intYgrid As Integer
Dim intDeltaX As Integer
Dim intDeltaY As Integer
Dim intGoal As Integer
Dim intFlag As Integer

'Loop control variable
Dim intCounter As Integer
```

```
'Corner identity array
Dim intCorner(4) As Integer

'Request dimensions of rectangle
intRows = InputBox("Enter number of rows", , , 6500, 5500)
intColumns = InputBox("Enter number of columns", , , 6500, 5500)

'Calculate corner values
intCorner(1) = 0
intCorner(2) = intColumns * 10
intCorner(3) = intColumns * 10 + intRows
intCorner(4) = intRows

'Initialise billiard ball
intDeltaX = 1
intDeltaY = 1
intXgrid = 0
intYgrid = 0
intFlag = 0

'Loop navigates rectangle
Do

'Move location
intXgrid = intXgrid + intDeltaX
intYgrid = intYgrid + intDeltaY

'Bounce off sides
If intXgrid = 0 Or intXgrid = intColumns Then
intDeltaX = -intDeltaX
End If

'Bounce off bottom or top
If intYgrid = 0 Or intYgrid = intRows Then

intDeltaY = -intDeltaY
End If

'Check if vertex is reached
For intCounter = 1 To 4
If intXgrid * 10 + intYgrid = intCorner(intCounter) Then
'Set flag to exit loop
intFlag = 1
'Identify vertex reached
intGoal = intCounter
End If
Next intCounter

Loop Until intFlag = 1

'State vertex reached
PicDisplay.Print Chr(intGoal + 64)

End Sub
```

Program documentation

The code begins, as usual, with a comment which indicates what the program does:

```
Option Explicit
Private Sub Command1_Click()
```

```
'Mathematical billiards
Cls
```

The user has of course to state how large the rectangle to be bounced around will be. This requires two integer variables which represent the number of rows and the number of columns involved:

```
'Variables defining rectangle dimensions
Dim intRows As Integer
Dim intColumns As Integer
```

As explained above the billiard ball is represented by four variables. Its position is defined by intGridX and intGridY. Its velocity is defined by intDeltaX and intDeltaY. All four variables are declared as integers:

```
'Grid variables for billiard ball
Dim intXgrid As Integer
Dim intYgrid As Integer
Dim intDeltaX As Integer
Dim intDeltaY As Integer
```

The program has to inform the user which vertex has been reached by the ball. This will require a further variable which will note, within a searching loop, which vertex matches the ball's position. The variable is named intGoal, for obvious reasons. (A possible alternative could be 'intPocket'!):

```
Dim intGoal As Integer
```

The loop which allows the billiard ball to move from point to point within billiard ball space will necessarily be a conditional loop. There is no way of determining in advance when the vertex will be reached. (More accurately, this is an entirely deterministic situation and so it would be perfectly possible to predict in advance how many times the ball would need to quantum hop from one point to another. This would, however, rather beg the question. The program is meant to be experimental, and not include the answer in its code.) As a conditional loop is being used, an exit condition will be required. This exit condition will involve the use of a flag, which is therefore declared now:

```
Dim intFlag As Integer
```

Embedded within the conditional loop which propels the ball around the rectangle there is a further loop which checks the ball's position against the vertex positions, via the parametic values explained earlier. This embedded loop will be unconditional. There are just four vertices to check. The loop therefore requires a loop control variable which will appear in the For and Next statements:

```
'Loop control variable
Dim intCounter As Integer
```

The array which holds the parametric values for the four vertices has to be declared:

```
'Corner identity array
Dim intCorner(4) As Integer
```

This ends the declarations.

The program now requests the size of the rectangle. The user's choice is assigned to intRows and intColumns:

```
'Request dimensions of rectangle
intRows = InputBox("Enter number of rows", , , 6500, 5500)
intColumns = InputBox("Enter number of columns", , , 6500, 5500)
```

Once these values have been entered the parametric values for the vertices can be calculated and placed in the intCorner() array. From Figure 3.53 it can be seen that the bottom left-hand corner is taken as the origin of the coordinate system and so both x- and y-coordinates will be zero. Multiplying the x-value by 10 and adding the y-value will give a parametric value of 0 for any rectangle. This is assigned to the array location intCorner(1):

```
'Calculate corner values
intCorner(1) = 0
```

The value for the bottom right-hand corner will depend upon the size of the rectangle. Obviously the y-coordinate will be zero, but the x-coordinate will equal the number of columns chosen by the user. This is intColumns. According to the rule explained above for calculating the parametric values, the x-coordinate must be multiplied by 10. This value is then assigned to intCorner(2):

```
intCorner(2) = intColumns * 10
```

The top right-hand corner will also have an x-coordinate equal to intColumns. Its y-coordinate will be equal to the number of rows chosen, intRows. Multiplying the x-coordinate by 10 and adding the y-coordinate leads to this assignment for intCorner(3):

```
intCorner(3) = intColumns * 10 + intRows
```

The top left-hand corner will have an x-coordinate of zero and a y-coordinate equal to the number of rows. The assignment for intCorner(4) is therefore:

```
intCorner(4) = intRows
```

These calculations have initialized the vertex array. Next the four variables defining the initial position and velocity of the ball have to be defined. At first the ball will be moving diagonally up and to the right. From Figure 3.53 it can be seen that this corresponds with values for both intDeltaX and intDeltaY of 1:

```
'Initialise billiard ball
intDeltaX = 1
intDeltaY = 1
```

The ball begins at the bottom left-hand vertex and so both intXgrid and intYgrid will be zero:

```
intXgrid = 0
intYgrid = 0
```

The exit flag is initialized:

```
intFlag = 0
```

At this point the conditional loop which moves the ball begins:

```
'Loop navigates rectangle
Do
```

The ball is moved by adding the appropriate velocity values to the coordinates:

```
'Move location
intXgrid = intXgrid + intDeltaX
intYgrid = intYgrid + intDeltaY
```

As soon as it has been moved, its new position has to be tested for either of two possible situations. The ball might have reached the boundary of the rectangle. Alternatively it might now be at a vertex, in which case the loop should stop repeating. The boundary conditions are tested first. There are two boundary conditions. The first deals with the case of the ball reaching the left- or right-hand side of the rectangle.

If it reaches the left-hand side this will be identified by the x-coordinate, intXgrid, becoming equal to zero. The value of intDeltaX will be –1, because the ball is travelling to the left, and it has to change to 1 so that the ball begins moving to the right.

If the ball reaches the right-hand side of the rectangle the *x*-coordinate will be equal to intColumns. The value of intDeltaX will be 1, because the ball is travelling to the right, and it has to be changed to –1 in order for the ball to begin moving to the left.

In either case, with the ball reaching the left- or right-hand side, the action that has to be taken is the same. The value of intDeltaX has to be reversed. This is done simply by multiplying it by –1:

```
'Bounce off sides
If intXgrid = 0 Or intXgrid = intColumns Then
intDeltaX = -intDeltaX
End If
```

Similar reasoning shows that if the ball arrives at the bottom or top of the rectangle the value of intDeltaY has to be reversed by multiplication by –1:

```
'Bounce off bottom or top
If intYgrid = 0 Or intYgrid = intRows Then
intDeltaY = -intDeltaY
End If
```

After the boundary conditions have been checked the position of the ball is examined to see if it has reached one of the vertices. As explained already this test is made by calculating the parametric position of the ball and seeing whether this matches the parametric values held in the corner array. As there are four vertices for which the ball's position has to be tested the governing loop has to repeat four times:

```
'Check if vertex is reached
For intCounter = 1 To 4
```

The ball's parametric value is calculated by multiplying its *x*-coordinate by 10 and adding its *y*-coordinate. This is then compared with each of the vertices' parametric values in turn:

```
If intXgrid * 10 + intYgrid = intCorner(intCounter) Then
```

If a match does occur the exit flag for the loop is set to 1:

```
'Set flag to exit loop
intFlag = 1
```

If a match has taken place the value of the loop control variable will inevitably identify which vertex has been reached. Recall that the vertices have been labelled A to D and that the parametic values placed in the intCorner() array have been inserted in the same sequence. If the loop control variable is 1 this means that vertex A has been reached. If it is 2 the vertex is B, and similarly for vertices C and D. It is therefore important to record the value of intCounter when a match occurs. This is done by assigning its value to the 'goal reached' variable, intGoal:

```
'Identify vertex reached
intGoal = intCounter
```

The condition then ends, and the For loop. By the end of this loop all four vertices will have been checked to see if the ball has arrived:

```
End If
Next intCounter
```

If the ball has fallen down one of the pockets the condition above will have set the exit flag to 1, and the loop moving the ball will end. If the ball still has not arrived at a corner the flag will remain as zero, and so the loop continues. All this is determined by the exit condition:

```
Loop Until intFlag = 1
```

When the loop has ended the value of intGoal will be 1, 2, 3 or 4. These values can be converted to the ASCII code of the appropriate capital letter to identify the vertex by adding 64. The letter can then be displayed:

```
'State vertex reached
PicDisplay.Print Chr(intGoal - 64)

End Sub
```

Animating the billiard ball

The program in the form detailed above does find the correct vertex reached according to the number of rows and columns entered by the user, provided that these values are kept in the range 1–9. It allows an investigation of the pattern. Probably by the time the student has worked through the computer solution they will be pretty aware of the pattern anyway, although possibly a really enthusiastic student could be encouraged to try the computer solution before investigating too much with pencil and paper. However, what the program does not do is the rather pretty part. It does not show the pattern produced by the path of the billiard ball.

This is rectified in the extended version of the program shown below. Here graphics routines have been included into the initial code. No program lines have been deleted, all of which remain in exactly the same order as before. Blocks of graphics programming have been inserted at relevant places, however.

```
Option Explicit
Private Sub Command1_Click()

'Animated mathematical billiards
Cls

'Variables defining rectangle dimensions
Dim intRows As Integer
Dim intColumns As Integer

'Variables determining individual square size
Dim intSizeR As Integer
Dim intSizeC As Integer
Dim intSize As Integer

'Variables determining rectangle size
Dim intXright As Integer
Dim intYbottom As Integer

'Coordinate variables for drawing rectangle
Dim intXcoord As Integer
Dim intYcoord As Integer

'Graphics variables for billiard ball
Dim intXstart As Integer
Dim intYstart As Integer
Dim intXstop As Integer
Dim intYstop As Integer

'Grid variables for billiard ball
Dim intXgrid As Integer
Dim intYgrid As Integer
Dim intDeltaX As Integer
Dim intDeltaY As Integer
Dim intGoal As Integer
Dim intFlag As Integer

'Loop control variable
Dim intCounter As Integer
```

```
'Corner identity array
Dim intCorner(4) As Integer

'Request dimensions of rectangle
intRows = InputBox("Enter number of rows", , , 6500, 5500)
intColumns = InputBox("Enter number of columns", , , 6500, 5500)

'Calculate corner values
intCorner(1) = 0
intCorner(2) = intColumns * 10
intCorner(3) = intColumns * 10 + intRows
intCorner(4) = intRows

'Calculate size of squares
intSizeR = Int(8000 / intRows)
intSizeC = Int(11600 / intColumns)
If intSizeR <intSizeC Then
intSize = intSizeR
Else
intSize = intSizeC
End If

'Draw rectangle as grid of squares
ForeColor = vbBlue
BackColor = vbCyan

'Draw vertical lines
intYbottom = 200 + intSize * intRows
For intCounter = 0 To intColumns
intXcoord = 200 + intCounter * intSize
Line (intXcoord, 200)-(intXcoord, intYbottom)
Next intCounter

'Draw horizontal lines
intXright = 200 + intSize * intColumns
For intCounter = 0 To intRows
intYcoord = 200 + intCounter * intSize
Line (200, intYcoord)-(intXright, intYcoord)
Next intCounter

'Initialise billiard ball
intXstart = 200
intYstart = intYbottom
intDeltaX = 1
intDeltaY = 1
intXgrid = 0
intYgrid = 0
intFlag = 0

'Select colour for path
ForeColor = vbRed

'Loop navigates rectangle
Do

'Move location
intXgrid = intXgrid + intDeltaX
intYgrid = intYgrid + intDeltaY

'Calculate graphics coordinates ending line
intXstop = 200 + intXgrid * intSize
intYstop = intYbottom - intYgrid * intSize
```

```
'Draw path of billiard ball
Line (intXstart, intYstart)-(intXstop, intYstop)

'Define graphics beginning of next line
intXstart = intXstop
intYstart = intYstop

'Bounce off sides
If intXgrid = 0 Or intXgrid = intColumns Then
intDeltaX = -intDeltaX
End If

'Bounce off bottom or top
If intYgrid = 0 Or intYgrid = intRows Then
intDeltaY = -intDeltaY
End If

'Check if vertex is reached
For intCounter = 1 To 4
If intXgrid * 10 + intYgrid = intCorner(intCounter) Then
'Set flag to exit loop
intFlag = 1
'Identify vertex reached
intGoal = intCounter
End If
Next intCounter

Loop Until intFlag = 1

'State vertex reached
PicDisplay.Print Chr(intGoal + 64)

End Sub
```

The program is shown in operation by the screen dump in Figure 3.60. The number of rows and columns that have been entered are 2 and 3. Two rows and three coloumns result in vertex D being reached.

In this second example of an actual program run five rows and eight columns have led to the ball reaching vertex B (see Figure 3.61).

The graphics code is now explained in the program documentation.

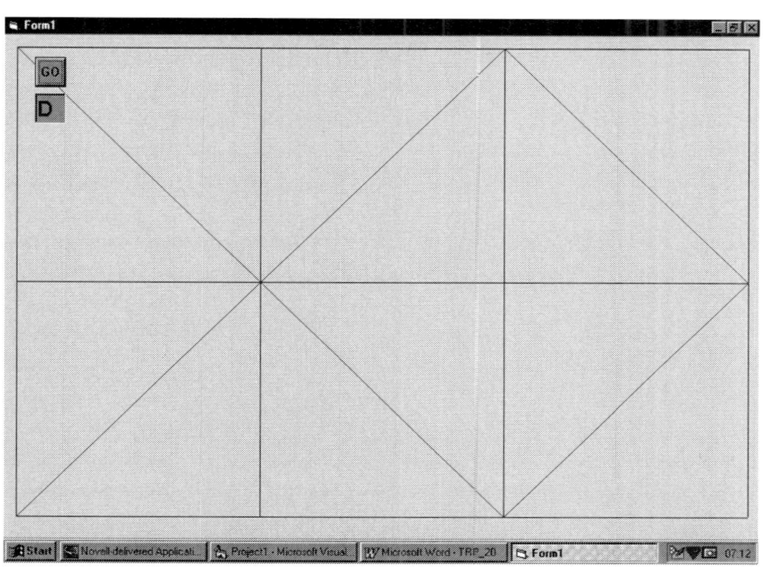

Figure 3.60

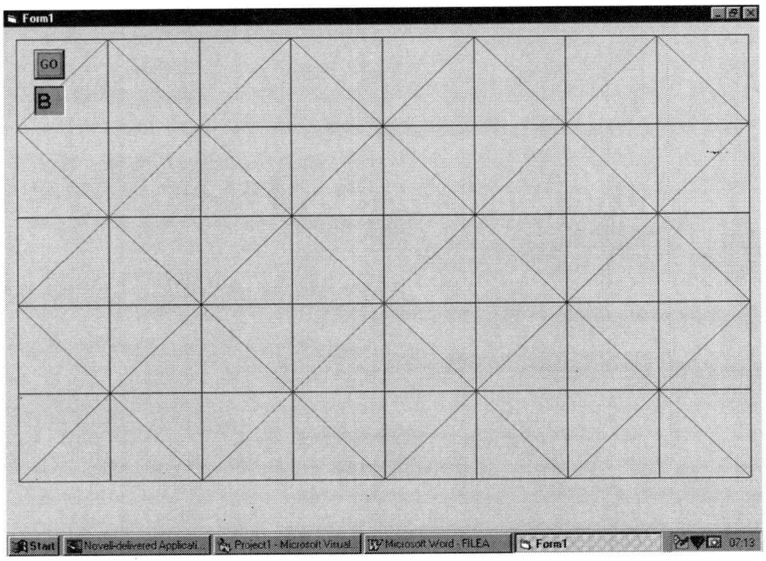

Figure 3.61

Program documentation

The initial comment indicates that this version of the program is animated:

```
Option Explicit
Private Sub Command1_Click()

'Animated mathematical billiards
Cls
```

The same variables used to define the ball's position are declared as before:

```
'Variables defining rectangle dimensions
Dim intRows As Integer
Dim intColumns As Integer
```

The program now requires the declaration of a series of variables required to produce the graphics. One of these is intSize, which will be the size of an individual side of the squares which will form the rectangle on the screen. In addition to this variable are intSizeR and intSizeC, which are needed in order that intSize can be made as big as possible.

This complication arises because there is a fixed area on the display which can be used to show the rectangle. This is set at a horizontal value of 11 600 across and a vertical value of 8000. What the program has to do is check the number of rows and columns that the user has entered and calculate what appropriate square size most closely matches this choice with the available screen area.

Suppose that the user has selected two rows and two columns. The width of the rows could therefore be (8000/2), or 4000. The width of the columns could be (11 600/2) or 5800. Which of these two numbers should be chosen for the square size? Well clearly if the square is going to have a side of 5800 the height of the overall grid of squares will be (5800×2), or 11 600. And this will not fit! Obviously what the program has to do is calculate the possible width of the rows, and the possible width of the columns, and then select the smaller of the two.

This will happen subsequently, but first the three variables are declared. These are the possible row width, intSizeR, the possible column width, intSizeC, and finally the actual square size chosen, intSize:

```
'Variables determining individual square size
Dim intSizeR As Integer
Dim intSizeC As Integer
Dim intSize As Integer
```

The size of the rectangle that appears on the screen obviously depends upon the size of the unit square and will need to be calculated. However, the *y*-coordinate of the top of the rectangle is fixed near the top of the display, and the *x*-coordinate of the left-hand side near the display's left. Meanwhile the bottom and the right-hand side will both depend upon the value of intSize. Variables are declared for the bottom and the right. Subsequently they will be assigned calculated values:

```
'Variables determining rectangle size
Dim intXright As Integer
Dim intYbottom As Integer
```

The grid of squares forming the rectangle will be drawn by For Next loops which calculate screen coordinates. Two variables are used inside these loops for the *x*- and *y*-coordinates involved:

```
'Coordinate variables for drawing rectangle
Dim intXcoord As Integer
Dim intYcoord As Integer
```

Additional coordinate variables are required for the billiard ball itself. We already have intXgrid and intYgrid which define its position in its own billiard ball space, but these are not the same as the coordinates which will plot its position on the screen. The ball's path is drawn as a series of short diagonal lines, each across a single square at a time. Every one of these lines has *x*- and *y*-coordinates for its start position and its stop:

```
'Graphics variables for billiard ball
Dim intXstart As Integer
Dim intYstart As Integer
Dim intXstop As Integer
Dim intYstop As Integer
```

The program then continues as in the previous version, up to the lines where the parametric values for the vertices are placed in their array:

```
'Grid variables for billiard ball
Dim intXgrid As Integer
Dim intYgrid As Integer
Dim intDeltaX As Integer
Dim intDeltaY As Integer
Dim intGoal As Integer
Dim intFlag As Integer

'Loop control variable
Dim intCounter As Integer

'Corner identity array
Dim intCorner(4) As Integer

'Request dimensions of rectangle
intRows = InputBox("Enter number of rows", , , 6500, 5500)
intColumns = InputBox("Enter number of columns", , , 6500, 5500)

'Calculate corner values
intCorner(1) = 0
intCorner(2) = intColumns * 10
intCorner(3) = intColumns * 10 + intRows
intCorner(4) = intRows
```

The size of the basic square is now calculated. As indicated above this is done by calculating two potential sizes first. The possible row width is found by dividing the display height of 8000 by the number of rows selected by the user, intRows. This gives a value for intSizeR. Then a similar process divides the display width by the number of columns chosen, intColumns, to give intSizeC:

```
'Calculate size of squares
intSizeR = Int(8000 / intRows)
intSizeC = Int(11600 / intColumns)
```

The smaller of these two values is then chosen to be the size of the grid square on the display:

```
If intSizeR <intSizeC Then
intSize = intSizeR
Else
intSize = intSizeC
End If
```

Once this basic dimension has been calculated the construction of the rectangle can begin. First screen colours are chosen:

```
'Draw rectangle as grid of squares
ForeColor = vbBlue
BackColor = vbCyan
```

The rectangle is now drawn as two sets of lines. The vertical set is drawn first. The value of the *y*-coordinate for the lower edge of the rectangle, intYbottom, is needed before these can be drawn. This will be equal to the number of rows, multiplied by the size of the square, and added to the offset of 200 chosen from the top of the screen:

```
'Draw vertical lines
intYbottom = 200 + intSize * intRows
```

A For loop controlled by intCounter now places the lines on the screen. This will have to repeat one more time than the actual number of columns chosen. (For example, four columns need five lines in order to appear as four columns.) The loop therefore begins at 0 rather than 1:

```
For intCounter = 0 To intColumns
```

All the points along a vertical line will have the same *x*-coordinate. This will equal the product of the loop control variable and the square size, again with the offset of 200 added:

```
intXcoord = 200 + intCounter * intSize
```

Using this value for the *x*-coordinate, each vertical line is now drawn from the top of the rectangle, where the *y*-coordinate is 200, to the lower edge, where the *y*-coordinate is intYbottom:

```
Line (intXcoord, 200)-(intXcoord, intYbottom)
```

By the time the For loop ends all of the vertical lines have been drawn:

```
Next intCounter
```

An analogous loop now draws the horizontal lines. This first requires the calculation of a value for the *x*-coordinate of the right-hand side of the rectangle, intXright. The For loop then repeats just one more time than the number of Rows and calculates the *y*-coordinate of each of the horizontal lines. These are then drawn from an *x*-coordinate of 200 to intXright:

```
'Draw horizontal lines
intXright = 200 + intSize * intColumns
For intCounter = 0 To intRows
intYcoord = 200 + intCounter * intSize
Line (200, intYcoord)-(intXright, intYcoord)
Next intCounter
```

The initial position of the ball, at the bottom left-hand corner, is then established:

```
'Initialise billiard ball
intXstart = 200
intYstart = intYbottom
```

The next five lines are the same as the first version of the program and define the velocity and position of the ball in its own space. The exit flag for the overall loop is also initialized:

```
intDeltaX = 1
intDeltaY = 1
intXgrid = 0
intYgrid = 0
intFlag = 0
```

The colour for the ball's path is then selected:

```
'Select colour for path
ForeColor = vbRed
```

The loop begins as in the previous version of the program:

```
'Loop navigates rectangle
Do
'Move location
intXgrid = intXgrid + intDeltaX
intYgrid = intYgrid + intDeltaY
```

After the new position of the ball has been calculated its graphic equivalent is found. This will be the screen coordinates for the end of the line which has to be drawn. The *x*-coordinate, intXstop, is simply the grid value multiplied by the square size. The offset of 200 must be added:

```
'Calculate graphics coordinates ending line
intXstop = 200 + intXgrid * intSize
```

The *y*-coordinate is slightly more involved. It has to be subtracted from intYbottom to take into account the way the screen coordinates are measured from the top of the display. The coordinates on the grid follow the more usual convention of the *y*-coordinate increasing from bottom to top:

```
intYstop = intYbottom - intYgrid * intSize
```

The path of the ball can now be drawn as a line from the start position to the stop:

```
'Draw path of billiard ball
Line (intXstart, intYstart)-(intXstop, intYstop)
```

Once the line has been drawn the start position of the next line is defined as the stop position of the line that has just ended. This keeps the pattern joined up!

```
'Define graphics beginning of next line
intXstart = intXstop
intYstart = intYstop
```

The remaining code is as in the earlier version:

```
'Bounce off sides
If intXgrid = 0 Or intXgrid = intColumns Then
intDeltaX = -intDeltaX
End If

'Bounce off bottom or top
If intYgrid = 0 Or intYgrid = intRows Then
intDeltaY = -intDeltaY
End If

'Check if vertex is reached
For intCounter = 1 To 4
```

```
If intXgrid * 10 + intYgrid = intCorner(intCounter) Then
'Set flag to exit loop
intFlag = 1
'Identify vertex reached
intGoal = intCounter
End If
Next intCounter

Loop Until intFlag = 1

'State vertex reached
PicDisplay.Print Chr(intGoal + 64)

End Sub
```

Advanced Exercise 6: Simple pattern recognition

> Like the previous exercise this is intended as more complicated material for students who have existing programming skills and who require a little stretching. It is a hard problem, but a stimulating one. The lecturer will need to judge carefully how much help is required for the individual student. Too little could make the exercise frustrating. Conversely too much would remove the excitement and the challenge.

Pattern recognition is an important area within computing research and has become one of the successes of artificial intelligence. Scanning an archived document and producing from it a soft, electronic copy which can be reworked is one of the many benefits of new technology. It is easy to use documents which have been scanned and converted in this way without even thinking about the considerable ingenuity of the software involved.

Similarly future planetary research is going to rely increasingly upon autonomous robotic vehicles, buggies on Mars, submersibles on Europa, which know where they are going. Computer vision systems will be increasingly sophisticated and the simpler task of pattern recognition will continue to be a hot field for some decades to come.

Pattern recognition is also a fascinating exercise for the rookie programmer. Can you write code that tells a 'T' from an 'X'? To make things easier students can be set a simplified exercise: If a simple geometic shape, a polygon like a square, a triangle, a rectangle or similar basic form, is presented to a computer as the coordinates of its vertices (corners), can you write a program which will be able to learn which is which?

Giving the coordinates of the vertices simplifies the problem a lot. Students are not going to be expected to deal with edge detection and other clever things. Their raw data will not be too raw.

This exercise could, perhaps, be presented to a group of Higher National students as a set of worksheets, each printed with a grid on which a simple shape has been superimposed, together with the coordinates of its vertices. Ideally the sheets should be arranged in some hierarchy of complexity. After students have looked at a series of right angled triangles located on different parts of the grid they could be shown bigger triangles, and then some which have been twisted around to a different angle. And they can be given squares and rectangles and perhaps some pentagons.

Brainstorming should ensue. Ideas which might arise could include:

Count the number of vertices
Calculate the lengths of the sides
Check whether all the sides are the same length
Check whether sides alternate in length
Calculate the angles at the vertices
Note whether all the angles are the same
Check whether angles occur in matched pairs
Compare the perimeter of the shape with its area

Promising ideas should be followed up. If, for example, the second suggestion above has been made, then the method for calculating lengths should be investigated.

Any workable algorithm, even one which solves only part of the problem, should be developed, coded and tested. People work most enthusiastically with their own ideas. Nevertheless an algorithm is given here which will allow a computer to learn and name different simple geometric shapes. Studying and testing this algorithm could be an exercise itself, as well as writing code for it. A coded version is, of course, provided, but alternatives are certainly possible.

The significance of this algorithm is that, although restricted to fairly simple polygons, it can identify a shape irrespective of its size or orientation. Once a particular example of a shape has been named by the user – for example, a small square is entered and described as being a 'square' – further examples of squares can be recognized, even if they are much bigger and twisted around so that they look like large diamonds.

A shape is first defined by the x- and y-coordinates of its vertices. This can be done by presenting a grid on computer display and letting the user type in what these coordinates are. The shape can then be drawn for confirmation. The precise method of entry is, of course, not critical for the algorithm. What matters is that vertex coordinates are provided.

At this point recognizing the shape seems to be made even more complicated. The distance between each vertex and all of the others is calculated in turn. This will lead to nine distances being worked out if there are three vertices, 16 if there are four, and generally n squared distances for a shape with n vertices.

In fact it is the square of the distance that is found, because the Pythagorean equation is used. If the coordinates of two points are (X1, Y1) and (X2, Y2) then the square of the distance between them is (X1 – X2) squared plus (Y1 – Y2) squared.

An important aspect of calculating the squared distances between all pairs of vertices is that 'extra sides' are automatically imposed upon the shape being considered. So, as far as the algorithm is concerned, a square is converted from a simple set of four lines to a more complicated shape consisting of four lines, equal in length, and another pair of lines, the two diagonals, which are equal to each other but longer than the other four.

This additional detail about the shape created by calculating all the inter-vertex distances makes it possible for the pattern algorithm to work. Clearly it is easier to distinguish between one shape and another if more information is available upon which to base a decision.

In particular an important fact about these extra lines is that they remove the need to involve the internal angles of a shape in the pattern recognition algorithm. (Working with angles would be difficult in any case.) A person asked to distinguish between a square and a rhombus would almost certainly think in terms of the fact that a square has all its angles equal, whereas a rhombus has two pairs of equal angles, one pair being bigger than the other. Designing a program to deduce this would be difficult. However, an algorithm which considers the distances between all pairs of vertices will easily distinguish a square as having equal diagonals but a rhombus having a long and a short diagonal. This fact will be immediately apparent from the set of squared inter-vertex distances shown in Figure 3.62.

It is not sufficient, however, to attempt to identify a shape just by using an unprocessed list of distances. Exactly the same shape would produce a different list if the coordinates of its vertices were typed in a different order. The shape would not be recognized the second time. Similarly the orientation of the shape would affect the list of squared inter-vertex distances. This problem can be solved by sorting all of the values into order. This means that whatever arbitary order of distances results from the orientation of the shape, the list of distances produced will be the same. In the program developed here a descending order is chosen, but an ascending order of squared distances could also be adopted.

Sorting the squared distances into order solves the problem of orientation. However, two polygons which are identical in shape, but which differ in size, would still produce different lists of numbers. This can be resolved if distances are reduced to a set of ratios, dividing all of the numbers generated by the smallest, non-zero, value. A big square and a little square, for example, will initially create quite different sets of distances but will go on to produce the same series of ratios.

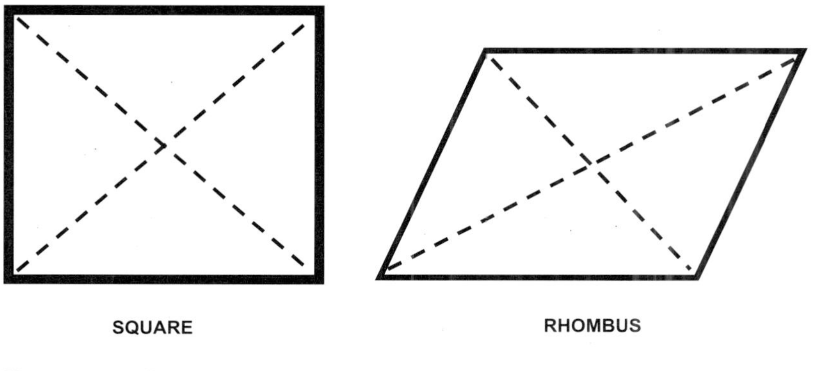

Figure 3.62 *Pattern recognition using inter-vertex distances*

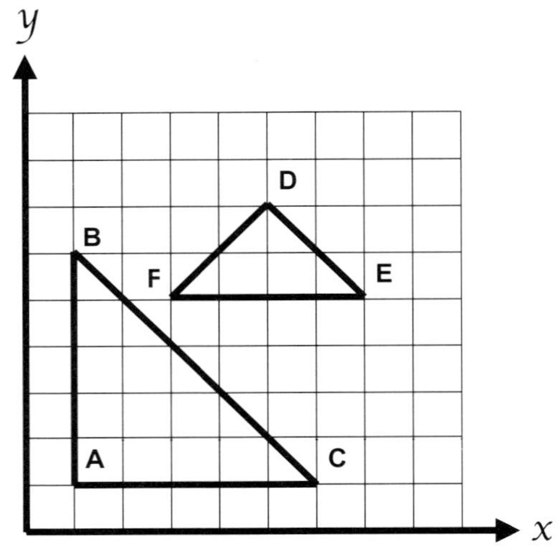

Figure 3.63 *Right angled isosceles triangles testing algorithm*

The algorithm as described informally above can now be tested by applying it in turn to two right angled isosceles triangles (see Figure 3.63). After that the algorithm will be stated more precisely and then coded into Basic.

The first triangle is lettered ABC. It has these coordinates for its vertices:

Vertex A = (1, 1)
Vertex B = (1, 6)
Vertex C = (6, 1)

Recall that the squared Pythagorean distance between two points is the difference in their *x*-coordinates squared plus the difference in their *y*-coordinates squared. Applying this to vertex A and vertex B of the triangle gives:

(Vertex A's *x*-coordinate – Vertex B's *x*-coordinate) squared = (1 – 1) squared

The squared difference in *x*-coordinates evaluates as 0.

(Vertex A's *y*-coordinate – Vertex B's *y*-coordinate) squared = (1 – 6) squared

The squared difference in *y*-coordinates evaluates as 25.
The sum is 0 + 25, or 25

All of the nine squared inter-vertex distances for the triangle can be calculated and made into the list shown below. The list is systematic, taking each vertex in turn and calculating the squared distance to each of the others, taken in the same order:

Squared distance from vertex A to vertex A = 0
Squared distance from vertex A to vertex B = 25
Squared distance from vertex A to vertex C = 25

Squared distance from vertex B to vertex A = 25
Squared distance from vertex B to vertex B = 0
Squared distance from vertex B to vertex C = 50

Squared distance from vertex C to vertex A = 25
Squared distance from vertex C to vertex B = 50
Squared distance from vertex C to vertex C = 0

The list of squared distances is therefore:

0, 25, 25, 25, 0, 50, 25, 50, 0

Sorting this list into descending order gives:

50, 50, 25, 25, 25, 25, 0, 0, 0

The smallest non-zero value is 25 and so this is divided into all the values to lead a set of ratios:

2, 2, 1, 1, 1, 1, 0, 0, 0

Finally these are concatenated into the string:

221111000

The algorithm is now tested again with the second right angled isosceles triangle, DEF. This has vertices:

Vertex D = (5, 7)
Vertex E = (7, 5)
Vertex F = (3, 5)

Squared distance from vertex D to vertex D = 0
Squared distance from vertex D to vertex E = 8
Squared distance from vertex D to vertex F = 8

Squared distance from vertex E to vertex D = 8
Squared distance from vertex E to vertex E = 0
Squared distance from vertex E to vertex F = 16

Squared distance from vertex F to vertex D = 8
Squared distance from vertex F to vertex E = 16
Squared distance from vertex F to vertex F = 0

These squared distances sorted into order are:

16, 16, 8, 8, 8, 8, 0, 0, 0

Dividing by the smallest non-zero value, 8, gives:

2, 2, 1, 1, 1, 1, 0, 0, 0

The string produced is:

221111000

It can be seen that the algorithm has produced the same code to identify the second isosceles triangle. The algorithm can now be stated more formally as follows:

1. Enter coordinates of vertices
2. Calculate the squared Pythagorean distance between all vertex pairs
3. Sort these distances into descending order
4. Divide all distances by the smallest non-zero value to produce ratios
5. Concatenate these ratios into a string
6. Compare string with known strings
7. If match found, state corresponding shape name
8. If no match, request shape name

The algorithm is now coded as the following program:

```
Option Explicit
Dim intCounter As Integer
Private Sub Command1_Click()
'Simple pattern recognition
```

```
'Declare vertex total
Dim intVertex As Integer

'Array for coordinates of vertices
Dim intGridX(5) As Integer
Dim intGridY(5) As Integer

'Graphics coordinates for side of shape
Dim intStartX As Integer
Dim intStartY As Integer
Dim intEndX As Integer
Dim intEndY As Integer

'Declare next vertex to join
Dim intJoin As Integer

'Declare loop control variable for pattern code
Dim intOther As Integer
'Declare array for pattern code
Dim intCode(25) As Integer

'Declare counter for pattern code
Dim intCodeCount As Integer

'Declare shape string
Dim strShape As String

'Declare pattern array
Dim strPattern(10, 2) As String

'Declare counter for pattern array
Dim intPatternNum As Integer
intPatternNum = 0

'Declare variables for sort routine
'and pattern recognition
Dim intCopy As Integer
Dim Flag As Boolean

'Declare minimum distance
Dim intMin As Integer

'Exit criterion
Dim strChoice As String

'Main program loop
Do

'Place grid on display
Grid

'Request coordinates for vertices
intVertex = InputBox("Enter number of vertices")
For intCounter = 1 To intVertex
intGridX(intCounter) = InputBox("Enter X- coordinate")
intGridY(intCounter) = InputBox("Enter Y- coordinate")
Next intCounter

'Add shape to grid
For intCounter = 1 To intVertex
```

```
'Boolean expression calculates next vertex to draw to
intJoin = intCounter + 1 + (intCounter = intVertex) * intVertex

'Calculate graphics coordinates for start of side
intStartX = intGridX(intCounter) * 400 + 100
intStartY = intGridY(intCounter) * 400 + 100
'Calculate graphics coordinates for end of side
intEndX = intGridX(intJoin) * 400 + 100
intEndY = intGridY(intJoin) * 400 + 100

'Draw side of shape from current vertex to next
ForeColor = vbBlack
Line (intStartX, intStartY)-(intEndX, intEndY)

Next intCounter

'Shape is now complete on grid
'Begin pattern recognition

'Calculate Pythagorean distances between vertices
'and place in pattern code array
intCodeCount = 0
For intCounter = 1 To intVertex
For intOther = 1 To intVertex
intCodeCount = intCodeCount + 1
'Calculate square of vertex distance
intCode(intCodeCount) = Int((intGridX(intCounter) - intGridX(intOther)) ^
2 + (intGridY(intCounter) - intGridY(intOther)) ^ 2)
Next intOther
Next intCounter

'Sort code array into descending order
Do
Flag = False
For intCounter = 1 To intVertex ^ 2 - 1
If intCode(intCounter) <intCode(intCounter + 1) Then
Flag = True
intCopy = intCode(intCounter)
intCode(intCounter) = intCode(intCounter + 1)
intCode(intCounter + 1) = intCopy
End If
Next intCounter
Loop Until Flag = False

'Find minimum non-zero distance
intMin = 1000
For intCounter = 1 To intVertex ^ 2
If intCode(intCounter) <intMin And intCode(intCounter)   0 Then
intMin = intCode(intCounter)
End If
Next intCounter

'Initialise shape string
strShape = ""
'Reduce code to ratios
'and place in shape string
For intCounter = 1 To intVertex ^ 2
intCopy = intCode(intCounter) / intMin
strShape = strShape + Str$(intCopy)
Next intCounter
```

```
'Check if pattern is recognised
intCounter = 0
Flag = False
Do
intCounter = intCounter + 1
If strShape = strPattern(intCounter, 1) Then
Flag = True
CurrentX = 0
CurrentY = 0
Print "Shape is "; strPattern(intCounter, 2)
End If
Loop Until Flag = True Or intCounter >= intPatternNum

'Add shape to array
If Flag = False Then
intPatternNum = intPatternNum + 1
strPattern(intPatternNum, 1) = strShape
strPattern(intPatternNum, 2) = InputBox("Please type name of shape")
End If

'End of main loop
strChoice = InputBox("Another shape Y/N?")
Loop Until strChoice = "N"

End Sub
Sub Grid()
Cls
'Show grid of squares
ForeColor = vbCyan
For intCounter = 100 To 8100 Step 400
'Draw vertical lines
Line (intCounter, 100)-(intCounter, 8100)
'Draw horizontal lines
Line (100, intCounter)-(8100, intCounter)
Next intCounter
End Sub
```

A series of screen dumps can now show the program in operation.

In the first a small right angled triangle has been entered by typing the coordinates:

(1, 1)
(5, 1)
(1, 5)

The program has then drawn the triangle, which appears in the top left-hand corner of the grid. It has not been recognized by the program and so a prompt has appeared, requesting that a name is given. The word TRIANGLE is entered (see Figure 3.64).

Immediately the screen clears and a fresh grid erases the triangle.

Now a very small square, the smallest possible in fact, is drawn by typing the coordinates:

(15, 16)
(16, 16)
(16, 17)
(15, 17)

This shape also is not yet known by the program and so again a request is made for a name to be given. The word SQUARE is typed in (see Figure 3.65).

The next shape is a second triangle, added to the grid by entering the coordinates:

(5, 19)
(11, 13)
(11, 19)

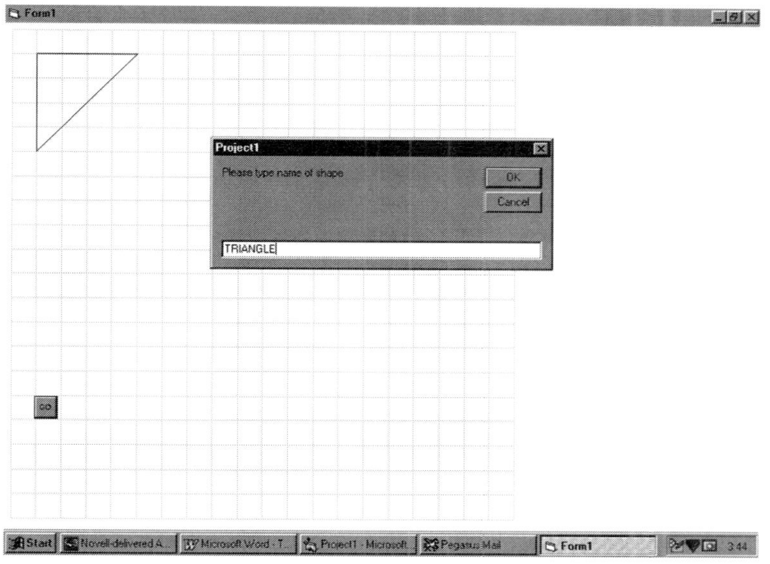

Figure 3.64

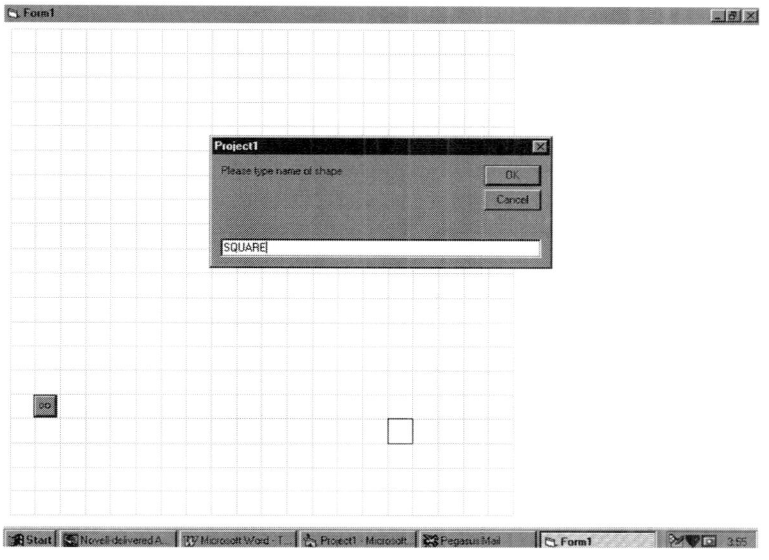

Figure 3.65

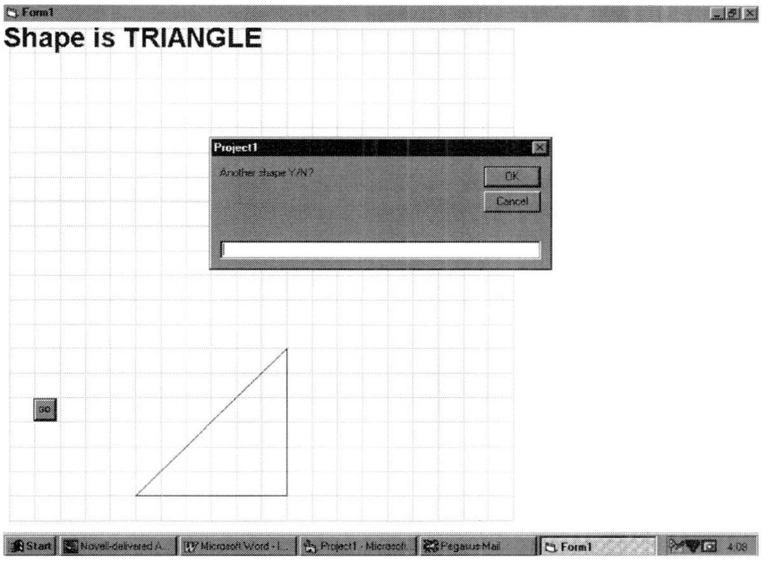

Figure 3.66

This triangle is right angled, like the previous one, but it is considerably larger and has been rotated through 180 degrees. Nevertheless the pattern recognition algorithm can see that it is essentially the same shape as the first triangle and so gives the appropriate name (see Figure 3.66).

Now another square is typed in. This has the coordinates:

(3, 11)
(11, 11)
(11, 19)
(3, 19)

The program names it correctly, despite the considerable difference in size to the previous example of a square (see Figure 3.67).

As a final example a square is typed in which has been rotated through 45 degrees to become a diamond shape, a trick which sometimes confuses people but not the algorithm used by the program. The coordinates for the square are:

(10, 11)
(14, 15)
(10, 19)
(6, 15)

The square is identified (see Figure 3.68).

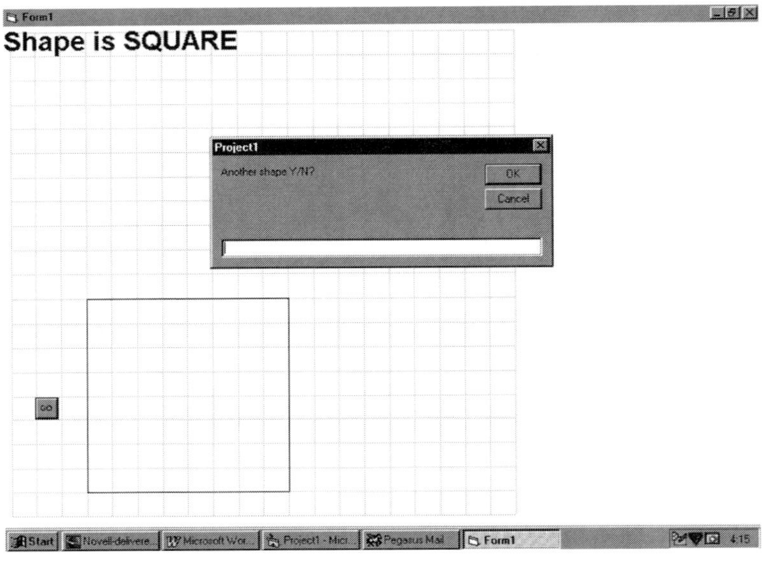

Figure 3.67

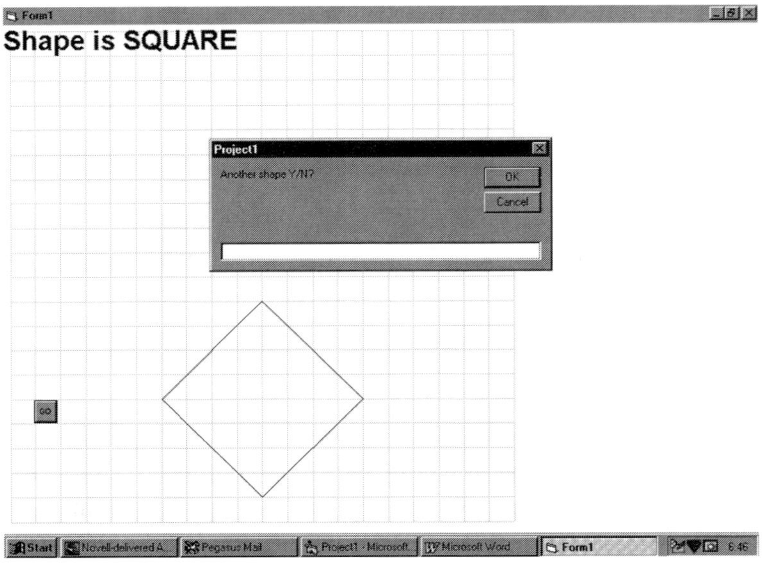

Figure 3.68

Program documentation

The loop control variable intCounter is used in two separate procedures and is declared immediately after Option Explicit:

```
Option Explicit
Dim intCounter As Integer
```

The first procedure then begins with a comment which indicates the problem that the program is designed to solve:

```
Private Sub Command1_Click()
'Simple pattern recognition
```

A variable, intVertex, is then declared which will store the number of vertices of the shape that the user draws on the screen:

```
'Declare vertex total
Dim intVertex As Integer
```

Two arrays are used to hold the coordinates of the vertices of the shape entered. These are intGridX() and intGridY(), for the x- and y-coordinates. These are coordinates on the 20×20 grid that appears on the screen, and not actual graphics coordinates on the Visual Basic form. This is reflected by the 'Grid' that appears in the two array names.

It is assumed that the shape will not be too complex and so both arrays are dimensioned to have five locations, ignoring the zeroth.

```
'Array for coordinates of vertices
Dim intGridX(5) As Integer
Dim intGridY(5) As Integer
```

Another four variables are then needed to draw each shape on the grid, line by line. These variables will represent actual graphics coordinates, calculated from the grid coordinates held in the two arrays, and so will be able to be used directly in the Visual Basic graphic primitive Line statement. The four variables correspond to the x- and y-coordinates of both the start position and end position for each side of the current shape being drawn on the grid. The coordinates of the start of each side are (intStartX, intStartY) and the coordinates of the end of the side are (intEndX, intEndY):

```
'Graphics coordinates for side of shape
Dim intStartX As Integer
Dim intStartY As Integer
Dim intEndX As Integer
Dim intEndY As Integer
```

The algorithm which draws each side of the shape requires a variable which identifies the end of the current side as the grid coordinates in the two arrays. This variable is intJoin, which will first be calculated by the algorithm as a common subscript in intGridX() and intGridY():

```
'Declare next vertex to join
Dim intJoin As Integer
```

Calculating the distances between the vertices of the shape at the beginning of the pattern recognition algorithm requires two nested loops. An additional loop counter must therefore be declared to supplement intCounter:

```
'Declare loop control variable for pattern code
Dim intOther As Integer
```

An array is then dimensioned to have 25 locations for the maximum possible combination of inter-vertex distances, which is 5×5 for a shape with five vertices. This array, intCode(), will hold integral values because as explained above the square of the Pythagorean distance is used for the identification code. It would be an unnecessary complication to calculate square roots in order to define the actual distance:

```
'Declare array for pattern code
Dim intCode(25) As Integer
```

Generating the squared distances to insert into the intCode() array will require a third counter to be incremented within the nested loops. This is the variable intCodeCount:

```
'Declare counter for pattern code
Dim intCodeCount As Integer
```

The array values held in intCode() will eventually be converted into a single string that identifies the shape. Using a string, rather than an array of values, makes it far easier to check whether this particular shape has been encountered before, or whether it is a fresh shape for which a name should be requested from the user. The shape-identifying string is declared as strShape:

```
'Declare shape string
Dim strShape As String
```

The shapes that the program learns have to be recorded. This is the role of a two-dimensional array, strPattern(), which is able to store both the identifying string and the name of up to 10 different shapes. The array has a set of 10 pairs of locations. In each pair the first position stores the shape string calculated by the pattern recognition algorithm. The second position in the pair holds the name of the shape, which initially has to be typed in by the user when a new shape is introduced but which subsequently is automatically identified by the program:

```
'Declare pattern array
Dim strPattern(10, 2) As String
```

The total number of shapes known at any given time by the program is held by the variable intPatternNum, which is initialized as zero:

```
'Declare counter for pattern array
Dim intPatternNum As Integer
intPatternNum = 0
```

One stage of the pattern recognition algorithm involves rearranging the squared inter-vertex distances in the intCode() array into descending order. This is achieved by a bubble sort. As in the earlier problem-solving exercise, 'Decoding secret messages' (Problem-solving Exercise 4), the bubble sort requires two additional variables. The first of these is intCopy, which enables the content of individual array locations to be exchanged. The second is the Boolean variable, Flag, which indicates when the sort routine is complete:

```
'Declare variables for sort routine
'and pattern recognition
Dim intCopy As Integer
Dim Flag As Boolean
```

The pattern recognition algorithm also requires the ratio of the inter-vertex distances to be determined. In order to do this, first the smallest non-zero distance must be found. The variable used for this is intMin:

```
'Declare minimum distance
Dim intMin As Integer
```

The last variable to be declared is strChoice, which permits exit from the main program loop:

```
'Exit criterion
Dim strChoice As String
```

The pattern recognition program can now begin. There is no limit to the number of shapes that the user can enter, although as explained above the number of individual shapes which can be entered is (arbitrarily) limited to 10. The program code is therefore all placed within one main conditional loop which will allow the user to continue entering shapes indefinitely:

```
'Main program loop
Do
```

Each time a new shape is investigated a fresh grid of 20 rows and 20 columns of small squares is placed on the display. This allows the user to design the required shape by entering the *x*- and *y*-coordinates of its vertices. The 20 × 20 grid is created by a call to the separate procedure, Grid:

```
'Place grid on display
Grid
```

The method for drawing the shape is extremely simple and just requires the user to enter the vertex coordinates directly. First the number of vertices is assigned to the variable intVertex. It would be a relatively minor modification to validate the user's entry at this point. An additional Do loop could check that the number of vertices did not exceed five. (As the program is written, an uncooperative user could easily crash it here):

```
'Request coordinates for vertices
intVertex = InputBox("Enter number of vertices")
```

The value of intVertex that has been entered is then used to control a For loop which assigns the user's input directly to the two arrays, intGridX() and intGridY(), that record the vertices of the shape. The range of each coordinate is 1–20, with the *y*-coordinate being measured from the top of the grid. This matches the way that *y*-coordinates increase from the top to the bottom of the display:

```
For intCounter = 1 To intVertex
intGridX(intCounter) = InputBox("Enter X- coordinate")
intGridY(intCounter) = InputBox("Enter Y- coordinate")
Next intCounter
```

Another For loop now draws the shape on the grid, according to the values that have just been placed into the intGridX() and intGridY() arrays. Again the loop control variable, intCounter, ranges from 1 to the value assigned to intVertex by the user:

```
'Add shape to grid
For intCounter = 1 To intVertex
```

Each repeat of this For loop adds just one side to the shape. The vertex at the start of the line, and the vertex at the end, must be identified for each repeat. For example, if a square or other quadrilateral is being drawn, the way in which the start and end vertex are related to the loop control variable will be like this:

First repeat:
intCounter = 1
Start vertex = 1
End vertex = 2

Second repeat:
intCounter = 2
Start vertex = 2
End vertex = 3

Third repeat:
intCounter = 3
Start vertex = 3
End vertex = 4

Fourth repeat:
intCounter = 4
Start vertex = 4
End vertex = 1

It can be seen that for each repeat of the loop the value needed for the start vertex is the same as the value of the loop control variable, intCounter. Similarly the value of the end vertex is just one more than the value of intCounter, except for the last repeat of the loop. For this the end vertex is 1.

It is quite easy to use a Boolean expression to calculate the value for the end vertex and assign it to the variable, intJoin. For all repeats of the loop, except the final one, intJoin is given by:

```
intJoin = intCounter + 1
```

Then, for the final repeat, the value must be 1.

This can be accomplished if an additional expression is added which has a value of zero for all loop repeats except the last one, at which point it should equal minus the value of intCounter and hence cancel it out to leave just the value of 1. A Boolean expression is clearly indicated and a little thought shows that the value of (intCounter = intVertex) has almost the property required. For all loop repeats except the last this expression will be false. Its value will be zero. For the last repeat, however, it will be true and so it will evaluate as (–1). If the expression is multiplied by intCounter, to give (intCounter = intVertex) * intCounter, precisely the behaviour required has been generated. This expression is zero until the final repeat. Here it is equal to –(intCounter).

The expression for intJoin can therefore be modified to:

```
'Boolean expression calculates next vertex to draw to
intJoin = intCounter + 1 + (intCounter = intVertex) * intVertex
```

The For loop can now use the values of the loop control variable, intCounter, and the value of intJoin to calculate the graphics coordinates of both ends of each side of the shape, and hence draw it using the Line statement.

Both intCounter and intJoin will act as subscripts for the grid variables held in the intGridX() and intGridY()arrays. The values found here then have to be converted into the coordinates required for the display. The grid variables for the start of the side will be intGriX(intCounter), which gives the *x*-coordinate of the starting vertex, intStartX, and intGridY(intCounter), which gives the *y*-coordinate of the start, intStartY. Both of these values are scaled up by multiplying by 400, and then a displacement of 100 is added to move the point diagonally down and across the display. These numbers, of course, match the way in which the grid is drawn in the separate procedure, Sub Grid():

```
'Calculate graphics coordinates for start of side
intStartX = intGridX(intCounter) * 400 + 100
intStartY = intGridY(intCounter) * 400 + 100
```

The *x*- and *y*-coordinates of the end of the side, intEndX and intEndY are now calculated by two expressions which are identical except for the substitution of intJoin in the place of intCounter:

```
'Calculate graphics coordinates for end of side
intEndX = intGridX(intJoin) * 400 + 100
intEndY = intGridY(intJoin) * 400 + 100
```

Now that values have been calculated for intStartX, intStartY, intEndX and intEndY, the side of the shape can be superimposed in black upon the grid. (This has been drawn in cyan by Sub Grid() and so the contrast is effective):

```
'Draw side of shape from current vertex to next
ForeColor = vbBlack
Line (intStartX, intStartY)-(intEndX, intEndY)
```

The For loop drawing the shape ends when all the sides are completed:

```
Next intCounter
```

At this stage in the program the shape has been drawn and the pattern recognition can begin. Comments indicate this fact in the listing:

```
'Shape is now complete cn grid
'Begin pattern recognition
```

The first step in the pattern recognition algorithm is to calculate the square of the distance between every possible pair of vertices of the shape that has been placed on the grid. For example, if a quadrilateral has been drawn there will be four vertices and so 16 pairs of squared distances (see Figure 3.69):

Square of the distance between vertex 1 and vertex 1
Square of the distance between vertex 1 and vertex 2
Square of the distance between vertex 1 and vertex 3
Square of the distance between vertex 1 and vertex 4

Square of the distance between vertex 2 and vertex 1
Square of the distance between vertex 2 and vertex 2
Square of the distance between vertex 2 and vertex 3
Square of the distance between vertex 2 and vertex 4

Square of the distance between vertex 3 and vertex 1
Square of the distance between vertex 3 and vertex 2
Square of the distance between vertex 3 and vertex 3
Square of the distance between vertex 3 and vertex 4

Square of the distance between vertex 4 and vertex 1
Square of the distance between vertex 4 and vertex 2
Square of the distance between vertex 4 and vertex 3
Square of the distance between vertex 4 and vertex 4

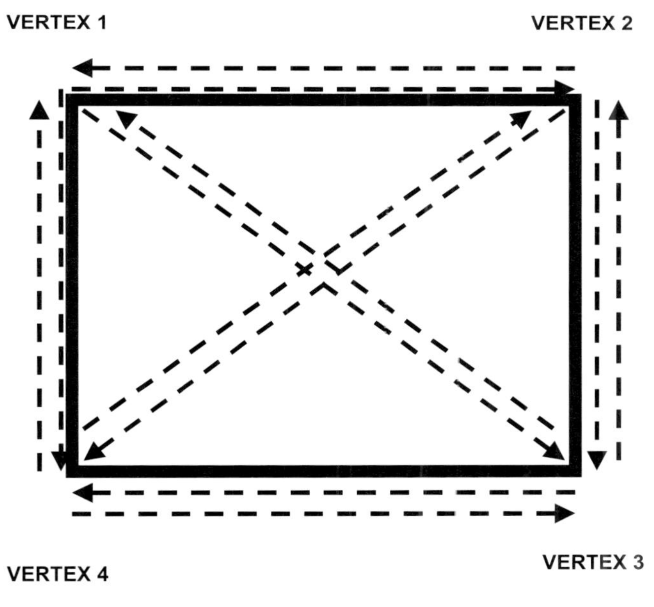

Figure 3.69 *Inter-vertex distances for a quadrilateral*

Four of these distances will be zero because each of the vertices naturally coincides with itself. (It would be a simple modification to the program to eliminate these distances by placing a conditional statement in the body of the nested loops in the code below.) The zero distances are naturally not indicated on the diagram.

The inter-vertex squared distances are placed in the intCode() array by the nested For loops which follow. At each repeat of the inner of these loops a squared distance is generated which needs a fresh array location to which it can be assigned. This location cannot be defined by either of the control variables for the nested loops. For example, if a triangle has been drawn the two control variables will both range from 1 to 3, whereas nine separate locations will have to be addressed in the intCode() array. In order to identify these locations a counter, int CodeCount, is incremented in the nested loop body. This will automatically be incremented just the correct number of times required to identify the array locations.

This counter is initialized as zero before the loops begin:

```
'Calculate Pythagorean distances between vertices
'and place in pattern code array
intCodeCount = 0
```

The two loops then begin. The outer For loop is controlled by intCounter and the inner loop by intOther. The range for both loops is from 1 to intVertex. This means that all possible combinations of vertices will be generated, as required by the pattern recognition algorithm:

```
For intCounter = 1 To intVertex
For intOther = 1 To intVertex
```

The counter for the array locations, intCodeCount, is then incremented:

```
intCodeCount = intCodeCount + 1
```

The squared distance between each pair of vertices is now calculated and assigned to the intCode() location identified by the counter, intCode(intCodeCount). The square of the distance is calculated by the Pythagorean expression: (Difference in x-coordinate) squared + (Difference in y-coordinate) squared.

The distances are calculated as grid values and not as actual screen coordinates. As one set of vertices is being identified by intCounter, and the other by intOther, the difference in x-coordinate is therefore intGridX(intCounter) minus intGridX(intOther). Similarly the difference in y-coordinate is intGridY(intCounter) minus intGridY(intOther). Squaring and adding these expressions and assigning the result to the intCode() array therefore gives:

```
'Calculate square of vertex distance
intCode(intCodeCount) = Int((intGridX(intCounter) - intGridX(intOther)) ^
2 + (intGridY(intCounter) - intGridY(intOther)) ^ 2)
```

The nested loops then end:

```
Next intOther
Next intCounter
```

There will be (intVertex ^ 2) values in the intCode() array. The pattern recognition algorithm then requires these squared distances to be arranged into descending order. A bubble sort is employed. (This type of sorting routine is explained in some detail in Problem-solving Exercise 4.) The routine uses two further nested loops. The outer is a conditional loop which keeps repeating until no further rearranging of individual pairs of locations is taking place. This is detected by the value of the Boolean variable, Flag, remaining as False:

```
'Sort code array into descending order
Do
Flag = False
```

The inner loop looks at each pair of locations in the intCode() array in turn, identified as intCode(IntCounter) and intCode(intCounter + 1). The range of the loop counter will therefore be from 1 to the square of intVertex, less 1, as the last pair of locations to be checked will be intCode(intCounter) and intCode(intCounter + 1). Obviously the second of these will have to be the same as intCode(intVertex ^ 2):

```
For intCounter = 1 To intVertex ^ 2 - 1
```

An exchange of array location content must take place if any pair of locations has a smaller value preceding a larger:

```
If intCode(intCounter) <intCode(intCounter + 1) Then
```

The flag value is changed to True to record the fact that an exchange has occurred:

```
Flag = True
```

The contents of the two array locations are then interchanged with the aid of a third variable, intCopy:

```
intCopy = intCode(intCounter)
intCode(intCounter) = intCode(intCounter + 1)
intCode(intCounter + 1) = intCopy
End If
```

The inner loop then ends:

```
Next intCounter
```

However, the outer loop keeps repeating until the value of Flag remains False. This means that no exchanges have occurred and that all the locations in intCode() have been placed in descending order:

```
Loop Until Flag = False
```

After the inter-vertex squared distances have been placed into descending order the algorithm needs them to be reduced to a series of ratios in which each squared distance is compared with the smallest, non-zero value. This involves first calculating what the smallest non-zero value in the intCode() array is. This can be done with a single For loop which inspects each location of the array in turn, comparing it with a constantly updated minimum value.

This minimum value, intMin, is initialized with a deliberately large integer:

```
'Find minimum non-zero distance
intMin = 1000
```

The For loop then repeats for the whole range of (intVertex ^ 2) locations in the intCode() array:

```
For intCounter = 1 To intVertex ^ 2
```

Each location in turn is compared with the value of intMin. If the location value is smaller, and at the same time not equal to zero, then it is assigned to intMin:

```
If intCode(intCounter) <intMin And intCode(intCounter)   0 Then
intMin = intCode(intCounter)
End If
```

This means that by the end of the For loop the value of intMin is equal to the smallest non-zero value in intCode:

```
Next intCounter
```

This smallest value is now used to create the set of ratios. The division required to do this takes place in a further loop which also converts the array values of intCode() into a single string, strString. Although an array had been required for the sorting and calculating of ratios which has now produced the unique code for the shape, once this code has been created it is easier to work with it as a string.

First strShape is initialized as an empty string:

```
'Initialise shape string
strShape = ""
```

A loop then checks the (intVertex^2) values in the intCode() array:

```
'Reduce code to ratios
'and place in shape string
For intCounter = 1 To intVertex ^ 2
```

Each value in the array locations is first converted to a ratio by division by intMin and this is then assigned to the variable intCopy:

```
intCopy = intCode(intCounter) / intMin
```

Next intCopy is converted to a string by the Str$ function and concatenated on to strShape:

```
strShape = strShape + Str$(intCopy)
```

By the end of the loop a unique string has been created, corresponding to the shape drawn by the user on the grid. It must be stressed here that this string is independent of the size of the shape because of the way that all the distances have been reduced to ratios of the smallest. The string is also independent of the orientation of the shape as a result of the distances being sorted into order:

```
Next intCounter
```

The program is now ready to check whether the shape that has been drawn by the user is one that has been encountered already. If it is, it will be named. If it is not, the program will request a name which it will then associate with the string generated for the shape:

```
'Check if pattern is recognised
```

The existing shapes known to the program are held in the strPattern() array. The pattern strings in this array are therefore checked against the current value that has been generated for strShape. This is done in a Do loop. First a counter for this loop is initialized as zero:

```
intCounter = 0
```

The Boolean variable, Flag, is initialized as False. This variable will be part of the exit condition from the loop. A value of False indicates that the shape has not been recognized. If it is recognized, Flag will be assigned a value of True:

```
Flag = False
```

The loop then begins:

```
Do
```

Immediately the counter for the loop is incremented:

```
intCounter = intCounter + 1
```

The pattern strings in the two-dimensional strPattern() array are held in the first position of the location pairs, with the associated name in the second position. The patterns are therefore identified in the loop as strPattern(intCounter, 1). The condition which indicates that a shape drawn by the user has been matched in the array is:

```
If strShape = strPattern(intCounter, 1) Then
```

If a shape is identified the flag must be reset to True:

```
Flag = True
```

The name of the shape can now be given. Coordinates are chosen to place the text at the top of the display:

```
CurrentX = 0
CurrentY = 0
```

The name is found in the second position of the array pair:

```
Print "Shape is "; strPattern(intCounter, 2)
```

The condition then ends:

```
End If
```

The Do loop which searches the strPattern() array exits when either the shape is identified, as shown by a value for the Boolean flag variable of True, or when the counter reaches the number of known shapes:

```
Loop Until Flag = True Or intCounter >= intPatternNum
```

Outside the Do loop a new shape can be named. This will be necessary when the loop has ended with value for Flag of False, which indicates that the shape is not already named in the strPattern() array:

```
'Add shape to array
If Flag = False Then
```

First the total number of shapes recorded in the strPattern() array is increased by 1 by incrementing the variable intPatternNum:

```
intPatternNum = intPatternNum + 1
```

Then the new shape code is assigned to the array location identified by the updated value of intPatternNum:

```
strPattern(intPatternNum, 1) = strShape
```

Finally the user is asked to name the shape. Whatever is typed at this point is assigned to the second position of the array pair selected by intPatternNum:

```
strPattern(intPatternNum, 2) = InputBox("Please type name of shape")
```

The condition then ends:

```
End If
```

The main loop of the program now ends with an exit condition which requires the user to make a deliberate choice of '*N*':

```
'End of main loop
strChoice = InputBox("Another shape Y/N?")
Loop Until strChoice = "N"

End Sub
```

The grid for the program is drawn by a separate procedure. First the display is cleared:

```
Sub Grid()
Cls
```

The colour chosen for the grid is cyan as this will allow the shapes drawn in black to be easily distinguished:

```
'Show grid of squares
ForeColor = vbCyan
```

The grid occupies a square situated between the points (100, 100), (8100, 100), (8100, 8100) and (100, 8100). The vertical lines which will divide up this area are drawn 400 apart horizontally and between the *y*-coordinate values of 100 and 8100. The lines are drawn in a For loop which steps from a value of 100 to 8100. The size of the step is 400 and the value of the loop control variable, intCounter, is used as the *x*-coordinate in a Line statement:

```
For intCounter = 100 To 8100 Step 400
'Draw vertical lines
Line (intCounter, 100)-(intCounter, 8100)
```

The same values for intCounter are also used as the *y*-coordinate in a similar Line statement which allows the horizontal lines to be produced:

```
'Draw horizontal lines
Line (100, intCounter)-(8100, intCounter)
```

The fact that both sets of coordinates are incremented by 400 at each repeat of the loop leads to small squares, sized 400 × 400, being produced by the end of the For loop. They create a grid of 400 squares on the larger square of 8000 × 8000.

```
Next intCounter
End Sub
```

Advanced Exercise 7: Maze solving

When microprocessors first became available to the general public there was great enthusiasm amongst hobbyists directed towards building robot 'mice' which could search a maze, turning and twisting through its corridors and junctions until they found the robot equivalent of cheese. Once it had been located by a blind search, the mouse could then navigate to its goal by a far more direct route. The computer controlling the mouse appeared to be intelligent.

A naive example of artificial intelligence like this one can be produced by quite simple programming techniques. In this final programming exercise a simulated robot searches a simulated maze and also learns how to simplify a random search into something far more direct.

Figure 3.70 shows a typical screen display with the robot searching a maze looking for its goal. Once this is found a more intelligent route is calculated.

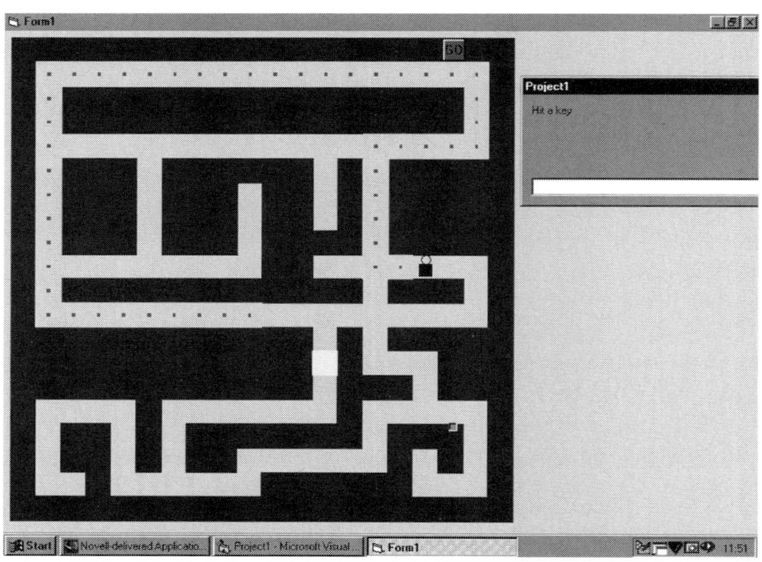

Figure 3.70

Program listing

```
Option Explicit
Private Sub Command1_Click()

'Maze

'Loop counters
Dim intX As Integer
```

```
Dim intY As Integer
Dim intCounter As Integer

'Coordinate variables for maze cells
'required to generate graphic
Dim intCellX As Integer
Dim intCellY As Integer

'Array to represent maze
Dim intMaze(20, 20) As Integer

'Strings for definition of maze walls
Dim strWall(20) As String

'Define maze walls as strings
strWall(1) = "11111111111111111111"
strWall(2) = "10000000000000000001"
strWall(3) = "10111111111111111101"
strWall(4) = "10111111111111111101"
strWall(5) = "10000000000000000001"
strWall(6) = "10111011111101011111"
strWall(7) = "10111011101101011111"
strWall(8) = "10111011101101011111"
strWall(9) = "10111011101111011111"
strWall(10) = "10000000001100000001"
strWall(11) = "10111111111111011101"
strWall(12) = "10000000000000000001"
strWall(13) = "11111111111101011111"
strWall(14) = "11111111111101000111"
strWall(15) = "11111111111101110111"
strWall(16) = "10000100000001000001"
strWall(17) = "10110101111111011101"
strWall(18) = "10110101100000010101"
strWall(19) = "10010000001111110001"
strWall(20) = "11111111111111111111"

'Transfer maze definition into main array
For intY = 1 To 20
For intX = 1 To 20
intMaze(intX, intY) = Val(Mid$(strWall(21 - intY), intX, 1))
Next intX
Next intY

'String for definition of adjacent cells
Dim strDirection As String
strDirection = "23322112"

'Arrays for definition of adjacent cells
Dim intAdjacentX(4) As Integer
Dim intAdjacentY(4) As Integer

'Transfer directions into arrays
For intCounter = 1 To 4
intAdjacentX(intCounter) = Val(Mid$(strDirection, (intCounter * 2 - 1),
1)) - 2
intAdjacentY(intCounter) = Val(Mid$(strDirection, (intCounter * 2), 1)) - 2
Next intCounter

'Total of vacant adjacent cells
Dim intVacant As Integer
```

```
'Arrays to record junction coordinates
Dim intJunctionX(10) As Integer
Dim intJunctionY(10) As Integer

'Total number of junctions encountered
Dim intJunctionT As Integer

'Current junction encountered
Dim intJunctionN As Integer
'Number of times junction visited
Dim intJunctionV(10, 4) As Integer

Dim intFlag As Integer

'Coordinates for robot's position
Dim intRobotX As Integer
Dim intRobotY As Integer
intRobotX = 10
intRobotY = 9

'Coordinates for goal
Dim intGoalX As Integer
Dim intGoalY As Integer
intGoalX = 13
intGoalY = 7

'Array stores possible directions
Dim intDirection(4) As Integer

'Initialise robot direction
Dim intForward As Integer
intForward = 3
Dim intReverse As Integer

'Array stores initial route
Dim intRoute(100) As Integer

'Distance travelled
Dim intDistance As Integer
intDistance = 1

'Loop counter for route pruning
Dim intJunctionC As Integer

'First and last occurrences of junction
'in route array
Dim intFirst As Integer
Dim intLast As Integer

'Array stores pruned copy of route
Dim intRouteCopy(100) As Integer

'Loop counter for copy of route
Dim intCopyCounter As Integer

'Enable next move
Dim NextMove As String
'Show maze
ForeColor = vbBlue
For intX = 1 To 20
```

```
For intY = 1 To 20
If intMaze(intX, intY) = 1 Then
intCellX = (intX - 1) * 400 + 100
intCellY = (21 - intY) * 400 + 100
Line (intCellX, intCellY)-(intCellX + 400, intCellY - 400), , BF
End If
Next intY
Next intX

'Show goal position
ForeColor = vbYellow
intCellX = (intGoalX - 1) * 400 + 100
intCellY = (21 - intGoalY) * 400 + 100
Line (intCellX, intCellY)-(intCellX + 400, intCellY - 400), , BF

'Maze search begins
Do

'Determine reverse direction
intReverse = intForward + 2 + (4 * (intForward > 2))

'Show robot's position

'Select appropriate cell
intCellX = (intRobotX - 1) * 400 + 100
intCellY = (21 - intRobotY) * 400 + 100
'Select colour
ForeColor = vbBlack
'Robot body
Line (intCellX + 100, intCellY - 50)-(intCellX + 300, intCellY - 250),
, BF
'Robot head
Circle (intCellX + 200, intCellY - 325), 75

'Count vacant adjacent cells
intVacant = 0
For intCounter = 1 To 4
If intMaze(intRobotX + intAdjacentX(intCounter), intRobotY +
intAdjacentY(intCounter)) = 0 Then
'Count vacant cell
intVacant = intVacant + 1
'Record direction
intDirection(intCounter) = intCounter
Else
intDirection(intCounter) = 0
End If
Next intCounter

'Determine direction for dead end
If intVacant = 1 Then intForward = intReverse

'Determine direction for straight path or bend
If intVacant = 2 Then
For intCounter = 1 To 4
If intDirection(intCounter)  0 And intDirection(intCounter)  intReverse
Then
intForward = intDirection(intCounter)
End If
Next intCounter
End If
```

```
'Determine direction for a junction
If intVacant > 2 Then

'Identify known junction
intJunctionN = 0
For intCounter = 0 To intJunctionT
If intJunctionX(intCounter) = intRobotX And
intJunctionY(intCounter) = intRobotY Then
intJunctionN = intCounter
End If
Next intCounter

'New junction
If intJunctionN = 0 Then

'Number new junction
intJunctionT = intJunctionT + 1
intJunctionN = intJunctionT

'Record junction coordinates
intJunctionX(intJunctionN) = intRobotX
intJunctionY(intJunctionN) = intRobotY

'Record available directions at junction
For intCounter = 1 To 4
intJunctionV(intJunctionN, intCounter) = intDirection(intCounter)
Next intCounter

'Remove direction junction approached
intJunctionV(intJunctionN, intReverse) = 0

End If

'Choose a direction to exit junction
intFlag = 0
For intCounter = 1 To 4
If intJunctionV(intJunctionN, intCounter)   0 And intFlag = 0
Then
intFlag = 1
intForward = intJunctionV(intJunctionN, intCounter)
intJunctionV(intJunctionN, intCounter) = 0
End If
Next intCounter

'Record route taken
intRoute(intDistance) = intJunctionN
intRoute(intDistance + 1) = intForward
intDistance = intDistance + 2

'Display route
PicDisplay.Cls
For intCounter = 1 To intDistance - 1
PicDisplay.Print intRoute(intCounter);
Next intCounter

End If 'End of if for whole of junction code

'Prompt for next move
NextMove = InputBox("Hit a key", , , 8200, 1000)

'Erase robot position
```

```
ForeColor = vbCyan
Line (intCellX, intCellY)-(intCellX + 400, intCellY - 400), , BF
ForeColor = vbRed
Line (intCellX + 180, intCellY - 180)-(intCellX + 220, intCellY - 220),
, BF

'Update robot coordinates
intRobotX = intRobotX + intAdjacentX(intForward)
intRobotY = intRobotY + intAdjacentY(intForward)

'Robot searches for goal
Loop Until (intRobotX = intGoalX And intRobotY = intGoalY)

'Prune unnecessary route

'Main loop checks each juntion in turn
For intJunctionC = 1 To intJunctionT
intFirst = 0
intLast = 0

'Inner loop checks for duplication of junction in route
For intCounter = 1 To intDistance - 1 Step 2
If intRoute(intCounter) = intJunctionC And intFirst = 0 Then
intFirst = intCounter
End If
If intRoute(intCounter) = intJunctionC Then
intLast = intCounter
End If
Next intCounter

'Route pruning required
If intFirst  0 And intLast  0 Then

'Delete intervening array values
intCopyCounter = 0
For intCounter = 1 To intFirst
intCopyCounter = intCopyCounter + 1
intRouteCopy(intCopyCounter) = intRoute(intCounter)
Next intCounter
For intCounter = intLast + 1 To intDistance
intCopyCounter = intCopyCounter + 1
intRouteCopy(intCopyCounter) = intRoute(intCounter)
Next intCounter

'Transfer shortened route back to array
For intCounter = 1 To intDistance
If intRouteCopy(intCounter)  0 Then
intRoute(intCounter) = intRouteCopy(intCounter)
intRouteCopy(intCounter) = 0
Else
intRoute(intCounter) = 0
End If
Next intCounter

'New route length
intDistance = intDistance - intLast + intFirst
End If

'End of main loop
Next intJunctionC
```

```
'Display pruned route
Picture1.Cls
For intCounter = 1 To intDistance - 1
Picture1.Print intRoute(intCounter);
Next intCounter

End Sub
```

Program documentation

The program begins with the usual comment giving the title:

```
Option Explicit
Private Sub Command1_Click()

'Maze
```

Three loop control variables are then declared:

```
'Loop counters
Dim intX As Integer
Dim intY As Integer
Dim intCounter As Integer
```

When the maze is drawn on the display it is constructed as a series of filled squares or cells. A typical square is defined by the *x*- and *y*-coordinates of its bottom left-hand corner. Two variables, intCellX and intCell, are declared as these coordinates:

```
'Coordinate variables for maze cells
'required to generate graphic
Dim intCellX As Integer
Dim intCellY As Integer
```

The maze itself is defined as a two-dimensional array, intMaze(). This will hold numerical values of 1 or 0. A value of 1 represents a single square section of maze wall. A value of 0 corresponds to free corridor space. The array is declared to allow 20 rows and columns for the maze. (The zero locations are ignored.)

```
'Array to represent maze
Dim intMaze(20, 20) As Integer
```

The array locations are filled with defining values of 1 and 0 from strings of appropriate digits held within the program code. These strings can be edited quite easily to produce a different maze. An alternative would be to have an input routine which allowed the user to define a fresh maze when the program was initially executed. The current method has been chosen for simplicity of coding, and also as it allows the same maze to be tested repeatedly.

There are 20 strings, each determining the filled and vacant maze positions of just one of the rows across the maze. The strings all belong to the same array, strWall(). This means that each row of the maze is referred to by a single subscripted variable. As a result the code which transfers the digits from the strings into the intMaze() array is uncomplicated.

The strWall() array is first declared:

```
'Strings for definition of maze walls
Dim strWall(20) As String
```

Individual assignments of the strings defining the maze are then made to each location of the strWall() array. An advantage of this method is that it is extremely easy to visualize the appearance of the maze from the lines of code for the strings. It is also quite simple to edit the strings to make minor adjustments to the arrangement of walls and corridors. New turns and junctions can be typed in very quickly and used to test the maze-solving algorithms used by the robot:

```
'Define maze walls as strings
strWall(1) = "11111111111111111111"
strWall(2) = "10000000000000000001"
strWall(3) = "10111111111111111101"
strWall(4) = "10111111111111111101"
strWall(5) = "10000000000000000001"
strWall(6) = "10111011111101011111"
strWall(7) = "10111011101101011111"
strWall(8) = "10111011101101011111"
strWall(9) = "10111011101111011111"
strWall(10) = "10000000001100000001"
strWall(11) = "10111111111111011101"
strWall(12) = "10000000000000000001"
strWall(13) = "11111111111101011111"
strWall(14) = "11111111111101000111"
strWall(15) = "11111111111101110111"
strWall(16) = "10000100000001000001"
strWall(17) = "10110101111111011101"
strWall(18) = "10110101100000010101"
strWall(19) = "10010000001111110001"
strWall(20) = "11111111111111111111"
```

The strings given here only demonstrate a typical maze and should be altered whenever required to test a different configuration of walls and corridors.

The information held in these strings is now transferred to the intMaze() array. This is done by two nested For Next loops using two of the loop control variables declared above. The outer loop, controlled by intY, reads down the list. There is a tiny sleight of hand here. The strings have been arranged in the intuitive way the user would expect. The pattern of the strings in the listing is the same as the appearance of the maze. This means that strWall(1) represents the top of the maze. However, in the intMaze() array the top of the maze will be defined by array elements with a y-subscript of 20. This accounts for the expression (21 – intY) which appears in the code below. There is no equivalent problem with the x-subscript.

The Mid$ function is used to remove each 1 or 0 from the strings. Val produces the numerical equivalent. This is then assigned to the appropriate array location as defined by intMaze(intX, intY):

```
'Transfer maze definition into main array
For intY = 1 To 20
For intX = 1 To 20
intMaze(intX, intY) = Val(Mid$(strWall(21 - intY), intX, 1))
Next intX
Next intY
```

The robot's position in the maze is represented by coordinates (intRobotX, intRobotY). These will correspond to the individual square cells of the maze and also to the array locations in intMaze(). Obviously the robot is only allowed to move into spaces that are vacant, and for which the value in intMaze() is zero. Conditions to make sure that it does not move into a wall, where intMaze() has a value of 1, are explained below. A prior problem to this, however, is knowing how to move the robot at all.

The robot is not permitted to move diagonally but only in the 'Up, Right, Down, Left' directions shown in Figure 3.71.

It can be seen that these moves will always consist of adding or subtracting 1, or simply leaving a coordinate the same. For convenience the four possible directions are numbered 1 to 4, beginning at 'North' and moving in a clockwise direction. It can be seen that the possible moves are then defined as:

Direction 1: Increase x-coordinate by 0, increase y-coordinate by 1
Direction 2: Increase x-coordinate by 1, increase y-coordinate by 0
Direction 3: Increase x-coordinate by 0, increase y-coordinate by –1
Direction 4: Increase x-coordinate by –1, increase y-coordinate by 0

It is useful for the code developed later in the program to regard the directions as numbered in this way. The number of the move can then act as a subscript for two arrays which define the increment (including negative values) required to the current robot coordinates in order to move in that direction.

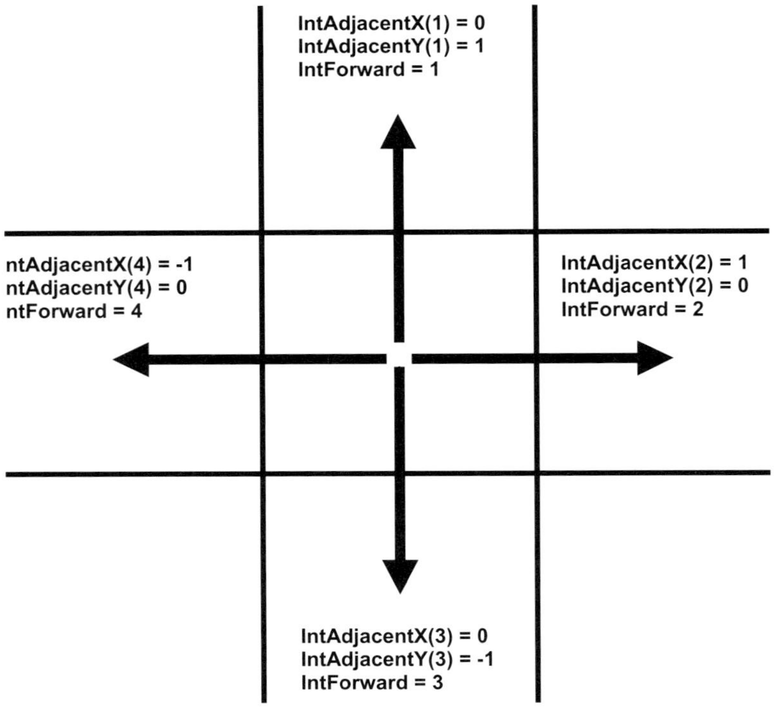

Figure 3.71 *Definition of adjacent maze cells*

Direction 1: Alter coordinates by increment in intAdjacentX(1), intAdjacentY(1)
Direction 2: Alter coordinates by increment in intAdjacentX(2), intAdjacentY(2)
Direction 3: Alter coordinates by increment in intAdjacentX(3), intAdjacentY(3)
Direction 4: Alter coordinates by increment in intAdjacentX(4), intAdjacentY(4)

The values required in the two arrays are then:

intAdjacentX(1) = 0
intAdjacentY(1) = 1

intAdjacentX(2) = 1
intAdjacentY(2) = 0

intAdjacentX(3) = 0
intAdjacentY(3) = –1

intAdjacentX(4) = –1
intAdjacentY(4) = 0

Eight lines of code, identical to these, in the program could make direct assignments to the intAdjacentX(), intAdjacentY() arrays. This is not the method adopted here. More compact code is introduced by defining all four directions as a single string and then using a For loop to insert the relevant parts of the string into the arrays.

The string is generated by first listing all the array values in the same order as the direction, with the *x*-value preceeding the *y*-value:

0, 1, 1, 0, 0, –1, –1, 0

The minus signs cause a problem and so 2 is added to all the values:

2, 3, 3, 2, 2, 1, 1, 2

Once all the values are positive they can be concatenated into a single string which holds in coded form all four directions:

23322112

This is placed in the program as strDirection:

```
'String for definition of adjacent cells
Dim strDirection As String
strDirection = "23322112"
```

The two arrays which will hold these increments are then declared:

```
'Arrays for definition of adjacent cells
Dim intAdjacentX(4) As Integer
Dim intAdjacentY(4) As Integer
```

A For loop now takes the coded directions from strDirection and places them in the arrays. The pattern to be followed is:

Direction 1: Characters 1 and 2 in strDirection
Direction 2: Characters 3 and 4 in strDirection
Direction 3: Characters 5 and 6 in strDirection
Direction 4: Characters 7 and 8 in strDirection

Clearly Mid$ can be used to obtain the correct pair of characters. The second argument in Mid$ must be one of the sequence of odd numbers 1, 3, 5 and 7 in order to match the pattern shown above. These can be generated by doubling the loop control variable and then subtracting 1. The relevant numerical values giving the increments are found with Val. Each must be reduced by subtracting 2, in a reverse of the earlier addition:

```
'Transfer directions into arrays
For intCounter = 1 To 4
intAdjacentX(intCounter) = Val(Mid$(strDirection, (intCounter * 2 - 1),
1)) - 2
intAdjacentY(intCounter) = Val(Mid$(strDirection, (intCounter * 2), 1)) - 2
Next intCounter
```

Part of the code which selects the direction for the robot to move involves counting the number of neighbouring empty maze cells. This number is assigned to the variable intVacant, which is declared here:

```
'Total of vacant adjacent cells
Dim intVacant As Integer
```

The maze navigation algorithms require that the junctions encountered by the robot are recorded. The *x*- and *y*-coordinates of the junctions are held in two arrays, intJunctionX() and intJunctionY(). An assumption is made here that a maximum of only ten junctions will be present in the maze. This is purely arbitrary and easily modified:

```
'Arrays to record junction coordinates
Dim intJunctionX(10) As Integer
Dim intJunctionY(10) As Integer
```

The total number of junctions encountered by a given stage of the robot's progress around the maze is held by the variable intJunctionT:

```
'Total number of junctions encountered
Dim intJunctionT As Integer
```

When the robot arrives at a junction it may be one of the junctions already traversed, or perhaps a new junction entirely. In either case it will be assigned a junction number, intJunctionN. This will be 1 for the first junction met, 2 for the second, up to a maximum of intJunctionT. As explained above this is the total number of junctions found. The variable intJunctionN is declared here:

```
'Current junction encountered
Dim intJunctionN As Integer
```

A further, two-dimensional array is declared which allows a record to be kept of the directions taken by the robot when it traverses a junction:

```
'Number of times junction visited
Dim intJunctionV(10, 4) As Integer
```

A flag is introduced which will be used in the routine which selects a direction to take from a junction:

```
Dim intFlag As Integer
```

The coordinates which define the robot's position in the maze are intRobotX and intRobotY. These correspond to the locations in the intMaze() array which defines the positions of walls and corridors. As a result each coordinate lies in the range 1–20. In this specfic example of a program listing the robot is given the initial coordinates (10,9). Naturally other starting positions for the robot are perfectly feasible. Care must be taken, though, not to place the robot in an impossible position. Locating it in the middle of a wall section would, in fact, not be disastrous but merely insert an extra junction into the maze. It could be possible, though, to locate the robot in a cell surrounded completely with other maze cells which were filled. This would trap it completely:

```
'Coordinates for robot's position
Dim intRobotX As Integer
Dim intRobotY As Integer
intRobotX = 10
intRobotY = 9
```

The robot has to search the maze for a goal. This is given coordinates intGoalX and intGoalY. Again it is a matter of choice where the goal is placed, and again it must be located in a corridor. The coordinates selected must correspond to a location in the intMaze() array with a value of 0. (It should be obvious that it is quite easy to set up accidentally a maze which will not lead to an effective program execution):

```
'Coordinates for goal
Dim intGoalX As Integer
Dim intGoalY As Integer
intGoalX = 13
intGoalY = 7
```

An essential part of the code which controls the robot's passage around the maze is a knowledge of the location of neighbouring vacant cells. Each time the robot moves to a new cell the adjacent positions are scanned and their status, vacant or filled, stored in the intDirection() array. This array is declared here:

```
'Array stores possible directions
Dim intDirection(4) As Integer
```

The direction currently adopted by the robot is defined by a single number. As shown on the earlier diagram, 'up' is represented by a value of 1, 'right' by 2, 'down' by 3 and 'left' by 4. The value of the direction is stored by the variable intForward. The variable is declared here and assigned an arbitrary value of 3. This means that this particular robot will initially move down, though of course the direction could easily be altered by changing the value assigned to intForward:

```
'Initialise robot direction
Dim intForward As Integer
intForward = 3
```

As well as the intForward variable it is also useful to have another variable which defines the reverse direction of the robot. For example, if the robot is moving to the right the value of intForwrd will be 2 and the reverse direction will be 4. This value is represented by the distinct variable intReverse, declared here. This does not need to be assigned a value because code further on in the listing calculates the value of intReverse from the value of intForward:

```
Dim intReverse As Integer
```

The robot's 'intelligent' maze solving requires a record to be kept of the junctions that it has travelled through and the direction taken at each junction. This information is stored in the intRoute() array:

```
'Array stores initial route
Dim intRoute(100) As Integer
```

The sequence of junctions encountered and directions taken, and hence the number of locations used in the intRoute() array, will gradually increase as the robot travels around the maze. The number of locations assigned values in intRoute() is held by the 'distance travelled' variable:

```
'Distance travelled
Dim intDistance As Integer
intDistance = 1
```

An additional loop control variable is used in the code which shortens the route taken to the goal by 'route pruning'. This produces a more sensible route by eliminating unnecessary directions taken in the initial blind search:

```
'Loop counter for route pruning
Dim intJunctionC As Integer
```

When the same junction has been visited more than once the blind search route is inefficient and needs pruning. This will be indicated by the duplication of the junction in the intRoute() array. Removing the unnecessary section of the route requires knowing where in intRoute the junction appears for the first and last time. These two positions are recorded by two separate variables:

```
'First and last occurrences of junction
'in route array
Dim intFirst As Integer
Dim intLast As Integer
```

Route pruning may take place more than once. A temporary copy of the new route generated at each pruning is placed in a second route array, intRouteCopy():

```
'Array stores pruned copy of route
Dim intRouteCopy(100) As Integer
```

The route pruning algorithm also needs another loop control variable:

```
'Loop counter for copy of route
Dim intCopyCounter As Integer
```

Dummy input is used to pause each cycle of the main control loop, halting the robot in each position it takes as it searches the maze:

```
'Enable next move
Dim NextMove As String
```

At this point in the listing all declarations have been made. The maze is now shown on the display. A colour is selected and then two nested For loops examine each location of the intMaze() array in turn:

```
'Show maze
ForeColor = vbBlue
```

```
For intX = 1 To 20
For intY = 1 To 20
```

If the array location is non-zero a section of wall needs to be shaded:

```
If intMaze(intX, intY) = 1 Then
```

The maze is built up as 400 individual cells. Each of these is, coincidentally, 400 by 400 units. The position of an individual cell is defined by graphic coordinates of the bottom left-hand corner, intCellX, intCellY.

The loop control variable intX has to range from 1 to 20. This matches the intMaze() array locations. In order to space the cells 400 apart intX will have to be multiplied by 400. However, beginning the maze 400 across the display will produce too wide a margin. The solution is to subtract 1 from intX before the multiplication takes place. This creates values of 0, 400, 800... for the *x*-coordinate of the bottom left-hand corner of each square. An extra 100 is added to move the maze slightly to the right:

```
intCellX = (intX - 1) * 400 + 100
```

The *y*-coordinate for the bottom left-hand corner of each cell is calculated in an almost identical fashion. The loop control variable intY is subtracted from 21 to take into account the way that graphic coordinates are measured from the top of the screen:

```
intCellY = (21 - intY) * 400 + 100
```

The shaded cell is then drawn with the Visual Basic Line statement. The second point for the line is offset by (400, 400). This is the top right-hand corner of the cell:

```
Line (intCellX, intCellY)-(intCellX + 400, intCellY - 400), , BF
```

The If statement and nested loops then end:

```
End If
Next intY
Next intX
```

The robot's goal is also shown by filling in one of the cells of the maze. A different colour is chosen so that it is clearly not simply another section of wall:

```
'Show goal position
ForeColor = vbYellow
```

The coordinates for the cell are calculated by the same expressions as in the nested loops:

```
intCellX = (intGoalX - 1) * 400 + 100
intCellY = (21 - intGoalY) * 400 + 100
```

The goal is then shaded by the Line statement:

```
Line (intCellX, intCellY)-(intCellX + 400, intCellY - 400), , BF
```

The robot then begins searching the maze. This takes place within one overall conditional loop which will not exit until the robot's coordinates match those of the goal. The search is blind, but an improved search strategy, the 'pruned route', is generated after the conditional loop ends.

The loop begins with Do:

```
'Maze search begins
Do
```

A value for the direction that the robot will take, intForward, has already been assigned before the loop begins. (The value will, of course, be regularly updated within the loop.) The reverse of this direction, intReverse, also has to be known in order to play a role in the route searching algorithms. Fortunately a single line of code is able to calculate intReverse from the value of intForward.

From Figure 3.71 the corresponding pairs of values are easily seen to be as follows:

intForward = 1 implies that intReverse = 3
intForward = 2 implies that intReverse = 4
intForward = 3 implies that intReverse = 1
intForward = 4 implies that intReverse = 2

This could be coded as:

If intForward = 1 Then intReverse = 3
If intForward = 2 Then intReverse = 4
If intForward = 3 Then intReverse = 1
If intForward = 4 Then intReverse = 2

These four separate conditions are not used in the program. Instead an alternative single line of code uses a Boolean expression to calculate intReverse from intForward in all four possible cases.

Devising this condition involves noticing that two of the correct values of intReverse are found simply by adding 2 to inForward. With the other two values of intForward, doing this gives a value of intReverse that is 4 more than required:

intForward = 1 gives value of 3; Value required = 3
intForward = 2 gives value of 4; Value required = 4
intForward = 3 gives value of 5; Value required = 1
intForward = 4 gives value of 6; Value required = 2

Hence adding 2, and then removing 4 when intForward is greater than 2, will give the required answer for intReverse. It is easy to find a Boolean expression which does this. When intForward is greater than 2 the expression (intForward > 2) evaluates as true, or –1. In other cases it is zero. Multiplying this expression by 4 therefore creates exactly what is required, the subtraction of 4 when intForward is more than 2.

The final expression for intReverse is:

```
'Determine reverse direction
intReverse = intForward + 2 + (4 * (intForward > 2))
```

Next the robot is drawn on the maze. It is placed in a single cell. The coordinates for this cell are calculated in precisely the same way, as graphic coordinates for the wall sections, and for the goal, have been generated from their maze coordinates. The maze coordinates for the robot are (intRobotX, intRobotY) and so the coordinates for the robot's cell are:

```
'Show robot's position

'Select appropriate cell
intCellX = (intRobotX - 1) * 400 + 100
intCellY = (21 - intRobotY) * 400 + 100
```

Figure 3.72 indicates how the robot is designed to fit inside a single cell. Each cell of the maze will be quite small on the display and so there is no need to have a detailed representation of a robot. Just a square with a circle on top is sufficient to depict body and head.

The body is a square with a side equal to 200. In order to fit centrally inside the maze cell of 400 there has to be a left and right margin of 100. This means that the graphics x-coordinate of the left-hand side of the square is (intCellX + 100) and the x-coordinate of the right-hand side is (intCellX + 300).

The body is not symmetrically placed in terms of y-coordinate. There needs to be a larger space at the top of the maze cell in order to leave room for the circular head. The square body is therefore offset by 50 from the bottom of the maze cell. As the y-coordinates are measured from the top of the display this leads to the y-coordinate of the bottom edge of the body as being (intCellY –50. Similarly the y-coordinate of the top is (intCellY –250).

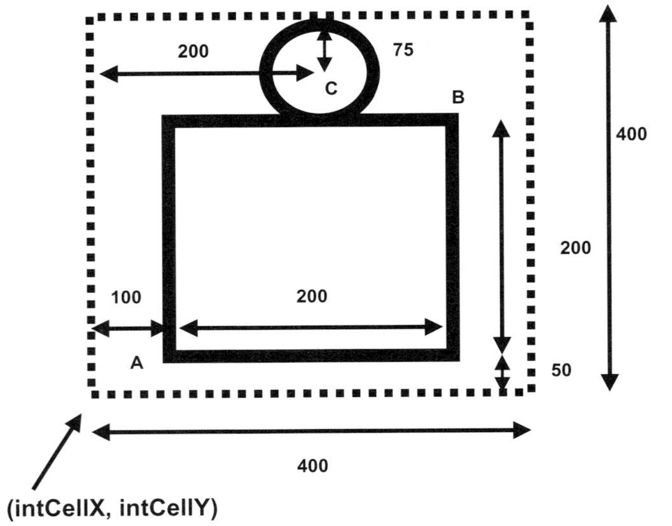

Figure 3.72 *Graphic coordinates for maze searching robot*

The coordinates of the bottom left-hand corner are therefore:

(intCellX + 100, intCellY – 50)

The coordinates of the top right-hand corner are:

(intCellX + 300, intCellY – 250)

These coordinates are used in the code which adds the body to the maze cell:

```
'Select colour
ForeColor = vbBlack
'Robot body
Line (intCellX + 100, intCellY - 50)-(intCellX + 300, intCellY - 250),
, BF
```

The distance between the top of the robot's body and the top of the maze cell is 150. The radius of the robot's head is therefore set at 75 in order to fill the space completely. The *x*-coordinate of the centre of this centrally placed circle is (intCellX + 200). The *y*-coordinate of the centre is 75 from the top of the cell, or 325 from the bottom. The value will therefore be (intCellY – 325). The Visual Basic statement which adds the head is:

```
'Robot head
Circle (intCellX + 200, intCellY - 325), 75
```

It is essential for the number of vacant cells surrounding the current robot position to be counted before any possible move can be planned. This is done by a single For loop which uses the increments held in the intAdjacent array to examine the four maze locations surrounding the current robot position and to which it could potentially move.

First the total of vacant neighbouring cells is reinitialized as zero. This prevents a running total being generated which includes the total of vacant neighbours from previous robot locations:

```
'Count vacant adjacent cells
intVacant = 0
```

The For loop then inspects the four directions around the current cell:

```
For intCounter = 1 To 4
```

Each value of the loop control variable will produce in turn the increments needed to define one of the four neighbouring positions. The increments needed to get to each position are intAdjacentX(intCounter) and intAdjacentY(intCounter). These have to be added to the robot's coordinates in the maze, (intRobotX, intRobotY). The location in the intMaze() array corresponding to the neighbouring cell that has been selected can then be checked. If this array value is zero then the neighbouring cell is vacant and the total number of vacant cells has to be incremented:

```
If intMaze(intRobotX + intAdjacentX(intCounter), intRobotY +
intAdjacentY(intCounter)) = 0 Then

'Count vacant cell
intVacant = intVacant + 1
```

In addition the location of the vacant cell is recorded in the intDirection() array. This is also required in deciding the route around the maze. If the neighbouring cell being examined is vacant, the direction of the cell, which will be identical to the value of the loop control variable, is placed in the corresponding location in the intDirection() array. If it is not vacant, which means that this cell is part of the maze wall, then a zero is placed in the intDirection() array instead.

This will be clear if diagrams are considered (see Figures 3.73 and 3.74).

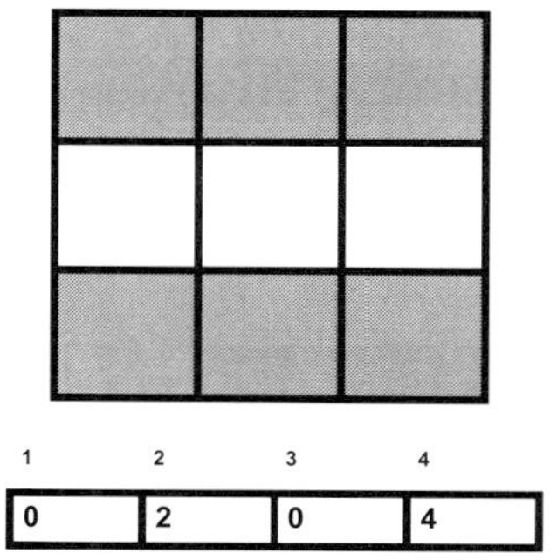

Figure 3.73 *Relation between neighbouring maze cells and the content of the intDirection() array*

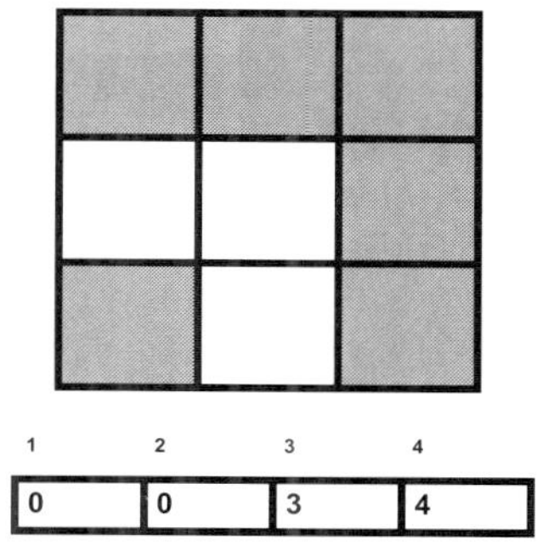

Figure 3.74 *Pelation between neighbouring maze cells and the content of the intDirection() array*

In this first example (Figure 3.73) the directions 1 and 3 are maze wall and directions 2 and 4 are corridor. This leads to these values for the intDirection() array:

intDirection(1) = 0
intDirection(2) = 2
intDirection(3) = 0
intDirection(4) = 4

In the second example (Figure 3.74) the directions 1 and 2 are maze wall and directions 3 and 4 are vacant corridor space. Wall sections are represented by 0 in the intDirection() array (note this is the reverse of the representation in the intMaze() array) and vacant corridor cells by the corresponding direction number. This means that the content of the intDirection() array is:

intDirection(1) = 0
intDirection(2) = 0
intDirection(3) = 3
intDirection(4) = 4

The direction is placed in the intDirection() array for corridor cells by this code:

```
'Record direction
intDirection(intCounter) = intCounter
```

A zero is placed in the array for wall sections by:

```
Else
intDirection(intCounter) = 0
End If
```

The loop which checks the neighbouring cells then ends:

```
Next intCounter
```

Once the number of vacant cells surrounding the robot has been obtained, and the intDirection() array filled, it is possible to select the robot's next move. This will be represented by a value, in the range 1 to 4, being calculated for intForward. From this new robot coordinates can be defined.

It is particularly easy to decide the new value for intForward if the value that has been found for intVacant is 1. If there is only one vacant cell adjacent to the robot's position then the robot has reached a dead end and must turn back (see Figure 3.75).

This is done easily. The opposite direction to the way the robot is moving through the maze is already known. It is intReverse. In order to make the robot back away from a dead end all that has to be done is assign the value of intReverse to intForward:

```
'Determine direction for dead end
If intVacant = 1 Then intForward = intReverse
```

The code becomes a little more complicated if the value of intVacant is 2. Choosing a value for intForward will require the use of the intDirection() array in this case, as explained below.

A value of intVacant = 2 can correspond to either of two possible situations. The robot might be travelling in a straight line. Alternatively it might be approaching a bend. Both types of situation are illustrated in Figures 3.76 and 3.77.

In Figure 3.76 the robot is moving in a straight line from left to right.

The current value of intForward for the robot is 2. This should also be the next value for intForward.

In Figure 3.77 the robot is moving in a straight line from right to left.

Here the current value of intForward is 4, and this should again remain the same for the next value of intForward.

However, simply retaining the same value for intForward does not work in the case of a bend (see Figure 3.78).

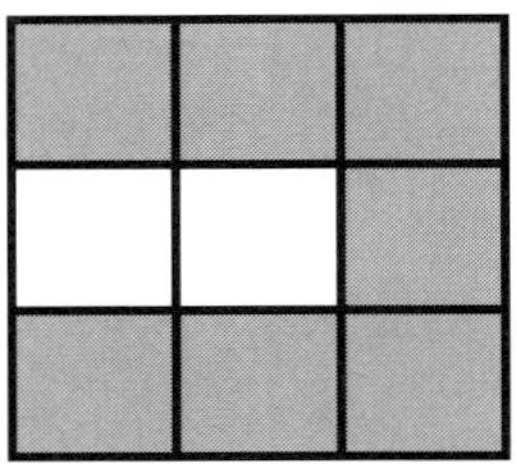

Figure 3.75 *Situation where robot must turn back: IntForward = intReverse*

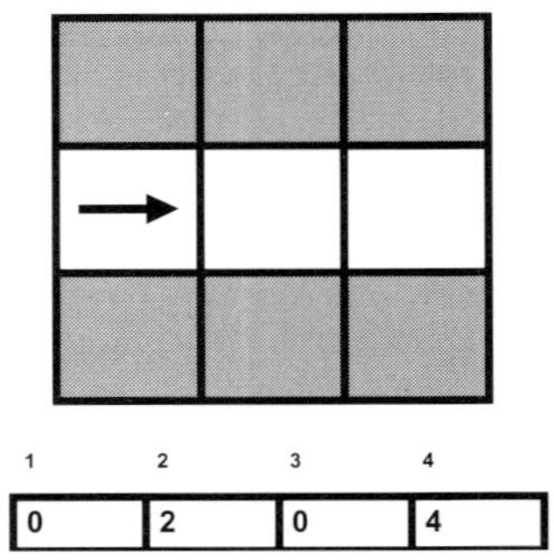

Figure 3.76 *Robot moving in a straight line from the left*

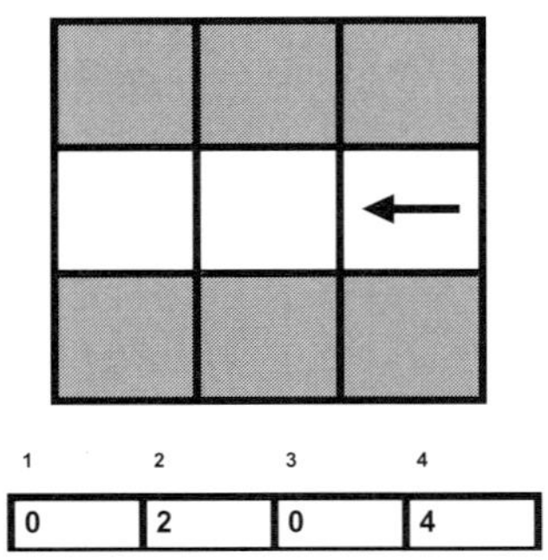

Figure 3.77 *Robot moving in a straight line from the right*

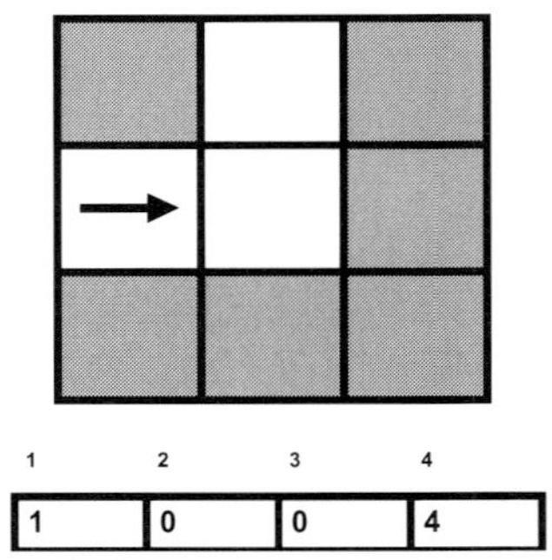

Figure 3.78 *Bend approached from the left*

The robot is approaching the bend from the left. When it arrives at the bend it has to change its value of intForward from 2 to 1.

Figure 3.79 shows the same bend approached from the top.

Now the robot has to change intForward from 3 to 4.

At first there does not appear to be a very obvious pattern here, but one emerges if values for intReverse and the intDirection() array are taken into account. The four examples we have considered are shown in Figure 3.80.

Figure 3.80 indicates the value of intForward and intReverse in each situation. It also displays the four values in the intDirection() array, as well as the new value for intForward that is required to move the robot, either in a straight line or round a bend. In all of these cases it can be seen quite readily that

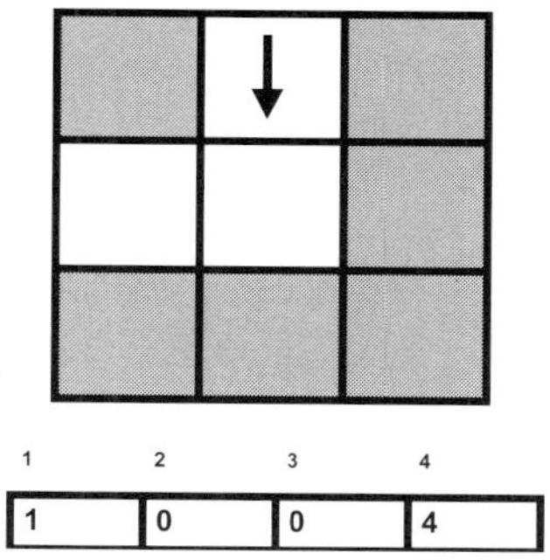

Figure 3.79 *Bend approached from top*

	Current intForward	Current intReverse	1	2	3	4	New intForward
Left to right	2	4	0	2	0	4	2
Right to left	4	2	0	2	0	4	4
Bend from left	2	4	1	0	0	4	1
Bend from top	3	1	1	0	0	4	4

Figure 3.80 *Using intDirection() array to select new robot direction*

the value required for the new intForward is simply the non-zero value in the intDirection() array which is not equal to intReverse. It is easy to code this into a For loop:

```
'Determine direction for straight path or bend
If intVacant = 2 Then
For intCounter = 1 To 4
If intDirection(intCounter)  0 And intDirection(intCounter)  intReverse
Then
intForward = intDirection(intCounter)
End If
Next intCounter
End If
```

Robot navigation becomes more complicated still if the value of intVacant is greater than 2. If there are more than two vacant adjacent cells the robot has reached a junction in the maze. A value of 3 indicates a T junction. A value of 4 corresponds to an X junction, a crossroad. Junctions play a particularly important role in solving the maze. At a junction different routes can be chosen. The robot initially does a blind search of the maze and so it is more than likely that inappropriate turns will be made. However, if a record is kept of the robot's past choices at all of the junctions it has visited, it is possible, with a relatively simple algorithm, to prune the route down to the most direct. This does simulate intelligent behaviour to a certain extent. It offers a good example of the way that AI techniques can create, in limited situations, the appearance of mind. Of course this is just trickery.

An important first stage in creating this intelligent route to the robot's goal is to identify whether or not the junction currently encountered has been visited previously. This is what happens in the first part of the code which is implemented when the number of vacant neighbouring cells is greater than 2:

```
'Determine direction for a junction
If intVacant > 2 Then
```

Each junction is given a number, intJunctionN. When the robot reaches a junction this number is initially set to zero before a check is made of known junctions to decide whether or not the current one has been visited previously. If it is a known junction the value of intJunctionN is changed to the appropriate value. First, however, intJunctionN is set to 0:

```
'Identify known junction
intJunctionN = 0
```

A For loop then searches through the known junctions. The total number of known junctions is represented by the variable intJunctionT and so this is set as the upper value for the loop control variable:

```
For intCounter = 0 To intJunctionT
```

The coordinates of all known junctions are held in two arrays, intJunctionX() and intJunctionY(). If these match the robot's coordinates as it reaches a junction then this indicates that the junction has been visited previously. It also means that the number that was assigned to the junction when it was first visited is the same as the current value of the loop control variable (since junctions are numbered sequentially). This value must therefore be assigned to intJunctionN:

```
If intJunctionX(intCounter) = intRobotX And
intJunctionY(intCounter) = intRobotY Then
intJunctionN = intCounter
End If
Next intCounter
```

If the loop does not manage to match the current junction with one already present in the intJunctionX(), intJunctionY() arrays, the value of intJunctionN will remain zero. When this is the case the new junction must be recorded. First the total number of junctions known, intJuntionT, is increased by 1:

```
'New junction
If intJunctionN = 0 Then

'Number new junction
intJunctionT = intJunctionT + 1
```

This then is the value which has to be assigned to intJunctionN:

```
intJunctionN = intJunctionT
```

The coordinates of the new junction have to be recorded. They will, naturally, be the same as the coordinates of the robot:

```
'Record junction coordinates
intJunctionX(intJunctionN) = intRobotX
intJunctionY(intJunctionN) = intRobotY
```

The available directions to take from the new junction are recorded by copying the intDirection() array for the robot's position to the intJunctionV() array. This is a two-dimensional array. The first subscript represents the junction number and the second subscript the four possible directions from it. A For loop assigns each value from intDirection() in turn:

```
'Record available directions at junction
For intCounter = 1 To 4
intJunctionV(intJunctionN, intCounter) = intDirection(intCounter)
Next intCounter
```

Of course the direction which the robot has approved the junction needs to be removed:

```
'Remove direction junction approached
intJunctionV(intJunctionN, intReverse) = 0

End If
```

Once the intJunctionV() array has been set up for a new junction a decision can be made about what direction the robot should take on leaving the junction. This decision will be based upon the content of the intJunctionV() array. This might be the set of array values that has just been set up for a new junction. Alternatively it could be the array content of one previously visited.

The direction at which the junction should be left is found by using a For loop to inspect each of the four values held in the intJunctionV() array. The loop selects the first non-zero value encountered, as this corresponds to a direction in which the robot can travel. Succeeding non-zero values in the array are ignored because a flag allows only one choice of direction to be made. In addition the value in the array itself is then reset to zero. This will prevent the same direction being taken again the next time the junction is visited.

First the flag is set to zero:

```
'Choose a direction to exit junction
intFlag = 0
```

The For loop then repeats four times, corresponding to the four directions in which the robot can move and to the four values in the intJunctionV() array:

```
For intCounter = 1 To 4
```

A condition looks for a non-zero value in the intJunctionV() array, but only if such a value has not already been found. The additional condition involving the flag prevents more than one choice being made:

```
If intJunctionV(intJunctionN, intCounter)   0 And intFlag = 0
```

If a non-zero direction is found the flag is set to 1. This means that the condition can now not be met a second time and so it will always be the first non-zero direction in the array that is chosen:

```
Then
intFlag = 1
```

The non-zero value in the array is now selected as the direction for the robot to take as it leaves the junction. This is done by assigning the array value to intForward:

```
intForward = intJunctionV(intJunctionN, intCounter)
```

The direction that has been chosen is then removed from the intJunction() array so that it cannot be chosen again. This involves setting the array location to zero:

```
intJunctionV(intJunctionN, intCounter) = 0
```

The condition and the loop end:

```
End If
Next intCounter
```

It is essential that both the junction number and the direction taken on leaving the junction are recorded. These two pieces of information, recorded at each junction passed by the robot, are sufficient to define the route it has taken through the maze. Once the goal has been reached, and exit made from the overall loop, this route can be examined and pruned down to the essential, most direct, route.

Both junction number and direction are recorded in the same array, intRoute(). They alternate in it, junction, direction, junction, direction, until the goal is found, at which point the route is complete. The subscript used in the intRoute() array is intDistance. First the junction number is assigned to the array using the current value of intDistance:

```
'Record route taken
intRoute(intDistance) = intJunctionN
```

The direction taken is then assigned to the next location in the array:

```
intRoute(intDistance + 1) = intForward
```

In order for the correct array location to be chosen the next time intRoute() has to be updated, the value of intDistance must be increased by 2:

```
intDistance = intDistance + 2
```

Note that the variable intDistance has to be thought of topologically, not metrically. It is the topology of the maze that has to be investigated, not how big it is. The robot has efficient batteries!

A loop allows the content of intRoute() to be displayed in order to help the user monitor its progress towards the goal:

```
'Display route
PicDisplay.Cls
```

```
For intCounter = 1 To intDistance - 1
PicDisplay.Print intRoute(intCounter);
Next intCounter
```

At this point the overall junction condition ends:

```
End If 'End of if for whole of junction code
```

The program is then delayed so that it is possible for the user to evaluate the route being taken by the robot:

```
'Prompt for next move
NextMove = InputBox("Hit a key", , , 8200, 1000)
```

The current robot position is now erased. This is done by filling the grid cell with a colour identical to the backgroud. The same Visual Basic Line statement is used as in the construction of the maze. The coordinates, intCellX, intCellY, still have their values from before:

```
'Erase robot position
ForeColor = vbCyan
Line (intCellX, intCellY)-(intCellX + 400, intCellY - 400), , BF
```

A small square dot is added at the centre of the cell so that the robot leaves a visible trace behind it:

```
ForeColor = vbRed
Line (intCellX + 180, intCellY - 180)-(intCellX + 220, intCellY - 220),
, BF
```

The new coordinates for the robot are now found by updating both the intRobotX and intRobotY coordinates with the increments found in the intAdjacentX() and intAdjacentY() arrays. The subscript used for both arrays is the direction that has been assigned to intForward:

```
'Update robot coordinates
intRobotX = intRobotX + intAdjacentX(intForward)
intRobotY = intRobotY + intAdjacentY(intForward)
```

The overall loop continues until exit is made possible by both *x*- and *y*-coordinates of the robot matching those of its goal:

```
'Robot searches for goal
Loop Until (intRobotX = intGoalX And intRobotY = intGoalY)
```

At this stage the robot stops moving and any unnecessary turns that it has made at junctions can be eliminated. The algorithm is quite simple, and depends upon locating duplication of junctions in the intRoute() array. This array will indicate quite clearly where wrong turns have been made.

This can be understood if a very obvious example of an incorrect turn is considered, as shown in Figure 3.81.

The diagram indicates a sample section of maze in which there are three junctions. The robot enters from the top left and encounters a junction after two cells. This will be junction 1. The intJunc-

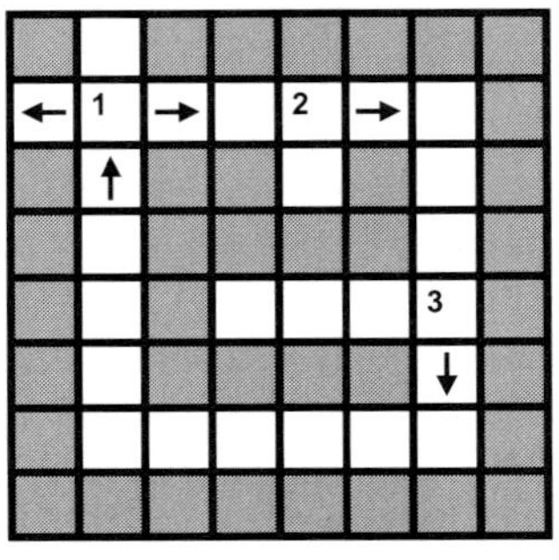

Figure 3.81 *Initial route: 1 2 2 2 3 3 1 4. Pruned route: 1 4*

tionV() array will have in its second locations the values (0,2,3,4). The robot takes the first non-zero direction 2. So at this stage the content of the intRoute() will be (1,2).

After another three cells the robot arrives at a second junction. This is junction 2 and the second location of the intJunctionV() array here has the four values (0,2,3,0). Again the robot will take direction 2. The intRoute() array is now (1,2,2,2).

Next junction 3 is reached. Here the intJunctionV() array has the values (0,0,3,4). The robot takes direction 3. The route it has taken up to this point is (1,2,2,2,3,3).

Finally the robot arrives back at junction 1. The intJunctionV() array for this junction will now be (0,0,0,4). The robot takes direction 4 and moves out of this section of the maze. The content of the intRoute() at this point is (1,2,2,2,3,3,1,4).

Clearly the robot should have taken direction 4 in the first place. The 'intelligent route' is (1,4):

Blind search route: (1,2,2,2,3,3,1,4)
Intelligent route: (1,4)

Note that there is an extremly simple way of generating the intelligent from the blind search route. The duplication of junction 1 in the array has to be detected. Then all the intervening values in the array must be eliminated.

This is the method by which route pruning is performed in the program. It involves two loops. The inner loop removes unnecessary occurrences of a specific junction from the intRoute() array. The outer loop then repeats this for each of the junctions in turn. When all junctions have been checked the resulting sequence of values in the intRoute() array represents the most efficient path to the goal that can be dervied from the blind search route.

First the outer loop checks for each junction in turn. The loop control variable is intJunctionC. It ranges up to the total number of junctions that have been found during the blind search, intJunctionT. The current junction being tested for repetition will be intJunctionC. This of course will become each of the known junctions in turn:

```
'Prune unnecessary route

'Main loop checks each junction in turn
For intJunctionC = 1 To intJunctionT
```

Two variables, intFirst and intLast, are set to zero. These will record the first and last occurrence of a particular junction in the intRoute() array:

```
intFirst = 0
intLast = 0
```

The inner loop now looks for where the current junction, intJunctionC, occurs in the route array, intRoute(). This loop is controlled by intCounter. It steps by two through the array so that it is only looking at the junctions and not the direction taken by the robot at each junction:

```
'Inner loop checks for duplication of junction in route
For intCounter = 1 To intDistance - 1 Step 2
```

If the value in the array matches the number of the junction, intJunctionC, the array location at which this occurs, intCounter, is assigned to intFirst. This records the first instance of the junction in the route. Further occurrences of the junction will be ignored as a result of the additional condition, intFirst = 0. This condition ensures that intFirst can only be assigned a value once in the loop. It inevitably records the first time the junction is identified:

```
If intRoute(intCounter) = intJunctionC And intFirst = 0 Then
intFirst = intCounter
End If
```

The last occurrence of the junction in the route is found by the single condition:

```
If intRoute(intCounter) = intJunctionC Then
intLast = intCounter
End If
```

The inner loop then ends:

```
Next intCounter
```

If the current junction has been repeated in the route array both intFirst and intLast will be non-zero and unnecessary values need to be deleted from intRoute():

```
'Route pruning required
If intFirst   0 And intLast   0 Then
```

Deletion from the array is achieved by using two For loops which copy only the relevant parts of intRoute() to the second array, intRouteCopy(). The first For loop copies values up to the first occurrence of the junction. The second loop copies the values which follow its last occurrence. This means that all the unnecessary values are removed.

An additional counter is required to identify the array locations in the second array, intRouteCopy(). This counter is intCopyCounter. First it has to be initialized as zero:

```
'Delete intervening array values
intCopyCounter = 0
```

The first For loop now copies the intRoute() array locations into the intRouteCopy() array. This copying goes up as far as intFirst.

```
For intCounter = 1 To intFirst
```

The counter for the intRouteCopy() has to be incremented:

```
intCopyCounter = intCopyCounter + 1
```

This value of intCopyCounter can now be used to transfer the content of intRoute() into intRouteCopy:

```
intRouteCopy(intCopyCounter) = intRoute(intCounter)
```

The first loop ends:

```
Next intCounter
```

The second For loop copies the remaining content of intRoute() to the second array, intRouteCopy. The range specified for the loop control variable means that none of the unnecessary route is copied across:

```
For intCounter = intLast + 1 To intDistance
```

Again the counter for the second array has to be incremented:

```
intCopyCounter = intCopyCounter + 1
```

The assignment is identical to the one in the first loop:

```
intRouteCopy(intCopyCounter) = intRoute(intCounter)
```

The second loop ends:

```
Next intCounter
```

Immediately the second route array is copied over the first. The range of the loop means that all of the locations that were originally filled in intRoute() are addressed again. However, the unnecessary values are overwritten by zero:

```
'Transfer shortened route back to array
For intCounter = 1 To intDistance
```

The overwriting by zero is controlled by the value in the intRouteCopy() array. If this is zero the original value is replaced by zero. Other values are just replaced by the new value in intRouteCopy. The content of the intRouteCopy array is itself erased in the process to avoid spurious values being transferred:

```
If intRouteCopy(intCounter)   0 Then
intRoute(intCounter) = intRouteCopy(intCounter)
intRouteCopy(intCounter) = 0
Else
intRoute(intCounter) = 0
End If
```

By the end of the loop the intRoute() array has had all unnecessary code removed for the junction being considered:

```
Next intCounter
```

It is essential that the total of the filled locations in intRoute() is truncated. The number of locations to be eliminated is (intLast – intFirst) and so the new value for intDistance is intDistance – (intLast – intFirst). Removing the bracket gives intDistance – intLast + intFirst:

```
'New route length
intDistance = intDistance - intLast + intFirst
```

The condition for route pruning then ends:

```
End If
```

Route pruning then continues for all junctions in the route. This is done by the overall loop:

```
'End of main loop
Next intJunctionC
```

When the route has been simplified as much as possible it is displayed (see Figure 3.82).

```
'Display pruned route
Picture1.Cls
For intCounter = 1 To intDistance - 1
Picture1.Print intRoute(intCounter);
Next intCounter

End Sub
```

It is left as an exercise to reanimate the robot from its starting position to the goal using the simpler route that has been generated.

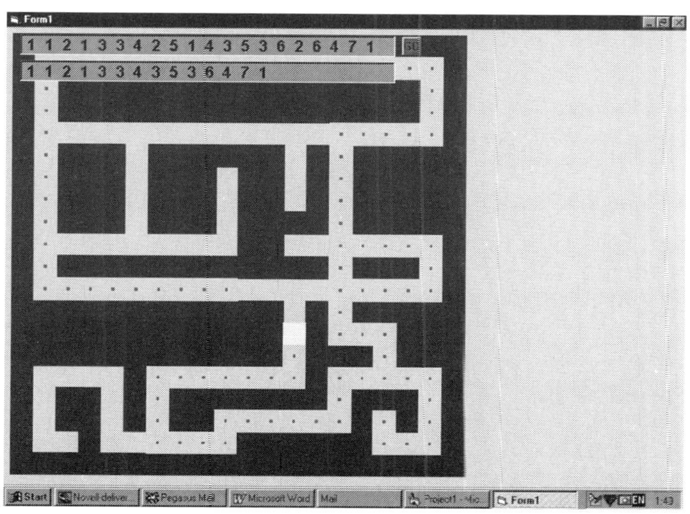

Figure 3.82

3.3 Problem-solving theory

Exercise 1: Pets problem

> It is relatively easy to devise simple puzzles which although they state a well-defined problem can be quite teasing to solve. The more of these that can be given to students the better, in order to introduce the idea of an initial state, a goal state and the operations required to reach the goal state.

Here is an example of the way a well-defined problem can be constructed and set as an exercise.

The pets problem

Seven children enter a pets' competition at a naval fête in the dockyard. The children are Mary, Susan, Janet, Jenny, Dave, Keith and Sandra. Their pets they take to the competition are a kitten, a goldfish, a hamster, a guinea pig, a tortoise, a chipmunk and a rabbit, but this is not necessarily the same order as the one in which the pets' owners have been given.

Clemency (the Admiral's daughter) notices that:

1. The owner of the tortoise and the owner of the hamster have the same initial.
2. Captain Carruthers, temporarily retricted to shore duties while his frigate is repaired, has put the pets into large mesh shaded cages with bedding and appropriate food and water. The cages are numbered 1–7. The pets have been placed into these cages in alphabetical order.
3. The cage number of Keith's pet is twice the number of the cage containing Mary's pet. Similarly Sandra's pet's cage number is twice Dave's.
4. The cages look secure but Clemency is worried that, should they escape, Janet's pet might eat Dave's.

The solution to the problem

There is no set method for a solution that will work with all problems. The example given here has been designed to encourage a little brainstorming at first before a more systematic approach is adopted. Various clues have been given which need to be investigated.

The statement that the tortoise and hamster are owned by children who have the same initial might appear at first to be a promising lead until it is realized that there are two pairs of children with shared initials. In fact the following four situations could all equally well apply:

Jenny owns the tortoise
Janet owns the hamster

Janet owns the tortoise
Jenny owns the hamster

Susan owns the tortoise
Sandra owns the hamster

Sandra owns the tortoise
Susan owns the hamster

It is better to ignore this piece of information until there is something else that it can be slotted in.

The information that Janet's pet might eat Dave's is more promising. An examination of the pets present shows that only one of them, the kitten, is likely to have strong non-vegetarian inclinations. And, whereas a fully grown cat might attempt to add almost any of the other pets to its diet, a kitten would be happiest with something small and succulent, like a goldfish. This strongly implies that Janet owns the kitten and Dave the goldfish.

At this point we can make use of Captain Carruthers' systematic approach to pet competitions and make an alphabetical list of pets in their numbered cages:

Cage 1. Chipmunk
Cage 2. Goldfish

Cage 3. Guinea pig
Cage 4. Hamster
Cage 5. Kitten
Cage 6. Rabbit
Cage 7. Tortoise

Adding Janet and Dave to the classification we have:

Cage 1. Chipmunk	
Cage 2. Goldfish	Dave
Cage 3. Guinea pig	
Cage 4. Hamster	
Cage 5. Kitten	Janet
Cage 6. Rabbit	
Cage 7. Tortoise	

Now we can use the fact that Sandra's pet's cage number is twice Dave's and modify the list to obtain:

Cage 1. Chipmunk	
Cage 2. Goldfish	Dave
Cage 3. Guinea pig	
Cage 4. Hamster	Sandra
Cage 5. Kitten	Janet
Cage 6. Rabbit	
Cage 7. Tortoise	

Next we note that the owner of the tortoise and the owner of the hamster have the same initial. As Sandra owns the hamster, Susan must own the tortoise.

Cage 1. Chipmunk	
Cage 2. Goldfish	Dave
Cage 3. Guinea pig	
Cage 4. Hamster	Sandra
Cage 5. Kitten	Janet
Cage 6. Rabbit	
Cage 7. Tortoise	Susan

In addition, Keith's pet's cage number is twice the number for Mary's pet. Inevitably this places Keith's pet in cage 6 and Mary's in cage 3:

Cage 1. Chipmunk	
Cage 2. Goldfish	Dave
Cage 3. Guinea pig	Mary
Cage 4. Hamster	Sandra
Cage 5. Kitten	Janet
Cage 6. Rabbit	Keith
Cage 7. Tortoise	Susan

Finally there is only one pet left for Jenny:

Cage 1. Chipmunk	Jenny
Cage 2. Goldfish	Dave
Cage 3. Guinea pig	Mary
Cage 4. Hamster	Sandra
Cage 5. Kitten	Janet
Cage 6. Rabbit	Keith
Cage 7. Tortoise	Susan

The owners of the pets are shown in Figure 3.83.

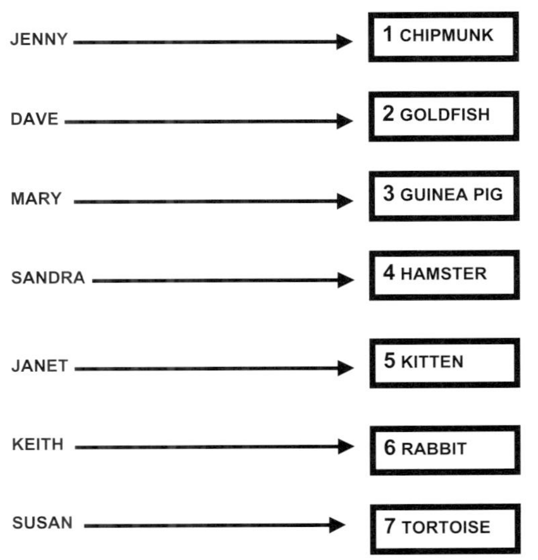

Figure 3.83

How similar problems can be devised

First two sets of associated entities have to be chosen so that there is a one-to-one correspondence between them. It might be people and the house number of where they live, or concert-goers and their favourite composer. The important thing is that specific pairings occur between the two sets.

Next there has to be some definite point at which the person solving the puzzle can 'break in'. For example, a clue might be 'Hilary likes listening to the composer of the Leningrad Symphony.'

After this the clues can become a little more cryptic, like 'Mr Brown's house number is the sum of Mr Jenkins and Miss Witchell's.'

The minimum number of clues should be given, just sufficient to solve the problem.

Once the set of clues has been checked, their order should be scrambled. They should not be given to the students in the same order as they were devised. This could make the solution too obvious.

Exercise 2: Cartesian Solitaire

Solitaire is a traditional game played on a special board consisting of holes and pegs. At the beginning of the game all of the holes, except the one at the centre, contain pegs. The object of the game is to remove the pegs one by one until only a single peg remains in the central hole.

A peg is removed by 'jumping' over one other peg into a neigbouring hole. The peg that has been jumped over is then taken from the board.

A variation of the game is considered in this exercise. 'Cartesian' solitaire uses counters on a draughtboard rather than the special board. The rules are the same as described.

The fact that a chessboard is eight by eight squares in size means that the missing counter will not be quite central. In Figures 3.84 and 3.85 the position is four across and four down from the top left-hand corner. Although this loses the pleasant symmetry of the original game it does not really affect the problem-solving aspect of solitaire.

The initial state for Cartesian solitaire will be a chessboard containing 63 counters, one per square, with one square left empty (see Figure 3.84).

The goal state for Cartesian solitaire is the same board, with just one counter located on the square which was empty in the initial state (see Figure 3.85).

The operations required to progress from the initial state to the goal state consist of repeated sets of the following three steps:

- Identify a counter which is two squares distant from an empty square and separated from it by a square which contains another counter.
- Move the counter to the empty square. The movement can be in any of the four possible directions, up, down, left, right and the four additional diagonal directions between them.
- Remove the counter located between the old and new positions of the counter that has been moved.

These steps should continue until the goal state is reached.

It is evident that the overall problem of Cartesian solitaire is not well defined. The initial and goal states are clear enough but there is no obvious way of specifying precisely how the set of steps should be implemented in order to reach the goal state. The game does involve skill, which is why it is felt worth playing. However, although the game as a whole is not well defined, specific areas of the board may pose a well-defined problem (see Figure 3.86).

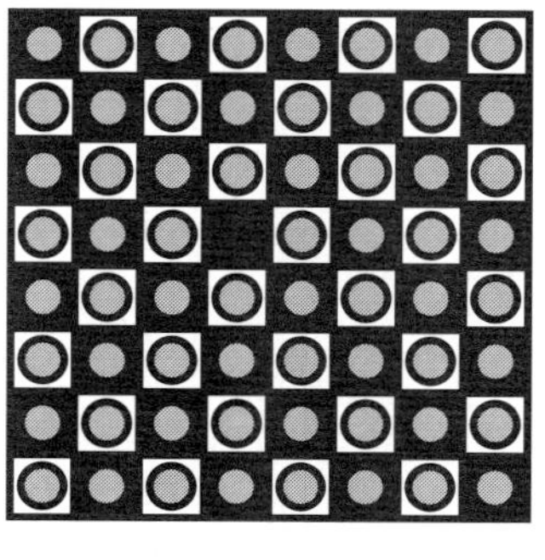

Figure 3.84 *Initial board for Cartesian solitaire*

Figure 3.85 *Final board for Cartesian solitaire*

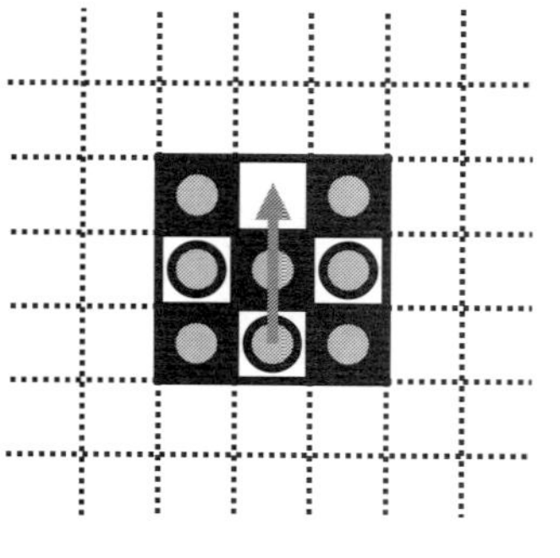

Figure 3.86 *Possible move in Cartesian solitaire*

If the set of nine squares shown in the diagram is considered then there is a very specific set of steps to follow. The counter in the middle of the bottom row is jumped into the middle of the top row, as shown by the arrow, and the central counter is removed.

Part of problem-solving strategy could be to examine the entire board in three by three segments, like the one shown in the diagram, to detect possible moves. Note that the diagram shows only one from a set of eight potential moves. Depending upon which counter is initially missing the moves could be:

Jump from top left square to bottom right square
Jump from top square to bottom square
Jump from top right square to bottom left square
Jump from right square to left square
Jump from bottom right square to top left square
Jump from bottom square to top square
Jump from bottom left square to top right square
Jump from left square to right square

All of these would result in the middle counter being removed.

Computer solution for Cartesian solitaire

The game does offer good opportunities for a computer solution, although one is not developed here. The computer solution is challenging and so would probably be suitable for more ambitious students who require extension material.

Specific aspects of the game which need to be considered include the following:

- There has to be an internal representation in the program of the state of the board. The most obvious choice here is a two-dimensional array. It must also be possible to update the representation so that the removal of counters from the board is recorded.
- Output to the user must indicate the current state of the board. Any display generated must be determined by the internal representation of the board and be adjusted whenever the data held in the representation alters.
- A method has to be found for allowing the user to specify what piece has to be moved. If a two-dimensional array has been chosen for the representation, the method of selection could be entry of the two relevant array subscripts. It is also necessary to state the direction in which the counter should jump as there can be situations in which the same counter can move in more than one direction.
- Validation of the user's choice of counter must be included. It should not be possible to select a counter which does not exist, nor a direction in which a counter cannot move. This becomes particularly difficult near the borders of the board. Here the number of directions available for jumping is reduced. Considerable care needs to be given to the way in which this validation can take place.
- The program code has to be able to identify when the goal state has been reached.

Exercise 3: Highest common factor

Finding the highest common factor of two numbers is an interesting exercise because it throws into sharp relief the difference between human methods for solving a problem and the algorithm more suited for a computer. The obvious approach for a person is quite distinct from the best method for a computer solution. Similarly the algorithm employed by a computer (ironically devised millennia before computers!) is extremely tedious for a person and would rarely be adopted.

The highest common factor (HCF) of a set of numbers is the largest number which will divide into all of them. Finding the HCF of various numbers is a traditional exercise in school fractions.

The HCF of 12, 20 and 16, for example, is 4. A larger factor of 12 is 6, but this will not divide into either 20 or 16. Likewise larger factors of 20 and 16 will not divide into the other numbers in the set.

Here for simplicity we restrict ourselves to the problem of finding the HCF of a pair of numbers, not a set of more than two. Suppose, for example, that we had to discover the HCF of 24 and 30. (The HCF is 6.) Most people can 'see' the answer immediately, but if we wish to produce a formal method we would probably think in terms of factorizing both numbers and then discovering which factors they had in common.

The factors of 24 are:

24 = 2 × 2 × 2 × 3

The factors of 30 are:

30 = 2 × 3 × 5

The common factors are 2 and 3, and so the HCF is (2 × 3), or 6. The factors of the two numbers can be thought of in terms of a Venn diagram, with the common factors forming the intersection of the two sets (see Figure 3.87).

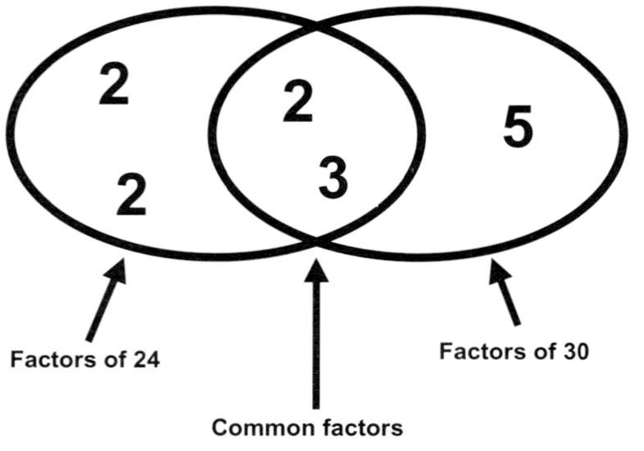

Figure 3.87

The algorithm that has been used can therefore be expressed as:

1. Factorize the first number to create a set of factors
2. Factorize the second number to create a second set of factors
3. Find the intersection of the two sets
4. Multiply the elements of this intersection together

However, even a casual inspection of this algorithm shows how difficult it would be to code as a computer program. Stepwise refinement would immediately highlight problems with both factorizing the numbers, to create sets, and then finding the intersection of the two sets.

An algorithm for factorizing a number, Number, could take this form:

1. Initialize Copy with value Number
2. Initialize Counter as 0
3. Initialize Factor as 2
4. If Factor does not divide exactly into Number go to 10
5. Increment Counter
7. Copy factor to array location defined by Counter
8. Reassign Number value of Number/Factor
9. Go to 4
10. Increment Factor
11. Factor is less than Copy/2 go to 4

This algorithm would need to be applied twice to create two arrays of factors. Then a second, moderately involved, algorithm would be needed to find the common elements between the two arrays. It should be apparent that this is not an efficient method for computer solution.

In contrast we can consider Euclid's algorithm for finding the HCF of two numbers, here slightly modified to make it easier to code as a computer program:

1. Determine the smaller of the two numbers
2. Initialize Factor as one greater than the smaller number
3. Decrement Factor
4. If Factor does not divide without remainder into the smaller number repeat from 3
5. If Factor does not divide without remainder into the larger number repeat from 3
6. Display Factor as the HCF

This algorithm can be coded as a very short program!

We can now apply Euclid's algorithm to the original problem of finding the highest common factor of 24 and 30. The smaller of the two numbers is 24, and so this is chosen as the initial value of the common factor.

Repeat number 1
Does 24 divide without remainder into 24? YES
Does 24 divide without remainder into 30? NO
Highest common factor not found
Reduce by 1

Repeat number 2
Does 23 divide without remainder into 24? NO
Does 23 divide without remainder into 30? NO
Highest common factor not found
Reduce by 1

Repeat number 3
Does 22 divide without remainder into 24? NO
Does 22 divide without remainder into 30? NO
Highest common factor not found
Reduce by 1

Repeat number 4
Does 21 divide without remainder into 24? NO
Does 21 divide without remainder into 30? NO
Highest common factor not found
Reduce by 1

Repeat number 5
Does 20 divide without remainder into 24? NO
Does 20 divide without remainder into 30? NO
Highest common factor not found
Reduce by 1

Repeat number 6
Does 19 divide without remainder into 24? NO
Does 19 divide without remainder into 30? NO
Highest common factor not found
Reduce by 1

Repeat number 7
Does 18 divide without remainder into 24? NO
Does 18 divide without remainder into 30? NO
Highest common factor not found
Reduce by 1

Repeat number 8
Does 17 divide without remainder into 24? NO
Does 17 divide without remainder into 30? NO
Highest common factor not found
Reduce by 1

Repeat number 9
Does 16 divide without remainder into 24? NO
Does 16 divide without remainder into 30? NO
Highest common factor not found
Reduce by 1

Repeat number 10
Does 15 divide without remainder into 24? NO
Does 15 divide without remainder into 30? YES

Highest common factor not found
Reduce by 1

Repeat number 11

Does 14 divide without remainder into 24?	NO
Does 14 divide without remainder into 30?	NO

Highest common factor not found
Reduce by 1

Repeat number 12

Does 13 divide without remainder into 24?	NO
Does 13 divide without remainder into 30?	NO

Highest common factor not found
Reduce by 1

Repeat number 13

Does 12 divide without remainder into 24?	YES
Does 12 divide without remainder into 30?	NO

Highest common factor not found
Reduce by 1

Repeat number 14

Does 11 divide without remainder into 24?	NO
Does 11 divide without remainder into 30?	NO

Highest common factor not found
Reduce by 1

Repeat number 15

Does 10 divide without remainder into 24?	NO
Does 10 divide without remainder into 30?	YES

Highest common factor not found
Reduce by 1

Repeat number 16

Does 9 divide without remainder into 24?	NO
Does 9 divide without remainder into 30?	NO

Highest common factor not found
Reduce by 1

Repeat number 17

Does 8 divide without remainder into 24?	YES
Does 8 divide without remainder into 30?	NO

Highest common factor not found
Reduce by 1

Repeat number 18

Does 7 divide without remainder into 24?	NO
Does 7 divide without remainder into 30?	NO

Highest common factor not found
Reduce by 1

Repeat number 19

Does 6 divide without remainder into 24?	YES
Does 6 divide without remainder into 30?	YES

Highest common factor found
Stop

All the stages have been displayed here to emphasize how tedious this approach is for a human. Computers, of course, are extremely good at number crunching. The computation involved is far outweighed by the simplicity of the code required to implement the algorithm.

Exercise 4: London visit decision tree

Mary decides to celebrate her recent promotion by taking her best friend, Jonathan, on a day's outing to London. Jonathan is unemployed and so Mary will pay for all the day's expenses as well as doing any driving.

If they go by rail instead, Mary's young niece, Michaela, who is a student studying horticulture, will join them. (Michaela has a tendency towards travel sickness in cars but enjoys the train.) If Michaela comes Mary will pay for her as well.

If the weather is fine when they arrive in London Mary has decided that they should have a trip on the Thames. However, the weather forecast says that there is a 30% chance of rain. This will not matter if Mary has driven because she and Jonathan can just eat their sandwiches in Mary's car, and hope to fit in a walk if the sky clears. However, if they have taken the train Mary thinks it will be more sensible to go to a concert at the Royal Festival Hall.

The train fare to London is £25 per person, with a 20% reduction for students. The cost of petrol for a return trip is £35. The price of a concert ticket is £15. A ticket for the river tour is £5.

The decision tree for this situation is shown in Figure 3.88.

Node 1 is the initial decision made by Mary about whether to travel by car or by train. Node 2 and Node 3 are chance nodes which will depend upon the weather. There are four terminal nodes: 4, 5, 6 and 7.

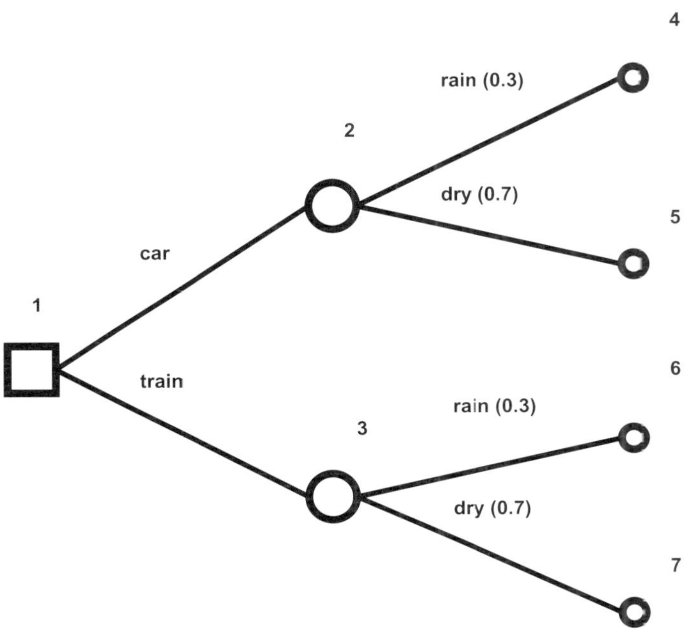

Figure 3.88 *Decision tree for London visit*

First we work out the cost to Mary for each of the possible paths through the tree structure:

Path 1, 2, 4
Mary decides to drive to London and so has to pay £35 for petrol. However, it rains and so she and Jonathan sit in the car eating sandwiches. There is no further expense.

Total cost for Node 4 = £35

Path 1, 2, 5
Again Mary decides to drive and pays £35 for petrol. As the weather is dry she and Jonathan take a trip on the river which means that Mary has to spend another £10 for the two tickets.

Total cost for Node 5 = £45

Path 1, 3, 6
Mary decides that they should go by train. She has to pay £25 for her ticket and Jonathan's, and 80% of this, or £20, for Michaela. The total for the rail fare will therefore be £70. The weather is

rainy when they arrive and so they go to the concert. Each ticket is £15 and so Mary has to spend another £45.

Total cost for Node 6 = £115

Path 1, 3, 7
Again Mary has to pay £70 for the rail tickets. As the weather is dry she, Jonathan and Michaela go on the river trip. The cost of three tickets for this is £15.

Total cost for Node 7 = £85

Once the cost of the terminal nodes is calculated we move back to the previous nodes, 2 and 3, and calculate their expected value. The expected value of a chance node is found by multiplying the value of each of the nodes leading from it by the probability that that node will be reached. All these products are then added together. This gives:

Expected value for Node 2 = (0.3 × £35) + (0.7 × £45)
= £10.50 + £31.50
= £42

Expected value for Node 3 = (0.3 × £115) + (0.7 × £85)
= £34.50 + £59.50
= £94

So the probable cost for Node 2 is £42 and for Node 3 it is £94. Assuming that Mary would wish to minimize her costs it makes sense for her to decide to go by car.

Note that in this example only one set of nodes has been involved between the initial decision and the terminal nodes but the same method applies for more complicated decision trees.

Exercise 5: Cliff's holiday decision tree

Cliff has three weeks' holiday.

He is considering going to Captain Nemo's World Domination Theme Park. The inclusive cost of being a resident is £80 per week. While he is there he might decide to contribute weekly articles about the holiday to the parish newsletter of his church, St Agnes of the Blessed Apparition, as Father Declan is currently short of copy. Although he will not be paid for his articles, Cliff knows that they will be automatically submitted to the *County Gazette*. Here they could win the £500 bursary for 'Most Promising Young Author of the Year'. As Cliff has considerable experience of writing for the popular taste, and has convinced most of the people who know him that he is under fifty, he believes that the probability of his winning (should he decide to enter) is 0.7.

If he goes to Wendy's Wonderland Holiday Camp he will have to pay £50 per week for accommodation, food and entertainment. At the holiday camp he knows that he is certain to enter the £250 'Bulging Biceps' competition. Cliff has been on steroids since Christmas and, as the rest of the campers tend to be chartered accountants, he is sure that he has an 80% chance of winning this prize.

Cliff might simply decide to stay at home and continue cramming for the Origami Finals at the town library. This competition offers considerable local status but no financial incentive.

Probably the more difficult aspect of using decision trees is the initial conversion of a situation which has been described in words into the graphical form required. Once this has been done it is relatively easy to follow the simple arithmetical rules which evaluate the tree.

Here the stages involved in constructing a tree are illustrated using the imaginary holiday options described above.

We begin the tree with a single node on the left. This is a decision node and so is shown as a rectangle. It is numbered as Node 1. Reading through the situation shows that Cliff can make three decisions. He can decide to take no holiday at all and instead practise his origami. Instead he might decide to go to Captain Nemo's World Domination Theme Park. A third possibility is that he stays at Wendy's Wonderland Holiday Camp. This means that there are three paths leading away from Node 1 (see Figure 3.89).

If he decides not to take a holiday this path will inevitably lead to a terminal node. This is shown in Figure 3.90 as Node 2.

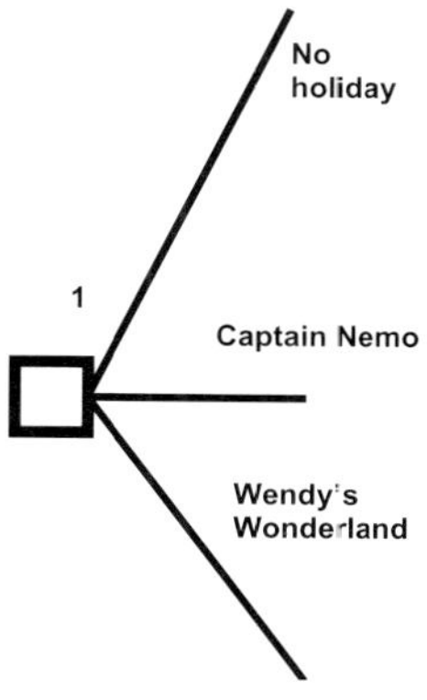

Figure 3.89

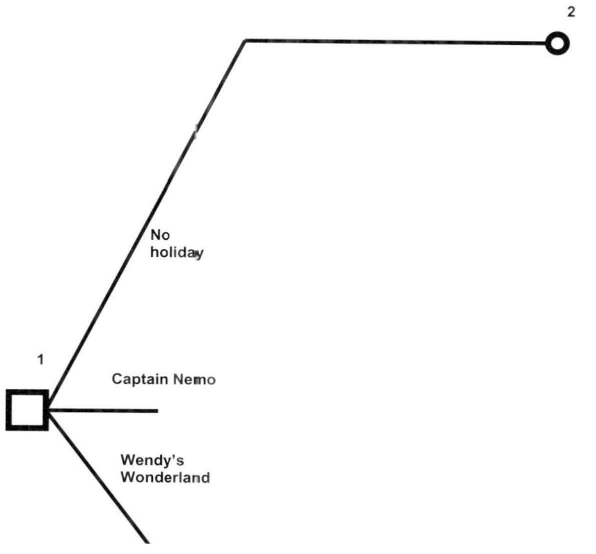

Figure 3.90

If Cliff decides to go to Captain Nemo's he might decide to write articles for the parish newsletter and so there will be another, rectangular, decision node. It is labelled as Node 3 on the tree and has two paths emerging from it representing whether or not he writes articles (see Figure 3.91).

If Cliff decides to write, this path will now lead to a circular chance node representing the possibility of his winning a bursary. This will be Node 4. Nothing further is said in the description of the situation about what will happen then and so both the paths leading from Node 4 will lead to terminal nodes, here called Node 5 and Node 6. The paths are labelled with the probabilities given (see Figure 3.92).

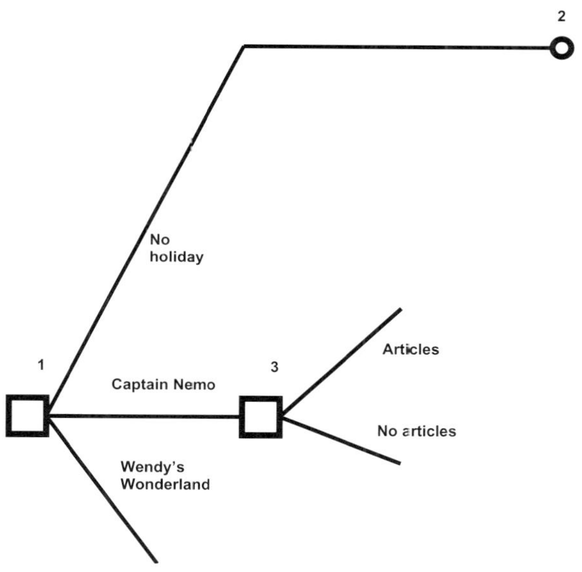

Figure 3.91

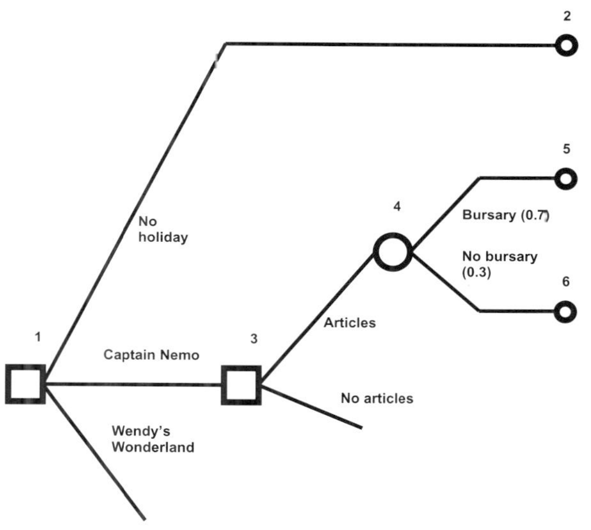

Figure 3.92

If he chooses not to write there will be a path from Node 3 directly to another terminal node, Node 7 (see Figure 3.93).

Finally we have to consider what will happen if Cliff decides to go to Wendy's Wonderland. He will enter the 'Bulging Biceps' competition. Note that there is no decision made here. The description of the situation makes it clear that his entering the competition is assured. That means the tree will have no decision node at this point but will have a chance node to reflect the possibilities of his winning or not winning. This is Node 8 (see Figure 3.94).

From this chance node paths will simply lead to the two final terminal nodes, 9 and 10 (see Figure 3.95).

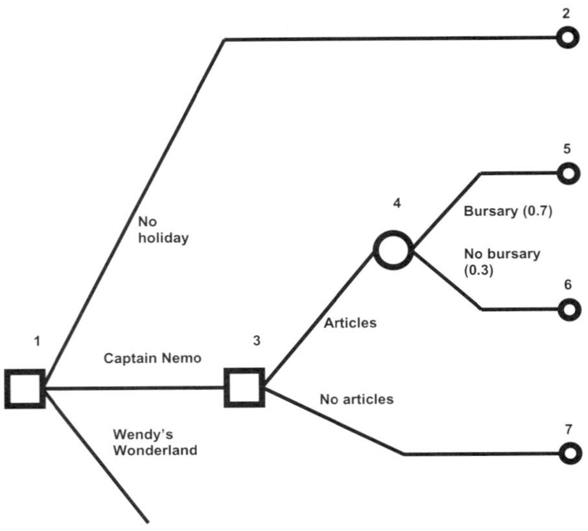

Figure 3.93

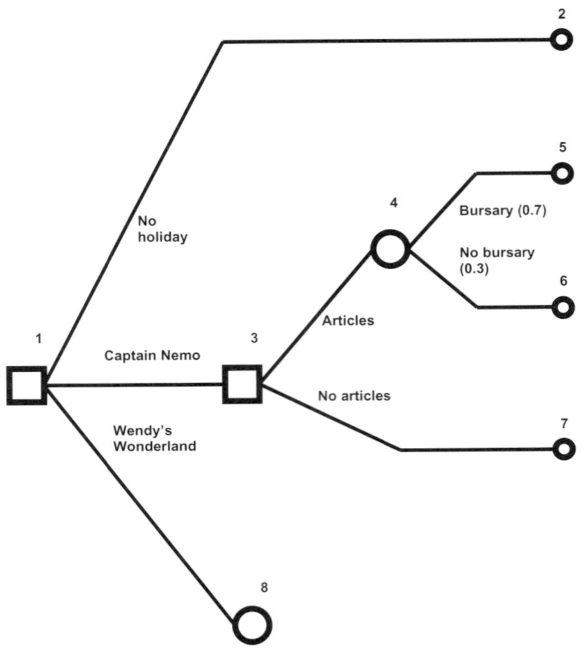

Figure 3.94

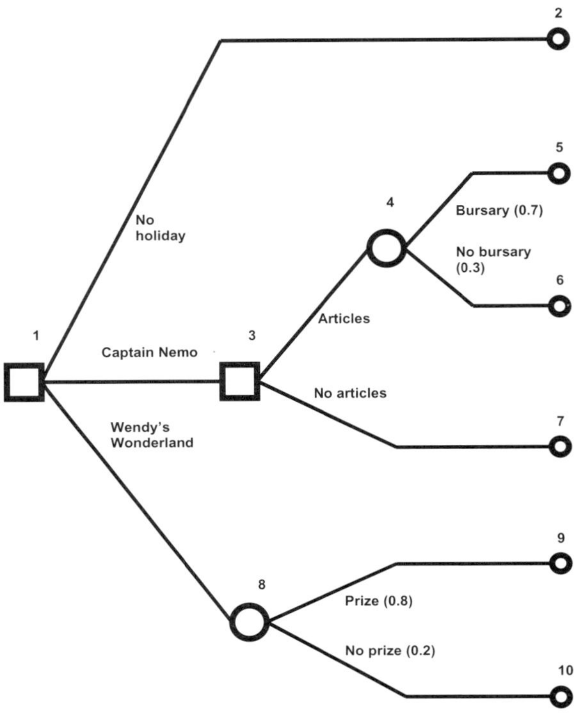

Figure 3.95 *Decision tree for Cliff's holiday*

Evaluating the decision tree

An overall decision tree has been constructed for the situation and can now be evaluated. This is done by calculating the total cost for each of the paths from Node 1 to a terminal node.

Path 1, 2

Cliff doesn't go on holiday and so there is no cost. (He uses scrap paper for his origami!)

Total cost for Node 4 = £0

Path 1, 3, 4, 5

Cliff goes to Captain Nemo's and so spends (3 × £80), or £240. However, he wins the *County Gazette*'s bursary of £500 for the articles he writes. This means that the total cost is (£240 – £500) or –£260. The minus sign indicates that he has made a profit!

Total cost for Node 5 = –£260

Path 1, 3, 4, 6
Cliff spends £240 to go to Captain Nemo's and still sends in his articles but does not win the bursary.
Total cost for Node 6 = £240

Path 1, 3, 7
Cliff goes to Captain Nemo's but does not bother to write.
Total cost for Node 7 = £240

Path 1, 8, 9
The cost of spending three weeks at Wendy's Wonderland is (3 × £50) = £150. However, Cliff wins £250 in the competition and so overall the cost is again negative, (£150 – £250).
Total cost for Node 9 = –£100

Path 1, 8, 10
Cliff spends £150 to stay at Wendy's Wonderland but does not win the competition.
Total cost for Node 10 = £150

The expected values for the chance nodes can now be calculated by multiplying the values of the nodes leading from them by the relevant probability and adding.

Expected value for Node 4 = (0.7 × –£260) + (0.3 × £240)
= –£182 + £72
= –£110

Expected value for Node 8 = (0.8 × –£100) + (0.2 × £150)
= –£80 + £30
= –£50

4 Computing solutions

4.1 Information and contemporary applications

Exercise 1: Report writing

> Word processing and desktop publishing make it very easy to produce professional looking documents but it should be remembered that software is a tool to complement traditional literary skills rather than a partial replacement for them. A formal report on a topic will be enhanced by access to IT tools but will still require the author to adhere to a recognized format and writing style.

Structure of a report

As a general guide a report should contain a number of specific features. Not all of the following will always be present but the majority will be contained by most reports:

- Title page
- Abstract
- Acknowledgements
- Contents page(s)
- Page numbers
- Tables and diagrams
- Conclusion
- Appendices
- Bibliography

Title page

A report should have a title page. This will show the name of the report, who has written it and the date of completion, or submission. It can also state the intended readership of the report and, perhaps, as an extension to the main title, a subtitle briefly explaining the area addressed.

Abstract

An abstract is a very brief summary of the area investigated by the report, including a concise account of its findings. The function of the abstract is to indicate to the potential reader whether or not the report is relevant to them. It lets them know in advance if the report is worth reading and saves them time if it is not.

The abstract must not take too long to glance through. It should fit on to less than a single, separate sheet of A4. (Published reports often tend to squeeze the abstract into a small box at the head of the main document by using smaller font.)

Acknowledgements

You may want to mention briefly particular people who have helped, by advice or by suggestions about additional research material. Such an acknowledgement section could be expanded into a Preface to the report if other details were included as well.

Contents page(s)
This will list the chapters of the report and show subtitles used within the chapters. It is conventional to adopt a decimal numbering system, so that Chapter 2 will contain sections with subtitles numbered 2.1, 2.2 etc. Further subdivisions within a section can be given an additional decimal place, like 2.2.3, which will of course be between 2.2.2 and 2.2.4.

This is a simple and elegant way of organizing a report. A large number of levels within the hierachy of sections and subsections does risk leading to something rivalling Wittgenstein's *Tractatus* in the number of decimal places required. (Nobody, as yet, has thought of converting his decimals to vulgar fractions, but it would be fun.)

Page numbers
A contents page will not work without page numbers. Word processing allows these to be added automatically to the report.

Tables and diagrams
These can add essential information in a way which is easily assimilated by the reader. Allow time for their creation as they can be deceptively simple in construction but lengthy to complete. This can be put to advantage as creating a diagram can be a restful break from long typing sessions.

Conclusion
The main points, recommendations and 'discoveries' of the report should be brought together in a concluding section. Do not be afraid of reiteration at this point. It is your responsibility to make everything clear, and you cannot rely upon the reader having made a mental summary, or marginal notes, as they read through the report. The essentials should appear again in one place where they can be easily identified.

Remember the fail-save advice to journalists. 'Say what you intend to say. Then say it. Then say what you have said.' Think of the early *Batman* television series, a tongue-in-cheek pastiche of the comic, unlike the grim profundity of the later movies. Wham! Blam! Ooof! Big letters on sheets of cardboard. Make it all really explicit.

Appendices
Relevant additional material which does not fit in easily with the main body of the report should be included as a series of appendices, usually named by the letters of the alphabet, and referred to, where needed, in the report. The important point here is that the material should be 'relevant'. It can be tempting to add weight, literally, by including shopping lists of unrequired information, but this should be resisted.

Bibliography
Books that have been used in the research for a report should be noted in the bibliography. The title, author's name and date of publication should be given. Similarly the publisher. The ISBN is not a recognized additional detail here. The reader is not expected to acquire copies of their own!

References should also be made to journals and websites that have been used.

Practical report writing

Some general factors should be taken into account in producing a report:

- Writing style
- Writer's block
- Proof reading
- Plagiarism

Writing style
You should write your report in a confident and informative fashion. The language used must be formal rather than familiar, but at the same time it should avoid being completely cold and dead. It must indicate the enthusiasm that you feel for the subject. If you have managed to get through all the research without building up too much enthusiam then proceed with caution. A report should not be ironic. (Except perhaps the final one before moving to the better job.)

An overfamiliar style can be quite annoying for the reader. Likewise humour. It is difficult to be James Thurber or the *Monty Python* team and humour often falls very flat.

A spoof account of an imaginary word processing package once had useful function buttons, like 'Plagiarize' and 'Insert long words'. The ideal report writing software would probably have a function which removed long words. The more simple and direct the language the better the report. Similarly, employ concise sentences as much as possible. You are not writing fiction, where the contrast between long and short sentences can have considerable dramatic effect. A report should be easy to read.

Often acronyms are inevitable but do not throw them around with too much abandon. The acronyms you do employ, unless really well known, should be defined in an additional appendix to the report.

Omit any slang terms and words which may offend. It is better to err on the side of caution here. There are people still around who find the stock phrase now used to refer to audience numbers in theatres either distasteful or an incomprehensible reference to tramps occupying benches in the park.

Also avoid words which are currently fashionable but which might date rapidly. It is quite amusing to estimate the age of unseen speakers on the radio simply by their verbal tendency to revert to their adolecence. Baby boomers have learnt to eliminate 'fab' from their formal vocabulary but it is interesting to note how many use 'encapsulate', which is equally linked with the same decade, and therefore burdened with the flavour of a bright future that never quite came.

Do not intrude in the first person unless it is completely unavoidable And never refer to yourself in the third person, which is ponderous beyond belief. Be transparent and let the document have its own life.

Writer's block

The parable of the centipede who was totally OK with walking, until somebody asked him how it all worked, could illustrate the problem of writer's block. It is quite possible to know exactly what has to be said and still be unable to say, or rather type, it. If you concentrate too closely upon the process of writing itself you can freeze. This is a situation in which authors of proposed reports frequently find themselves. Irrespective of the quality of their research, or the detail of the outline that they have prepared, the actual writing of the report itself becomes an impossible obstacle to overcome.

The solution is simply to write. Write a little every day and add bulk. It does not matter too much at first if what is being written is not completely relevant or correct. You will rework your material in any case, and once you have sufficient words in the document you will not worry too much about the paragraphs you remove entirely. The human brain is alleged to develop a huge number of neurons in the womb and then starts discarding them as the individual begins to emerge with memories and consciousness. A sculptor might cast a large block of plaster before attacking it with hammer and chisel to lever out whole chunks and create an artistic form within the original rectangular outlines. It is much easier to whittle down excess than to stick together little pieces. Writing any document should be regarded in the same way. The minimalist approach – 'Yesterday I added a comma: today I took it out' – works for an Oscar Wilde, but is a hopeless strategy for anybody prone to writer's block.

Proof reading

Make sure you have allowed yourself time to read through your report before the agreed deadline for its delivery.

It is better to proof read from hard copy than from the screen. Underline mistakes and typos in a contrasting colour. Red is quite a good choice. Hand write modifications to sentences in the margin or in gaps between paragraphs. Then use this corrected hard copy to produce a revised electronic version.

If possible ask somebody else to read through for you. You can become blind to glaring errors simply through overexposure to them.

Do not become too dependent on the auto-correct facilities of your software. A spell check is great for typos but sometimes fatal for spelling and sense.

Plagiarism

Plagiarism is the unacknowledged use of another person's material. Electronic copy has made it very easy for even the honest student to lapse into plagiarism. You only have to forget which files, saved months previously and from which you are now quoting, were not actually your own. Nevertheless the penalties exacted are harsh. As a result of plagiarism becoming so easy colleges feel obliged to act decisively on those who are discovered.

Plagiarism can be avoided in two ways.

You are unlikely to be an Einstein or Goethe. Nobody is expecting you to produce something of striking originality. Accept the fact that your work is only going to be your own perspective of what has gone before, and not something that is a masterpiece of creativity, with fresh ideas and concepts spilling out of every paragraph. You have done your research, read scores of sources. Now you have to produce your own piece of work, drawing upon all these sources, but in your own imaginative and idiosyncratic way.

Never work with copies of your initial source documents in front of you. You will find it almost impossible not to reproduce word-for-word phrases of somebody else's material. Instead rely upon your memory.

Think about what you have read and understood. Now pretend that you are explaining it to somebody else, perhaps a person slightly less endowed intellectually than you are. Your explanation will be elegant but simple, and, most important of all, in your own language. There will be no unsightly joins with spliced in pieces. Your document will not be a literary Boris Karloff with the stitching plain for all the villagers to see in the light of their torches.

Sometimes a quote is inevitable. It's hard to say 'e equals m c squared' without it being a bit obvious. So, when you do have to quote, admit that this is what you are doing. Come clean and it's not plagiarism.

Case study: The early American space programme

In this exercise you have to prepare a brief report about the early American space programme. To research for your report you use the Internet and download three documents. These are shown below as 'Source A', 'Source B' and 'Source C'. You realize that to avoid plagiarism you must not copy and paste from these documents but it is acceptable to:

- Explain the material briefly in your own words.
- Quote brief excerpts, provided that you indicate clearly where you obtained the material. For example: 'Training Your Cat to Play Chess' by Espeth Higgs, Publisher: Nutter Books (1992).

Prepare the material that you might present for your talk. Produce your own summary of Source A (roughly one side of A4 assuming business style font, size 12) and include one acknowledged quote from Source B and a further, similarly acknowledged, quote from Source C. Remember that Internet material is sometimes suspect! Be on your guard.

Source document A

Title: One Small Step: The Apollo Space Programme
Author: Benedict Bulstrode
Publisher: Extraordinary Press
Date of publication: 1985

Chapter One: The Quest Begins!

After the trauma of the Second World War many people looked forward to a bright new future. In the United Kingdom the ascent to the throne of a beautiful young queen led many British people to believe that they were entering a new Elizabethan age, the achievements of which would mirror the success of that earlier Elizabeth and reassert the authority of Britain in Europe after the terrors of the recent Nazi past.

In the United States of America a different pride was felt. The war had led to the emergence of America as the World's first superpower, with only the distant threat of a similar power developing in the Soviet East.

The Americans had benefited from the traditional spoils of war. In particular they had inherited many A4 rockets which had been captured when Yankee forces overran the German slave factories. Also eagerly shipped to the States were the ex-Nazi designers of these terror machines, better known to their English targets as the dreaded V2 vengeance weapon.

Chief among these fleeing German scientists was Werner von Braun who willingly adopted American citizenship. Cruelly mocked in a later, 1960s popular song as 'the man whose allegiance is ruled by expedience', von Braun was only interested in building giant liquid-fuelled rockets in order to achieve his childhood dream of space travel. Naive to an extreme, this was why he had willingly helped Adolf Hitler by constructing the V2 rocket. Von Braun did not have the time to investigate too closely the morality of his decision.

In 1958 von Braun launched the first successful American satellite using the Jupiter rocket he had built for the US Army. Many believed that this satellite would easily have beaten the Soviet 'Sputnik' satellite into orbit (October 1957) and become the first man-made object in space. However, the American authorities had baulked at the thought of sending a military machine into space. The territory 'up there' should be neutral, they believed, and not tainted by war. Their Russian opponents were not so squeamish.

Horrified by the Soviet success, the Americans immediately formed an organization to coordinate their space research. This was the National Aeronautics and Space Administration. Within months NASA was planning a man-in-space policy. First single 'spacemen', or astronauts (from the Latin 'star sailor'), would be launched in the tiny Mercury spacecraft. If Project Mercury proved successful it would be followed without delay by Project Gemini. The Gemini spacecraft would carry two astronauts.

Both Mercury and Gemini spacecraft were designed to fly in Earth orbit. However, the next step in NASA's space plans was Project Apollo. The Apollo spacecraft was capable of reaching the Moon. In fact there were two separate Apollo spacecraft which would be launched simultaneously by the same giant rocket. These two spacecraft were referred to as 'modules'. The Command Module would only orbit the Moon, but the Lunar Module would land. After exploring the surface the two Lunar Module astronauts would take off and rejoin their fellow crewman in lunar orbit. Then all three would return to Earth in the Command Module and splash down in the Pacific Ocean.

The first successful Moon landing was made in 1969. The astronauts were Neil Armstrong, Buzz Aldrin and Michael Collins.

Chapter 2: Martian Base Discovered on Lunar Farside

Consternation spread worldwide when the first evidence of an alien presence on the Moon was obtained by...

Source document B

Title: The Rocket Catalogue
Author: Mavis Blackberry
Publisher: Channel 4 Productions
Date of publication: 1998

Launch vehicle: Vanguard
Spacecraft carried: Small early satellites
Comments: Many initial failures with this low-powered rocket.

Launch vehicle: Jupiter
Spacecraft carried: Explorer satellite
Comments: Van Allen radiation belt discovered.
Launch vehicle: Redstone
Spacecraft carried: Mercury
Comments: Alan Shepherd and Virgil Grissom made non-orbital flights.

Launch vehicle: Atlas
Spacecraft carried: Mercury
Comments: First American in orbit was John Glenn.

Launch vehicle: Titan
Spacecraft carried: Gemini
Comments: Highly successful missions. First American spacewalk.

Launch vehicle: Saturn
Spacecraft carried: Apollo
Comments: First man on Moon was Neil Armstrong.

Source document C

Title: Senior School Latin
Author: Erasmus Pinchpenny
Publisher: Victoria and Albert Impress
Date of publication: 1893

Exercise 5
Learn by heart these first declension nouns:

Agricola: farmer
Astra: star
Mensa: table
Nauta: sailor
Puella: girl

Also memorize these first conjugation verbs:

Amo: I like or I love
Guberno: I steer
Porto: I carry

Case Study: The Europan Exploitation Consortium

In this case study you are given a series of source documents related to the future imaginary Europan Exploitation Consortium.

Read through these and produce a brief report on the EEC.

Source document A

The Europan Exploitation Consortium (EEC)

The EEC is a multi-planetary organization with mining interests on the Moon, Mars and Europa, as well as an involvement with those areas of the Earth which are not yet depleted of all mineral resources.

The EEC has become the major supplier of edible organics to three quarters of the Earth's population. This role followed largely from the discovery that the pre-biotic slime covering the surface of Jupiter's fourth satellite could be processed into foodstuff only slightly less palatable than the convenience food already marketed by the EEC on Earth.

The historical origin of the Consortium is obscure and convoluted. Like many organizations it can find its ancestry in a variety of smaller concerns which merged and mutated. Seeking a single beginning, an event in time, is therefore like an explorer hacking through a jungle in search of the river's source. Which rivulet is most distant from the ocean?

Nevertheless many would assert that the first glimmer of the EEC lies in the enterprise of a small business in mid-twentieth century Britain. In the economic doldrums which, surprisingly, followed victory in the war against Austrian warlord Adolf Hitler, a grocer with a keen eye for the main chance decided to adopt American-style merchandizing of food. The supermarket arrived in the UK!

Expansion was rapid. Acquisition of smaller rival chains led within a few decades to a massive company before which local politicians and planning committees quailed. International conquest followed in the twenty-first century, leading in turn to political power on a global scale. Earth's bounds themselves were broken with the unexpected takeover of the American National Aeronautics and Space Administration (NASA) in 2081.

Initially the Consortium simply offered funding for interplanetary research after Congress refused to endorse Presidential support for the International Mars Station in 2075. At first welcomed by the American government and public, this British involvement was later viewed with suspicion when subsequent changes in management led to a gradual shift in NASA policy.

It was felt that NASA's direction had been lost. Critics argued that the idealistic vision of space pioneers had been corrupted. The courage of John Glenn (and his predecessor in orbit, Yuri Gargarin), the steely determination of President Kennedy to see an American on the Moon before 1970, the cute photos of Buzz Aldrin at the Sea of Tranquility (making sure that Neil Armstrong had the only camera), the Space Shuttle, the international cooperation in space which followed the end of the Cold War, the development of the 'moderately warm' fusion drive, all of this, they said, had been sacrificed for the 'get it cheap, sell it dear' marketing policy of the EEC. The new management, it was claimed, saw only the economic benefit of space research. World Currency Units replaced ideals.

In the wake of the death of the last of the 'old guard' NASA administrators in a freak accident on a launch pad, NASA was officially renamed as the Europan Exploitation Consortium. Within a few months a new research programme had been adopted. Gone were both the Mars Station and Lunar Farside laboratories. In their place was a commercial policy directed principally towards the economic potential of the distant satellite of Jupiter. Before the EEC's interest, Europa had hosted a single research base, an unmanned station controlling a small fleet of robot submarines investigating the subterranean ocean of the little planet. Now, in contrast, plans were in place for shipping vast quantities of organic chemicals mined from Europa's icy crust.

United Nations' objections that the Europa development could hinder the search for extra-terrestrial life foundered after an unexpected leak of 20 000 litres of rocket fuel into the only region of the Europan surface with the combination of nutrients and light required for life to thrive.

After this further objections to the economic development of the Jovian satellite were discounted with the results that everybody is now familiar.

Source document B

The Italian scientist Galileo Galilei discovered the four largest satellites of Jupiter, Ganymede, Callisto, Io and Europa. These cannot be observed with the naked eye and so were unknown before the telescope.

Galileo made his own telescope from a verbal description of the invention in Holland. He realized its potential for astronomy and soon began making discoveries, like the cratered surface of the Moon and the phases of Venus. He also discovered what are now called, in his honour, the 'Galilean' satellites of Jupiter.

He noticed that very close to Jupiter were some new stars. Galileo first assumed that he was seeing faint stars that just happened, accidentally, to be in the same line of sight as Jupiter. This is like the way a distant cathedral spire might seem to be close to a cottage from one point of view although not really close to it at all. However, when Galileo continued watching Jupiter night after night he realized that something odd was happening.

The faint stars lay in a straight line passing through Jupiter. (This is because the satellites are all in approximately the same orbital plane about the planet.) Their relative position along this imaginary line altered from night to night. In addition they followed Jupiter as it gradually moved across the night sky. The most obvious explanation was that the stars were in fact small planet-like bodies in orbit around Jupiter.

The significance of this discovery was not lost on Galileo. The fact that newly discovered 'stars' could orbit around Jupiter was clear evidence against the traditional picture of the Universe in which everything went around the Earth.

The names for the four satellites were suggested by Simon Marius, who also claimed to have seen them before Galileo. Marius chose names from classical mythology which reflect the irregular social life of Jupiter.

Source document C

Table from EEC Traveller's Guide

Mass	4.8 e 22 kg
Diameter	3 138 km
Density	3.01 gm/cm^3
Surface gravity	0.135 g
Escape velocity	2.02 km/sec
Mean distance from Jupiter	670 900 km
Mean distance from the Sun	5.203 AU
Orbital period about Jupiter	3.55 days
Rotational period	3.55 days

Source document D

Commodities traded by Europan Exploitation Consortium (World Currency Units)

	USA	*Brazil*	*EU*	*China*	*Africa*	*Antarctica*
Methane	345	101	158	300	152	23
Volatiles	237	99	67	101	80	15
Organics	403	200	204	302	95	32
Infotainment	2133	1023	1352	1504	801	402
Microchips	1923	678	898	1082	673	98
Tourism	104	76	98	47	15	2

Source document E

Distribution of personnel in four main divisions of EEC

	Earth	*Moon*	*Mars*	*Europa*
Administration	904	230	134	98
Astronauts	120	457	386	219
Rocket scientists	502	394	98	65
Software engineers	287	130	47	34
Marketing	850	34	50	12

Source document F

Logo for EEC

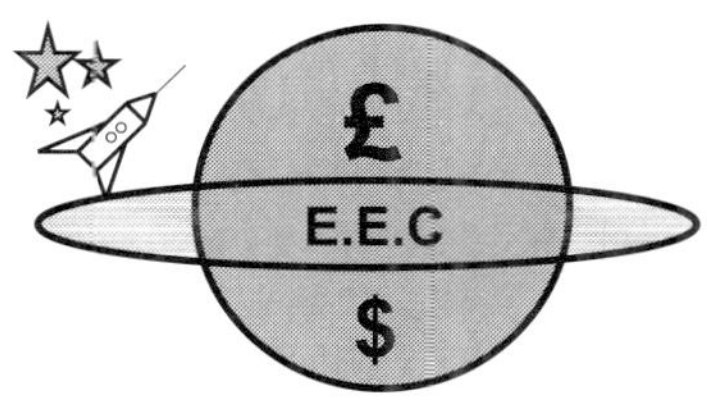

Figure 4.1

Source document G

Tragic accident at Cape Canaveral

Dr Shaun O'Cassidy, last of the original senior management team at NASA, was fatally injured in a freak accident at Cape Canaveral on Tuesday afternoon.

Dr O'Cassidy, or 'Meddlin' Micky' as he was affectionately known by members of the launch team at historic pad 29, had maintained his traditional pre-launch inspection of the launch site despite his 92 years and artificial left leg. This, as regular visitors to the Cape will recall, suffered from an intermittent software glitch which caused it to bend forwards at the knee. O'Cassidy revealed his wry humour on such occasions. 'Old Bill will get me yet,' he used to cackle, briskly hitting the offending joint to reverse its direction. (His leg's software was the last code written by the Microsoft Corporation before its absorption into the Macdonald's conglomerate.)

On this occasion luck looked the other way.

O'Cassidy had declined help as he climbed the steps to the gantry's elevator, unaware that a rocket umbilical had become detached and lay across the steel platform. His leg's software crashed at just the wrong moment, jerking his foot into an exposed socket. Doctors later estimated that 95% of the prelaunch automatic sequencer code downloaded into the leg's RAM.

He was rushed to hospital but did not recover consciousness.

Vice President Fulham Clinton has sent her sympathy to Dr O'Cassidy's widow.

Exercise 2: Setting up a database

One application of information technology that has invaded practically every aspect of modern life is the relational database, used in nearly every imaginable situation from requesting a bank overdraft to planning an A level project. Databases are inescapable.

The way in which a relational database can be used to help organize a business organization is illustrated by the following case study of a (hypothetical) tour company.

South Pacific Safari is a small specialist tour operator which offers unique holidays tailored to the needs of its clientele. It prides itself on being able to provide 'the vacation of a lifetime' to its customers, principally as the result of buying a tropical island, Xanadont, from the estate of the late Chief Mongane of the Isepi tribe, a people and land little known to anthropologists and *terra incognita* for most aspiring cartographers and nineteenth century colonists. Inspired by H.G. Wells' *The Island of Dr Moreau*, the company arranged for massive landscaping and the importation of genetically modified species. This has now permitted South Pacific Safari to offer, without question, tours unrivalled anywhere in the world.

Loyal tourists return year by year but, following an unfortunate incident involving a London taxi driver and gorilla/polar bear hybrid, South Pacific Safari's CEO decides that it is time that the business is computerized. A database is hastily set up and implemented on a PC installed in company HQ.

The information held in this database comprises four tables. The first of these lists the company's tourists, giving their personal details, where they are staying, and the length of their holiday on the island:

Tourists

1st name	*2nd name*	*Nationality*	*Occupation*	*Hotel*	*Duration of holiday*
Helena	Sefton	British	Dentist	Regal	14 days
Brian	Hume	British	Taxi driver	Sunshine	7 days
Ludwig	Leibniz	Austrian	Photographer	Regal	7 days
Jo	Laplace	American	Architect	Hamilton	21 days
Sandra	Everton	Canadian	Mathematician	Sunshine	3 days
Lulu	Stockhausen	German	Welder	Regal	14 days
Spencer	Bland	Nigerian	Teacher	Hamilton	3 days
Willum	Katze	American	Journalist	Sunshine	10 days
Francis	Flower	Canadian	Florist	Regal	3 days
Celeste	Martin	French	Data entry clerk	Sunshine	14 days

The second table gives essential facts about the local tribesmen employed as tour guides:

Guides

Name	*Experience*	*Recommended tip*
Fernando	15 years	£10
Mr Jeremy	20 years	£25
Toddy	10 years	£5
Silas	12 years	£10

A third table records the different standard one-day tours run by the company:

Tour

Tour name	*Location*	*Distance covered*	*Cost*
Scenic	Green Mountains	27 km	£45
Verdant	Creepy forest	15 km	£30
Seaside	River delta	10 km	£20
Cultural	Old City	10 km	£20
Sultry	Badlands	20 km	£35

The fourth table shows which tours have been selected by tourists. As these tours are highly individualized, tourists are permitted to choose their own guide. Note that South Pacific Safari are not particularly concerned about the dates on which tours are conducted. This is left according to the weather and individual arrangements between tourist and guide.

Bookings

1st name	*2nd name*	*Tour name*	*Guide*
Jo	Laplace	Verdant	Toddy
Sandra	Everton	Scenic	Mr Jeremy
Celeste	Martin	Sultry	Mr Jeremy
Jo	Laplace	Seaside	Fernando
Brian	Hume	Cultural	Silas
Celeste	Martin	Scenic	Toddy
Willum	Katze	Verdant	Silas
Brian	Hume	Scenic	Fernando
Helena	Sefton	Sultry	Toddy
Francis	Flower	Cultural	Mr Jeremy

These tables can be saved in Microsoft Access and then linked to allow data to be drawn from them to create queries

Here are the stages involved, in Access, to set up the first table of data.

First you need to load Access. Once it is loaded click on File and select New Database. As we are going to type in several tables of data we need to create a relational database in which this data can be held.

A name has to be chosen for the database. Here SPS is chosen, for South Pacific Safari. Once the name has been entered click on Create.

The first table has to be entered into the database. Select the Tables tab and click on New. Then choose Design View and click on OK. This allows you to decide what the field names for the table should be and also the data type. (Note that the data type for the field will default to Text unless you choose something different from the drop down menu.)

In design view you can now select the field names and data types appropriate for the table of information above. An additional 'Tourist ID' field is added. (AutoNumber is selected as the data type for this field.) The other field names are as shown above.

It is vital that you also choose the primary key at this point. The primary key will allow one table to be associated with another. Primary keys are so vital to the concept of a relational database that if you do not choose one Access will create one all by itself. But you wish to remain in charge.

The primary key you should select for this table is Tourist ID. Highlight this now and click on the little picture of a key at the top of the screen.

Your screen should look like Figure 4.2.

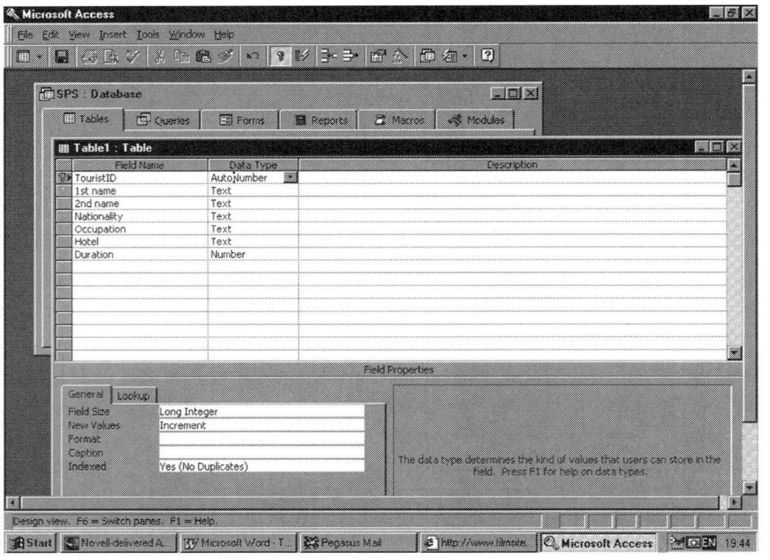

Figure 4.2

After this you need to save this new, though empty, table. Click on File, select Save and then enter a filename. This name is arbitrary but here it is assumed that you have called it 'tbl Tourists'.

You can now close or minimize the current window to return to the initial screen. Select Tables again and double click on tbl Tourists. You will now see an empty table. The field names appear at the top. Type in the information from the original information above. When you get to the end of each record the cursor automatically goes to the next record of the table. Note that you do not have to resave. This takes place automatically.

When all the data has been entered your display will look like Figure 4.3.

In the same way a table is set up for the guides (see Figure 4.4).

A third table holds the tour details (see Figure 4.5).

The fourth table will store bookings. At this point the way a computer relational database views things and the human approach part company fairly drastically. Automated searching, and the various algorithms employed by database software, will go hopelessly wrong if duplicated data is contained within the database. There is too much room for error. In the human method – displayed earlier in the bookings table – data has been repeated from the previous tables. For example, tourist names appear in both the Tourists table and in the Bookings table. This must not occur in the computer version. Instead the same information – which tourists have booked which tour and with which guide – can be stored simply in terms of the Tourist ID, Tour ID and Guide ID fields. The new table could be written out manually like this:

Tourist ID	*Tour ID*	*Guide ID*
4	2	3
5	1	2
10	5	2
4	3	1
2	4	4
10	1	3
8	2	4
2	1	1
1	5	3
9	4	2

Figure 4.6 shows how it will apppear in Access.

Once the data for South Pacific Safari has been entered as these four tables, links have to be established between them in order to allow different data items to be related to one another. In this way meaningful information can be extracted as queries on the database. The links are set up as follows:

Click on Tools then Relationships
The Show Table dialogue box appears
Click on each table in turn and then click on Add
Close Show Table

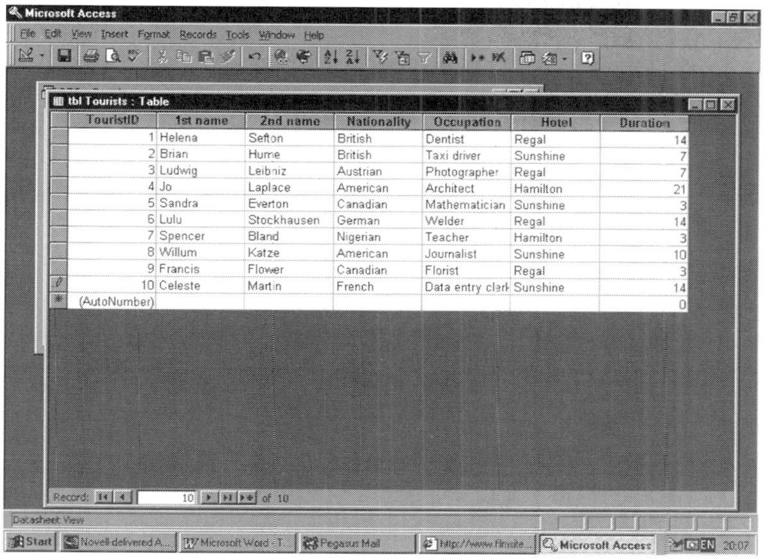

Figure 4.3

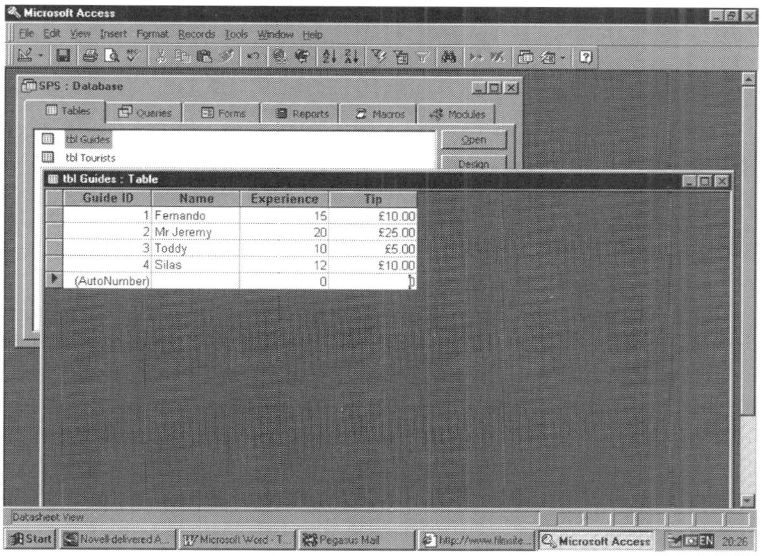

Figure 4.4

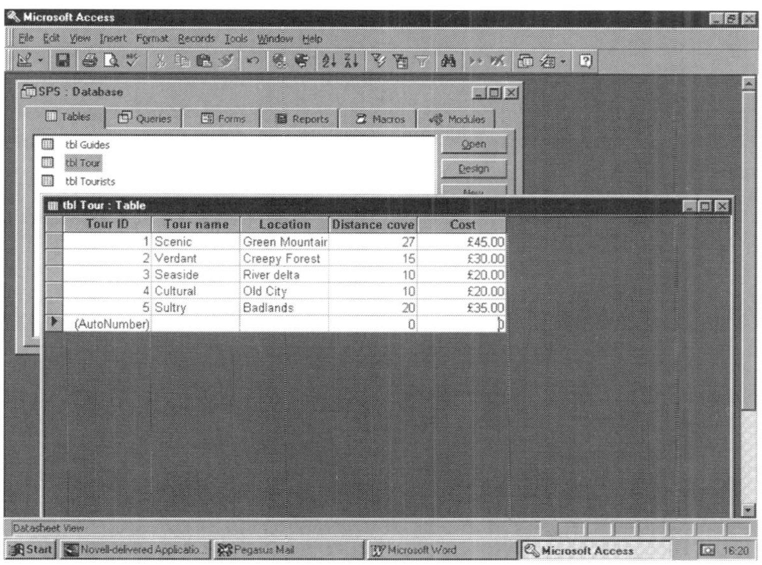

Figure 4.5

In the Relationships window the four tables will be shown, indicating the names of the fields in each of them. It may be easier at this point to drag the tables around the window to clarify the view of the links that are established between them.

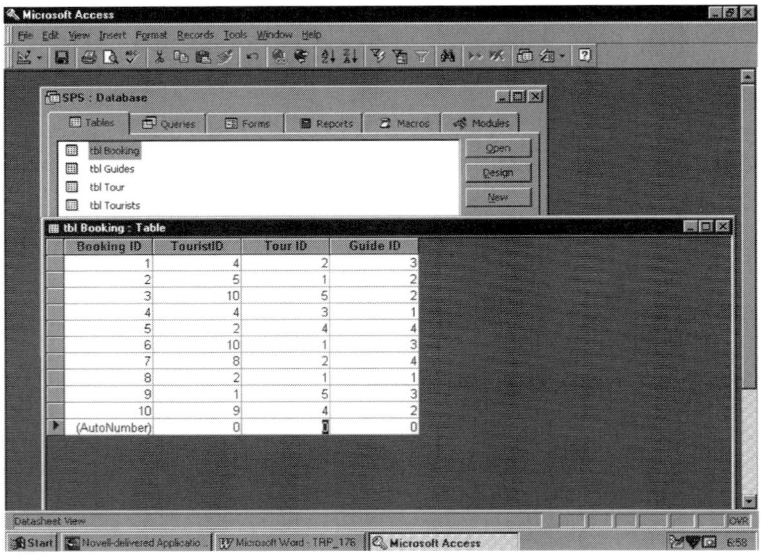

Figure 4.6

Set up the links between the tables as shown in Figure 4.7. Do this by clicking and holding on a relevant field in one table and dragging on to the same field in the other table. For each link check the Enforce Referential Integrity box and then click on Create.

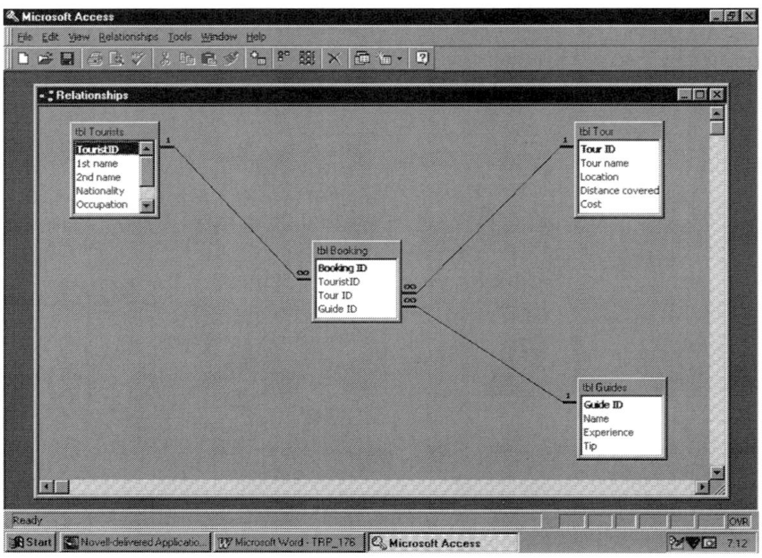

Figure 4.7

Now that the tables have been linked, queries can be designed to extract information. In the examples given here it is assumed that tourists want to know how much they are going to be expected to pay in tips to guides. The information which will allow this query to be constructed lies in three of the four tables we have set up. These tables are Tourists, Guides and the Bookings table, which holds the vital additional information of which tourists will be involved with which guides. So these three tables have to be incorporated into the query.

In the Database window select Queries and New
Select Design View

In the Show Table window select the three tables. The display will now appear like Figure 4.8.

The query will have to show the names of the tourists and the tips they pay. This means that the field's 1st name (from table Tourists), 2nd name (from table Tourists) and Tip (from table Guides) must be chosen, as indicated in Figure 4.9.

Finally the query has to be saved. In Figure 4.10 the name Gifts has been chosen. Clicking on Gifts now shows the information required.

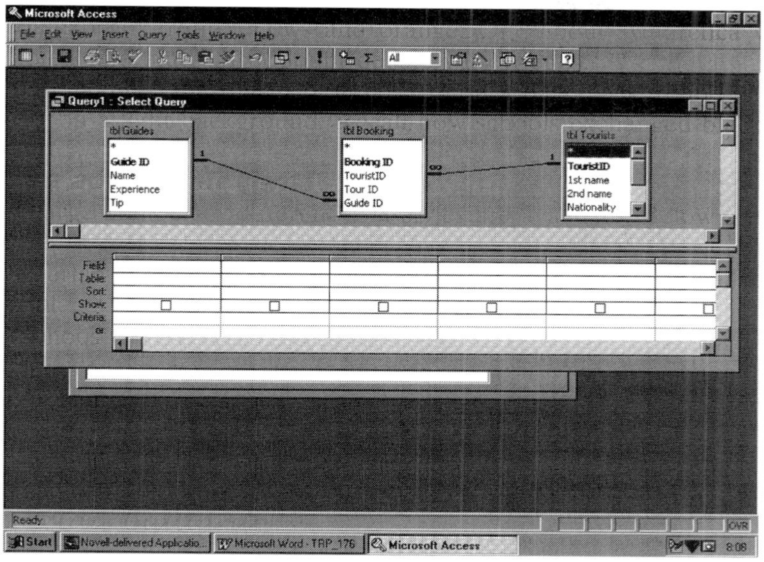

Figure 4.8

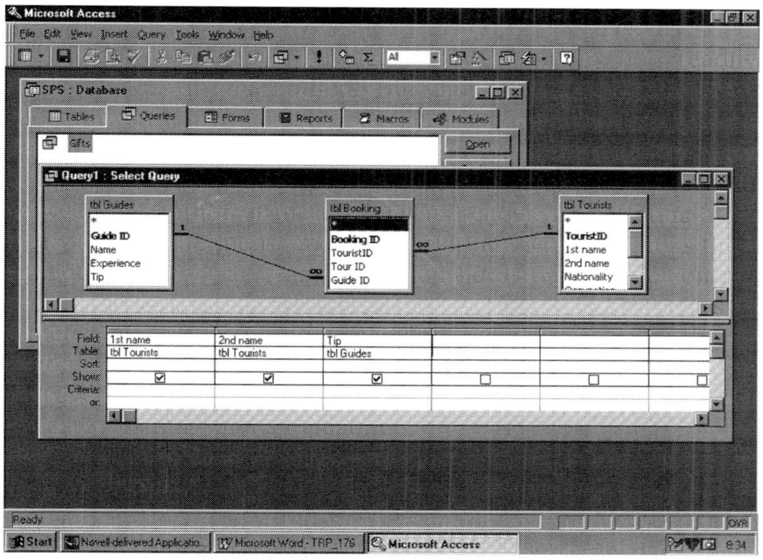

Figure 4.9

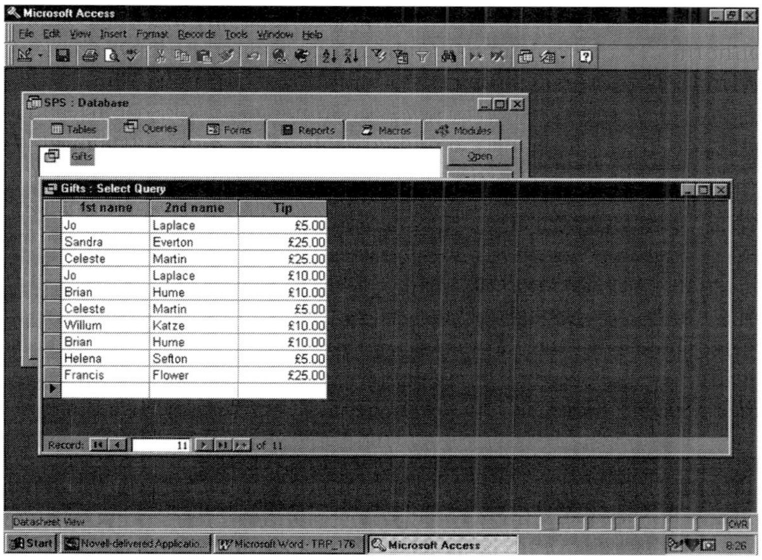

Figure 4.10

4.2 Information processing tools

Exercise 1: Human resources and profiling software

A personnel department has the difficult task of making sure that applicants seeking a post are correctly matched with available positions within the organization. This will be particularly taxing in a situation in which redeployment is being carried out.

The assumption in the following exercise is that posts have to be filled from employees already belonging to an organization. As a consequence of natural wastage, and of a management decision to use this opportunity to reduce the size of the overall workforce, it has become necessary to reassess professional skills amongst the current staff and to decide which of the available posts a particular employee best suits.

This exercise is carried out, in a theoretical organization, by staff in personnel conducting a series of interviews, psychometric tests and other assessment exercises upon the 'floating' members of staff. By doing this they are able to produce a percentage score for staff in a number of areas, as shown in Table 4.1.

Table 4.1

	Numeracy	*Literacy*	*Org. skills*	*Comm. skills*	*Fitness/strength*	*Empathy*
Doreen Sorrel	75%	43%	83%	49%	67%	23%
Marcel Penny	34%	75%	60%	80%	47%	78%
Ann Henshaw	21%	34%	40%	39%	96%	43%
Percy Hogkins	56%	67%	99%	78%	66%	79%
Prudence Smith	98%	87%	76%	80%	41%	69%
Helena Sutton	77%	88%	22%	67%	54%	85%
Sandra Sidley	89%	55%	45%	67%	99%	55%
Harrison Foreman	87%	67%	77%	65%	56%	88%
Harriet Hopeman	55%	67%	24%	33%	55%	41%
William Wincel	34%	44%	23%	56%	65%	45%

The posts that have to be filled in the organization are:

Receptionist
Accounts clerk
Caretaker
Deliveries van driver
Wages clerk
Cleaner
Production line worker

For each of these the personnel department constructs a 'skills' profile', or weighting for each skill relative to a particular post. This weighting will indicate the importance which personnel believe a skill has for the post considered. Hence, at the risk of being politically incorrect (and making the assumption that the Estates Dept. at the author's college does not read this material!) a putative skills profile for the post of caretaker in the organization could be as shown as below. A scale of 1–5 has been used, 1 representing low importance and 5 high:

Numeracy = 3
Literacy = 3
Organizational skills = 5
Communication skills = 2
Fitness/strength = 5
Empathy = 1

Assuming this profile, the overall weighted total for a given member of staff being redeployed can be calculated by multiplying each of their scores by the weighting factor. The overall total of these products is then obtained. Applying this to the data for Harriet Hopeman in Table 4.1 gives this calculation:

$(55 \times 3) + (67 \times 3) + (24 \times 5) + (33 \times 2) + (55 \times 5) + (41 \times 1)$
$= 165 + 201 + 120 + 66 + 275 + 41$
$= 868$

In a similar way, overall scores can be obtained, using the skills profile to weight the way in which individual skills contribute, for each of the staff being considered. An assumption is then made that the highest score identifies the most appropriate person for the post specified by the profile.

This mechanism may appear a little crude but it does allow rapid assessment of staff over a range of chosen skills and for a variety of posts. It is versatile and can be used in a broad range of applications, depending upon the data available.

These ideas are now developed as a program in Basic.

A program which allows different skills profiles, corresponding to a range of posts, to be matched against the proficiencies of applicants is given below. Typical screen displays are shown here as well. The first (Figure 4.1) illustrates how the program display will appear initially when the series of weights for a particular post is being entered. The user (assumed to be a personnel officer in the Human Resources department of an organization) is being prompted to enter a weighting for the first skill, Numeracy (see Figure 4.11). All the data in this example is taken from Table 4.1.

When the relevant weighting for all six skills have been entered for the chosen post, a comparison is made with the skills attributed to each of the 10 candidates and the person with the best match suggested (see Figure 4.12).

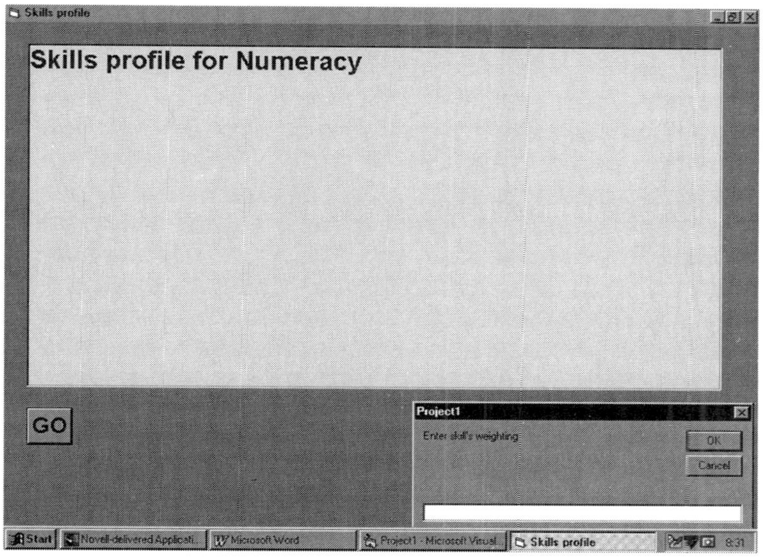

Figure 4.11

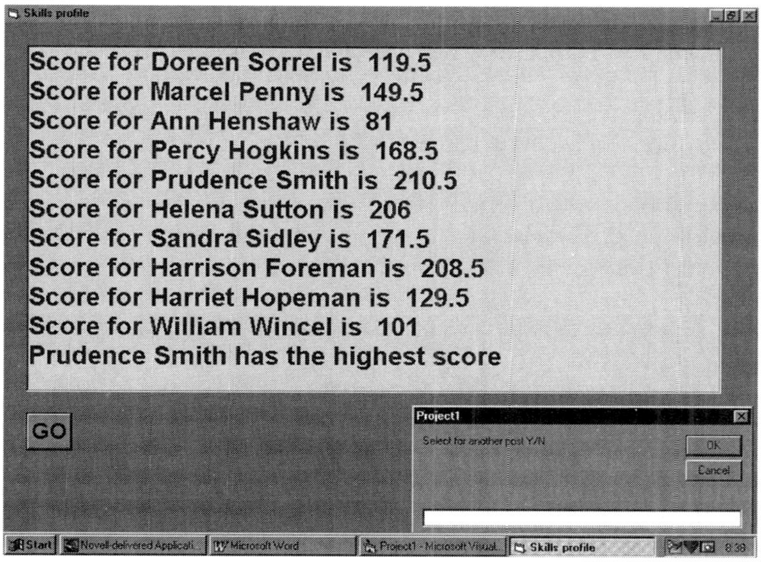

Figure 4.12

Program listing

```
Option Explicit

Private Sub Command1_Click()

'Skills profiling case study

'Array holds names of skills
Dim strSkillName(6) As String

'Array holds skills' weightings (assigned at run time)
Dim sngWeight(6) As Single

Rem Array holds names of applicants
Dim strPerson(10) As String

Rem 2D array holds applicants' scores in skills assessment
Dim intSkill(10, 6) As Integer

'Array holds applicants' data
Dim strData(10) As String

'Declare position in strData()
Dim intPosition As Integer

'Declare applicant's score
Dim sngTotal As Single

'Declare maximum score
Dim sngMaximum As Single

'Declare matching subscript
Dim intMatch As Integer

'Exit variable
Dim strAnswer As String

'Declare loop control variables
Dim intCounter1 As Integer
Dim intCounter2 As Integer

'Assign names of skills to array SkillNames$()
strSkillName(1) = "Numeracy"
strSkillName(2) = "Literacy"
strSkillName(3) = "Org skills"
strSkillName(4) = "Comm skills"
strSkillName(5) = "Fitness/Strength"
strSkillName(6) = "Empathy"

'Assign applicants' names to array strPerson()
strPerson(1) = "Doreen Sorrel"
strPerson(2) = "Marcel Penny"
strPerson(3) = "Ann Henshaw"
strPerson(4) = "Percy Hogkins"
strPerson(5) = "Prudence Smith"
strPerson(6) = "Helena Sutton"
strPerson(7) = "Sandra Sidley"
strPerson(8) = "Harrison Foreman"
strPerson(9) = "Harriet Hopeman"
strPerson(10) = "William Wincel"
```

```
'Data for applicants
strData(1)  = "75, 43, 83, 49, 67, 23"
strData(2)  = "34, 75, 60, 80, 47, 78"
strData(3)  = "21, 34, 40, 39, 96, 43"
strData(4)  = "56, 67, 99, 78, 66, 79"
strData(5)  = "98, 87, 76, 80, 41, 69"
strData(6)  = "77, 88, 22, 67, 54, 85"
strData(7)  = "89, 55, 45, 67, 99, 55"
strData(8)  = "87, 67, 77, 65, 56, 88"
strData(9)  = "55, 67, 24, 33, 55, 41"
strData(10)  = "34, 44, 23, 56, 65, 45"

'Assign applicants' skills assessment to intSkill() array
For intCounter1 = 1 To 10
For intCounter2 = 1 To 6
intPosition = intCounter2 * 4 - 3
intSkill(intCounter1,intCounter2) = Val(Mid$(strData(intCounter1),
intPosition, 2))

Next intCounter2
Next intCounter1

'Loop permits different posts to be analysed
Do

'User enters each skill's weighting
For intCounter1 = 1 To 6
PicDisplay.Print "Skills profile for ";
PicDisplay.Print strSkillName(intCounter1)
sngWeight(intCounter1) = Val(InputBox("Enter skill's weighting", , ,
6500, 6500))
PicDisplay.Cls
Next intCounter1

'Reinitialise maximum value
sngMaximum = 0

'Reinitialise matching applicant
intMatch = 0

'Loop calculates scores
For intCounter1 = 1 To 10

PicDisplay.Print "Score for "; strPerson(intCounter1); " is ";
sngTotal = 0
For intCounter2 = 1 To 6
sngTotal = sngTotal + intSkill(intCounter1, intCounter2) *
sngWeight(intCounter2)
Next intCounter2
PicDisplay.Print sngTotal

Rem Find greatest score
If sngTotal > sngMaximum Then
sngMaximum = sngTotal
intMatch = intCounter1
End If

Next intCounter1

'Indicate best match to skills profile
PicDisplay.Print strPerson(intMatch); " has the highest score"
```

```
'Loop exit condition
strAnswer = InputBox("Select for another post Y/N", , , 6500, 6500)
PicDisplay.Cls
Loop Until strAnswer$   "Y"

End Sub
```

Program documentation
A number of arrays are required by the program. The first of these is strSkillName() which holds the names of the six skills analysed by this program. In the current version of the code the array is dimensioned to have six locations (ignoring the zeroth) but, as with all the arrays and data, incorporated into the listing, this number could be adjusted to adapt the code to different situations:

```
Option Explicit

Private Sub Command1_Click()

'Skills profiling case study

'Array holds names of skills
Dim strSkillName(6) As String
```

A second array will store the individual weighting that will be entered for each skill. This is the array sngWeight(). It too is dimensioned to allow for six skills to be examined. The numerical data type chosen, single, permits the program to calculate with fractional values if necessary. This will allow the personnel officer to define the weights over a range 0–1, if desired. No error trapping (user validation) has been included in the program and so any range of weightings can be chosen. This makes the program more versatile:

```
'Array holds skills' weightings (assigned at run time)
Dim sngWeight(6) As Single
```

A third array, strPerson(), will hold the names of the 10 applicants:

```
Rem Array holds names of applicants
Dim strPerson(10) As String
```

The program needs to be able to hold the table, given above, in which the 10 rows show the 10 applicants and the sixth column their corresponding scores for the different skills that have been assessed. A two-dimensional array, intSkill(), is used here to store this data. An alternative approach would be to work with six one-dimensional arrays, but the code would be longer and less elegant:

```
Rem 2D array holds applicants' scores in skills assessment
Dim intSkill(10, 6) As Integer
```

The numerical data which will be placed into the two-dimensional array, intSkill(), is intially held as a set of 10 separate strings in the array strData():

```
'Array holds applicants' data
Dim strData(10) As String
```

The algorithm which processes the data in the strData() array, and then transfers the processed numbers into the intSkill() array, requires a working variable, intPosition, to calculate precisely where in the strings of data the required numbers are located. This can be declared as an integer variable:

```
'Declare position in strData()
Dim intPosition As Integer
```

In order to decide who amongst the 10 applicants best matches the skills profile for a particular post, a total has to be calculated for each person. This is represented by the variable sngTotal. It does not need to be subscripted as an array because once the value is displayed on the screen, and used to determine the best match, it is no longer required by the program:

```
'Declare applicant's score
Dim sngTotal As Single
```

Determining the applicant whose skills most suit them to a particular post requires a routine involving two further variables, sngMaximum and intMatch:

```
'Declare maximum score
Dim sngMaximum As Single

'Declare matching subscript
Dim intMatch As Integer
```

A dummy variable is used in an exit condition:

```
'Exit variable
Dim strAnswer As String
```

Two loop control variables are required as a result of the program using a two-dimensional array:

```
'Declare loop control variables
Dim intCounter1 As Integer
Dim intCounter2 As Integer
```

The names of the six skills analysed by the program are directly assigned to the array strSkillName(). As already stated, this choice is quite arbitary and the program can be easily modified to work with other names and with a different number of skills:

```
'Assign names of skills to array SkillNames$()
strSkillName(1) = "Numeracy"
strSkillName(2) = "Literacy"
strSkillName(3) = "Org skills"
strSkillName(4) = "Comm skills"
strSkillName(5) = "Fitness/Strength"
strSkillName(6) = "Empathy"
```

Similarly the names of the ten applicants are assigned to strPerson():

```
'Assign applicants' names to array strPerson()
strPerson(1) = "Doreen Sorrel"
strPerson(2) = "Marcel Penny"
strPerson(3) = "Ann Henshaw"
strPerson(4) = "Percy Hogkins"
strPerson(5) = "Prudence Smith"
strPerson(6) = "Helena Sutton"
strPerson(7) = "Sandra Sidley"
strPerson(8) = "Harrison Foreman"
strPerson(9) = "Harriet Hopeman"
strPerson(10) = "William Wincel"
```

The numerical data from the table is directly assigned to the 10 locations of the strData() array in a way which is intended to make the listing simple to modify. Hence the otherwise unnecessary use of spaces and commas. Purists should object at this point to the way the program has been constructed (If they have not done so already!) because clearly it is mixing program and data in a way which is contrary to the spirit of programming: keep program code and data distinct. However, it was felt inappropriate to introduce file handling. At the same time it would be excessively taxing to retype all the details every time the program was executed. And so this compromise is introduced:

```
'Data for applicants
strData(1) = "75, 43, 83, 49, 67, 23"
strData(2) = "34, 75, 60, 80, 47, 78"
strData(3) = "21, 34, 40, 39, 96, 43"
strData(4) = "56, 67, 99, 78, 66, 79"
strData(5) = "98, 87, 76, 80, 41, 69"
strData(6) = "77, 88, 22, 67, 54, 85"
strData(7) = "89, 55, 45, 67, 99, 55"
strData(8) = "87, 67, 77, 65, 56, 88"
strData(9) = "55, 67, 24, 33, 55, 41"
strData(10) = "34, 44, 23, 56, 65, 45"
```

The data is now transferred to the two-dimensional array. Examining the data strings shows that successive pairs of digits begin at positions 1, 5, 9, 13, 17 and 21 within each string. These numbers are significant and need to be related to the sequence of numbers 1, 2, 3, 3, 5, 6 representing each skill in the table. It is often helpful to use a diagram to help identify arithmetical patterns like this:

Skill number	*Position in data string*
1	1
2	5
3	9
4	13
5	17
6	21

It can be seen that the increments in the second column are 4. This suggests multiplying the first column by 4 to give the series 4, 8, 12, 16, 20, 24. Subtracting 3 from each of these numbers then creates the series required for the second column.

In the nested loops below the 'second column' of Table 4.1 is defined by the loop control variable intCounter2. The expression which calculates the position in the data string, intPosition, is therefore intCounter2 * 4 – 3.

The range of the control variable for the outer loop, intCounter1, corresponds to the 10 applicants. The range of the control variable for the inner loop, intCounter2, represents the six skills of the original table.

Numbers can now be copied from the 10 data strings using the value calculated for intPosition together with the Mid$ function. These numbers are assigned to the intSkill() array. Appropriate array locations are determined by the two loop control variables:

```
'Assign applicants' skills assessment to intSkill() array
For intCounter1 = 1 To 10
For intCounter2 = 1 To 6
intPosition = intCounter2 * 4 - 3
intSkill(intCounter1,intCounter2) = Val(Mid$(strData(intCounter1),
intPosition, 2))
Next intCounter2
Next intCounter1
```

At this point the program can compare applicants' skills with the skills' profile entered by the personnel officer for a specific post. This is done by multiplying and summing values from the two-dimensional intSkill() array and the one-dimensional sngWeight() array. (Essentially this is multiplying a matrix with a vector.) An overall loop permits the program to be repeated to match the candidates with other posts:

```
'Loop permits different posts to be analysed
Do
```

First the skills profile for the post is entered into the sngWeight() array. This needs a For loop which repeats six times:

```
'User enters each skill's weighting
For intCounter1 = 1 To 6
```

Each time the loop repeats, the name of the current skill being entered is shown by using the strSkillName array:

```
PicDisplay.Print "Skills profile for ";
PicDisplay.Print strSkillName(intCounter1)
```

The personnel officer's chosen value is then assigned to the sngWeight() array by the InputBox function:

```
sngWeight(intCounter1) = Val(InputBox("Enter skill's weighting", , ,
6500, 6500))
PicDisplay.Cls
Next intCounter1
```

The sngMaximum and intMatch variables are initialized:

```
'Reinitialise maximum value
sngMaximum = 0
'Reinitialise matching applicant
intMatch = 0
```

An outer For loop then repeats 10 times to calculate an overall score for each applicant:

```
'Loop calculates scores
For intCounter1 = 1 To 10
```

The name of the applicant is displayed:

```
PicDisplay.Print "Score for "; strPerson(intCounter1); " is ";
```

The applicant's score is reinitialized:

```
sngTotal = 0
```

After this nested, inner For loop turns sngTotal into a running total of the product of the applicant's skills and the weightings for the post. The former is identified as intSkill(intCounter1, intCounter2). The latter is sngWeight(intCounter2):

```
For intCounter2 = 1 To 6
sngTotal = sngTotal + intSkill(intCounter1, intCounter2) *
sngWeight(intCounter2)
```

When the inner loop ends the applicant's score is displayed:

```
Next intCounter2
PicDisplay.Print sngTotal
```

This is not sufficient. The greatest of all 10 scores must be found. This is done by comparing each score for the current applicant, identified by the outer loop control variable, with the value of intMaximum. If the score is greater, intMaximum is reassigned this value. As a result, by the last repeat of the loop intMaximum will be equal to the greatest score achieved by any applicant. This is coded as an If Then End If structure:

```
Rem Find greatest score
If sngTotal > sngMaximum Then
sngMaximum = sngTotal
```

What is important, of course, is not the greatest score itself but which applicant was awarded the greatest score. The identity of this successful applicant is recorded by assigning the value of the loop control variable to intMatch within the conditional structure:

```
intMatch = intCounter1
End If

Next intCounter1
```

Once the loop has ended sngMaximum will record the highest score and intMatch the person who obtained this score. The value of intMatch can therefore be used to display this applicant's name:

```
'Indicate best match to skills profile
PicDisplay.Print strPerson(intMatch); " has the highest score"
```

A simple exit condition allows the personnel officer either to enter a new skills' profile or to exit the program:

```
'Loop exit condition
strAnswer = InputBox("Select for another post Y/N", , , 6500, 6500)
PicDisplay.Cls
Loop Until strAnswer$ <> "Y"

End Sub
```

Exercise 2: Applications of expert systems

A very simple introduction to the concept of expert systems can be given, without involving the complexity of inference engine and knowledge base, by illustrating how a very simple tree structure can combine a hierarchy of questions to give a reasonably 'intelligent' output.

A binary tree structure in particular leads to an easily visualized data structure which nevertheless proceeds, through a series of increasingly refined questions, to a more specific definition of the outcome. This type of structure can even be used to demonstrate the concept of machine learning.

A binary tree is a data structure used in some programs which need to store information in an (upside down) tree-like pattern. Information, which can include questions, is held in 'nodes'. Each node is linked to two nodes in the next level of the tree by 'arcs'. One arc represents a 'yes route', the other a 'no route'. Figure 4.13 shows a binary tree being used in a pet animal guessing game.

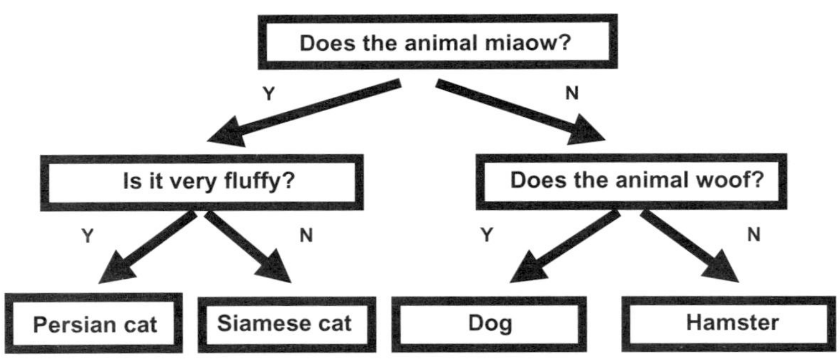

Figure 4.13

The next level of the tree would contain eight nodes, and the next level 16. This pattern continues, the number of nodes doubling at each successive level. This can be seen by applying a binary tree structure to this problem:

A small travel agency offers eight different holidays, as described on the forms below. Using a binary tree as your data structure, write a program in Basic which, by asking the user relevant questions, is able to recommend an appropriate choice of holiday.

Holiday Name	Edinburgh holiday
UK/Abroad	UK
Location	North of the country
Feature	Famous for its Festival

Holiday Name	Liverpool holiday
UK/Abroad	UK
Location	North of country
Feature	Beatles museum

Holiday Name	London holiday
UK/Abroad	UK
Location	South of country
Feature	Excellent theatre and concerts

Holiday Name	Bournemouth holiday
UK/Abroad	UK
Location	South of country
Feature	Traditional English seaside

Holiday Name	Paris holiday
UK/Abroad	Abroad
Location	Europe
Feature	Superb cultural traditions

Holiday Name	Berlin holiday
UK/Abroad	Abroad
Location	Europe
Feature	Exciting city now redeveloping its past culture

Holiday Name	Florida holiday
UK/Abroad	Abroad
Location	USA
Feature	Space Shuttle launches

Holiday Name	Chicago holiday
UK/Abroad	Abroad
Location	USA
Feature	Home city of Nobel prize winning novelist Saul Bellow

Analysis of this information about the holidays suggests a binary tree structure as shown in Figure 4.14.

A program which codes this structure as Visual Basic is given here:

Program listing

```
Option Explicit
Dim strAnswer As String
Private Sub Command1_Click()
Print
Print
```

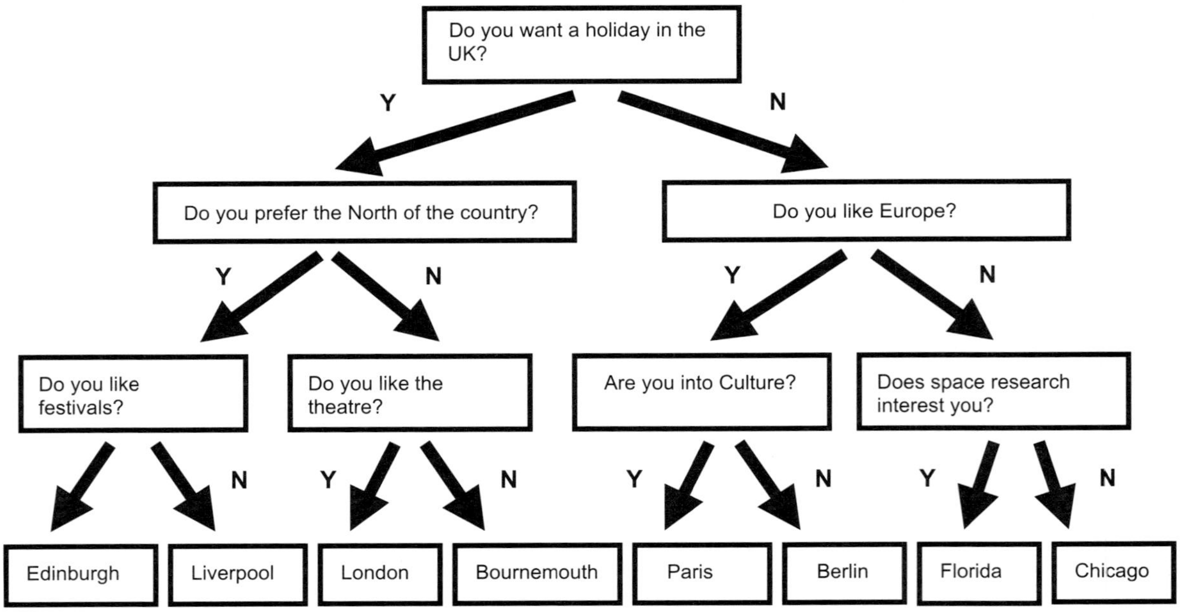

Figure 4.14 *Holiday selection as a binary tree*

```
Print "Do you want a holiday in the UK Y/N?"
strAnswer = InputBox("Enter Y or N", , , 6500, 5500)
If strAnswer = "Y" Then
Home
Else
Away
End If
End Sub

Sub Home()
Print "Do you prefer the North of the country?"
strAnswer = InputBox("Enter Y or N", , , 6500, 5500)
If strAnswer = "Y" Then
North
Else
South
End If
End Sub

Sub Away()
Print "Do you like Europe?"
strAnswer = InputBox("Enter Y or N", , , 6500, 5500)
If strAnswer = "Y" Then
Europe
Else
Usa
End If
Print
End Sub

Sub North()
Print "Do you like festivals?"
```

```
strAnswer = InputBox("Enter Y or N", , , 6500, 5500)
If strAnswer = "Y" Then
Edinburgh
Else
Liverpool
End If
End Sub

Sub South()
Print "Do you like the theatre?"
strAnswer = InputBox("Enter Y or N", , , 6500, 5500)
If strAnswer = "Y" Then
London
Else
Bournemouth
End If
End Sub

Sub Europe()
Print "Are you into Culture?"
strAnswer = InputBox("Enter Y or N", , , 6500, 5500)
If strAnswer = "Y" Then
Paris
Else
Berlin
End If
End Sub

Sub Usa()
Print "Does space research interest you?"
strAnswer = InputBox("Enter Y or N", , , 6500, 5500)
If strAnswer = "Y" Then
Florida
Else
Chicago
End If
End Sub

Sub Edinburgh()
Print
Print "Your recommended holiday is..."
Print "Holiday name: Edinburgh"
Print "UK/Abroad: UK"
Print "Location: North of country"
Print "Feature: Famous for its Festival"
End Sub

Sub Liverpool()
Print
Print "Your recommended holiday is..."
Print "Holiday name: Liverpool"
Print "UK/Abroad: UK"
Print "Location: North of country"
Print "Feature: Beatles Museum"
End Sub
```

```
Sub London()
Print
Print "Your recommended holiday is..."
Print "Holiday name: London"
Print "UK/Abroad: UK"
Print "Location: South of country"
Print "Feature: Excellent theatre and concerts"
End Sub

Sub Bournemouth()
Print
Print "Your recommended holiday is..."
Print "Holiday name: Bournemouth"
Print "UK/Abroad: UK"
Print "Location: South of country"
Print "Feature: Traditional English seaside"
End Sub

Sub Paris()
Print
Print "Your recommended holiday is..."
Print "Holiday name: Paris"
Print "UK/Abroad: Abroad"
Print "Location: Europe"
Print "Feature: Superb cultural traditions"
End Sub

Sub Berlin()
Print
Print "Your recommended holiday is..."
Print "Holiday name: Berlin"
Print "UK/Abroad: Abroad"
Print "Location: Europe"
Print "Feature: Brilliant Norman Foster bits"
End Sub

Sub Florida()
Print
Print "Your recommended holiday is..."
Print "Holiday name: Florida"
Print "UK/Abroad: Abroad"
Print "Location: USA"
Print "Feature: Space Shuttle launches"
End Sub

Sub Chicago()
Print
Print "Your recommended holiday is..."
Print "Holiday name: Chicago"
Print "UK/Abroad: Abroad"
Print "Location: USA"
Print "Feature: Nobel prize winning Saul Bellow"
End Sub
```

When the program is run the user is presented with a series of three questions, each corresponding to a shift down to the next level of the tree. The questions are written so that a Yes/No answer is appropriate. This reflects the binary structure of the tree.

In the typical display shown in Figure 4.15 the third of these questions is about to be answered.

As soon as a third answer has been provided the holiday recommendation is shown in Figure 4.16.

Program documentation

The program reflects the tree structure as a series of procedures which can call further procedures as indicated in Figure 4.17.

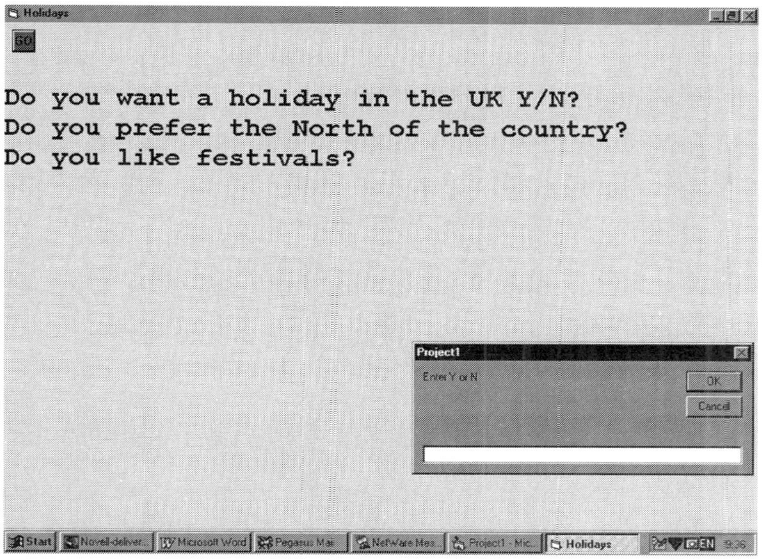

Figure 4.15

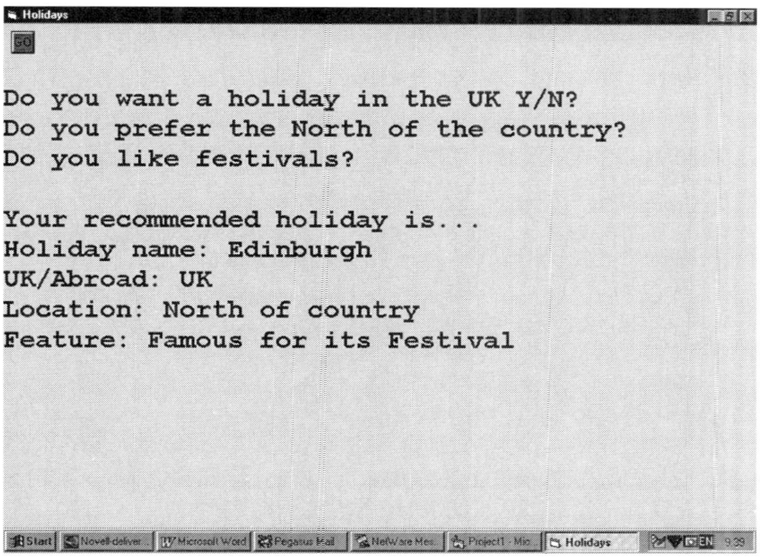

Figure 4.16

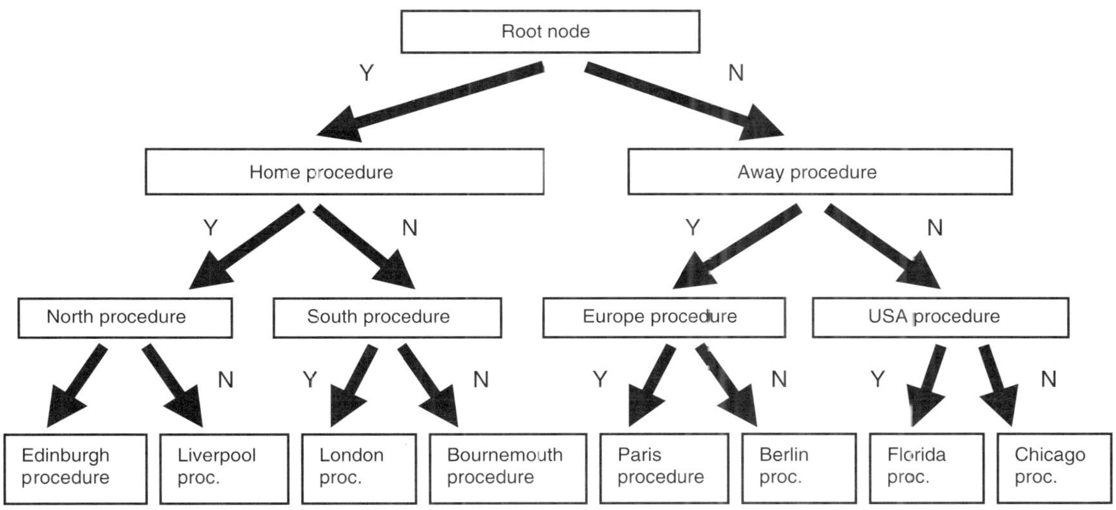

Figure 4.17 *Procedures called for holiday selection*

The user's response to the questions which appear on the screen will be represented by the variable strAnswer. This is used in all of the procedures and so is declared in the general declarations area:

```
Option Explicit
Dim strAnswer As String
```

The first procedure corresponds to the root node of the tree structure. It therefore has to ask the question contained by this node, 'Do you want a holiday in the UK?'

```
Private Sub Command1_Click()
Print
Print
Print "Do you want a holiday in the UK Y/N?"
```

The user's response is assigned to strAnswer by the InputBox function:

```
strAnswer = InputBox("Enter Y or N", , , 6500, 5500)
```

If the user answers positively the left-hand child node must be selected. This is done by calling the procedure Home, as indicated by the diagram:

```
If strAnswer = "Y" Then
Home
```

Alternatively if anything other than Y is entered the procedure Away is called instead. (Note that no attempt has been made to error trap user entry. This means that the Away procedure is called when any entry occurs which is not a single capital letter Y.)

```
Else
Away
End If
```

This main subroutine then ends:

```
End Sub
```

The structure of the first procedure is then repeated for all of the subsequent procedures in the main structure of the tree. Only the 'leaf' nodes at the bottom of the structure do not ask a question for which a yes or no answer is assumed. For example, the Home procedure, called in response to the main procedure above, will in turn call either the procedure North or the procedure South:

```
Sub Home()
Print "Do you prefer the North of the country?"
strAnswer = InputBox("Enter Y or N", , , 6500, 5500)
If strAnswer = "Y" Then
North
Else
South
End If
End Sub
```

Similarly the Away procedure calls either the procedure Europe or the procedure Usa:

```
Sub Away()
Print "Do you like Europe?"
strAnswer = InputBox("Enter Y or N", , , 6500, 5500)
If strAnswer = "Y" Then
Europe
Else
Usa
```

```
End If
Print
End Sub
```

By the time that program execution has reached this stage the third level of the tree has been encountered, with any one of four procedures, North, South, Europe and USA, now selected. Each of these third level procedures will ask a final question to distinguish between pairs of leaf nodes in the fourth level. The North procedure will call either Edinburgh or Liverpool:

```
Sub North()
Print "Do you like festivals?"
strAnswer = InputBox("Enter Y or N", , , 6500, 5500)
If strAnswer = "Y" Then
Edinburgh
Else
Liverpool
End If
End Sub
```

The South procedure will determine either London or Bournemouth as the final node:

```
Sub South()
Print "Do you like the theatre?"
strAnswer = InputBox("Enter Y or N", , , 6500, 5500)
If strAnswer = "Y" Then
London
Else
Bournemouth
End If
End Sub
```

Europe distinguishes between Paris and Berlin procedures:

```
Sub Europe()
Print "Are you into Culture?"
strAnswer = InputBox("Enter Y or N", , , 6500, 5500)
If strAnswer = "Y" Then
Paris
Else
Berlin
End If
End Sub
```

USA selects either Florida or Chicago:

```
Sub USA()
Print "Does space research interest you?"
strAnswer = InputBox("Enter Y or N", , , 6500, 5500)
If strAnswer = "Y" Then
Florida
Else
Chicago
End If
End Sub
```

The final level of the tree consists of leaf nodes which simply display the information about each holiday. The Edinburgh procedure uses Print statement to show on screen the information that was initially presented on the holiday forms:

```
Sub Edinburgh()
Print
```

```
Print "Your recommended holiday is..."
Print "Holiday name: Edinburgh"
Print "UK/Abroad: UK"
Print "Location: North of country"
Print "Feature: Famous for its Festival"
End Sub
```

Similarly the Liverpool and other procedures show the relevant holiday information:

```
Sub Liverpool()
Print
Print "Your recommended holiday is..."
Print "Holiday name: Liverpool"
Print "UK/Abroad: UK"
Print "Location: North of country"
Print "Feature: Beatles Museum"
End Sub

Sub London()
Print
Print "Your recommended holiday is..."
Print "Holiday name: London"
Print "UK/Abroad: UK"
Print "Location: South of country"
Print "Feature: Excellent theatre and concerts"
End Sub

Sub Bournemouth()
Print
Print "Your recommended holiday is..."
Print "Holiday name: Bournemouth"
Print "UK/Abroad: UK"
Print "Location: South of country"
Print "Feature: Traditional English seaside"
End Sub

Sub Paris()
Print
Print "Your recommended holiday is..."
Print "Holiday name: Paris"
Print "UK/Abroad: Abroad"
Print "Location: Europe"
Print "Feature: Superb cultural traditions"
End Sub

Sub Berlin()
Print
Print "Your recommended holiday is..."
Print "Holiday name: Berlin"
Print "UK/Abroad: Abroad"
Print "Location: Europe"
Print "Feature: Brilliant Norman Foster bits"
End Sub

Sub Florida()
Print
Print "Your recommended holiday is..."
Print "Holiday name: Florida"
Print "UK/Abroad: Abroad"
Print "Location: USA"
```

```
Print "Feature: Space Shuttle launches"
End Sub

Sub Chicago()
Print
Print "Your recommended holiday is..."
Print "Holiday name: Chicago"
Print "UK/Abroad: Abroad"
Print "Location: USA"
Print "Feature: Nobel prize winning Saul Bellow"
End Sub
```

Alternative listing

This alternative version of the program uses an array to ask the questions rather than this being done by separate procedures. The array locations correspond with the nodes of the binary tree.

A pointer indicates the current node that has been reached. It begins with a value of 1 to show the first node and question. The next node, as can be seen from Figure 4.18, will always be twice the value of the current node for a Yes answer and twice the value plus one for a No answer.

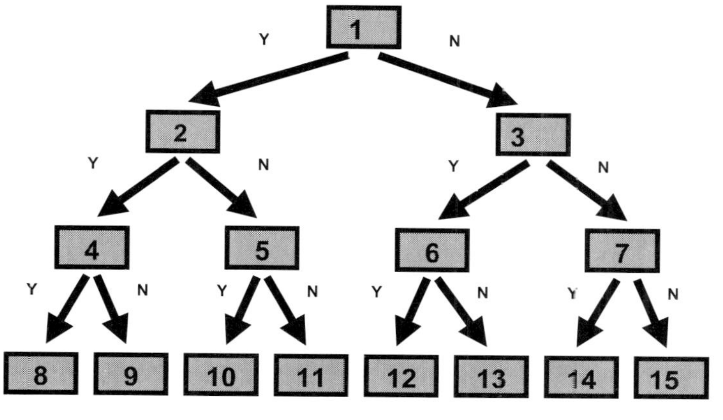

Figure 4.18 *Node numbering for binary tree algorithm*

This calculation of the next node is performed by the Boolean expression given here:

```
intPointer = intPointer * 2 - (strAnswer = "N")
```

If the answer is No the expression in brackets evaluates as minus 1. Subtracting this from the value of twice the pointer then gives the required node.

Similarly if the answer is Yes the expression evaluates as zero and hence again the required node is given.

The final value of the pointer at the leaf nodes of the tree is used in a Select Case structure to call the appropriate procedure.

```
Option Explicit
Private Sub Command1_Click()
'Holiday selection program
Dim strNode(7) As String
Dim intPointer As Integer
intPointer = 1
Dim strAnswer As String

'Node content
strNode(1) = "Do you want a holiday in the UK Y/N?"
strNode(2) = "Do you prefer the North of the country?"
strNode(3) = "Do you like Europe?"
strNode(4) = "Do you like festivals?"
strNode(5) = "Do you like the theatre?"
strNode(6) = "Are you into Culture?"
strNode(7) = "Does space research interest you?"
```

```
Print
Print
Do
'Ask question
Print strNode(intPointer)
strAnswer = InputBox("Enter Y or N", , , 6500, 5500)
'Calculate next node
intPointer = intPointer * 2 - (strAnswer = "N")
Loop Until intPointer > 7

'Adjust pointer value for use in select case
intPointer = intPointer - 7

'Display selected holiday
Select Case intPointer
Case 1
Edinburgh
Case 2
Liverpool
Case 3
London
Case 4
Bournemouth
Case 5
Paris
Case 6
Berlin
Case 7
Florida
Case 8
Chicago
End Select
End Sub

Sub Edinburgh()
Print
Print "Your recommended holiday is..."
Print "Holiday name: Edinburgh"
Print "UK/Abroad: UK"
Print "Location: North of country"
Print "Feature: Famous for its Festival"
End Sub
Sub Liverpool()
Print
Print "Your recommended holiday is..."
Print "Holiday name: Liverpool"
Print "UK/Abroad: UK"
Print "Location: North of country"
Print "Feature: Beatles Museum"
End Sub

Sub London()
Print
Print "Your recommended holiday is..."
Print "Holiday name: London"
Print "UK/Abroad: UK"
Print "Location: South of country"
Print "Feature: Excellent theatre and concerts"
End Sub
Sub Bournemouth()
```

```
Print
Print "Your recommended holiday is..."
Print "Holiday name: Bournemouth"
Print "UK/Abroad: UK"
Print "Location: South of country"
Print "Feature: Traditional English seaside"
End Sub
Sub Paris()
Print
Print "Your recommended holiday is..."
Print "Holiday name: Paris"
Print "UK/Abroad: Abroad"
Print "Location: Europe"
Print "Feature: Superb cultural traditions"
End Sub
Sub Berlin()
Print
Print "Your recommended holiday is..."
Print "Holiday name: Berlin"
Print "UK/Abroad: Abroad"
Print "Location: Europe"
Print "Feature: Brilliant Norman Foster bits"
End Sub
Sub Florida()
Print
Print "Your recommended holiday is..."
Print "Holiday name: Florida"
Print "UK/Abroad: Abroad"
Print "Location: USA"
Print "Feature: Space Shuttle launches"
End Sub
Sub Chicago()
Print
Print "Your recommended holiday is..."
Print "Holiday name: Chicago'
Print "UK/Abroad: Abroad"
Print "Location: USA"
Print "Feature: Nobel prize winning Saul Bellow"
End Sub
```

Exercise 3: Producing an invoice

> The production of an invoice can be simplified by the use of a spreadsheet. This can contain all the text required to clarify the entries on the invoice, numerical data indicating different items, and the equations allowing subtotals to be calculated.

The basic structure of the invoice can be planned in terms of input, process and output variables, as shown in the following example.

Ballantine Park is a holiday theme park in Scotland. It is a large area of open moorland that has been divided into distinct attractions.

The most significant of these is the Castle, where guests sleep and can watch television and videos when the weather is unsuitable for outside activities. The Castle is some distance from the Lodge, where guests eat. Although a modern building, the Lodge has been constructed in mock-Gothic style and is situated on a rocky escarpment approached by a footpath overlooking the glass roof of the Lagoon, an enclosed heated pool supervised by qualified lifeguards. Some distance across the moor is the Glen, an outdoor theatre where *son et lumière* tableaux of Scottish history are presented after dusk. These tableaux have achieved a considerable reputation for their authenticity, and guests often wish to purchase 'spin-off' merchandise, like dolls in historically verified costume and illustrated pamphlets. On arrival guests leave their cars at an underground car park at the Castle, and can travel between Park attractions in small electric buggies which they hire. All staff at the four attractions have access to the Park's computer network, and can update guest accounts according to services provided and purchases made.

Guests are charged according to how many nights they stay at the Castle, the number of meals eaten at the Lodge, the hours spent in the Lagoon, the number of performances attended at the Glen and the distance in miles driven in a buggy. Incidental purchases can be paid for on leaving as well. A discount scheme is in operation to encourage guests to eat more frequently at the Lodge; if the cost of the meals purchased by a guest exceeds £120 all performances attended at the Glen become free of charge. (This acts retrospectively and includes the cost of performances attended before the cost of meals passes the threshold figure.) A further potential discount is also offered. If the total charge to a guest exceeds £350 they are offered a 10% discount on future holidays at Ballantine Park. This offer is automatically printed on an invoice presented to guests before they leave.

The finance department of the park keeps a guest file which stores details of customers and the park attractions they have frequented during their holiday. It allows the production of the invoice.

> Using appropriate spreadsheet software design an invoice will be presented to customers when they leave the theme park indicating how they are being billed.

In the screen shot of a typical invoice (see Figure 4.19) the cost of meals is not more than £120 and so the charge for *son et lumière* is not discounted. Also as the overall total does not exceed £350 no future discount has been offered to the guest.

When the guest increases the number of meals eaten at the Lodge so that their total charge is greater than £120, the invoice automatically removes any payment for *son et lumière* performances. Note that the guest still does not qualify for a future discount (see Figure 4.20).

Finally if the number of days attended, meals eaten and other expenses lead to an overall total greater than £350 the automatic discount for a future visit is displayed (see Figure 4.21).

The model for the invoice design is developed here. The invoice has to indicate an overall total for the guest to pay. This will be the main output variable for the spreadsheet model:

Output variable
Total Overall charge to guest

In calculating this total there will be constant values involved as listed below:

Constants

Night_Cost	Charge for one night's accommodation in the Castle
Meal_Cost	Cost of a single meal at the Lodge
Swim_Cost	Charge for one hour in the Lagoon
Theatre_Cost	Admission to a performance at the Glen
Miles_Cost	Charge per mile for electric buggy

The values, which will vary from guest to guest according to the length of their stay, and how they spend their time at the theme park, form this set of input variables:

Input variables

Nights	Number of nights spent in the Castle
Meals	Number of meals eaten at the Lodge
Swim	Number of hours spent swimming in the Lagoon
Theatre	Number of performances attended at the Glen
Miles	Number of miles travelled in an electric buggy
Incidentals	Total spent on additional purchases

The process variables for the model will actually be placed on the invoice as subtotals:

Subtotals (process variables)

Subtotal_Castle	Total charge for accommodation
Subtotal_Lodge	Total charge for meals
Subtotal_Lagoon	Total charge for swimming
Subtotal_Glen	Total charge for *son et lumière*
Subtotal_Buggy	Total charge for electric buggy

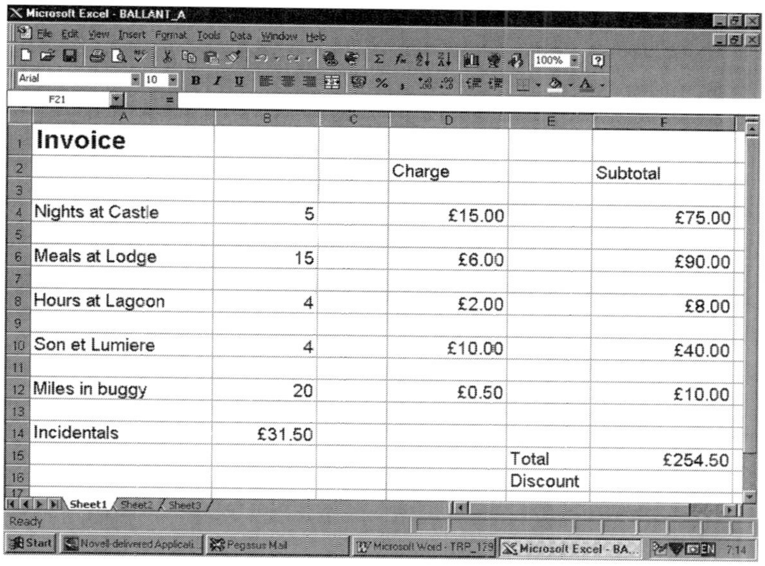

Invoice					
			Charge		Subtotal
Nights at Castle	5		£15.00		£75.00
Meals at Lodge	15		£6.00		£90.00
Hours at Lagoon	4		£2.00		£8.00
Son et Lumiere	4		£10.00		£40.00
Miles in buggy	20		£0.50		£10.00
Incidentals	£31.50				
				Total	£254.50
				Discount	

Figure 4.19

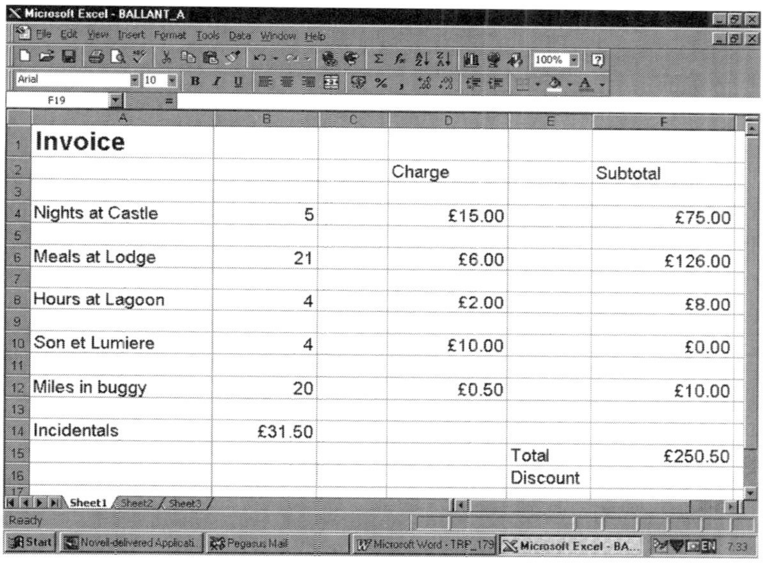

Invoice					
			Charge		Subtotal
Nights at Castle	5		£15.00		£75.00
Meals at Lodge	21		£6.00		£126.00
Hours at Lagoon	4		£2.00		£8.00
Son et Lumiere	4		£10.00		£0.00
Miles in buggy	20		£0.50		£10.00
Incidentals	£31.50				
				Total	£250.50
				Discount	

Figure 4.20

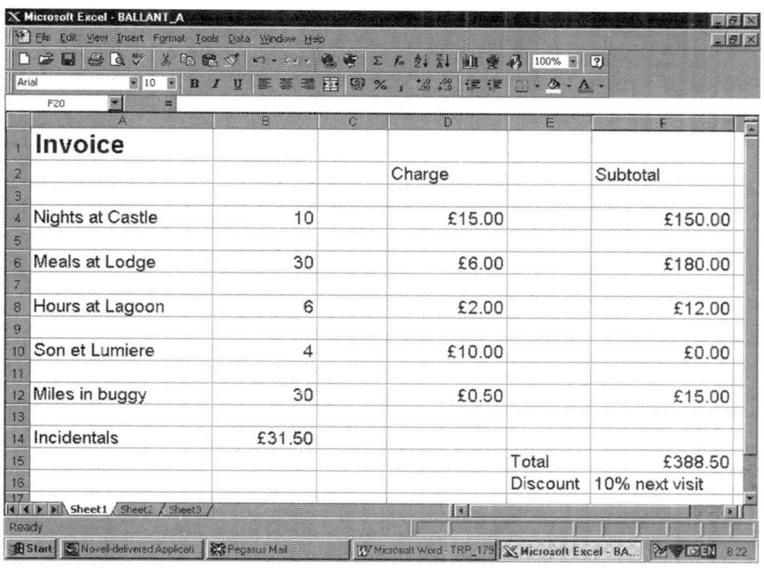

Invoice					
			Charge		Subtotal
Nights at Castle	10		£15.00		£150.00
Meals at Lodge	30		£6.00		£180.00
Hours at Lagoon	6		£2.00		£12.00
Son et Lumiere	4		£10.00		£0.00
Miles in buggy	30		£0.50		£15.00
Incidentals	£31.50				
				Total	£388.50
				Discount	10% next visit

Figure 4.21

Equations to calculate these subtotals, and the overall charge, are as shown:

Equations
Subtotal_Castle = Night * Night_Cost
Subtotal_Lodge = Meal * Meal_Cost
Subtotal_Lagoon = Swim * Swim_Cost
Subtotal_Glen = Theatre * Theatre_Cost
Subtotal_Buggy = Miles * Miles_Cost
Total = SubTotal_Castle + SubTotal_Lodge + Subtotal_Lagoon + Subtotal_Glen + Subtotal_Buggy + Incidentals

Two conditions are involved in the model. One reduces the subtotal for theatre performances to zero if the subtotal for meals exceeds £120. The other condition generates a discount for a further visit if the overall total passes £350:

Conditions
If Subtotal_Lodge > 120 Then Subtotal_Glen = 0
If Total > 350 Then Display discount

The model for the invoice involves assumptions, some of which are listed:

Assumptions
The invoice is produced for an individual guest and would require modification for groups of guests.

All meals are the same price.

The model is complete at this point and can be coded.

The main heading for the invoice is placed in cell A1.

Standard charges are indicated in column D of the sheet. These are identified by placing 'Charge' in cell D2 and then adding the constants for the spreadsheet in cells D4, D6, D8, D10 and D12. These correspond to identifying text placed in cells A4, A6, A8, A10 and A12.

The relevant input variables are then located in cells B4, B6, B8, B10 and B12. After this the equations of the model can be added to the sheet, using appropriate cell references to replace variable names. The equations initially become:

B4 * D4 which is placed in F4
B6 * D6 which is placed in F6
B8 * D8 which is placed in F8
B10 * D10 which is placed in F10
B12 * D12 which is placed in F12

The input variable for incidental purchases is not involved in any calculation for a subtotal. It is placed in cell B14.

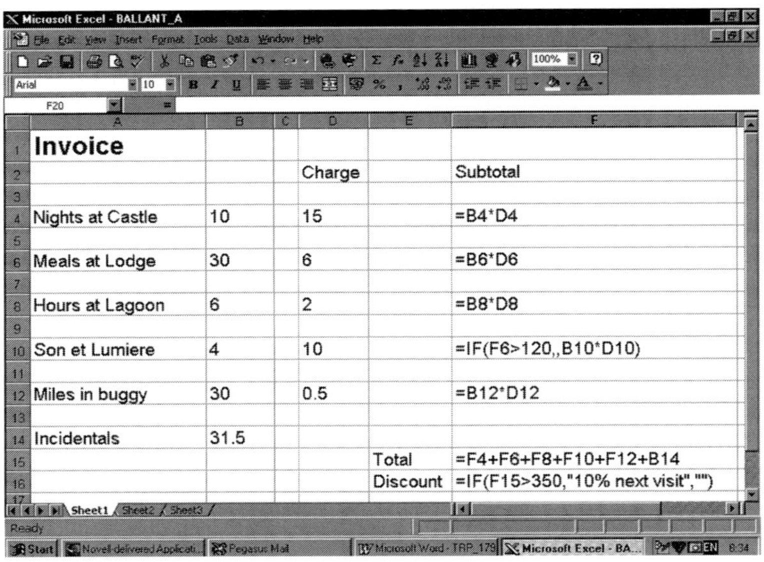

	A	B	C	D	E	F
1	Invoice					
2				Charge		Subtotal
3						
4	Nights at Castle	10		15		=B4*D4
5						
6	Meals at Lodge	30		6		=B6*D6
7						
8	Hours at Lagoon	6		2		=B8*D8
9						
10	Son et Lumiere	4		10		=IF(F6>120,,B10*D10)
11						
12	Miles in buggy	30		0.5		=B12*D12
13						
14	Incidentals	31.5				
15					Total	=F4+F6+F8+F10+F12+B14
16					Discount	=IF(F15>350,"10% next visit","")

Figure 4.22

The fourth of these equations, in cell F10, needs to be modified by the first condition. If the subtotal cost for meals is greater than £120 the subtotal for *son et lumière* must be zero. The subtotal for meals is calculated in F6 and so the cell content for F10 becomes, in Microsoft Excel, the condition:

```
If (F6 > 120, , B10 * D10 )
```

Here the condition is the first term in the brackets, followed by the action (no calculation) if the condition is true as the second term. The third term is evaluated if the condition is not satisfied, and so the original equation, B10 * D10, is placed here.

The overall total is placed in F15. It is found by adding together all the subtotals in column F and including the cost of incidentals in cell B14 to give F4 + F6 + F8 + F10 + F12 + B14. A condition is then based upon the value in F15 and displays a discount if the overall total is more than £350:

```
If (F15 > 350, "10% next visit", "")
```

The cell content for the sheet appears as indicated in Figure 4.22.

Exercise 4: Writing specific code

There are occasions when a particular application can best be approached by a unique piece of code specially written for the purpose, rather than using an off-the-shelf application package. Naturally such occasions will be hard to predict, and the programming language likewise will be very much a matter of individual choice (frequently dependent upon the skills of staff available to an organization). Such a situation is considered in this exercise.

As an example, a very short program is considered here. It could be regarded as a very tiny database, a program which simply allows the user to keep track of small debts owed by various friends belonging to the same club. With modification it could be developed into a petty cash program to be used instead of a grander spreadsheet application. Sometimes old machines get left in corners of offices and can be related to the role of performing odd, one-off processing. Here an elderly PC is used to keep track of borrowing by members of the club.

Friends' names and their debts are recorded by the program, which has a simple menu-driven structure allowing data to be entered into arrays, displayed and updated. Two arrays are employed (see Figure 4.23).

In keeping with the character of the application a traditional procedural language is used, the one always present on old, redundant PCs. Program documentation is provided internally in the form of comments:

```
REM Demonstration of pseudodatabase
REM written using arrays in QBasic

REM Declare an array to hold names of five friends
DIM Friend$(5)
```

Array location	Content	Array location	Content
Friend$(1)	Bert	Owed(1)	5
Friend$(2)	Ted	Owed(2)	10
Friend$(3)	Claudia	Owed(3)	45
Friend$(4)	Bruno	Owed(4)	4
Friend$(5)	Amaryllis	Owed(5)	3

Loop control variable s range is 1 - 5

Figure 4.23 *Use of arrays in simple data retrieval program*

```
REM Declare second array to hold debts
DIM Owed(5)

REM Screen 7 is a display mode which allows decent sized font
SCREEN 7

REM The COLOR [sic] statement selects foreground and background colour
COLOR 1, 3

REM An overall loop allows the program to repeat
REM until 4 is chosen on the menu
DO

  REM The LOCATE instruction fixes screen coordinates for
  REM position of a PRINT statement immediately following
  REM The syntax is SCREEN Y, X where Y is the number of lines
  REM down the screen and C the number of character spaces across

  REM The menu is displayed by alternating LOCATE statements
  REM with appropriate coordinates and PRINT statements

  CLS
  LOCATE 4, 18
  PRINT "MENU"
  LOCATE 6, 10
  PRINT "Enter members.....1"
  LOCATE 7, 10
  PRINT "Display members...2"
  LOCATE 8, 10
  PRINT "Alter details.....3"
  LOCATE 9, 10
  PRINT "Quit program......4"

  REM User's choice is assigned to the variable MenuValue%
  REM The % sign indicates that an integer variable is being employed
  REM here. An integer variable can only be assigned integral values
  REM and so the user can't enter values like 3.57. This is part of
  REM of the validation process for the menu selection.

  REM The input takes place within a DO loop the exit condition
  REM for which limits the possible values for MenuChoice% to
  REM just 1, 2, 3 or 4, thus matching the range stated on the
  REM displayed menu.

  DO
    LOCATE 11, 10
    INPUT MenuValue%
  LOOP UNTIL MenuValue% > 0 AND MenuValue% < 5

  REM This clears the menu from the screen
  CLS

  REM The SELECT CASE structure allows choice to be made on the value
  REM of the variable MenuChoice%

  SELECT CASE MenuValue%
  CASE 1
  GOSUB Enter
  CASE 2
  GOSUB Display
```

```
  CASE 3
  GOSUB Alter
  END SELECT

  REM This pauses the display before returning to the menu
  LOCATE 20, 1
  PRINT "Press return to see menu or exit program"
  INPUT DummyValue%

REM This is the end of the main loop.
REM It exits when the user chooses 4 on the menu.
LOOP UNTIL MenuValue% = 4

END

Enter:

  REM This is the subroutine called when 1 is selected
  REM on the menu. It fills the two arrays, Friend$() and Owed()
  REM with data.

  REM Note how subroutines in QBasic begin with a label followed by
  REM a colon. (The colon is NOT used when the subroutine is called in
  REM a GOSUB.)
  REM In this version of the subroutine the assumption
  REM is made that you don't want to keep typing in
  REM fresh data. However if you do the only change
  REM required is to replace READ with INPUT.

  REM The RESTORE statement places the data pointer at the beginning
  REM of the data. It's only needed here to avoid 'Out of Data' errors
  REM if the user hits 1 twice on the menu.
  RESTORE

  FOR Counter = 1 TO 5
    READ Friend$(Counter)
    READ Owed(Counter)
  NEXT Counter

REM Subroutines always end with a RETURN statement.
RETURN

Display:

  CLS

  REM This subroutine is called when 2 is chosen on the menu.
  REM It displays the data in the arrays.

  FOR Counter = 1 TO 5

    REM This LOCATE statement uses the value of the loop
    REM control variable to calculate a suitable
    REM position on the display for the data
    REM The use of semicolons then places everything else
    REM at end of previous text.

    LOCATE Counter * 2 + 5, 3
    PRINT Friend$(Counter);
    PRINT " owes you ";
```

```
    PRINT Owed(Counter);
    PRINT " pounds."
  NEXT Counter

RETURN

Alter:

  REM The name of the record to be updated is chosen by
  REM the user entering a value for the variable Request$.
  LOCATE 3, 3
  PRINT "Enter name of friend"
  LOCATE 4, 3
  INPUT Request$
  REM A variable Found is used to identify the friend found
  REM in the array Friend$(). Initially Found is assigned a value
  REM of zero.
  Found = 0

  REM A counter is required for the DO loop. It begins
  REM with a value of zero.
  Counter = 0

  REM This is the beginning of the DO loop
  REM which searches the Friend$() array.
  DO

    REM The counter has to be incremented so
    REM that it does count for the loop.
    Counter = Counter + 1

    REM If a match is found the variable Found is
    REM given the value of the loop control variable.
    IF Request$ = Friend$(Counter) THEN Found = Counter

    REM A double exit condition is used
    REM for the DO loop. It exits either if
    REM (i) The friend is found, which means that the
    REM variable Found will no longer be zero, or if
    REM (ii) The value of Counter shows that all 5 records
    REM have been checked.
  LOOP UNTIL Found  0 OR Counter = 5

  IF Found = 0 THEN

    REM Display error message in contrasting colour
    REM if friend not located in data.
    REM Then return colour to previous values.
    LOCATE 5, 3
    COLOR 4
    PRINT "This friend is not known"
    COLOR 1

  REM If friend is located call another subroutine, Update,
  REM which will allow the debt to be given a new value.
  ELSE
    GOSUB Update
  END IF

RETURN
```

```
Update:
  REM This subroutine is called from the Alter subroutine
  REM when a friend's name is matched. It allows a new
  REM debt to be entered into the Owed() array.

  LOCATE 5, 3
  PRINT "Enter new debt"
  LOCATE 6, 3

  REM The array location is identified by a subscript
  REM equal to the value of the variable Found. This results
  REM from the way the searching loop was written in the
  REM Alter subroutine.
  REM A new value is placed in the array simply by assigning
  REM it via the INPUT statement.
  INPUT Owed(Found)
RETURN

REM Here DATA lines have been used to save constantly re-entering
REM all the details. However READ and DATA are
REM fairly idiosyncratic and only found in early versions
REM of procedural Basic.

DATA Bert, 5, Ted, 10, Claudia, 45, Bruno, 4, Amaryllis, 3
```

4.3 Evaluation measures

Exercise 1: Investigating an e-commerce site

The effectiveness of an e-commerce site will depend upon a number of factors, many of which are subjective. Evaluation of a particular site becomes easier if a large number of sites are visited. Subjective impressions can be related to specific features which begin to be repeated between different sites. Sufficient exposure to different techniques and styles can then help to establish a benchmark to aid evaluation of a new site.

Some issues in evaluation of an e-commerce site

- Is the site easy to navigate?
- How convenient is it for the potential purchaser to evaluate services offered by the site?
- Is sufficient information supplied about the products?
- What visual information is given for products?
- What help is given to the customer in searching for a particular item? Is there access to catalogues or to a range of catalogues?
- Does the site indicate a running total of items added to the cart? Are discounts calculated?
- What degree of security is offered for credit card transactions?
- Generally, how is the customer encouraged to buy?

Does the e-customer obtain the service they require?

Research has indicated that a high proportion of customers visiting an e-commerce site will in fact want to engage in offline service help. Rather than rely solely upon the site content available online, or being satisfied with e-mailed responses from staff, customers like being able to speak in real time with a human being at the end of a phone line. This does seem somewhat contrary to the purposes of setting up an e-commerce site. In investigating a site it is worthwhile making a note of whether enquiries can be handled adequately online.

A possible solution here is the use of instant messaging, although this does of course have implications regarding staffing levels at the site.

If the site has a complete range of frequently asked questions (FAQs) available then customer satisfaction is likely to increase. Regular updating of this facility is therefore advisable. Access to FAQs will not, however, be a solution for the unusual, singular query for which some kind of specific, human response may be necessary.

Implications of the Stanford–Poynter study

An apocryphal tale in marketing is of the advertising campaign launched for a new detergent brand. Large billboards displayed a triptych. On the left-hand panel, a happy, dirty boy in mud-ingrained football shirt and shorts. In the middle a more than life-size packet of the touted washing powder, parent and machine ready in the background to accept the soiled garments. On the right-hand panel the child was ready to race on to the pitch again, now in pristine, gleaming kit. The campaign was a brilliant success, simple and to the point. Sales went through the ceiling. And then the same advertisement, with its Western cultural assumptions, was released in a country where the eye had been trained from childhood to read from right to left.

We do make such assumptions, and assumptions should be challenged when designing an e-commerce site.

A successful challenge resulted from an original study launched as the combined effort of Stanford University and the Poynter Institute. This research investigated precisely how people reacted when they encountered a new web page. What did they look at first? How did their eye travel across the screen? Where did it linger? How could the page be redesigned to maximize its impact?

The results obtained were unexpected.

Before the study the perfectly reasonable assumption had been made that the addition of photographs and graphics to a web page would automatically draw the eye. After all that is where people look first when presented with the printed page. 'A picture is worth a thousand words' is the mantra of the rookie journalist. However, this proves not to be the case when it comes to the information that gushes on to our PCs from the Internet. Our eye instinctively, without conscious control, leaps to the text. The fancy photos are missed out, only visited as a subconscious second choice. The implications of this for site design are significant.

How was this result established?

Volunteers wearing special eye-tracking equipment visited various web pages. Low-power lasers beamed at the eyeball could detect precisely where the person's attention was focused as they encountered each new page.

General conclusions were that:

- As stated earlier it is text, rather than graphics, that first attracts attention.
- Banner advertisements on web pages are effective. These automatically draw the gaze of the user for at least a second. Such time is long enough for the brief slogan to register, and perhaps to influence future choice of purchase.

Width of screen

The designer of an e-commerce web page has to anticipate the size of the shopper's screen. There is little point in placing important details at the edge of a page if this means that the information will be lost as a result of the customer's PC having a narrower width than had been assumed.

Current (2001) typical screen sizes (figures taken from TheCounter.com) are as shown. It can be seen that the most popular is 800 × 600 pixels, which means that web pages wider than 800 will require the customer to scroll horizontally. This could deter.

Screen size in pixels	*Percentage of users*
800 × 600	53%
1024 × 768	32%
640 × 480	5%
1280 × 1024	3%
1152 × 864	2%

It is possible to use JavaScript to recognize the user's screen size and adjust the web pages accordingly. However, many Internet users deliberately disable JavaScript.

Practical evaluation exercise

The form adopted in this exercise for the evaluation of an e-commerce site is shown below.

Feature	*Satisfaction 5–1 (5 = very satisfied 1= very dissatisfied)*
1. Appropriate address	
2. Speed of access	
3. Ease of navigation	
4. Appropriate content	
5. Aesthetic appeal	
6. Suitable colours	
7. Reliability of service	
8. Security of credit details	
9. Assessing customer service	
10. Links to related sites	

The features selected here for assessment are:

1. Appropriate address
Does the site have an easily memorized address? Does the address clearly indicate the nature of the site? This is in fact not always the case. It is sadly only too easy to think of e-commerce sites that are not clearly defined by their address. This has led to otherwise unnecessary advertising in the traditional media. Sadly even then the subtlety of the advertising has often defeated its purpose!

2. Speed of access
It is tempting for the designers of an e-commerce site to display their programming skills. Unfortunately a very clever, but overblown, site with plenty of bells and whistles can overtax the potential customer's ability to download. This oversight caused the collapse of several promising dotcoms in the late 1990s.

3. Ease of navigation
For a site to become popular it must be easy to navigate to the required pages. Sensibly designed links, with a succinct hierarchy that ensures that the customer is only a few clicks from their desired purchase, are essential.

4. Appropriate content
Ease of navigation inevitably implies that pages should involve concise and relevant content.

5. Aesthetic appeal
Rating aesthetic appeal is perhaps contentious. Who has not fumed when a critic has roundly condemned a favourite novelist or composer? Nevertheless it is reasonably safe to say that an animated cartoon character will probably not enhance the sales of a chiropractor.

6. Suitable colours
'Blue and green should never be seen' was once the chorus of assistants in men's outfitters, but this advice has ebbed since they started getting out into the countryside more often. Choosing colours is again subjective but clearly does have an impact on a site's appeal.

7. Reliability of service
This is hard to judge until a service has actually been bought and the results road tested. Word of mouth may help.

8. Security of credit details
As above, this information might arrive too late!

9. Assessing customer service
How much attention the individual customer will receive from the site proprietor can be deduced to a certain extent from the site itself. Will e-mail be answered promptly? Is there a telephone helpline? Does the site attempt to build up a loyal customer base?

10. Links to related sites
Some e-commerce sites are sufficiently confident about the quality of their service and do not fear comparison with other sites. This is a good sign for the potential customer.

Each feature is marked on a scale of 1–5. On this scale 1 indicates that this feature of the site was found very dissatisfying. A mark of 5 indicates that it was very satisfying. A chart produced for the exercise is shown in Figure 4.24.

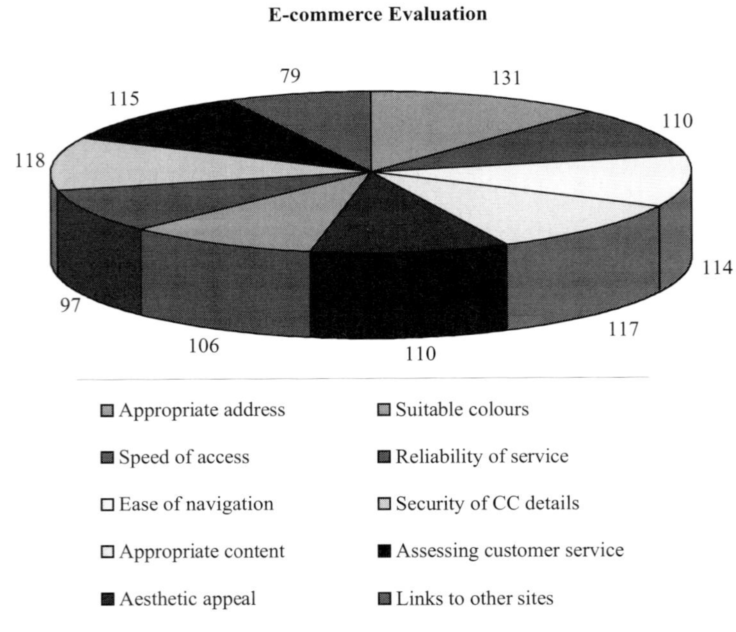

Figure 4.24

Exercise 2: Practical website design

> Good website design depends upon a combination of imagination and creativity, technical proficiency, and the application of some commonsense skills.

People using the Internet to research a topic do not have the advantage of a person sitting at a large table in a well-stocked library. It is easy to skim through books quickly to find relevant information at the right level of detail. Even a momentary glance can indicate whether a particular book is appropriate. The size of the font, the diagrams and photographs included, even a brief sample of the style of language used, can let the reader decide almost intuitively whether or not to proceed further. If the book doesn't feel right, choose another. It is not this easy when trying to assess the content of a website. Here it is rather like attempting to read a book through a sheet of cardboard in which a small rectangular opening has been excised. The reader is now permitted only to see a few sentences at a time. It is far more difficult to judge the whole.

This should always be remembered when constructing a website. A successful site will make it clear whether or not the information held is likely to be of use as early as possible. Although there is no sure way of organizing a site to meet these goals in all situations, there are a number of guidelines which can be followed.

Gain attention

A good novel engages with the reader immediately. So should a good website. The visitor to the site should immediately want to delve deeper. Of course if the site is not relevant to the search they are conducting that should also be immediately obvious to them to avoid wasting their time.

Planned use of font, colour, layout, some graphics and, most important of all, clear navigation, makes a website appealing and useful.

Use neutral colours

It is important to make sure that pages can be read easily. Contrast between text and background is important. The ideal is probably white and black, although for aesthetic reasons it is likely that other combinations will be appealing. The important factor is that sensible use of colour can aid a site enormously. Use of colour should be planned carefully.

Colour appreciation is subjective. Combinations which attract one person may deter another. Nevertheless some general ideas probably apply to the majority. A website about the geology of the Sahara could profit from yellows and orange. One about Antarctica would seem more appealing in whites, violets and blues. If in doubt debate with friends.

Remember that light coloured text on a dark background is often more difficult to read than dark text on a light background. Recall how schools exchanged blackboards for whiteboards.

Use appropriate font

A large number of different font styles are available. Below are just a few examples:

Algerian
Arial
Bauhaus
Courier
Elephant
Forte
Garamond
Helvetica
Lucida Calligraphy
Onyx
Rockwell
Times New Roman
Verdana

The font chosen for a passage of text will affect how readily it can be read. Some fonts are simply clearer to identify than others. But choice of font decides more than mere legibility. It says something about the way in which the passage is intended to be read. It makes an implicit statement about the content, even before it is assimilated. A passage written using Forte is going to have a different impact to one written in Times New Roman. Font choice also says something about the presumed relationship between the author of the text and its reader. By selecting a particular font the author is indicating the type of person he/she is, and also declaring the assumptions that are being made by the author about the intended reader. Care can be needed here. Will the person reading a page be as 'switched on' as the writer? (Choose whatever linguistic preference exists for a synonym of 'switched on', and regard this sentence as demonstrating its content, a 'performative' in the sense of Austin's concept of speech act.)

Font size is equally important. Random variations should be avoided. Use the size of font to indicate the level at which the reader is within the document being displayed. Larger or emphasized fonts should indicate headings and subheadings.

Provide relevant detail

Not too much text should be present on any one page. This means that individual pages should be concise, saying what is required elegantly and briefly. Nevertheless a careful distinction has to be drawn between concise and terse. Too little information will make it more difficult for the visitor to the page to know what else will be found further on.

Further details should be found lower in the hierarchy of pages entered from the home page and reached by clear naviagtion paths.

Avoid where possible the current fashion for drawing attention to a particular point just for effect.

It is quite common, especially in some magazines, for a fairly irrelevant phrase to be copied from an article and repeated prominently, with different font, font size and colour somewhere else on the page. Although this does have the advantage of making a person glancing through pay more attention at this point, the summary often seems to have been done at random, almost, one suspects, by software instructed to extract a few consecutive words from anywhere in the passage. For example, a paragraph with serious content, like:

> Conservationists are concerned about the plight of the hairy nosed wombat. This rare marsupial could easily become victim of the same lack of concern for the environment that has led to the demise of many species, like the Great Auk or the Dodo. These creatures, once common, are now known only as museum exhibits and as faded sketches executed by naturalists in the nineteenth century. A special fund has been set up in Victoria to enable a research programme into the feeding habits of the threatened wombat in the hope that it might still be saved.

might be graced with a bright red 20pt banner in Elephant font saying:

> Executed by naturalists

Despite the tendency even for heavyweight journals to adopt this approach towards précis, it is not a technique suited to any website.

Design clear navigation

It should be possible for the visitor to gain 'in-depth' information within a few clicks. This means that there should not be too many vertical levels within a website. The site should spread horizontally as much as possible. It follows that on each separate page there should be a reasonable number of links to other pages. Suppose that a site allows five links from each page. One level down from the home page there will be five pages. Another level down there will be 25. A third click leads to 125 pages. Now compare this with a site where each page only has two links. Three mouse clicks will lead to a mere eight pages (see Figure 4.25).

Good navigation should also make it easy to return to the initial page with a single click.

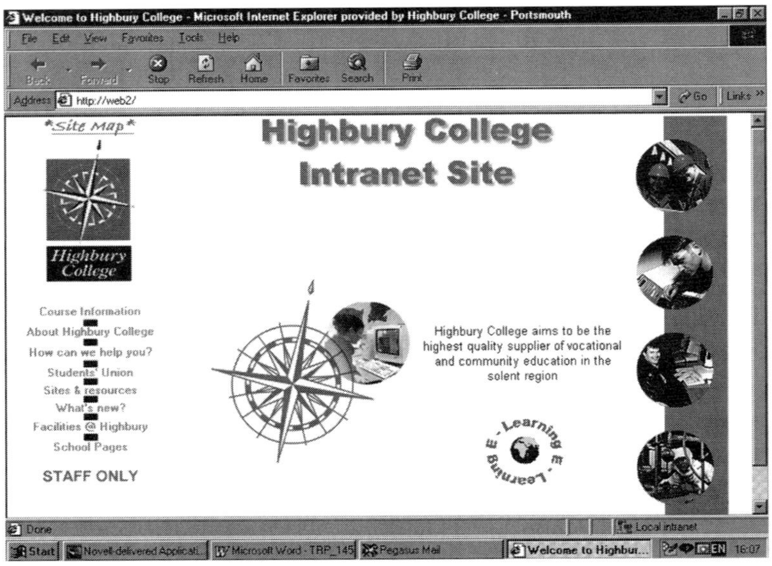

Figure 4.25 *Example of web page displaying clear navigation*

Provide links with other sites

Where related sites are relevant, links should be provided. This will involve the designer in a fair degree of research but the results will reward this effort.

> Imagine that you have to design a website for the information outlined below. Produce a 'storyboard' indicating the type of information that you would present on successive pages of your site. You should indicate schematically the links between pages, thus establishing a hierarchy in your design.
>
> 'Candy's Cactus' supplies cactus plants as presents. The sender can request a specific cactus from the catalogue and this is then forwarded by courier post to the friend who has been named.
>
> A number of different services are provided. A cactus can be sent as a birthday present, a Christmas present or as a get-well offering. According to the choice made, a suitably decorated box can be provided, for an additional charge. The exterior of the box is inscribed with an appropriate message.
>
> An alternative present is a gift-wrapped miniature bottle of tequilla. This can be supplied alone, or with a small book explaining the origin and manufacture of this enchanting drink.
>
> The person ordering a cactus for a friend has to supply the name, address and postcode of the recipient, as well as credit card details for payment. The sender's address is also required so that a receipt can be forwarded.
>
> The price for individual cacti depends upon the size of the plant and its rarity. As many people are unfamiliar with cacti the site provides a number of photographs and descriptive information. This includes hints for the best ways of ensuring healthy and prolonged growth.
>
> Links are also provided to a number of national and international sites devoted to cactus.

5 Quality management principles

Rationale

By way of an introduction students will:

- learn about the analysis and design tools used within the Software Development process. They will use CASE tools to produce graphical and text-based analysis and design models. The syntax and semantics of the model will be tested to ensure the quality of the product conforms to the stated requirements
- learn the techniques of traditional life cycle models and object-oriented models, and how they are developed, documented and quality assured for a simulated customer specification
- use the concepts of project management to ensure the development process is planned and implemented within prescribed deadlines and checked at various milestones to ensure the verification and validation processes
- need to determine the maintenance requirements for a given software product. The need for a software maintenance contract and how 'change' can be implemented and its effects on the documentation
- need to be introduced to the basic concepts of 'quality assurance' and how it interacts across a software development project. Estimating and costing factors need to be considered along with the timing and testing issues for a software product under development
- need to develop the quality assurance tools used throughout a developing software project. They will need to hold reviews, walkthroughs and inspections and be able to produce recognized quality assurance documents
- need to be aware of the legal implications surrounding the development of a product and its associated staff. For example, the Software Project Manager needs to approach health and safety in a strictly systematic way by assessing the risks and hazards in the workplace and taking steps to ensure that their house is in order. Also the manager needs to be aware of the issues involving storage of 'Data', i.e. recorded information

Professionalism and standards are key issues developed by any successful manager. Students need to understand the importance of these issues and how they are implemented within a quality development programme. The concept of professionalism implies taking responsibility, accounting for one's work and performing work to the highest standards. Factors like ISO, British Standards, training (CPD) etc. need to be considered in the quest for producing quality professional software development personnel.

5.1 System analysis and design tools

Further information on data dictionaries

Usage: Within analysis models like data flow and entity-relationship diagrams

Generally these are computer based and provide a central repository for all the information contained within a modelling process. They are used to provide automatic analysis and checking of entries that are applied in the development of a proposed model.

From the System Analysis Unit we can see that a special notation is used within a data dictionary based on the BNF (Backus–Naur Format) syntax.

@BNF syntax

The BNF clause is used in the data dictionary to describe the data components of data flows and stores. It uses the following syntax:

+	means AND
[I]	means EITHER-OR, i.e. select one of the options
()	means enclosed component is OPTIONAL
{}	means ITERATIONS OF enclosed component
" "	means enclosed component is a LITERAL value
\\	encloses a textual description

The iteration braces {} are often annotated with lower/upper limits. For example:

3{ dog }7	between 3 and 7 iterations of dog
1{ cat }	one or more iterations of cat
{horse}3	up to 3 iterations of horse

The BNF expression can contain a mix of these operators:

@BNF = [lion I cat + 2[dog]2 + (horse) I danger]

Further examples:

@NAME = MESSAGE
@TYPE = Discrete Flow
@BNF = \ single character A-Z in either upper or lowercase \
@NAME = OCTAL DIGIT
@TYPE = Discrete Flow
@BNF =["0"I"1"I"2"I"3"I"4"I"5"I"6"I"7"]

Note that the '+' sign should not be confused with the arithmetic use of the symbol. It is used to represent a combination of data components into a composite structure. It can be considered as an 'and' operation with the '[I]' taking the 'or' equivalent.

Be a little careful with the 'or' statement as the whole expression that is to be included in the comparison must be included inside the square brackets, i.e. [aFlow I bFlow I cFlow] is an inclusive or statement based on the three flows.

Data flow diagram example

Figure 5.1 shows two group nodes that need to be specified using correct BNF notation. A data dictionary for the 'readings' data flow is outlined below.

Data Flow: readings
readings = temperature + pressure + speed
Notes: all the readings need to be converted in order to produce the required code settings
Alias:

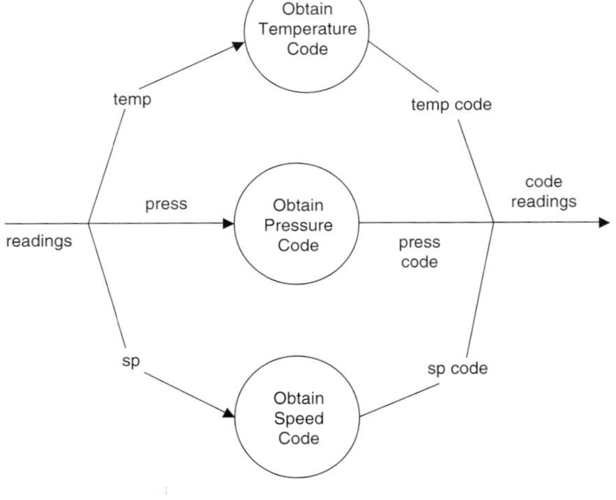

Figure 5.1

temperature =
 * temperature in Celsius expressed as a real number *
Notes:
Alias: temp

pressure =
 * pressure in Pascal's expressed as a real number *
Notes:
Alias: press

speed =
 * speed in revs/min expressed as a real number *
Notes:
Alias: sp

Looking at the Yourdon Select CASE tool package (using the Bess and Bailey Kennel System example), the dictionary shows the components as shown in Figure 5.2.

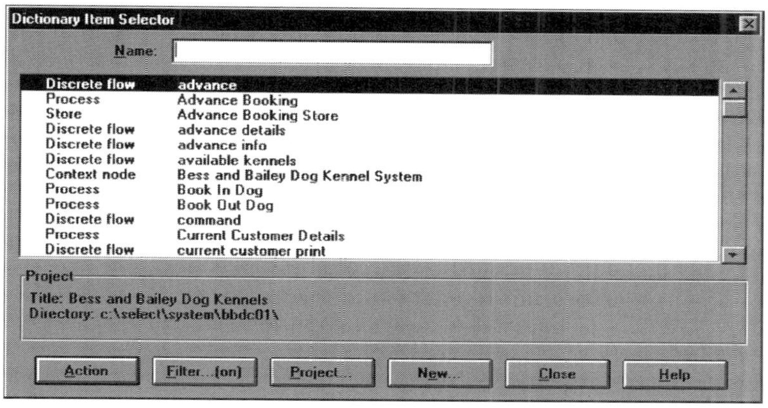

Figure 5.2

Looking at the valid command data flow (group node input) and selecting edit results in Figure 5.3.

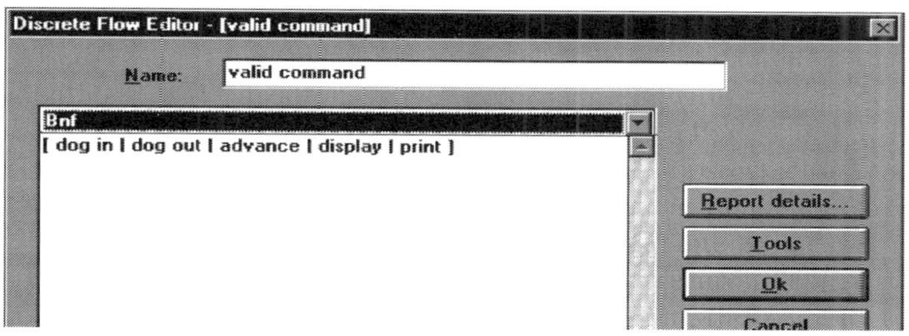

Figure 5.3

Which shows the appropriate BNF syntax (inclusive 'or' outputs) and the report contains

Project: C:\SELECT\SYSTEM\BBDC01\
Title: Bess and Bailey Dog Kennels
Date: 10-Apr-2001 Time: 13:4

Name: valid command
Type: Discrete flow
Bnf: [dog in | dog out | advance | display | print]
This item is used on the following diagrams:
 DOG2.DAT Bess and Bailey Dog Kennel System
 DOG3.DAT Process Receptionist Command
Last changed: DEFAULT 19-Dec-2000 19:06:01

---- End of report ----

Note: To add comments and other information like appropriate units select the options arrows to the right of the BNF term (see Figure 5.4).

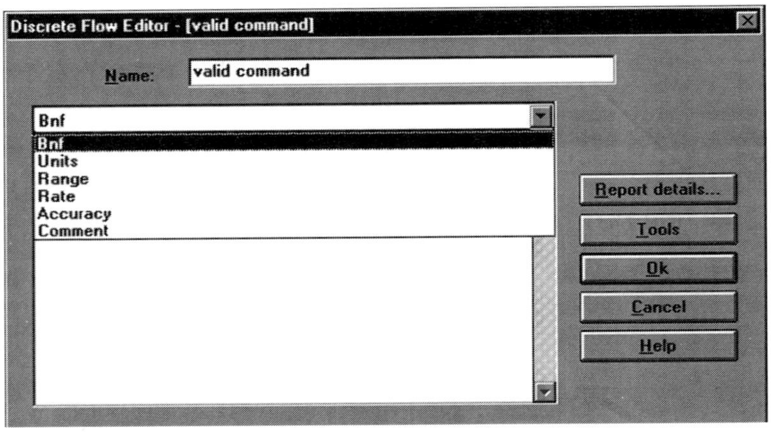

Figure 5.4

The data dictionary can be used to express more precise information, for example the field structures within the stores and the maximum number of records to be held.

Additional student exercise – data dictionaries

Produce data dictionary entries for the data described in the statement of requirements extract outlined below:

> The system needs to display personal information about current students. This should include full name, address, date of birth and telephone number. Students can be classified as undergraduates or postgraduates. The system also needs to determine the next of kin to include their names, addresses and telephone numbers.

The following definitions are to apply:

> A name is composed of 1..20 characters i.e. 1, { Character } 20.
> An address is composed of a house number or name, street, town, county and a postcode.
> The date-of-birth is made up of day (2-digit number), month (2-digit number) and year (4-digit number). i.e. for somebody born on the 13th March 1979 the actual date requirement is: 13 03 1979.
> The telephone numbers are to be between 8 and 11 digits to cater for local and non-local students and next-of-kin, i.e. 8 { Digit } 11.
> Student classification will be composed of 14..15 characters, where 14 characters are required for a postgraduate student and 15 characters are required for an undergraduate student.

Complete a data dictionary to model the above requirements.

Suggested solution

Data Flow: Student
Student =
Student Name + Student Address + Date Of Birth + Student Telephone + [Under-Graduate | Post-Graduate] + Next Of Kin Name + Next Of Kin Address + Next Of Kin Telephone
Notes: Required student details to be displayed
Alias:

Student Name:
1 { Character } 20
Notes: Current student name
Alias: SName

Student Address:
[House Number | House Name] + Street + Town + County + Post Code
Notes: Current student address
Alias: SAddress

Date Of Birth:
2 { Digit } 2 + 2 { Digit } 2 + 4 { Digit } 4
Notes: Student's date of birth expressed as a day, month and year, i.e. 12 05 1981
Alias: DateOfBirth

Student Telephone:
8 { Digit } 11
Notes: Current student telephone number. For local numbers 8345 6789 can be used as 8 continuous digits or 020 8322 1111 as 11 continuous digits for non-local numbers.
Alias: SPhone

Undergraduate:
15 { Character } 15
Notes: Undergraduate student classification
Alias: UGrad

Postgraduate:
14 { Character } 14
Notes: Postgraduate student classification
Alias: PGrad

Next Of Kin Name:
1 { Character } 20
Notes: Emergency contact name for the next of kin to be informed in an emergency
Alias: NOKName

Next Of Kin Address:
[House Number | House Name] + Street + Town + County + Post Code
Notes: Address of the next of kin
Alias: NOKAddress

Next Of Kin Telephone:
8 { Digit } 11
Notes: Emergency telephone number for the next of kin
Alias: NOKPhone

Control aspects – suggested solution to Exercise 5.1.1 – Bailey Comfortable Room Company

Context diagram

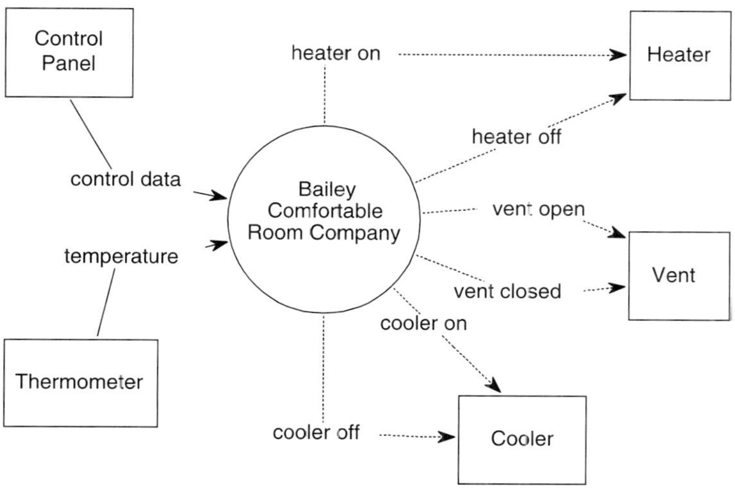

Figure 5.5 *CONTEXT Bailey Comfortable Room System*

DFD refinement

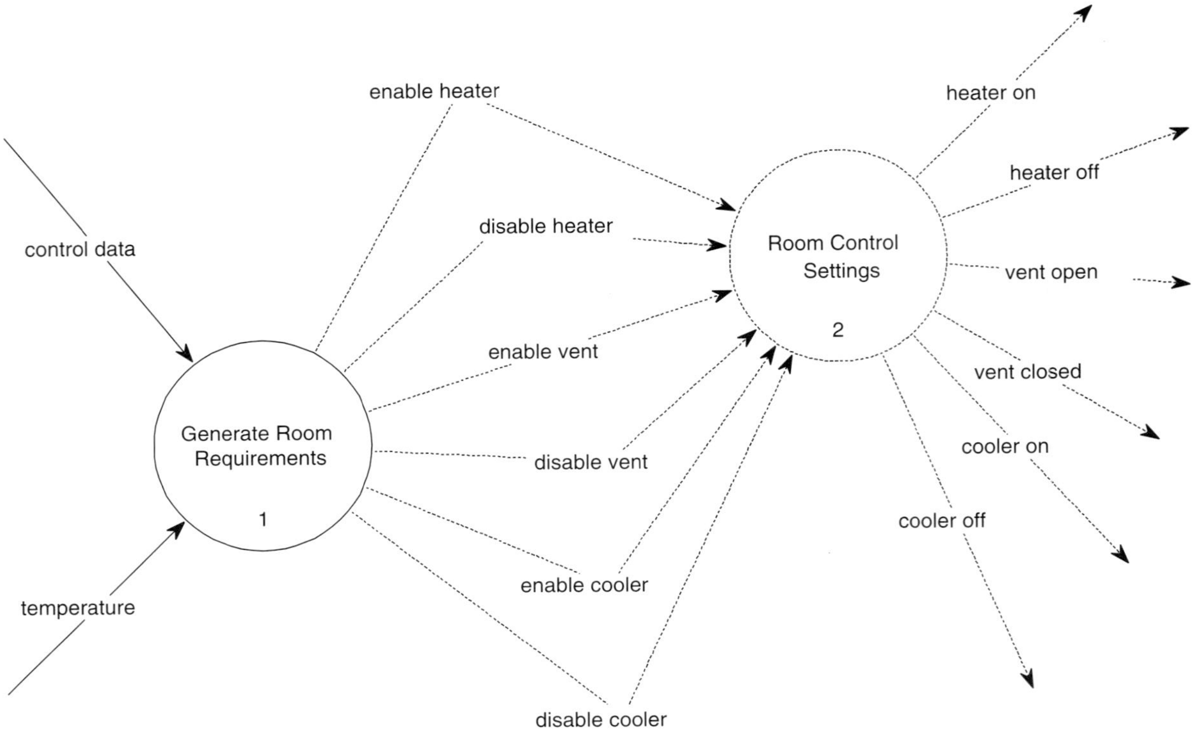

Figure 5.6 *Bailey Comfortable Room Company*

Remember a state transition diagram is a child of a control process:

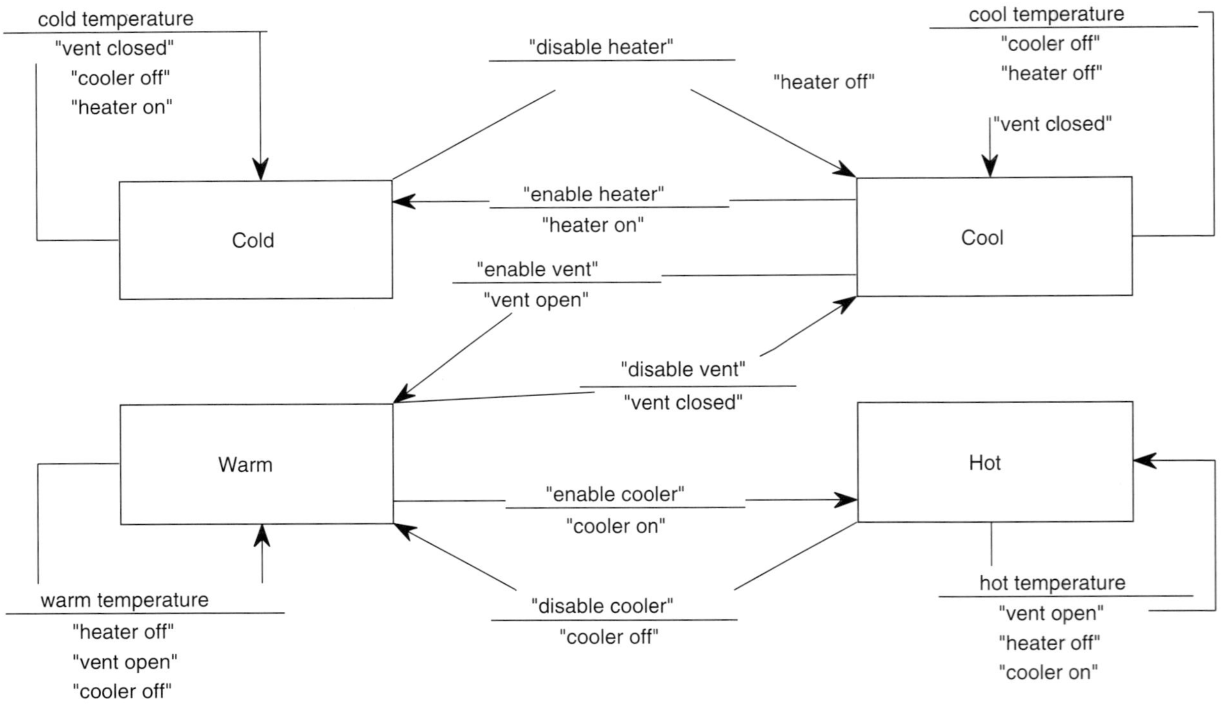

Figure 5.7 *Room control settings*

Syntax consistency check:

Project: C:\SELECT\SYSTEM\ROOM1\
Title: Bailey Comfortable Room Company
Date: 17-Apr-2001 Time: 17:1

Report: Diagram Consistency checking

This report contains a consistency check of all the diagrams in the project.

Checking ROOM1.DAT
    No Errors detected, No Warnings given.

Checking ROOM2.DAT
    No Errors detected, No Warnings given.

Checking SROOM3.DAT
    No Errors detected, No Warnings given.

---- End of report ----

Additional example

Susie South West Train Company train level crossing control system

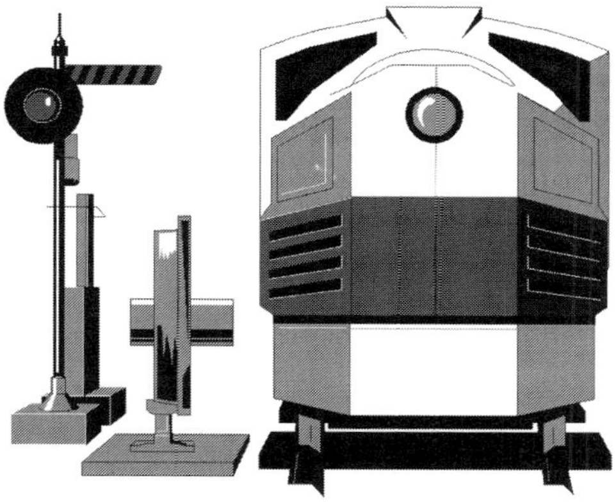

Figure 5.8

Below is part of a specification for the Susie South West Train Company.

The Susie South West Train Company requires a computerized control system for one of its single-track railway routes. The system is to control an unmanned level crossing point where the railway crosses a main road. A sensor will detect the approach of a train which first starts the warning lights flashing and then drops down the barriers. The crossing is now closed to all road vehicles. A second sensor will then detect when the train is leaving the level crossing which first opens the barriers and then stops the lights flashing. The crossing is now open to all road vehicles.

From the above specification complete:

1. A data flow context diagram.
2. A refinement for the context diagram to include the required control process and associated control flows.
3. Create a child of the control process to produce a state transition diagram showing the dynamic aspects of the level crossing system.
4. Produce a consistency test to ensure that the correct parent–child balancing is maintained and the diagrams are syntactically correct.

Note that you are to complete the above requirements using a suitable CASE tool application.

Suggested solution

Context diagram:

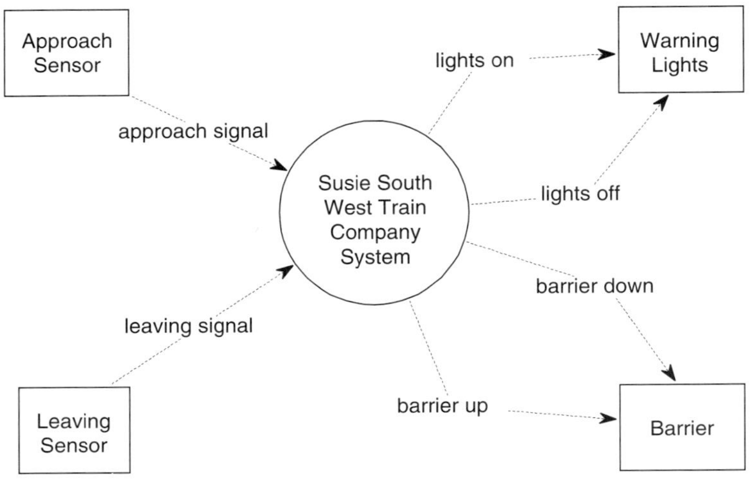

Figure 5.9 *CONTEXT Susie SW Train System*

Control refinement:

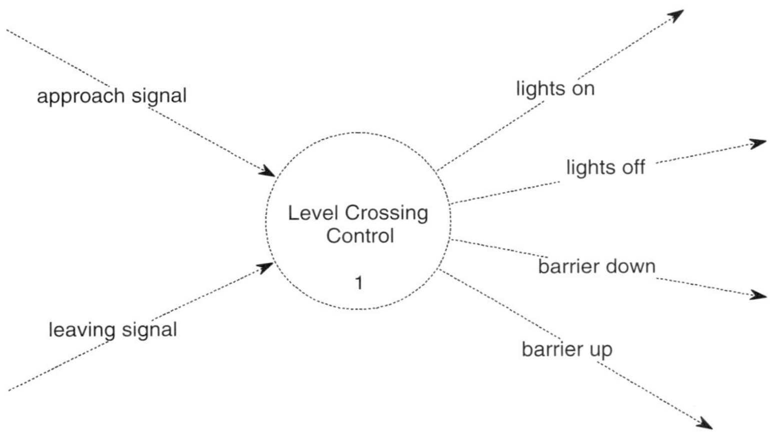

Figure 5.10 *Susie SW Train Company System*

State transition diagram:

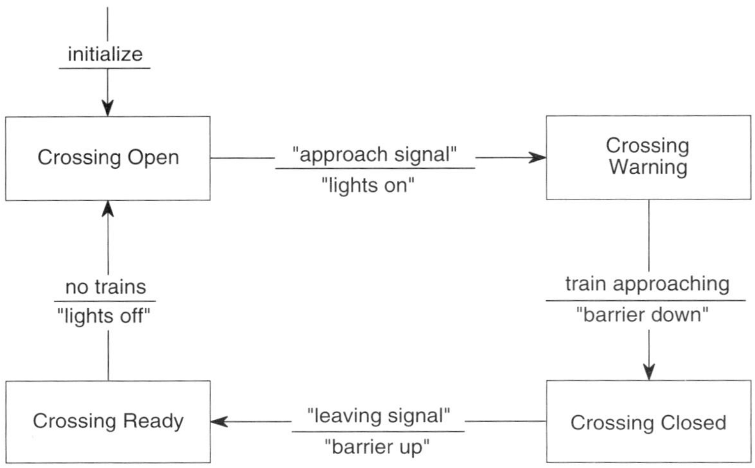

Figure 5.11

Consistency check:

Project: C:\SELECT\SYSTEM\TRAIN1\
Title: Susie SW Train Company
Date: 18-Apr-2001 Time: 19:1

Report: Diagram Consistency checking

This report contains a consistency check of all the diagrams in the project.

Checking STRAIN1.DAT
    No Errors detected, No Warnings given.

Checking TRAIN1.DAT
    No Errors detected, No Warnings given.

Checking TRAIN2.DAT
    No Errors detected, No Warnings given.

---- End of report ----

Implementation modelling – some important considerations

To improve the quality of a product a good software designer needs to follow the analysis process with sound design principles. An implementation model represents the concrete features of a system as opposed to an abstract one. The developer will need to consider the structure in detail and base the resulting model on the organizational requirements for the end product A good implementation model will be based on the following three phases:

- model the physical processes involved
- model the software environment in which the software system is to exist
- model the structure of the software to be produced

The first two phases may involve modifications to the analysis documentation. Data flow and other development diagrams may need to be modified to take into account the requirements of the system in its operational environment. For example, it may be necessary to link the new system with the company's central computer in order to obtain essential client data.

The third phase translates the implementation-oriented documentation into a system design process using structure charts to represent required program modules. For an object-oriented system the design document will detail the classes required, their variables and method headings. In order to ensure the project is being developed correctly to meet its original aims a thorough verification and validation process must be adopted. This will ensure that the original functionality is maintained and no new functionality added.

Coupling and cohesion

In order to produce a structure chart the developer needs to split the software into component modules. Such modules can be implemented as C functions, BASIC subroutines or PASCAL procedures (or functions). The control of these modules needs to be carefully considered and the complexity of the model kept to a minimum. This is best achieved by designing a system where the main section of the program controls a few modules only and other modules are controlled by them (see Figure 5.12).

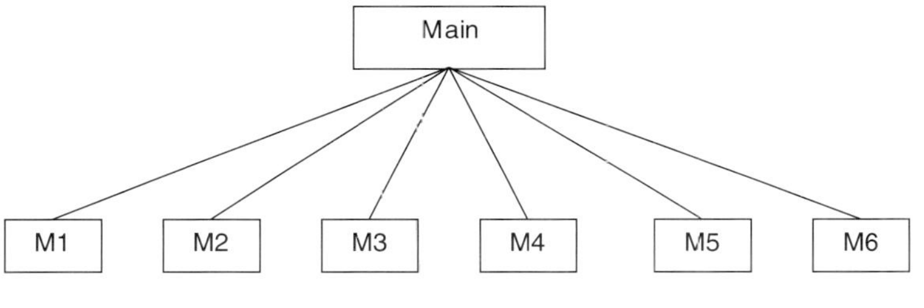

Figure 5.12 *Highly coupled system – main controls six modules directly*

Coupling is the measure of the degree in which modules depend on each other. High coupling generally implies high complexity and reduced reliability. This can eventually lead to high maintenance costs and difficulties in tracing and correcting semantic or logical errors. Low coupling generally implies lower complexity, improved reliability, lower maintenance costs and easier debugging activities.

Figure 5.12 shows a main process directly controlling six modules. It needs to know the precise interface requirements, the actual parameters being passed and what modules are being accessed. This design does not allow for each module to know about the existence of the other modules or their associated interfaces.

Figure 5.13 outlines a system with improved coupling.

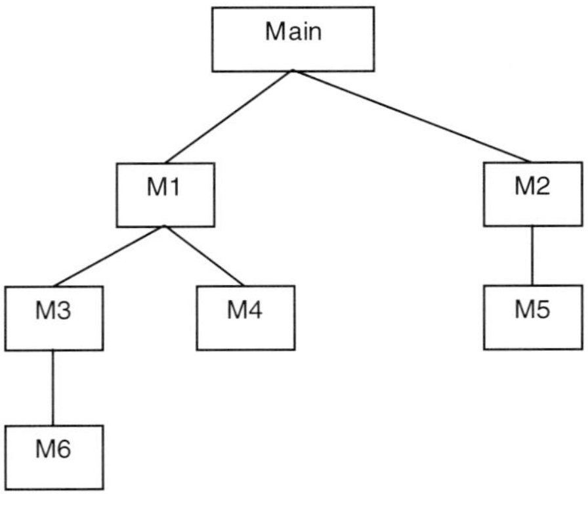

Figure 5.13 *Improved coupling*

As the main section does not have to control as many modules its complexity is reduced. Although modules M1 and M2 have a more complex role as they now have control of subordinate modules. But this approach of reducing complexity from within modules has proved to provide more reliable software with lower maintenance overheads.

Cohesion

This is the measure of how closely the parts of a module correspond to a single function of the software. If any given module is totally concerned with achieving exactly one aim, then cohesion is said to be high. A module is said to exhibit low cohesion if there is not much of a relationship between the elements inside. For example, if a module is designed to ask the user for their name, gets the current date, displays a message and prints an account balance then the module is said to show low cohesion as each of the module aims are not related.

Therefore a good design should show: LOW COUPLING and HIGH COHESION.

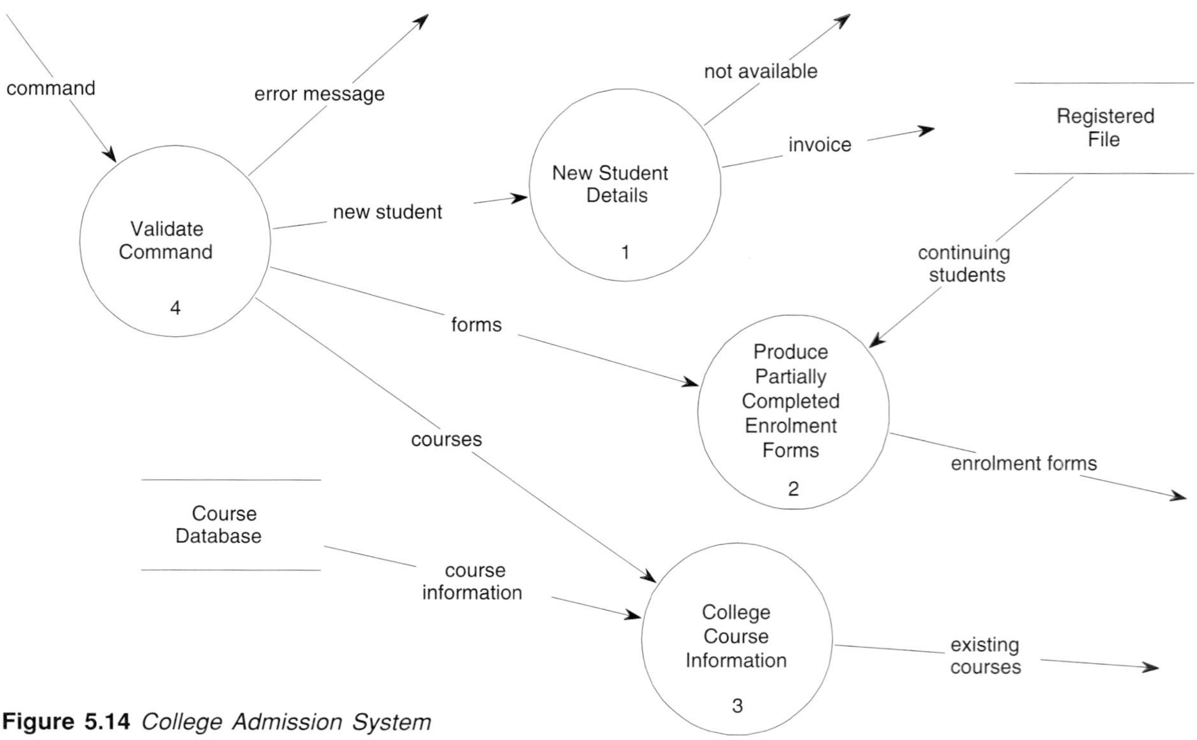

Figure 5.14 *College Admission System*

Structure chart example – College Admission System

Figure 5.14 is a data flow diagram that represents a College Admission System
Complete the following activities:

1. Determine the afferent (input), central transformation, and efferent (output) processes from the diagram above.
2. Show how the data flows are to be intersected for the input, central and output requirements suggested in 1. Use Figure 5.14 to show these.
3. Complete a structure chart using an appropriate CASE tool to represent the above system.
4. Check the diagram is syntactically correct.

Suggested solution

1. Position of processes

Afferent (input) processes	*Central transform*	*Efferent (output) processes*
Validate Command	New Student Details Produce Partially Completed Enrolment Forms College Course Information	

2. The flows are split as shown in Figure 5.15.

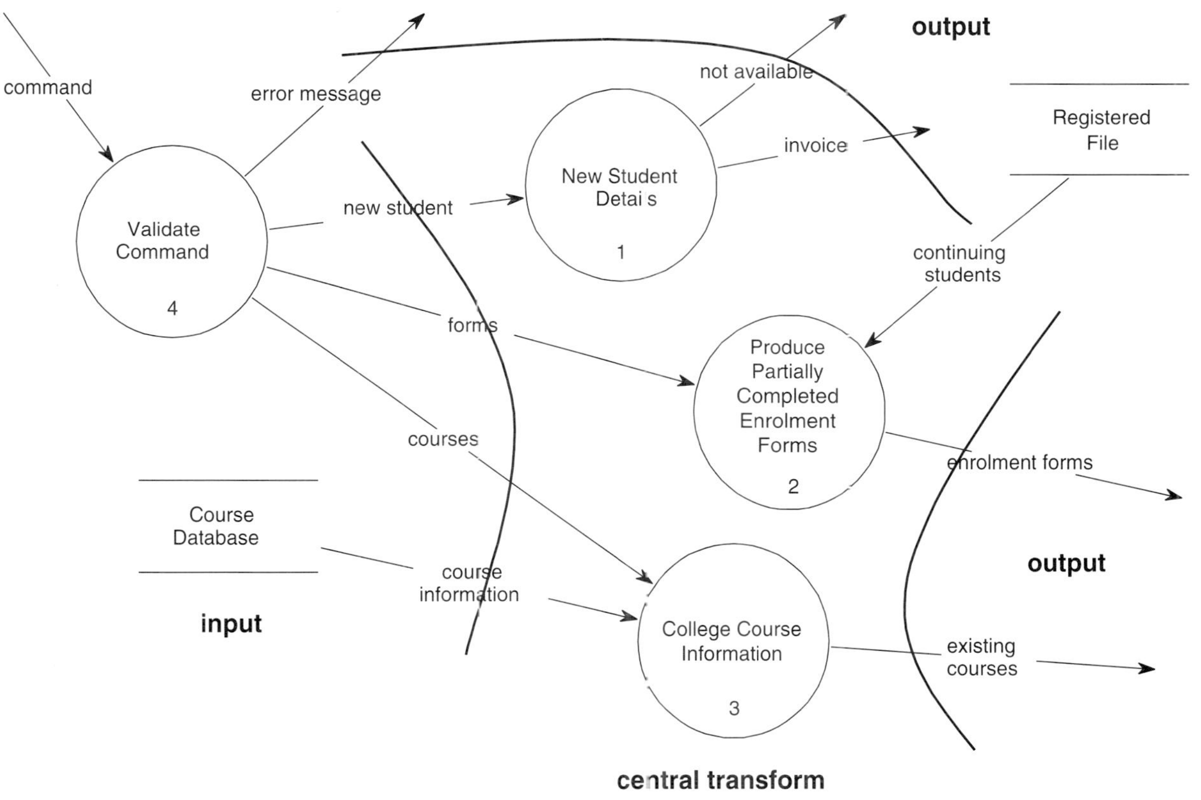

Figure 5.15 *College admission system*

See Figure 5.16 for the structure chart.

3. Structure chart

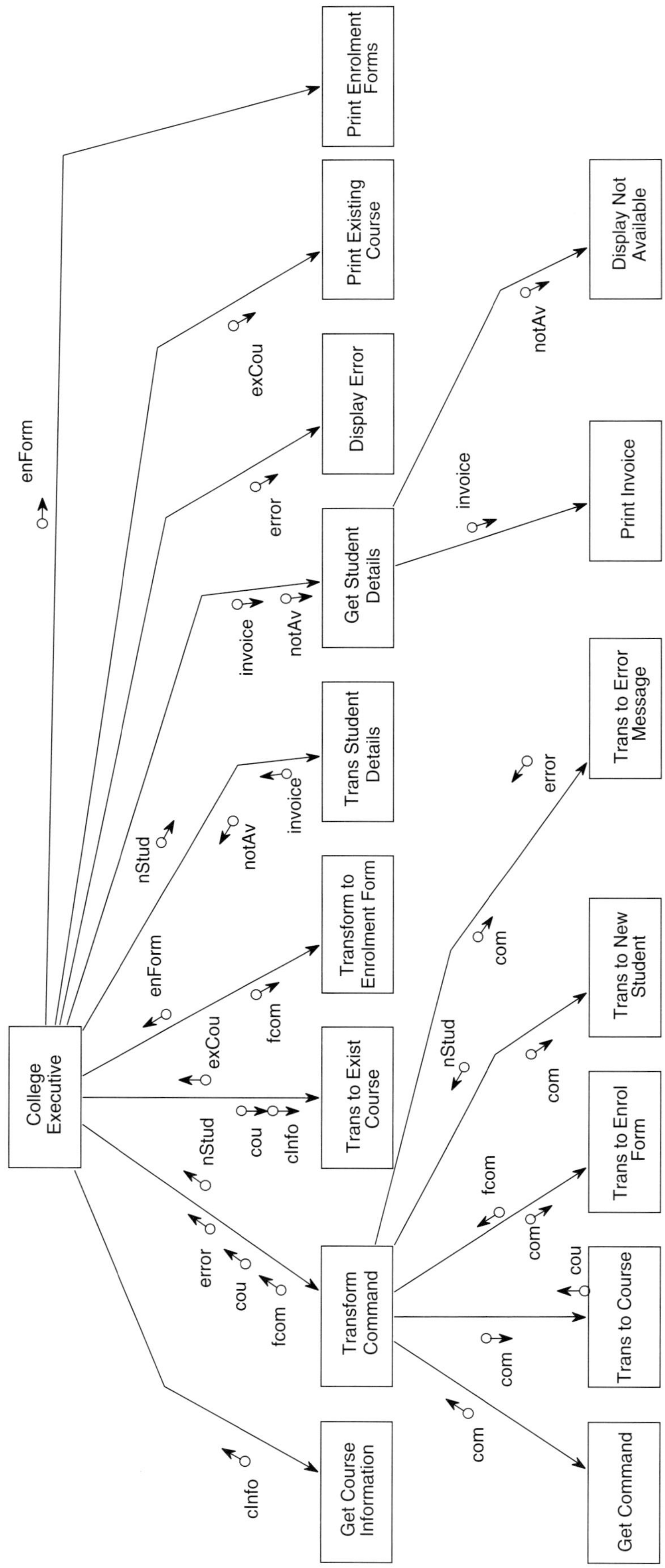

Figure 5.16 *Structure chart representation – College Admission System*

4. Syntax test

Project: C:\SELECT\SYSTEM\COLLEGE\
Title: College Admission System
Date: 19-Apr-2001 Time: 13:2

Checking CADMIN1.DAT

No Errors detected, No Warnings given.

---- End of report ----

Object-oriented analysis and design

It has been proved that the quality of a software product is vastly improved with the use of object-oriented techniques. This is mainly due to the way object concepts lead themselves to real world entities and the construction of the class library where developed code can be reused time and time again within given applications.

'Reuse' concerns using or adapting existing software components which are initially provided by the class library supplied with the object system and supplemented by the components constructed by earlier software developments.

Figure 5.17 shows an example from the Java class library showing the Button class.

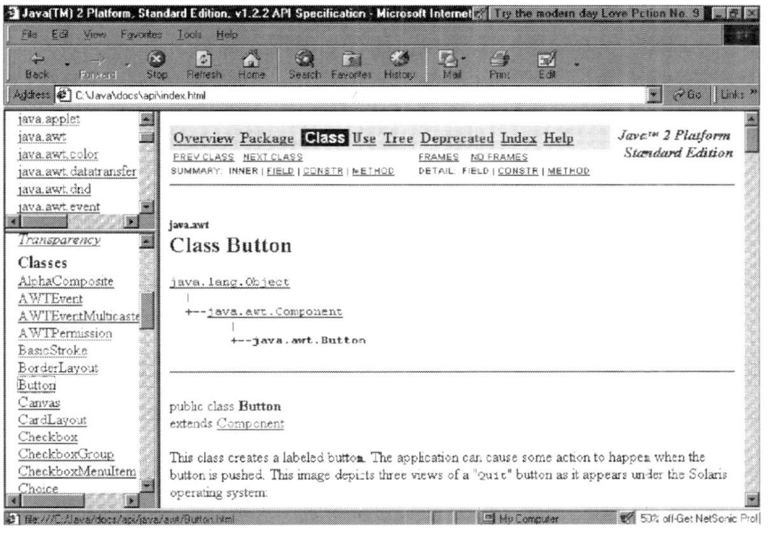

Figure 5.17

For the development of Java classes the Java 2 (version 1.3) platform is an essential tool for code development. Note that the top class of the hierarchy is Object and all classes below this can inherit its internal components.

Determining the classes from a given specification was developed in Chapter 2 using textual analysis. This also showed that class structures were the fundamental building block of object development. This is outlined in Figure 5.18.

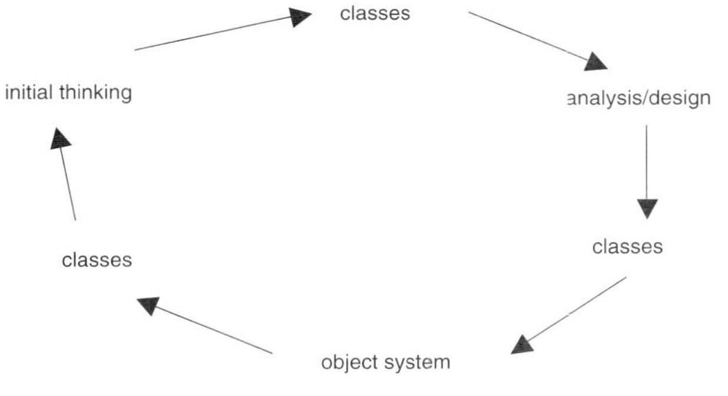

Figure 5.18

Remember a class is an implementable base for objects. Below are some outlines of high level examples of class structures:

C++

```
class MyData
{
        private:
                int value;
                char name[20];
        public
                MyData()
                {

                }
                int calculate(int data)
                {

                }
};

void main()
{

}
```

Java

```
public class MyData
{
        private int value; // instance variable
        private static String name;
                                // class variable
        MyData() // constructor
        {

        }
        // an instance method
        public int calculate(int data)
        {

        }
        // main method
        public static void main(String args[])
        {

        }
}
```

data is an instance of the MyData class, it is an object

```
MyData data;
```

```
MyData data = new MyData()
```

To sum up:

- A class describes the behaviour of a set of objects of some kind.
- Objects (which are instances of some class) are related to other objects (mostly, but not necessarily, instances of other classes). The relationships between objects are represented as associations between the classes of which the objects are instances.
- The behaviour of a class of objects can be described in terms of the responsibilities that are assigned to the class. There are two forms of responsibilities, for recording information and for doing something (i.e. taking action).
- Objects fulfil their responsibilities by means of collaborations with other objects. Hence the Class–Responsibility–Collaboration (CRC) method used as a development method within object-oriented software development.

Full details of this method can be found in the *Designing Object-Oriented Software* by Rebecca Wirfs-Brock, Brian Wilkerson and Lauren Wiener published by Prentice Hall. The processes involved in this method are outlined in the table below:

Development stage	*Activity*
Analysis	This initial stage takes a statement of requirements that has been negotiated with the customer and is analysed to obtain an understanding as to what the system is to do. The aim is to provide an initial understanding of the classes, associations, responsibilities and collaboration. Here the initial class-association diagram will be developed possibly using techniques like UML with an appropriate CASE tool which provide checking facilities to ensure quality is built into the model from the start.
Design	This stage is concerned with producing a design document that specifies how the object model may be represented by software components. The design document will detail the classes required, their method heading and the associated variables. This stage moves away from real world entities and events to objects such as software components. An example table format outlining the CRC method and variable class requirements is shown below.
Implementation	This stage takes the design activity and essentially produces the appropriate object code. For example, C++, Smalltalk or Java.
Component and integration testing	The individual components are tested first to ensure their internal protocol is correct. Then the components are brought together to form the complete working system. During this stage integration testing is carried out to ensure the components correctly link together and all message calls between classes are correctly structured.

Class design table

Class: MyData			*Superclass: SuperData*
Responsibility	Type	Collaborator	Variables and methods
Records the data details	record	YourData	variables:
Calculate the data fee	action	None	methods:

Note: The number of responsibilities contained within a class should be kept to a minimum. An average figure is normally around two, with four being the maximum.

At the design stage we need to think carefully about the class protocol (the methods) and their associated variables. Most modern object-oriented languages classify their variables and methods as being 'class' or 'instance'.

The piece of Java code shown previously contains examples of these. Another example is shown below:

```
private static char letter;                    // class variable

public static int myMethod(String name) // class method
{
        ....................;
        ....................;

        return ( );

}
```

These are specified as being a 'class variable' and a 'class method'. This is defined within Java by the use of the static term.

If we have:

```
private double balance;                // instance variable

public void setData(String data)       // instance method
{

}
```

So what are the differences?

Instance variable – These hold unique values for each instance of the class created. For example, if we have a class called Account, which has an instance variable called balance, and we create two instances of the class (objects), baileyAccount and bessAccount then each can have a unique balance value.

Class: Account

Instances of the class (objects)	*Instance variable*	*Value*
baileyAccount	balance	579.23
bessAccount	balance	23.57

Generally instance variables can only be directly accessed from the methods of the class in which they are defined and from the methods of its subclasses.

Instance method – A method is the implementation of the message that has the same name. A method is the code that is executed when the corresponding message is sent to an object. These may be used as 'accessor methods' for the instance variables. For example:

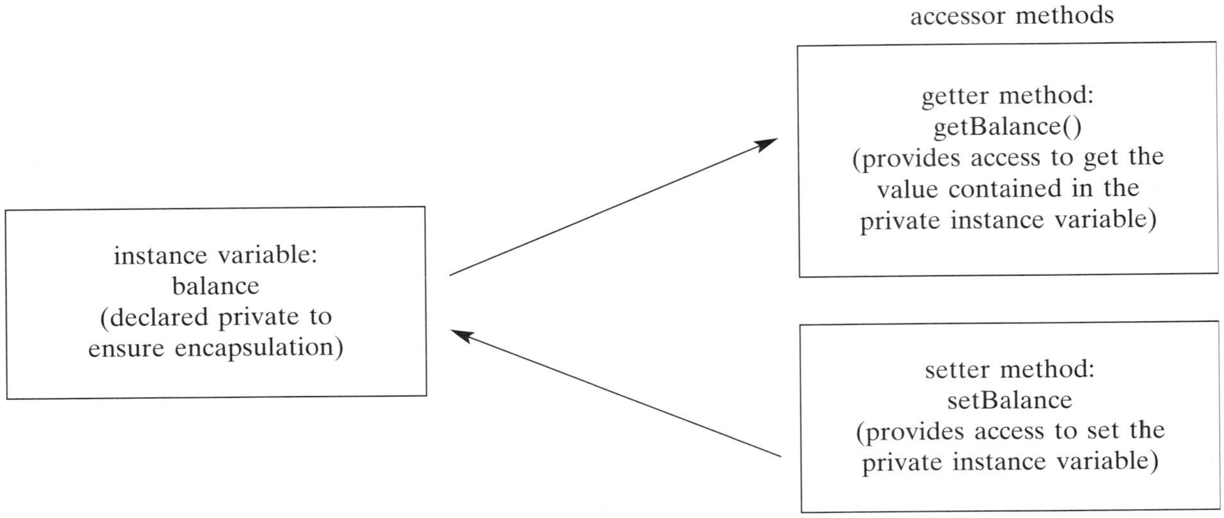

Note: An instance method is sent to an instance of a class (i.e. an object), i.e.

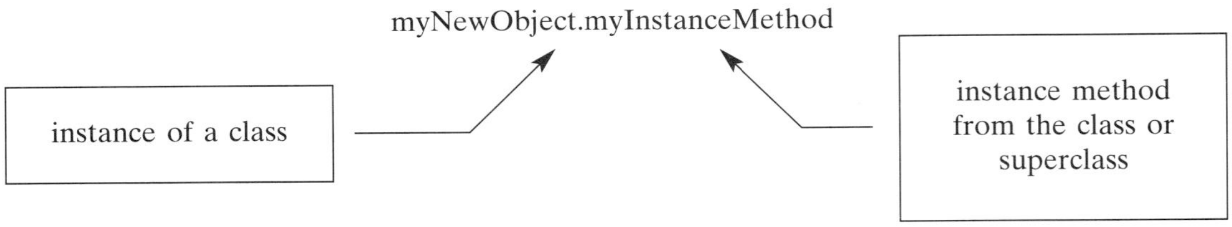

Class variable – This is the most common means by which classes can have state associated with them. These variables are visible to and can be used directly by the class and instance methods of the class, its subclasses, instances of the class and instances of any subclasses. Hence they allow the class state to be shared by all instances, subclasses, and their instances. A class variable is similar to a global variable in that all instances of the class share its same common state.

Class method – Class methods can be used in a similar way as instance methods for providing 'assessor routines' for the class variables. They can be used without creating an instance of a class. A class method is defined for a message sent directly to a class. For example:

MyClass.myClassMethod

Note: Instance methods can also access class variables, but class methods cannot directly access instance variables. Instance methods can also access class methods from within their code structure.

Object-oriented example – airline booking system

Below is an extract from a negotiated statement of requirements:

> An airline booking system is required that can take passenger reservations for specific flights. The system needs to keep track of many airlines each with their own respective flights. It will handle all bookings and cancellations made by customers it has, or will service. Each flight will contain many passengers that are made up of first class, business class and tourist class. Also each flight will need to keep track of its flight number and destination plans.

1. Analyse the statement of requirements to establish the required classes.
2. Using a suitable CASE tool construct an outline class-association diagram and check its syntactic correctness.
3. Develop the class text structures that represent the diagram outlines in 2 above.
4. Consider any invariants that may need to be documented.
5. Carry out a 'walkthrough' to ascertain the responsibilities and collaborations.
6. Develop any aspects of inheritance that may be explicit in the analysis model.
7. Complete a design table to represent the classes to include their variables and methods. The type of responsibility needs to be included along with the collaborators established during the 'walkthrough'.
8. Modify the class diagram to include the variables and methods (operations).
9. Complete a basic Java object-oriented programming implementation of the analysis and design model to contain part of the AirlineBookingSystem that is able to create two new airline objects and one tourist class passenger object. You will need to complete four classes: AirlineBookingSystem, Airline, Passenger (abstract) and TouristClassPassenger (which inherits from Passenger). Remember, to create a new tourist class passenger object you need the following code structure: TouristClassPassenger newPassenger = new TouristClassPassenger();
10. Thoroughly test the classes by adding a test harness (main program section) in the AirlineBookingSystem class, and finally document the execution results.

Note: Remember the CRC (Class–Responsibility–Collaboration) method provides a basis for us to get started. The problem specified above would be a massive coding project, but we are just looking at the structures contained in the extract (i.e. showing collaboration and inheritance). Do not go beyond the specification as this may lead to an overcomplicated solution.

For implementation the responsibilities and collaborators will enable you to determine the variable structures and their supporting methods. Each class will require a constructor that will set the initial values of the instance variables.

As this is not an object-oriented programming course (full details in the unit of the same name) keep the storage structures simple. For example, use array structures and not complicated data storage techniques. Remember that Passenger is an abstract class in which no instances need to be created; its subclasses (TouristClassPassenger, FirstClassPassenger and BusinessClassPassenger) all inherit from the superclass.

Suggested solution

1. By using the process of textual analysis we have:

> An <u>airline booking system</u> is required that can take <u>passenger reservations</u> for specific <u>flights</u>. It will handle all bookings and cancellations made by <u>customers</u> it has, or will service. Each <u>flight</u> will contain many <u>passengers</u> that are made up of <u>first class</u>, <u>business class</u> and <u>tourist class</u>. Also each <u>flight</u> will need to keep track of its flight number and destination plans.

From the main candidates for class structures are:

- Airline Booking System (AirlineBookingSystem)
- Airline
- Flight
- Passenger
  - Passenger First Class (FirstClassPassenger)
  - Passenger Business Class (BusinessClassPassenger)
  - Passenger Tourist Class (TouristClassPassenger)

Note: Customers are future passengers so a class for them is not required.

2. Outline class structure

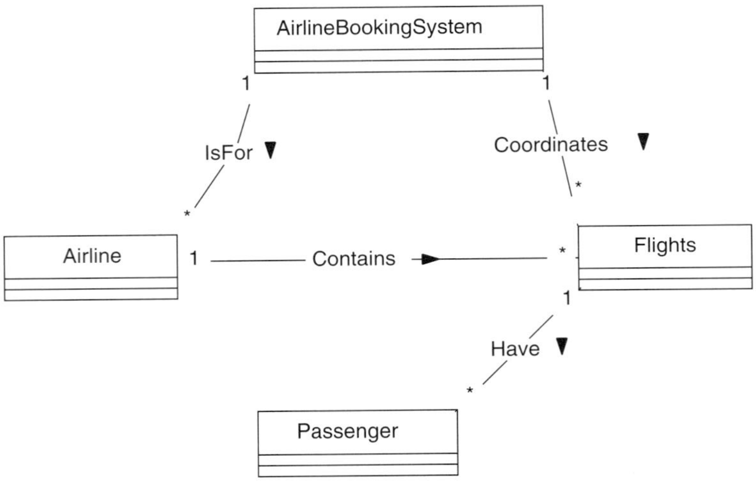

Figure 5.19

Note: Figure 5.19 was completed using Select Enterprise© CASE tool.

To ensure quality is installed from the outset, the diagram was checked for semantic correctness. At the moment it is an outline only and may require modifications as the model develops.

3. Develop the class text structures that represent the diagram outlined in 2 above

Class: AirlineBookingSystem
Handles all the booking requirements for the particular airlines and passengers'

Class: Airline
'Provides overall control for all its flights'

Class: Flight
'Provides details about particular flights'

Class: Passenger
'Passengers travel or make booking to travel'

Class: FirstClassPassenger
'A type of passenger that only travels first class'

Class: BusinessClassPassenger
'A special type of passenger that only travels business class'

Class: TouristClassPassenger
'A passenger who travels by the cheapest rate'

4. Consider any invariants that may need to be documented

Invariant
Any given instance of Flight is associated with a set of Passenger instances via the contains association. Each instance of passenger is either: First Class, Business Class or Tourist Class.

5. Carry out a 'walkthrough' to ascertain the responsibilities and collaborations:

Walkthrough
Stage 1: Understanding in application area terms

What information is the system provided with?
1. Passenger details (name, address, travel requirements, etc.)
2. The Airline and Flight details

What must the system do with that information?
1. Record the passenger information
2. Record that a passenger is booked onto a flight associated to a particular airline

Stage 2: Understanding in terms of instances of classes and associations
Processing the booking of a passenger for a flight requires the following actions:
1. Locating the instance of Flight corresponding to the scheduled flight.
2. Navigating via the contains association to those instances of Passenger that correspond to those passengers belonging to that flight.
3. For each such instance of Passenger, obtain the value corresponding to the passenger's name.

Stage 3: Understanding in terms of responsibilities and collaborations

Class: AirlineBookingSystem
Responsibilities:
    Keeps track of the airlines under its control
    Keeps track of the passengers it has or will service
    Handles passenger bookings
Collaborators:
    Airline, Passenger

Class: Airline
Responsibilities:
    Records the airline name
    Keeps track of the scheduled flights
Collaborators:
    Flight

Class: Flight
Responsibilities:
    Records the flight name
    Keeps track of the passengers in a flight
    Records the route and flight times
Collaborators:
    Passenger, Airline

Class: Passenger
Responsibilities:
    Records the passenger name, address and telephone number
Collaborators:
    None

Class: FirstClassPassenger
    'A subclass of passenger'
Responsibilities:
    Records the passenger's special requirements
Collaborators:
    None

Class: BusinessClassPassenger
    'A subclass of passenger'
Responsibilities:
    Records the passenger's company name
Collaborators:
    None

Class: TouristClassPassenger
    'A subclass of passenger'
Responsibilities:
    Records the passenger's travel company
Collaborators:
    None

6. Develop any aspects of inheritance that may be explicit in the analysis model

From the class structure above we can see that passenger is a prime candidate for a superclass of Business Class Passenger, First Class Passenger and Tourist Class Passenger. As passengers can only be of one type only Passenger can be defined as abstract as no instance of it needs to be created.

All the three subclasses can inherit the methods created in Passenger as they are common to all of them. The layout is shown in Figure 5.20.

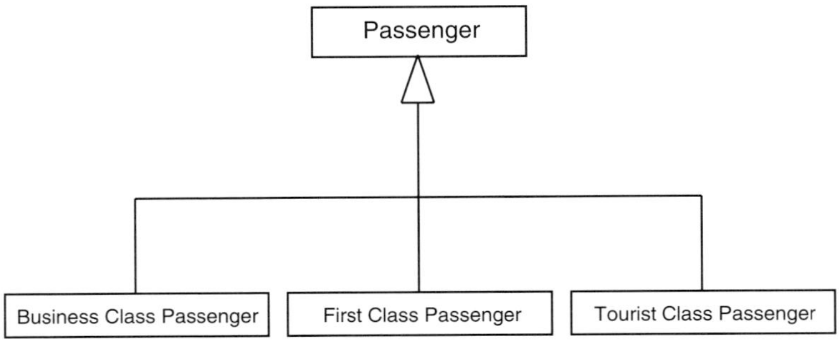

Figure 5.20

7. Complete a design table to represent the classes to include their variables and methods. The type of responsibility needs to be included along with the collaborators established during the 'walkthrough'

Class: AirlineBookingSystem			*Superclass: Object*
Responsibilities	*Type*	*Collaborators*	*Variables and methods*
Keeps track of the airlines under its control	record	Airline	Instance variables: airlines passengers
Keeps track of the passengers it has or will service	record	Passenger	Instance methods: addAirlines() addPassengers()
Handles passenger bookings	record	Passenger	bookPassenger()

Class: Airline			*Superclass: Object*
Responsibilities	*Type*	*Collaborators*	*Variables and methods*
Records the airline name	record		Instance variables: airlineName flights
Keeps track of the scheduled flights	record	Flights	Instance methods: setAirline() getAirline()

Class: Flight			*Superclass: Object*
Responsibilities	*Type*	*Collaborators*	*Variables and methods*
Records the flight name	record		Instance variables: flightName flightPassengers
Keeps track of the passengers in a flight	record	Passenger	route flightTimes
Records the route and flight times	record		Instance methods: setFlightName() getFlightName() addPassengers() getPassengers() setRoute() getRoute(0 setFlightTimes() getFlightTimes()

Class: Passenger			*Superclass: Object*
Responsibilities	*Type*	*Collaborators*	*Variables and methods*
Records the passenger name, address and telephone number	record	none	Instant variables name address phone Instance methods getName(), setname() getAddress(),setAddress() getPhone(), setPhone()

Class: BusinessClassPassenger			*Superclass: Passenger*
Responsibilities	*Type*	*Collaborators*	*Variables and methods*
Records the passenger's company name	record	none	Instance variables: companyName Instant methods: setCompanyName() getCompanyName()

Class: FirstClassPassenger			*Superclass: Passenger*
Responsibilities	*Type*	*Collaborators*	*Variables and methods*
Records the passenger's special requirements	record	none	Instance variables: specialRequirements Instant methods: setSpecialRequirements() getSpecialRequirements()

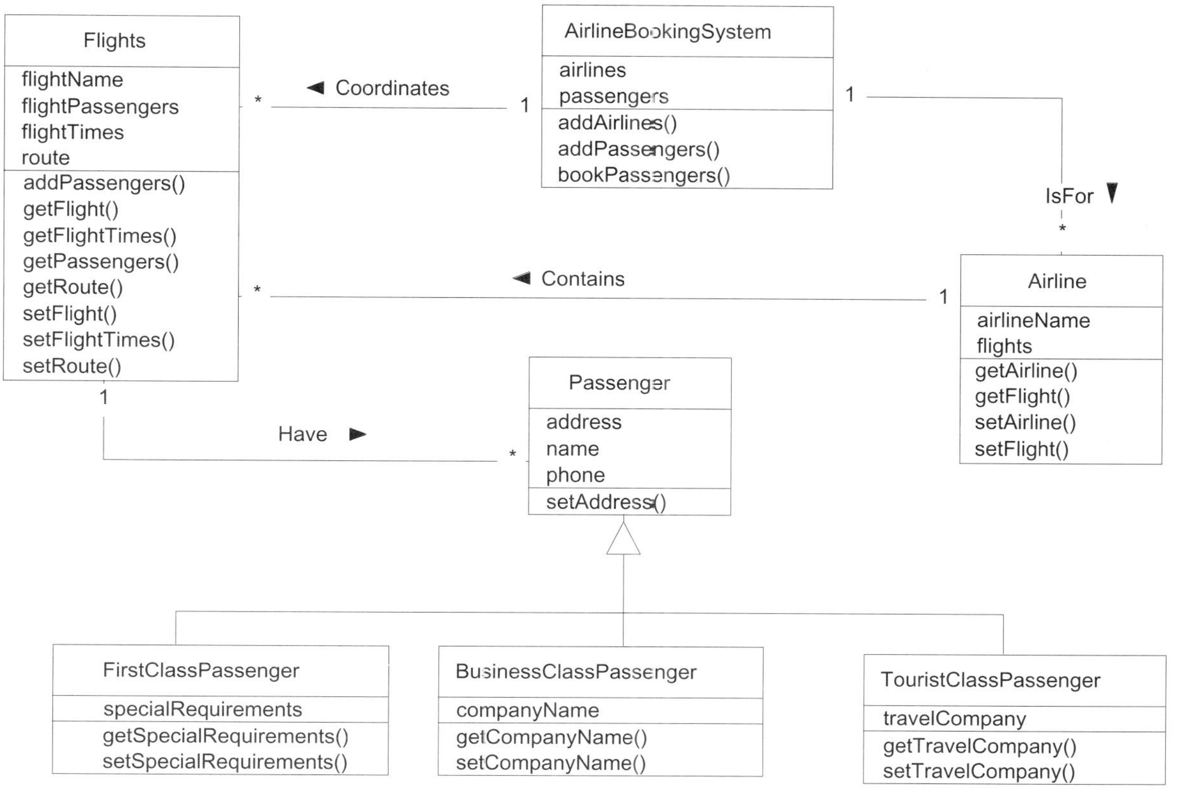

Figure 5.21

Class: TouristClassPassenger			*Superclass: Passenger*
Responsibilities	*Type*	*Collaborators*	*Variables and methods*
Records the passenger's travel company	record	none	Instance variables: travelCompany Instant methods: setTravelCompany() getTravelCompany()

8. Modify the class diagram (developed in 2) to include the variables (attributes) and methods (operations)

Syntax check

```
Project: N:\MYWORK\SELECT\SYSTEM\AIR1\
Title: Airline Booking System
Date: 7-Jun-01 Time: 11:40

Checking AIR1.DAT

No Errors detected, No Warnings given.
```

9. Complete a Java object-oriented programming implementation of the analysis and design model developed so far

Outline Class Structures:

```
/* Airline Booking System main class
   AirlineBooking System.java
*/
public class AirlineBookingSystem
{
      // instance variables
      private String airlines[];
      private String passengers[];
      // class variables - required for input control
      static byte buffer[];
      static String inString, trimString;

      AirlineBookingSystem()  // constructor
      {
            airlines = new String[10];
            passengers = new String[10];
      }

      public void addAirlines()
      throws java.io.IOException
      {
            String anAirline;
            //create two airline objects by collaborating with Airline
            Airline newAirline1 = new Airline();
            Airline newAirline2 = new Airline();
            //enter first airline name
            System.out.println("\nAdd new airlines: \n");
            System.out.print("Create first new airline name: ");
            buffer = new byte[80];
            System.in.read(buffer);
```

```
        inString = new String(buffer);
        trimString = inString.trim();
        airlines[1] = trimString;
        newAirline1.setAirlineName(airlines[1]);
        //enter second airline name
        System.out.print("Create second new airline name: ");
        buffer = new byte[80];
        System.in.read(buffer);
        inString = new String(buffer);
        trimString = inString.trim();
        airlines[2] = trimString;
        newAirline2.setAirlineName(airlines[2]);
        // test objects have been successfully created
        System.out.println("\n\nThe following airlines have been
        created:\n' + newAirline1.getAirlineName()+" and "+
        newAirline2.getAirlineName());
}
public void addPassengers()
throws java.io.IOException
{
        //create new tourist class passenger object (newPassenger)
        //note the collaboration with the Passenger class
        TouristClassPassenger newPassenger = new
        TouristClassPassenger();
        String newPhone, newAddress, newTravelCompany;
        System.out.println("\nAdd new passenger details: \n");
        //enter the passengers name and store in an array for
        //future use
        System.out.print("Enter the passengers name: ");
        buffer = new byte[80];
        System.in.read(buffer);
        inString = new String(buffer);
        trimString = inString.trim();
        passengers[1] = trimString;
        newPassenger.setName(passengers[1]) ;
        //enter the passengers address
        System.out.print("\nEnter the passengers address: ");
        buffer = new byte[80];
        System.in.read(buffer);
        inString = new String(buffer);
        trimString = inString.trim();
        newAddress = trimString;
        newPassenger.setAddress(newAddress);
        //enter the passengers phone number
        System.out.print("\nEnter the passengers phone number: ");
        buffer = new byte[80];
        System.in.read(buffer);
        inString = new String(buffer);
        trimString = inString.trim();
        newPhone = trimString;
        newPassenger.setPhone(newPhone);
        //enter the travel company
        System.out.print("\nEnter the passengers travel company:");
        buffer = new byte[80];
        System.in.read(buffer);
        inString = new String(buffer);
        trimString = inString.trim();
        newTravelCompany = trimString;
        newPassenger.setTravelCompany(newTravelCompany);
```

```
            //test the new passenger has been created
            System.out.println("\nCheck of new passenger object: ");
            System.out.println("\nPassenger Name: " +
            newPassenger.getName());
            System.out.println("\nPassenger Address: " +
            newPassenger.getAddress());
            System.out.println("\nPassenger Phone: " +
            newPassenger.getPhone());
            System.out.println("\nPassenger Travel Company: "
                                + newPassenger.getTravelCompany());
      }

      //test harness to check the above methods
      public static void main(String args[])
      throws java.io.IOException
      {
         int check;
         AirlineBookingSystem aSystem = new AirlineBookingSystem();
         do
         {
            System.out.print
                  ("\nSelect 1 for Airlines or 2 for Passengers (3 to
                  end): ");
            buffer = new byte[80];
            System.in.read(buffer);
            inString = new String(buffer);
            trimString = inString.trim();
            check = Integer.parseInt(trimString);
            if ( check == 1 )
            {
             aSystem.addAirlines();
            }
            else
             if ( check == 2 )
             {
                aSystem.addPassengers();
             }
         }
         while ( check != 3 );
         System.out.println("\n\nEnd of Program .................. ");
      } // end main

}
```

Airline class:

```
/* Airline class for Booking System
   Airline.java
*/

public class Airline
{
      // instance variables
      String airlineName, flights;

      Airline()    //constructor
      {
            airlineName = null;
            flights = null;
      }
```

```
        //basic instance methods for the airline name i.e. Canada Air
        public void setAirlineName(String aName)
        {
                airlineName = aName;
        }

        public String getAirlineName()
        {
                return airlineName;
        }

}
```

Passenger class:

```
/* Passenger class to maintain customer that is entered
   via the AirlineBookingSystem class
   Passenger.java
*/

abstract class Passenger
{
   // instance variables
   private String name;
   private String address;
   private String phone;

   Passenger()     //constructor
   {
      name = "name";
      address = "empty address";
      phone = "no phone";
   }

   // instance methods
   public String getName()
   {
      return name;
   }

   public void setName(String aName)
   {
      name = aName;
   }

 public String getAddress()
   {
      return address;
   }

   public void setAddress(String anAddress)
   {
      address = anAddress;
   }

   public String getPhone()
   {
      return phone;
   }
```

```
    public void setPhone(String aPhone)
    {
        phone = aPhone;
    }
}
```

Tourist class:

```
/* This is a sub-class of Passenger for
   the tourist class passengers.
   TouristClassPassenger.java
*/

public class TouristClassPassenger extends Passenger
{

        // instant variable
        private String travelCompany;

        TouristClassPassenger() //constructor
        {
                travelCompany = "Travel Company";
        }

        // instance methods
        public void setTravelCompany(String aCompany)
        {
                travelCompany = aCompany;
        }

        public String getTravelCompany()
        {
                return(travelCompany);
        }
}
```

10. Thoroughly test the classes by adding a test harness (main program section) in the AirlineBookingSystem class, and finally document the execution results

```
C:/Java/bin>java AirlineBookingSystem

Select 1 for Airlines or 2 for Passengers (3 to end): 1

Add new airlines:

Create first new airline name: Canada Air
Create second new airline name: West Pacific

The following airlines have been created:
Canada Air and West Pacific
```

```
Select 1 for Airlines or 2 for Passengers (3 to end): 2

Add new passenger details:

Enter the passenger's name: Fred Smith
```

Enter the passenger's address: 22 West Side Lane, Surbiton, Surrey

Enter the passenger's phone number: 020 8766 6565

Enter the passenger's travel company: Sunshine Tours

Check of new passenger object:

Passenger Name: Fred Smith

Passenger Address: 22 West Side Lane, Surbiton, Surrey

Passenger Phone: 020 8766 6565

Passenger Travel Company: Sunshine Tours

Project management

Further information – 'why projects go wrong'

The example below outlines some of the main causes of why projects do not meet their required stated objects:

> The National Health Service (NHS) decided to set up Information Systems across hospitals in the UK. It went ahead with one project despite high costs and risks. Even the suppliers did not think it was feasible. It chose three pilot projects within just two months. The hospitals selected were not prepared and no business mechanisms were established.

This example along with many other such cases are outlined in the Committee of Public Accounts Report titled 'Improving the Delivery of Government Projects' (ISBN 0 10 204700 6). The document includes information on 25 projects, the problems, the impact of the problems and the lessons learned.

On the issue of project management the report states that managers need more than a thorough grounding in the principles and practices, plus relevant experience. To be successful they need imagination and well-conceived risk management.

The 'lessons learned' outlined in the report are:

- Analyse and understand the full implications of proposed systems
- The specification must take into account the business needs and user requirements
- Look at the scale and complexity to assess if the project can be achieved
- Make sure senior management are involved
- High quality project management is essential
- Risk management and contingency plans are vital
- Develop close relationships with suppliers, but avoid undue reliance on them; retain ownership of progress
- Pay detailed attention to drawing up and managing contracts
- Plan in resources for staff training, do not underestimate this task
- Review projects so that lesson learned can be applied next time

The report states that projects can be overtaken by technological changes because of delays. Senior management should be aware of the importance of halting a project that has been overtaken by events. An example is outlined below:

> A defence intelligence system was written off at a cost of £41m after it fell more than two years behind schedule and was overtaken by technology. The team did not recognize the complexity at the start, relied too much on contractors, without enough involvement and should have introduced the system in phases.

In addition, project plans should be flexible enough to allow new technologies to be included where relevant. Organizations need to develop close relationships with suppliers in which they are able to share the same business vision.

Solution to Exercise 5.1.3

Activity	*Estimated duration*	*Maximum span*	*Total float*
A1	16	20	4
A2	10	14	4
A3	12	16	4
A4	14	14	0
A5	7	20	13
A6	8	21	13
A7	5	5	0
A8	23	23	0

The critical path lies along the line where the TOTAL FLOAT is ZERO.
Therefore the critical path lies along the line A4, A7, and A8.
This is outlined in Figure 5.22.

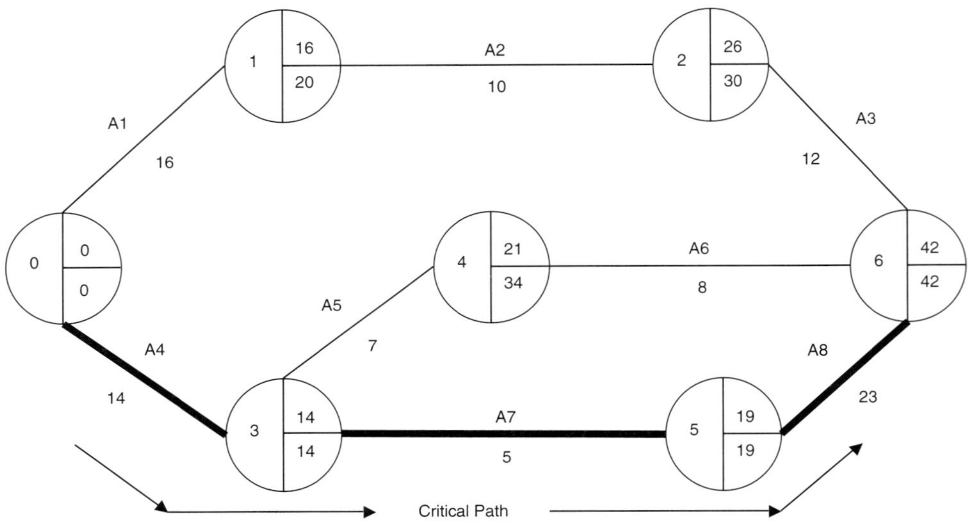

Figure 5.22 *Outline network diagram*

Additional exercise – critical path analysis

Figure 5.23 represents a series of software development activities that are all carried out by a single software engineer. The duration in days is included on the diagram.

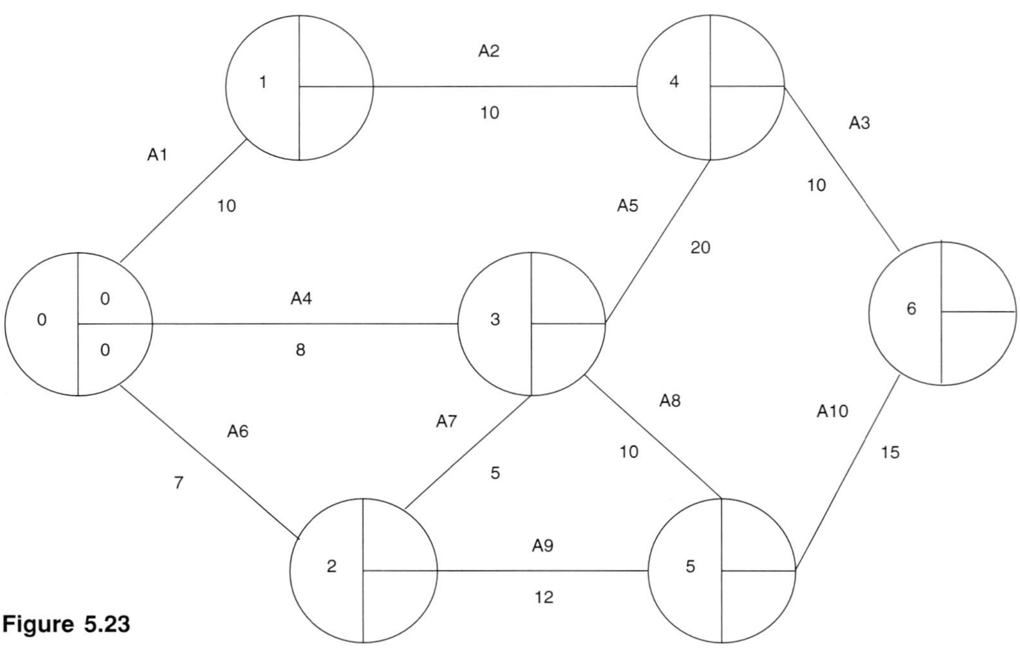

Figure 5.23

(i) Complete the missing Earliest Estimated Times (EET) and Latest Allowable Times (LAT) by filling in the missing spaces on the diagram.

(ii) Create a table that specifies the maximum span and total floats and from this specify the critical path.

(iii) The activities in the diagram are now to be rescheduled to a team of software engineers. Activities A1, A2 and A3 are allocated to software engineer 1, activities A4, A8 and A10 are allocated to software engineer 2, activities A6, A7 and A5 are to be allocated to software engineer 3 (all these activities start work on day 0). A fourth software engineer is to be brought in at the earliest possible date to undertake activity A9. Prepare a Gantt chart to represent this schedule. Can all 10 activities be completed by fewer than four software engineers?

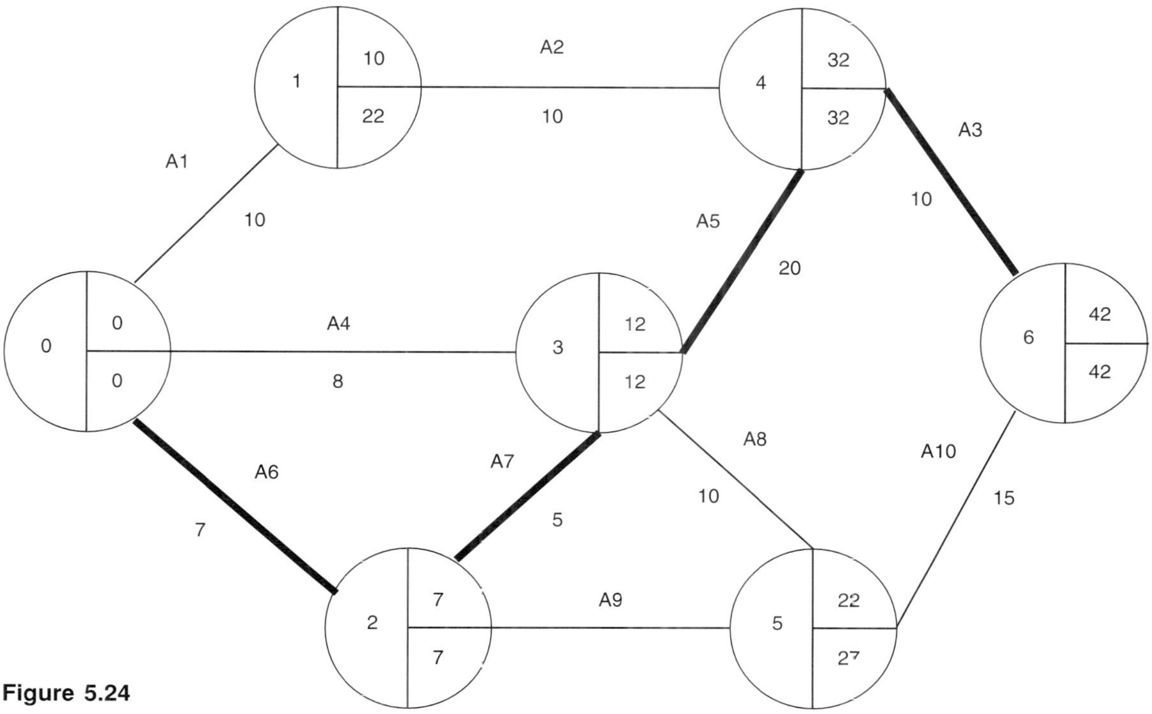

Figure 5.24

Further solutions

Activity	*Estimated duration*	*Maximum span*	*Total float*
A1	10	22	12
A2	10	22	12
A3	10	10	0
A4	8	12	4
A5	20	20	0
A6	7	7	0
A7	5	5	0
A8	10	15	5
A9	12	20	8
A10	15	20	5

Activities with a total float of 0 identify the critical path, in this case A6, A7, A5 and A3.

The critical path has 42 days. The total programming time is 107 days so three software engineers could complete the task with 19 slack days.

Staff	*Activities*	*Free days*
Software Engineer 1	A1, A2, A8	with 12 days free
Software Engineer 2	A4, A9, A10	with 7 days free
Software Engineer 3	A6, A7, A5, A3	no free days

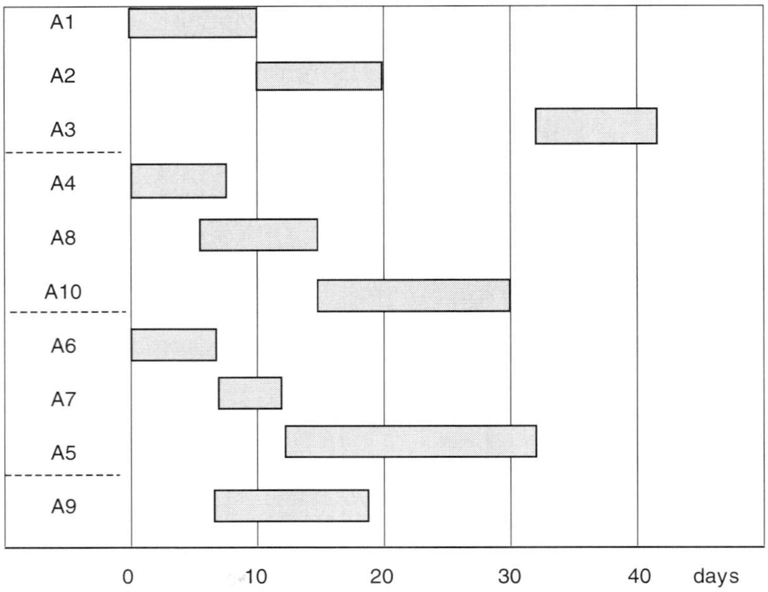

Figure 5.25

Tools for project management

Microsoft Project

Microsoft Project 2000 is a powerful, flexible tool designed to help you manage a full range of projects. Schedule and closely track all tasks – and use Microsoft Project Central, the Web-based companion to Microsoft Project 2000, to exchange project information with your team and senior management.

Some main features:

IMPROVE TEAM PRODUCTIVITY

1. Collaborative planning with Microsoft Project Central

Personal Gantt chart

Render Gantt views like those in Microsoft Project to outline each team member's own tasks across multiple projects.

New task

Team members can create tasks which a project manager can then approve before adding them to the project plan.

Task delegation

Once assigned by the project manager, tasks may be delegated from team leaders to team members or from peer to peer. The Delegation feature can also be disabled if desired.

Show Microsoft Outlook tasks

Team members can display entries from their task list in the Microsoft Outlook(r) messaging and collaboration client so they can see all their project and non-project tasks in a single location.

View non-working time

Team members can report non-working time to the project manager, such as vacation or sick leave, and also report work time that cannot be devoted to the project.

Workgroup

Project managers can assign task responsibilities and track project status across workgroups to keep the project on track.

2. Collaborative tracking with Microsoft Project Central

Auto-accept rules

Managers can reduce time spent in administrative activities by establishing rules to automatically accept actual hours, percentage completed, or any information in a custom field.

Status reports

Create custom report formats and request or receive team member status updates, which Microsoft Project Central automatically rolls into a group report.

Administration module

Project administrators can gain more control over definitions of non-project time, views, formatting styles, and security to ensure consistency in management approaches and organization structure.

Timesheet
Team members can see their assignments across projects, enter updates, and easily send them to the project manager.
Actual hours and per cent complete tracking
Team members can track and report actual hours spent on each assigned task, or estimate what percentage of the task is complete when tracking is difficult or deemed unnecessary.

3. Easy access to project information
Views
Senior executives, managers, and team members can access different views of projects, such as View Your Portfolio, View Your Project, and View Assignments.
Offline capabilities
Team members can take their timesheets and status reports offline and continue working on them from any location.

INCREASE DATA USEFULNESS
4. Flexible viewing
Grouping
Quickly categorize and view task and resource information in any grouping that is most useful to you.
Outline codes
Define outline codes instead of having to tie them to the outline structure of a project.
Graphical indicators
Associate graphical indicators with the data in a custom field, so a particular image can be displayed in place of the actual data to easily spot potential problems.
Fiscal year in timescale
Independently set the use of the fiscal year for both major and minor timescales to display data in a specific timescale combination.
Network diagram
Customize network diagrams with new filtering and layout options, increased formatting features, and enhanced box styles (formerly the PERT Chart).
Rollup Gantt
Display Gantt bars for all subtasks on a single task summary line.

5. Flexible analysis
Task calendars
Create schedules with task-specific calendars that affect only selected tasks.
Materials resources
Specify consumable resources such as lumber or concrete and assign them to tasks.
Deadline dates
Remind your team of deadlines and alert them visually if deadlines cannot be met.
Cross-project critical path
Calculate the critical path within individual or across all inserted projects to see a single critical path for the overall master project.
Custom fields: value lists
Define pick-lists to restrict the values that can be entered into a custom field and simplify data entry with just a mouse click.
Custom fields: formulas
Add custom formulas for arithmetic calculations, conditional testing, and functions to be applied to custom field data.
OLE DB
Share Microsoft Project 2000 data with other applications and integrate data across the enterprise using OLE DB.
Estimated durations
Indicate a tentative duration for a given task by simply entering a value for the duration followed by a question mark; then return to the task at a later time to enter a confirmed duration.
Month duration
Microsoft Project now supports months as a unit of duration.
Contoured resource availability
Create plans that incorporate time-phased resource availability information.

Clear baseline
Clear the baseline or interim plan data for selected tasks or an entire project.

6. Easier reporting
Scaling and printing
Print documents more efficiently and easily with new and improved printing and scaling options.
Copy picture
Create higher quality images with larger allowable sizes and better scaling.

7. Enhanced user confidence
HTML help
Enables easier interaction between the procedures found in HTML Help, Microsoft's new standard help system, and your work in Microsoft Project 2000.
Adaptive menus
Just as in Office 2000, only the items that you use most often are prominently featured on the menu.
Templates
Create and access Microsoft Project templates easily.
Variable row height
Drag the row line between tasks to set individual rows to the height you want.
In-cell editing
View the context of a task while editing it.
Fill handle
Select the cells you want to populate, and use the Fill Handle feature to easily copy information or repeat patterns in several locations.
AutoSave
Set Microsoft Project 2000 to automatically save work at chosen time intervals to avoid losing valuable data if your computer is inadvertently shut down.
Office server extensions support
Save to a Web server just as easily as you save to network locations.
Single document interface
Similar to Office 2000 applications, Microsoft Project 2000 supports the single document interface.
Default save path and format
Specify a default save path and format to save project data where and how you want it.
Accessibility
Get support for third-party accessibility aids through Microsoft Active Accessibility programming interfaces.
Project open and save
The open and save dialog boxes now feature the same look and functionality as those in Office 2000.
Hyperlinks
Easily link to frequently browsed Web pages or commonly used files with the new Office 2000 Hyperlink dialog box.

EXTEND PROJECT MANAGEMENT
8. Improve capacity and performance
Database performance
Get improved performance and access to data with changes to the Microsoft Project database.
Resource pooling
Improve network performance by using a resource pool.
Inserted projects
If you ever need to move a project, all the links from master projects to subprojects will automatically be maintained.

9. Keep users up and running
Install on demand
Install only the components you need – when you need them.
Roaming user support
Enhanced portability lets you log on to any computer in a networked environment and maintain personal settings and preferences.
Windows terminal server support
Microsoft Project 2000 can now run on Microsoft Windows Object Model.
The outline (see Figure 5.26) shows a typical Gannt chart display with a list of associated tasks.

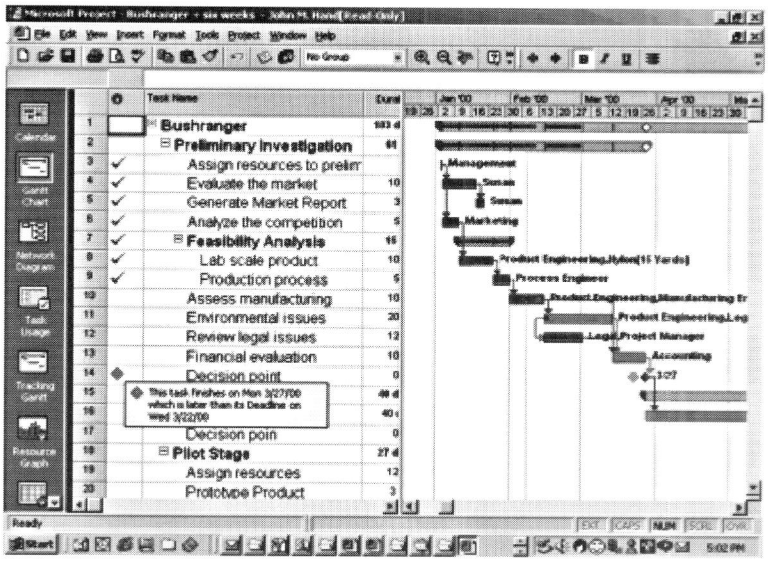

Figure 5.26 *Microsoft Project 2000 pictorial outline*

Microsoft Project books

Microsoft Project 2000 Step by Step with CD-ROM by Carl S. Chatfield and Timothy D. Johnson. Published by Microsoft Press

Using Microsoft Project 2000 by Tim Pyron. Published by Que

Microsoft Project 2000 for Dummies by Martin Doucette. Published by International Data Group Incorporated

Effective Executive's Guide to Project 2000: The Eight Steps for Using Microsoft Project 2000 to Organize, Manage and Finish Critically Important Projects by Stephen L. Nelson, Pat Coleman and Kaarin Dolliver. Product Code (ISBN): 0967298113

Further information

A lot of additional information, including tutorials, downloads, trial software, case studies, training and certification, support etc. can be found at:

http://www.microsoft.com/office/project/default.htm

Software maintenance

Further information

When any physical component goes into use, for example a car, a washing machine, a vacuum cleaner or a personal computer, one would expect that very little change would be required. The change is only intermittent and this is usually to replace parts that are worn out or need modifying. This is not the same with software systems; from the moment they are validated they tend to change. Policies need to be introduced whereby the decisions to effect these changes can be made. Often these are commercial decisions that are designed to emit new versions of software systems that:

(a) are less wrong
(b) require improved features and functionally for end users.

Change is potentially a major source of loss of original quality during the development of software systems. Many systems have undergone many changes and become so patched up that it is a wonder they serve any useful purpose.

Software evolution

Evolutions of software are things like new features, or modifications to existing ones that come about for a number of reasons. The customer may require new additions to be added to a working system as his/her business evolves due to natural expansion. These could include; greater use of IT within the organization, the system needs to be more economically viable, make the system more user friendly as more staff are to be involved with its use etc.

Lehman's laws of software evolution

1. *The law of continuing change.* Programs concerning real world requirements either undergo continual change, or become progressively less useful. This continues until it is judged more economic to replace the system than to change it.
2. *The law of increasing complexity.* Changes to software systems increase the complexity of their construction and, commensurately, reduce their degree of good structure with detriment in quality. That is unless explicit work is done to maintain the degree of good structure, or improve it and, thereby, preserve or reduce the level of complexity and thereby enhance quality.
3. *The law of program evolution.* Program evolution is subject to a dynamic process that makes it, and measures of its development and system properties, self-regulating with statistically determinable treads and invariance.
4. *The law of invariant work rate.* During the active life of a program, the overall activity rate in associated programming tasks is statistically invariant.
5. *The law of perceived complexity.* During the active life of a program, the change content (changes, additions and deletions) of successive releases of the evolving program is statistically invariant.

It goes without saying that changes to 'safety-critical' software should undergo severe testing and debugging routines to ensure that the modified product still meets its original high specification requirements.

For further information see *A Study in Software Maintenance* by Dart, Christie and Brown.

PDF and PostScript files can be found at:

http://www.sei.cmu.edu/publications/documents/93.reports/93.tr.008.html

Version control

One of the main considerations of maintaining a configuration management system in practice is in the documentation process. We have stated highly in this chapter that all development aspects should be documented, but control on this documentation is essential. Outlined below are two possible (perhaps exaggerated) examples of potential problems:

1. There may be a free-for-all by developers to the documents that are being produced during the development of a system. Such an unrestricted access to write to the deliverable documentation files can lead to a divergence between system requirements, source code or data elements. In the worst case major changes to one document may occur without a collateral updating of another document which could give rise to problems with the source and objects codes and the documentation not corresponding to either of them.
2. There may be highly restrictive access to the development documentation. This could involve security checks or software hardware password keys being required which add to the problems of accessing the documentation. Such restricted access can also be placed on attempts to modify a master copy of the source code.

The second method stated above has both technical and managerial advantages, as full control is placed on both the documentation and the source code. In some cases the organization may select a nomination of authorized staff, along with security measures to complete the system of restricted access. These fairly extreme conditions occur in a surprising number of instances with managers unaware of the possible consequences.

If a company is not using an electronic version control system then an alternative system needs to be put into place. An example client/product table is outlined below:

Client	*Product*	*Version*	*Document file name (key)*
Bernese Dog Food Ltd	BERDOG	2.1	BERDOG.2.1
Bailey Brewery Ltd	BAIBRE	1.7	BAIBRE.1.7
Morgan Freight Assoc.	MORFRE1	3.4	MORFRE1.3.4
	MORFRE2	1.2	MORFRE2.1.2
Tia & Susie Dance Studio	TIASUS	1.4	TIASUS.1.4

Whatever method is employed a successful version control system is essential for the success of the configuration management process.

Suggested solution to Exercise 5.1.4 – version control

This has been completed using the Component Software RCS (Revision Control System) which monitors changes made in files that are accessed by stand-alone or networked workstations.

This system can be downloaded free for single workstations or purchased under licence for network use. It can be found at:

http://www.componentsoftware.com/

A simple example of document control using CS-RCS revision control system:

Step 1 *Getting started*
Save a simple text file with some simple lines of text in it. Call it MyTest1.txt.

Step 2 *Add a file to the repository*
Select the file in windows and right click the mouse button (see Figure 5.27).

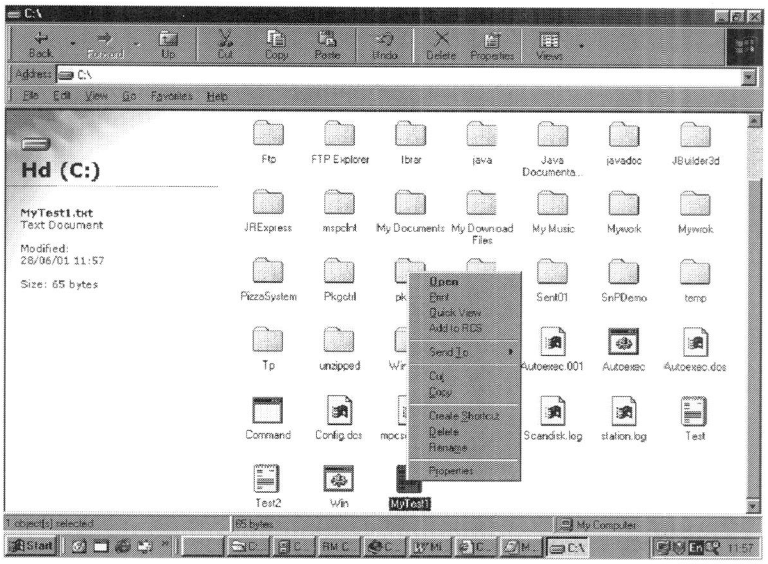

Figure 5.27

The dialog display contains RCS components required to handle the control of the document. From this select the Add to RCS. A message box appears asking to confirm this. Click yes. Then click OK. The file has now been added to the repository.

Step 3 *Checking the file*
To check whether MyTest1.txt changed since it was last added to the Repository:

From the Windows Explorer, right click MyTest1.txt. The right-click menu appears (see Figure 5.28).

Note: As long as MyTest.txt is unchanged, the Check-in menu entry is disabled. If you installed ComponentSoftware as Personal, the Check-out menu entry is also disabled.

Next click on the RCS Status and the message shown in Figure 5.29 appears.
Select OK.

Step 4 *Editing the file*
Edit the file MyTest1.txt by adding some more lines. Then save the file. Then check and view the file changes in the repository:

Right click the file in Windows Explorer
Select RCS Status
The message shown in Figure 5.30 appears.
Click yes.

The file is displayed with the modifications and deletions noted (see Figure 5.31).

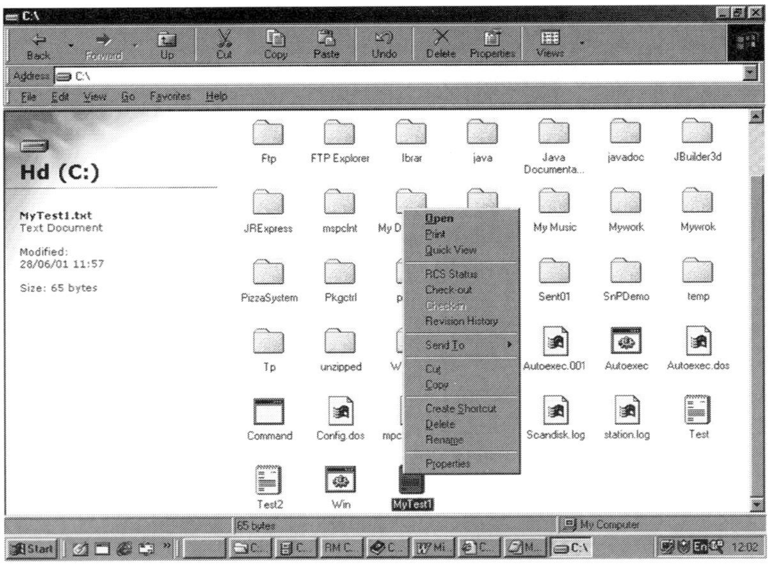

Figure 5.28

Figure 5.29

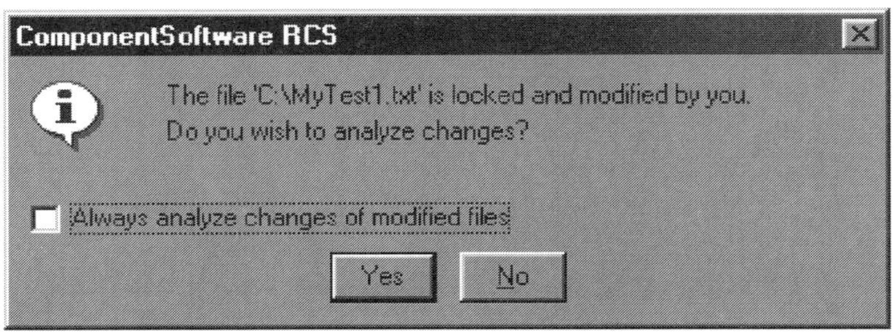

Figure 5.30

Step 5 *Checking out a file*
By checking out a file, you can undo all the changes you made to a file since it was last added to the Repository. When you check out a file, you are retrieving the latest revision of a file.

Right click on the file MyTest1.txt

Select Check-out

The screen shown in Figure 5.32 is displayed.

Ensure Retain Lock is selected then select Review Changes. The document is now back in its original state.

Step 6 *Checking in a new revision*
Modify the document MyText1.txt by adding and deleting a line. Right click the mouse button over the file in Windows Explorer and select Check-in. The screen shown in Figure 5.33 appears.

You can now enter a description about the changes and an appropriate change title. Then click OK.

Note: To allow other users to edit the file uncheck Retain Lock.

Step 7 *Review the Revision History*
Right click on the file in MyTest1.txt in Windows Explorer shown in Figure 5.34. Select Revision History from the menu. The page shown in Figure 5.34 is displayed.

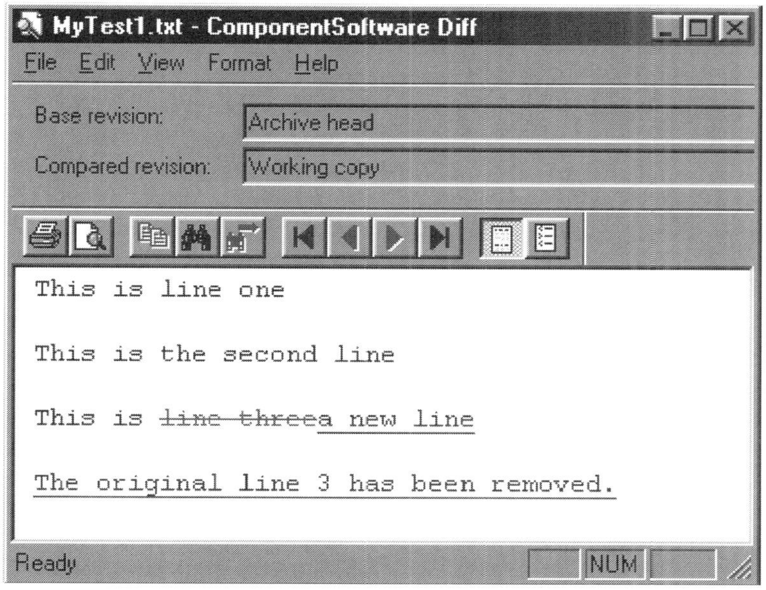

Figure 5.31

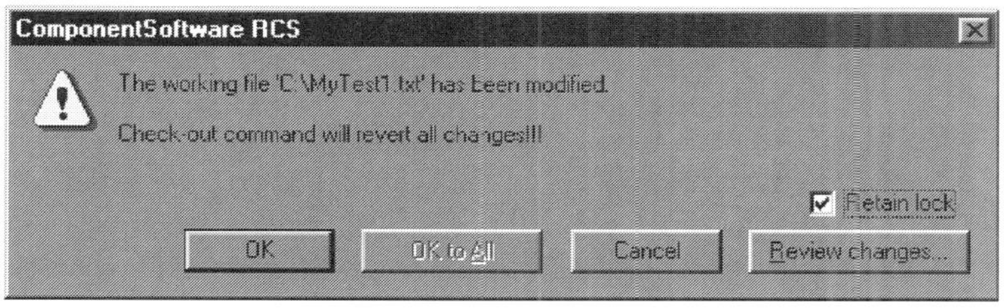

Figure 5.32

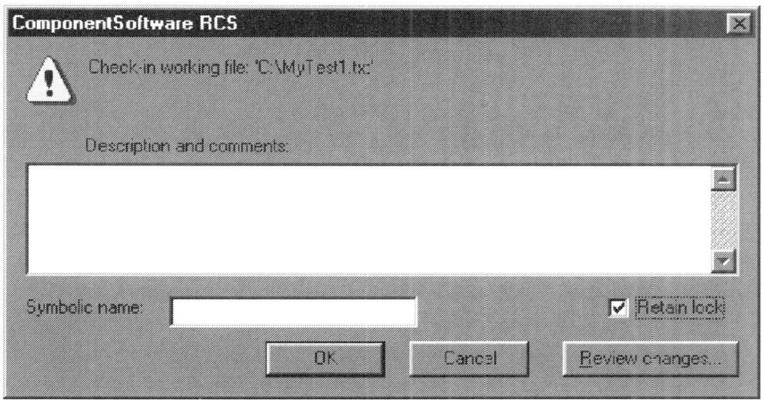

Figure 5.33

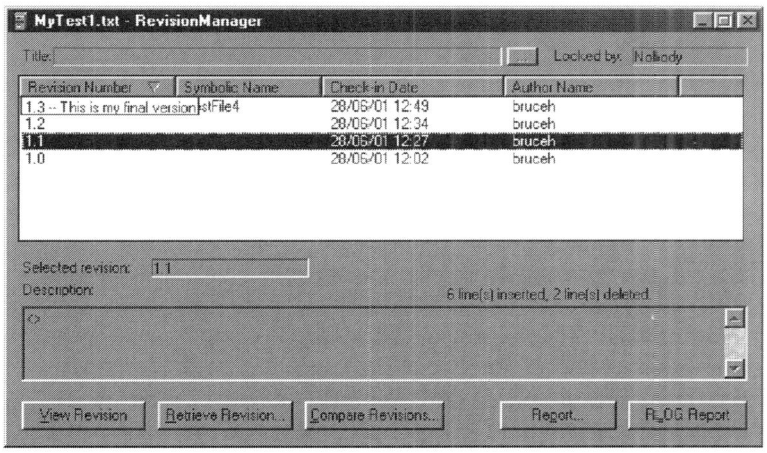

Figure 5.34

Several options are available for checking and comparing revisions.

Note: You can see the revision by double left clicking on the required version.
Step 8 *The Document Explorer*
The Document Explorer allows you to view and organize all documents that are checked into the Repository, as well as view general information about them. From the Document Explorer's Project menu, you can create projects, project milestones, branching, merging, and generate reports (see Figure 5.35).

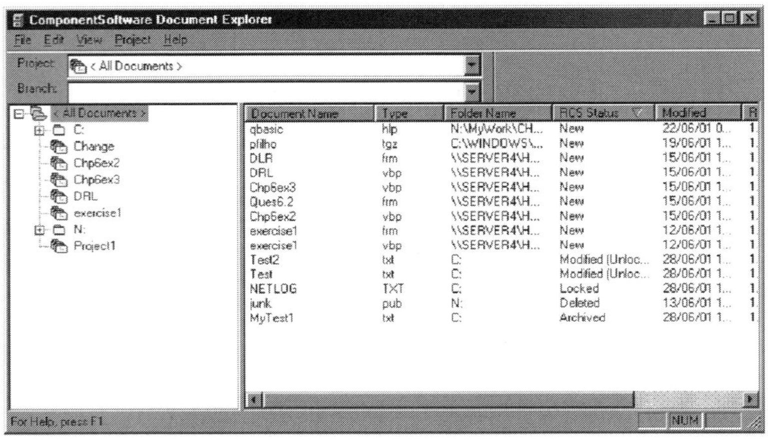

Figure 5.35

5.2 Software quality assurance

Further information

Whatever design methodology is used when developing a software system, they all need to incorporate the following main activities:

Management	→ Planning, controlling and directing
Software engineering	→ Analyse, design, implement and structure
Quality assurance	→ Ensures the product meets all its requirements

Example of quality assurance activities:

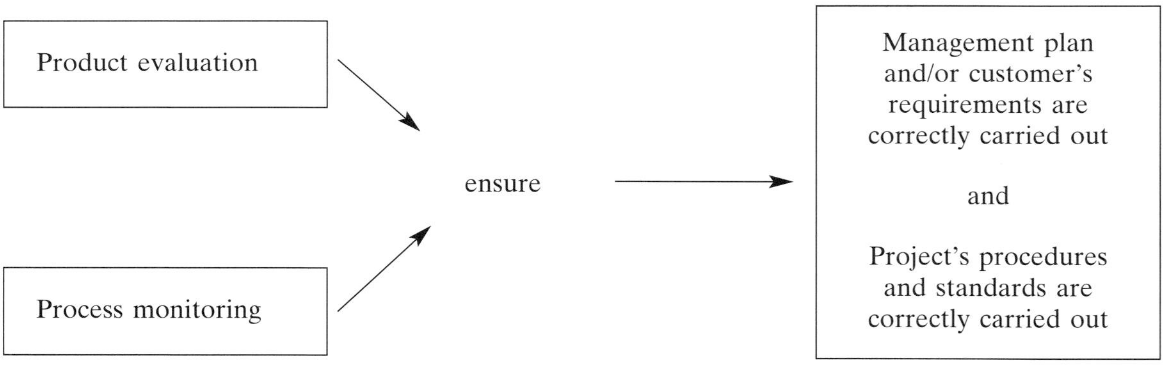

Product evaluation ensures that standards are being followed. In an ideal situation the first products being monitored by software quality assurance should be the project's standards and procedures. The process ensures that acceptable standards exist and that compliance of these is maintained. Evaluation assures that the software product reflects the requirements of the standards as outlined in the initial plan.

Process monitoring is a quality assurance activity that ensures the correct steps are being carried out (verification) to develop the product. This activity compares the actual steps taken with those in the original documentation to ensure they correspond.

Further Information on ISO standards.

Further information see: http://satc.gsfc.nasa.gov/assure/agbses1.txt (also agbsec2 & 3)

Solution to Exercise 5.2.1 – ISO standards update

An example of research into the latest ISO standards.

Below are two examples from the latest standards that directly effect quality management systems

A. Quality management principles

This document introduces the eight quality management principles on which the quality management system standards of the revised ISO 9000:2000 series are based. These principles can be used by senior management as a framework to guide their organizations towards improved performance. The principles are derived from the collective experience and knowledge of the international experts who participate in ISO Technical Committee ISO/TC 176 Quality Management and Quality Assurance which is responsible for developing and maintaining the ISO 9000 standards.

The eight quality management principles are defined in ISO 9000:2000, Quality management systems Fundamentals and vocabulary, and in ISO 9004:2000, Quality management systems Guidelines for performance improvements.

Principle 1 *Customer focus*
Organizations depend on their customers and therefore should understand current and future customer needs, should meet customer requirements and strive to exceed customer expectations.

Principle 2 *Leadership*
Leaders establish unity of purpose and direction of the organization. They should create and maintain the internal environment in which people can become fully involved in achieving the organization's objectives.

Principle 3 *Involvement of people*
People at all levels are the essence of an organization and their full involvement enables their abilities to be used for the organization's benefit.

Principle 4 *Process approach*
A desired result is achieved more efficiently when activities and related resources are managed as a process.

Principle 5 *System approach to management*
Identifying, understanding and managing interrelated processes as a system contributes to the organization's effectiveness and efficiency in achieving its objectives.

Principle 6 *Continual improvement*
Continual improvement of the organization's overall performance should be a permanent objective of the organization.

Principle 7 *Factual approach to decision making*
Effective decisions are based on the analysis of data and information.

Principle 8 *Mutually beneficial supplier relationships*
An organization and its suppliers are interdependent and a mutually beneficial relationship enhances the ability of both to create value.

B. Implementing your ISO 9001:2000 quality management system

1. *Identify the goals you want to achieve*

Typical goals may be:

- Be more efficient and profitable
- Produce products and services that consistently meet customer requirements
- Achieve customer satisfaction

- Increase market share
- Maintain market share
- Improve communications and morale in the organization
- Reduce costs and liabilities
- Increase confidence in the production system

2. *Identify what others expect of you*
These are the expectations of interested parties (stakeholders) such as:

- Customers and end users
- Employees
- Suppliers
- Shareholders
- Society

3. *Obtain information about the ISO 9000 family*

- For general information, look to this brochure
- For more detailed information, see ISO 9000:2000, ISO 9001:2000 and ISO 9004:2000
- For supporting information, refer to the ISO website
- For implementation case studies and news of ISO 9000 developments worldwide, read the ISO publication ISO 9000 + ISO 14000 News

4. *Apply the ISO 9000 family of standards in your management system*
Decide if you are seeking certification that your quality management system is in conformance with ISO 9001:2000 or if you are preparing to apply for a national quality award.

- Use ISO 9001:2000 as the basis for certification
- Use ISO 9004:2000 in conjunction with your national quality award criteria to prepare for a national quality award

5. *Obtain guidance on specific topics within the quality management system*
These topic-specific standards are:

- ISO 10006 for project management
- ISO 10007 for configuration management
- ISO 10012 for measurement systems
- ISO 10013 for quality documentation
- ISO/TR 10014 for managing the economics of quality
- ISO 10015 for training
- ISO/TS 16949 for automotive suppliers
- ISO 19011 for auditing

6. *Establish your current status, determine the gaps between your quality management system and the requirements of ISO 9001:2000*
You may use one or more of the following:

- Self-assessment
- Assessment by an external organization

7. *Determine the processes that are needed to supply products to your customers*
Review the requirements of the ISO 9001:2000 section on Product Realization to determine how they apply or do not apply to your quality management system including:

- Customer related processes
- Design and/or development
- Purchasing
- Production and service operations
- Control of measuring and monitoring devices

8. *Develop a plan to close the gaps in step 6 and to develop the processes in step 7*
Identify actions needed to close the gaps, allocate resources to perform these actions, assign responsibilities and establish a schedule to complete the needed actions. ISO 9001:2000 Paragraphs 4.1 and 7.1 provide the information you will need to consider when developing the plan.

9. *Carry out your plan*
Proceed to implement the identified actions and track progress to your schedule.

10. *Undergo periodic internal assessment*
Use ISO 19011 for guidance in auditing, auditor qualification and managing audit programmes.

11. *Do you need to demonstrate conformance?*
If yes, go to step 12
If no, go to step 13
You may need or wish to show conformance (certification/registration) for various purposes, for example:

- Contractual requirements
- Market reasons or customer preference
- Regulatory requirements
- Risk management
- To set a clear goal for your internal quality development (motivation)

12. *Undergo independent audit*
Engage an accredited registration/certification body to perform an audit and certify that your quality management system complies with the requirements of ISO 9001:2000.

13. *Continue to improve your business*
Review the effectiveness and suitability of your quality management system. ISO 9004:2000 provides a methodology for improvement.

Suggested outline example solution to Exercise 5.2.2 – software failure

Some suggested examples:

Three Mile Island

This near disaster, which occurred in 1979, nearly caused a meltdown in the nuclear reactor. When the fault occurred this caused nearly 100 alarms to go off at the same time virtually overloading the system. There was no clear prioritization of the alarms by the computer system. The fault was caused by a pressure relief valve being stuck open allowing coolant to escape and the core to overheat. The emergency system did cut in and provide extra coolant, but in the confusion the operators misunderstood the information displayed in the control room and shut off the emergency system. So without adequate cooling the core started to melt. Fortunately the emergency system was turned back on and a catastrophe was avoided. During the inquiry that followed much attention was focused on the poor user interface of the control panels. Below are two points from the inquiry:

- a light on the control panel indicated that the pressure relief was still closed when in fact it was open
- the light signalling that the emergency system was off was obscured by a maintenance tag

Patriot missile

Failures of Patriot missiles to intercept Scud missiles have been attributed to an accumulation of inaccuracies in the internal time keeping of a computer. The system was meant to be turned off and restarted often enough for the accumulated error never to become dangerous. The smallest possible perturbation (disturbance) to the state of a digital computer (changing a bit from 0 to 1, for instance) may produce a radical response.

Atlas rocket

A single incorrect character in the specification of a control program for an Atlas rocket, carrying the first US interplanetary spacecraft, Mariner 1, ultimately caused the vehicle to veer off course. Both rocket and spacecraft had to be destroyed shortly after launch. In addition to unintentional design bugs, flaws deliberately introduced to compromise a system can cause unacceptable system behaviour.

Airbus
A Lufthansa Airbus A320 crashed after landing at Warsaw Airport, killing two and injuring 54. Safeguards in the user interface delayed the pilot's attempt to activate the spoilers and reverse thrust to avoid overrunning the runway.

Tornado
Two Royal Air Force Tornado fighter planes collided in the UK in August 1988. Four crew were killed. Both planes used autopilots that used pre-programmed cassettes; they were given identical tapes, resulting in both planes reaching the same point at the same instant.

See also *Software Failure: Avoiding the Avoidable and Living With the Rest* by Leslie Hatton. Published by Addison Wesley, January 1998.

Further example of the estimation quality factor (EQF)
From the table below:

(a) Complete a graph that represents the data contained in the table
(b) From the graph calculate the EQF
(c) Comment on the results (i.e. are they acceptable or not)

Estimate number	*Date*	*Cost of estimate (£m)*
1	1-4-2000	2.25
2	1-7-2000	2.50
3	15-10-2000	4.25
4	1-2-2001	4.00
Actual	1-4-2001	3.75

Suggested solution:
(a) The graph:

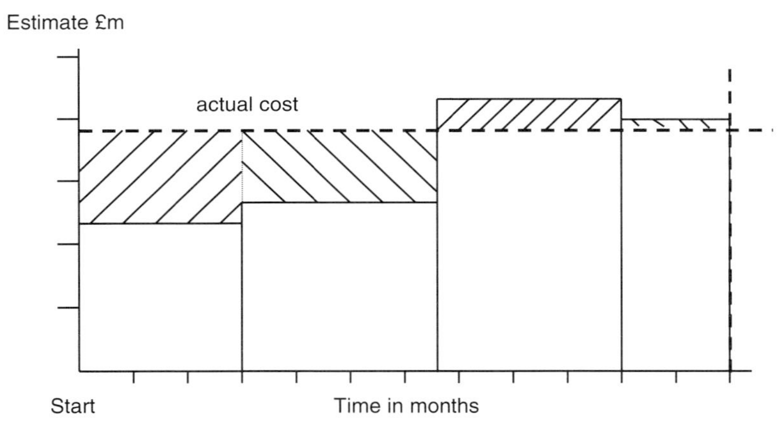

Figure 5.36

(b) Calculation:

Area of the shaded area:	(3×1.5) + (3.5×1.25) + (3.5×0.5) + (2×0.25)	
	= 4.5 + 4.375 + 1.75 + 0.5	= 11.125
Total area under the actual cost line	= 12 × 3.75	= 45

Therefore EQF = 45/11.125 = 4.045

(c) This is only just an acceptable EQF as 4.045 is only just greater than 4 which is the minimum figure set by DeMarco as a quality standard.

Total quality management (TQM) – some more views

Total quality management is a structured system for satisfying internal and external customers and suppliers by integrating the business environment, continuous improvement, and breakthroughs with development, improvement and maintenance cycles while changing organizational culture.

One of the keys to implementing TQM can be found in this definition. It is the idea that TQM is a structured system. In describing TQM as a structured system, I mean that it is a strategy derived from internal and external customer and supplier wants and needs that have been determined through Daily Management, Hoskin, Hoskin Management and Cross-Functional Management.

Pinpointing internal and external requirements allows us to continuously improve, develop and maintain quality, cost, delivery and morale. TQM is a system that integrates all of this activity and information.

Hoshin is a one-year plan for achieving objectives developed in conjunction with management's choice of specific targets and means in quality, cost, delivery and morale. Accordingly, Hoshin can be described as follows.

Hoshin = Targets + Means

A target statement can be established by combining at least one direction word, performance measure, target value for the performance measure and time period. The following table shows two elementary examples for target statements. The first example target statement reads Decrease new product development cycle from 8 to 4 months by December 1999.

Items	*Direction word*	*Performance measure*	*Target value*	*Time period*
Example 1	Decrease	new product development cycle	from 8 to 4 months	by December 1999
Example 2	Decrease	new product development defects	from 7 to 2%	by December 1999

After determining a target based on this rule, the means for achieving the target should be determined. For example, to accomplish decreasing the new product development cycle from 8 to 4 months by December 1999, the means may be:

- Establish an effective development process
- Develop documentation for the product development
- Implement QFD within the quality assurance system

Depending on the particular organization, the means will differ from other organizations that share the same targets. Customarily, there are a few means for each target. It is consequential to determine both the targets and means for Hoshin. The hierarchical management levels, such as top management and middle management, need to determine the Hoshin according to the above rules.

Some additional useful points

The guiding principle:

- Successful total quality management requires both behavioural and cultural change
- A successful TQM system brings two other management systems together with a behavioural and cultural commitment to customer quality
- Thus, TQM becomes a system within itself by default or by choice
- These three management systems must be aligned in a successful TQM initiative:
  - OM (organizational management) system,
  - HRM (human resource management) systems and
  - TQM (total quality management)

Two implementation approaches of TQM:

- *Traditional management approach.* This is the most common. A TQM is overlaid (some say forced) upon the other two systems. This approach represents the 80% failure of TQMs. In this approach TQM never becomes an accepted reality by either organizational or human resource management. It is usually seen as competition, or 'something to be tolerated'. The TQM system consumes valuable resources needed by the other systems and rejection begins to occur.

- *Integrated management approach.* This is the least common. A TQM is blended and balanced with existing cultural initiatives in both organizational and human resource management systems. This represents the 20% success rate of TQMs. Whether both organizational management and human resource management systems take on a 'quality management commitment' or 'join a quality management team' is not important. The principles of quality management are attended to as an important third system that blends, integrates, aligns and maximizes the other two systems to beat competition in world class quality performance. This approach can often be divided into two subchoices, depending upon managerial resources, readiness, acceptance and competencies.

Summary

Total quality management is based on the belief that the people who are closest to the job best understand what is wrong and how to fix it. Management has the responsibility at all levels to work on the systems in which goods or services are produced.

For further information see:

http://www.goalqpc.com/RESEARCH/TQMwheel.html

Validation requirements

The quality plan would specify how validation requirements for a system are to be identified, expressed and accepted by the customer or end user. The fundamental concept of providing effective quality assurance testing techniques is to ask the question:

> How can I develop a test that ensures that this particular requirement is met by the system that we are developing?

The validation requirements are formally extracted at the end of the requirements analysis phase of the development process, but they may be expressed informally at the start of the project.

Some basic points for validation requirements:

- Validation requirements are to be extracted from the system specification by the quality assurance staff assigned to the project
- The validation requirements suggested by the quality assurance staff must be discussed at the system specification review and between the development staff and the quality assurance staff
- Where possible, validation requirements and any test subsequently derived from them must be expressed in a decision table format (see below). Each row must contain the command being tested, the conditions under which it is being tested, for example the value of any relevant parameters, and the output expected from the test
- If the table format is not possible for any reason, then the validation requirements must be expressed in clear, concise and unambiguous English

Below is an extract from a negotiated statement of requirements and a decision table:

> The following command is provided for the signal operators
> The CHECKSTATUS command. When the signal operator invokes this command the system checks that the line is clear and no trains are within a five mile radius of the junction. The system will respond with either a clear message (no trains in the area) or no clear warning signal that trains are in the vicinity of the crossing. The response must be immediate in case a train is approaching on the wrong track.

Command	*Conditions*			*Output*
	Command	*Input signal*	*Response time*	
CHECKSTATUS	correct	no trains	correct	correct – no trains message
CHECKSTATUS	correct	trains in area	incorrect	warning – response time to slow

Software metrics – further information

We have seen that software metrics provide numerical measures of the products and processes that make up the software product. Traditionally metrics have been applied at the later stages of a software project, but this limits their usefulness in predicting the course it takes and monitoring the controlling processes.

For metrics to be fully useful as a quality assurance tool they should be used throughout the life cycle of the development process. Two examples of metrics that may be applied at the early stages of development are outlined below:

- Function-point analysis which concentrates on extracting information from the system specification to measure productivity and to predict product cost
- Maintenance analysis which concentrates on extracting information from the system's architecture, produced during system design to minimize the cost of system design

A selection of where to possibly obtain measurable metrics is outlined below:

- The number of decisions in the detailed design of a program unit
- The length of a program unit or object class
- The number of discovered errors in a software system during the first 12 months of operation
- The amount of effort put into a project
- The number of classes in an object-oriented design diagram for a software system

These are not all useful, and the following three tests should be applied to any potential metric:

- The purpose of a metric should be clear and concise
- The model that the metric is to be used on should be tested for suitability
- When applied the metric should be analysed to ensure it is the most suitable method

Some main characteristics of a software metric:

- A software metric must be measurable
- A software metric must be independent
- A software metric must be accountable
- A software metric must be precise

A software metric should be based on facts not opinions, it should not be possible for project team members to alter its value without affecting the quality of the software. Details about how the metric was measured should be documented and the level of tolerance allowed when measuring it should be specified.

Examples of metrics

- *Size metrics* – Relates to the size of the software code.
- *Data structure metrics* – This analyses data in the form:

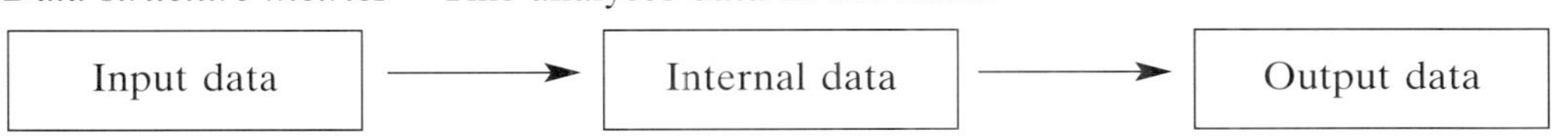

- *Logic structure metrics* – How the program allows different operations dependent upon different input data or intermediate calculations.
- *Composite metrics* – This looks at both size and logic structure metrics to form an order hierarchy based on complexity.
- *Effort and cost metrics* – This can be used to model the project by bringing in the proposed costs and estimates that may occur. It may also be used to outline errors in calculations by comparing 'Results metrics' against 'Predictor metrics', see Figure 5.37.

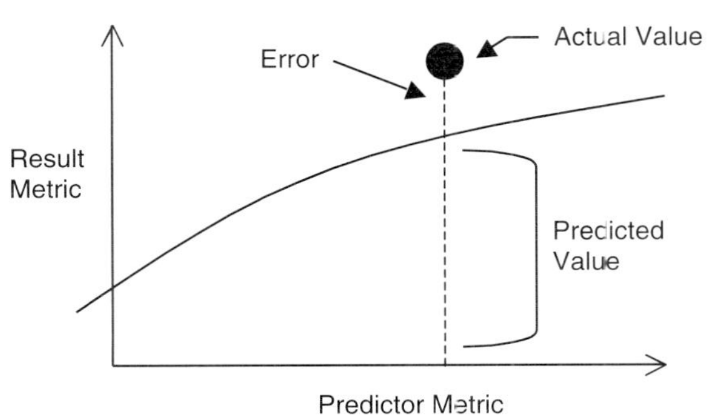

Figure 5.37

Error = Actual Value – Predicted Value
The historical prediction errors are used to estimate the model.

- *Design metrics* – In general program complexity increases with program size. Design metrics are used to encourage program modularization, i.e. ensure a structured approach by partitioning work at an early stage. Design metrics can be used to analyse structure charts and data flow diagrams (DFDs).

Further example – McCabe's cyclomatic complexity metrics

Consider the following program fragment:

```
int total = 0;
int index = 1;
int count = 0;
do
{
        leave = false;
        jindex = 1;
        do
        {
                if ( temp[index] = ignore[jindex] )
                {
                        leave = true;
                }
                jindex ++;
        }
        while ( jindex <= 10 );
        cout << "Test Output: " << index;
        if ( !leave )
        {
                total += temp[index];
                count ++;
        }
        index ++;
}
while ( temp[index] != -1 );
cout << "Total: " << total
if ( index > 1 )
{
        average = total/count;
}
cout << "Average: " << average;
```

Questions:

1. Draw a graph to represent the code structure.
2. Calculate its cyclomatic complexity.
3. Comment on the complexity of the design.

Cyclomatic complexity example

Suggested solution:

1. Graph

2. Cyclomatic complexity:

Arcs – Nodes + 2
16 – 12 + 2 = 6

Cyclomatic complexity: 6

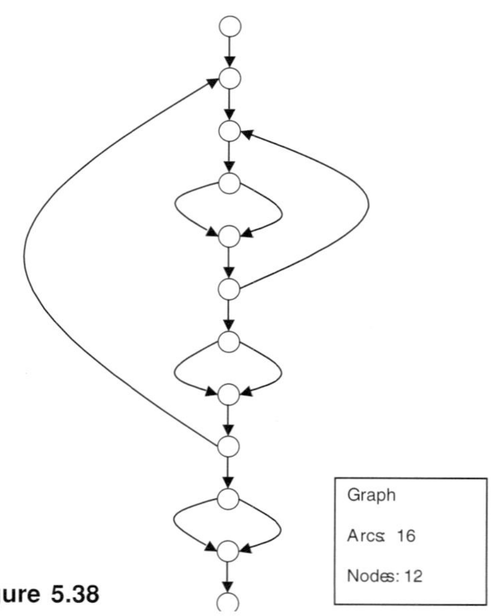

Figure 5.38

3. The design is fairly complex but as the cyclomatic complexity is <10 it does not warrant any redesigning. This is based on the research carried out by McCabe and backed up with experimental evidence.

Impact matrices

Impact matrices are used to help determine the amount of resource that a particular system is going to use during the process of maintenance. A project manager wants to know as early as possible in the development process the risk factors that may affect the software system during its lifetime.

An impact matrix is used to display the change (impact) of one unit (or method within an object-oriented class structure) on another. The matrix is a two-dimensional table that shows the probability that a modification of one unit will directly lead to the need to change another unit. The configuration manager, possibly using CASE tool analysis, usually determines the probabilities.

The main aim at this stage is the interaction and use of the probabilities, not how they were derived at.

Example:

Impact matrix

	V	W	X	Y	Z
V	1.0	0.3	0.2	0.1	0
W	0.3	1.0	0.4	0	0
X	0.2	0.4	1.0	0	0.1
Y	0.1	0	0	1.0	0.3
Z	0	0	0.1	0.3	1.0

The matrix is assumed to be symmetrical. For example, a change in unit 'V' affects unit 'W' by 0.3 (30%), and the reverse is true, a change in unit 'W' affects unit 'V' by the same amount (0.3 or 30%). This may not always be the case in all applications, but for this example we are considering the matrix to be symmetrical.

The second row shows that if there is a change to 'W' then there is a probability of 0.3 that, as a direct result of a change in 'W', there will be a change to 'V'. A probability of 0.4 that there will be a change to 'X' and no change to 'Y' or 'Z'.

Note that there must be a probability of 1.0 (100%) of a change to a unit affecting itself.

This can be represented as a block diagram (see Figure 5.39).

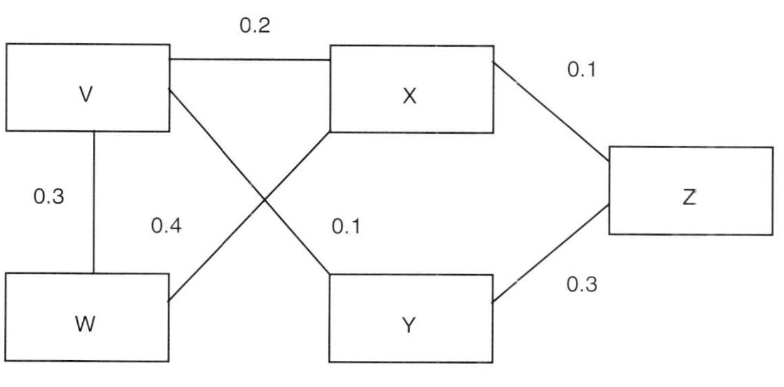

Figure 5.39

From the diagram it is easy to see that the unit 'V' can affect unit 'X' indirectly as well as directly via unit 'W'. The probability of this second-order effect from 'V' to 'X' is calculated as follows:

- A change in program unit 'V' has a probability of 0.3 of affecting program unit 'W'
- A change in program unit 'W' has a probability of 0.4 of affecting program unit 'X'
- Hence a change to program unit 'V' will have a probability of affecting program unit 'X' by means of a second-order effect of $0.3 \times 0.4 = 0.12$

Question

Calculate the probability of a change in program unit 'V' affecting program unit 'Z' as a result of second-order effects.

Suggested solution

There are two second-order effects of 'V' on 'Z':

1. First via 'X' ('V' to 'X' with a probability of 0.2 and 'X' to 'Z' with a probability of 0.1). This gives a total second-order effect of 0.02.
2. Second via 'Y' ('V' to 'Y' has a probability of 0.1 and 'Y' to 'Z' has a probability of 0.3). This gives a total second-order effect of 0.03.

This gives a total second-order effect of a change to unit 'Z' affect unit 'Z' of 0.02 + 0.03 = 0.06.

Note that there are other higher-order effects, for example 'V' to 'W' to 'X' then 'Z' and in complex systems these would need to be considered. This process is outlined in the following example.

Let us now consider the overall effect of 'V' on 'X'. From Figure 5.39 it can be seen that 'X' is affected directly from 'V' (first-order effect) and indirectly through 'W' (second-order effect). The probabilities are 0.2 and 0.12 (see above). Units 'V' and 'X' also interact via 'Y' (giving a third-order effect) this has the probabilities of 'V' to 'Y' 0.1, 'Y' to 'Z 0.3 and 'Z' to 'X' 0.1, giving $(0.1\times0.3\times0.1) = 0.003$. This figure needs to be calculated in the overall value. In order to do this the following formula is used:

$$P(VX) = P(VX_1) + P(VX_n) - P(VX_1)\,P(VX_n)$$

This gives a total possibility of change from 'V' to 'X' of:

$$\begin{aligned} P(VX) &= P(VX_1) + P(VX_n) - P(VX_1)\,P(VX_n) \\ &= 0.2 + (0.12 + 0.003) - (0.2\times(0.12 + 0.003)) \\ &= 0.2 + (0.123) - (0.2\times0.123) \\ &= 0.323 - 0.0246 \\ &= 0.2984 \\ &= \text{Total probability of change between units 'V' and 'X'} \end{aligned}$$

The total probability of all possible interactions is finally displayed on a dependency matrix. The steps taken to achieve this are outlined below:

- Identify any second- or higher-order effects between units or methods whose dependency is represented on the block diagram
- Calculate the probability associated with each of the second- or higher-order effects. There may be more than one
- Calculate the total probability of a change in one unit or method on another using the formula outlined above
- Construct a dependency matrix

Below is the dependency matrix with the changes in 'V' affecting 'X' added:

Dependency matrix

	V	W	X	Y	Z
V	1.0		0.2984		
W		1.0			
X	0.2984		1.0		
Y				1.0	
Z					1.0

Note: It is easy to make a mistake with the calculations. The result must be slightly larger than the original impact matrix figure if second- or higher-level effects are taken into account.

Question

Calculate the effects of a change to 'V' affecting 'Y' and add the results to the dependency matrix.

Suggested solution

There are two higher-level routes from 'V' to 'Y':

1. V - X - Z - Y = $(0.2\times0.1\times0.3) = 0.006$
2. V - W - X - Z - Y = $(0.3\times 0.4 \times 0.1 \times 0.3) = 0.0036$

Therefore: $P(VY) = 0.1 + (0.006 + 0.0036) - (0.1\times (0.006 + 0.0036))$
$= 0.1 + 0.0096 - (0.1 \times 0.0096)$
$= 0.1096 - 0.00096$
$= 0.10864$

Dependency matrix

	V	W	X	Y	Z
V	1.0		0.2984	0.10864	
W		1.0			
X	0.2984		1.0		
Y	0.10864			1.0	
Z					1.0

The rest of the dependencies can then be calculated to complete the table.

5.3 Professional standards

The Data Protection Acts (further information)

History of Data Protection Acts 1984 and 1998

- The Data Protection Act 1984 grew out of public concern about personal privacy in the face of rapidly developing computer technology.
- The Data Protection Act 1998 (the new Act) was passed in order to implement a European Data Protection Directive. This Directive set a standard for data protection throughout all the countries in the European Union and applies to personal data held in a structured way in any medium (paper, computer, microfiche, tape etc.). The new Act extends the rights of individuals and increases the responsibilities of data controllers.

Data Controller, i.e. the person or persons who determine the purposes and manner in which personal data is processed, need to be aware of the following components inherent within the data protection act:

1. *Data.* Information which is being processed by a computerized system, or which is recorded with the intention that it will be processed in this way. In addition, any information kept as part of a 'relevant filing system' (i.e. structured either by reference to individuals or by reference to criteria relating to individuals so that the data is readily accessible), or which is recorded with the intention that it will be processed in this way, is also data. Data can be written information, photographs, or information such as fingerprints or voice recordings.
2. *Personal data.* Information which relates to a living individual who can be identified from those data, or from those data and other information which is in the possession of or is likely to come into the possession of the data controller and includes any expression of opinion about the individual and any indication of the intentions of the data controller or any other person in respect of the individual. So, for example, application forms marked only with a number will not identify an individual and will not be deemed personal data, but put together with the list of numbers and names will do so, and so will be deemed personal data.
3. *Processing.* Anything which can be done with data, i.e. obtaining, recording, holding, organizing, adapting, altering, retrieving, consulting, disclosing, aligning, combining, blocking, erasing, destroying and so on.
4. *Data subject.* An individual who is the subject of personal data. For example, within a college this will include: staff, students, suppliers of goods and services, business associates, prospective students, delegates who attended a conference/course run by your School/Division/Centre etc., survey respondents etc.
5. *Data processor.* Any person (other than an employee of the data controller) who processes the data on behalf of the data controller.
6. *Recipient.* Any person to whom the data are disclosed who is an employee or agent of the data controller, a data processor or an employee or agent of the data processor.
7. *Third party.* Any person other than the data subject, the data controller, the data processor or other person authorized to process data for the data controller.

What are the main changes between the 1984 and 1998 Acts?

1. Wider definition of processing – anything which can be done with personal data is now caught by the new Act. Includes obtaining, organizing, adapting, altering, amending, storing, browsing and deleting. Processing by reference to surname, student number, postcode, county etc. is also included within the new Act. Restrictions imposed on processing personal data and processing sensitive personal data.
2. The new Act applies to personal data held on computers and personal information held in 'relevant filing systems', i.e. information held in a structured way. This can mean any medium such as paper, database, videotape, microfiche etc.
3. There are new 'fair processing' principles.
4. Personal data may be transferred to non-EEA nations only if certain conditions are met.
5. The use of automated decision-making processes on their own to make significant decisions with regard to individuals is subject to restrictions.
6. Directors, managers, secretaries or similar officers of a body corporate, including HE institutions, can be held liable for offences committed by their institutions.
7. Individuals can go directly to court if they believe that their rights under the Act have been breached.
8. The rights of staff and students have been enhanced.
9. Some types of processing are specifically excluded from the regulations, e.g for journalism or artistic purposes.
10. New rules for enforcement have been introduced.
11. The data protection principles have been extended from seven principles under the 1984 Act to eight principles under new Act.
12. Statements of intention as well as opinions about an individual will be classed as personal data.
13. Wider grounds for claims for compensation from individuals have been introduced.
14. A simplified notification system will replace the registration system.
15. The Data Protection Registrar will be known as the Data Protection Commissioner.

Background to the 1998 Act

The Act came into force at the beginning of March 2000. Key changes under the Act include:

- Extending the provision to include manual records
- A new definition of Sensitive Personal Data
- An individual right to prevent processing likely to cause damage or distress
- An individual right to prevent processing for the purpose of direct marketing
- New exemptions from notification and registration
- A direct requirement on data controllers to comply with the data protection principles whether they are required to notify under the Data Protection Act or not
- The Data Protection Registrar will now be called the Data Protection Commissioner and has powers of enforcement, a new duty to promote good practice and a power to issue codes

Rights of the individual

Individuals have extensive rights in relation to personal data held about them. In particular, they may have the right to:

- be notified if, what, why and by whom personal data is being processed
- prevent processing likely to cause damage and distress
- prevent processing for the purposes of direct marketing
- ensure that no decision which affects them significantly is being automated
- compensation where damage or distress is suffered
- have inaccurate or damaging data corrected or destroyed
- ask the Commissioner to make an assessment on compliance

Right of access to information

The 1998 Act significantly extends the range of information held by a data controller on a data subject which must be supplied at the request of the data subject. If personal data is being processed, the data subject must, on request, be given a description of the nature of the data held, the purposes for which it is to be processed and the persons, or categories of person, to whom it may be disclosed.

The data controller must also give information as to the source of this data. In addition, where decisions affecting the subject are likely to be taken solely on the basis of automated processing, the data subject must also be supplied with information regarding the 'logic involved in that decision taking' provided that the data controller will not need to disclose any information which constitutes a trade secret.

The data controller is obliged only to respond to requests which are made in writing and which enclose any fee required by the controller. The data controller will then have 40 days to respond satisfactorily to the request.

Exemptions

The legislation recognizes that in certain circumstances the strict application of these rules is inappropriate – because the interests of the state and/or the public outweigh the threat to individual privacy, or because compliance with the law would be burdensome for data controllers and of little benefit to data subjects. Data processed for domestic purposes is completely exempt. Further examples are the suspension of subject access rights to confidential references given by the data controller, and (often) personal data which also identifies another individual. Restrictions on disclosure do not generally apply to, for example, disclosures for the purposes of preventing crime or where disclosure is required by a court order. Journalists have the benefit of a wide exemption where it is reasonably believed that publication of the personal data is in the public interest and that compliance with data protection rules would be incompatible with journalistic purposes. Exemptions are, however, often limited in scope and, broadly speaking, the obligation to comply with the rules should be assumed.

Some additional links:

http://www.dataprotection.gov.uk/transbord.htm
http://www.hmso.gov.uk/acts/acts1998/19980026.htm

Exercise

Get the students to review how your college/university handles the Data Protection Act, for example what are their rights, what information is available to them, how can they access this information etc.

Copyright, Designs and Patents Act 1988

Suggested solution to Exercise 5.3.1

This Act made it clear that unauthorized copying of software is illegal. Copyright law protects software authors and publishers, just as patent law protects inventors.

Copyright law makes no distinction between duplicating software for sale or for free distribution. Penalties include unlimited fines and jail terms of up to two years.

Within an organization the following are examples of software theft:

- Copying company owned software onto privately owned computers
- Copying privately owned software onto company computers
- Copying a single copy of software onto multiple machines without buying additional licences
- Putting a single copy of software onto a LAN server without paying for additional licences

Examples of infringements under the Act are:

1. Software pirate gets maximum sentence – July 1999

As a direct result of their investigations, FAST and Kingston Trading Standards ensured a custodial sentence for a software fraudster for nine counts of copyright and trademark infringements. He had offered computer software at very low prices in a leading trade magazine under a bogus company name. When they raided his home address they discovered two CD writers and 500 pirated CDs. When he appeared in court in July 1999, the magistrates decided he should be remanded to the Crown Court for sentencing. He was eventually convicted and sentenced to two years' imprisonment.

2. Software piracy, police bust AOL UK – November 1998

Red-faced executives at AOL's London offices were busted for using illegal software after the BSA moved following an anonymous tip-off. The UK arm of AOL was caught red-handed using unlicensed copies of Adobe PhotoShop and Illustrator software at the company's office in London. The BSA has been quick to point out that AOL's misdemeanour was not premeditated. Instead, AOL was the victim of its own bad systems management, which allowed their software usage to increase without securing enough licences.

The company held up its hand to the infringement and agreed to pay an undisclosed settlement to the BSA.
For additional information see:

http://www.hmso.gov.uk/acts/acts1988/Ukpga_19880048_en_1.htm
http://www.patent.gov.uk/copy/tribunal/triabissued.htm

Professional standards – further information

The importance of continued professional development (CPD)

In a modern working environment, especially within the computing and IT industry, all employees need to be aware of the need to update their technical and managerial skills. This updating can be gained in many ways and many employers are turning to a formal system of Continued Professional Development (CPD). One of the main characteristics of CPD is that of recording the additional skills that have been obtained, but this process is often off-putting as it places an additional time constraint on the employee. In an article on the growing importance of CPD by Tome Kennie, he specifies six main reasons why CPD is vital for professional success:

- *Competence:* Knowledge gained at the start of one's career has a short lifespan. If you want to progress along your career you have to continually update that knowledge and add new skills.
- *Consumerism:* Consumers are simply far more sophisticated and demanding than ever before. New skills have got to be acquired if these demands are to be met.
- *Litigation:* Claims of negligence are at an all-time high, and one way to cut back is to keep professionals up to date with current codes of practice.
- *Standards:* Standards of competence are safeguarded by the professional bodies, and CPD is one way of making sure that members understand and comply with such standards.
- *Quality Management System:* There is now a great emphasis on QMS and continuous improvement. CPD ensures the training and education vital to these processes.
- *Competitiveness:* Modern businesses are now even more competitive, and there is a focus on service quality and technological innovation. Again there is a need for the development of people.

CPD is a requisite for membership of an associated professional institution and registration with the Engineering Council. The Engineering Council states that registration with it, and membership of a professional institution, obligates members to maintain and develop their professional competence. Its three point code of practice maintains that members must:

1. Demonstrate commitment to maintaining professional competence through self-managed CPD. This includes being aware of and understanding your requirements for evidence, what kinds of evidence are available and appropriate, and the need for the availability of said evidence.
2. Take responsibility for and manage CPD. This includes knowing your development needs, their benchmarks, how to carry out your development action plan, recording achievements and evaluating them against needs.
3. Support the learning and development of others. This includes providing support and sharing expertise with others, staying involved with the activities of your institution and making sure that your employer is also aware of the importance of CPD.

See also:

www.engc.org.uk

Additional information from the BCS

The British Computer Society is a valuable source of information for the computing professional. For example, through its BCS Review 2001 there is company and corporate information ranging from technological issues to legal requirements. The Disability Discrimination Act (DDA) is an example outlined currently, with information on what it is, Disability Rights Commission (DRC) and why it is important to you.

There is also a large section on training that includes the Industry Structured Model (ISM). The ISM is a definitive set of performance, training and development standards for the information systems industry. This is aimed at companies and helps to identify staffing requirements, create job descriptions, access competence of IS staff, plan training and more. It has measurable benefits and its use can result in:

- increased effectiveness
- improved quality levels
- better focused, more cost-effective training
- significant savings in both time and money.

The ISM is recognized worldwide as the most authoritative reference and forms the basis of the European Informatics Skills Structure (EISS). The latest release, ISM3.2, was developed and updated after several months of consultation with professionals from all areas of IS.

Under the section for Continued Professional Development (CPD) the BCS outlines a measurement strategy for people updating skills. This strategy specifies a points system for updating skills, examples are:

- Courses of study leading to a successful examination, for example Microsoft Certification qualification. 1 CPD unit per hour of study
- Interactive training where both knowledge and skills are acquired and demonstrated. 3/4 CPD unit per hour of study
- Structured self-study that does not contain a formal examination. 1/2 CPD unit per hour of study
- Preparation of a professional paper or article. 5 CPD units
- Production and (first) delivery of a professional presentation or lecture where this is NOT part of normal work duties. 5 CPD units per hour of presentation
- Attendance only CPD, i.e. lecturers, seminars, workshops etc. 1/2 CPD units per hour
- Other useful CPD activities (other than normal work duties). 1/2 CPD units per hour

As a guide, the BCS recommends that members should seek to achieve an average of at least 20 CPD units per year.

See also:

www.bcs.org.uk

Outline suggestions to Exercise 5.3.2

1. *BCS – Student member*

To be eligible for Student membership you must be studying a course at HNC level or higher. Once you have successfully completed a course at this level you will be eligible for Graduate membership of the Society.

Student Fees: £49*

- *Student membership fees:* There is an abated rate of £14 for full-time students in colleges and universities. (*Note:* To qualify for Student membership you must be studying a course at HNC level or higher.) There is also a one time fee covering the full duration of your course (max. 4 years) £26. Correct at August 2001.

For professional development see previous information on the BCS.

2. *Alternative institution: Institute of Analysts and Programmers*

This institution is the premier body dealing specifically with the needs of the working analyst or programmer. Membership is drawn from all sectors of the industry and from all sizes of business. Membership grades are:

- Student and Graduate membership (GradIAP)
- Associate membership (AMIAP)
- Member (MIAP)
- Fellow (FIAP)

The Institution's main purpose is to promote vocational skills and professionalism. Thus, in the past examinations have played a secondary role in the admission criteria. The view has been that theoretical knowledge is principally the preserve of the educational establishment, and that the Institution should concern itself more with what a programmer can do rather than what he is supposed to know. While the Institution does not wish to get 'bogged down' in a complex system of examinations, it is proposing to become more active in sponsoring courses which will teach the fundamentals of programming and analysis, and provide a sound foundation on which the novice can begin to build a professional career. There has been increasing demand for such courses since the Institution began to phase in more rigorous methods for assessing the competence of potential new recruits. While the decision to seek a Royal Charter may have been the initial impetus behind these changes, they are in the interests of everyone. As a professional body, the Institute of Analysts and Programmers will stand or fall on the professional quality of its members.

See also:

www.iap.org.uk

6 Networks

6.1 Impact of communications technology

Exercise 1: High Altitude Long Endurance platforms

Long distance communications currently rely upon cables, microwave links or satellite. An alternative to any of these is the High Altitude Long Endurance (HALE) platform, an aerial vehicle which is able to remain airborne for very long periods and which can also achieve very great altitudes. Although flying in the atmosphere, such a platform has many of the practical characteristics of a satellite in terms of relaying signals. HALE platforms are currently the subject of considerable research and will undoubtedly play a major role in future telecommunications.

As part of the espionage carried out during the Second World War, specially equipped RAF Mosquito aircraft were sometimes used as aerial relay stations, allowing short range transmissions made by French resistance fighters to be received and then retransmitted to other allied personnel operating in secret in occupied territory. (The technology developed for this incidentally led to cellular radio networks decades later.) It is perhaps not too fanciful to see these aircraft acting as a precursor of High Altitude Long Endurance (HALE) platforms.

HALE platforms would fly in the stratosphere at an altitude range of 15 to 30 km and be airborne for periods measured in weeks rather than days. They would carry all the electronics required to receive ground transmission and rebroadcast it over the large area that was within the distant horizon resulting from the platform's extreme height. A HALE platform circling above a city would in effect be the equivalent of a local satellite, constantly available for all telecommunications.

A diagram can indicate the operational height of HALE in contrast with Low Earth Orbit and Geostationary satellites (see Figure 6.1). (The latter are investigated in a subsequent exercise.)

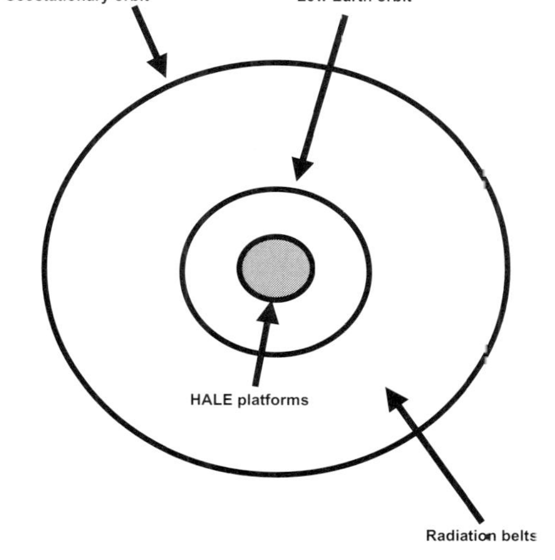

Figure 6.1

HALE platforms are only now beginning to emerge as a serious technological possibility. A number of factors have caused the sudden interest in HALE. One is the development of very light, but strong, composite materials like carbon fibre, Kevlar (perhaps better known for its use in bullet-proof protective clothing), styrofoam, and graphite epoxy. This has made possible the design of the lightweight airframes required for an aircraft flying with minimal power.

Solar cell technology has also improved considerably. Early solar cells, of the type first developed for satellites, used a glass substrate to support the semiconducting crystalline material that generated power from sunlight. The glass added significant weight to the device and such cells had little potential for powering aircraft. New cells now use a light polymer for their base, thus reducing the weight involved.

In addition, developments in electronics have created very small and light computers as well as reliable autonomous navigational systems.

The role of the military in the development of HALE platforms is also an important factor. Very real advantages are provided by unmanned, and therefore expendable, small aircraft in situations in which the military are likely to be deployed. Significantly the first study of the HALE concept was carried out by the US Navy in their High Altitude Superpressurized Powered Aerostat (HASPA) programme in 1978.

Possibly one of the reasons why attention is being directed towards HALE platforms is the problem encountered by the Iridium network of Low Earth Orbit satellites. Launched at considerable expense, these satellites were expected to provide worldwide direct communication between special satellite phones. Unfortunately the scheme did not prove a financial success. Perhaps it was attempted slightly too early and did not achieve the reliability required for telecommunications simply because of this. Irrespective of the technological and organizational problems the network encountered, however, it did leave a slight bitter taste in the mouths of investors.

Advantages of HALE platforms

HALE platforms possess two significant advantages when compared with either category of communication satellite.

One of these is expense. The cost of launching satellites is still very high. The Shuttle had been expected to reduce cost into orbit to reasonable levels but, despite everything that the Shuttle programme has achieved, cheap satellites are still a long way into the future. (This is discussed in the separate exercise.)

The second advantage of HALE platforms is that repairs, or upgrading, can be done, if not on the wing – for after all the platform would need to be landed to permit repairs to be carried out – then considerably more easily than repairing a satellite. Admittedly astronauts attending to the Hubble Space Telescope made the headlines, and more recently regular 'housekeeping' with the International Space Station involved astronauts donning suits and exiting though one of the air locks to work outside. This, however, would be an unrealistic approach to maintenance of Low Earth Orbit satellites. It would hardly be worth the effort as these re-enter the atmosphere relatively soon anyway. In contrast a HALE platform, whether unmanned aircraft or balloon, could be brought the short distance down to Earth quite readily for minor or even major repairs, provided that the latter had not compromised the control required to land.

Other HALE applications

Telecommunications is not the only potential use to which these platforms could be put.

They could also be used in any situation where ground surveillance is required. Traffic density could be monitored to produce congestion reports then relayed to motorists. Crop yields could be monitored and advance warning produced for drought relief. Police security could be an obvious application. Already police spotter planes, equipped with thermal imaging equipment, are a common sight in the night sky over some cities. HALE platforms would simply remove this monitoring to a higher altitude, and perhaps become more effective as a result of not alerting wrongdoers in the way that the low whine of engines reveals the presence of overhead law enforcement.

HALE platforms could have a significant impact upon the effectiveness of emergency relief when a natural disaster occurs. Flood or fire or refugee crises could all be monitored more readily if a HALE platform were present to aid in reconnaissance missions. In such situations previous local communications are frequently disrupted and so the platform could be used to provide temporary support.

The unfortunate military events that had to follow the September 2001 terrorist atrocities also show how HALE platforms, specifically UAVs (Unmanned Aerial Vehicles), have a military role which is unlikely to diminish in the future.

These additional roles for a HALE platform could naturally be combined with its primary function of telecommunications relay.

Types of HALE platform

Two types of HALE platform are being investigated. Airships are one possibility. With modern technology these can be made in a way that minimizes the mass of the airframe and thus maximizes the payload capacity. The rigid metal framework of an early twentieth century airship is not required. Instead a modern airship is more like a blimp, relying on internal pressure to maintain structural integrity. Helium would be used as the lifting gas.

The HALE airship would carry an engine to allow it to be placed in the correct location and which would also allow it to remain stationary despite any wind that was encountered. Power for the engine could be made available by covering the upper portion of the airship with solar cells. (The application of solar power is described later.) A maximum altitude of 20 km would probably be adopted to avoid the stronger winds present at greater heights.

This version of the HALE concept is being explored by the European Space Agency, which has granted research funding to Daimler-Chrysler Aerospace and Lindstrand Balloons in order to investigate the feasibility of a HALE platform to fly at 70 000 feet with a 600 kg payload. This could be used for mobile phone communications, surveillance, weather observations or other sensors.

The other type of HALE platform is the small autonomous aircraft. There are two areas of research related to this type of HALE platform. Each has its own acronym. Unmanned Aerial Vehicles (UAVs) could be unkindly regarded as advanced model aircraft but have been the focus of intense research, especially by the military. The minute size and light weight of modern electronics means that even very sophisticated capabilities can be designed into extremely small aircraft. The possibilities for both scientific research and military applications are obvious. Many would regard the use of UAVs in war as disturbing, but the probable eventual deployment of related aircraft in the future robotic exploration of Mars will provide immense scientific knowledge of the planet.

Development of UAVs is linked with work in the Environmental Research Aircraft and Sensor Technology (ERAST) programme. This is especially concerned with the use of onboard sensors on small unmanned aircraft both to contribute to control and navigation of the aircraft and to return useful data back to a ground station.

Obviously there is a considerable amount of technology in common between all three research areas, HALE, UAV and ERAST, with only the objectives differing. HALE is primarily concerned with telecommunications.

Power for a HALE platform

If an aircraft is going to be able to stay in the air for long periods, attention has to be directed towards an efficient energy supply which will be able to power the aircraft for the long periods required.

Internal combustion engines which can operate efficiently in the oxygen poor atmosphere found at high altitude have been developed for military purposes. An example of this is the experimental Condor aircraft which has flown at heights exceeding 20 km for over 48 hours.

An obvious disadvantage of any HALE platform which uses conventional hydrocarbon fuel is the fact that, regardless of how efficient the engine is and how light the airframe is, at some point the platform will have to replenish its fuel tanks. It will have to land, unless some system of mid-air refuelling can be adopted.

Landing for fuel will mean that another HALE platform will need to be positioned in order to continue to act as a telecommunication relay station. The very act of landing itself could be viewed as a disadvantage, risking damage to a relatively fragile craft.

Solar power

Solar power has the advantage of unlimited fuel. At the heights at which HALE platforms are intended to fly there would be few problems with cloud cover. Weather tends to happen fairly close to the ground most of the time. Towering thunderheads would be a problem of course but it would be unwise to fly a HALE platform into such conditions in any case. The savage air currents inside such storms have been known to rip gliders apart, and a HALE platform flying under solar power would suffer similar danger.

Interruption of sunlight can be countered by including efficient lightweight batteries in the airframe. Fuel cell technology would need to be involved here. Excess electrical power generated during periods of strong and continual sunlight could be used to split apart appropriate chemical substances into constituent elements. These then reproduce the electricity when allowed to recombine. Fuel cell research is also an important area of research because of the drive to create energy efficient, less polluting, transport for towns and cities.

Solar arrays for HALE platforms would therefore most certainly be combined with fuel cells which would chemically store surplus energy produced during the hours of sunlight and then convert it back into electricity to drive the platform's propellers when sunlight was not available.

Fuel cell technology

The first fuel cell was built by Sir William Groves, a nineteenth century Welsh lawyer who also went on to develop a parallel career as a professor of Physics. He appears to have been the first scientist with a clear concept of the principle of conservation of energy, but a major part of his work was devoted to the new subject of electricity. Here he devised a number of different types of electrical cell, including a zinc, platinum and sulphuric acid battery which was chosen to operate early telegraph systems in the United States. The 'gas voltaic' battery which he invented in 1839 was subsequently developed in the second half of the twentieth century to become the modern fuel cell. The fact that the first fuel cell was constructed by a Welsh scientist inspired the much-reiterated claim by the Press during the early days of American spaceflight that the Gemini and Apollo spacecraft were, naturally, 'powered by a British invention'. The term 'fuel cell' itself was devised in 1889 by two later scientists, Mond and Langer, who also experimented with the new technology and who tried to produce a working prototype for eventual commercial use.

The basic concept of the fuel cell is fairly easy to understand and the underlying chemistry can, in part, be demonstrated by a very simple home experiment. Water made conductive with traces of an electrolyte will pass a current of electricity. What is more interesting, and capable of demonstration with even a Heath Robinson home experiment in the kitchen using a battery, jam jar and lengths of electric flex, is that the electricity passing through the water is capable of splitting its molecules into their component atoms of hydrogen and oxygen. Hydrogen ions have a positive charge and so are attracted towards the piece of wire attached to the negative pole of the battery. This is known technically as the 'cathode'. Conversely oxygen ions have a negative charge and so are drawn to the positive wire or 'anode'. At the two electrodes (collective name for cathode and anode) the ions recombine to form the two gases, hydrogen and oxygen, which form tiny bubbles on each wire and rise to the surface.

An even more interesting fact is that the process can be reversed. Hydrogen and oxygen can be combined in a fuel cell to produce water and electricity. The reversibility of this reaction under the right conditions means that a fuel cell can act as a reservoir for electricity, taking it in to create the two gases, storing these and then using them to produce fresh electricity again when it is required.

In practice a fuel cell consists of a stack of individual cells, each of which only produces approximately 0.7 volts. A schematic diagram of a typical cell is shown in Figure 6.2.

Hydrogen and oxygen are introduced on opposide sides of the cell, hydrogen at the anode and oxygen at the cathode. (Note that this is the opposite way to the electrodes at which the two gases are released in the electrolysis described above.) Both gases need to be moist and are distributed evenly over the surfaces of the anode and cathode through a system of fine channels. The electrodes are coated with a catalyst of powdered platinum which splits up the hydrogen and oxygen creating positively charged hydrogen ions and electrons on one side of the cell and single oxygen atoms on the other.

Between the electrodes is a 'proton exchange membrane'. This is a hydrated polymer which will allow the passage of positive ions, but not electrons. It is this one-way system which is responsible for the cell generating electricity. The hydrogen ions can pass through and react with the oxygen atoms to produce water, while the surplus electrons create the electric current that flows from the cell.

In a HALE platform this electricity would power the electric motors connected to propellers at night and the water produced by the fuel cell would be stored. Then the following day when sunlight was plentiful again the same water would be electrolysed into hydrogen and oxygen using the excess electricity not required to keep the platform airborne. The two gases would be stored, just as the water had been previously.

The conversion of water plus electricity into hydrogen and oxygen, alternating with the combination of hydrogen and oxygen to give water plus electricity, can continue cycling for long periods, allowing a HALE

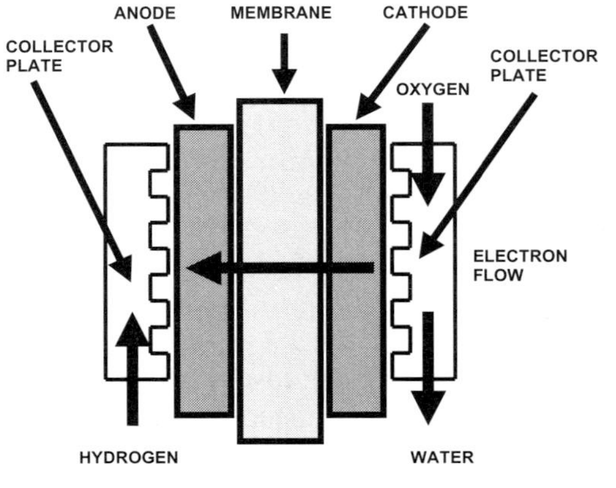

Figure 6.2 *Schematic diagram of a hydrogen/oxygen fuel cell*

platform to remain aloft and relay unbroken telecommunication links. This technology is being investigated in the NASA Helios programme described later. (Incidentally, different combinations of chemicals have been investigated for fuel cells, and cells using alternative fuels could help to ease the burden of supplying domestic electricity in the future. Solid oxide and molten carbonate cells operate at high temperatures but could be used to supplant the large turbines and generators of stations supplying the Grid. Alternatively fuel cells using a 'reformer' to extract hydrogen from a conventional hydrocarbon, like methanol, propane or natural gas, could become the major component of tomorrow's road vehicles. They might even be the power source for portable home appliances, like laptops and mobile phones.)

Microwave power

Another possibility is that a HALE platform could be kept aloft via microwave power beamed from the ground. This would operate by having a large ground array close to a city where a HALE platform was required. Electrical power provided by dedicated generators, or just from the grid, would be converted into a focused beam of microwaves and transmitted, ideally vertically, to the platform. Here it would be converted back into electricity and used to drive propellers.

A problem with this solution would be the cost of the ground stations and also the potential danger faced by anything flying into the beam near its focus at the platform. Fortunately birds would be unlikely to fly at this altitude, and human pilots should be aware of the location of the ground stations.

Looking a long way ahead, the potential of beaming power could have significant implications for future science. It might be one way in which exploration of other solar systems becomes possible. A NASA spokesman had suggested that giant lasers could be used to power interstellar spacecraft: 'If you make a powerful enough laser and can aim ... we could beam light to a spaceprobe halfway to Alpha Centuri.'

The Helios programme

Helios is a 'flying wing' unmanned aircraft under development by NASA, which commissioned the independent commercial organization AerVironment to carry out design studies and practical construction of a prototype ERAST aircraft. Helios is an excellent example of the type of HALE platform which will act as a telecommunications relay station in the near future. The immediate goals for Helios are that it should achieve altitudes of 100 000 feet and be able to remain airborne for a minimum of four days. Once the technology is successfully demonstrated, successor aircraft based upon design principles tested by Helios will be able to achieve the altitude and flight duration necessary for a viable HALE platform.

Helios has almost no fuselage. It is a mere 12 feet in length compared with the aircraft's wing, which is 8 feet wide and 247 feet from wing tip to wing tip. Incorporated into the wing are 14 electric motors, each powering a propeller and giving the craft a cruising speed of 25 mph.

For its initial test flights Helios has been powered by batteries, but a subsequent stage of development will replace these with the hydrogen/oxygen fuel cells described earlier.

> What advantages do HALE platforms have over satellite communications? What disadvantages could these platforms possess?
>
> Contrast the potential effectiveness of the two approaches to HALE: lighter-than-air platforms and UAV.
>
> Investigate the potential for microwave power transmission and contrast this with the use of fuel cells.
>
> Identify developments in electronics which have permitted serious consideration of HALE platforms.

Exercise 2: Launch vehicle economics and Low Earth Orbit satellites

> The future of telecommunications and the information 'superhighway' depends upon the ready availability of satellites able to act as relay stations redirecting network traffic beamed from the surface of the Earth beneath. Future expansion will depend upon reducing the cost of inserting satellites into orbit.

The information superhighway

Continued growth of the Internet will be affected by the methods adopted for placing communication satellites into orbit. Cheaper ways of providing satellites are required if the intended broadband data transmissions to all parts of the globe will be achieved. And yet it is generally agreed that a discrepancy has appeared between the rapid development of electronics and computing and the more sedate evolution of space technology.

Ironically both the growth of electronics, and relative stagnation of space technology, could be regarded as resulting from the 'space race' of the 1960s. America, fearing it had been humiliated by the Soviet Union launching the first Earth satellite, Sputnik, in October 1957, moved with incredible determination. Just three months later von Braun placed America's own first satellite into orbit. Three years after this initial step, on 25 May 1961, President Kennedy announced the decision to stage a manned lunar mission before the end of the decade.

There can be little doubt that the enormously funded research and engineering that produced the Apollo Spacecraft and their onboard miniaturized computers revolutionized the world of computing and advanced it far beyond previous estimates. Indeed personal computers were being marketed only five years after the last Apollo flight. At the same time it seems that complacency after beating the Soviet Union to the Moon led to America losing the will to continue developing spaceflight. Von Braun's plans for manned missions to Mars were quickly discarded and a policy for a gradual investigation of space adopted instead. Only now is the true economic significance of space technology reaching the wider commercial world. The Internet could return the good deed of 1960s space research and provide the incentive to enthuse over space again.

For the Internet to continue to grow satellite technology is essential. Voice, video and other broadband data will all be transmitted by 'constellations' of satellites in Low Earth Orbit (LEO). It must be admitted that the market has suffered initial problems. The Iridium constellation of LEO satellites, although technically successful, failed to obtain the userbase that had been anticipated. The technology was earlier than the demand. As a result Iridium decided to sell its satellites, although at first it was even considered necessary to deorbit them. Nevertheless it seems inevitable that broadband communications in areas where surface networks are unavailable will depend upon the use of satellite constellations. It is a more feasible option than a vast number of fibre-optic links. These are not a realistic alternative in many regions where the terrain is unsuitable. Note that Low Earth Orbit satellites are also important in many other applications, in addition to telecommunications. These include mapping, sensing and monitoring of resouces, as well as military requirements.

Telstar, the first communications satellite

The birth of communications satellites can be dated with historical accuracy. The first actively relayed signal, as opposed to the earlier test signals reflected off Echo, an inflated, metallic space balloon, was sent on 10 July 1962 via the Telstar satellite. This had been placed into orbit only a few hours before by a Thor-Delta rocket. This first phone conversation, relayed by Telstar, was between Frederick Kappel, Chairman of AT&T, in Andover, Maine, to Vice-President Lyndon Johnson in Washington. A little later transatlantic signals were sent to a British receiving station on Goonhilly Downs, Cornwall, and to another in Brittany.

Telstar was purely an experimental satellite, placed in a low orbit, but it was soon followed by other communication satellites which were intended for serious commercial use. Very soon satellites like Early Bird were making international telecommunication via satellite commonplace.

The concept of satellite communications

However, the idea of telecommunication via satellite first appeared in print in the October 1945 edition of the journal Wireless World. The article was written by a young scientist, soon to become a science fiction giant, Arthur C. Clarke, and had the title: 'Extra terrestrial relays: Can rocket stations give world-wide radio coverage?' This article appeared shortly after the Nazi bombardment of England using V2 rockets, but Clarke was more aware of the practical future uses of rocketry. Specifically he saw the potential of artificial satellites as a way of transmitting television signals over large distances. Television had been introduced just before the Second World War. Now that peace would allow television services to develop quickly, Clarke knew that a solution would need to be found for long distance transmission. Rapidly dismissing the possibility of a vast number of closely spaced repeater stations on the Earth's surface, he proposed the construction of artificial space stations in orbit around the Earth. These could receive signals beamed from future television transmitters and redirect them over the large area of the Earth beneath the immensely high space station.

He realized the novelty of his idea and made a brief apology for it:

> Many may consider the solution proposed in this discussion too far fetched to be taken very seriously.

His discussion of the concept went into considerable technical depth, combining the mathematical precision of his scientific training with the imaginative descriptive writing that would later appear in his popular stories. He knew that research would need to be carried out into space technology. Writing at a time when use of captured V2 rockets for upper atmosphere research in America had yet to begin he suggested:

> Direct evidence could be obtained . . . by V2 rocket technique, and it is to be hoped that someone will do something about this soon as there must be quite a surplus stock somewhere!

Arthur Clarke assumed that the relay stations would not be automatic. Electronic equipment of the period required constant attention. Vacuum tubes (Clarke would have used the British term 'valve') were hot and burnt out regularly. A chap with soldering iron and replacement parts was an essential part of the system. And so the Clarke communication satellite was a full blown Flash Gordon piece of space Art Deco, with mirrors concentrating sunlight to boil the water of a low pressure steam engine. This would generate the electrical power required by a station supporting human occupants. Clarke did actually add that 'photoelectric developments' might later make this unnecessary, so perhaps the windmill-like appearance of Skylab, Mir and the International Space Station was not a surprise for him.

> It would be possible to construct a 'space-station' in such an orbit . . . provided with living quarters . . . and everything needed for the comfort of its crew . . . The technical problems involved in the design of such a station are extremely interesting but only a few can be gone into here.

Later in the same paper Clarke's optimism sadly exceeded the actual developments of the decades that followed. With the then typical, and with hindsight slightly touching, enthusiasm of the immediate post-atomic bomb period, he appears to have expected a universal technological panacea in the form of nuclear energy:

> It seems unlikely that we will have to wait as much as 20 years before atomic-powered rockets are developed.

Nuclear rockets, but electronics so unreliable that it requires the full-time supervision of TV repair men – even sending them 22 000 miles into space (by nuclear rocket of course). Well, perhaps the best futurologists, like Arthur C. Clarke, are allowed the occasional wobbly . . .

Geostationary orbit

What Arthur C. Clarke had realized was the significance of a particular type of orbit about the Earth. The further away a satellite is, the slower it needs to move in order to balance its reduced weight with the centripetal force required to deflect it from a straight line into an ellipse about the Earth. For example, an orbit close to the Earth can be completed in about 80 minutes, whereas the Moon takes a whole month. Clarke reasoned that between these values would be an orbit that would have an orbital period of precisely one day. Such a satellite would just keep pace with the Earth's rotation and hover in exactly the same place in the sky. In a 'geostationary orbit' a satellite appears to levitate by magic. A geostationary orbit confers great advantages. The dish-shaped domestic TV aerials required to receive signals from a satellite only need to be aligned just once. They are permanently locked on to the one unmoving point in the sky where their satellite is poised, unlike the earliest satellite dishes used for Telstar. In addition to their great size these earlier satellite dishes had to track the satellite as it moved rapidly from horizon to horizon.

Geostationary orbits have to be above the equator. This is the reason why satellite dishes on house walls point grazingly at our horizon. Britain is far north in the Northern hemisphere and the aerials remind us of our distance from the equator.

A rough calculation can be made for the radius of a geostationary orbit by applying Kepler's Third Law of Planetary Motion. Kepler deduced his three laws, published in 1609 and 1619, by analysing the pre-telescopic observational data obtained by Tycho Brahe, and he used them to explain the way in which the planets moved around the Sun. Later they became a mathematical inevitability, deducible from Newton's new physics. And they apply equally to the description of the way in which satellites orbit the Earth.

Kepler's third law says that the period of an orbit, the time a satellite takes to orbit its parental body once, is related to its size. For a circular orbit this means that the square of the period is proportional to the cube of the radius. We can apply the law to estimate the height of a geostationary satellite by using the Moon as a source of data for a second orbit. Then by comparing the Moon's orbit with the orbit of a geostationary communication satellite we can deduce the size of the latter.

First, data on the Moon:

Moon's period, MP, is 29.5 days.
Radius of Moon's orbit, MR, is 238 000 miles.

Initially all that is known about the geostationary orbit is its period. Its radius will be just the algebraic variable GR:

Geostationary orbit's period, GP, is one day.
Radius of geostationary orbit is GR thousand miles.

Applying Kepler's third law about the proportionality of the square of an orbit's period and the cube of its radius gives:

MP squared/MR cubed = GP squared/GR cubed

Rearranging the equation leads to:

GR cubed = GP squared * MR cubed/MP squared

Inserting the values given above then gives:

GR cubed = 1 squared * 238 cubed/29.5 squared
GR cubed = 1 * 13 481 272/870.25
GR cubed = 15491

Taking the cube root gives an approximate value of 25 000 miles. Allowing for the radius of the Earth this is not too far, given the approximate nature of the calculation, from the accepted figure of 22 300 miles for the height of a satellite in geostationary orbit.

More correctly such an orbit is 'geosynchronous'. To create a properly geostationary orbit occasional correction using onboard thrusters is required to take into account the way in which the Earth's gravitational field does not match that of a perfectly spherical distribution of mass. Note that a geosynchronous 'transfer orbit' is an elliptical orbit with a 24 hour period and the highest point of which ('apogee') is at the correct height for a geostationary orbit. Further boosting of a satellite would be required for insertion into the geostationary orbit.

Expendable launch vehicles

Arthur C. Clarke's giant space stations in geostationary orbit have yet to appear. So what is the true situation regarding launching communication satellites?

The rockets currently used as an alternative to the Shuttle for placing satellites into orbit are referred to as Expendable Launch Vehicles (ELVs) because no part of them is returned to the ground intact for future use. In contrast the Shuttle lands in one piece, and its solid fuel rockets parachute back to the sea, where they can be recovered and refurbished for later missions. Only the large external fuel tank is lost. All early satellites were launched by expendable rockets. It was generally believed that these would be entirely replaced by the Shuttle, which would simply release satellites into orbit from its payload bay. However, the Shuttle fleets simply cannot satisfy the demand for satellites to be placed into orbit and so expendable rockets are still used as well. The Challenger disaster also had an adverse effect on the use of the Shuttle for commercial satellite launches.

Some of the American ELVs are:

Atlas-Centaur

This is an example of an early American launch vehicle which has remained in service far longer than originally anticipated as a result of fewer launches taking place via the Shuttle. The Atlas first stage dates from the 1950s and an Atlas launch vehicle was used to place the first American, John Glenn, into orbit on 20 February 1962. However, with the high energy Centuar second stage, fuelled like the Shuttle with liquid hydrogen and liquid oxygen, the combined vehicle is capable of placing eight 200 pound payloads into geosynchronous orbit. The Atlas exists in versions II, IIA and IIAS.

Development of the Atlas has continued over the years. As late as 2000 an updated Atlas III was produced by Lockheed Martin and the Atlas V will become available for satellite launches in 2002.

Atlas launches take place from Cape Canaveral.

Delta

Delta is a large launch vehicle produced by Boeing, and at a height of 240 feet exceeds the Shuttle and its external tank. Delta has liquid fuelled first and second stages, a solid fuelled third stage and large additional solid fuelled strap-on boosters. Delta III and Delta IV versions can place payloads into geosynchronous transfer orbit. Over 29 000 pounds can be placed into such an orbit by Delta IV. Delta launches take place from Cape Canaveral.

Titan

The original Titan II was used to place the two-astronaut Gemini spacecraft into orbit in the 1960s. Titan III launched the Viking Mars probes and Voyager spacecraft and Titan IV has also been used to launch an interplanetary probe, the Cassini spacecraft to Saturn. Titan II is still used in satellite launches while Titan IV can place a 13 000 pound payload in geosynchronous orbit.

Athena

This is a solid fuelled launch vehicle produced by Lockheed Martin. It exists in two versions, Athena I and Athena II, and has been launched from a number of different sites including the new Kodiak launch complex in Alaska.

Taurus

This is an example of private enterprise entering into space technology. Taurus was developed by Orbital Sciences of Dulles, Virginia, which has supplied launch vehicles for NASA. Taurus is a four stage rocket, using solid fuel, and can place two 200 pound payloads into Low Earth Orbit. Taurus launches take place from Vandenberg Air Force base.

Pegasus

The majority of satellites are launched into orbit from the ground. There is a great advantage in getting a 'flying start' by launching a satellite with a rocket that is already in the air. Much of the work of the first stage of a launch vehicle will already have been performed by the parent aircraft and the rocket itself can be relatively small. The Pegasus launch vehicle, also a product of Orbital Sciences, adopts this approach. It is carried to an altitude of approximately 39 000 feet by a specially converted Lockheed L-1011 aircraft. The three stage solid-fuelled Pegasus can then place a satellite into Low Earth Orbit. Payloads of 970 pounds are possible.

Pegasus does not require extensive ground facilities and can be based at any conventional airfield. The Lockheed parent has flown successfully from a variety of American launch sites including Cape Canaveral, Wallops Island and Vandenberg.

Launch sites

The ideal place to launch most satellites into orbit is from the equator. Here the full benefit of the Earth's rotation will be added to the velocity acquired by the rocket boosting the satellite. Some satellites though need particular orbits for which this is not a necessary advantage. For example, an orbit that passes over the North and South Pole, will not benefit. (A polar orbit like this is useful since it means that the satellite will eventually pass over all parts of the Earth's surface, which is convenient for various types of monitoring and remote sensing.)

A number of launch sites have been developed.

Eastern Range

The Eastern Range is better known as Cape Canaveral, the Florida location of the Project Mercury, Gemini and Apollo missions, and now the launch site for the Space Shuttle. It also includes the Patrick Air Force Base.

It has two separate areas from which rockets can take off. These are known as launch complexes because they consist of a number of separate facilities, like launch pads, blockhouses for protection of personnel when a launch vehicle takes off, workshops, and various other facilities required to prepare a rocket for launch. Cape Canaveral launch complexes are number 17 and number 36. Launch complex 17 is used for the Boeing Delta II and Delta III vehicles. Launch complex 36 is used for the Lockheed Martin Atlas series.

Western Range

The Western Range is associated with Vandenberg Air Force Base in California. It is a military base and was, at one time, intended to be an additional launch site for Space Shuttle missions for the military. Various USAF groups are based at Vandenberg.

However, it does act as a launch site for commercial flights by Titan II and Titan III launch vehicles, Pegasus, Taurus and Delta II.

Kodiak Island
The Kodiak Launch Complex in Alaska is a recent addition to the United States space facilities, achieving its first launch in 1998.

Kwajalein Atoll
The United States Army's Regan Test Site is based at Kwajalein, an atoll in the Marshall Islands. Pegasus launches have been based here.

Wallops Island
The Wallops Island base is on the coast of Virginia, about three hours' drive from Washington DC. It is a very early launch site, set up at the end of the Second World War, and is used mainly for 'sounding rockets'. These do not place satellites into orbit but instead follow ballistic trajectories which take the rocket far out into near Earth space to conduct scientific experiments. Such experiments date from the research programme carried out from the late 1940s at the White Sands Proving Ground with commandeered V2 rockets. (Later renamed White Sands Missile Range, this is a large desert area in New Mexico, 100 by 40 miles in extent.)

Sounding rockets conduct suborbital research into areas like, optical and ultraviolet astrophysics, high energy astrophysics, geospace science and microgravity research. A large number of different sounding rockets have been launched from Wallops Island, all using solid fuel motors. These include the Super Arcas, Terrier Malemute, Orion, Nike-Orion, Taurus-Orion, Nike-Black Brant, various other rockets in the Black Brant series, the Viper Dart, Terrier Orion and Terrier Lynx. The rockets, which should not be described as launch vehicles, range in length from the Orion at 6 metres to the largest of the Black Brant series at 20 metres. Compared with satellites, which remain in orbit until either deliberately deorbited or brought down by the cumulative effect of the minute amount of atmosphere still present in Low Earth Orbit, sounding rockets only spend a brief time in space. The Orion remains above an altitude of 100 km for just 100 seconds. The largest Black Brant remains this high for 14 times as long, but still ventures only briefly into space. Sounding rockets do compete with satellites in terms of distance from the Earth's surface. Orion's apogee (highest point reached) is 100 km. Black Brant reaches 16 times this figure. Sounding rockets do not have any potential for telecommunications.

Future developments in space transportation

From the dawn of the space age in the 1950s to the present, research and development of all spacecraft has been the sole domain of governments. From the immensely successful programmes developed by NASA in America and by the (then) Soviet Union, the faltering and sadly stalled British space effort culminating in the launch of a single satellite in the Black Arrow project and the immediate curtailing of funds by the UK Government, to the continuing French involvement via ESA and the burgeoning space programmes of China and Japan, every major development in space has been the result of central planning and funding.

It appears that this is now due to change, and that private organizations will exploit the financial potential of space exploration. Encouraged by the relative lack of success of national policy in creating cheaper access to space, ordinary commercial concerns are investigating novel techniques which could substantially reduce the price per kilo of payload in Low Earth Orbit. A grand prize is seen. The future of telecommunications will rest largely upon methods for placing telecommunication satellites in orbit. A secondary goal of eventual space tourism, already witnessed by the sojourn of Dennis Toto on the International Space station, is a further incentive to produce more inexpensive ways of getting into orbit.

As observed earlier, business speculators have noted the mismatch between rapid advances in computing and telecommunications and the oddly archaic way in which the necessary satellites are placed in orbit. Leading industrialists wonder if space policy has become fossilized in governments' minds. The colossal investments that have been made in establishing the existing space technology may, indeed, be acting as a barrier to a more radical approach. It is suspected that new approaches could lead to genuinely reusable launch vehicles that do not inherit the Shuttle's limitations, and hence to the real economic potential of Earth orbit. The Shuttle, of course, does not qualify as a fully reusable space vehicle because of its reliance on its very large external fuel tank (actually separate tanks of fuel and oxidizer but appearing a single entity from outside). This is discarded at every launch and crashes into the Atlantic.

Additional time since the development of the Shuttle has allowed a new generation of space scientists to think of alternative ways of solving basic problems. The Shuttle programme itself began in the

1970s. Dramatically its political approval was announced to Apollo astronauts on the Moon at the time. This gives some idea of the age of the basic Shuttle design concept. Improvements have been implemented in recent years, like an improved rocket engine, and the introduction of modern computer avionics, when individual Shuttles have been given major overhauls, but these have not significantly affected the spacecraft's efficiency in terms of payload into orbit.

Fascinating future possibilities are to be found in the proposals of two independent organizations, Kelly Space and Technology and Kistler Aerospace, each with a vision for space.

Kelly Space and Technology

Kelly Space and Technology is a Californian-based organization founded in 1993. It hopes to develop a series of innovative spacecraft which will reduce the price of placing payloads, typically telecommunications satellites, into orbit. The hope is to reduce costs to approximately 40% of current values.

Kelly Space is investigating the potential of both orbital and sub-orbital spacecraft. The latter category, like the early Project Mercury flights of Alan Shepard (later the first man to play golf on the Moon!) and Virgil Grissom, would follow high ballistic paths arching out of the Earth's atmosphere without actually entering orbit.

The major project of Kelly Space is the Astroliner. This is a large vehicle with a shape not wholly unlike the Shuttle, but quite different in concept. The Astroliner would take off horizontally from a normal runway, not under its own power but towed behind a Boeing 747 airliner. At a height of 20 000 feet, and already travelling at Mach 0.8, the Astroliner would detach from the tow and fire its own rocket engines. Powered flight would then continue until an altititude of 350 000 feet was reached. The rocket engines would then shut down and the Astroliner coast to 400 000 feet. The internal second stage would then be released from the nose of the Astroliner and fire its own engine, taking a satellite into orbit. The Astroliner then re-enters the atmosphere. When low enough, jet engines allow a powered landing at an airport.

The Astroliner has a number of advantages when compared to a spacecraft like NASA's Shuttle:

- The Astroliner's first stage is fully reusable. It does not have an external tank to discard. (The Astroliner's second stage is not recovered, but this is a far cheaper component of the overall craft.)
- The Astroliner scores over the Shuttle because unlike the latter it does not actually enter orbit itself. As a result there is no need for expensive shielding from the heat of re-entry. This heat is considerable, as it represents the equivalent energy required to put a Shuttle into orbit in the first place. Any spacecraft returning from orbit, and relying upon friction against the atmosphere to reduce its kinetic energy, is going to have heat shielding and suffer as a result from a weight and cost burden. Kelly Space's Astroliner avoids this. Saving weight on shielding leads to a direct increase in payload.
- An additional advantage of the Astroliner is that even if its rocket engine should fail after separation from the Boeing 747 this does not seriously affect the spacecraft, or cause loss of its payload. It can simply glide back to a safe landing with satellite intact. Such a possibility does not exist for an expendable launch vehicle. Loss of valuable satellites was witnessed, for example, in the first Ariane V launch for the European Space Agency.
- The horizontal configuration of the Astroliner before it takes off makes it far easier to load satellites and to conduct various maintenance. It does not require the expensive use of gantries and elevators and reduces risk of injury to ground crew.
- The Astroliner would not require a dedicated spaceport from which to operate. It could be towed from, and subsequently land at, any airport with an appropriate runway. (As with any launch system, of course, the nearer to the Equator the more the Astroliner's second stage would benefit from the Earth's rotation.)
- Development costs for the Astroliner would be kept to a minimum by employment of existing engineering and avionic components where possible.

Confidence in Kelly Aerospace was confirmed by a contract awarded by NASA itself in January 2001 for a design study into next generation space transport systems.

Kistler Aerospace

Kistler Aeropspace is another commercial organization that is seeking to develop reusable launch vehicles which could be used to place telecommunication satellites in orbit. Kistler hopes to be able to deliver payloads into both Low Earth Orbit and High Energy Orbits (HEO). Low Earth Orbit missions could include the transport of crew and supplies to the International Space Station.

The Kistler 'K1' rocket would be a two stage launch vehicle, both stages being recoverable. The two stages use an existing rocket engine, the Russian NK33/43. The first stage of the vehicle would use three engines and the second stage just one. Parachutes, combined with airbags to soften impact, are intended to be used for recovery of the vehicle. Launch sites for the KI are planned in Nevada and in Woomera, Australia.

Advantages of Kistler's proposal include:

- Rapid deployment of new satellites into a particular orbit when required, in contrast to the long delays common with expendable launch vehicles. This would make unnecessary the current practice of launching 'spare' satellites into the same orbit to be activated should the primary satellite fail.
- Provision of services for the US Government as well as for private organizations.

In August 2000 Kistler Aerospace was awarded a contract by NASA to investigate how the K1 launch vehicle could be used to deliver supplies to the International Space Station. A fleet of five K1 vehicles was proposed.

Venture Star/X-33

A NASA project for the development of a new launch vehicle ran into problems with US Government funding. This was the Venture Star programme, the plan for a replacement for the Shuttle fleet.

In its initial conception the project consisted of two separate vehicles, the Venture Star itself and an approximate half scale version of the Venture Star, called the X-33. Both would take off vertically, but land horizontally, in the same way as the Shuttle. The X-33 was to be a suborbital craft, whereas the Venture Star would achieve orbit. The X-33 was intended to reach an altitude of approximately 60 miles.

The Venture Star, had it been produced, would have achieved the long awaited status of a Single Stage To Orbit (SSTO) vehicle, regarded as a major milestone in the development of space technology.

The decision to proceed with the X-33 was announced on 2 July 1996. Unfortuntately, perhaps, the news was broken by (then) Vice President Al Gore. Possibly his support was a bad omen as it was the X-33 that lost political support.

Incidentally both vehicles would have been smaller than the Shuttle, which would tower over the X-33, and even top the Venture Star, should all three, hypothetically, be seen side by side. The X-33's length (or perhaps height) was 69 feet and it would have been remarkably chubby in appearance with a maximum width of 77 feet.

The *raison d'être* for the research project was twofold:

- To produce new technologies required for more sophisticated launch vehicles.
- To demonstrate that commercial applications of these vehicles were feasible. This would require the production of a machine that could be readied for another flight within days, in constrast with the stately turnaround time preferred by the ageing Shuttle.

The X-33 was intended to demonstrate the feasibility of the Venture Star design. It would show that the Venture Star was technically possible and could provide access to space that was more economic than the Shuttle, using a reusable launch system that was routinely available. The hope was that the cost of a pound of payload in orbit would drop from the $10 000 of the Shuttle to $1000, thus increasing commercial use of space.

The X-33 was under development at various locations around the United States when it was abandoned, including the famous Lockheed Martin Skunk Works, home of many of the country's more adventurous projects, like the U2 spy plane and the later F-117 'Stealth' fighter aircraft. Initially it was hoped that the craft would make its first flight in March 1999.

Unlike the Shuttle, with its external fuel tank, the X-33 contained all fuel and oxidant (liquid hydrogen and liquid oxygen) internally to its elegant wedge-shaped aeroframe, held in separate tanks of revolutionary lightweight construction. These used an innovatory mixture of graphite epoxy composite and an alloy of lithium and aluminium. (Those who remember the periodic table in school chemistry laboratories will recognize the low density of both of these metals.) Other advanced features of the X-33 included a lifting body, wingless overall design, differing from the winged Shuttle. The X-33 did not require the high-maintenance ceramic tiles used by the Shuttle to resist the heat of re-entry. In addition it was to use two aerospike rocket engines, prototyped by Rockwell Rocketdyne. This type of engine is an imaginative departure from the conventional engine design inherited from the early days of von Braun. Instead of a large bell-shaped exhaust nozzle the aerospike engine vents its combusted gases alongside the rocket exterior, down the exterior walls of a tapering ramp. Such a design has been technically recognized for a long time as a better alternative, maximizing thrust at all altitudes as well as permitting vectoring of the thrust without the need for moving parts.

It was problems with the tank design that played a major part in the withdrawal of funding for the development programme. The X-33 also suffered from considerable financial problems, exceeding its planned budget and failing to meet the optimistic time schedule initially proposed for the project.

Distinguish between Low Earth Orbit and Geostationary Orbit for communication satellites. How do these relate to the type and number of satellites required?

Investigate the impact of the 'space race' on subsequent telecommunications.

How is the future of telecommunications likely to be affected by developments in space transportation?

What role is private funding likely to play in the creation of 'satellite constellations'?

What evidence is there that wider political considerations affect the creation of telecommunications systems?

6.2 Cost and security

Exercise 1: Home networking

Reliable technology is beginning to appear which will allow networks to be set up within individual homes, connecting appliances with one another and, via the Internet, to the outside world. Such home networks are likely to use the existing domestic power supply rather than requiring the installation of additional cables.

It will be possible in the near future for houses to incorporate networking technologies which will link various appliances. Food packaging, for example, could have sophisticated labels containing microchips, which would indicate what had been placed in the refrigerator. Similarly food items could be automatically logged when they were removed. This information would be of little use if restricted to a microprocessor in the fridge. But if the refrigerator were networked to other devices in the home then the information could become more useful. Via the Internet the fridge could even be accessed by mobile phone while out shopping.

One way in which a home computer network can be created is by using the existing electrical power supply to act as the cabling between the different networked devices. Although the power supply is carrying a large current, at a far higher voltage than present in computer circuitry, network signals can still be transmitted as well, provided that devices are connected to the power line via dedicated adapters. Currently a separate lead is used to supply power to the device, but combined data and power leads are likely in the future.

Different organizations have experimented with versions of this technology in the past. Now a standard is emerging backed by the HomePlug Powerline Alliance. The data transfer rate currently capable of being achieved is approximately 8 Mbps, which is sufficient for a feasible home network.

The fact that the network makes use of wiring that is already in place leads to ease of installation. All that is required is a power line network adapter for each device, which can then be plugged into any of the multitude of sockets already in place around the house. This means that individual appliances in the home can be linked, and, in addition, the home network can be connected to the Internet, allowing remote access to domestic appliances (see Figure 6.3).

Likely applications of home networks

One potential use of home networking has already been noted, knowing the contents of your fridge while out shopping. Obviously with an emerging technology it is hard to make precise predictions. In the past it has often been an unexpected application of new technology which has succeeded beyond expectation. It is reasonably safe, though, to suggest that home networks could find a role in at least some of the following:

Sharing computer resources

A home network can offer the same type of advantage as a LAN operating in an office environment. Children doing homework in separate rooms will be able to use the same printer and other hardware resources, rather than separate equipment being purchased for each child.

Adjusting central heating before arrival

Sometimes it is hard to decide in advance when you will return home. If the second act of a ballet is cancelled unexpectedly as the result of a fracas in the green room you may suddenly wish that you had set your central heating to power up a couple of hours earlier. A home network could resolve this situation.

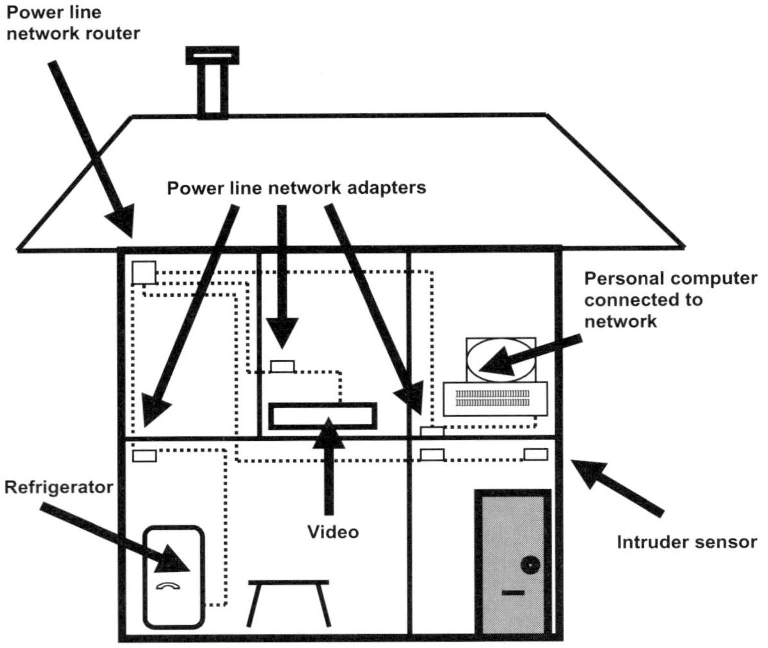

Figure 6.3 *Home networking links appliances together and to the external world*

Setting video to record

If you have only just realized that an overlooked channel is rebroadcasting *High Society* or the *Creature from the Black Lagoon* (perhaps in a special compilation edition) then home networking resolves the problem, even if you are on the beach.

Assessing computing files remotely

If you concentrate best when away from home then being able to access files on the computer in the study via a laptop and modem, on the table in front of you in the library/pub, will be a decided advantage.

Electronic games

Children can play interactive games from separate bedrooms, thus preventing virtual violence from finding its counterpart in the real world.

Future intelligent home appliances

As home networking is something which will affect future homes its use in association with proposed new domestic appliances should be considered. These might easily include robot cleaners. The robot vacuum cleaner has featured in cartoons for at least the last 50 years, but it now does at last appear to be emerging in reality. Already (2002) home trials are being conducted on the Dyson DC06, a small robot which employs 50 sensors and three microprocessors to allow it to construct its own internal representation of the room which it is cleaning. The robot does not need to be trained but operates in a wholly autonomous way. Obstacles that are encountered are stored in the robot's map of the room and used to make sure that all areas are cleaned uniformly. This contrasts with some early robot lawnmowers which succeeded in navigating around objects in their way, but did this in a random fashion. As a result both bald and long patches of grass could develop over time. It is not inconceivable that similar cleaners could be incorporated into a home network and activated by a decision made remotely.

Home monitoring

A home network allows the possibility of a house becoming autonomous and monitoring its own status. A freezer about to fail could alert a service engineer, for example.

Rival home technologies

There are three other choices for home networking. These do not use the power supply line:

- Wireless network
- Internal telephones
- Ethernet

Wireless network
It is possible to communicate between different appliances using radio frequencies. Network data is transmitted and received by including radio devices in each appliance. Compared with home networking through the power supply this is an expensive choice. The dedicated equipment required is not as versatile and cheap as power line network adapters. Some potential users are also worried about the risk of neighbouring houses' wireless networks intercepting private traffic, perhaps through error in the use of encryption.

Wireless networking is considered in more detail in a separate exercise.

Internal telephones
Those homes which have an internal phone system can use the phone wires to connect networked devices using the Home Phoneline Networking Alliance (Home PNA) standard. Setting up a system can be difficult, however, and adds to the cost of construction of new houses. Another problem is that it is unlikely that the majority of houses will have existing phoneline connections in all rooms. This contrasts with power line sockets which will be present in nearly every room.

Ethernet
There are homes where computing enthusiasts have gone ahead with conventional technology and installed Ethernet connections between personal computers and other equipment located in different rooms around the house. This is very unlikely ever to become the accepted technique for home computer networks. One reason is price. Another is the fact that the newer technologies are being specifically aimed at the types of devices and appliances found in the domestic situation.

Potential problems with power line connections

There are potential problems with power line connections:

- Appliances drawing power from the electricity supply will create interference.
- Additional interference can be created by the house wiring acting as a receiving aerial for radio broadcasts.
- The power wiring in a house does not carry all the frequencies normally required.
- The wiring inside a house does not form a distinct unit. A circuit apparently within the house can actually involve a transformer some distance away. This means that home network traffic can have much further to travel than might initially be expected.
- The physical implementation of the home network will not be constant. As switches are reset, and different appliances switched on and off, the electrical characteristics will alter.

Some of these problems can be avoided by designing the network to operate at unusually high frequencies. Network packets can also be subdivided into even smaller 'symbols' which can be transmitted between electrical noise on the power line. A technique called Orthogonal Frequency Division Multiplexing (OFDM) is used to send information over 76 separate channels. These are constantly monitored to see which should momentarily be closed as a result of an unacceptable level of noise.

The Haines family live in a large house in the suburbs.

Mr Haines is currently unemployed. He spends much of the day meditating in the garden shed, but also plays computer chess with his father-in-law, who is permanently confined to bed in the granny flat.

Mrs Haines has a temporary job working in a supermarket checkout. Her wages are low but offset by a 20% reduction in the cost of some of the supermarket's commodities. She tends to leave home in a rush every morning.

Their eldest daughter is at university studying law, but in her spare time works in the faculty library writing a novel on her laptop. Her fiction is largely autobiographical and draws heavily upon her diary, which she has written on the personal computer in her bedroom since the age of 12.

Their twin sons are both studying for GCSEs and have coursework which often misses teachers' deadlines. As a result they tend to complete unfinished work in the school prep room. They frequently forget to bring files from home on floppy disk.

Discuss how home networking would help individual members of the family.

Investigate the different technologies that could be used to implement a suitable home network, and research the cost of installation.

Exercise 2: Wireless LAN

The limitations imposed by the fixed physical layout of a conventional LAN can be avoided if radio frequency signals are instead used to replace the normal wiring. Such a wireless LAN can have many advantages, depending upon the physical environment in which the network is installed.

What a wireless LAN achieves

In a conventional LAN individual workstations are linked to the hub via permanent cables, built into the structure of the LAN's environment, typically in ducts placed beneath flooring or attached to nearby walls. This results in a workplace which is inflexible. Desks remain in position because that was where it was first decided they should be placed. This will not necessarily reflect future needs of users.

In contrast to wired connections a wireless LAN connects stations via radio frequency transmission and reception. An employee's computer does not have to remain where they first find it. If another part of the office is quieter, more comfortable or simply nearer other required resouces (perhaps the water cooler!) the employee can move, shifting their computer at the same time. All the network resources are still available. Files can be retrieved and documents printed, just as they can be from a fixed position.

In practice, wireless technology is usually combined with a conventional LAN. The wireless link adds extra flexibility for the user, permitting them to roam within the range permitted by the wireless connection to the wired LAN.

A wireless card installed in a laptop computer then connects to the wired LAN via an 'access point', a transceiver which can transmit and receive data, as well as storing a certain amount of data in its own memory to buffer input/output from the wired LAN. The antenna for the access point is usually mounted as high as possible in the physical environment to improve reception of signals. The range between access point and laptop can be in excess of a 150 metres indoors, or twice this distance in the open. A typical access point can provide network access for as many as 50 users' laptops.

Ideally access points are arranged throughout the site so that users will have continuous network connection. In addition to access points extension points can be used. Unlike access points these are not hard wired into the LAN. Instead they function as relays, transmitting and receiving network traffic from users' mobile machines and helping to forward such traffic directly or indirectly to an access point.

The throughput of a wireless LAN is well within the range of acceptability. A typical bit rate is of the order of 1.5 Mbps, more than sufficient for normal LAN traffic, like Internet usage, e-mail and accessing database files.

Different wireless technologies are available: narrowband transmits and receives signals over a small frequency range. This ensures privacy but can require licensing. Spread-spectrum transmission uses a wider frequency range. It can involve frequency-hopping, in which transmitter and receiver switch from frequency to frequency in a synchronized way. An alternative is direct sequence spread spectrum, or DSSS.

Infrared light can also be used to establish wireless connections in a LAN. Infrared radiation is of a much higher frequency, and therefore shorter in wavelength, than radio waves. In fact infrared is just slightly longer in wavelength than visible light. The way in which electromagnetic waves propagates mean that the short wavelength radiation does not conveniently 'bend round corners'. Objects are also opaque to infrared and so line of sight is usually essential between access point and computer, although some diffuse reflection of signal can occur in room interiors. Infrared LAN connections are normally restricted to fixed wireless connections over short distances within buildings and are unsuitable for mobile users.

Accepted acronyms for wireless LAN are WLAN (Wireless Local Area Network) and the more easily pronounced LAWN (Local Area Wireless Network).

Who uses wireless LAN?

- Educational establishments benefit particularly from the use of wireless LAN. A lecturer can retain access to a college network, for example, whether in their office, a department library, laboratory or even lecture theatre. Files on students can be accessed during tutorials irrespective of the location chosen. Research can be continued in the staff room. The potential for wireless LAN is tremendous.
- Information can be made available to committee members in boardrooms or in other semi-formal situations in which a wired workstation would be intrusive.
- Similarly a wireless LAN is extremely useful in warehouses. In a situation like this the people who need access to the network are also going to have to move about a great deal as they fetch items that are required. This is an obvious area in which wireless LAN offers advantages.

- In hospitals doctors and nurses can have immediate access to patient files, even as they move from ward to ward.

Advantages of wireless LAN

- Wireless LANs are designed to be compatible with existing networking standards.
- Users can access the network anywhere within the organization. This improves productivity of employees. For example, research might be carried out within a library if access is required to information only available as books or printed files. Early archived material, predating the introduction of any information technology into the organization, can be easily retrieved. The alternative to the wireless LAN would be physically moving volumes and files to the nearest workstation with a wired connection, and this might not be realistic.
- A wireless LAN can be installed far more quickly than a conventional LAN requiring wired connections. This results quite simply from the fact that holes do not have to be drilled through walls, nor does ducting need to be attached to ceilings and walls or under floors. The installation of a wireless LAN is quick, efficient and painless. It can be particularly useful in an older building where the physical cost of installing cables through thick Victorian masonry can be very high.
- In addition a wireless LAN is extremely flexible and is less constrained by the geographical layout of rooms within a building or buildings on a site complex.
- Networks can be expanded easily as wired connections do not have to be provided.
- The network topology can be altered quickly. For example, a small peer-to-peer network can be rapidly expanded into a network permitting a far larger number of users to access a full range of network services.
- The security of wireless LAN connections is not a problem, partly due to the influence of the military in the development of wireless technologies. Secure encryption techniques make illicit interception of LAN traffic extremely difficult and unlikely to occur.

Disadvantages of wireless LAN

- Initial costs of the installation of a wireless LAN can be higher than for a wired network. However, over a period of time this is outweighed by cost benefits.
- Infrared LAN connections are usually limited to line of sight.
- Radio interference is a possible problem, though less so in the type of physical environment in which a wireless LAN will be likely to be installed. Possible souces of interference are other wireless LANs and microwave ovens.
- The use of different standards (frequency hopping or direct sequence) by different suppliers of wireless hardware could be a problem for the unwary network administrator.
- Depending upon the country involved, and national legislation currently implemented, there could be the need to acquire a licence for the frequencies with which a particular wireless LAN was intended to operate.

Case Study: The Research Institute for Forestry Innovation and Development

An independent scientific body, the Research Institute for Forestry Innovation and Development, has been awarded Government funding for a crash programme to avert the worst effects of global warming. The Institute's brief is to develop genetically modified olive trees that will have the ability to absorb a far higher proportion of carbon dioxide from the air than occurs with other vegetation. It is hoped that large plantations of such artificially created trees will result in a significant decrease in atmospheric carbon dioxide and eventually reverse the worse environmental effects of climate change.

The newly inserted genes will lead to rapid growth in the plant tissue and, incidentally, the production of large fruiting bodies rich in hydrocarbons. Several commercial organizations have already displayed interest in the possibility of harvesting this crop for low-grade cattle fodder. Polymerization of the extracted plant oil to produce a range of thermosetting plastics suitable for domestic appliances is also a possibility.

Political sensitivity over genetically modified organisms, and the fear of terrorism, has led to the development of a new research centre for the Institute in a fairly unpopulated region in the north of Scotland. A dedicated ISDN link is proposed with two universities involved in parallel research in the Home Counties, and it is deemed essential that all scientists involved with the project have permanent e-mail access to one another.

The scientific staff are housed in an accommodation block inside a compound protected by the military. Temporary guardhouse and barracks are established alongside the only road leading from the A6423 into the complex. The commanding officer and his staff also have access to the site network for security purposes.

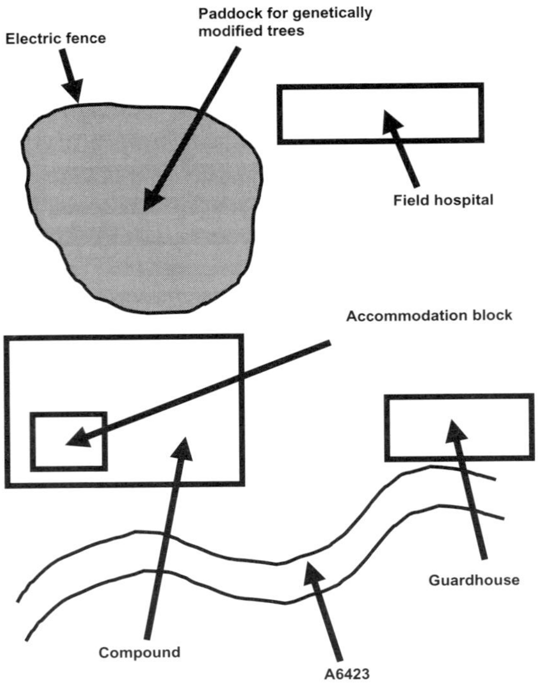

Figure 6.4 *The Research Institute for Forestry Innovation and Development*

At a fairly late stage in the construction of the research centre it is discovered that some of the modified trees are acquiring the ability to retract their roots and move slowly about the experimental woodland site. While this development is being investigated a specially fortified paddock, with triple electric fence, is hastily erected and the trees relocated.

Scientists working in the paddock need to keep in constant contact with their colleagues in the tissue laboratory. Later the RAF loans a field hospital when the trees begin to show signs of spitting venom if researchers approach within range.

The final layout of the site is as shown in Figure 6.4.

Discuss the use of wireless, and conventional, networking for the Research Institute for Forestry Innovation and Development.

Exercise 3: Encryption algorithms

Commercial security requires the use of sophisticated encryption, like the RSA algorithm. However, the very necessity for security involves intensive calculation which makes such methods difficult for illustrative use with students. An alternative is to develop concepts of encryption with algorithmic methods that lack the complexity that would be required in the real world. Such a method is developed in this exercise. It depends upon the behaviour of the exclusive OR operation, XOR, when it is combined with an encryption key. This can be compared with the use of a public (though not a private) key in commercially viable encryption.

The method of encryption shown here depends upon the properties of the logical operation exclusive OR. (Exclusive OR appears in books as either XOR or EOR, the latter presumably the preferred form for A.A. Milne's readership.) It is defined by the truth table:

p	q	p XOR q
0	0	0
0	1	1
1	0	1
1	1	0

It can be seen that exclusive OR is the same as inclusive OR except that it has a value of False if both p and q are true. In other words it really is exclusive. It means p is the case or q is the case, but not both of them are the case simultaneously.

It is interesting to see what happens if we attempt an extended truth table in which a fourth column has been added. In this column we perform a second exclusive OR, this time between the truth values (1 or 0) of the result (p XOR q) and q itself. This is equivalent to taking an XOR between p and q and then repeating it with q again. Initially the fourth column will be blank but we can fill it in by working systematically with the truth values of (p XOR q) and q that are already present in the other columns of the table.

We begin with a table like this:

p	q	p XOR q	(p XOR q) XOR q
0	0	0	
0	1	1	
1	0	1	
1	1	0	

First we shall decide what value should be filled in for the top location of the last column. For this row of the truth table the value of (p XOR q) can be seen to be 0 and the value of q is also 0. We know, from the truth table for XOR shown originally, that 0 XOR 0 is 0. So this is the value to add to the top of the column:

p	q	p XOR q	(p XOR q) XOR q
0	0	0	0
0	1	1	
1	0	1	
1	1	0	

Now we look at the second row and decide what value should be placed in the fourth column. For this row we can see that the value of (p XOR q) is 1 and the value of q is 1. So we have to work out the value of 1 XOR 1. The original table for XOR shows that this is 0. So we add 0 in the second row of the fourth column:

p	q	p XOR q	(p XOR q) XOR q
0	0	0	0
0	1	1	
0	1	0	1
1	1	0	

Next we check the third row. Here the value of (p XOR q) is 1 and the value of q is 0. So we have to work out 1 XOR 0. This is 1 and so this is the value that must be added to the third row of the fourth column:

p	q	p XOR q	(p XOR q) XOR q
0	0	0	0
0	1	1	0
1	0	1	1
1	1	0	

Finally we examine the fourth row of the truth table. For this row the value of (p XOR q) is 0 and the value of q is 1. This means we have to find the truth value of 0 XOR 1. This of course is 1. So 1 is the last value to add to the table:

p	q	p XOR q	(p XOR q) XOR q
0	0	0	0
0	1	1	0
1	0	1	1
1	1	0	1

At this point we compare the first and last columns of the table. They are identical. The truth table has shown that the truth values of p and of the apparently complicated expression (p XOR q) XOR q are identical in all cases. The expression is completely equivalent to just p by itself.

What does this mean in practice, and what significance does it have for encryption?

Well, in practical terms we can XOR a First number with a Second number to get a Third number. But then if we XOR the Third number with the Second number we get back to the first. Confused? This really does follow on from the result established by our truth table. Here it is shown with a pair of numbers 25 and 61. We shall XOR 25 with 61 and then XOR the result of this with 61 again. And we shall see that the result of the second exclusive OR is to return us to our initial value of 25.

In order to perform the exclusive OR using the truth table the decimal numbers must first be converted to binary.

If we convert 25 to binary we obtain:

25 = 16 + 8 + 1
   = 0001 1001

Next we convert the encryption key of 61 to binary:

61 = 32 + 16 + 8 + 4 + 1
   = 0011 1101

With both numbers in binary notation we can now combine them, bit by bit, in a 'bitwise' operation. First we find the XOR of the two bits 7, one from each binary number. Then we repeat with all the other pairs of bits: bits 6, bits 5 ... bits 0. For each pair we perform an exclusive OR to produce a new bit for the encrypted code. These bits can then be combined to created the new, coded number:

XOR-ing bit 7

Bit 7 in the number 25 = 0
Bit 7 in the encryption key 65 = 0
0 XOR 0 = 0
Bit 7 in the encrypted code = 0

XOR-ing bit 6

Bit 6 in the number 25 = 0
Bit 6 in the encryption key 65 = 0
0 XOR 0 = 0
Bit 6 in the encrypted code = 0

XOR-ing bit 5

Bit 5 in the number 25 = 0
Bit 5 in the encryption key 65 = 1
0 XOR 1 = 1
Bit 5 in the encrypted code = 1

XOR-ing bit 4

Bit 4 in the number 25 = 1
Bit 4 in the encryption key 65 = 1
1 XOR 1 = 0
Bit 4 in the encrypted code = 0

XOR-ing bit 3

Bit 3 in the number 25 = 1
Bit 3 in the encryption key 65 = 1
1 XOR 1 = 0
Bit 3 in the encrypted code = 0

XOR-ing bit 2

Bit 2 in the number 25 = 0

Bit 2 in the encryption key 65 = 1
0 XOR 1 = 1
Bit 2 in the encrypted code = 1

XOR-ing bit 1

Bit 1 in the number 25 = 0
Bit 1 in the encryption key 65 = 0
0 XOR 0 = 0
Bit 1 in the encrypted code = 0

XOR-ing bit 0

Bit 0 in the number 25 = 1
Bit 0 in the encryption key 65 = 1
1 XOR 1 = 0
Bit 0 in the encrypted code = 0

Summarizing:

Bit 7 of encrypted code = 0
Bit 6 of encrypted code = 0
Bit 5 of encrypted code = 1
Bit 4 of encrypted code = 0
Bit 3 of encrypted code = 0
Bit 2 of encrypted code = 1
Bit 1 of encrypted code = 0
Bit 0 of encrypted code = 0

Encrypted code = 0010 0100
= 32 + 4
=36

This shows that the result of performing an exclusive OR between 25 and 61 is to produce a new, encrypted, number of 36. For this to be a useful discovery we now have to show that, as claimed earlier, a second exclusive OR between 61 and 36 now gives us 25 again:

36 = 32 + 4
= 0010 0100

XOR-ing bit 7

Bit 7 in the encrypted code 36 = 0
Bit 7 in the decryption key 61 = 0
0 XOR 0 = 0
Bit 7 in the decrypted code = 0

XOR-ing bit 6

Bit 6 in the encrypted code 36 = 0
Bit 6 in the decryption key 61 = 0
0 XOR 0 = 0
Bit 6 in the decrypted code = 0

XOR-ing bit 5

Bit 5 in the encrypted code 36 = 1
Bit 5 in the decryption key 61 = 1
1 XOR 1 = 0
Bit 5 in the decrypted code = 0

XOR-ing bit 4

Bit 4 in the encrypted code 36 = 1
Bit 4 in the decryption key 61 = 0
1 XOR 0 = 1
Bit 4 in the decrypted code = 1

XOR-ing bit 3

Bit 3 in the encrypted code 36 = 0
Bit 3 in the decryption key 61 = 1
0 XOR 1 = 1
Bit 3 in the decrypted code = 1
XOR-ing bit 2

Bit 2 in the encrypted code 36 = 1
Bit 2 in the decryption key 61 = 1
1 XOR 1 = 0
Bit 2 in the decrypted code = 0

XOR-ing bit 1

Bit 1 in the encrypted code 36 = 0
Bit 1 in the decryption key 61 = 0
0 XOR 0 = 0
Bit 1 in the decrypted code = 0

XOR-ing bit 0

Bit 0 in the encrypted code 36 = 0
Bit 0 in the decryption key 61 = 1
0 XOR 1 = 1
Bit 0 in the decrypted code = 1

Summarizing:

Bit 7 of decrypted code = 0
Bit 6 of decrypted code = 0
Bit 5 of decrypted code = 0
Bit 4 of decrypted code = 1
Bit 3 of decrypted code = 1
Bit 2 of decrypted code = 0
Bit 1 of decrypted code = 0
Bit 0 of decrypted code = 1

Decrypted code = 0001 1001
= 16 + 8 + 1
= 25

So the double use of XOR has encrypted 25 into 36 and then decrypted 36 back to 25. Of course a single example is not quite the same as proof, but the general idea should be clear: by choosing a number, and an encryption key, and performing a series of XORs, numbers can be coded into an unrecognizable form. Then with the same number being used as a decryption key the coded numbers can be converted back again into their original form.

Once it is appreciated that letters can be encrypted, via the ASCII codes, by this method we have a way of concealing the content of a message to anybody who does not know what the decryption is.

For example, the capital letter T has an ASCII code of 84. In binary this is:

84 = 64 + 16 + 4
= 0101 0100

Suppose that 42 is chosen as the encryption key. In binary this is:

42 = 32 + 8 + 2
   = 0010 1010

If a bitwise XOR is carried out between 0101 0100 and 0010 1010 we obtain:

0 XOR 0 = 0
1 XOR 0 = 1
0 XOR 1 = 1
1 XOR 0 = 1
0 XOR 1 = 1
1 XOR 0 = 1
0 XOR 1 = 1
0 XOR 0 = 0

The new encrypted number is 0111 1110. Converting this code into decimal gives:

0111 1001 = 64 + 32 + 16 + 8 + 4 + 2
          = 126

So encrypting T with 42 as the key leads to 126 as the code.

Finally the conversion of 126 back into an ASCII code should be demonstrated:

126 = 64 + 32 + 16 + 8 + 4 + 2
    = 0111 1110

0 XOR 0 = 0
1 XOR 0 = 1
1 XOR 1 = 0
1 XOR 0 = 1
1 XOR 1 = 0
1 XOR 0 = 1
1 XOR 1 = 0
0 XOR 0 = 0

The decrypted number is therefore 64 + 16 + 4. Converting this into decimal gives 64, which is the ASCII code for capital T.

The method of encryption does work.

As an example of encryption using exclusive OR a short message (familiar to those taught to read by the phonics method, though not to the Fluff and Nip generation) is given below. The encryption key is again 42.

126, 98, 111, 10, 105, 107, 126, 10, 121, 107, 126, 10, 101, 100, 10, 126, 98, 111, 10, 103, 107, 126.

Encryption program

It is relatively easy to write a very short program which converts individual letters of a text message into coded numbers by performing an XOR between the ASCII codes of the letters and a selected key number. In the program illustrated here this simple program is extended in order to show the way in which the XOR-ed code is produced by a bitwise operation on the individual binary digits.

A typical screen display is shown in Figure 6.5.

The program listing is shown below.

Program listing

```
Option Explicit
Dim intDecimal As Integer
Dim intBinary1(7) As Integer
Dim intBinary2(7) As Integer
Dim intCounter1 As Integer
Dim intCounter2 As Integer
```

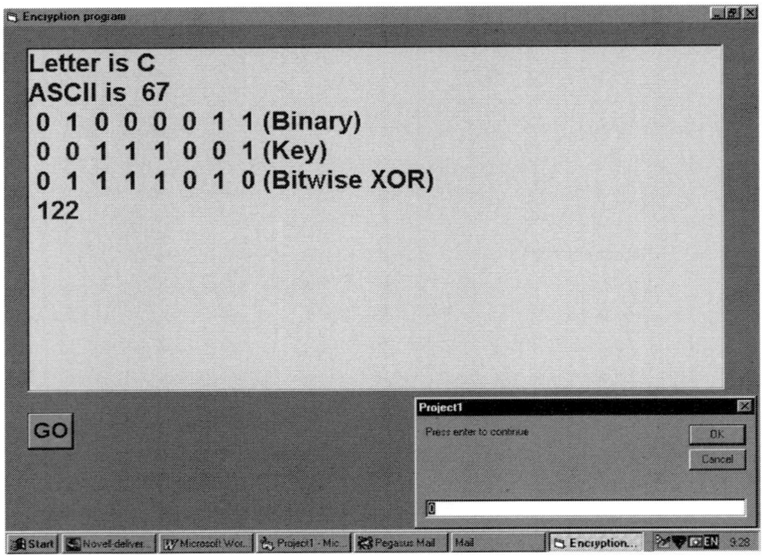

Figure 6.5

```
Private Sub Command1_Click()
'Encryption program
Dim intKey As Integer
Dim strTextstring As String
Dim strLetter As String
Dim intCode As Integer
Dim intDummy As Integer

'Enter number for key
intKey = InputBox("Enter number for key", , , 6500, 6400)
'Convert key into binary form
intDecimal = intKey
Convert1

'Enter text for encryption
strTextstring = InputBox("Enter text for encryption", , , 6500, 6400)

'Loop encrypts characters

For intCounter1 = 1 To Len(strTextstring)

strLetter = Mid$(strTextstring, intCounter1, 1)
intCode = Asc(strLetter)

'Show current letter in string entered
PicDisplay.Print "Letter is "; strLetter

'Show its ASCII code as decimal
PicDisplay.Print "ASCII is "; intCode

'Show code converted to binary
intDecimal = intCode
Convert2
For intCounter2 = 7 To 0 Step -1
PicDisplay.Print intBinary2(intCounter2);
Next intCounter2
PicDisplay.Print "(Binary)"
```

```
'Show key for encryption
For intCounter2 = 7 To 0 Step -1
PicDisplay.Print intBinary1(intCounter2);
Next intCounter2
PicDisplay.Print "(Key)"

'Show bitwise exclusive OR
For intCounter2 = 7 To 0 Step -1
If intBinary1(intCounter2)   intBinary2(intCounter2) Then
PicDisplay.Print 1;
Else
PicDisplay.Print 0;
End If
Next intCounter2
PicDisplay.Print "(Bitwise XOR)"

'Show encrypted decimal
PicDisplay.Print intCode Xor intKey

'Pause for next character
intDummy = InputBox("Press enter to continue", , 0, 6500, 6400)
PicDisplay.Cls
Next intCounter1

End Sub
Sub Convert1()

'Routine converts number used as key
'into bits held in an array to simulate
'a binary number

For intCounter1 = 7 To 0 Step -1
'Set bit if required
If intDecimal >= 2 ^ intCounter1 Then
intDecimal = intDecimal - 2 ^ intCounter1
intBinary1(intCounter1) = 1
End If
Next intCounter1

End Sub
Sub Convert2()

For intCounter2 = 7 To 0 Step -1
'Clear existing array location
intBinary2(intCounter2) = 0
'Set bit if required
If intDecimal >= 2 ^ intCounter2 Then
intDecimal = intDecimal - 2 ^ intCounter2
intBinary2(intCounter2) = 1
End If
Next intCounter2

End Sub
```

Program documentation

Several variables used in the program are declared in the general declarations area of the listing because they are present in a second procedure called by the main program. There are five variables used in this way. They are as follows.

The integer variable intDecimal is used to hold the value of a conventional decimal number which will be converted into a simulated binary format by the procedures Convert1 and Convert2. Actual binary numbers are not used by the program despite the intention to demonstrate to the user the bitwise binary operation, XOR. This dichotomy is resolved by creating values of 1 and 0 in integer arrays in a way which is superficially equivalent to actual binary. The technique is explained in detail later in this documentation:

```
Option Explicit
Dim intDecimal As Integer
```

Two integer arrays are used to hold the simulated binary values. These are intBinary1(), which represents the key used for the encryption, and intBinary2(). The latter stores the binary values for the ASCII code of each character of the input text in turn. Both arrays are declared in the general declarations area of the program:

```
Dim intBinary1(7) As Integer
Dim intBinary2(7) As Integer
```

Part of the program code involves nested For loops. The loop control variables for these are intCounter1 and intCounter2. Both are declared as integers:

```
Dim intCounter1 As Integer
Dim intCounter2 As Integer
```

Further declarations take place within the main procedure. The integer variable intKey is used to represent the encryption key entered by the user and the string variable strTextstring the passage of text that then has to be encrypted:

```
Private Sub Command1_Click()
'Encryption program
Dim intKey As Integer
Dim strTextstring As String
```

A separate variable, strLetter, is used for the individual letters of the message as they are extracted from the text string:

```
Dim strLetter As String
```

The ASCII code for each letter is assigned to a distinct variable, the integer variable intCode:

```
Dim intCode As Integer
```

Finally a 'dummy' variable is used to permit the program's execution to be stepped through. This allows the user to examine each bitwise operation in turn:

```
Dim intDummy As Integer
```

A prompt is given for the encryption key, which is then assigned to the integer variable intKey by the InputBox function. Note that, as a result of the adoption of 8-bit representation for the simulated binary numbers, the encryption key should not exceed 255. (No error trapping is included to prevent illicit values.):

```
'Enter number for key
intKey = InputBox("Enter number for key", , , 6500, 6400)
```

The encryption key is immediately converted to simulated binary form. The value of intKey has first to be copied to the additional variable intDecimal before the conversion procedure, Convert1, is called. After program execution has returned from this procedure the encryption key is present, in simulated binary form, in the array intBinary1():

```
'Convert key into binary form
intDecimal = intKey
Convert1
```

When the key has been entered the user is prompted to type in the passage which has to be encrypted. The InputBox is used to assign the passage to the variable strTextstring:

```
'Enter text for encryption
strTextstring = InputBox("Enter text for encryption", , , 6500, 6400)
```

The main program loop which converts the characters in strTextstring into encrypted form, using exclusive OR, now begins. As the number of characters in the passage is known in advance a FOR loop can be used. The upper limit of the loop is the number of characters in the passage. This number is determined by using the Len function:

```
'Loop encrypts characters
For intCounter1 = 1 To Len(strTextstring)
```

Each character in the entered string is temporarily assigned to the variable strLetter by using the Mid$ function:

```
strLetter = Mid$(strTextstring, intCounter1, 1)
```

The ASCII code of strLetter is then assigned to the integer variable intCode:

```
intCode = Asc(strLetter)
```

The program is intended to be as informative as possible, and to show each stage of the encryption process. This means that it is appropriate for each letter in turn to be shown on the display. The current letter will, of course, be held in the variable strLetter:

```
'Show current letter in string entered
PicDisplay.Print "Letter is "; strLetter
```

The next stage in explaining the process of encryption is to show the ASCII code of the letter. This is done by displaying the value of intCode:

```
'Show its ASCII code as decimal
PicDisplay.Print "ASCII is "; intCode
```

Next the letter's ASCII code must be converted into binary so that the bitwise exclusive OR can be illustrated. The ASCII code is converted to simulated binary form by first assigning the value of intCode to the variable intDecimal and then calling the procedure Convert2. This places the binary form of the ASCII code into the intBinary2() array:

```
'Show code converted to binary
intDecimal = intCode
Convert2
```

Once the conversion has taken place the ASCII code can be displayed again, this time as the binary equivalent to the decimal value which has already been shown. A For loop is used to print out all of the array locations in intBinary2(). Note that the second loop control variable, intCounter2, must be used because this code is nested inside the outer loop controlled by intCounter1.

The use of a semicolon in the loop means that all of the simulated bits will be placed on the same line of the display. The loop steps from 7 to 0 as a result of the way that the conversion to binary has taken place in Convert2. This will be explained subsequently:

```
For intCounter2 = 7 To 0 Step -1
PicDisplay.Print intBinary2(intCounter2);
Next intCounter2
```

An explanatory "Binary" makes the display easier to follow. (As well as tidying up the effect of the final semicolon in the loop!):

```
PicDisplay.Print "(Binary)"
```

The encryption key, in its binary form, is displayed beneath the ASCII code, and in-line with it, in order to make it clear how the bitwise XOR functions. The key is displayed in exactly the same way as the ASCII code of the letter. A For loop steps from 7 to 0, this time taking values from the intBinary1() array. The explanation "Key" is placed after the sequence of simulated binary digits:

```
'Show key for encryption
For intCounter2 = 7 To 0 Step -1
PicDisplay.Print intBinary1(intCounter2);
Next intCounter2
PicDisplay.Print "(Key)"
```

The display is now ready for the bitwise operation. A further For loop steps from 7 to 0, this time comparing the pairs of simulated bits in both the intBinary1() and intBinary2() arrays. A simple rule is used to produce the exclusive OR. If the corresponding bits are different a value of 1 is displayed. If the bits are the same a 0 is shown instead:

```
'Show bitwise exclusive OR
For intCounter2 = 7 To 0 Step -1
If intBinary1(intCounter2)   intBinary2(intCounter2) Then
PicDisplay.Print 1;
Else
PicDisplay.Print 0;
End If
Next intCounter2
```

The text "Bitwise XOR" is placed at the end of the simulated byte:

```
PicDisplay.Print "(Bitwise XOR)"
```

After the encrypted value is shown as binary it is repeated as a decimal. This is the coded output of the program and the user is expected to write it down. In its present form, the program does not record any continuous output.

The decimal code is not found, of course, by converting the simulated binary digits. Instead the calculation reverts to the initial decimal values of both the ASCII code, intCode, and the encryption key, intKey, and performs an exclusive OR operation directly between the two. This is possible because XOR is available in Basic:

```
'Show encrypted decimal
PicDisplay.Print intCode Xor intKey
```

The program execution is then delayed so the user can study how the encrypted value has been (apparently) produced by the bitwise operation. The delay is produced by a spurious request for an input. All this does is use the InputBox function to assign a default value of zero to the unrequired variable intDummy:

```
'Pause for next character
intDummy = InputBox("Press enter to continue", , 0, 6500, 6400)
PicDisplay.Cls
```

The For loop which has examined all of the characters in the text string, and the main procedure, then both end:

```
Next intCounter1

End Sub
```

The first of the two procedures used to create the simulated binary numbers then begins. This procedure, Convert1, produces the binary form for the encryption key that has been entered and places the bits into the intBinary1() array:

```
Sub Convert1()

'Routine converts number used as key
'into bits held in an array to simulate
'a binary number
```

The way in which the binary number is found is by a process of attempted subtraction, from the decimal, of decreasing powers of 2: 128, 64, 32, 16, 8, 4, 2 and 1. It relates directly to the fact that decimal numbers can be expressed as a suitable addition selected from this range of numbers. (Note that here we are deliberately restricting the decimal numbers to those that can be represented by 8-bit binary.)

As an example we take 201 as the number to be converted into binary. It can be seen that 201 is the sum of these powers of 2:

200 = 128 + 64 + 8 + 1

The way in which a conversion to binary can be achieved by repeated subtraction of powers of 2 from a number can be illustrated, using 201, as follows:

Stage 1: Power of 2 = 128
Decimal number being tested: 201
Can 128 be subtracted?
Yes. Record 1 to indicate this; current 'binary' is 1
Perform subtraction: 201 – 128 = 73
Decimal number is now 73

Stage 2: Power of 2 = 64
Decimal number being tested: 73
Can 64 be subtracted?
Yes. Record 1 to indicate this; current 'binary' is 11
Perform subtraction: 73 – 64 = 9
Decimal number is now 9

Stage 3: Power of 2 = 32
Decimal number being tested: 9
Can 32 be subtracted?
No. Record 0 to indicate this; current 'binary' is 110
Do not perform subtraction by 32
Decimal number is still 9

Stage 4: Power of 2 = 16
Decimal number being tested: 9
Can 16 be subtracted?
No. Record 0 to indicate this; current 'binary' is 1100
Do not perform subtraction by 16
Decimal number is still 9

Stage 5: Power of 2 = 8
Decimal number being tested: 9
Can 8 be subtracted?
Yes. Record 1 to indicate this; current 'binary' is 11001
Perform subtraction: 9 – 8 = 1
Decimal number is now 1

Stage 6: Power of 2 = 4
Decimal number being tested: 1
Can 4 be subtracted?

No. Record 0 to indicate this; current 'binary' is 110010
Do not perform subtraction by 4
Decimal number is still 1

Stage 7: Power of 2 = 2
Decimal number being tested: 1
Can 2 be subtracted?
No. Record 0 to indicate this; current 'binary' is 1100100
Do not perform subtraction by 2
Decimal number is still 1

Stage 8: Power of 2 = 1
Decimal number being tested: 1
Can 1 be subtracted?
Yes. Record 1 to indicate this; current 'binary' is 11001001
Perform subtraction: 1 – 1 = 0
Decimal number is now 0

It can be seen that this method does produce the required binary, just by recording a 1 for a successful subtraction and a zero when a subtraction cannot take place.

Note also that at the end of this process the decimal number has become zero. This is why it is important to work with a copy of the original number.

In the program the algorithm described above is implemented in a For loop. By stepping the control variable from 7 to 0, the required powers of 2 for the repeated subtraction are generated simply by raising 2 to the power of the control variable to give 2 ^ intCounter1. An If Then structure then assigns a 1 to the appropriate array location in intBinary1() depending upon whether the power of 2 has been subtracted or not. The array location is identified by the value of the loop control variable:

```
For intCounter1 = 7 To 0 Step -1
'Set bit if required
If intDecimal >= 2 ^ intCounter1 Then
intDecimal = intDecimal - 2 ^ intCounter1
intBinary1(intCounter1) = 1
End If
Next intCounter1

End Sub
```

A second binary conversion procedure is used to produce the simulated binary for the ASCII code of each letter. This procedure is almost identical to the previous one, and it uses the same algorithm. The simulated binary bits have, of course, to be placed in the separate array intBinary2(). In addition this array needs to have all its locations reset to zero before the attempted subtraction of the power of 2. This is because values of 1 from an earlier letter could still be present:

```
Sub Convert2()

For intCounter2 = 7 To 0 Step -1
'Clear existing array location
intBinary2(intCounter2) = 0
'Set bit if required
If intDecimal >= 2 ^ intCounter2 Then
intDecimal = intDecimal - 2 ^ intCounter2
intBinary2(intCounter2) = 1
End If
Next intCounter2

End Sub
```

Decryption program

It would be possible to decode the encrypted numbers produced by the last program by hand. It is far more convenient, though, to have a program which does the decryption automatically. A program which does this is given below.

Also here is a screen dump showing decryption corresponding to the previous diagram (see Figure 6.6). There the capital letter C became an encrypted code of 122 using an encryption key of 57. In the second screen dump the reverse takes place. A decryption key of 57 has been entered followed by the code 122. As intended this value decrypts and reverts to capital C.

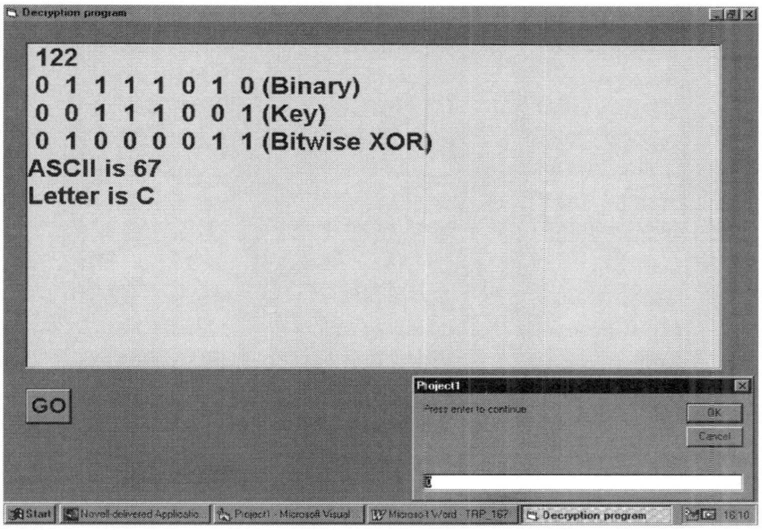

Figure 6.6

Program listing

```
Option Explicit
Dim intDecimal As Integer
Dim intBinary1(7) As Integer
Dim intBinary2(7) As Integer
Dim intCounter1 As Integer
Dim intCounter2 As Integer

Private Sub Command1_Click()
'Decryption program
Dim intKey As Integer
Dim intCode As Integer
Dim intDummy As Integer

'Enter number for key
intKey = InputBox("Enter number for key", , , 6500, 6400)

'Convert key into binary form
intDecimal = intKey
Convert1

'Loop decrypts codes

Do

intCode = InputBox("Enter code number", , , 6500, 6400)

If intCode   999 Then

'Show code number
PicDisplay.Print intCode
```

```
'Show code converted to binary
intDecimal = intCode
Convert2
For intCounter2 = 7 To 0 Step -1
PicDisplay.Print intBinary2(intCounter2);
Next intCounter2
PicDisplay.Print "(Binary)"

'Show key for decryption
For intCounter2 = 7 To 0 Step -1
PicDisplay.Print intBinary1(intCounter2);
Next intCounter2
PicDisplay.Print "(Key)"

'Show bitwise exclusive OR
For intCounter2 = 7 To 0 Step -1
If intBinary1(intCounter2)   intBinary2(intCounter2) Then
PicDisplay.Print 1;
Else
PicDisplay.Print 0;
End If
Next intCounter2
PicDisplay.Print "(Bitwise XOR)"

'Show decimal value
PicDisplay.Print "ASCII is";
PicDisplay.Print intCode Xor intKey

'Show decoded letter
PicDisplay.Print "Letter is ";
PicDisplay.Print Chr$(intCode Xor intKey)

'Pause for next character
intDummy = InputBox("Press enter to continue", , 0, 6500, 6400)
PicDisplay.Cls

End If

Loop Until intCode = 999

End Sub
Sub Convert1()

'Routine converts number used as key
'into bits held in an array to simulate
'a binary number

For intCounter1 = 7 To 0 Step -1
'Set bit if required
If intDecimal >= 2 ^ intCounter1 Then
intDecimal = intDecimal - 2 ^ intCounter1
intBinary1(intCounter1) = 1
End If
Next intCounter1

End Sub
Sub Convert2()

For intCounter2 = 7 To 0 Step -1
'Clear existing array location
```

```
intBinary2(intCounter2) = 0
'Set bit if required
If intDecimal >= 2 ^ intCounter2 Then
intDecimal = intDecimal - 2 ^ intCounter2
intBinary2(intCounter2) = 1
End If
Next intCounter2

End Sub
```

Program documentation

The decryption program is very similiar to the previous listing. It performs the same operations but in a different order. The encypted code is entered, one number at a time, by the user. The program then performs an exclusive OR to recreate the ASCII code of the original letter. This is displayed, followed by the letter itself. The process of the bitwise exclusive OR is shown by displaying simulated binary digits, just as in the earlier program.

The program listing repeats much of the previous code, although the order of sections is different. In addition some detail, like entering the text to be encrypted, is omitted.

As before an integer variable, intDecimal, is declared to be used in conjunction with the Convert1 and Convert2 procedures. Two integer arrays, intBinary1 and intBinary2, are declared for the two binary simulations and two loop control variables, intCounter1 and intCounter2, are declared. All of this is in the general declarations area of the program:

```
Option Explicit
Dim intDecimal As Integer
Dim intBinary1(7) As Integer
Dim intBinary2(7) As Integer
Dim intCounter1 As Integer
Dim intCounter2 As Integer
```

Further variables are declared for the decryption key, intKey, for the individual code numbers to be decrypted, intCode, and for the dummy variable used to step through the program, intDummy:

```
Private Sub Command1_Click()
'Decryption program
Dim intKey As Integer
Dim intCode As Integer
Dim intDummy As Integer
```

The user is prompted to enter the decryption key:

```
'Enter number for key
intKey = InputBox("Enter number for key", , , 6500, 6400)
```

This is then converted into binary and placed in the intBinary1() array by the Convert1 procedure:

```
'Convert key into binary form
intDecimal = intKey
Convert1
```

A loop then begins which will convert each coded number individually. The program structure differs here from the encryption program above. In that program the entire passage to be encrypted was entered before coding began. This meant that the exact number of characters to be coded was known in advance. As a result the main controlling loop was an unconditional For. In contrast it is assumed that when the decryption program is run the user will not know how many coded letters are present in the encrypted message. He/she will just keep entering the numbers until the end of the message is reached. This means that the controlling loop is a conditional Do. The exit condition for the loop is a value of 999 entered by the user. (The user has to know this. No screen prompt has been provided!):

```
'Loop decrypts codes

Do
```

The user enters the coded number as the variable intCode. If this is not 999 the decryption takes place within an If Then code block:

```
intCode = InputBox("Enter code number", , , 6500, 6400)

If intCode   999 Then
```

First the code itself is displayed:

```
'Show code number
PicDisplay.Print intCode
```

This decimal number is then converted to simulated binary by calling the procedure Convert2. This places the simulated bits into the intBinary2() array:

```
'Show code converted to binary
intDecimal = intCode
Convert2
```

A For loop then displays these array values and the text "Binary" is added at the end:

```
For intCounter2 = 7 To 0 Step -1
PicDisplay.Print intBinary2(intCounter2);
Next intCounter2
PicDisplay.Print "(Binary)"
```

A similar loop shows the decryption key as binary:

```
'Show key for decryption
For intCounter2 = 7 To 0 Step -1
PicDisplay.Print intBinary1(intCounter2);
Next intCounter2
PicDisplay.Print "(Key)"
```

As in the encryption program, a further loop calculates the bitwise XORed values by comparing the corresponding values in the intBinary1() and intBinary2() arrays. If they are different a 1 is displayed. If they are the same a 0 is shown instead:

```
'Show bitwise exclusive OR
For intCounter2 = 7 To 0 Step -1
If intBinary1(intCounter2)   intBinary2(intCounter2) Then
PicDisplay.Print 1;
Else
PicDisplay.Print 0;
End If
Next intCounter2
PicDisplay.Print "(Bitwise XOR)"
```

The true decrypted value, as opposed to the simulated binary value, is then calculated by performing an XOR between intCode and intKey. This is the ASCII of the letter:

```
'Show decimal value
```

```
PicDisplay.Print "ASCII is";
PicDisplay.Print intCode Xor intKey
```

Next the letter itself can be shown:

```
'Show decoded letter
PicDisplay.Print "Letter is ";
PicDisplay.Print Chr$(intCode Xor intKey)
```

As in the encryption program a delay is created by waiting for a value to be assigned to intDummy:

```
'Pause for next character
intDummy = InputBox("Press enter to continue", , 0, 6500, 6400)
PicDisplay.Cls
```

The If Then block then ends:

```
End If
```

The conditional loop will end when 999 is entered:

```
Loop Until intCode = 999

End Sub
```

The creation of binary values is achieved as in the encryption program by the procedures Convert1 and Convert2:

```
Sub Convert1()

'Routine converts number used as key
'into bits held in an array to simulate
'a binary number

For intCounter1 = 7 To 0 Step -1
'Set bit if required
If intDecimal >= 2 ^ intCounter1 Then
intDecimal = intDecimal - 2 ^ intCounter1
intBinary1(intCounter1) = 1
End If
Next intCounter1

End Sub
Sub Convert2()

For intCounter2 = 7 To 0 Step -1
'Clear existing array location
intBinary2(intCounter2) = 0
'Set bit if required
If intDecimal >= 2 ^ intCounter2 Then
intDecimal = intDecimal - 2 ^ intCounter2
intBinary2(intCounter2) = 1
End If
Next intCounter2

End Sub
```

6.3 Tutor's resources

Internet search on bridges, routers, hubs and switches etc.
Useful Internet glossaries

Network hardware	
Practically Networked	Router? Bridge? Switch? Hub? What's the difference? http://www.practicallynetworked.com/networking/bridge_types.htm
Surecom	HUB/Switch FAQ http://www.surecom-net.com/support/faq/faq-hubs.htm#q2
Surecom	Internet Router FAQ http://www.surecom-net.com/support/faq/faq-internet.htm
Surecom	NIC FAQ http://www.surecom-net.com/support/faq/faq-nic.htm
Daryl Banttari	Daryl's TCP/IP Primer http://www.tcpipprimer.com/section.cfm
JV Fields	James's TCP/IP FAQ – Understanding Network Hardware http://www.camden411.com/tcpipfaq/hardware.html
Wright State University	LAN Refresher http://www.cs.wright.edu/~pmateti/Courses/499/LAN/
Back Office Systems	Hubs and switching http://backofficesystems.com/tips/network/router.htm
Back Office Systems	Internet Protocols http://backofficesystems.com/tips/ip/Default.htm
Brian Brown	Networking Fundamentals http://www.cit.ac.nz/smac/networks/default.htm

Glossaries	
HDT Team spa – High Design Technology for Telecommunications	Computing Glossary http://www.hdtteam.it/glossario/a.htm
CNET.com	CNET glossary http://www.cnet.com/Resources/Info/Glossary/
Internet.com	webopedia http://www.pcwebopedia.com/
University of Chicago	A Glossary of Computer Related Terms http://www-ccs.uchicago.edu/technotes/misc/Glossary/

6.4 Network assignment

What you are required to do

As an independent IT consultant, you have been asked to advise on a network connection to suit a small company. This company is outlined below. After an unhappy experience with an ISP, they have decided to run their own Internet connection and servers. Rather than specify a single solution, you are asked to provide the pros and cons of different solutions and to present these at a meeting with the company, where the decision about the next step will be made. It is not intended at this stage to decide on the final solution, simply to present to the company the main options before a specialist network company is employed.

Hammer and Tong Co. Ltd

Birmingham-based Hammer and Tong Co. Ltd supplies small tools to the engineering industry. They were set up in 1896 and the firm has been in the same family ever since. Their distribution is almost exclusively mail order. In 1998 they had an e-commerce package put together for them by an external company, this web-based system generally works very well and Hammer and Tong have come to rely on this form of business. Employing 30 people, they do not have a dedicated IT specialist on site but five of the staff are able to update databases and to carry out day-to-day running of a computer system. They already have a peer-to-peer LAN that connects to their old ISP using a single modem, used mainly for e-mail and updating the e-commerce database. Currently all the network traffic is handled by their ISP but unfortunately they have recently become unreliable. They had started to blame the e-commerce package for a series of failures but Hammer and Tong believe that the fault lies with the ISP. Hammer and Tong have decided not to rely on a third party for what has become a core part of their business so they require a system to provide the following performance:

1. On average, 40 orders are processed each day, the peak being approximately 100 orders on a Monday morning reducing to about five on a Friday afternoon. Previous experience shows that for every order, potential customers refer to their website at least 10 times giving an average hit rate of 400 hits per day but a peak of 1000 hits on a Monday morning.
2. The website software has been designed to load quickly so has a low bandwidth requirement, a typical 'look' at the website requiring about 80 kb of data including images. High-resolution images of products are available but most customers are regulars so these are not called upon very often. These images are on average 140 kb each.
3. Hammer and Tong use a third party banking house to collect on-line payments but they are concerned that hackers could gain entry to their system so a good level of security is required.
4. Profitability in the engineering sector has been lower than previous years. Whilst the cost of the network link is not the first priority, it will be examined very carefully before any decision is made.

What you must deliver
1. Recommendations about the network connection to the outside world.
2. Recommendations on security.

Possible solutions
High bandwidth network connection possibilities:

- Cable
- ISDN
- DSL
- Satellite
- Leased line

Cable

Speed. The cable system was designed and installed for one-way TV signal delivery, the download bandwidth is high but uploading data is often difficult, not due to the cabling bandwidth but design difficulties with the installed equipment at the cable company. There are specifications such as MCNS (Multimedia Cable Network System) and DOCSIS (Data over Cable Service Interface Specification) but not all cable companies can offer these. Most are able to supply good bandwidth for download but require a modem for uploads. This situation will change, possibly in the near future, but the cable companies have been slow to offer high-speed net access.

Security. To connect to a client, most cable companies use the 75 ohm coaxial cable that is similar to the old 'thick' Ethernet cable. Cable modems generally use 10 baseT (Ethernet) and run TCP/IP over what is in effect a small LAN. This means that one connection is shared with other users, creating a security risk so a firewall would have to be used to avoid this risk (see Figures 6.7 and 6.8).

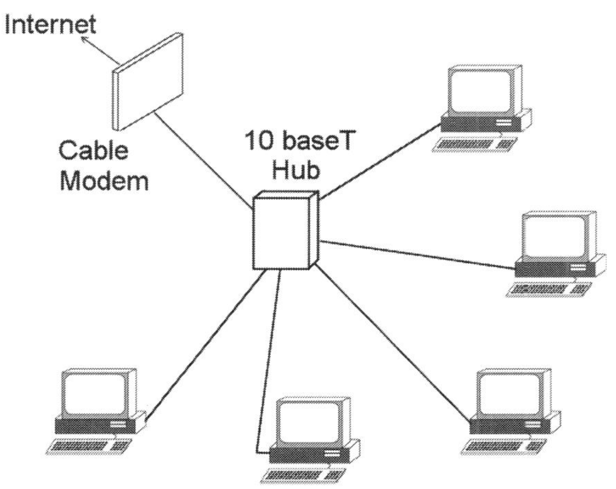

Figure 6.7 *Insecure cable connection*

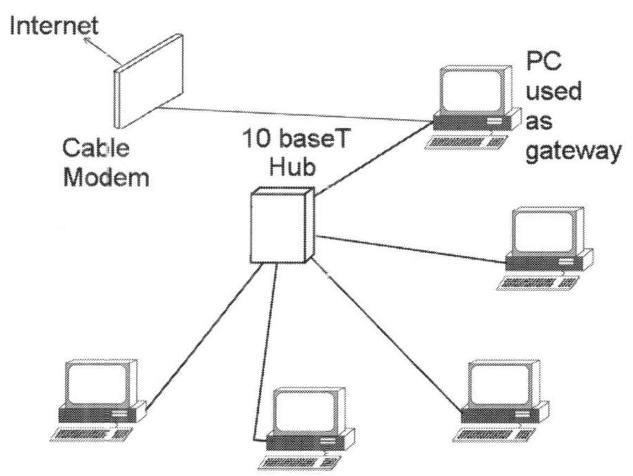

Figure 6.8 *Secure cable connection*

Effect on the LAN topology. A cable modem connection will allow several computers to be connected (often not allowed with xDSL). This would be insecure if it was done simply via a 10 baseT hub, a better solution would be to attach a PC to act as a gateway and to attach this to a hub. The gateway can act as a firewall.

Cable is aimed at heavy 'home' use and many cable providers will block the TCP/IP ports used to run web servers etc. Currently a cable connection is not a viable solution but may be in the future particularly in those areas where the cable laid into premises was fibre.

ISDN

ISDN was designed as a digital telephone system but has been adopted to run data communications. It requires that 'calls' are set up for each communication session so is not suitable for running a web service.

DSL

The POTS (Plain Old Telephone System) was designed for a bandwidth of about 3 kHz. This bandwidth applies to the whole channel, i.e. the connection from one telephone to the next. It was realized that the 'local loop', i.e. the copper wire from the exchange to the subscriber, had a far higher bandwidth provided it is short (a few kilometres depending on which DSL standard is used). DSL or xDSL is the name given to a range of communication standards designed to carry voice and data traffic over the local loop. It is not available in all areas, a check can be run at www.bt.com/adsl to find out. The current xDSL standard that is becoming available in the UK is ADSL and the best business package will provide a bandwidth of 1 Mbit/sec download and 256 kbits/sec upload but some providers will block the TCP/IP ports used to run web servers etc.

Satellite

Although download speeds can be as high as 4 Mbits/sec, the upload speed of a satellite link is usually via a normal modem so is not suitable for running a web server.

Leased line

Speed. A leased line is a permanently made, 'always on' connection; the leasing is usually from a telecommunications company. It is normal to have a line to an ISP that is in turn connected via high bandwidth leased lines to the rest of the Internet backbone.

The most basic leased line will provide 64 kbits/sec increasing in 64 k increments. More expensive lines running SONET (Synchronous Optical Networking) run at 51.84 Mbits/sec and increase in 51.84 Mbit increments. Unlike DSL and cable modems, leased lines are aimed squarely at businesses and usually come with a range of permanent TCP/IP addresses and fixed domain names.

Security and its effect on the LAN topology. To achieve a reasonable degree of security a firewall is required. If this is placed between the router and the rest of the internal network, it would not be practical to run a web server. The better but more expensive option is to have a 'demilitarized zone' as in Figure 6.10. Here the web and e-mail servers are outside the firewall that protects the internal LAN but are under the protection of a dedicated firewall of their own. This will result in 'public' and 'private' parts of the network. One of the higher costs associated with a DMZ is the requirement to have specialized security experts set up the entire network; it is not a trivial task.

The main recommendation would be to invest in a 128 kbits/sec leased line, the additional hardware of firewalls, servers etc. and to budget for specialized people to configure the whole system. From the

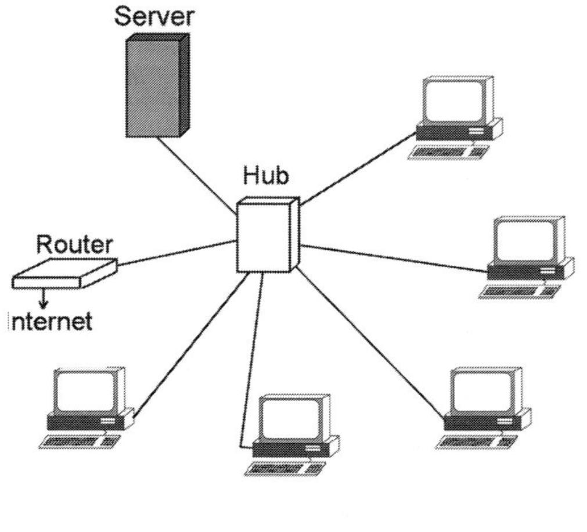

Figure 6.9 *Insecure leased line connection*

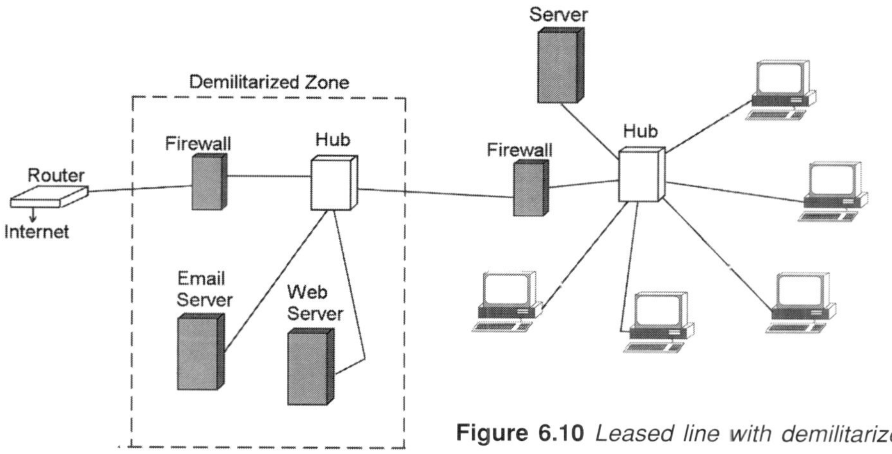

Figure 6.10 *Leased line with demilitarized zone*

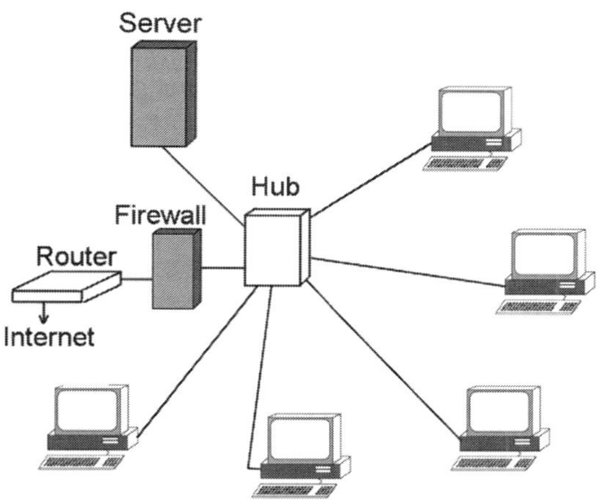

Figure 6.11 *Basic secure leased line connection*

figures describing the likely hit rate on the website, it would seem logical to provide a minimum bandwidth of 64 kbits/sec. This is calculated from the peak hit rate of 1000 hits in a morning translating into 250 hits per hour or about 4 hits per minute. If each hit requires the upload over the network of 80 kb of data (800 kbits) then $4 \times 800 = 3200$ kbits per minute or 53 kbits/sec is required.

This figure of 53 kbits/sec is close to the maximum bandwidth of the line and does not take into consideration any other traffic occurring at this peak time such as customers requiring the higher resolution image etc. If the e-business is to grow it is vital that potential customers very rarely find they have a slow response. For this reason it would be better to specify 128 kbits/sec as the minimum bandwidth and to take an option on increasing this to 256 kbits/sec when required.

Appendix A: Hex, binary and other number bases

As with many ideas in mathematics, practice makes perfect. Whilst the *HNC Computing* units do not specifically require fluency with number conversions, most people will find that such fluency is very useful. The idea of the sections presented here is to provide sufficient practice to achieve this fluency.

In 'normal' numbers, the value 137 equals $(1 \times 10^2) + (3 \times 10^1) + (7 \times 10^0)$ or $100 + 30 + 7$. Set out as numbers by position we get:

10^2	10^1	10^0
1	3	7

Each column represents the next power of 10. We only use 10 because people are born with 10 fingers, the system works just the same with any positive integer. If we use 8 as the number base (octal numbers), the columns will have the values 8^3, 8^2, 8^1, 8^0 so octal 137 would be $(1 \times 8^2) + (3 \times 8^1) + (7 \times 8^0)$ or, $64 + 24 + 7 = 95$ in decimal. As another example, if we used numbers to the base 12, each column would have values 12^3, 12^2, 12^1, 12^0 so 137 to base 12 in decimal would be $(1 \times 12^2) - (3 \times 12^1) + (7 \times 12^0)$ or $144 + 36 + 7 = 187$. Remember that any number to the power 0 is 1, so $9^0 = 1$ etc.

For a given number base, the same number of symbols are required so in decimal we use the 10 symbols 0–9, in octal we use 0–7, etc. The use of number bases over 10 is sometimes seen as awkward as we have to use letters as number symbols. Hexadecimal (or hex) numbers use 0–9 and A–F, giving a total of 16 symbols. Once you get used to this idea, seeing numbers written as 5DA is not a problem as it simply means $(5 \times 16^2) + (13 \times 16^1) + (10 \times 16^0)$ or $(5 \times 256) + (13 \times 16) + (10 \times 1) = 1498$ in decimal. The trick is to remember that A = 10, B = 11 etc. Binary numbers are simply to the base 2 so we need only two symbols, 0 and 1, the system of numbers by position is exactly the same. The binary value $100110 = (1 \times 2^5) + (0 \times 2^4) + (0 \times 2^3) + (1 \times 2^2) + (1 \times 2^1) + (0 \times 2^0)$ or 38 decimal.

Exercise 1

Complete the values in the correct number base. Answer shown at the end of this section.

Binary	*Octal*	*Decimal*	*Hex*
111111011	773		1FB
10100001	241		A1
10111000	270	184	
11000100	304	196	
111001111	717	463	
100111010			13A
110001100			18C
111100001	741		
10011000	230		
	637	415	19F
	6471	3385	D39
			C0C
			209
110110011010			
100010101101			
		1197	
	2132		
	10054		
110011010110			
			98EF
	21657		
		39780	
			5AAD
11100010110000			
		33247	

There is no point in using a calculator to do the calculations but using one to check your answers is a good idea. Most calculators will not convert decimal to binary for numbers above 511, this includes Excel 97 using the DEC2BIN function. The calculator that comes with Windows 98, if set to 'Scientific' mode, will work in binary for numbers up to 2^{32} or 4 294 967 295. This is 11111111111111111111111111111111 in binary!

Exercise 2

There are no errors in the additions below. What number base is used in each case? Answer shown at the end of the section.

A. 2 + 7 = 10
B. 2 + 4 = 10
C. 325 + 170 = 515
D. 121 + 212 = 1110

Direct conversion of hex to binary to hex

You should practice converting binary to hex and hex to binary directly. Binary to hex is very easy, simply split the binary number into groups of four digits starting at the right-hand side then convert each group into the hex digit.

Example: 101101010000111010 split into groups is 10 1101 0100 0011 1010. This is shown on the table:

10	1101	0100	0011	1010
2	D	4	3	A

so 101101010000111010 binary = 2D43A hex

Going the other way is just as easy, write down the binary for each of the hex digits.

3EB5A is 11111010111011010

Hex	3	E	B	5	A
Decimal	3	14	11	5	10
Binary	11	1110	1011	101	1010

Direct conversion of octal to binary to octal

The same system as above works for octal numbers, only split the binary into groups of 3 instead of 4.

(This will work for numbers to base 4; in this case, split the binary into groups of 2. The more general case is to work number bases to integer powers of 2, i.e. 2, 4, 8, 16, 32, etc. To work with number base 32, split into groups of 5, i.e. $2^5 = 32$.)

Conversion using successive division

As shown in the *HNC Computing* book, numbers can be converted by successive division. Here is another example:

The number 3823 = 111011101111 in binary, looking from the bottom of the remainder column.

		Base	*Quotient*	*Remainder*
Number =	3823	2	1911	1
Previous quotient	1911	2	955	1
""	955	2	477	1
""	477	2	238	1
""	238	2	119	0
""	119	2	59	1
""	59	2	29	1
""	29	2	14	1
""	14	2	7	0
""	7	2	3	1
""	3	2	1	1
""	1	2	0	1

The previous table was made using a simple Excel spreadsheet. If the number 3823 is placed in cell A2, the formulas are:

	A	*B*	*C*	*D*
1	Decimal	Base	Quotient	Remainder
2	3823	2	=INT((A2/B2))	=MOD(A2,B2)
3	=C2	2	=INT((A3/B3))	=MOD(A3,B3)
4	=C3	2	=INT((A4/B4))	=MOD(A4,B4)
5	=C4	2	=INT((A5/B5))	=MOD(A5,B5)
6	=C5	2	=INT((A6/B6))	=MOD(A6,B6)
7	=C6	2	=INT((A7/B7))	=MOD(A7,B7)
8	=C7	2	=INT((A8/B8))	=MOD(A8,B8)
9	=C8	2	=INT((A9/B9))	=MOD(A9,B9)
10	=C9	2	=INT((A10/B10))	=MOD(A10,B10)
11	=C10	2	=INT((A11/B11))	=MOD(A11,B11)
12	=C11	2	=INT((A12/B12))	=MOD(A12,B12)
13	=C12	2	=INT((A13/B13))	=MOD(A13,B13)

Simply changing the base value to 8 to use octal numbers, you get from the same spreadsheet:

Decimal	*Base*	*Quotient*	*Remainder*
3823	8	477	7
477	8	59	5
59	8	7	3
7	8	0	7

So 3823 decimal is 7357 octal.

To use this spreadsheet for number bases higher than 10 you would have to wrap the formulas in the right-hand column with the DEC2HEX function like this: =DEC2HEX(MOD(A2,B2)). Using this you get:

Decimal	*Base*	*Quotient*	*Remainder*
3823	16	238	F
238	16	14	E
14	16	0	E

So 3823 decimal = EEF hex. This gets over any number restrictions in Excel.

Answers

Exercise 1

Binary	*Octal*	*Decimal*	*Hex*
111111011	773	507	1FB
10100001	241	161	A1
10111000	270	184	B8
11000100	304	196	C4
111001111	717	463	1CF
100111010	472	314	13A
110001100	614	396	18C
111100001	741	481	1E1
10011000	230	152	98
110011111	637	415	19F
110100111001	6471	3385	D39
110000001100	6014	3084	COC
1000001001	1011	521	209
110110011010	6632	3482	D9A
100010101101	4255	2221	8AD
10010101101	2255	1197	4AD
10001011010	2132	1114	45A
1000000101100	10054	4140	102C
110011010110	6326	3286	CD6
1001100011101111	114357	39151	98EF
10001110101111	21657	9135	23AF
1001101101100100	115544	39780	9B64
101101010101101	55255	23213	5AAD
11100010110000	34260	14512	38B0
1000000111011111	100737	33247	81DF

Exercise 2

A. 2 + 7 = 10 uses number base 9
B. 2 + 4 = 10 uses number base 6
C. 325 + 170 = 515 uses number base 8 (octal)
D. 121 + 212 = 1110 uses number base 3

Appendix B: ASCII and Unicode

Whilst the *HNC Computing* units do not specifically require fluency in ASCII, most people will find that such fluency is very useful. The idea of the sections presented here is to provide sufficient practice to achieve this fluency.

Below is the famous part of a poem called *For the Fallen* by Laurence Binyon. A file containing just this text was created using Notepad under Windows.

They shall grow not old, as we that are left grow old;
Age shall not weary them, nor the years condemn.
At the going down of the sun and in the morning
We will remember them.

A hex dump of this file is shown below. The 16 left-hand columns show the hex values of each byte in the file, the right-hand 16 characters show printable text or "." for non-printable or CTRL characters.

```
09 54 68 65 79 20 73 68 61 6C 6C 20 67 72 6F 77  .They shall grow
20 6E 6F 74 20 6F 6C 64 2C 20 61 73 20 77 65 20   not old, as we
74 68 61 74 20 61 72 65 20 6C 65 66 74 20 67 72  that are left gr
6F 77 20 6F 6C 64 3B 0D 0A 09 41 67 65 20 73 68  ow old;...Age sh
61 6C 6C 20 6E 6F 74 20 77 65 61 72 79 20 74 68  all not weary th
65 6D 2C 20 6E 6F 72 20 74 68 65 20 79 65 61 72  em, nor the year
73 20 63 6F 6E 64 65 6D 6E 2E 0D 0A 09 41 74 20  s condemn....At
74 68 65 20 67 6F 69 6E 67 20 64 6F 77 6E 20 6F  the going down o
66 20 74 68 65 20 73 75 6E 20 61 6E 64 20 69 6E  f the sun and in
20 74 68 65 20 6D 6F 72 6E 69 6E 67 0D 0A 09 57   the morning...W
65 20 77 69 6C 6C 20 72 65 6D 65 6D 62 65 72 20  e will remember
20 74 68 65 6D 2E                                 them.
```

The poem shows a TAB character at the start of each line. TAB is ASCII character 9. Each line ends with a Carriage Return and Line Feed pair. The Carriage Return (CR) is character 13 decimal or 0D hex, Line Feed (LF) is character 10 decimal or 0A hex. After the word 'old' at the end of the first line, you can see the four hex bytes 3B 0D 0A 09. These are ";" CR LF and TAB. You can see them in the hex byte section but they cannot be printed in the text section because CR, LF and TAB all cause an action, they do not result in printed characters. That is why they are shown as dots.

Showing ASCII in hex is more efficient than using decimal. In hex, the character A is 41. Any other capital letter can be worked out by using 40 + its position in the alphabet so F is 40 + 6 = 46 hex. Lower case a is 61, i.e. "A" + 20 so f is 46 + 20 = 66. By following these rules, you can work out any of the letter bytes in the hex dump. A space is character 20.

Exercise

From memory, write down the text and appearance of what would be output on a standard ASCII printer if the following hex bytes were sent to it.

Remember the point is only to achieve some fluency. There is little point continuing to the end once you have done this. Answer shown at the end of this section.

57 69 74 68 20 70 72 6F 75 64 20 74 68 61 6E 6B 73 67 69 76 69 6E 67 2C 20 61 20 6D 6F 74 68 65 72
20 66 6F 72 20 68 65 72 20 63 68 69 6C 64 72 65 6E 2C 0D 0A 45 6E 67 6C 61 6E 64 20 6D 6F 75 72
6E 73 20 66 6F 72 20 68 65 72 20 64 65 61 64 20 61 63 72 6F 73 73 20 74 68 65 20 73 65 61 2E

The same poem text as above was saved in a Unicode file using the Unicode option under Wordpad. The resulting hex dump shows what has happened. Each character is stored as 2 bytes because Unicode uses 16 bits per character.

```
FF FE 09 00 54 00 68 00 65 00 79 00 20 00 73 00 ÿ_..T.h.e.y. .s.
68 00 61 00 6C 00 6C 00 20 00 67 00 72 00 6F 00 h.a.l.l. .g.r.o.
77 00 20 00 6E 00 6F 00 74 00 20 00 6F 00 6C 00 w. .n.o.t. .o.l.
64 00 2C 00 20 00 61 00 73 00 20 00 77 00 65 00 d.,. .a.s. .w.e.
20 00 74 00 68 00 61 00 74 00 20 00 61 00 72 00 .t.h.a.t. .a.r.
65 00 20 00 6C 00 65 00 66 00 74 00 20 00 67 00 e. .l.e.f.t. .g.
72 00 6F 00 77 00 20 00 6F 00 6C 00 64 00 3B 00 r.o.w. .o.l.d.;.
0D 00 0A 00 09 00 41 00 67 00 65 00 20 00 73 00 ......A.g.e. .s.
68 00 61 00 6C 00 6C 00 20 00 6E 00 6F 00 74 00 h.a.l.l. .n.o.t.
20 00 77 00 65 00 61 00 72 00 79 00 20 00 74 00 .w.e.a.r.y. .t.
68 00 65 00 6D 00 2C 00 20 00 6E 00 6F 00 72 00 h.e.m.,. .n.o.r.
20 00 74 00 68 00 65 00 20 00 79 00 65 00 61 00 .t.h.e. .y.e.a.
72 00 73 00 20 00 63 00 6F 00 6E 00 64 00 65 00 r.s. .c.o.n.d.e.
6D 00 6E 00 2E 00 0D 00 0A 00 09 00 41 00 74 00 m.n.........A.t.
20 00 74 00 68 00 65 00 20 00 67 00 6F 00 69 00 .t.h.e. .g.o.i.
6E 00 67 00 20 00 64 00 6F 00 77 00 6E 00 20 00 n.g. .d.o.w.n. .
6F 00 66 00 20 00 74 00 68 00 65 00 20 00 73 00 o.f. .t.h.e. .s.
75 00 6E 00 20 00 61 00 6E 00 64 00 20 00 69 00 u.n. .a.n.d. .i.
6E 00 20 00 74 00 68 00 65 00 20 00 6D 00 6F 00 n. .t.h.e. .m.o.
72 00 6E 00 69 00 6E 00 67 00 0D 00 0A 00 09 00 r.n.i.n.g.......
57 00 65 00 20 00 77 00 69 00 6C 00 6C 00 20 00 W.e. .w.i.l.l. .
72 00 65 00 6D 00 65 00 6D 00 62 00 65 00 72 00 r.e.m.e.m.b.e.r.
20 00 74 00 68 00 65 00 6D 00 2E 00             .t.h.e.m..
```

Answer to exercise

With proud thanksgiving, a mother for her children,
England mourns for her dead across the sea.

This is the first line of the poem *For the Fallen* by Laurence Binyon used at the start of this section.

Searching the Internet

Most people use search engines to find what they want on the net. Many have a favourite search engine on the grounds that it gives them what they want. The best advice is: don't have a favourite. You should realize that there are different kinds of search engine and each will (may!) find what you want depending on what that is. It is not unreasonable to use six or more search engines in a particular search.

This difference is not so much in the subject area, it is more on how you look and exactly what you want. Broadly, search engine indexes (the things that are actually searched) are either built by humans or by 'spider' software. Although the actual picture is a little more complex than this, it is worth remembering when you search. For example, the search engine www.yahoo.com uses indexes mainly built by people so when someone submits a web address to Yahoo, a real live person decides on where to put it in the index. If you use www.go.com, you will be searching through an index created by software that looks for keywords in the web pages it 'spiders'. Many search engines now use multiple indexes and some even use indexes of different types but the fact remains that different engines will give different results from the same search. Use more than one.

If you search for the words 'history' and 'computer', you could get references to a file that contains the string '... he was playing with his computer during the history lesson...' simply because it contains the correct keywords. If you had used a human categorized search engine, you are less likely to have come across this problem. On the other hand, if keywords are what you want, a keyword search engine is better. For example, if you want information on 'colossus' and Alan Turing, you would be better off with a keyword engine as neither colossus nor Alan Turing are 'subjects'. As a clear demonstration of the power of keyword search engines, try looking for a single line in a famous poem. Try looking for 'if you can keep your head when all about you' in both www.yahoo.com and www.go.com, making sure you put the string in quotes, you may be surprised at the different hits returned. (It is the first line in a poem called *If* by Rudyard Kipling voted 'the most popular poem in England'.) Even more impressive is looking for computer components. On a motherboard in the author's office, a chip was found with just the number 'ms62256h' printed on it. The Altavista Advanced search engine returned six hits to data sheets about this SRAM chip.

Another consideration is search syntax. Use Boolean expressions. These contain logic symbols or statements like + , –, OR and AND. If you search for the words 'computer' and 'history' you should enter + computer + history, the + signs meaning that the word must be present. If you don't use the plus signs, some search engines will do a logical OR operation and search for either computer OR history. It is well worth your trouble looking at the search engine tutorial at completeplanet.com/tutorials/index.asp, it will add much power to your searches. You will know when you are getting good at searching the net when the number of hits you get from a search is less than 100. A search that gives a million hits is unlikely to be of much use. You can also use the – sign to mean do not include, e.g. + history + computer -mainframe to avoid the word 'mainframe'.

Metasearch engines will search other engines for you and give good results. A problem with this approach is that they do not always pass on the full syntax to each client search engine, so carefully constructed Boolean searches do not always work.

If you do not have time to read the tutorial or the web address of the tutorial has changed since this was printed, use these guidelines:

- Do not use CAPITAL letters in searches. Different engines use different rules about capital letters but lower case nearly always works.
- Put strings that contain spaces in quotes, e.g. 'if you can keep your head when all about you'.
- Use + and – signs routinely, some engines use OR and AND but most take + and –.
- Use the 'advanced' or 'power' searches. Some search engines only allow Boolean expressions in the advanced search page. You can then search for specific items such as 'stored program' AND electronic AND semiconductor AND silicon AND 'alan turing' AND 'blaise pascal'. On a recent trail with Altavista Advanced, this gave less than 40 hits and some interesting information (note no capital letters in the search string).
- Use plenty of keywords to narrow down a search, try + history + computer + microprocessor + intel instead of just + history + computer, the first returned 22 hits, the second over 2000 hits on a recent trial.
- Try putting the string in a different order. Some engines assume the first word is more important than the second so + history + computer may give different results from + computer + history.
- Use the * character as a wildcard, e.g. a search for comput* will find the words computer computers, computing, computation etc.
- Avoid plurals such as computers as it will miss the word computer. It is better to use a wildcard like computer* which will find both.
- Use either site: or domain: to filter for different countries. In various engines, try + history + computer + pentium + site:uk. It should only give sites in the UK (but will miss those with a .com at the end).

Some subjects are hard to research and there are several reasons for this. Some commercial information is only available for a payment, for instance current business performance, stock prices, etc. are not generally available free of charge. Other information is swamped by commercial interests, e.g. try looking for + pentium + computer and you will find hundreds of companies trying to sell you their oh so cheap yet oh so fast computers. These are areas that will test your searching skills, often the solution is to use a Boolean search that includes a technical term not often found in sales literature. The search string + pentium + computer + silicon returned 90 mainly non-commercial hits whereas just + pentium + computer returned over 4000 hits that were mainly adverts.

Finally, do a search, using different engines, for the expression + search + engine*. You will find much information that will aid your use of the fantastic resource called the Internet. Computing is one of the fastest changing subjects yet known and it is often difficult to keep up to date. One of the most profitable parts of your study time will be to polish your searching skills.